BED & BREAKFAST
IN NEW ENGLAND

"For all the answers. . . . The Book to get."
—*Evening Magazine*, WBZ-TV, Boston, MA

". . . the most detailed and extensively researched guidebooks available."
—*Country Almanac*

"The travel philosopher. . . "
—*Spy* **magazine**

"Unprecedented personal and logistical data about the hosts and their accommodations. . . [Chesler's] style reinforces the concept of bed and breakfast as a warm, person-to-person accommodation."
—**The American Bed & Breakfast Association's** *Shoptalk*

"Your book is by far the best *and most fun to read."*
—**Gail Sanderson, Stonecrest Farm, Wilder, Vermont**

"Your book was very helpful and informative. All of the places we chose from your book were exactly as described."
—**Gloria and Patrick Johnson, Michigan**

"Like reading a best-seller. I couldn't put the book down."
—**Dorothy Traverse, Massachusetts**

"The amount and quality of information provided to the reader are unmatched in any other guidebook."
—**The American Country Collection**

"We just returned from a wonderful trip to New England. We spent 10 days and traveled 1600 miles. We carried your book and stayed in eight bed and breakfasts recommended by you. Your book is a wonderful guide. The inns we stayed at were just like you described. It would not be easy to pick a favorite as they were all excellent."
—**Wayne and Delores Knapp, Illinois**

"Purchased four different B&B publications. . . . We found your guide to be outstanding and far superior to the other books. The information was wonderfully comprehensive, and the map format was invaluable."
—**Howard R. Katz, Maryland**

"Your guidebook was a very helpful tool for us, making our vacation in the U.S. very enjoyable."
—**Iris Ehgartner, Vienna, Austria**

Other books by Bernice Chesler

Editor and Coordinator
The ZOOM Catalog
Do a ZOOMdo
People You'd Like to Know

Coauthor
The Family Guide to Cape Cod

Author
In and Out of Boston with (or without) Children
Mainstreaming through the Media
Bed & Breakfast Coast to Coast
Bed & Breakfast in the Mid-Atlantic States

Bed & Breakfast in New England

Connecticut, Maine, Massachusetts, New Hampshire, Rhode Island, Vermont

Third Edition

by Bernice Chesler

A Voyager Book

Old Saybrook, Connecticut

Prior to revision, some of the material in this book appeared in *Bed and Breakfast in the Northeast*.

Library of Congress Cataloging-in-Publication Data

Chesler, Bernice.
   Bed & breakfast in New England / by Bernice Chesler. — 3rd ed.
   p. cm.
   "A Voyager book."
   Includes index.
   ISBN 1-56440-029-8 : $14.95
   1. Bed and Breakfast accommodations—New England—Guide-books.
2. New England—Description and travel—1981- —Guide-books. I. Title.
II. Title: Bed and breakfast in New England.
TX907.3.N35.C47 1992
647.947403—dc20
                                                      91-45188
                                                         CIP
Editorial-Production Services: Editorial Inc. of Rockport, Massachusettts
Cover design: Hannus Design Associates
Cover photo: Shelburne Museum, Shelburne, Vermont. Photograph by Ken Burris
Text design: Penny Darras-Maxwell
Composition done in Meridien on the Ventura 3.0 system
Maps composed on CorelDRAW! 2.0
Primary compositor: Hagop Hagopian
Production editor: Jeanne Ryer
   Manufactured in the United States of America.
   Third Edition / Second Printing

To David

CONTENTS

What Is Bed & Breakfast
_____ All About? _____

From the author's mailbag:

Guests from Canada wrote:

"We spent three days at a Maine B&B last month and would have been happy to stay longer. The host has created a beautiful home for herself and her guests—a home, not a museum, even though it is full of books, pottery, photos, and other treasures that make it a pleasure to spend some quiet hours indoors.

"Breakfasts were a treat, partly for the excellent and abundant food and coffee, but mostly for the chance to get to know our host. She gave us a lot, just by being herself—warm and funny and interested in all sorts of things, from poetry and fairy tales to health care systems and Canadian geography. She was interested in us, too, and made us feel like Very Important Visitors. She happily answered our many questions and helped us choose what turned out to be excellent destinations for our cycling trips.

"I learned a lot in those three short days—about Maine, certainly, but even more importantly about enjoying life fully, wherever I happen to be. Bravo!"

The host commented:

"This will be my eleventh season. Last night about ten o'clock I had a telephone call from Hong Kong, a 'how are you, we're keeping in touch' call from B&B guests who have been coming here regularly for a long time. It made me feel very cosmopolitan, as well as touched by their thoughtfulness. So you can be hidden away here on the coast of Maine, but, lo and behold, someone is thinking about you on the other side of the world. What a business. I still love it."

INTRODUCTION

"Those hosts would be great for a documentary film," I said to my husband. We were leaving a Vermont bed and breakfast, a genuine farmhouse; the farmer had offered me cow salve to soothe leg muscles that ached from pedaling over the hilly terrain.

That was a decade ago. (I had been working as a documentary film researcher for public television.) Who would have guessed then that bed and breakfast was to become the hottest trend in American travel? The acceptance of B&Bs on this side of the ocean came at just the right time for us—just as our youngest left for college, just as we were to discover the joys of pedaling from B&B to B&B, and from one interesting experience to another in what is now a total of 14 states and 6 countries.

In the 1990s bed and breakfast has come to be recognized for its personalized style, for hosts who help to give a sense of place. Now many B&B hosts have plotted back-road routes for guests. With the advent of bed and breakfast reservation services, bed and breakfasts are in the city and suburbs as well as in rural areas. In addition, B&Bs have opened in restored everything—from churches to schoolhouses, from beach cottages to mansions.

To distinguish private homes from inns, this book has introduced a symbol (✿) for private homes that have one, two, or three guest rooms. B&B inns are likely to be larger, are a full-time profession, and in some cases have one or more hired staffers. Other symbols—in answer to travelers' requests—will lead you (quickly) to a romantic place, a spot that is great for kids, or a B&B where your group, family, or colleagues might book the entire place. See the key to symbols that appears at intervals throughout the book.

In documentary film style, *Bed & Breakfast in New England* tries to focus as much on the memorable hosts as on their homes and B&B inns. In addition, each description aims to save travelers' time by anticipating questions: Located on a main road? What time is breakfast? Sample menu? Size of bed? What floors are rooms on? Shower *and* tub? Is smoking allowed? Any pets in residence? What's the difference between the $60 and the $90 room?

Research for my first B&B guide began in 1980. Seven B&B books and about 1,500 interviews later, this latest edition reflects the wide range of possibilities that fit into my original interpretation of bed and breakfast: a home setting with an owner in residence; a maximum of about 10 rooms; a common room; breakfast included in the rate, but no public restaurant or bar on the premises.

So what's changed? New owners are in residence. Lots of new places have opened. Many gazebos are on the outside. Many more private baths are on the inside. New layers of regulations have added to costs and rates. Old-timers (more than five years in business) find themselves adding a few rooms to keep B&B economically viable. Some move across the street or next door. They learn to hire an inn-sitter now and then. And always, there is a steady stream of dreamers who see B&B—after all, it's only breakfast, they say—as a fantasy lifestyle.

And what about you, the traveler? "Adventuresome and flexible, interesting and appreciative—a very special breed," hosts say. The feeling is mutual. The art of letter writing is alive! Excerpts from some of the thousands of enthusiastic letters written to me are included in this book. There really is a letter of the day, usually one that reinforces the concept of a people-to-people program—and makes you feel good all over.

Accuracy is a hallmark of this book. Every detail was confirmed just before press time. But please keep in mind that successful hosts sometimes make *changes in rooms, beds, menu, or decor—and yes, in rates too.*

My thanks go to Lourdes Alvarez, who, with great cheer and efficiency, has handled more than 30,000 pieces of paper, deciphered floor plans, and decoded hieroglyphics. It is a pleasure to work with Jay Howland, my editor who remembers everything and everyone. Additional support and encouragement have come from my agent, Laura Fillmore, and the staff of Editorial Inc., including Jeanne Ryer, Hagop Hagopian, and MaryEllen Oliver. Penny Darras-Maxwell, who created the new design for this book, died just before the book went to press. We remember her with fondness and her work with gratitude and respect. And once again, David, my husband, has planned all our trips by plane, car, and bicycle. He listens, offers judgment when I solicit objectivity, and acts as my computer expert in residence.

Suggestions about people and places are welcome for consideration in the next edition. Please address them to me at The Globe Pequot Press, P.O. Box 833, Old Saybrook, Connecticut 06475.

Answers to Frequently Asked Questions

What is bed and breakfast?

It is a package arrangement that includes overnight accommodations and breakfast. Although many American B&Bs feature embellishments (amenities), the keynote is hospitality. Think of bed and breakfast as a people-to-people program. (And be aware that package pricing, sometimes *labeled* "B&B," is now offered by many hotels and motels.)

Are baths shared?

Some are. But, depending on the number of guests, a shared bath could be private for you. Many American B&Bs have followed the trend to all private baths, sometimes with a shower but no tub, sometimes with a whirlpool bath and a sauna too.

Is B&B like a hotel?

Not at all! It's not intended to be. You are greeted by a family member or an assistant, or occasionally by a note. Every room is different in size, layout, and decor. A B&B may not provide the privacy—or the loneliness—of a hotel. There's no elevator service. Television is not an important feature. Now that business travelers have discovered B&Bs, however, there may be a phone jack (occasionally a private phone) in the room.

If you must have things exactly as they are in the hotel you usually go to, go to the hotel!

Is B&B for everyone?

Many B&Bs are just right for unwinding and a change of pace. Many first-time B&B guests are won over by the experience. If you seek anonymity, however, B&B probably isn't for you. As one Vermont host said, "Guests who come to B&Bs screen themselves: They are outgoing; they want to be sociable and learn about you and the area."

Among all the wonderful guests, a few hosts can recall the occasional "memorable" demanding guest; sometimes I think that it is the same person going from B&B to B&B. And I have heard of a first-timer who appeared with considerable luggage—cumbersome indeed on the narrow steep stairs to the third floor of the historic house.

Tastes and interpretations differ. Take charm, for example. "Tell me," said the older guest, "What's so charming about a tub on legs? I was so glad when built-ins finally became the fashion."

Recommendation: Tell the host if this is your first time at a B&B. When making the reservation, if privacy is a real concern, say that too. Hosts' listening skills are usually well tuned.

How much do they cost?

B&B rates for two people, including breakfast, range from $35 to well over $100. The season, location, amenities, food, length of ownership, maintenance costs, taxes—all affect the rate. Nothing is standardized at B&Bs!

In this book, check under each B&B's "Rates" to see what credit cards are accepted there. Many small places prefer cash or travelers' checks. And it's a good idea to check on deposit requirements; refund policies differ. Required local and/or state taxes vary from place to place and are seldom in the listed rates.

Suggestion: Consider paying upon arrival. The good-byes can be that much smoother, and you really do feel as if you have visited friends.

To tip or not?

In a private home, tipping is not a usual practice, *but* times may be changing. In a private home where B&B is rather constant, owners realize that extra help helps. Those B&B owners also know that some remembrance is appreciated by the part-time folks who contribute to your memorable stay.

In a B&B inn, treat staff as you would in a hotel. *Some inns, particularly those in resort areas, add gratuities to the tab*—or else they couldn't keep their help!

An interesting phenomenon: An amazing number of travelers write heartfelt thank-you notes to surprised and delighted hosts.

How do B&Bs on this side of the Atlantic differ from those in the British Isles or other countries?

The B&B-and-away-you-go idea is not necessarily the norm in North America. Although there are B&Bs with just one room and many where you are expected to leave for the day following breakfast, guests are often invited to spend more time "at home"—by the pool or fireplace, on the hiking trails or on borrowed bicycles. Even hosts are amazed at what they do when they get involved in others' lives. They worry about late arrivals. They have been known to drive someone to a job appointment or to do laundry for a businessman whose schedule changed or to prevail upon the local auto mechanic when the garage was closed.

Can I book through travel agents?

Many travel agents have caught on to the popularity of B&Bs. In this book B&Bs with ♦ in the "Rates" section pay commissions to travel agents. And some agents will make arrangements for you, whether or not they receive a commission from the B&B.

Do B&Bs welcome children?

Some B&Bs provide everything from the sandbox to the high chair—and a babysitter too. (Check the "Plus" section in the descriptions in this book.) And then there are B&B hosts who have been known to say (tactfully), "Children find us tiresome."

Consider the facilities, the room and bath arrangements, and the decor. Are your kids enticed by candlelit breakfasts? Are they used to being around "don't touch" antiques? Do they enjoy classical music? Are rooms limited to two persons? Is a crib provided? Are there lots of animals on the farm? Is there a built-in playmate, perhaps an innkeeper's child? Remember what you looked for B.C. (before children). Be fair to yourself and your children, to other guests, and to the host/chef/gardener/interior designer/historian—who really does love children. In this book B&Bs with the symbol ♣ are always happy to host children. Some B&Bs without the symbol also welcome children, though not necessarily a houseful!

Are there facilities for physically handicapped persons?

Some. (Not many.) Rooms that are handicapped accessible are noted in the detailed "Bed and bath" item of each B&B description in this book. In addition, each writeup mentions the floor locations of guest rooms.

Are there B&Bs that prohibit smoking?

Many do. (Note the ✄ symbol in this book.) Among the B&Bs that do allow smoking, many limit it to certain areas or rooms.

If you like people and enjoy company and cooking, isn't that enough to make you a happy host?

It helps. But experienced hosts all comment on the time and work involved. Guests who ask, "Is this all you do?" would be surprised to realize that there *is* more to hosting than serving tea and meeting interesting people. Even I have fallen into the trap of multiplying a full house by the nightly rate, only to hear my husband say, "Never mind, that's 600 sheets!"

What do you recommend to those who dream about opening a B&B?

For starters, attend one of the workshops or seminars given by adult- education centers, extension services, innkeepers, or B&B reservation services. Apprentice, even for a weekend, or sign up with a reservation service and host in your own home.

Many prospective innkeepers attend Bill Oates and Heide Bredfeldt's seminar, "How to Purchase and Operate a Bed & Breakfast or Country Inn." Contact Oates & Bredfeldt, P.O. Box 1162, Brattleboro, VT 05302, 802/254-5931. For a free Aspiring Innkeepers'

Kit that includes a list of innkeeping workshops conducted in various parts of the country, contact the Professional Association of Inn-keepers International, P.O. Box 90710, Santa Barbara, CA 93190, 805/569-1853, fax 805/682-1016.

Every host in this book enjoys what they call "the great emotional rewards of a stimulating occupation." Some remind couples who wish to make hosting a vocation that it helps to have a strong marriage. One who encourages prospective innkeepers to "Just do it!" adds, "but be aware that you have to be more gregarious than private. You have to learn to carve time out for yourself. Hosting requires a broad range of talents (knowledge of plumbing helps), a lot of flexibility, an incredible amount of stamina, and perseverance. And did I mention you might need some capital?"

Can a host or reservation service pay to be in this book?

No. All selections are made by the author. There are no application fees. And all descriptions are written by the author; no host or service proprietor can write his or her own description.

A processing fee is paid after each selected B&B or reservation service reviews its writeup. The fee offsets the extensive research that results in highly detailed writeups reflecting the individual spirit of each B&B.

The processing fee for an individual B&B is $125. (For those with one or two rooms and a top rate of $50, it is $100.) The fee for a fully described reservation service is $125; for a reservation service host, $40. The author pays for all her stays.

What are some of your favorite B&Bs?

Even when you stay in hundreds, you tend to remember the hosts of each B&B more than the place. We have arrived on bicycles and been greeted with the offer of a car to go to dinner. There's the horticulturist, a septuagenarian, whom we could hardly keep up with as she toured us through her spectacular gardens. There's the couple who built their own solar house. Multifaceted retirees. History buffs who filled us in on the area and recommended back roads. Literary buffs who suggested good books. Hosts in a lovely residential section just minutes off the highway. Hosts we have laughed with. Yes, even some we have cried with too. Great chefs. People who are involved in their communities and trying to make this a better world. People whose home has been a labor of love and who love sharing it with others. We have enjoyed rather luxurious settings and some casual places too. It *is* true that each B&B is special in its own way. All together, the list of thankful guests numbers well into the millions. The place to stay can be the reason to go. It's wonderful.

B&B RESERVATION SERVICES

A reservation service is in the business of matching screened hosts and guests. Although it can be a seasonal operation, in some areas the service is a full-time job for an individual, a couple, partners, or a small group.

For hosts, it's a private way of going public, because the host remains anonymous until the service (agency) matches host and guest. This unique system allows hosts in private homes to have an off-and-on hosting schedule.

Listings may be in communities where there are no overnight lodging facilities, or they may provide an alternative to hotels or motels. Although most services feature private homes, others include B&B inns with 6–10 guest rooms. And some services now offer stays in unhosted homes.

Each service determines its own area and conducts its own inspections and interviews. A service may cover just one community, or a metropolitan area, or an entire region.

Advance notice is preferred and even, with many services, required. Length-of-stay requirements vary. Some services stipulate a one-night surcharge; some require a minimum of two nights.

Rates are usually much less than at area hotels and motels. The range may cover everything from "budget" to "luxury." Deposits are usually required. Refund policies, detailed with each reservation service description in this book, differ.

Fee arrangements vary. Many services include their commission in the quoted nightly rate. For public inns the service's quoted rate may be the same as what the inn charges, or it could be a total of the inn's rate plus a booking fee of $5–$15.

Write for printed information or maybe, better yet, call. Before calling think about bed and bath arrangements, parking, smoking, pets, children, air conditioning—whatever is important to you.

A reservation service acts as a clearinghouse and frequently provides an opportunity to stay at a B&B that would not be available any other way.

KEY TO SYMBOLS
- ♥ Lots of honeymooners come here.
- ♣ Families with children are very welcome. (Please see page xiii.)
- ♠ "Please emphasize that we are a private home, not an inn."
- ♣ Groups or private parties sometimes book the entire B&B.
- ♦ Travel agents' commission paid. (Please see page xii.)
- ✕ Sorry, no guests' pets are allowed.
- ✗ No smoking inside *or* no smoking at all, even on porches.

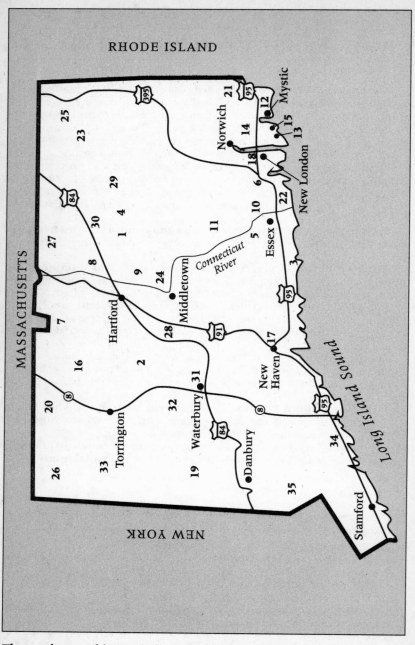

The numbers on this map indicate the locations of B&Bs described in detail in this chapter.

CONNECTICUT

__ Connecticut Reservation Services __

Bed and Breakfast, Ltd.

P.O. Box 216, New Haven, CT 06513

Phone: 203/469-3260 During the academic year, 5–9:30 p.m. weekdays; anytime weekends or summer months.

Listings: Over 125. "From elegantly simple to simply elegant." Located throughout Connecticut. Some listings in Massachusetts and Rhode Island; new listings constantly added. Mostly private residences. A few inns and unhosted private residences.

Reservations: For one day or up to three months. Same-day service usually available. "A quick phone call encouraged to discuss availability and appropriate placement."

Rates: $45–$50 singles, $50–$75 doubles. Suites and deluxe accommodations slightly higher. ◆

Jack Argenio emphasizes variety—in types of homes as well as in price range. Many are historic residences filled with antiques. He selects knowledgeable and congenial hosts and tries to personalize matches to suit guests' needs and budget.

Plus: In-ground pools, Jacuzzis, gourmet dinners, hiking trails. Some hosts meet guests at airports or train stations.

Covered Bridge

Maple Avenue, P.O. Box 447, Norfolk, CT 06058-0447

Phone: 203/542-5944, 9 a.m.–6 p.m. daily; other times, answering machine.

Listings: 70. Most are hosted private residences in Connecticut's Litchfield County and shoreline communities, in the Berkshires of Massachusetts, in Rhode Island and New York towns bordering Connecticut, and in Southern Vermont. A few are unhosted and some are inns. A free sample list is available. Directory (booklet), $3.

Reservations: One to two weeks' advance notice preferred. Two-day minimum for weekends, three for holidays.

Rates: $50–$150. Some family, senior citizen, and weekly rates available. Prepayment in full is required. Cancellations received at least 10 days before expected arrival date will be refunded less a $15 handling charge. With less than 10 days' notice, entire prepayment may be forfeited unless room is rebooked. ◆

Hank and Diane Tremblay, former corporate executives, are experienced travelers and innkeepers (Manor House, page 23) who work with travelers on an individual basis to try to accommodate their needs. Most of their selected hosts live in antiques-furnished historic homes that are sometimes featured in major national publications. Many are in idyllic settings. Hearty breakfasts are a feature, as is the "free to come and go" atmosphere.

Nutmeg Bed & Breakfast Agency

P.O. Box 1117, West Hartford, CT 06127-1117

Phone: 203/236-6698, Monday through Friday, 9:30–5, year round; machine at other times.

Listings: 200. Located throughout Connecticut—near all major cities and towns, along the shore, and in the Berkshire foothills of Massachusetts and New York. Hosted private residences and some inns. Directory ($5.00) has general characteristics of each area as well as house descriptions.

Reservations: One week's advance notice preferred. Two-night minimum on holidays and graduation weekends and at other times at some locations.

Rates: $40–$125 single, $45–$135 double; average $65–$85. Family and weekly rates available. AMEX, MC, VISA to hold reservations. $15 charge for confirmed cancellation. One night's lodging charged if notice received less than 7 days before expected arrival; 14 days for holidays and special events. Five percent credit card fee. ◆

Michelle Souza, a former insurance executive who has traveled extensively, offers quality accommodations for tourists and business travelers. Her well-established service specializes in finding temporary and permanent housing for relocating executives; she also works with colleges, private schools, and hospitals to provide lodging for visiting faculty, parents, and patients in private homes. Short-term and unhosted housing is also available.

Other reservation services with some B&Bs in Connecticut:
Bed & Breakfast/Inns of New England, page 257
Pineapple Hospitality, page 106

Do you have to get up for breakfast?
There's no one rule. Check each description in this book for the various arrangements. More than one guest has been enticed by the aroma of fresh muffins. If you are on business or want to catch the morning ferry, eat-and-run is just fine. If, however, cuisine is a feature, plan on appearing at the specified time!
Vacationers (not skiers) find breakfast a very social time. One hostess says that even when guests say they want to be on the road early, they often linger over breakfast for hours. If hosts join you, please understand when they leave the table after a while.

_____ Connecticut B&Bs _____

Jared Cone House   203/643-8538
25 Hebron Road, Bolton, CT 06043

Hosts: Jeff and Cinde Smith
Location: Fifteen miles east of Hartford in the country with farms and woodlands. In a community of 5,000 people. Fine cuisine nearby. Two miles from Bolton Lake; 15 miles to University of Connecticut. Near pick-your-own farms, hay and sleigh rides. Seven miles west of Caprilands Herb Farm.
Open: Year round. Reservations requested.
Rates: Single, $45 shared bath, $55 private. Double, $60 shared bath, $70 private. Rollaway $10.

The Palladian window in the second-floor hallway is a dramatic introduction to the guest floor in this traditional post-and-beam center hall Georgian colonial, which has wide board floors and a kitchen with a huge hearth. Architecture buffs are delighted with an invitation to see the hand-hewn beams in the attic and the hand-stacked rock foundation in the basement. Jeff, a furniture maker, and Cinde purchased their treasure in 1985. Built by a wealthy farmer in the late 1700s and once the library and the town's post office, the house is now registered with the U.S. Department of Interior Office of Archeology and Historic Preservations.

The spacious rooms in the historic home have print wallpapers, antiques and reproductions, and a light, airy, uncluttered look. This is the land of antiquing (right here at the B&B, if you'd like), fall foliage, and canoeing (with the hosts' canoe).

In residence: In family quarters on first floor—Julie, age six, and Drew, age three. Two cats, Groucho and Wilma.
Bed and bath: Three second-floor rooms, each with a queen bed. One with private full bath en suite. Two share a full bath. Crib and twin-sized rollaway available.
Breakfast: Usually 8–10. Juice, homemade pumpkin bread, cream cheese, jellies and marmalades. Eggs with toast, pancakes or French toast with homemade maple syrup. Fresh fruit in the summer. Served in dining room or on the porch.
Plus: Upstairs sitting area next to the Palladian window. Porch and patio. Use of bicycles, stroller, playpen.

Six weeks *after* one B&B opened, a neighbor inquired: "I need lodging for visiting relatives. When are you going to open?" This was the same neighbor who, during a zoning hearing, had expressed great concern about traffic and noise that a B&B would create!

Chimney Crest Manor   203/582-4219

5 Founders Drive, Bristol, CT 06010

Hosts: Dan and Cynthia Cimadamore
Location: On a hilltop overlooking Farmington Valley. In historic Federal Hill area, one-quarter mile from Bristol Clock Museum, one mile from New England Carousel Museum. Eight minutes from Lake Compounce Festival Park; 20 minutes west of Hartford, 15 minutes east of Waterbury.

Open: Year round. Two-night minimum stay on holiday weekends and in foliage season.
Rates: $65–$95 single, $75–$105 double. Rose Garden Suite $90 double occupancy, $10 per child. Weekly and monthly rates available. Corporate, senior citizen, and Lovers' Weekend (two-night stay) discounts.
♥ ✄ ✂

British royalty, honeymooners, and many business travelers have walked along the 40-foot-long arcade in this sprawling 32-room Tudor mansion. There's a cherry-paneled library, a Spanish-tiled sun room, six handcrafted fireplaces, and ornate plaster ceilings. Much of the house is carpeted; furnishings are traditional.

When a television crew filmed a B&B segment here, they pointed the camera at the tile roof, arches, gardens, and multiflue chimneys. Then they came into the huge dining room, where a roaring blaze was in the fireplace and the table was beautifully set. The estate was built in 1930 by the Barnes family, known locally for specialty steels and springs. Since Cynthia's parents bought the house in the mid-1950s, it has seen use as a preparatory school. After the second Cimadamore child was born, Cynthia was ready for "something else to do at home." The residence for three generations became a B&B offering privacy, warm hospitality, large full guest suites, and meeting-room space.

In residence: Diana, 15, and Dante, 7. Buffy is the family's bichon frise.
Bed and bath: Five suites. On first level, full apartment. On lower level, large suite with living room, bedroom, kitchen, rolltop bar, exercise room. Three on second floor, each with private bath, two with full kitchens. Living room and queen bed in each two- or three-room suite. One large room has fireplace. Private guest entrance.
Breakfast: Full, 7–8; continental until 9. Fruit salad, homemade breads plus yogurt pancakes, French toast or eggs. Served with linen, china and crystal in the large fireplaced dining room. Dan or Cynthia joins guests.
Plus: Bedroom air conditioning. Fan, clock radio, television, telephone in each suite. Garden. Large patio.

> From New Jersey: *"Our first B&B experience and we are won over. Cynthia was terrific, the food excellent, and the rooms immaculately clean."*

People are funny.
From Cape Cod: "One guest said the house needed a cat. The next day another lady said, 'I hope you don't have cats. I'm allergic to them.'"

Captain Dibbell House   203/669-1646

21 Commerce Street, Clinton, CT 06413-2107

Hosts: Ellis and Helen Adams
Location: Two blocks from harbor, on an historic residential street. One mile south of I-95, just off Route 1. Two miles to Hammonasset State Beach; 10 to Essex; 40 to Mystic; 23 to Yale University; 3 to Salt Meadow National Wildlife Refuge.

Open: February–December. Reservations appreciated.
Rates: $60 single, $75 double. After three nights, $5 less per night. Weekly, senior, corporate, and off-season (November–May) rates. AMEX, MC, VISA.
♥ ❀ ◆ ✖ ✄

A triumph! For three consecutive years, the hosts of this three-guest-room B&B have won first prize in *Yankee* magazine's Great New England Inns Apple Pie Contest. Their restored 1866 Victorian, "not the ornate kind," is furnished with family pieces and auction finds. Much of the original artwork is done by "up and coming" traditional artists. Classical music is almost always playing.

"After spending summers in the area on our sailboat, we knew this would be a marvelous place to open our kind of B&B, a small friendly place in a small friendly coastal town. Here we have a special appreciation for the winter sunsets viewed from the beach." And so it has been for the Adamses since they left their Poughkeepsie, New York, area jobs as child welfare caseworker and public health inspector. "Now, five years later, we have hosted some of the greatest people in the world. Some breakfasts last more than two hours, and people who arrived here as strangers to us and to the other guests leave as friends."

In residence: Ruffles, 9-year-old Briard (French sheepdog), "willingly poses for pictures." Two cats, "very shy" Mister Max and Susie Two, age 20.
Bed and bath: Three second-floor rooms; private shower baths. Two queen-bedded rooms. One with two twin beds, convertible to king.
Breakfast: 8:30–10. An egg dish or baked treat such as scones or breakfast version of the prizewinning pie. Juice, fresh fruit, teas, and freshly ground coffee. In summer, served in gazebo bordered by gardens and brick walk.
Plus: Bedroom ceiling fans. Fruit. Flowers. Freshly baked snack. Champagne for newlyweds and anniversary couples. Guest refrigerator. Lawn games. Rainy-day guide. Borrowables include bicycles, beach chairs with umbrella, cooler, rain umbrella.

Maple Hill Farm Bed & Breakfast

365 Goose Lane, Coventry, CT 06238-1215   203/742-0635

Hosts: Tony Felice and Mary Beth Gorke-Felice
Location: Rural. Four miles from I-84 and from Caprilands Herb Farm, 7 miles from University of Connecticut, 20 miles east of Hartford. On seven acres with apple orchard, stone fences, birds, flowers.

Open: Year round. Two-night minimum stay on University of Connecticut's graduation, homecoming, and parents' weekends.
Rates: $50 single, $60 double, $5 crib, $10 extra person. MC, VISA.
♥ 🐚 ❀ ◆ ✖ ✄

A real B&B. An experience. A trip through 260 years. In back, there's still a three-seat outhouse; the original dwelling, which predates the house; and a well. And there are horses, an in-ground swimming pool, hammocks, and a picnic area under a huge maple tree, alongside an English garden. Inside the Cape-style house there are gunstock posts, wide board floors, and lots of collectibles and family memorabilia, all blending with skylights and a solarium with hot tub and huge winter-flowering jade. In 1991 the keeping room was recreated, complete with beehive oven in cook-in fireplace built with original hearthstone and lintel. "When the children left, we felt that the space was meant to be shared," explains Mary Beth, an independent pediatric nurse practitioner. For the curious (and most guests are), Tony, an industrial salesman, and Mary Beth share fascinating and fun information about the history of the house and its former owners. All this, with breakfast by candlelight accompanied by classical music.

In residence: Brandy Alexander, "an extremely affectionate miniature poodle."
Bed and bath: Four good-sized second-floor rooms share two full baths. One room with two twin beds. Of four double-bedded rooms, one has skylight; one also has a single bed and another, a crib and a dollhouse.
Breakfast: 7:30–9. "A feast." (If you'd like, coffee in kitchen while Tony cooks.) Fresh fruit dish. Homemade bread. Their own farm-fresh eggs. Bacon or ham, French toast or hot cakes. Cereals. Served on heirloom china, crystal, and silver.
Plus: Complimentary wine. Tour of house. VCR movies with fresh popcorn. Board games. Therapeutic massage by appointment.

> Many guests wrote: *"Relaxing . . . beautiful countryside . . . hosts who embrace guests with open arms and warm hearts . . . highly recommended."*

Riverwind   203/526-2014
209 Main Street, Deep River, CT 06417-1704

Hosts: Barbara Barlow and Bob Bucknall
Location: Adjacent to the town green, in a small Connecticut River Valley village between Essex and Chester. Minutes to Goodspeed Opera House, Gillette Castle, Hammonasset Beach; half-hour to Mystic Seaport.

Open: Year round.
Rates: Per room. $85 (the one with unattached bath) to $145 ("Champagne and Roses"). $20 extra bed. MC, VISA.
♥ ♣ ✈

Perfect for *Country Living*, a wonderful spread in *Country Inns* magazine, and a "ten best country inns" award. Guests often use the words "charm, relaxing, and warm hospitality." Romance, too, plays a part in this inn's history.

Barbara, a Virginia junior high school learning-disabilities teacher who had experience restoring three other houses, came north for a week, found, and bought the abandoned 1850 house. She uncovered fireplaces, hand sanded floors, wired, tiled, and stenciled. In 1984 she drove a truck from

(Please turn page.)

Smithfield, Virginia, filled with family and other country antiques. Placed throughout the inn, they show a love of folk art, a sense of display, imagination, and whimsy. A garden rake handle holds the hanging over one mantel. Carpenters' tools are towel racks. Pig items acknowledge the innkeeper's growing years on a farm in the ham capital of the world. Color schemes are taken from quilts.

When it was time to expand, Barbara planned an authentically styled 18th-century keeping room along with four more guest rooms, some quite luxurious. She hired Bob Bucknall, a local contractor and Deep River native. And in fairytale fashion, they fell in love, they married (in Virginia), and Bob became full-time co-innkeeper.

In residence: Miss Hickory, "an affectionate tabby."
Bed and bath: Eight rooms on first and second floors. All private baths. Each room quite different. Some canopied beds. Some four-posters. Most are double; one queen-sized. "Champagne and Roses" features mahogany pencil-post canopied bed, bath with Japanese steeping tub, separate shower, private balcony, complimentary champagne.
Breakfast: Usually 9–10:30. (Coffee and tea for early risers.) A southern buffet in fireplaced dining room. Hot entree, Smithfield ham, pig-shaped biscuits, fruit compote, coffee cake, juices, coffee, tea.
Plus: Bedroom air conditioning and ceiling fans. Welcoming drink. Game room. Library. Guitar. Sherry. Mints. Flowers. Piano; old sheet music. Plant- and wicker-filled wraparound (glassed-in) porch—with ceiling fans. Bocci. Badminton. Croquet. Hibachis. Picnic baskets.

The Red House   203/739-5327
365 Boston Post Road, East Lyme, CT 06333-1402

Hosts: Harlan and Joan Sturgis
Location: A rural setting on three acres. On a two-lane road, 5 minutes to I-95, 3 to the shore, 20 to Essex and Mystic. Midway between New York City and Boston.

Open: Year round. Reservations preferred.
Rates: $50 single, $65 double. $7 for cot. Special rates for families using both rooms. MC, VISA.
🏠 🐾 ♦ ✄ ✂

> From Rhode Island guests: *"Great people. Harlan (justifiably) takes great pride in the berries he grows and serves for breakfast . . . Joan's wonderful too . . . their 1760s house, a real charmer."*

A gem of a B&B is another way of putting it. The Sturgises bought the 1760 center chimney colonial, all restored, in 1982. Inside you'll find wainscoting, small-print wallpapers, seven (nonworking) fireplaces, and, in the living room, exposed ceiling beams and a beehive oven. Part of the family room is a greenhouse where most of the plantings are started. It also has a wood stove and sliding doors to a welcoming wood deck.

Outside are thriving gardens, stone walls, two "mugs," a goose pen, and circular rock outcroppings, all with stories. Archeologists think the mugs, or outdoor cellars, are similar to caves discovered nearby, carbon tested to circa 900 B.C.

Harlan, a selectman and retired school principal, has lived in town for over 40 years. Joan, a native, is a massage therapist (right here, if you'd like). They share good hints for interesting back roads to area attractions.

In residence: Sherman, "a large, friendly black-and-white long-haired cat."
Bed and bath: Two rooms. A first-floor room with king/twins option has an adjoining bath, wide board floors, exposed beams. Second-floor room with heirloom double bed is next to full bath (shared with hosts). Nonworking fireplace in each room. Cot available.
Breakfast: 6:30–9:30 weekdays, Sundays until 10. Coffee for early risers. Menu varies. Often, Harlan's blueberry pancakes with buttermilk and his blueberries. Served with sausages or bacon or French toast made from Joan's sourdough bread. Homemade jams. Unlimited coffee. Hosts usually join you in the sunny dining room overlooking the gardens, or on the deck.
Plus: Refreshments. House and garden tour. Sometimes, opportunities to pick raspberries. Family room with TV and wood-burning stove. Bedroom window fans. Passes to private beach. Outdoor hot/cold shower. Laundry facilities (extra charge).

Nutmeg Bed & Breakfast Agency Host #442
Granby, CT

Location: Rural. Across from 3,400-acre game refuge with trails for riding, cross-country skiing, and birding. Six miles west of Bradley International Airport, 15 miles from Hartford, 20 minutes from I-91. Close to Westminster and Ethel Walker schools and historic Old Newgate Prison.

Reservations: Available year round through Nutmeg Bed & Breakfast Agency, page 5.
Rates: $55 single, $65 double. (Extra for trail rides.) Overnight stabling arranged for horses.

It's about ten years since the hostess, a B&B fan, took her first horseback riding lesson and started collecting country antiques. Four years ago, when she spotted the huge barn on the property with this 1930s fieldstone house, she knew she had found the perfect place "in a great small community" for combining all of her interests. Here she shares the ambiance of that community with "B&B for you and your horses"; hospitality—even brunch for small wedding parties or reservations for three-hour canoe trips; restaurant menus—"I love to eat"; and trail rides for adults. Every antique is for sale. "If you buy one, I'll replace it with another."

The living room has a cathedral ceiling and floor-to-ceiling stone fireplace. The hostess, a computer salesperson (also), welcomes first-timers and some who now "come for an annual pilgrimage."

In residence: One outdoor cat. Six horses.
Bed and bath: Three bedrooms in private guest wing. Separate exterior entrance for two rooms (one is queen and one is double) across from one another, one full bath plus access to main house full bath also, and sitting room with TV, desk, and double futon. On lower level, with private entrance,

(Please turn page.)

large room with twin beds, double sleep sofa, wood stove, TV, half bath, shared full bath in main house area.

Breakfast: 7–9:30. Fruit, cereal, homemade muffins, popovers, homemade jams, juice, coffee, tea, milk.

Plus: Afternoon beverage, cheese and crackers. Turndown service. Mint on pillow. Picnic lunches prepared.

The Stephen Potwine House   203/623-8722

84 Scantic Road, East Windsor, CT 06088

Hosts: Bob and Vangy Cathcart
Location: Between Hartford, Connecticut, and Springfield, Massachusetts, five minutes from I-91, on a country road with farms and animals. Overlooks a pond, sweeping lawn, willow trees. Adjoins 100 acres of undeveloped state property. Near cider mills, antiques shops, dinner theater.
Open: Year round. Reservations required.

Rates: Main house room—$65 single, $75 double. Guest wing—$35–$50 single with shared bath depending on bed size. $10 more with private bath. $55 double with shared bath. $95–$135 suite (two or three bedrooms, sitting room, private bath).
♥ ✕ ⅋

Weddings have been held by the pond. Some honeymooners have opened their presents in the living room. Other travelers return for rest and renewal weekends scheduled periodically by Vangy, a career and stress-management counselor who teaches yoga. Her career switch, from retailing and fashion, coincided with empty-nest time. Husband and cohost (and chef) Bob is an insurance sales manager.

The homestead, built in 1831 for Stephen Potwine and occupied by Potwine family members until 23 years ago, is the Cathcarts' sixth restoration. (Others have been in Rochester, New York, and in Hartford and Boston.) In 1986 Vangy stenciled walls, curtains, and "charming crooked floors." She repaired Grandmother's crocheted bedspreads, hung family portraits, and arranged country collectibles. And one Mrs. Potwine, a 91-year-old East Windsor resident, came to tea.

From Virginia: *"We were treated like friends in a beautiful home and peaceful setting."*

In residence: Chaun-see, "a very friendly Himalayan cat who is not allowed in guest quarters."
Bed and bath: Four second-floor rooms. One in main house has queen bed, air conditioning, nonworking fireplace, private full bath with Jacuzzi. In guest wing, reached through carriage house, two double-bedded rooms (one is air conditioned) and one with a twin bed share a full bath with claw-foot tub. Suite option includes sitting room.
Breakfast: 7–9. Garnished with Vangy's herbs. Juices, eggs, granola, cereal, cottage cheese, homemade muffins, bagels, English muffins. "Healthy eating encouraged!" Served in keeping room with working fireplace or on screened porch.

Plus: Picnic table, canoe, TV, VCR. Cross-country skiing, ice skating, and fishing right here.

Butternut Farm 203/633-7197

1654 Main Street, Glastonbury, CT 06033-2962

Host: Donald Reid
Location: On two wooded and land-scaped acres. "Within 90 minutes of most of Connecticut." Ten minutes from Hartford by expressway; 1.6 miles south of Glastonbury Center to Whapley Road. Enter by first hole in the bushes on left, and "don't run over the chickens, please."
Open: Year round.
Rates: $65 room. $74 suite. $83 apartment. AMEX, MC, VISA.
♥ ♠ ⁂ ✗ ✂

Don restored this 1720 center entrance architectural gem with its eight wide fireplaces, pumpkin pine floors, and paneled walls while he was a banker. (Then he was a schoolteacher for seven years.) Along the way, in the 1970s, he was asked to accommodate a neighbor's guests. Ever since, he has been sharing his home with travelers—including famous chefs.

Everywhere you look, there's an 18th-century treasure—a cherry high-boy, a gateleg table, banister-back chairs, and English Delft, in addition to hand-hammered hinges, exposed beams, and 12-over-12 windows. Outside, there are tulips in the spring, herb gardens, and Adirondack chairs on a stone patio. And those animals. All appreciated by "lovely people from all over the world."

In residence: "Abyssinian cats Chester, Rupert, and Millie crave attention." Fifteen goats with names, 50 pigeons without names, 50 chickens "with eggs!"
Foreign languages spoken: French, some German and Italian.
Bed and bath: Two rooms; one with two twin "hired man's" beds and one with a canopied double bed share two full baths. Two suites—one with a four-poster double, private full bath; one with double sofa bed, shower bath, private entrance. Barn apartment has canopied double bed, full bath, kitchen, private garden.
Breakfast: Usually 8:30; flexible for business travelers. Juice and fruit. Fresh-from-the-barn eggs and milk. Toast. Homemade jam. Cheeses. Coffee, tea. Don serves in intimate breakfast room or in early 18th-century dining room.
Plus: Air conditioning. Individual thermostats. Private phone and TV in some rooms. Late-afternoon wine or soft drinks. Robes. Guest refrigerator. Apples. Sherry in rooms. Several common rooms.

---

*I*s B&B like a hotel?
How many times have you hugged the doorman?

Hidden Meadow

203/434-8360

40 Blood Street, Lyme, CT 06371

Hosts: Karen and Jim Brossard
Location: In a quiet country area, good for walking. Near antiques shops, fine restaurants. Three miles to Old Lyme village, 15 minutes to Essex, within half hour of Mystic, Stonington, state beaches.

Open: Year round. Two-night minimum on holiday weekends and during fall foliage.
Rates: Per room. $90–$110 king, queen, or twin beds.
🛏️ ❄️ ✕ ✔️

There's even room to stable your horse here on the property. The house began in 1760; additions were made by well-known Lyme residents, a Broadway actor, and an author who specialized in New England historic houses and barns. The changes in the 1930s resulted in a colonial with Georgian entry, circular driveway, multiple stone terraces, iron railings, and reflecting pool. And there are lawns, gardens, stately trees, a small orchard, two horse barns (tours given), and other small buildings.

Jim, a marketing/advertising executive and professional old-house renovator, and Karen, a U.S. Pony Clubs riding instructor (and tennis player), have lived here since 1986. They started B&B in 1991 by "spoiling guests," using china, silver, and linens in a fireplaced dining room decorated with antiques, chintzes, and still-life paintings. They mark maps and give touring suggestions—all to appreciative "new friends."

In residence: In hosts' quarters, Kate age 13. One dog, Nutmeg, is "our hostess with the mostest." Dusty, a Labrador, enjoys wading in the reflecting pool. Four horses.
Foreign language spoken: French—a little by Karen, fluently by daughters Lucie, Anne, and Nancy, college students who visit frequently.
Bed and bath: Three second-floor rooms, attached private full baths. Two could be a suite: one with king bed and fireplace, one with twin four-poster beds/king option and sitting area. One with queen bed.
Breakfast: 8:30–10. Fresh fruit, homemade breads, muffins. Brandy French toast; farm-fresh eggs; country sausage or bacon; blueberry pancakes; walnut waffles. In dining room or on covered terrace.
Plus: Tea, sherry, or lemonade. Homemade cookies. Living room with fireplace and beehive oven. Library. Help yourself to raspberry crop (in July). Turndown service. Fresh flowers. Thick towels. Mints. Window fans.

KEY TO SYMBOLS
♥ Lots of honeymooners come here.
🛏️ Families with children are very welcome. (Please see page xiii.)
🛏️ "Please emphasize that we are a private home, not an inn."
❄️ Groups or private parties sometimes book the entire B&B.
♦ Travel agents' commission paid. (Please see page xii.)
✕ Sorry, no guests' pets are allowed.
✔️ No smoking inside *or* no smoking at all, even on porches.

The Fowler House

203/873-8906

P.O. Box 432, Plains Road, Moodus, CT 06469

Hosts: Barbara Ally and Paul Seals
Location: On the Moodus town green. Four miles north of antiques shops, restaurants, shops, Goodspeed Opera House, Gillette Castle. Half hour from Hartford and Wesleyan University; 40 minutes to Mystic Seaport; one mile to Johnsonville.

Open: Year round. Two-night minimum stay on weekends and holidays.
Rates: Double occupancy. Shared bath, $65 weekdays, $70 weekends. Private bath, $75–$85 weekdays, $80–$90 weekends. $10 additional guest. MC, VISA.
✹

The small town "with country warmth and Victorian elegance" attracted these hosts, whose inn is the only Connecticut house in the book *Daughters of Painted Ladies*. Their decor was featured in a *Better Homes & Gardens Decorating Ideas* magazine, and they were a runner-up in a Burlington House "tough window treatment" contest.

Barbara and her husband, Paul, together with another couple, restored— all the way to the top of the turret—the 1890 Victorian, which features six stained glass windows, even a stained glass skylight, hand-carved woodwork, and eight working (coal-burning) fireplaces. Furnishings are period pieces and family antiques. The fireplaced library is carpeted. Oriental rugs are in the living and dining rooms. Some guest rooms have painted and stenciled floors.

Before innkeeping, Barbara was an office manager in Hartford. Paul has his own appliance repair business.

In residence: Ian Ally Seals, age 12. Sophie, the dog, and Fluffy, the cat, are not allowed in guest areas.
Bed and bath: Six large rooms, including one in turret. Four private baths; two full, two shower only. The first-floor room has a double bed, working fireplace, original light fixture, private adjoining bath with claw-foot tub. Upstairs, queen (brass), double, or two twin four-poster beds. Extra bed available.
Breakfast: 8:30–10. Fruit. Freshly squeezed juice. Home-baked goods with Fowler House jams. Homemade granola. In dining room or, if preferred, in the guest's room.
Plus: Afternoon tea. Turndown service. Chocolates on the pillow. Bedroom window or ceiling fans. Complimentary champagne for special occasions. Guest refrigerator. Wraparound porch. Lawn chairs.

---

*A*ccording to many hosts:
*"Guests come with plans and discover
the joys of porch sitting."*

Nutmeg Bed & Breakfast Agency Host #513

Mystic, CT

Location: On 1½ acres, surrounded by stone walls and fruit trees. Half mile off I-95, along the street that leads into Mystic. Five-minute drive to Mystic Seaport; 20 to Rocky Neck Beach in New London.

Reservations: Year round except Thanksgiving week through Nutmeg Bed & Breakfast Agency, page 5. Two-day minimum for holiday weekends.

Rates: Per room. $90 private bath. $75 semiprivate bath. Third person, $15 adult, $10 child.

Outside there's a Scottish flag, sign of the hospitality offered inside by a Scottish-born hostess and her Connecticut-born husband, a mechanical engineer who is looking forward to becoming a full-time host.

During one of their many trips to Mystic, after having lived all over the country, they chanced upon a FOR SALE sign in front of this rambling 15-room Victorian (with attached barn and outbuildings), which had been meticulously restored two years earlier. The house deed, dated in the mid-1800s with Charles Hancock's signature, hangs in the hall. Was he a relative of John Hancock? Such research is ongoing—as is the search for "just the right antique."

Someday this house, a meeting place for many guests from New York and Boston, may be the setting for a novel. The hostess, a writer, has formed an area writers' workshop.

In residence: One son in his twenties. One dog and two cats.

Foreign language spoken: "A little high school French."

Bed and bath: Five rooms. One first-floor queen-bedded room with working fireplace, private full bath en suite. Upstairs, room with two twins and a daybed and a room with a double bed share a full bath. Room with king bed and another with two twins and a daybed share a shower bath. Rollaway available.

Breakfast: 8:30–9:30. Fruit compote. Eggs, bacon, sausage, muffins or nut breads. Bagels and cream cheese. Served in large, many-windowed dining room or in garden.

Plus: Beverages. Candy. Garden flowers. Bedroom window fans. TV room, books, games, VCR (lots of movies). Chairs under dogwood tree. Sun porch.

Can't find a listing for the community you are going to? Check with a reservation service described at the beginning of this chapter. Through the service, you may be placed (matched) with a welcoming B&B that is near your destination.

Shore Inne
203/536-1180

54 East Shore Road, P.O. Box 3487, Groton Long Point, CT 06340-8040

Hosts: Judy and Harold Hoyland
Location: Overlooking a tranquil harbor, "where the sound of seagulls and the sunrise over the islands are the major attractions." Three beaches within walking distance; one has a diving dock and separate fishing pier. Half mile to area conservation lands for bird-watching and walking. Five miles to Mystic Seaport or Groton, 10 to New London.

Open: April 1 through November 1. Two-night minimum in July and August and on holiday weekends.
Rates: $85 per room in July and August, all Fridays and Saturdays, and three-day holidays. Other times, $60–$85 depending on bath arrangements and ocean view, or single-person rate. MC, VISA.
♥ 🛏 ❊ 🐾 ✄

The setting here gives guests the feeling of being residents rather than tourists. It's a comfortable colonial home, a quiet place, with an interesting origin. Around 1920 vaudeville performers, owners of the summer home next door, had so many guests that they built this as an inn, using beach stones for the fireplace.

Since the Hoylands became, in 1991, the innkeepers of this well-established B&B, they have painted throughout and installed blue carpeting "the same color as the ocean" in most rooms. They have a special appreciation for both the view of the coast—"imagine living with that view all the time!"—and the opportunity to share it with travelers.

Both Judy's and Harold's mothers were innkeepers many years ago. And Judy had innkeeping experience in Vermont and New Hampshire. In addition, she has worked with the Chamber of Commerce in Mystic and New London. Harold has just retired from his position as school counselor.

Bed and bath: Seven second-floor rooms, three with private full bath. Four share two baths. Queen, double, or twins/king beds. Sorry, no cots or cribs available.
Breakfast: 8–9:30. Juice, cereal and bananas, homemade muffins and corn bread, marmalades and jams. Coffee, tea, cocoa.
Plus: Air-conditioned dining room. Bedroom window fans. Guest refrigerator. Down quilts. Fresh flowers from Judy's garden. Fireplaced living room. TV in sun porch/library. Lawn chairs. Picnic table. Fitness walking/biking trail nearby.

Applewood Farms Inn
203/536-2022

528 Colonel Ledyard Highway, Ledyard, CT 05339-1608

Hosts: Frankie and Tom Betz
Location: On 33 acres. A colonial farm surrounded by stone walls, lawn, and a neighboring farm breeding prize Arabians. Five miles north of Mystic.

Open: Year round. Two-day minimum on weekends.
Rates: Double occupancy. $65–$95. $25 third person in room. MC, VISA (but check or cash preferred).
♥ ❊ ♦

(Please turn page.)

Thank goodness. Thank the Betzes, and many do, for buying this farm, which was considered for condominiums in the 1980s. A guest from New Hampshire dubbed it "a real discovery," one that is now on the National Register of Historic Places. Five generations of Gallups lived in the 1826 house until it became a horse farm in 1964. When the Betzes bought it in 1985, they restored everything. Most walls are simulated whitewash. Stenciling abounds. There are hand-hewn chestnut floor boards. And antiques, primitives, a grandfather clock, and a large pewter collection. Next door there are about 50 horses, and the Betzes have two of their own.

Tom's farming days started at age 11, long before he had a marine electronics business (and a home in Mystic with a greenhouse). Here he wears a cowboy hat, rides a tractor, grows vegetables and roses, and dreams up special Valentine's Day arrangements. Tom and Frankie, known for her elderberry jam, are the grandparents of four and share interests in horticulture, birding, and travel.

In residence: Milton, a Hungarian sheepdog.
Bed and bath: Six rooms, four with working fireplaces. Three private baths; one shared bath with oversized shower. Rooms are on second and third floors and have king, canopied four-poster double, or double bed.
Breakfast: 8–10. Juice, tropical fruit dish with sherbet, eggs with bacon and toast. "Other surprises." Hot beverages. Can last as long as two hours.
Plus: Beverages. Air conditioning in some bedrooms. Three common rooms. Parlor baby grand piano. Fruit, mints, seasonal wildflowers. Hiking trails. With advance notice, courtesy car pickup at stations or Groton–New London Airport. "Polite pets welcomed; kennel and stable provided."

The Palmer Inn   203/572-9000

25 Church Street, Noank, CT 06340-3611

Host: Patricia White
Location: In a quiet fishing village, two miles southwest of Mystic. One block to Long Island Sound beach. Within walking distance of tennis, art galleries, and a renowned casual lobster-in-the-rough restaurant.

Open: Year round. Two-night minimum on summer and fall weekends.
Rates: $115–$135 third floor; $125–$165 second floor; $165–$175 room with fireplace.
❄ ✈

"Connecticut's best" in a *Yankee* magazine apple pie contest is also almost famous for two miniature dachshunds, Dickens and Arthur. In their honor one returnee, a Long Island baker, brought cakes shaped like dachshunds and decorated with "authentic" faces.

Pat, a sailor, lives in a Southern plantation–like house located on just an acre of land. It has 30-foot pillars in front and a main hall with 13-foot ceilings, mahogany beams, brass fixtures, and original wallcovering.

Until 1984 Pat was director of a nonprofit agency. Here, surrounded by family heirlooms and antiques, she offers holiday theme weekends, a crackling fire, the evocative sound of a foghorn, a nearby winery, dinner sails, and hot-air ballooning.

In residence: Dickens and Arthur, "real charmers."
Bed and bath: Six (large, some huge) second- and third-floor rooms, some with water views. King, queen, and twin beds available. All private full baths.
Breakfast: 8:30–9:30. Fresh fruit salad. Homemade granola, muffins—especially banana walnut—and breads, jellies, jams. In the Grand Salon, "our parlor."
Plus: Tea or sherry, 4–6. Ceiling fans in all rooms. Library. Games. Fresh flowers year round. Veranda. Bicycles.

Cobble Hill Farm   203/379-0057
Steele Road, New Hartford, CT 06057

Host: Jo McCurdy
Location: On 40 magnificent acres. Two hours from Manhattan and Boston, 20 minutes to Litchfield, 30 to antiques shops on Route 7, 40 to Great Barrington or Lake Waramaug.

Open: May–December. Advance reservations required.
Rates: $75 single. $95 double. $170 suite.
♥ 🏡 ⚶ ✗ ✄

> Guests wrote: *"We felt like we were dreaming. . . . My husband says that the breakfast alone is worth the drive . . . a little piece of paradise."*

A *Country Living* magazine spread featured the old cooperage, now a summer house, and the grounds. Those grounds! Filled with gardens, paths, privacy, and a sense of freedom. No wonder that some guests enjoy a walk, sit by the spring-fed pond, or relax on the patio "where you can hear the chatter of the birds and the rush of the water over the dam."

The McCurdys brought up five children—"I loved that role," Jo says—here in this marvelous 1796 house filled with interesting antiques. When you finally move from the country kitchen cum attached greenhouse (I took many pictures right there), you'll see Jo's decorating skills in beautiful rooms without clutter or formality but with warmth and wonderful themes and colors. When husband Don returns from his business (controlling heat and air conditioning by computers) he, too, enjoys the farm and guests.

In residence: Bingo, a Jack Russell terrier. Buddy, a black Labrador. Horses, chickens, and other barn animals.
Bed and bath: Five very private second-floor rooms; some can be suites. All private baths. One with queen waterbed, shower bath. Four-poster canopied double bed, shower bath. High double bed, tub bath. Room with queen canopied bed and room with twins/king option, full bath.
Breakfast: 9:30. An event. Fresh fruit or baked apple, homemade muffins, bacon and fresh eggs, toast and homemade jam; maybe custard with raspberry sauce, pumpkin bread, raspberry-filled French toast. Juice, coffee, tea. Served by dining-room fireplace, on screened porch, or on flower-filled terrace by pond.
Plus: Swimming in pond. Gather your own breakfast eggs. Fireplaces in guests' living room and library. Bedroom floor fans. Big bath sheets. Teakettle and cookies in room.

Covered Bridge Host #2NH

New Hartford, CT

Location: Secluded. In Litchfield County, near quiet Farmington River village. Thirty minutes from Bradley Airport and Hartford.
Reservations: Year round through Covered Bridge, page 4. Two-night minimum on weekends, three on holidays.

Rates: Suite $95 for two, $150 for four. Canopied bed $85 shared bath, $90 private. King $80 shared bath, $90 private.
 ⚓ ✈

"No one knows each other to begin with. Often we hear laughter in the dining room. People are great. They come for everything from tubing to antiquing to skiing—all in scenic Litchfield County."

When the host retired from the Air Force and the children were grown, the parents looked for a way to stay in this wonderful 15-room Victorian house ("our hobby") with 12-foot ceilings. "Of course the doing over never stops—nor does the collecting of antiques—Victorian, early American, Queen Anne, and Oriental."

Bed and bath: On second floor, a two-room suite (two kings or twin beds) with private full bath plus a canopied double-bedded room and a room with king/twins option sharing a full bath.
Breakfast: Usually before 10. Juices, fresh fruit platter, cereals, homemade muffins, coffee, tea. Served in formal dining room or on one of three porches.
Plus: Welcoming beverage. Fireplaced living room. Sitting room with TV. Sun and open porches overlooking grounds.

Nutmeg Bed & Breakfast Agency #210

New Haven, CT

Location: A quiet neighborhood of late 19th-century homes, one-half block from buses and Yale shuttle. Half mile from Yale's science campus.
Reservations: Year round through Nutmeg Bed & Breakfast Agency,

page 5. Three-day minimum on Yale graduation and parents' weekends.
Rates: Suite, private bath, $90 for 3; $80 double, $70 single. $55 double, $50 single, semi-private bath.
 ⚓ ✈ ✂

In addition to guests who come for nearby Yale University, "many, especially foreign travelers, come to this 'gateway to New England' before going to the coast, to Cape Cod and on up to Maine. They enjoy our symphony, theater, museums, antiques shows, and concerts."

The host is prepared with maps, books about New Haven—many on architecture—and some on New England too. The century-old house is attractively and comfortably furnished.

In residence: Two cats.
Bed and bath: Third-floor suite has room with antique iron double bed, alcove with single bed, private full bath. One second-floor room with brass-and-iron double bed, shared bath.

Breakfast: Fresh fruit salad, baskets of homemade breads and muffins, cereals, coffee, tea, milk. Buffet style, with flowers and linens, in formal dining room.
Plus: *New York Times*. Beverages. Bedroom window or table fans. Front porch. Rear deck overlooks large perennial garden.

Queen Anne Inn

203/447-2600
800/347-8818

265 Williams Street, New London, CT 06320-5721

Hosts: Ray and Julie Rutledge
Location: In a residential neighborhood, one-quarter mile from I-95. Within walking distance of restaurants, Connecticut College, and the Coast Guard Academy. Ten-minute drive to Mystic Seaport, Eugene O'Neill Theater, Nautilus Museum.
Open: Year round. Two-night weekend minimum, May–October.

Rates: Double occupancy. $94–$120 (depending on room size), private bath. $130 with wood-burning fireplace. $150 two-room suite; $200 three-room suite. Single $5 less. Extra person $15. AMEX, Diners, Discover, MC, VISA.
♥ ♣ ♦ ✕ ✄

A restoration award winner. Recognized in 1985 by the New London Landmarks Commission. Among the architectural features in this turreted 1880 Queen Anne Victorian are the many fireplaces, a paneled foyer, intricate oak woodwork, and stained glass windows at the circular landing.

All those details were taken care of by the time Ray and Julie, CPAs, were "looking to buy or redo." While they were both with large firms (communications and international accounting) in San Antonio, Texas, they spent four years traveling and searching. So, here they are, surrounded by Victorian antiques and a collection of nautical artwork—pampering honeymooners, tourists, dignitaries who are visiting the Coast Guard, and visiting professors at Connecticut College.

In residence: "Our two cats and two birds live in our quarters only."
Bed and bath: Eight rooms, including two suites. On three floors. All private baths. Some with wood-burning or freestanding fireplace. Bridal room also has a balcony. Twin/king, queen, and double beds. Several antique four-posters and canopied beds. Rollaway available.
Breakfast: 8:30 and 9:30. Ever-changing menu. Fruit, freshly made breads, muffins. Maybe fruit or vegetable crepes, quiche, apple cinnamon waffles or orange vanilla French toast. Presented at individual tables by fireplace in parlor.
Plus: Jacuzzi on third floor, sign-up basis. Air-conditioned bedrooms. Private phone, desk, TV in some rooms. Fruit. Flowers. Nominal charge for use of nearby pool and health club. High tea at 3, Sundays, late fall–early spring.

B&Bs offer the ultimate concierge service.

The Homestead Inn

203/354-4080

5 Elm Street, New Milford, CT 06776

Hosts: Rolf and Peggy Hammer
Location: In the village center, near village green, shops, restaurants, movie theater.
Open: Year round. Two-night minimum holiday and May–October weekends.

Rates: In the inn, $65–$75 single, $75–$85 double. In motel, $58–$65 single, $65–$75 double. AMEX, Discover, MC, VISA.
♦️ ♦

Unique! This inn, discovered by business travelers as well as vacationers, is really two buildings, an 1850 Victorian house and a neighboring motel.

With restoration experience that included two other older homes over 25 years, here, in 1985, the Hammers refurnished and redecorated using antiques, reproductions, wallpaper, and traditional fabrics. Outside, they planted perennial gardens.

Before becoming an innkeeper, Rolf had been in corporate sales and marketing. Peggy, a physical therapist, has recently completed massage therapy school. Both hosts are experts on hiking trails, scenic drives, wineries, historic sites—"so much in these beautiful Litchfield Hills!"

In residence: Kerley, a golden retriever not allowed in guest rooms.
Bed and bath: All private baths; most are tub and shower. Eight inn rooms on two floors. Rooms have one or two twin beds, one or two double beds, or a double and one twin. Motel rooms have queen, two doubles, or one double and one twin. Rollaway and crib available.
Breakfast: Buffet 8–10 weekends; 6:30–9 weekdays. Fresh fruit, juice, English muffins, cereals, dark bread, coffee cake, yogurts, cheese.
Plus: Air conditioners, telephones, TV in bedrooms. Wicker-furnished porch. Soft drinks and ice in guest refrigerator. Dogs allowed in motel only.

From Massachusetts: *"In all our travels, one of the best for cleanliness, atmosphere and service . . . warm, friendly hosts . . . a successful 'inn' experience!"*

Covered Bridge Host #2NOR

Norfolk, CT

Location: Secluded estate on five acres. Ten-minute walk to town center, Yale School of Music; 20 to Music Mountain, 40 to Tanglewood. Near lakes, antiquing, skiing.
Reservations: Available year round

through Covered Bridge, page 4. Two-night minimum on holiday weekends.
Rates: Queen bed $90–$110. Double bed $85–$100. Suite $125–$150.
♥ 🧺 ⚹ ✈ ✗

A horse and carriage will pick you up under the stone-pillared portico and take you along the circular driveway and the gorgeous grounds to the quiet tree-lined street and a restaurant on the other side of the town green. The hostess, who arranges the garden flowers—iris, peonies, and lilacs—will make

custom bouquets. And lined picnic baskets, co
available to guests in this 1903 colonial reviva

The English country look—throughout—w
ily heirlooms, and auction finds through the
who works in interior design and her husban
painter.

Bed and bath: Two suites plus two rooms. On th
room with king/twins option, sitting room, d
(two-room) bath. On second floor, spacious gar   with double-
bedded room, working fireplace in sitting room, private full bath. Peach room
has queen bed, fireplace, private full bath. Blue room has double bed, private
full bath.

Breakfast: 8:30–11. Full. Maybe omelets or eggs Benedict with bacon or sausage, homemade muffins and breads, fresh fruit and juice. Served in guest rooms.

Plus: Welcoming beverage. Fireplaced living room. Spacious sun porch.
Terrace. Candy. Silver beverage bucket. Robes. In each room, tape player,
radio, (hidden) alarm clock. Special occasions acknowledged.

From New York: *"Don't tell. We want to keep this for ourselves."*

Manor House   203/542-5690

Maple Avenue, P.O. Box 447, Norfolk, CT 06058-0447   **800/488-5690**

Hosts: Diane and Hank Tremblay
Location: On five beautifully landscaped acres, within walking distance of quiet village, historical society, antiquing, Yale chamber music
concerts. On a side street off Route
44. Twenty miles to Tanglewood.
Open: Year round. Two-day minimum on weekends, three-day minimum holiday weekends.

Rates: Double occupancy. $135–
$160 with fireplace. $95–$120 twins
or king bed. $90–$120 queen bed.
$80 double bed. $20 additional person.
Less in March and April. Midweek
discounts. $10 one-night surcharge.
AMEX, MC, VISA.
♥ ❖ ♦ ✈

The hosts, who "spoil their guests with unflappable affability" (*Philadelphia Inquirer*), live in a very large antiques-furnished English Tudor built in 1898 by Charles Spofford, designer of London's underground system. Often dubbed "romantic and elegant," the inn has the original cherry paneling, Tiffany stained glass windows—and, for one guest room, a private elevator. Another baronial-sized guest room has a king-sized lace-canopied bed, a sitting area, a working fireplace, and a balcony. Manor House may also be the only B&B in the world that offers free accommodations with the purchase of a harpsichord.

Beekeeper, gardener, and chef Hank talks about being "a corporate graduate." Until 1985 both hosts (the staff) were executives with a large Connecticut-based insurance company. Their commitment to personalized quality B&Bs carries over to their reservation service (page 4) for other B&Bs in the area.

(Please turn page.)

e: "Mineau is our friendly and affectionate cat."
anguage spoken: French.
d bath: Nine rooms on second and third floors. All with private bath; have shower without tub; one has two-person soaking tub. King, queen, uble, or two twin beds; some rooms with daybed too. Some with private balcony.
Breakfast: Usually 8:30–10. Blueberry pancakes, orange waffles, stuffed French toast or poached eggs with lemon chive sauce. Homemade muffins and Hank's yeast breads; Tremblays' honey; local maple syrup; homegrown vegetables, herbs, and berries; special teas and coffee brewed with spring water. Served in dining room, on porch, or in bed!
Plus: Bedroom ceiling fans. Piano. Library. Collection of 78-rpm records. CDs (most were produced by a guest). Flannel sheets, down comforters, huge bath towels. Those garden flowers. Guest refrigerator. Town lake passes. Christmas sleigh rides. Horse-drawn historic tours. Possible tour of harpsichord builder's studio.

Antiques and Accommodations   203/535-1736

32 Main Street, North Stonington, CT 06359

Hosts: Ann and Tom Gray
Location: In a village center with 18th- and 19th-century homes and a meandering stream (where children fish). Fifteen minutes to Mystic, Stonington, and Watch Hill (Rhode Island) beaches. Four miles to casino opened early 1992.
Open: Year round. Two-night mini-mum on summer and fall weekends.
Rates: Victorian—bath en suite $125–$145 weekends; $95–$110 midweek; private bath off kitchen $95. Cottage—suite $185 weekend night, $125 weekday; room $125 weekend, $95 weekday.
♥ ♯ ❖ ♦ ✖ ✄

"Just wrap it all up!" Wishful thinking expressed by more than one guest when the hosts opened this 1861 Victorian in 1988. Ann and Tom, antiques dealers and appraisers, filled the B&B with 18th- and 19th-century antiques gathered during 15 trips to England. Then they acquired the neighboring 1820 center chimney colonial, their "garden cottage" with stenciled curtains and furnishings and floor-length curtains. Separating the two houses are brick-lined gravel paths and gardens with flowers, raspberries, strawberries, and blackberries. Many international travelers stay at this B&B, which has become known as both a romantic place and perfect (in the cottage) for families.

In residence: Two outdoor cats, Bonnie and Merlin. Britt, a black Labrador.
Foreign language spoken: Elementary German.
Bed and bath: Three rooms and two suites. In Victorian, private baths (one full, one shower only) for two air-conditioned second-floor rooms, each with a canopied double bed. (Plus a single available only as part of a suite.) First-floor room with double four-poster bed and working fireplace shares hosts' full bath. In cottage—a first-floor suite with kitchen, living room, two bedrooms (one is fireplaced), bath; two second-floor double-bedded rooms, private full baths.

Breakfast: 8:30–9:30. Full. Ever-changing menu. Eggs fresh from the chickens next door. Fresh fruits. Juice. Quiches, omelets, French toast with pecans. Homemade muffins and jams. By candlelight. With classical music.
Plus: Complimentary sherry. Plant-filled porch. Courier service for touring shops. Fresh flowers (wild ones in season). In cottage, crib, high chairs, toys. Sometimes, babysitting.

Helen and Donald Janse   203/434-7269
11 Flat Rock Hill Road, Old Lyme, CT 06371-1503

Hosts: Helen and Donald Janse
Location: On a quiet country road lined with stone walls and old maple trees. Ten minutes from I-95. Twenty minutes from Goodspeed Opera House, half hour west of Mystic Seaport.

Open: Year round. Reservations suggested.
Rates: $60 single. $75 double. $15 rollaway for third person. AMEX, MC, VISA.
♥ ⬛ ♦ ✈

The first guests came here as overflow from the local inn. Built just 18 years ago, the Williamsburg-style saltbox was designed for world travelers and antiques collectors who were retiring. Since the Janses purchased the wonderful property 14 years ago, they have not only maintained the parklike acre but developed extensive gardens that have become the basis for mail-order marketing of their own crafts, foods, and how-to books. "Wreath making is our most popular one." They also have a shop in the garage with their own items, such as ornaments, preserves, and wood products.

Inside there's an unhurried gracious atmosphere with artwork everywhere, Orientals, and antiques. Don recently retired as director of cadet musical activities at the Coast Guard Academy. He now teaches music and drama, part time, at Fishers Island School. He is a poet and a published composer. Helen, how-to book coauthor, is a retired executive secretary of Kodak and IBM.

In residence: Both hosts smoke. Twinkle, "a blond cocker, gentle, friendly, affectionate."
Bed and bath: One room with double bed, adjoining private full bath. Four windows provide views of the grounds and adjacent woodlands. Rollaway available.
Breakfast: Juice or seasonal fruit, sausage, ham or bacon, eggs, toast, freshly baked muffins and homemade jams, coffee. Served in dining room or on the porch or patio.
Plus: Air conditioning throughout. Beverages. Fireplaced living room. Library/den. Fresh bouquets. Garden tour. Annotated list of restaurants (reservations made) and sightseeing attractions.

*T*o *tip or not?*
(Please turn to page xii.)

Clark Cottage at Wintergreen   203/928-5741
354 Pomfret Street, Pomfret Center, CT 06259

Hosts: Doris and Stan Geary
Location: Quiet. On parklike grounds in this semirural New England town. Set way back from Routes 44 and 169, a half mile south of Pomfret School and Rectory School. Thirty minutes to Sturbridge Village, Worcester, Providence; 45 to Hartford, New London, and Mystic Seaport. Six minutes to Golden Lamb Restaurant; necessary advance reservations (months, sometimes) made by Gearys.
Open: Year round.
Rates: Double occupancy. Private bath $65, with fireplace $70. Shared bath $60. MC, VISA.
♥ ✈

Four acres of rolling lawns and extensive oft-photographed gardens surround the 18-room house, once part of the 1,000-acre Clark estate. Although many guests come for the area private schools, the hosts of this B&B, an 1885 Victorian with six fireplaces and five porches, introduce other travelers, including antiques dealers and those looking for a getaway, to an unspoiled area—a place with marvelous old homes, lots of open space, and wonderful valley views.

Stan, an Oyster Bay, Long Island, native and sailor (now business manager at Rectory School), was in business in New York and in other Connecticut towns before he and Doris moved here seven years ago. The grandparents of five have been restoring the house "room by room." Furnishings include 18th- and early 19th-century antiques.

> Guests wrote: *"I would go out of my way to stay in this place . . . very private setting . . . wonderful breakfasts . . . lovingly restored . . . immaculately maintained . . . amicable hosts . . . good directions to Brimfield . . . felt at home."*

Bed and bath: Four large second-floor rooms. One with Italian antique queen bed, working fireplace, private adjoining shower bath. One with queen, hall shower bath. One with two twin beds, working fireplace, hall full bath. One with queen brass bed, nonworking fireplace, private bath. Rollaway available.
Breakfast: Until 9. Fresh fruit. Freshly baked bread or muffins. Pancakes, stuffed French toast, omelets, or bacon and eggs. In breakfast or dining room, or on screened porch.
Plus: Air-conditioned bedrooms. Ceiling fans. Desk, private phone, and (in three rooms) TV. Tea, wine, or cocktails. Down comforters, flannel sheets. Robes. Fresh fruit. Turndown service. Guest refrigerator. Garden flowers. Adirondack chairs. Spectacular sunsets.

The tradition of paying to stay in a private home—with breakfast included in the overnight lodging rate—was revived in time to save wonderful old houses, schools, churches, and barns all over country from the wrecking ball or commercial development.

The Croft

203/342-1856

7 Penny Corner Road, Portland, CT 06480-1624

Host: Elaine Hinze
Location: On a residential street in a rural community. On four acres with open fields, barns, and gardens. Three miles to Wesleyan University on the other side of Connecticut River; 20 minutes to Hartford; 40 to beaches. Within 30 minutes of Goodspeed Opera House, Valley Railroad (steam train).

Open: Year round. Reservations required.
Rates: Larger suite, one bedroom, $75 double, $60 single; two bedrooms, $85 two people, $105 three people. Smaller suite, $55 double, $45 single, $15 rollaway or trundle.

Although Wesleyan is a major draw, Elaine's guests come to stay in this old shipbuilding and quarrying (brownstone) town. "They relax on the grounds, take day trips, and come 'home' to their own comfortable quarters."

Elaine, "a gentlewoman farmer" who is an administrative assistant at Wesleyan, redid—from insulating to tiling and stenciling—her low-ceilinged Federal colonial. Built in 1822 as the first house on the street, it has had many changes and additions, including a small solar greenhouse "where I keep my rose geraniums going from cuttings." She grows her own herbs and bay (for bay leaves) and has an extensive perennial flower garden on the property that winds behind the neighboring houses. And many of her guests seem to enjoy gathering eggs.

In residence: Amy, college-age daughter, during vacations. Corigan is a sable collie. Ten chickens.
Bed and bath: The entire second floor: two suites with private exterior entrances. Larger suite has one room with double bed, one with twin bed, sitting/dining room, kitchen with microwave, full bath. Other suite has double bed, dining nook, private shower bath. Trundle bed and portacrib available.
Breakfast: In your own quarters. In larger suite, stocked refrigerator. Juice. Bagels, sweet buns, English or homemade muffins, breads. Cream cheese, jams. Eggs and Canadian bacon. Tea, milk, coffee, herbal teas. In smaller suite, tray with juice, fruit, heated sweet breads or muffins, cereals, coffee and teas.
Plus: A good area orientation. Refrigerator, private telephone, and TV in each suite. Down or polyester pillows. Flannel sheets. Hair dryer. Setups provided. Window fans. Off-street parking.

> From South Africa: *"Extremely convenient to Wesleyan. . . . We felt like we were going into our own home . . . totally private."*

The Felshaw Tavern

203/928-3467

Five Mile River Road, Putnam, CT 06260-3104

Hosts: Herb and Terry Kinsman
Location: In rural country known as "Connecticut's quiet corner." On Route 21, 3½ miles from Putnam, 1½ miles from Route 395, 2 miles from Route 44. Sturbridge is 30 miles away; Mystic, 50; Boston, 65. Within 10 minutes of Pomfret, Rectory, and Marianapolis schools.
Open: Year round.
Rates: $75 per room, includes tax.

The magnificent restoration is worth a thousand pictures. Still, it is the hospitality that is remembered by business people, honeymooners, travel writers, many poets . . . and at least one young man who subsequently booked a weekend for his parents.

Thanks to an *Antiques* magazine advertisement, the Kinsmans found this center chimney colonial with five working fireplaces. Built in 1742 as a tavern, it had seen many changes by 1979, when Terry and Herb, after 30 years in Los Angeles, "fled east."

The hosts greet you on the granite steps at the handsome mahogany raised-panel front door made by Herb. Among the many rooms in the large, gracious home furnished with fine antiques is the Keeping Room with beehive oven. The skylit breakfast room, the English oak-paneled study, and the recently completed 28-by-17-foot "library/music room/run-away-from-the-world room with leaded and stained glass, French doors, and a Palladian window" are also Herb's creations. And it is hard for the untrained eye to tell that his slant-front mahogany desk or black walnut lowboy are reproductions. On the grounds there's a stone wall, a pergola leading to an enclosed gazebo, and a high fence with perfectly scaled finials.

What a setting for Terry to write copy for classical record liner notes! What a setting "for rediscovering oneself and each other"—and the Kinsmans with their global concerns.

Bed and bath: Two very large second-floor rooms, each with queen four-poster bed, sitting area, working fireplace, private bath. One full bath; one shower bath.
Breakfast: Full. Served at guests' convenience (within reason!) in breakfast room overlooking meadow and woods. Perhaps eggs scrambled with cheese, beef sausages, homemade muffins, coffee or tea.
Plus: Welcoming beverage. Books, periodicals, and TV. Tour of house. If you'd like, Herb's expertise, backed by examples of pitfalls and experiences. Suggestions for tour routes by foot, bicycle, or car, for a lake in Woodstock or an historic home in Canterbury.

Innkeepers are sharers. One recalls the guest who arrived for a wedding only to find he'd left his dress pants at home. The innkeeper wore the same size. The guest appeared at the wedding properly dressed in borrowed pants.

Thurber House

203/928-6776

78 Liberty Way, Putnam, CT 06260-3113

Hosts: Betty and George Zimmermann
Location: Rural and quiet. On a hill overlooking the village common and white spired church. Good cycling and hiking area. Ten minutes to Putnam and Pomfret, 30 to Worcester, 45 to Sturbridge.

Open: Year round.
Rates: Per room. $75 private bath, $65 shared bath. Tax included.
🐾 ✖️

Some extraordinary sunsets are enjoyed from the back porch of this handsome Federal colonial house—but the Zimmermanns haven't forgotten the guests who tarried so long watching the celestial performance that they were late for the wedding that brought them to town.

"The Kinsmans of Felshaw Tavern [page 28] suggested that we would like hosting, and they were correct. Many come for area private schools, to enjoy the countryside, Sturbridge Village and antiquing."

Originally a summer place built in the early 1800s for artist T. J. Thurber's family, the house became a year-round residence around 1870. Twenty-five years ago, the hosts bought it—in need of complete restoration. Throughout there are fine antiques, Oriental rugs, drapes and swags on the windows, and many Thurber paintings. And the porch overlooks gardens and long vistas, as well as many a long-remembered sunset.

In residence: Elsie, the cat.
Bed and bath: Two second-floor rooms with working fireplaces. Larger room with two twin four-poster beds. One room with double four-poster. Baths are private or, sometimes, shared.
Breakfast: 7–9. Fresh fruit, juice, "and a hearty main dish and home-baked goods." In semiformal dining room; sometimes on porch.
Plus: Piano. Bicycles for guests' use. Window fans. Usually, afternoon hot or cold drink, evening wine, cheese and crackers.

> From Louisiana: *"Warm, accommodating hosts . . . immaculate and comfortable house . . . fabulous food."*

Nutmeg Bed & Breakfast Agency Host #324

Salisbury, CT

Location: Rural, with lake frontage; three minutes' drive to launch area, eight to swimming. On 36 acres in Berkshire foothills. Tanglewood, 45 minutes; Catamount and Butternut ski areas, 12 miles; half hour to Music Mountain, Norfolk, and Yale Music Festival; 15 minutes to Lime Rock Park racetrack. Two hours northwest of Manhattan.

Reservations: Year round through Nutmeg Bed & Breakfast Agency, page 5. Two-night minimum preferred on weekends and holidays.
Rates: Double occupancy. $85 semiprivate bath. $130–$150 private bath.
🐾 ✖️ 🍴

(Please turn page.)

"There's something compelling about the land in this area," said the host, a writer who covers a wide range of topics—from taxes to art. Before opening the B&B, this Ohioan's jobs included one that took her to 48 states.

The wonderful house, furnished with English, German, and American antiques, is a 1780s Federal with an 1830s Georgian/Victorian addition. The front door, framed by leaded glass fan and side lights, has the original key and bolt. And then there's that land—with the lake, the sheep in the pasture, and the blooms in the gardens.

In residence: One dog, a midsize (45-pound) Australian shepherd.
Bed and bath: A variable combination of five rooms; some overlook gardens and lake. Option of private or semiprivate bath. Suite arrangement; queen, double, or twin beds.
Breakfast: 8:30–9:30. Fruit, coffee, toast and muffins or croissants, cereals. Served under chandelier in fireplaced dining room.
Plus: Down pillows. Blankets woven of wool from host's sheep. Screened porch. Fireplaced library. Picnic baskets.

Yesterday's Yankee   203/435-9539

Route 44 East, P.O. Box 442, Salisbury, CT 06058

Hosts: Doris and Dick Alexander
Location: On the edge of a colonial village in Berkshires foothills. Forty minutes' drive to Tanglewood. Near antiques shops, fine restaurants, outdoor activities, old cemeteries, and historic sites.
Open: Year round. Two-night weekend minimum on weekends, Memorial Day–October 31.

Rates: $65 smaller queen room; $70 large. $70 twin beds. $75 king. $20 rollaway. Seventh consecutive night free. Ten percent less for three-night midweek (Sunday–Thursday) and for senior citizens midweek (no minimum stay). AMEX, MC, VISA.
♥ ❖ ◆

From New York: *"I wish I could stay on, permanently! . . . Dick and Doris make everyone feel so comfortable . . . everything, every detail, is 'right' . . . a peaceful atmosphere . . . delicious breakfasts . . . an extensive library . . . interesting conversations about Early American antiques . . . help with travel plans. If I were an artist I would love to capture the lilac at the front door, the herb garden (fresh breakfast garnishes), the large, old trees, the flower beds."*

Dick, who restores and builds fine furniture, and Doris, a calligrapher who taught junior high English, have lived in town for 28 years. They're volunteers with the library, the travel commission, Dial-a-Ride, the local historic home. Seven years ago they restored this treasure and started B&B. The only original (1744) Cape Cod-style home in Salisbury, it has wide board floors, whitewashed walls, small-paned windows. Throughout there are collections—many antiques, books, silhouettes, and mirrors. Braided rugs are in the guest rooms. And the acclaimed hosts may offer a suggestion for a private spot with panoramic sunset view.

Bed and bath: Three second-floor rooms share one full modern bath. One with queen bed. One with queen and rocking chairs in sitting area. One with twins/king and rocking chairs in sitting area.
Breakfast: 6–9. "Prepared with an eye toward healthful living." Four courses may include juice without added sugar, peach soup, figs with lime cream, 20-grain porridge, homemade granola, Norwegian "munka," fresh herb omelet, French toast, ham and apple bake, homemade breads. Dick serves by the 250-year-old fireplace in the keeping room.
Plus: Air-conditioned bedrooms. Thick towels. Robes. Fruit, cheese, candy. Bocci court. Lawn croquet. "Games and books galore."

The Old Mill Inn

203/763-1473

63 Maple Street, Somersville, CT 06072-0443

Hosts: Ralph and Phyllis Lumb
Location: On a main street, surrounded by lawns, huge sugar maple trees, shrubs, and flowers. Two houses past waterfall and Old Mill, now being renovated for retail shops and condominiums. Minutes from I-91, between Hartford, Connecticut, and Springfield, Massachusetts.
Open: Year round.
Rates: $50 single or double, shared bath; $55.55 with private bath. $15 rollaway.

Pure enjoyment for guests and hosts alike. Guests write about the immaculate inn, where iced tea is available in the summer and windshields are cleared in the winter: "The Lumbs provide newspapers, maps, make dinner and theater reservations, take messages . . . remarkable hospitality." The hosts remember "great people who come for a getaway, for graduation, weddings, while en route to visit relatives. . . ."

In this 1850 Greek Revival, which has had several renovations and additions, the president of the mill raised 7 children. The Lumbs, grandparents to 11, transferred their professions from Virginia to this location in 1986. Ralph is a nuclear fuel consultant; Phyllis, an out-of-print book dealer.

Bed and bath: In guest wing, four second-floor rooms, each with ceiling fan and air conditioner. Option of shared or private full bath. Three double-bedded rooms. One with two twin beds. Rollaway and crib available.
Breakfast: Generally 7–9. Juices, fruit, cereals, Danish, toast, donuts, jelly and jams, coffee, tea, milk. Served at tables set for two, four, or eight in dining room that has hand-painted murals and a windowed wall overlooking the terrace.
Plus: Fireplaced living room. Sitting room on each floor with desk and stationery. Guest refrigerator. Cable TV. Stereo. Front porch. Terrace. Mints. Flowers.

Innkeeping may be America's most envied profession. As one host mused, "Where else can you get a job where, every day, someone tells you how wonderful you are?"

Chaffee's B&B   203/628-2750

28 Reussner Road, Southington, CT 06489-3310

Hosts: Milton and Kay Chaffee
Location: In a quiet residential area, two miles from I-84. Ten minutes from the Mount Southington (downhill) ski area and 15 from Lake Compounce Festival Park. Minutes from four large Southington apple orchards.
Open: Year round except Christmas. Reservations preferred.
Rates: $40 single, $50 double.
✈ ✄

According to Milt and Kay, they used my first B&B book for their own travels, then came home and observed that the Southington area was lacking in personalized accommodations. Their family is grown, and Kay enjoys crafts, cooking and baking. Milt, a retired banker, has been an active amateur radio operator for over half a century. Since 1985 they have been offering a relaxed environment in their six-room colonial ranch house located in an area that is "s-o-o quiet."

Bed and bath: Room on first floor with two twin beds, private full bath.
Breakfast: Usually about 8:30. Juice, fruits, eggs any style, cereal, and Kay's specialty, muffins. Served in dining room overlooking the large yard, or on screened porch. Hosts join guests.
Plus: Central air conditioning. Hosts' living room with books, organ, cable television.

> From Maryland: *"More than a place to stay. . . . From the moment we walked into their home, Milt and Kay made us feel welcomed . . . concern for guests showed in the many conveniences provided in our large, private room and bath."*

Storrs Farmhouse on the Hill   203/429-1400

418 Gurleyville Road, Storrs, CT 06268

Hosts: William and Elaine Kollet
Location: Rural. Less than 2 miles to University of Connecticut campus, 7 miles to Caprilands Herb Farm, 15 to Sturbridge Village.
Open: February–December. Advance reservations required.
Rates: $35 single. $55 double. $15 rollaway or crib.

Although many guests come with a planned agenda, this is a place where you may help feed the sheep (whose wool has been woven into guests' blankets), feed chickens, and collect eggs. The Kollets, grandparents of six, feel that they could fill a book with stories about memorable guests who have come from all over the world. One who stayed here during a sabbatical wrote, "Warmth, care and love are what the Kollets offer."

Elaine, a hotel and food management graduate and a former town council and zoning board member, and Bill, a retired insurance company electrical engineer, built most of their center chimney Cape farmhouse 18 years ago. (As a youngster, Elaine learned from her father about carpentry, bricklaying, and tiling.) They furnished with some antiques, a grandmother clock, and Oriental rugs. One room has huge tropical plants hanging from a half-glassed roof and many windows that look out on sheep pastures and flower gardens—and, in the spring, bluebirds.

In residence: Chables, a golden retriever. Seventeen Columbian sheep.
Bed and bath: Four large rooms. All private baths (some full, some shower only). Two double-bedded rooms on first floor. On second, one room with two twin beds, one with double bed.
Breakfast: 7–9. Almost-famous muffins. Fresh eggs. Cereals. Fruit. Plenty of coffee or tea. Served in "white and bright" kitchen, on sun porch, or in dining room. High chair available.
Plus: Wool mattress pads. Flannel sheets in winter. Guest refrigerator. Coffee and tea almost anytime. Loan of bicycles and canoe. Greenhouse exercise room with hot tub, exercise equipment, plants.

> From New York: *"Great! Comfortable. Immaculate. Friendly. Breakfast included the best muffins I have ever had."*

The Tolland Inn   203/872-0800

P.O. Box 717, 63 Tolland Green, Tolland, CT 06084-0717

Hosts: Susan and Stephen Beeching
Location: Facing the village green. Three minutes from I-84. Steps from country store and genealogical library. Seven miles to University of Connecticut, 20 to Hartford and Old Sturbridge Village, 22 to vineyard, 6 to Caprilands Herb Farm.
Open: Year round. Two-day mini-mum stay on some key spring and fall weekends.
Rates: $50 double, shared bath; $60 private bath. $40 single, shared bath; $50 private bath. Suite $90 with use of kitchen, $70 without. AMEX, MC, VISA.
♦ ✈ ✂

A perfect match. Susan, a teacher of special education, is a third-generation innkeeper, with experience at a family guest house on her native Nantucket Island. Steve, a designer and maker of custom fine furniture—using, primarily, American hardwoods—has examples of his work throughout the inn. And he is happy to show commissions in progress to guests.

When the Beechings moved from Boston in 1985, they bought The Steele House, known for its lodging accommodations from the 1800s until 1959, the year it was sold as a private home to its last registered guests. They renovated and refurbished and renamed the white clapboard inn. One guest wrote in detail about the peaceful ambiance, the menu, and the tour of Steve's workshop, then concluded, "I was totally enchanted."

The hosts find time to do some antiquing and to volunteer at a soup kitchen.

Bed and bath: Seven rooms, five private baths. On first floor, double bed, shower bath, strobe fire alarm for the hearing impaired. Upstairs, two double-bedded rooms; one with "an amazing curved wall" and one with exposed-beamed ceiling share a full hall bath. Room with two twin beds, beamed ceiling, private shower bath. One with a high handmade double bed, one with brass double bed; each with private shower bath. Two-room suite

(Please turn page.)

overlooks gardens; double bed, full kitchen, sitting area, private shower bath, Rollaway available.

Breakfast: 8–10. "Susan's fabulous orange rolls." Juices, seasonal fruit, muffins, breakfast cakes. Inn-made jams include grape made with inn's arbor fruit. Brewed coffees; tea. Served at trestle dining room table or on wicker-furnished sun porch.

Plus: "Books everywhere—for readers of any sort." Classical music. Beverages.

House on the Hill

92 Woodlawn Terrace
Waterbury, CT 07810-1929

203/757-9901
800/348-HOUSE
(4687)

Host: Marianne Vandenburgh
Location: High on a hill in historic residential district. One mile from I-84 and Route 8. Within ten minutes' drive of Teikyo Post University, Westover and Taft schools, Cheshire Academy. Ninety miles from Manhattan, 20 miles from Litchfield.

Open: Year round.
Rates: $65 shared bath. $75 suite; $100 suite with queen bed, fireplace. Romantic dinner, custom-designed menu, presented by fire or on a silver tray in your room; by arrangement only, $150 for two.
♥ ❖ ♦ ✂

This B&B is putting Waterbury on the map. Painted in six colors (the neighbors sent thank-you notes), the 20-room Victorian is surrounded by glorious perennial gardens. Inside, the natural woodwork—mahogany in the library, cherry in the main parlor, oak in the main entrance—has never been painted since the house was built in 1888 by Wallace Camp, a brass manufacturer and inventor.

From the wicker-furnished arched porches (grand for a wedding) all the way to the turret suite, there is a sense of joy. Its creator is Marianne, a Renaissance woman who has an eye for display and color—a home economist/former Soho antiques shop owner and elderly services administrator turned house restorer/caterer/freelance decorator/garden designer/community activist. Throughout, there's an interesting mix of crafts, antiques, and modern pieces. Go and experience. I did, for one night, during a B&B promotion tour. Jane Fonda did, for several weeks, during a filming. *Connecticut* magazine came and produced a cover feature. Business travelers and house hunters also appreciate the welcoming environment.

Bed and bath: Suites. On second floor, canopied double bed, sitting area, tub bath, porch; two double-bedded rooms with full baths can be a suite. On third floor, double bed, full bath, kitchen. Turret suite has queen bed, fireplace, full bath.

Breakfast: Flexible timing. Most frequently requested menu: pancakes (made with cornmeal ground by hand by Marianne's father on his Ohio farm), smoked sausages, homemade four-berry/rhubarb sauce, orange juice, coffee (freshly ground beans) or tea. Prepared in country kitchen, often a gathering place. Served in fireplaced Victorian dining room with built-in curved buffet.

Plus: Refreshments upon arrival. Mints or cookies on pillow. Flannel sheets. Turndown service. Extensive library. Window fans.

The Clarks

203/274-4866

97 Scott Avenue, Watertown, CT 06795-2518

Hosts: Richard and Barbara Clark
Location: One block from the main street in Watertown. Three blocks from the Taft School; within a 10-minute drive of Routes 8 and 84.

Open: Year round except February and July.
Rates: $35 per room.
🏃 🛥

This traditional B&B filled a need. Taft School parents were having difficulty finding accommodations in the area, so the Clarks began hosting in 1983. Since then, others—particularly business people and those "passing through"—have also found the Cape-style home a convenient and comfortable stopping point.

Barbara is a retired elementary school teacher. Richard established his current home-improvement business after retiring from 33 years with Uniroyal. They are both active in community and church activities. As for B&B, "Each guest is different. We have been privileged to meet so many interesting people. It is fun!"

Bed and bath: Two rooms. One large first-floor room with two twin beds, adjoining guest den, private half-bath, separate entrance, large deck. One second-floor double-bedded room. Both share second-floor shower bath with hosts.
Breakfast: 6–8 weekdays, 6–9 weekends. Usually a continental menu, but eggs are also available. Served in the dining room.
Plus: Afternoon or evening beverages. Use of entire house, including kitchen and laundry facilities, front and back porches, barbecue grill.

> From Massachusetts: *"We felt like we were visiting friends and staying in their guest room. For $35 we had a clean bed and bath . . . coffee and Danish. Amazing!"*

Covered Bridge Host #2WC

West Cornwall, CT

Location: On a 64-acre wooded estate with breathtaking views of mountains and valley. Three miles to Marvelwood School; about 10 to Hotchkiss, Kent, Salisbury, and South Kent schools; 1½ miles from historic covered bridge, unspoiled village, antiquing, and restaurants—including one with deck overlooking a "delightfully noisy (babbling)" brook.
Reservations: Available year round through Covered Bridge, page 4. Two-night minimum on holiday and fall weekends.
Rates: $95 per room.
♥ ✈ ✂

First there's the 200-degree, 75-mile all-the-way-to-the-Catskills view. One-nighters have been known to take a look and ask to stay for a week. The setting is complete with a sharp drop, amidst pine, hemlock, oak, ash, birch, hickory, and walnut trees—and wild turkeys too. Then there's that stone (inside and out) library, built in 1930 by the host's father, who traveled extensively and lived in China for several years. And all the wonderful

(Please turn page.)

antiques, rugs, and chandeliers collected by the host while he restored large Victorian residences in Washington, D.C. Since making the family homestead his permanent residence seven years ago, this host has become full-time tree surgeon/road repair man/bottle washer/bell captain/butler.

Area residents search for miles around and feel as if they have discovered this place in their own backyard. One couple who came in search of lodging for wedding guests decided that this would be their honeymoon site.

Bed and bath: In a guest wing with private exterior entrance, two double-bedded rooms without a common wall, each with private full bath and air conditioning.
Breakfast: 7–9:30. Freshly squeezed orange juice, freshly ground coffee, Grand Marnier French toast or blueberry pancakes with bacon. By wide stone library fireplace or on 50-foot-long flagstone terrace.
Plus: Living room. Sun room. Lots of books. The terrace with wrought iron furniture—and that compelling vista.

The Cotswold Inn   203/226-3766
76 Myrtle Avenue, Westport, CT 06880

Hosts: Richard Montanaro and Lorna Smith
Location: Not visible from the road but right in town, amidst historic homes. On a small lot surrounded by gardens. Five- minute walk to shops, restaurants, Westport Country Play-house. Five-minute drive to Long Island Sound beach; 75-minute drive from Manhattan.
Open: Year round.
Rates: Per room. $175–$225 depending on size. AMEX, MC, VISA.
♥ ✿ ✈

Pure luxury. In a gabled English cottage that Richard built with authentic materials (wide plank maple floors and used brick for fireplaces) on a vacant lot in 1982. Now it has a guest book filled with well-known names (many of actors who have performed at the Westport Country Playhouse), honeymooners, business travelers, "and plenty who come for and seem to get relaxation."

Considered a sophisticated, elegant version of "country," the intimate inn is furnished with fine reproductions—Chippendale and Queen Anne wing chairs, love seats, and sofas; highboys; four-poster beds. The rooms, "all romantic," were decorated with the help of the Laura Ashley folks in New York and Westport.

Richard, who has lived in the area all his life, has built many large beautiful homes in Westport and New Canaan. Lorna is in marketing research. For peaceful walks, they'll direct you to Devil's Den, a 1,500-acre wildlife sanctuary that has hiking (and cross-country ski) trails.

Bed and bath: Four soundproofed, air-conditioned second-floor rooms, each with individual thermostat, telephone, desk, cable TV, clock radio. All with queen bed (two with canopy), private full bath; one room also has a single sleigh bed and working fireplace.

Breakfast: 8–10:30. Earlier by request. Fresh fruit salad, orange juice, cereals, bagels and pastries, yogurts. In kitchen with sliding doors leading to garden patio. "Can last up to three hours!"
Plus: Flower arrangements everywhere. Specialty soaps and shampoos. Evening cognac and wine. Mints and Godiva chocolates. Access to health facility, two blocks away.

Nutmeg Bed & Breakfast Agency Host #119
Wilton/Ridgefield area, CT

Location: Secluded. In woods overlooking pond, stream, and waterfalls. Near fine restaurants, antiquing, tennis and racquetball, hiking trails. An hour from Manhattan.

Reservations: Available year round through Nutmeg Bed & Breakfast Agency, page 5.
Rates: $90 for two.

Maybe you'll arrive to the romantic scene of candles and kerosene lamp at the end of the path. The Oriental pavilion-like cottage, created from a rustic cabin, was designed by the host with a carpenter friend. Almost hidden from the main house three seasons of the year, it has glass-sided cupolas and a 16-by-24-foot main room with cedar ceiling and oak floor. Glass walls and wide decks overlook a suspension bridge, waterfalls, woods with deer, phlox in the spring, flaming colors in the fall. Furnishings are a blend of contemporary and antiques. The kitchen has a Mexican tile floor and granite counters.

Explore the area or stay right here. The well-traveled hosts, a hospital administrator and a school administrator, know that it's a great place to "just hang out." They are avid gardeners who also enjoy cooking, sports, and photography. Here they have had the fun of seeing newlyweds arrive in bridal clothes. A budding cartoonist who arrived with a unique idea (that, subsequently, he worked on with the host) has returned several times with reports of "close to a contract." And some guests take advantage of the glass-topped private spa room on the property, just up the hill.

Bed and bath: Queen-sized bed plus a double futon, skylit shower bath.
Breakfast: Full. Your choice. Gourmet meal prepared and delivered to you; prepare your own with provided items you've requested; or join hosts in their spectacular kitchen.
Plus: Welcoming beverage. Swimming. Use of float, tennis racquets, bicycles. Hiking trail map. Restaurant discount book.

Can't find a listing for the community you are going to? Check with a reservation service described at the beginning of this chapter. Through the service, you may be placed (matched) with a welcoming B&B that is near your destination.

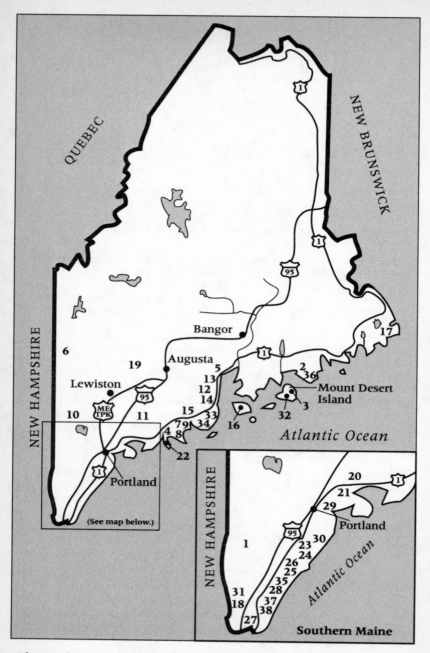

The numbers on this map indicate the locations of B&Bs described in detail in this chapter.

MAINE

KEY TO SYMBOLS
♥ Lots of honeymooners come here.
⚤ Families with children are very welcome. (Please see page xiii.)
⚑ "Please emphasize that we are a private home, not an inn."
♣ Groups or private parties sometimes book the entire B&B.
♦ Travel agents' commission paid. (Please see page xii.)
✶ Sorry, no guests' pets are allowed.
✄ No smoking inside *or* no smoking at all, even on porches.

_____ Maine Reservation Services _____

Bed & Breakfast Down East, Ltd.

Box 547, Macomber Mill Road, Eastbrook, ME 04634

Phone: 207/565-3517, Monday–Friday, 10–5.

Listings: 90 in about 80 communities. "They are all over the state in every possible setting—oceanfront, lakeside, beach, mountain, rural, coastal village, city, suburban, inland village, on working farms, wilderness lodge. . . ." Mostly hosted private residences. A few inns. Directory (45 pages, $4) is organized according to region with full description and detail.

Reservations: Advance notice of three to four weeks preferred, but will try to accommodate last-minute callers. Some hosts—particularly those in resort areas—require two-night minimum weekends, especially during the summer months.

Rates: $40–$70 single. $45–$105 double. Deposit equivalent to one night's stay required. $10 surcharge, July–October 15, for one-night stay. Deposit less $10 processing fee refunded on cancellations with at least two weeks' notice. With less notice, a refund is at the host's discretion. AMEX, MC, VISA.

With a very traditional view of B&B, filled with down-home hospitality, good value, and an opportunity to "meet the locals," Sally Godfrey began her service in 1983. A bit of a phenomenon among B&B services, she personally handles an incredible volume—still knowing all her (varied) hosts. It is very much a full-time commitment, matching travelers with compatible hosts in surroundings of comfort and hospitality.

Plus: Some homes offer babysitting, laundry, or other services. Some will pack lunches. "Most offer the spectacular Maine scenery, clean air, peace and quiet."

Bed & Breakfast of Maine

32 Colonial Village, Falmouth, ME 04105

Phone: 207/781-4528. Live weekday evenings and all day on weekends. Answering machine at other times. Closed December 24–January 2 and during a three-week period in the winter or spring.

Listings: 70 in 27 communities. Most are hosted private residences; three are inns. Located mostly along 250 miles of coast, but few are actually on the waterfront. Some in Portland; some in mountains, near lakes, and on working farms. Directory ($1) is about six pages of descriptions with rates.

Reservations: Two weeks' advance notice suggested; two months' notice for July and August, busy months that also have minimum stay requirements in resort areas.

(Please turn page.)

Rates: $35–$65 single, $45–$150 double. Some weekly rates available. Deposit equal to first night's lodging required in most cases. A few resort places have $5 or $10 one-night surcharge. Cancellations made within one week of reservations receive refund less $10 service charge. MC, VISA.

Peg Tierney observes, "Although each year my list has newcomers, most of the hosts have been with me for four or five years. Nearly all of their homes are 'older' and many are historic. All are inspected, clean, and pretty, and they offer a friendly atmosphere. Most have two or more guest rooms, some with a private bath. And the hearty breakfasts are a trademark. I often assist travelers in planning trips."

Other reservation services with some B&Bs in Maine:
  Bed & Breakfast/Inns of New England, page 257.
  Pineapple Hospitality, page 106.

Maine B&Bs

Clover Hill Farm   207/490-1105
RR 1, Box 241A, Alfred, ME 04002-9758

Hosts: Margit and Leif Nordberg
Location: On 100 acres of hills and
woodland. Two hours from Boston.
Five miles from the village center "in
old Shaker country," 20 to
Kennebunkport. Within 30 minutes
of beaches, fishing, antiquing.
Open: Year round.

Rates: Memorial Day–Columbus
Day/Christmas–New Year, $50 dou-
ble bed, $60 twin beds. $45 single.
$15 extra bed. $10 crib. Off-season
and five-night stay, Sunday–Thursday, 20 percent less. VISA.
♣ ⌂ ❄ ✕ ✁

A Ph.D. physicist and professor of radiology (Margit) and a computer specialist
(Leif) left big-city life (Philadelphia) to start this organic farm. Since buying
the property in 1986, they have "rescued" the huge 1889 dairy barn and have
been joined by another couple, cross-country cyclists, who want to learn to
live off the land. Guests sleep in simple, comfortable, clean rooms; wake up
to the rooster; have a bountiful and healthful breakfast; and, often, take a
tour of the farm with its lambs and chicks, gardens, and young orchard. You
are welcome to hike, cross-country ski, and bird watch right here. Margit is
active in the Baha'i faith. Leif is a volunteer librarian.

Foreign languages spoken: Swedish, Finnish, German, and Spanish.
"French, Korean, and Japanese when daughter and son-in-law are here."
Bed and bath: Three second-floor rooms. Two double-bedded. One
twins/king. Two shared full baths; one nearby, one on first floor (a fair
distance). Crib and rollaway available.
Breakfast: At 8. Eggs, home-baked breads and muffins, berries, jam, mint
tea. Juice, hot cereal, coffee. Served country style in kitchen; eaten at large
dining room table "where sometimes we solve the world's problems."
Plus: Window fans. Fresh flowers. Flannel sheets. Wood stove in dining room.

Green Hill Farm   207/422-3273
RR 1, Box 328, Ashville, ME 04607-9731

Hosts: Ted and Nuna Cass
Location: In a rural coastal community, 17 miles northeast of Ellsworth,
45 minutes to Acadia National Park.
Open: Year round. Advance reservations required October–May.

Rates: $30 room with ¾ bed. $35
twin beds. $5 more mid-May
through mid-October. $5 third per-
son in room.
⌂

Intentionally an informal place, this is a traditional B&B, "sharing our home"
style. Before coming here six years ago, Nuna, a spinner and knitter, worked

(Please turn page.)

as an historic home guide and with a New Hampshire logging museum. Ted, the gardener, originally from Iowa, served in the Merchant Marine and the Peace Corps and was a Spanish teacher. A lantern helps to identify the house for latecomers. Sag-wagon service is provided for cyclists "who misjudge distances or energy."

In residence: Junior, a reasonably friendly black cat. Three sheep. Ted is "a pretty well-trained pipe smoker." (Smoking area restricted.)
Foreign languages spoken: Fluent Spanish and Danish; French and German "on a make-do basis."
Bed and bath: Two second-floor rooms—one with antique ¾ cannonball bed and one with two twin beds—share modern shower bath. Rollaway available in twin room.
Breakfast: Juice or fruit. Hot or cold cereal, eggs, homemade muffins, toast, blueberry/oatmeal pancakes, French toast. In kitchen at table set with flowers.
Plus: Window or floor fans. Tea, coffee, or cocoa. Flannel sheets. Clothes dryer.

> From New York: *"An unpretentious, eclectically furnished Maine farmhouse with charming antiques, old wallpapers, modern plumbing, delicious breakfasts. Perhaps the nicest feature is the Casses themselves . . . feeling of staying with family."*

Black Friar Inn   207/288-5091
10 Summer Street, Bar Harbor, ME 04609

Hosts: Barbara and Jim Kelly
Location: On a quiet in-town street, 1½ blocks from Frenchman's Bay.
Open: May through October. Two-night minimum July 1–Columbus Day.

Rates: Double occupancy. $85–$98 in season; $68–$85 off-season. Singles slightly less. Enroute, MC, VISA. ♥

"A little like the home everybody wishes they had," wrote one guest, who liked "to hang around the kitchen and chat. As a New Yorker, I can't tell you what a balm this was to my soul. . . . Jim and Barbara suggested the hike to Bar Island at low tide. I think they consider themselves permanent tourists." Other guests added comments about the food, the immaculate inn, its convenient location, and the innkeepers (again and again).

As Barbara says, "It seemed natural—after years of traveling throughout Maine and after careers in the textile business—to choose innkeeping (in 1986) when we decided to do something together in a place we really love."

Architectural features from old Bar Harbor mansions were used when this Victorian house was completely rebuilt in the early 1980s. In one room there's a mantel used as a headboard. The pub was a private library. The wicker-furnished sun room has cypress and tin walls that came from a Maine church.

The place to stay has become the reason to go.

Bed and bath: Six queen-bedded rooms on second (Victorian decor) and third (Laura Ashley patterns) floors. One with skylights. All private baths; some down the hall. Pedestal sinks in three rooms.
Breakfast: 8–9:30. Entree could be surprise French toast or Belgian waffles. Baked apples, cereals, eggs or omelets, breakfast meats, cinnamon buns, homemade breads and muffins. Served in sun room.
Plus: Guided kayaking and fly-fishing programs. Ceiling or window fans. Cozy third-floor rear sun deck. Robes for hallway baths. In summer, flowers in rooms and window boxes; afternoon refreshments.

Castlemaine Inn
39 Holland Avenue, Bar Harbor, ME 04609

207/288-4563
800/338-4563

Hosts: Norah O'Brien and Terry O'Connell
Location: On a quiet street, two blocks from waterfront. Five-minute walk to shops and restaurants. One mile from Acadia National Park and Bluenose ferry terminal.
Open: May–October. Two-night minimum July and August and on holiday weekends.

Rates: Double occupancy. $85 or $100 double bed. $105 queen, $115 with fireplace or balcony. $135 two-room suite, canopied queen, fireplace, air conditioning. $25 third person. Less May, June, September, and October. MC, VISA.
♥ ✳ ✄

> Guests wrote: *"Warm, charming, tastefully decorated . . . gives 'eat off the floor' cleanliness new meaning . . . congenial hostess . . . delightful breakfast spread . . . lace curtains . . . personal touches . . . when my wife needed medical care in Bar Harbor, I felt loved and at home in Castlemaine."*

The walk is canopied now that all the major interior changes—including baths and fireplaces—have been made in this rambling Victorian house, which the hosts converted to a B&B in 1981. They knew the area from vacations. When they lived in Ohio, Norah was a teacher. Terry, who worked with a construction company for 20 years, cohosts full time or, when commuting to Chicago, on weekends.

Bed and bath: Ten air-conditioned rooms, most with canopied queen beds, on three floors. All private baths; most have tub and shower. Some rooms with working fireplace and a private balcony. One suite on first floor. Third-floor suite has two bedrooms—one queen, one with two twin beds—and parlor with VCR, balcony, one shower bath, and a half bath.
Breakfast: 8–9:30. Muffins, coffee cake, scones, cereal, homemade bread, fresh fruit bowl, bagels with cream cheese, preserves, cheese, juices, imported teas, gourmet coffee. Buffet in breakfast room with starched Irish linens, in fireplaced parlor, or on veranda.
Plus: Wicker-furnished front porch. TV in each room.

"Guests arrive as strangers, leave as friends."

Graycote Inn

207/288-3044

40 Holland Avenue, Bar Harbor, ME 04609-1432   **800/GRA-COTE**

Hosts: William and Darlene DeMao
Location: On an acre of land on a quiet side street. Two blocks to waterfront. Five-minute walk to village.
Open: May–October. Two-night minimum June 15–October 15.

Rates: Per room, double occupancy. June 15–October 15, $85–$120. May 1–June 15 and after October 15, $75–$95. $20 third person. Singles' discount. MC, VISA.
♥ ⅍

It's a lifestyle that many dream of. In 1986 this was an old-house lover's dream: "We found bundles of ceiling moldings in the basement rafters and oak flooring strips in the attic. An old cupboard was filled with antique lace-trimmed and embroidered linens which we now use."

That was when Bill and Darlene came from Pittsburgh to be in the Bar Harbor they knew from vacations—"with its great hiking possibilities, waterfalls, even a cave." They left their jobs in a corporation transportation department and with an accounting firm and began to transform the 1881 Victorian, which had been an inn since the 1930s. They refinished antiques and decorated with pastel backgrounds, with country and Victorian furnishings, and with flair. Among the long list of returnees: a young couple who were married in the living room.

Bed and bath: Ten carpeted rooms on three floors. All private baths, some full, some shower without tub. Beds are king or queen; most are canopied. Amenities vary: balcony with "treetop ocean view," sun porch, skylight, sitting room with daybed, working fireplace, air conditioning, window or ceiling fans.
Breakfast: 8–9:30. Buffet featuring quiche, pancakes, stuffed French toast and blueberries, peach cobbler, apple dumplings, or raspberry crunch. Always granola, fresh fruit, bagels. With china and crystal. On sun porch with ceiling fans.
Plus: Evening refreshments. Fireplace flanked by Victorian sofas. A "borrow or exchange" library. Guest refrigerator. Microwave. TV. Porch rockers. Garden flowers. Yard. Picnic table under shade trees. Bicycle storage.

Hearthside Inn

207/288-4533

7 High Street, Bar Harbor, ME 04609-1816

Hosts: Barry and Susan Schwartz
Location: On a quiet side street. Two blocks from the waterfront. Five-minute drive to Acadia National Park.
Open: Year round. Two-night minimum July and August and on holiday weekends.

Rates: Per room. First floor, queen bed, fireplace, ceiling fan, porch, $110. Upper floors, $75, $80, $95, $110 depending on room size, amenities. MC, VISA.
♥ ⬤ ⅍

The couple who, five years ago, just "upped and moved from New Jersey," where Barry was a corporate executive and Susan was a teacher, are pretty happy with their decision. So are their guests, who are responsible for Hearthside's number three placement in a nationwide "best of the B&Bs" contest.

A before-and-after album chronicles the restoration efforts in this 1907 house, originally built as a doctor's home. Winston Churchill, Romeo and Juliet, Queen Victoria, and Emily Dickinson are some names of the guest rooms. The carpeted inn is furnished with Victorian and country antiques. As for suggestions, "There is one place we send our honeymoon couples to, and I'd be in a lot of trouble if it ever got into print!" says Susan.

In residence: Pennie, 13, and Josh, 11.
Bed and bath: Nine queen-bedded rooms on three floors; some with working fireplace and/or private porch. All private baths; some full, some shower only.
Breakfast: 8–9:30. Buffet style. Hot dish may be pancakes, French toast, or eggs. Fruit salad, strawberry or other homemade breads, maybe poppyseed cake, muffins, bagels, homemade granola, hot/cold cereal, juice, tea, coffee.
Plus: Afternoon tea or evening refreshments.

> From New Mexico: *"A wondrous tapestry is woven by combining charming, clean, delightfully apppointed rooms with touches of Victoriana . . . vivacious conversation, good suggestions . . . we have been recommending it to everyone."*

Nannau–Seaside B&B   207/288-5575

P.O. Box 710, Lower Main Street, Bar Harbor, ME 04609-0710

Hosts: Ron Evers and Vikki Erickson Evers
Location: A mile from town center, down a long private driveway in a quiet wooded area adjoining Acadia National Park.
Open: May–October. Two-night minimum.

Rates: Double occupancy. $105 bath en suite, $85 private nonadjoining bath, $65 shared bath. Singles $5 less. MC, VISA.
♥ ✖ ✂

If you have ever wanted to stay in one of the area's famed summer "cottages," here is your chance. From the grand front hall your eyes focus ahead to the enormous full-length window with ocean views. To the left is the living room with huge fireplace (with crackling fire many mornings and most nights) and walls covered with a wonderful coral-colored hand-printed William Morris paper.

With prompting, Ron and Vikki, the first year-round residents of the house built in 1904, will share their unlikely experience of taking a hike eight years ago, seeing an empty house without a "for sale" sign, and finally buying the place, which was "way too big for the two of us." The art history major turned researcher and fine wallpaperer, together with her husband, a talented carpenter and baker, have done all the restoration work except the plumbing. The house, now on the National Register of Historic Places, has a growing collection of period pieces and newly upholstered auction finds as well as Japanese and 20th-century Maine woodblock prints.

(Please turn page.)

Guests who walk through the lovely winding wooded trail to the private beach return with treasures, smooth flat rocks. "Wax them and they'll look like wet ones," Ron advises. He and Vikki can also tell you about hikes where you can swim on top of a mountain or enjoy spectacular scenery away from summer crowds.

In residence: Misty, their mixed terrier.
Bed and bath: Four queen-bedded rooms with sitting areas and ocean views. Each bath has marble sink, claw-foot tub, hand-held shower. Two second-floor rooms (one with bay window); each with private bath, working fireplace. Two third-floor rooms share one bath.
Breakfast: 8–9. Maybe omelets and homemade croissants, almond-filled French toast with maple syrup, eggs Florentine with English muffin, or Belgian waffles with whipped cream, fresh berries.
Plus: Down comforters. Feather pillows. Screened porch. Croquet court.

Fairhaven Inn   207/443-4391
North Bath Road, RR 2, Box 85, Bath, ME 04530-9304

Hosts: George and Sallie Pollard
Location: Quiet. On 24 acres of trees, meadows, lawns, bordered by the tidal Kennebec River. Birding, snowshoeing, and cross-country skiing right here. Five-minute drive to town center and Maine Maritime Museum, 20 minutes to Freeport. Twelve miles to beach, eight to Bowdoin College.

Open: Year round. Two-night minimum on holiday weekends.
Rates: $45–$60 single. $55–$70 double. Special rates for stays longer than three nights and for whole-inn bookings. Cross-country ski packages. MC, VISA.
♥ ❖ ♦ ✄

> From Pennsylvania: *"Lovely . . . nicely decorated, meticulously clean . . . spacious and comfortable common rooms . . . breakfasts are delicious, imaginative, and plentiful. The combination of Sallie's infectious enthusiasm and George's dry wit, plus their friendliness and helpfulness, left us with warm, happy feelings that lasted for the rest of our vacation."*

As 1988 guests who were looking for land, the Pollards expressed their love of this inn, its quiet country setting with birds and wildflowers—and its nearby beaches with sand, dunes, and tide pools. "Why don't you buy it?" asked the previous owners. Within two months the Pollards sold their home of 30 years in Wilbraham, Massachusetts, where Sallie was a human service program director and George a manufacturer's representative. The inn, restored in the 1970s, is a 1790s shingled Georgian colonial furnished with antiques and country pieces.

In residence: Host smokes a pipe occasionally. Two cats.
Bed and bath: Six rooms. First-floor queen-bedded room has private bath. Five second-floor rooms; three with private baths, two rooms share one bath. Choice of double, queen, or twin beds. Rollaway available.

Breakfast: 8–9 (coffee available at 7). Fruited hot cereals, yogurt or granola, blintzes with bananas/strawberries, fruit soups, baked grapefruit. Served in fireplaced dining room with view of the river.

Glad II

207/443-1191

60 Pearl Street, Bath, ME 04530

Host: Gladys Lansky
Location: In historic area. Eight-minute walk from center of town; 1½ miles to Maritime Museum. Ten minutes to Bowdoin College, 20 to Freeport, 40 to Boothbay Harbor; 25 to Popham Beach or Reid State Park; 45 minutes north of Portland.

Open: Year round. Reservations appreciated. Two-day minimum on holiday weekends.
Rates: $45 per room. AMEX, MC, VISA.

"I worked for a large insurance company in New York City as an administrative assistant, and I also gave piano lessons for many years. I have stayed in B&Bs and can't think of a nicer thing to do. Since opening here in 1984, it has proven to be exactly what I had hoped for." Her only regret? Not having taken pictures of the "before" with its layers of wallpaper. She painted the walls of the Victorian house white and added cheery accents in primary colors and a blend of furnishings. Now Gladys is giving piano lessons again. And she has compiled a bed and breakfast cookbook for the Bath B&B Association.

At the suggestion of this enthusiastic hostess, guests spend hours, even whole days at the Maritime Museum, by including a visit to the working shipyard where you can take a boat ride down the river. Gladys suggests beaches, a state park with varied topography, picnic places and playgrounds, classical music performances, local band concerts, and festivals.

In residence: Nicholas, "four-legged dog person." Knack, the parakeet "who walked here one day."
Foreign languages spoken: "A bit of French and Spanish."
Bed and bath: Two carpeted second-floor rooms share one full bath. One large room has double bed. The other room has two twin beds with wicker headboards.
Breakfast: 7:30–9. Juice, fruit, cereal, homemade muffins and jam, beverage. Served in dining room or on screened porch.
Plus: Air conditioning. Grand piano, cable TV. Parlor. Bedroom window fans. Porch.

From Maine: *"A warm, hospitable, knowledgeable hostess whom we returned to while looking for a home in this area."*

"It's been a great season—filled every night," said the happy but tired innkeeper. As I began to calculate $60 times seven nights times. . . my husband quipped, "Forget it, that's 600 sheets."

Packard House   207/443-6069
45 Pearl Street, Bath, ME 04530

Hosts: Vincent and Elizabeth Messler
Location: In historic district, one block from the Kennebec River. Within walking distance of shops and restaurants. One and one-half miles from the Maine Maritime Museum; 15 minutes from Bowdoin College; 20 from L. L. Bean; 40 from Portland.

Open: Year round. Two-night minimum weekends, July–October. Reservations required January–March.
Rates: Double occupancy. $65 queen or twins. $80 suite. $15 third person in suite sitting room. MC, VISA.
🛏 ✂

Since moving from Connecticut seven years ago, the Messlers have hosted receptions for the Maritime Museum and have become involved with many organizations—from the Chamber of Commerce to Hospice to a bed and breakfast association. Their enthusiasm for Bath results in a long, varied, and unusual list of things—"all wonderful"—to see: wildlife sanctuaries, lighthouses, historic homes, the launching of a ship, performances, antiques shops, and galleries.

Their B&B, once the home of Benjamin F. Packard, an illustrious Bath shipwright, is a "dream come true" in the state where Elizabeth's family had spent many summers. Host/chef Vincent, a former health insurance executive, sells real estate and refinishes furniture and collectibles. Elizabeth enjoys painting, interior decorating, and, most of all, walking the beaches. The 1800s Georgian house is furnished with antiques, reproductions, historic paintings, and family heirlooms.

In residence: Basset hound named Benjamin Basset who stays in rear of house.
Bed and bath: Three second-floor rooms. One with queen four-poster and one with two twin spool beds share a full hall bath. Suite includes room with queen cannonball bed, adjoining private shower bath, sitting room with love seat/twin bed.
Breakfast: 8–8:30; usually 8:30–9 in winter. "Special" French toast; blueberry buttermilk pancakes; baked Swiss eggs with bacon or homemade sausage and homegrown herbs, applesauce, toasted Irish soda bread, a family tradition. Served in formal dining room.
Plus: Music room with baby grand piano. English garden in enclosed courtyard. Dinners—if guests are snowed in!

From Florida: *"What a haven and heaven . . . warm, friendly, caring."* From California: *"A gracious welcome, even aromatic lilacs."*

Can't find a listing for the community you are going to? Check with a reservation service described at the beginning of this chapter. Through the service, you may be placed (matched) with a welcoming B&B that is near your destination.

1024 Washington B&B   207/443-5202

1024 Washington Street, Bath, ME 04530

Host: Michele Valdastri
Location: In a mansion-lined historic district. Five-minute walk
through park overlooking river to
shops, galleries, and restaurants.
Open: Year round. Two-night minimum Friday–Sunday.

Rates: $65 shared bath, $80 private,
$125 suite. Off-season, $50 shared,
$60 private, $90 suite. MC, VISA.
♥ ✵ ♦ ✈

Four gorgeous *Colonial Homes* pages pictured the restored brick Italianate
mansion decorated with Victorian antiques. Leaded windows, cherry dining
room wainscoting, a light and bright parlor—all are part of the B&B opened
in 1987 by Michele, who moved here from Florida with her husband, a
consultant for an international corporation. She grew up in a family of
innkeepers and has been cooking "since I was old enough to stir the sauce.
Here, I think breakfast is absolutely magic. People—some timid, some gregarious, all strangers—leave as friends." Many write thank-you notes, often
expressing thanks for Michele's suggestion to slow down and not miss "the
good stuff, the real Maine, the hideaway spots."

In residence: One dog not allowed in guest areas. Two birds, Tweeter and
Woofer.
Bed and bath: Five second-floor rooms plus a two-room suite with working
fireplace, seven-foot tub. All with 12-foot ceilings, ornate wood floors, air
conditioning, individual heat control. Queen bed in five rooms; one room
with two twin beds. Five private baths.
Breakfast: Presented 8:30–10. Crepes, gourmet egg "McMuffin," croissants,
fresh fruit mix, Italian frittata. Served on antique china in breakfast room
overlooking gardens. Background chamber music.
Plus: Mints. Robes. Fresh flowers. TV (hidden in cabinet) in guest rooms.
Guest refrigerator. Special occasions acknowledged. Babysitting.

> From Massachusetts: *"A special place . . . elegant, gracious, and pleasant . . .
> warm, delightful, enthusiastic hostess."*

The Horatio Johnson House   207/338-5153

36 Church Street, Belfast, ME 04915

Hosts: Helen and Gene Kirby
Location: In historic district, a
neighborhood of lovely old homes,
20 miles north of Camden. Five-minute walk to shops, antiques centers,
restaurants, and waterfront.

Open: Year round. Reservations recommended.
Rates: $40 single, $45 double. $10
third person.
♥ ⌂ ✵ ♦ ✈

"It's seven years since we remodeled our 1842 home into a B&B that would
reflect American hospitality to travelers arriving by land, sea, air, or stage-

(Please turn page.)

coach. Return guests seem to have photographic memories and want 'their room' with photos, quilts, and other items unchanged."

Helen was a university administrative assistant and Gene a superintendent of a Massachusetts vocational school "in our other life." Now Gene makes animal and Santa Claus carvings that are sold in shops from Camden to Bar Harbor.

Their suggested local walking tour includes architectural gems and a Paul Revere bell. At "home" (where Jefferson Davis was a guest in 1858), you'll see the punched tin cabinet doors Gene made in the kitchen, which is complete with wood stove, beamed ceiling, and hanging baskets. The Kirbys share all their expertise and can tell you about making a bathroom out of three closets or teach you the ways of counted cross stitching—all in a very relaxed welcoming atmosphere.

Bed and bath: Three large rooms, all with private baths. One with twin beds; one with queen; another with queen has adjoining room with single bed.
Breakfast: 8–8:30. Fresh fruit. Homemade granola, egg-free muffins and dishes. Hosts usually join guests.

The Jeweled Turret Inn   207/338-2304
16 Pearl Street, Belfast, ME 04915-1907   in Maine **800/696-2304**

Hosts: Carl and Cathy Heffentrager
Location: Residential. Two blocks from Victorian downtown. Half mile from "super park overlooking ocean," 17 miles north of Camden, within 20 miles of four state parks.

Open: Year round.
Rates: Double occupancy. July–October, $55–$75. November–June 30, $45–$65. Singles $5 less. $10 third person.
♥ ❖ ◆ ✕ ⅊

"A bed and breakfast vacation in beautiful historic Maine" is the answer to "What brought you from Anchorage, Alaska, where you were born and raised?" Several trips and years later, the young couple, still in their twenties, found Belfast, a "stepping-back-in-time town with this house and its stone verandas and gables and turrets." Now on the National Register of Historic Places, the house has been restored—all the woodwork too—by Carl, who grew up doing carpentry and construction, and Cathy, a piano teacher. They have filled the house with Victorian antiques, lots of lace, and their knick-knack collections.

In residence: Daughter Megan, age 10. Renegade, a Yorkshire terrier, "a toy dog who occasionally introduces himself."
Bed and bath: Seven rooms on first and second floors, private baths. (Ceiling fans in two rooms.) Queen-bedded rooms with shower bath. Double-bedded rooms with full bath. One room with queen bed, fireplace, full bath, hand-held shower. One with two twin beds, shower bath. Rollaway available.
Breakfast: At 8 and 9. Poached cinnamon pears, fruit cup, or baked apples. German pancakes, sourdough gingerbread waffles, Belgian waffles, quiche, or French toast. Scones are house specialty. Teas and freshly ground gourmet coffee.
Plus: Victorian tea at 3 p.m. Mints. Verandas. Garden.

Guests wrote: *"A magnificent grand old Victorian lady. . . . Memorable breakfasts . . . spotless . . . I'll always remember the sun streaming through, throwing colorful prisms on the wall."*

Chapman Inn   207/824-2657
Corner Church & Broad Streets, P.O. Box 206, Bethel, ME 04217-0206

Hosts: Sandra and George Wight
Location: Facing the town green, in an historic district. Across from cross-country trails, 18-hole championship golf course, historical society. Ten minutes to Sunday River and Mount Abram ski areas.
Open: Year round. Two-night minimum on winter weekends.
Rates: Include use of sauna and, in summer, private pond beach four miles away. For winter weekends and vacation weeks, add $10. Private bath, $55 single, $65 double, $20 extra adult, $10 child under 12. Shared bath, $45 single, $55 double, $15 extra adult, $5 under 12. AMEX, MC, VISA.
♯ ❀ ◆

This casual, homey, and friendly place is a big 1860 Federal-style home, originally built by a sea captain. It became an inn in 1984 when Robin and Douglas Zinchuk recognized the need for lodging in this historic town, once chosen for a Hallmark Christmas card commercial. Returnees—and there are lots of them, especially families in the winter—enjoy the changes, even the amenities, that have come with the popularity of B&B. The Zinchuks now live nearby with their four children, ages three to nine. You may meet Robin or Doug; but currently the Wights, long-time Bethel residents, are full-time innkeepers.

Bed and bath: Eight inn rooms. Two first-floor two-room suites, each with kitchen and private bath. Second- and third-floor rooms that share two baths (one room also has half bath) have either a double bed or both a double and a single bed.
Breakfast: 7–9. Gourmet entree—with fruits in season. Homemade muffins. Juices, coffees, teas. Special diets accommodated.
Plus: Bedroom fans. Beverages. Fresh seasonal flowers. Game room, TV room, two saunas in converted barn. Use of canoe and beach chairs. Group dinners arranged. Babysitting with advance request. Toys, cribs, booster chairs. A Maine touch, a souvenir. Some pets allowed.

From Maine: *"We are fussy about clean comfortable accommodations and were delighted. They made us feel right at home."*

"I'll just sleep in the morning," said one college-age son, until the next day when he smelled the muffins.

The Douglass Place

207/824-2229

HCR 61, Box 90, Bethel, ME 04217-9501

Hosts: Dana and Barbara Douglass
Location: On Route 2, a mile north-east of the village. Six miles to Maine downhill ski areas, 30 to foot of Mount Washington in New Hampshire; 72 miles from Portland, 180 to Montreal.

Open: Year round except for two weeks in April and last two weeks in October. Two-night minimum on holiday weekends.
Rates: $40 single, $50 double. $15 cot. $5 crib.

Good timing! Barbara had thought about her B&B stays in the British Isles. And she thought, just about the time she retired from a career as a social worker for the state of Maine, that the idea might be a good solution toward meeting the terrific oil bills. One of the first B&B guests, who has become an annual visitor, wrote, "What a joy to stay at the Douglasses', my old ancestral home. It is changed just enough to make it convenient and comfortable."

The Douglasses brought up four daughters in this house built in the early 1800s by the Twitchells, successful farmers whose descendants put on a Victorian addition in the 1880s. Those flower gardens, the hobby of Dana, a semiretired land surveyor, are the reason that some tour buses stop here. "Sharing this 20-room home is a marvelous way to meet people from all over the world," says Barbara, the daughter of a Boston interior decorator. Visitors from England summed it up, "The friendliest welcome to strangers, a lovely house, comfortable beds, an interested host and hostess—just a half mile from Bethel center."

In residence: Husband occasionally smokes ("Shouldn't!").
Foreign language spoken: A little French.
Bed and bath: Four twin-bedded rooms share two second-floor full baths plus a half bath downstairs. In addition, a large second-floor living room includes queen sleep sofa and twin bed. TV in all rooms. Cot and crib available.
Breakfast: 7–9:30. Beverage, fruit in season, dry cereals for children, homemade muffins and preserves.
Plus: Gazebo. Tour of huge pegged barn. Game room with piano and pool table. Cross-country ski trail starts in backyard. Cookies and cool drinks; hot tea or cocoa for skiers. "Hiking trails and antiques shop for our summer guests."

All the B&Bs with this ◀ symbol want you to know that they are a private home set up for paying guests and that they are not an inn. Although definitions vary, these private home B&Bs tend to have one to three guest rooms. For the owners, people who enjoy meeting people, B&B is usually a part-time occupation.

The Hammons House   207/824-3170

Broad Street, P.O. Box 16, Bethel, ME 04217

Hosts: Sally Rollinson Taylor and Richard Taylor
Location: In historic district, 1½ blocks from Main Street. On a tree-lined street, across from an 18-hole golf course and groomed ski trails. Six miles to downhill and cross-country ski areas.
Open: Year round. Advance reservations required. Two-night minimum on holidays and school vacation weeks.

Rates: Holidays and school vacation weeks: $60 single, $75 double, $135 suite. Weekends and ski season: $50 single, $65 double, $120 suite. Midweek off-season (April until week before Christmas, except for one week in October): $40 single, $50 double, $75 suite. Additional person $25; $20 ages 10–16, $12 age 10 and under. MC, VISA.
♥ ⌂ ⁂ ✗ ⚄

Perfect for peace, tranquillity—and special occasions. Since Sally opened this B&B in 1986, her perennial gardens have been the site for several beautiful weddings, including her own in the summer of 1991. Dick teaches English, Latin, and German at Gould Academy, where he is also running and cross-country ski coach.

The Greek Revival house, built for the Honorable David Hammons, member of the thirteenth Congress, is on the National Register of Historic Places. It is decorated with soft colors, traditional prints and furnishings, and braided rugs, a craft Sally teaches. A plant-filled conservatory overlooks the mountains. In winter, a fireplace beckons. As for the one-of-a-kind special events, Sally reports that "the Hammons House Novel-in-Progress is being written by guests. It's getting pretty interesting! . . . Our recent winter film festival, representing four decades, is held in the adjacent 1920s theater-now-antiques shop. Anyone who brought two logs for the wood stove fire got free popcorn."

In residence: Rif, "a small version of a Maine coon cat, very lovable and quiet disposition."
Bed and bath: Four rooms. One corner room with two twin beds and one large room with a double and one twin bed share sitting area and full bath. Two-room corner suite with private stairway and full bath, window seats; one room with two twins, one with extra-long double bed. Rollaway available.
Breakfast: 8–9. Baked apples, French toast, whole wheat pancakes or cheddar omelets. Homemade muffins, lemon or brown sugar corn bread. Fresh fruit. Juice, coffee, tea. Served in dining room or conservatory.
Plus: Heat lamps in baths. Beverages. Lots of books. Shaded porches. Open patios. Summer wedding receptions.

From New York: *"Tastefully restored and immaculate. . . . A gracious hostess . . . superb and beautiful breakfasts."*

From Bernice's mailbag: "And then there was the classmate from 1935, whom I hadn't seen in 50 years, who read about us in your book. He's been here twice."

Kenniston Hill Inn

207/633-2159
Route 27, P.O. Box 125, Boothbay, ME 04537-0125   800/992-2915

Hosts: Susan and David Straight
Location: Two miles north of bustling Boothbay Harbor, set back from the road on a hill, surrounded by maple and oak trees.
Open: Year round.

Rates: Double occupancy. $65–$75 double beds, $85 twin beds, $85–$95 queen or king beds. Fireplaced queen-bedded $90–$95, king-bedded $95. MC, VISA.
♥ ♦ ✈ ⊱

The beamed living room with Oriental rugs has a huge hearth flanked by wing chairs. Period wallpapers, stenciling, and wainscoting are in some rooms. David, a cabinetmaker (reproduction early country pieces), and Susan, who was working in banking, ended their search in 1990 when they found this handsome 200-year-old center chimney Georgian colonial, an established inn. The contented innkeepers—"Why did we wait so long?"—love to go antiquing. And they have become experts on rainy-day suggestions, seal-watching sites and lobster restaurants.

In residence: Jack, a Yorkshire terrier, "a good napper."
Bed and bath: Ten rooms, all private attached baths. Three rooms with private exterior entrance. Arrangements include rooms with working fireplaces and full baths (other baths are shower, no tub). King, queen, double, or two twin beds (many four-posters) available. Queen and one twin bed in carriage house.
Breakfast: Coffee/tea at 8. Full at 9. Perhaps bacon-and-three-cheese pie, ham and Swiss wrapped in puff pastry, eggs Benedict, peaches and cream French toast. Fruit. Home-baked goods. Family style on fine china in fireplaced dining room. Table surrounded by handcrafted Windsor chairs.
Plus: Special occasions acknowledged. Fans. Option of five-course fireside dinner in winter.

Seawitch Bed & Breakfast

207/633-7804
Route 27, Box 27, Boothbay, ME 04537-9807

Hosts: Claire and Bill Hunt
Location: Secluded. On 10 wooded acres on a country road halfway between Route 1 and Boothbay. A short walk to quiet cove where seals visit. Ten-minute drive to harbor.

Open: Year round.
Rates: Double occupancy. $105 Memorial Day–Labor Day. $95 September–October. $85 rest of year. $15 third person.
♥ ⚬ ✈

While this expanded Cape Cod-style sea captain's house that the Hunts designed was being built, they stayed a total of 100 days at a Boothbay B&B, the inspiration for Seawitch. Since moving here from Grosse Pointe, Michigan, two years ago, Bill has been working in his wood shop and Claire has exchanged her hat as director of special education programs for the hats of full-time house- and groundskeeper. They both enjoy sharing their love of the area and their home filled with antiques, ship prints, and artifacts from all over the world.

Foreign languages spoken: French and German.

Bed and bath: Two spacious double-bedded (one is a four-poster) second-floor rooms, each with attached private full bath, working fireplace, sitting area. Private guest entrance. Rollaway available.

Breakfast: Usually at 9. Almond crepes with raspberry puree, Spanish omelets, thick slab French toast, or eggs and cheese pie. In dining room with pewter-filled cupboard. Table set with Battenburg lace linens, crystal, fine china, antique silver.

Plus: Late-afternoon beverage with hors d'oeuvres in Library. Coffee and juice at 7:30 a.m. Fresh flowers. Candy. Amenities basket. "Piles of pillows." Down comforters. Flannel sheets. Lace and cutwork duvet covers in summer.

Five Gables Inn   207/633-4551

Murray Hill Road   (outside Maine) **800/451-5048**
East Boothbay, ME 04544

Hosts: Ellen and Paul Morissette
Location: On a hill overlooking a lobstering bay. On a narrow road off Route 96. In a small shipbuilding village, four miles from Boothbay Harbor.
Open: May through mid-November. Two-night minimum on holiday weekends.

Rates: Double occupancy. On first and third floors, $80 double bed, $90 queen bed. Fireplaced rooms $100 or $110 with queen bed, $120 with king bed. MC, VISA.
♥ ❖ ◆ ✄

Here they are—the Morissettes, who in 1983 created Boothbay's Kenniston Hill Inn from a 200-year-old house that had become apartments. (Previously, Paul had been a renowned Vermont restaurant owner and chef for a quarter century.) When Ellen and Paul learned that the region's only remaining Victorian hotel, built in 1845 and last used in 1978, was about to meet the fate of similar structures, they, together with extended family members, took on the two-year restoration. A before-and-after album is in the large common room. Twenty-two guest rooms and six baths were made into 15 rooms with private baths. Ellen's daughter decorated with reproduction pine, wicker, and cherry furnishings. Once again the wide veranda with hammock, Lifecycle Bike, and lots of wicker, is filled with guests who enjoy the view and serenity. Some take a lovely walk through the woods to the summer community of Bayville. And should you come by sea, the inn has two moorings.

Bed and bath: Fifteen rooms (five with working fireplace) on three floors. All private baths; some with tub and shower, some shower only. King, queen, double, twins available.
Breakfast: 8–9:30. Eggs Florentine, chili-cheese strata, homemade muffins, fresh fruit, homemade granola, juices, meats. In dining room or on porch. (Lasts for up to two hours.)
Plus: No TV. Fresh flowers. Glycerine soap. Recipes shared.

Anchor Watch   207/633-2284

3 Eames Road, Boothbay Harbor, ME 04538-1005

Hosts: Captain Bob and Diane Campbell

Location: One hundred feet from ocean, facing lighthouses, islands, lobster boats, and yachts. On a dead-end street, a five-minute walk into town with shops and restaurants.

Open: Year round except mid-January to mid-February.

Rates: Double occupancy. $65–$85 (view of the ocean determines rate). $15 third person. MC, VISA.

Rave reviews have come from a CEO who had never stayed in a B&B before—"We usually stay in The Williamsburg Inn (Virginia) or The Greenbrier Hotel (West Virginia)"—and from guests who have slept in every room, guests from England, guests who have returned with in-laws and babes-in-arms. They remember "the pink light of morning reflected off the ocean," fresh flowers, neat plantings, spotless everything, hot breakfast breads, the wicker-furnished porch, and the abundant evidence that "Diane, who has a warm and friendly touch, likes what she does."

About six years ago, the Campbells left their jobs as English teacher and design engineer to return to the town where they grew up. To accommodate passengers who take Bob's ferry to Monhegan and Squirrel islands, they bought the house next door, decorated in country cottage style, and became innkeepers. In summer, Diane's dad is official porch greeter.

In residence: Two outside cats, Skeesix and Smokey.

Bed and bath: Four uncluttered rooms on second and third floors. All private baths; one full, the rest shower without tub. Third-floor rooms have ocean views, shared deck, and air conditioning. Views of ocean or garden from second-floor rooms. Two queen-bedded rooms. Two with both a double and a twin bed.

Breakfast: Usually 8–9. Could be apple pancakes and blueberry muffins; orange/pineapple or blueberry blintzes and bran muffins; banana/strawberry popovers with warm applesauce and rhubarb muffins. Served in breakfast nook with ocean view; in summer, tray tables for porch or deck.

Plus: Late-afternoon tea. Pillow favors. In season, discount coupons for ice cream and harbor tour. Laundry facilities.

Can't find a listing for the community you are going to? Check with a reservation service described at the beginning of this chapter. Through the service, you may be placed (matched) with a welcoming B&B that is near your destination.

The Noble House   207/647-3733
37 Highland Ridge Road, P.O. Box 180, Bridgton, ME 04009-0180

Hosts: Dick and Jane Starets and family
Location: On scenic Highland Lake, near Sabbathday Shaker Village. Minutes' walk to antiques shops. "Near romantic restaurants." Five miles to Shawnee Peak ski area, 30 to North Conway, N.H., outlet shopping.

Open: Year round. Two-night minimum on weekends June 15– October 15.
Rates: $70 shared bath, $80–$115 private bath. Third person, $15 child, $25 adult. No charge for portacrib.
♥ ♠ ❀ ◆ ✕ ✂

Guests paint the sunset. They fall asleep in the lakeside hammock. They write to me about the family that came from California in 1984 to the house built for a senator in 1903: "Like having a fairy godmother for the weekend. . . . A fulfillment of how I thought New England would be."

When the Staretses bought the big Queen Anne-style house from Dr. Noble, the town dentist for 40 years, little restoration was needed in the main house. When they converted the carriage house, Jane decorated with wicker and antiques, comforters and color-coordinated linens.

Dick is a commercial airline pilot. Jane has been a special education teacher in three states.

In residence: (Varies with school schedules.) Rich, 22; Tim, 20; Heather, 19, and Jonathan, 10. One smoky gray coon cat.
Bed and bath: Nine rooms. Queen four-poster or double bed in three second-floor rooms that share a large full bath and porch. Huge third-floor suite with two twin beds and a double bed, private shower bath. In converted barn, two adjoining ground-level rooms; one with queen bed and Jacuzzi; one with two twin beds, private shower bath. Lake-view honeymoon suite has queen brass bed, whirlpool bath. Rollaway and bassinet available.
Breakfast: 8–9. Freshly squeezed orange juice, fruit, eggs, homemade bread. Cheese strata, blueberry or whole-wheat pancakes with Noble's own maple syrup, or rum raisin French toast. By fireplace in Victorian dining room.
Plus: Grand piano. Antique organ in fireplaced parlor. Porch rockers. Special attention for honeymooners. Use of pedal boat and canoe. Swimming, ice skating.

Middaugh Bed & Breakfast   207/725-2562
36 Elm Street, Topsham, ME 04086

Hosts: Mary Kay and Dewey Nelson
Location: In the historic district, one mile from downtown Brunswick and Bowdoin College. Ten miles from Freeport and L. L. Bean, 30 miles north of Portland. The yard adjoins the Topsham Fairgrounds.

Open: Year round. Advance reservations preferred.
Rates: $50–$60 per room. $10 hide-a-bed. MC, VISA.
♠ ✕

(Please turn page.)

The Nelsons found most of the interior restoration done when they bought the Federal/Greek Revival house in 1987. Their own decorating touches include stenciling and swags. "Our search for background has taken us back to 1820. We have been gathering oral history documentation too. And gardening has become a great hobby. With the aid of a chart given to us by the woman who arranged the gardens, we are having fun working on the iris, daylilies, peonies, roses, quince, lilacs, and honeysuckle."

Dewey, a retired aviator, is a contractor, Historic District Commission member, and full-time host. Mary Kay teaches second grade, enjoys walking, and assists guests in planning coastal Maine day trips.

In residence: K.C., a senior in college, and Jake, a senior in high school. Giorgio, the "very friendly six-year-old black and white cat." Molly, an "aloof three-year-old springer spaniel."
Bed and bath: Two large second-floor rooms, one with a king bed and one with a queen, each with private full bath. Hide-a-bed available on first floor. Crib available.
Breakfast: 7–9. Homemade breads and muffins. Entree could be blueberry pancakes, waffles, or French toast. Fruit. Served in dining room or on sun porch.
Plus: Fireplaced living room with plenty of reading material. Family room with TV and games. Mints. Bedroom ceiling fans. Large yard.

Blackberry Inn   207/236-6060
82 Elm Street, Camden, ME 04843-1907

Hosts: Vicki and Ed Doudera
Location: On U.S. Route 1 with good view of Mount Battie. Within easy walking distance of harbor.
Open: Year round. Two-day minimum on holiday weekends.
Rates: Double occupancy. July–October, $80–$90 queen, $75–$80 double, $80 twins. $100 carriage house (more than two people, muffins and coffee only). Off-season, $45–$70 double or twin beds; $55–$80 queen, $60–$80 carriage house. Third person, $15 adult, $10 child. MC, VISA.
♥ � ✕ ⅙

There's a sense of place in this restored Victorian, which was featured in Pomada and Larsen's book, *Daughters of Painted Ladies: America's Resplendent Victorians*. It has polished parquet floors, antiques of the 1800s, some country pieces, and ceilings with intricate plaster decorations. The friendly attention-to-detail innkeepers are former Bostonians who love the Camden area with its theater and chamber concerts, its opportunities to sail, ski, and hike. Ed, the creative chef, is a lawyer, a hospital trustee, and organizer of Camden's Affordable Housing Committee. Vicki, food and travel writer as well as Chamber of Commerce vice-president, helped to save the old Camden post office.

In residence: Matthew, age four; Nathan, age two. Mookie, a lovable black Labrador retriever, "everyone's favorite innkeeper!"
Foreign language spoken: Fluent French.

Bed and bath: Eight rooms; four with private full baths, four with private half baths. Queen, double, or twin beds. First-floor double-bedded room has working fireplace, private half bath, upstairs shower (robes provided). On first floor of carriage house, queen bed, sofa bed, full bath, full kitchen, color TV. Rollaway available.

Breakfast: 8–9. In Ed's repertoire—cheese blintzes with blackberry sauce, brie souffle, and apricot crunch toast. Breads, muffins, coffee cakes, fresh fruit, juices, yogurt, granola. Freshly ground blended coffee. In courtyard or fireplaced dining room.

Plus: Blackberry candies. Wood stove. Fireplace. Beverage and cheese in winter. Pickup at Owls Head Airport or Camden bus stop. Air conditioning in two rooms. Special occasions acknowledged.

Edgecombe–Coles House   207/236-2336

HCR 60, Box 3010, 64 High Street, Camden, ME 04843-3501

Hosts: Louise and Terry Price
Location: Overlooking the ocean. Set back from Route 1, behind a huge hedge. A half mile north of the center of Camden.
Open: Year round. Two-day minimum on July, August, and fall weekends. Reservations required weekdays November–May.

Rates: July–October, double $100, twin $110, queen $120, king $135/$150. Rest of year, double $70, twin $80, queen $85, king $90/$105. Third person, $25. AMEX, Diners, MC, VISA.
♥ ❖ ♦

The ocean view—with or without the porch telescope—is remembered almost as much as the innkeepers. The Prices found the property on their way to Bar Harbor, on their way to a lifestyle change; their find was a New England farmhouse that had become the gatehouse to a mansion that is no more.

Terry, an engineer/designer, and Louise, an illustrator/designer, had already restored 12 houses in California. Since coming to Camden in 1982, they have spent several winters restoring other houses, which they sold. Because they are avid collectors, the inn is filled with various types and styles of antique furniture, Oriental rugs, and original art—all admired by guests, both "people who require lots of attention and others who wish privacy."

In residence: Three show dogs—"the very friendly one greets guests."
Bed and bath: Six second-floor rooms; three with ocean views; all with private en-suite baths. King, queen, double, or twin four-posters. Twin room has a shower bath; all others have a tub and shower. Cot available.
Breakfast: 8:30. (Coffee available at 7:30.) Juice, fresh fruit, home-baked muffins and bread, eggs, bacon or sausage, homemade jams, tea, freshly ground and brewed coffee. Some days Terry makes omelets, sour cream blueberry pancakes, waffles, or Dutch babies. In dining room or on porch.
Plus: Fireplaces. Bicycles. Chocolates. Flowers. Imported toiletries. Special occasions acknowledged. Afternoon beverages. Window fans. Transportation from Camden bus or Rockland/Owls Head Airport. Local laundry service provides next-day return. Option of dinner during severe weather. "No pipes or cigars, period!"

Hartstone Inn

207/236-4259

41 Elm Street, Camden, ME 04843-1910

Hosts: Elaine and Peter Simmons
Location: On U.S. Route 1, "one block from the harbor in a village with the mountains behind and the huge bay in front." Minutes' walk to shops, restaurants, and parks.
Open: Year round. Two-night minimum in August and all summer weekends.

Rates: Double occupancy. June–October 15, $75 or $90. Off-season, $60–$65; with fireplace, $75 or $90. Picnic baskets ($5–$10/person). Weekend dinner by reservation for inn guests only, $15–$20 per person, January–May and November–December. AMEX, Discover, MC, VISA.
♥ ♣ ♦

"When we decided to get married, we wanted a business we could do together. We were both widowed and had demanding jobs—in retailing and with the state lottery. In 1986 we came to Camden, where we enjoy our guests and sailing. This Federal style-turned-Victorian was owned by a Dr. Stone and then by Dr. Hart. (Yes, we have collected some history and anecdotes too.) It is light and airy; most rooms have high ceilings and several windows. We furnished with many antiques from both our families and selected other pieces for comfort."

Peter is on the town harbor committee and Rotary. Sunny is on the Opera House (restoration) committee and the Women's Club. Among their favorite suggestions: quiet, beautiful spots.

In residence: Amanda, a Shetland sheepdog.
Bed and bath: Eight rooms, two with working fireplaces, all private baths. First-floor room has two twin beds. On second and third floors, queen or double (and two housekeeping suites). Most beds are Victorian; some are four-poster and canopied. Rollaway and crib available.
Breakfast: 8–9:30. (Coffee at 7:30.) Fruit. Juices. Homemade muffins, coffee cake, or breads. Egg and nonegg specials. Coffees and teas. At individual tables in fireplaced dining room. Option of continental breakfast in bed.
Plus: Off-street parking. Afternoon tea. Nighttime cookies. Robes. Window fans. Library/common room with TV, games, music. Fireplaced parlor. Free tickets to Civic Theater with dinner package. Transportation from Rockland airport or bus. Guests' pets are allowed in suites.

The Maine Stay

207/236-9636

22 High Street, Camden, ME 04843-1735

Hosts: Peter and Donny Smith and Diana Robson
Location: On Route 1, among homes on the National Register of Historic Places. Two blocks from the harbor.

Open: Year round.
Rates: $65–$86 double. $45–$64 single. MC, VISA.
♥ ♣ ♦ ✂

There's an antique coal stove in the country kitchen. A deck outside the dining room looks out onto parkland and Mount Battie. Period furnishings,

Oriental rugs, wide board floors are here too. What to do? Printed suggestions that may win a prize some day. Activities measured in blocks and miles from the door. A walking tour. Gardens. Places you've heard a lot about. Places you've never heard a word about. And hints: "Don't sit next to the foghorn." Bicycle tours. Driving tours. Stitchery weekends. Maps. Small-business meeting arrangements. Recipes at the touch of a computer key. Occasionally, by request only, singing at breakfast. (Peter sang with barbershop quartets. His wife, Donny, a registered nurse, and her twin sister, Diana, a music major and librarian, have competed in Sweet Adelines groups.) It all happens in a house that began in 1802 and continues to this day to see changes. Peter says that the inn is well on its way to having all private baths. And he comments, "After 36 years in the Navy, we wanted to drop anchor in a nice spot and let the world come to us." Guests have summed it up: "Delightful."

Bed and bath: Eight rooms on second and third floors. "Currently five baths (three are private), but we have plans for more." Queen, twins, double, or, in adjoining rooms, a double bed and a twin bed.
Breakfast: Usually 8:30, as early as 6:30, as late as 10:30. Fresh fruit. Egg dish, waffles, French toast, or whole-wheat pancakes. Breads, muffins or popovers. Served on English china, sterling silver and crystal.
Plus: Afternoon tea. Freshly baked cookies. Flannel sheets. Some ceiling fans. Five rooms with individual thermostats. Transportation to/from airport. Two fireplaced parlors. TV room. Pets may stay in barn, storeroom, or local kennel.

The Spouter Inn   207/789-5171

U. S. Route 1, P. O. Box 176, Lincolnville Beach, ME 04849-0176

Hosts: Paul and Catherine Lippman and sons Matthew and Grant
Location: On the main road, across from sandy beach and small harbor in center of village. Five minutes from Camden.
Open: Year round. Two-night minimum on weekends, June 15–October 15.
Rates: Double occupancy. June 15–October 15, $75 double, $85 queen, $125 suite. Off-season, $45 double, $65 queen, $95 suite. MC, VISA.
♥ ❄ ✕ ⊁

> From Massachusetts: *"Amazing restoration work . . . beautiful hardwood floors and cherry stairs . . . charming. . . impeccable. . . great breakfast. . . felt at home."*

Porch rockers face Penobscot Bay. Two interior stairways have been replaced by a central one and seven new bathrooms installed. There are original lighting fixtures, floorboards, and windows. Everywhere there are signs of Paul's creative thinking and Catherine's decorating. It feels like a well-kept old house; but the inside is all redesigned and rebuilt by the Lippmans, a couple who in 1986 were looking for a place to live. In Pennsylvania, Paul was an engineer and Catherine a registered nurse. "We could see that this house, in a great location, had possibilities for blending our interests, experiences (which include catering), and goals."

(Please turn page.)

Now they are at home—for work and school. Matthew, age 11, and Grant, age 9, who have always been home taught, are involved with Little League and soccer.

Bed and bath: Four second-floor rooms with ocean views and private baths. Two rooms, each with antique double bed. One with queen four-poster, working fireplace. Suite with double bed, queen sofa bed, full kitchen, deck overlooking mountains and ocean. Rollaway available.

Breakfast: 8–9. Quiche, crepes, omelet, puffed pancakes, or strata. Fresh fruit dish, homemade pastries, juice, coffee, tea. In dining room. Hosts join guests.

Plus: Window fans. Individual thermostats. Fresh flowers. Mints on pillow. Beverages. Two common rooms. Fireplace and wood stove. Directions to favorite picnic spot at the end of a dirt road.

Bed & Breakfast of Maine Host #32

Rockport, ME

Location: Serene. High on a ledge overlooking the harbor. Two miles from Camden.
Reservations: Year round through Bed & Breakfast of Maine, page 41.

Rates: $85 double with shared bath. $175 king. $115 for two on the sloop with stocked galley. Less in off-season.

♥ 🛏 ❄ ✈ ✂

Rare and wonderful. It was built four years ago, and from the street the exterior resembles a dormered Cape Cod-style clapboard house. From the harbor it's a spectacular structure with towering gables, lots of glass, balconies, and gardens. Stone terraces lead all the way down to the water where the hostess's 30-foot sloop is moored. (The sloop is available for overnights that include a stocked galley, and for day sails and week-long charters.) The house has wood floors, Oriental rugs, and period furnishings. And the pièce de résistance: in the center of the house, a cool, windowless screening room with an entire wall, 9 feet by 12 feet, waiting for your video selections.

The hostess is a film scriptwriter who has traveled extensively for location filming and for seminars she teaches.

Foreign languages spoken: French and Spanish.
Bed and bath: Double with shared bath, French doors leading onto the terrace and hammocks. King with private bath, Jacuzzi, working fireplace, balcony.
Breakfast: Full. With that view, of course, from circular deck.

The place to stay has become the reason to go.

Brannon–Bunker Inn   207/563-5941

HCR 64, Box 045C, Route 129, Damariscotta, ME 04543-9503

Hosts: Jeanne and Joe Hovance
Location: Rural with spectacular sunsets. Five-mile drive from Route 1 on the road to Christmas Cove. Five miles to Damariscotta, 15 minutes to Pemaquid Point, 45 to Camden.
Open: Year round. Advance reservations preferred.

Rates: Double $50 shared bath, $60 private, $70 suite. Singles $5 less. Third person, $10 adult, $5 children. $110 four in suite. AMEX, MC, VISA.
♥ ♨ ♨ ❀ ♦ ✄ ✃

The layout of the barn-turned-inn is fascinating. It is attached to a Cape-style house and has a wide interior staircase and a low ceiling on the first floor, creating a wonderful gathering area in the Publyck Room with its huge fieldstone fireplace. Actually, the first conversion of the barn was as a 1920s dance hall called "La Hacienda."

Everyone asks the Hovances about their pre-inn (before 1984) lifestyle. Joe—host, antiques dealer (with shop at the inn), and refinisher, who also does caning and other seat repair—was director of an environmental center and historic sites in New Jersey. Jeanne, an experienced house restorer, has decorated each "deliberately old-fashioned" room with antiques of a different era and with stenciling, print wallpapers, homemade quilts, and country crafts. One sitting area reflects Joe's interest in World War I military collectibles. The hosts welcome children ("we know what it is like to travel with them") and offer lots of suggestions, everything from restaurants to "a gem of a canoeing place."

In residence: In summer, Michael, a theater major at Sarah Lawrence College. Teenager Beth is active in the Naval League Sea Cadet program. Jamie, age eight, enjoys all guests, especially those with families.
Bed and bath: Eight rooms; four with private bath. Queen, double bed, or twin beds. Two handicapped-accessible rooms; one has a queen bed, the other has twin beds; shower bath, kitchenette. In second-floor suite, one double-bedded room, one with twin beds, living room area, kitchen. Cot and crib available.
Breakfast: 8–9:30. Early-bird special available. Juices or fresh fruit, homemade muffins, toast, cereal, coffee, tea, or milk.
Plus: TV, games, and books. Picnic table and outdoor seating. Kitchen facilities. Babysitting.

Wedding guests love to stay at a B&B. One innkeeper tells of the bride who asked to have relatives booked on different floors. "Be forewarned, my aunts haven't spoken for 15 years."

Bed & Breakfast of Maine Host #58

Deer Isle, ME

Location: Rural. On an island. Quiet. Minutes' drive to Blue Hill, concerts, Haystack School of Crafts, sailing, sea kayaking, galleries, trips to other islands.
Reservations: May–December

through Bed & Breakfast of Maine, page 41. Two-night minimum.
Rates: Per room. $60 shared bath. $80 double bed, private bath. $90 queen suite, private bath. Less in off-season.
♥ 🏠 ❄ 🚫 ✄

Come over the bridge, drive down to the end of a lane to this very large restored 1850s farmhouse with landscaped grounds, orchards, and its own private beach. From the Great Room there's a 180-degree view of the ocean, of sailboats, of serenity—with no other houses in sight. The host had such a good time redoing this house that he has changed careers and become a contractor. He and his wife and two young children live in their own private quarters.

Bed and bath: In guest wing, seven antiques-filled rooms, all with private baths. Throw rugs on highly polished floors. Queen, double, and twin beds.
Breakfast: Continental. Varies. Perhaps freshly squeezed juice, fruit cup, blueberry bread pudding, beverages.

Todd House   207/853-2328

1 Capen Avenue, Eastport, ME 04631-1001

Host: Ruth McInnis
Location: At Todd's Head on Passamaquoddy Bay in this coastal fishing village.
Open: Year round.
Rates: $35 single, $40 smaller dou-

ble, $50 double with fireplace, $65 or $75 queen with private bath and furnished kitchenette. $10 additional person. $5 less on stays of more than six days.
♥ 🏠

From Ohio: "A most felicitous place . . . always a native Mainer stopping by to chat. . . . The rooms are exquisite—all the modern conveniences in a 200-year-old setting. . . . And where does the coffee smell better than 100 feet from the Bay of Fundy?"

With advice from the Maine Historic Preservation Commission, Ruth has become a restoration expert. When the chimney was rebuilt, she learned that this house was, in 1775, a cabin before becoming a Cape. You can almost follow the history of the house through the Indian Room, the Cornerstone Room, and other named guest rooms on to the recent addition. "As the house is on the National Register, the street side of the addition looks almost as it did years ago, but the water side is all glass. And now there's an eight-foot-tall fieldstone barbecue and a deck, all taking advantage of the view."

Until 1980, when she returned to Eastport to teach in her hometown, Ruth taught in Portland. As she did in a *Yankee* magazine feature on the changing (developing) scene, she'll share her perspective with guests; B&B is her way of sharing her love of old houses, history, and Eastport.

In residence: Kitty, the cat, "a hit with many guests." (Well-behaved guests' pets are welcome; the "most unusual" award goes to a large parrot.)
Bed and bath: Six rooms on two floors. First-floor queen-bedded room with private bath. One second-floor room with a queen and a twin bed, private bath. The four that share two baths have a double or two twin beds. Some have working fireplaces, cable TV, sitting areas, view of water. Some on first floor are handicapped accessible. Two trundle beds.
Breakfast: 7:30–10. Juices, coffee, tea, milk, cereals, homemade muffins, fruit. Served at antique table with views of the ocean, next to huge fireplace with bake-oven.
Plus: Tours of the house and area. Books on local history. Will meet guests at airport or bus. Kitchen privileges. Cookout equipment.

Weston House Bed & Breakfast 207/853-2907
26 Boynton Street, Eastport, ME 04631-1305

Hosts: Jett and John Peterson
Location: On a hill overlooking Passamaquoddy Bay and Campobello Island. In easternmost U.S. city, seven miles southeast of Route 1.

Open: Year round.
Rates: Per room. $60 king, $50–$55 queen, $45 double, $40 single. $15 extra bed.
♥ 🖼 ✿ ✕ ⚥

Acclaimed Vermont innkeepers wrote: "Worth traveling to the end of the earth for." That's just what the Petersons thought when they came from northern California to this well-maintained 1810 Federal-style house listed on the National Register of Historic Places. They learned its history and furnished with a mixture of antiques and family treasures, with antique clocks and Oriental rugs. They experimented with orchids. And watched a lemon tree flourish in the living room.

John was with the U.S. Forest Service. Jett, a former junior high school teacher, supervised legal caseworkers in the district attorney's office. Moving to the East Coast has meant more time to work with foods and needlepoint; to do woodworking and gardening; to offer (by reservation) high tea in December or candlelight dinners for special occasions. "The real joy is meeting people from all over the world who come here for business or pleasure."

In residence: Fala Delano II, a Scottish terrier. Landseer is a West Highland white terrier.
Bed and bath: Five large second-floor rooms share two full baths. King-bedded room has working fireplace, color cable TV, bay view. Two rooms each with a queen bed. One double-bedded room. One room with single brass bed. Rollaway available.
Breakfast: "A holiday every day." Accompanied by classical music. Could be Dutch baby pancakes with spiced grape compote or smoked salmon frittata with sour cream and smoked salmon caviar. Wild blueberry or cranberry

(Please turn page.)

walnut muffins. Freshly ground coffee. Steeped tea with milk. In dining room or on porch.

Plus: Afternoon tea. Mints. Flowers. Kitchen wood stove. Fireplaced living room. Croquet. Lawn chairs. A list of 16 reasons to come to Eastport.

High Meadows   207/439-0590
Route 101, Eliot, ME 03903-1210

Host: Elaine Raymond

Location: A wooded country hill-side. Four miles from Kittery/Route 1 factory outlets. Six miles to Portsmouth, New Hampshire.

Open: April through October.

Rates: $50 shared bath, $60 private bath.

♥ 🏠 ❖

Can't think of a better reason to go off the beaten path. Even the approach, up a shaded lane, gives a sense of anticipation. There are meadows, a tree growing through an old wagon wheel, granite from a barn foundation made into a wonderful stone wall. And perennial gardens and manicured lawns and, everywhere, views. Guests stay in an antiques-filled home built in 1736 by a merchant shipbuilder and captain. "I tell them about camping with the children here in 1960 when there was no water, no electricity, no roadway," says Elaine, who designed and planned the restoration of all 11 rooms. She made all the curtains, she hooked rugs, and she furnished with handsome period and country pieces. Kitchen cabinets are made from 200-year-old attic floorboards. What started out to be "a place to keep my horses" has become a haven, a B&B since 1981, where occasionally Elaine, a justice of the peace, officiates at small weddings. Her husband, Ray, is genial cohost and grounds-keeper.

Bed and bath: Five rooms. On first floor, queen bed, private full bath. Upstairs, a private shower bath for room with a queen and another with two twins. Two double-bedded rooms share a shower bath.

Breakfast: 8–9. Entree varies. Fruit, pancakes or quiche, homemade muffins and breads, beverage. In summer, on large screened porch or patio facing woods.

Plus: Large terrace. Barn porch with rockers. Living-room fireplace that is high and shallow and draws beautifully. Half-hour walking trail with wild raspberries in July.

> From Massachusetts: *"Renewed our appreciation for life, the elegance of simplicity, delicateness and detail."* From Illinois: *"My bride of 48 years and I found love at first sight for Elaine, her family, the place. In Germany, they would say 'Ausgezeichnet!'"*

---

*T*o tip or not? (Please turn to page xii.)

Home-Nest Farm   207/897-4125

Baldwin Hill Road, Fayette, ME
Mailing address: Box 2350, Kents Hill, ME 04349

Hosts: Arn and Leda Sturtevant
Location: In hill and lake country
with a 65-mile panoramic view to
White Mountains. Eighteen miles
west of Augusta, 1½ miles from
Route 17, "beyond a small stretch of
gravel, a small annoyance that
blesses us with relative isolation."

Open: Year round except March and
April. Reservations required.
Rates: Double occupancy. Breakfast
included. $50 per room main house.
$80 The Red Schoolhouse. $95 Lilac
Cottage. Some weekly rates available.

More than an experience, Home-Nest gives the feeling of discovery—all
because of Mainers who share their "love of history and one of the prettiest
spots on planet Earth with new friends." Arn is a sixth-generation resident;
the family homestead restorer; a retired bank president; a farmer; and a
cofounder of Norlands, a nearby living history museum where you can churn
butter, cut ice, milk cows. He and Leda can direct you to waterfalls, to
abandoned orchards in woods, or to private local swimming holes. If you'd
like, they'll show you slides of all the possibilities and help plan day trips. You
are invited to picnic in the meadow, pick berries, fish, ski from the door, enjoy
their sheep. It's no wonder that guests speak of "an oasis" and "down-home
hosts."

In residence: Two riding horses; Bilbo, the cat; 25 sheep (each has a name).
Bed and bath: Five rooms in three antiques-furnished historic buildings,
each with kitchen and oil and electric heat. In hosts' residence, on second
floor—queen canopied bed, private tub bath, private living room, working
fireplace, separate entrance. Lilac Cottage (1800s Cape)—three bedrooms (on
two floors), two baths, wood stove. The Red Schoolhouse (1830 Greek
Revival)—a large bedroom (double), a twin sleeper couch in living room,
shower bath, wood stove. Rollaway available.
Breakfast: In hosts' residence only, full buffet 7:30–10; otherwise prepared
by guests from well-stocked larder that includes fresh berries, muffins made
with homegrown blueberries, fresh eggs, homemade bread and oatmeal,
jellies and jams.
Plus: Window fans. Laundry facilities. Canoes (no charge) at nearby lakes.
Yacht club beach privileges. Sailboat rentals.

From the country: " Rural living is great. Did I tell you about the night
the cows came? A farmer neighbor up the road had left a gate unlatched.
About 10 p.m. I had 22 Holsteins and one bull milling around the back
yard, peering in the windows, mooing and munching! The guests loved
it. (The garden didn't.)"

The Bagley House

RR 3, Box 269C
Freeport, ME 04032-9408

207/865-6566
800/765-1772
fax 207/353-5878

Host: Sigurd A. Knudsen, Jr.
Location: Rural. On Route 136, six miles from downtown. On six acres of woods and blueberry fields. Surrounded by perennial gardens and century-old maple trees.
Open: Year round. Two-night minimum on holiday weekends.

Rates: Double occupancy. $95 May–October. $80 November–April. Room with fireplace $110 September–October, $95 November–April. Singles $15 less. $15 third person. Infants free. AMEX, Discover, MC, VISA.

♥ ⚓ ❄ ♦ ✈ ⚕

From California: *"I found a gem ... a study in attention to detail ... immaculately clean ... hearty yet beautifully presented breakfasts ... a piece of rural Maine where guests are pampered."*

Both overnight guests and small groups (for weddings or meetings) understand why Sig chose to live "out" here. He loves to suggest lighthouses, beaches, parks, and nature sanctuaries. Except for 10 years in Alaska, where he was director of a high school dormitory for 174 teenagers, Sig has almost always lived in Freeport. In 1987 he was a social services agency administrator when he bought this 1772 colonial Greek Revival house from a young couple who had spent five years on meticulous restoration. He furnished it with antiques, wing and rocking chairs, botanical prints and Eskimo artifacts. One bed made by a local craftsman was featured on the cover of *Fine Woodworking*. Sig's sister, Karen Parent, made the quilts for all the antique beds and stenciled the walls and rugs. And Sig became an acclaimed B&B chef.

In residence: Henry Mark, from Alaska, works in accounting. Chappy, a black Labrador retriever, "entices guests to play ball." Arp is "an extremely seductive, long-haired gray feline who frequently greets guests' cars, begs to be picked up and carried indoors."
Bed and bath: Five rooms; private baths. First-floor room—double bed, adjoining full bath. Second floor—two queen-bedded rooms, one with working fireplace, shower baths. One double-bedded room, full bath. One skylit room with a double and a ¾ bed, shower bath.
Breakfast: 7:30–9. "Decadent." Could be French toast made with croissants, cream, and fresh eggs or Belgian waffles piled high with Maine wild blueberries and yogurt. Fresh fruit, homemade granola and muffins. In front of huge fireplace with beehive oven.
Plus: Individually controlled room heat. Electric blankets. Window fans. Guest refrigerator with natural fruit beverages. Evening beverage. Fireplaced living room. Library. Croquet. Barbecue. Cross-country skiing or hiking through woods.

Did you hear about the salesman who left a B&B breakfast with five good leads?

181 Main Street B&B   207/865-1226
181 Main Street (U.S. Route 1), Freeport, ME 04032-1418

Hosts: Ed Hassett and David Cates
Location: On a quiet end of Main Street. A five-minute walk to L. L. Bean and outlets.

Open: Year round.
Rates: Double occupancy $95. Third person $15. MC, VISA.
♥ ❊ ✖ ⊁

> Guests wrote: *"We like as many comforts as possible. 181 Main Street has them all. . . . The innkeepers know where to get bargains, what to see and do, where to find a garage (and dentist) in an emergency. . . . And they can cook, too."*

Ed, a former mental health administrator, hadn't been in Freeport in 20 years when "the search" (300 houses in five states) brought him to town. His "worst shape of all" discovery opened in July 1987 as a totally renovated—from roof to furnace, from baths to in-ground pool—B&B. A lot of help came from David's energetic parents, Clair and Adeline, once they got over the shock of this "find." Now David, a former flight attendant, is a full-time innkeeper.

The Greek Revival Cape house, featured in *Country Home,* is furnished with many country and Empire antiques, Maine oil paintings, local crafts, and hand-hooked rugs. Wide pine floors are refinished. But the real conversation pieces are the many quilts (some with dates sewn into them)—all made by David's mother.

In residence: Mae, a golden Labrador, "loves to walk with guests."
Foreign languages spoken: French. Very little Spanish.
Bed and bath: Seven second-floor rooms, each with double or queen bed (canopied or four-poster) and private shower bath.
Breakfast: 7:30–9. (Tea and coffee at 7.) Could be heart-shaped French toast or house frittata, garnished with fruit or fresh flowers. Fresh fruit, juices, lime and other homemade breads. In adjoining dining rooms with a table for each guest room. A very sociable time.
Plus: Parking. In-ground 18-by-36-foot pool, brick deck. Large backyard, Adirondack chairs. Perennial gardens. Bedside homemade goodies.

Porter's Landing Bed & Breakfast
70 South Street, Freeport, ME 04023-6426   207/865-4488

Hosts: Peter and Barbara Guffin
Location: A quiet country setting with woods and a small stream. Less than a mile from downtown.
Open: Year round.

Rates: Double occupancy. $90 Memorial Day weekend–October. $75 off-season. Singles $10 less. MC, VISA.
♥ ❊ ♦ ✖ ⊁

The Guffins from New Jersey fell in love with Maine on their camping honeymoon in 1974. They returned to the state when they bought their 1830 Greek Revival house in 1985. With fond memories of British Isles B&B experiences (on a bicycling trip), they renovated the 1870 attached carriage house as a B&B. In the large living/dining room there's a photographic documentation of their efforts, which have been acclaimed for attention to historic and architectural detail. A loft library is over the second-floor bed-

(Please turn page.)

rooms. Throughout, there are traditional furnishings, Oriental rugs, some balloon shades, some swags and jabots.

Peter is a lawyer and president of the Freeport Area B&B Association. Barbara, a quilter and school volunteer, is full-time innkeeper. Frequently they answer questions about renovating, decorating, a sandy beach, hiking trails—and shopping bargains too.

Bed and bath: Three rooms. One with queen four-poster bed and another with a double bed each have a private shower bath. One double-bedded room with full bath. Rollaway available.
Breakfast: 8:30. Could be pancakes—blueberry or baked sausage and apricot; Belgian waffles; or raisin bread French toast. Fresh fruit salad. Homemade breads and muffins. Granola. Fresh ground/brewed coffee.
Plus: Living-room Rumford fireplace. Afternoon tea or lemonade with homemade breads, cheese and crackers, or fresh fruit. Floor fans. Phone jack. Flannel sheets. Forgotten items basket. Guest refrigerator.

White Cedar Inn 207/865-9099

178 Main Street, Freeport, ME 04032-1320

Hosts: Carla and Phil Kerber
Location: Two blocks north of L. L. Bean.
Open: Year round. Two-night minimum on holiday weekends.
Rates: Double occupancy. Memorial Day weekend–November 1, $75 shared bath, $95 private. Off-season, $60 shared bath, $75 private. $15 third person in room year round.
♥ ⅓

> From Maryland: *"The L. L. Bean shopping was fun, but the real treat was staying with Phil and Carla. This young couple has turned an older home into a comfortable and warm place to stay."*

As Phil tells it, "We've always wanted to run an inn, so I sold my restaurant in Berkeley Springs, West Virginia, and bought this century-old house that had belonged to Arctic explorer Donald MacMillan when he accompanied Robert Peary to the North Pole. Carla is a nurse at the Maine Medical Center. To our interests of skiing, hiking, fishing, and snowshoeing, we can safely add—after 13 months of renovating—carpentry and wallpapering. The decor here is enhanced by my mother's quilts and my sister's paintings. Innkeeping is enhanced by the friendly guests, people who make us feel as if we have one of the world's largest extended families."

In residence: In hosts' quarters, Alice, four, and Robin, three.
Bed and bath: Six rooms with antique brass or painted white iron beds—queen, double, or double and a twin. Two first-floor rooms, each with private shower bath. Upstairs, two rooms with private full bath; two share a full bath.
Breakfast: 7:30–9. Juices, homemade muffins and jams, fresh fruit, wild Maine blueberry pancakes, French toast, scrambled eggs, bacon or sausage or ham, waffles, coffee cake, coffee. Served in sun porch with floor-to-ceiling windows facing town and spired church.
Plus: Common room with wood stove and TV. Picnic table. Outdoor grill.

Atlantic Seal B&B   207/865-6112

25 Main Street, P.O. Box 146, South Freeport, ME 04078-0146

Hosts: Captain Thomas and Gaila Ring
Location: Overlooking Harraseeket Harbor. Quiet neighborhood. Five-minute drive to L. L. Bean.
Open: Year round.
Rates: Double occupancy. Shared bath, $65 double, $85 queen. Private bath, $100 queen, $125 (double or queen) with Jacuzzi. $15 third person. December–May 1, shared bath, $55 double, $65 queen; private bath, $85 queen, $100 with Jacuzzi.

♥ ✍ ❖ ◆ ✕ ✂

> Guests wrote: *"A homey atmosphere . . . overlooking the sea . . . liked it so much we decided to make it our base camp for day trips . . . joined Tom on excursion to Eagle Island and watched him unload a lobster trap, saw seals. . . . And the food! Took a walk in the morning (with their dog) just to work up an appetite . . . served on antique china . . . warm and friendly hosts."*

This 1850s Cape Cod-style house furnished with family antiques—spinning wheel, sleigh bed, Victorian sofa in old-fashioned parlor—is the "ticket booth" for Tom's 28-passenger excursion boat, for island visits and lobstering demonstrations. Because so many passengers asked if it was also a B&B, Gaila, who was working as a dental assistant, decided to change to a home-based job. Captain Tom, a Freeport native, is a Maine Maritime Academy graduate who is experienced with tugboats all over the world.

In residence: Samantha, an English springer spaniel who "loves people and boat rides with Tom." Sadie, a black cat, "loves bird watching and wood stoves."
Bed and bath: Three second-floor rooms, all with water view. Room with a queen and a double, Jacuzzi for two, shower, cable TV. One double-bedded room shares full bath with a room that has queen four-poster, window seat. Rollaway available.
Breakfast: Usually 8–9:30. Lobster omelet is house specialty. Fresh fruit, sausages, homemade muffins, orange juice, fresh-brewed coffee, teas. In dining room or on deck.
Plus: Phone jacks. Fans. Afternoon beverage and cheese. Homemade candies. Down comforters. Flannel sheets. Turndown service. Guest refrigerator. Picnic table. Beach towels. Rowboat. Transportation to Freeport (free) or to airport (charge).

Coveside–Five Islands B&B   207/371-2807

North End Road, Georgetown, ME 04548

Hosts: Tom and Judy Ewing
Location: Off the beaten path. Just off Route 127. Where the Sheepscot River meets the Atlantic Ocean. A short drive to Reid State Park beaches.
Open: Year round. Two-night minimum on weekends.
Rates: $85 per room. November–May, $10 less. $25 rollaway. MC, VISA.

♥ ✍ ❖ ◆ ✕ ✂

(Please turn page.)

There's an expansive lawn that meets the serene cove at this B&B, a remodeled century-old lobsterman's house with a new wing and large deck against a backdrop of five wooded acres. It's a quiet cove, with rocky shore, ducks, loons, blue herons, and lobster boats. Guests may use the Ewings' canoe. Take boat tours of the islands. Walk to the picturesque fishing village of Five Islands. Or be mesmerized right here in this private setting.

Tom, Maine-born, was with the FAA before he and Judy, who worked in advertising in Massachusetts, restored this property. The project took from 1986 until 1988; everyone asks who did the work. They furnished with New England antiques. As hosts, they recall seeing a bride being carried over the threshold by the groom. And then there was the father who rowed his daughter in from an anchored schooner for a wedding ceremony and clambake reception on the lawn.

In residence: Four cats "not allowed in B&B areas."
Bed and bath: Three rooms, each with private shower bath, water views. On first floor, queen brass bed. On second floor, one room with antique four-poster double bed, one with two twins/king.
Breakfast: Usually 8–9. Freshly ground/brewed coffee at 7. Hot entree, perhaps sausage with cinnamon-raisin French toast with maple syrup or strawberry sauce. Fresh fruit. Homemade breads. On deck or in country kitchen.
Plus: Sauna on deck. Robes. Evening beverage. Beach towels. Books. Games. Stereo. Fans available. Phone jack. Homemade candies on pillow. Wood stove in winter.

The Alewife House   207/985-2118
1917 Alewife Road, Kennebunk, ME 04043-9739

Hosts: Maryellen and Tom Foley   **Open**: Year round.
Location: Pastoral. On Route 35, on   **Rates**: Double occupancy. $65–$75.
six acres of gardens, with meadows,   MC, VISA.
woods, and a babbling brook.   🐾 ◆ ✖ ✄

> Guests wrote: *"Absolutely charming . . . with pre-Revolutionary trappings . . . spacious guest rooms . . . decorated with a magnificent collection of fine and country antiques from all over the world . . . a splendid pair of innkeepers . . . spotless . . . gave us the grand tour, punctuated with anecdotes . . . good information about the area . . . made us feel like family."*

The large 1756 house of post-and-beam construction, owned by the same family for 200 years, was purchased by the Foleys in 1986. Tom is a bank personnel director and retired army officer who has worked in the computer industry. Maryellen, a curator for the Kennebunkport Historical Society, is a teacher and writer, and she has an antiques shop on the premises. Their guests have included a business school dean, a Soviet author, professional musicians, and a foursome who arrived in their own plane—all "people who make us glad to be here in Maine." Among the Foleys' touring suggestions: a nearby waterfall, art galleries, beaches, restaurants, and the president's summer home.

In residence: Michael Brian, 18. Marchesa, "a friendly retired (greyhound) racer, experiencing 'couch potato' stage."
Bed and bath: On second floor, two double-bedded rooms. One with working fireplace and private bath with shower only. The other has a private bath with tub and hand-held shower.
Breakfast: Usually 8–9. Fresh fruits, homemade muffins, vanilla yogurt, freshly brewed coffee, tea. On sun porch overlooking gardens and forest.
Plus: Window fans. Beach passes. Fresh flowers in season. Expansive rear lawns. Turndown service upon request.

Lake Brook Bed & Breakfast Guest House

57 Western Avenue, Lower Village,   207/967-4069
Kennebunk, ME 04043-2865

Host: Carolyn A. McAdams
Location: On a tree-lined street. One mile from beach, half mile from Kennebunkport's Dock Square. Facing a tidal brook that ebbs and flows. "Quite an array of wildlife; a moose last Thursday at 6:30 a.m.!"
Open: Year round. Two-night minimum and advance reservations re-quested on Memorial Day, Labor Day, Columbus Day weekends only.
Rates: Late June–October and Christmas season, $60–$80. November–June, $60–$70. $15 third person in first-floor room only. Singles, $10 less, year round.

♥ ♨ ❈ ◆ ✖ ✁

> From Massachusetts: *"A peaceful B&B . . . homey . . . wonderful conversations . . . our hideaway . . . a different, creative menu each day."* From 'Benjamin Franklin' (Bill Meikle): *" . . . (over)indulging with but a modicum of chagrin in her estimable comestibles. Indeed, despite the press of business, I have yet to stay less than two days."*

When he is performing in the area, you, too, might have the company of the Emmy award-winning actor, now known for his one-man shows and Boston walking tours. His chosen B&B has, many say, the most spectacular gardens in town. And then there's Carolyn, a former Peace Corps member who changed the floor plan, added baths, and hung Maine seacoast watercolors in this colonial farmhouse. She returned to Costa Rica in 1988 and stayed with some of the same families she had lived with 20 years earlier. "In many ways, the Peace Corps (and B&B too) makes us realize we are all the same."

In residence: Calli, a "very friendly double-pawed calico cat."
Foreign language spoken: Spanish.
Bed and bath: Four rooms, three with private baths. Room with a double and a twin bed, on first floor, shares bath with hostess. On second floor, three rooms, all with private entrance. One with a queen brass bed and tub bath; two double-bedded rooms with shower baths.
Breakfast: 8–9. Fresh fruit, juice, Carolyn's own special blend coffee, tea. Repertoire includes homemade English muffins, breads, quiche, crepes, Mexican torte, baked French toast, asparagus/cheese strata. In dining room or on wraparound porch overlooking tidal brook.
Plus: Porch rockers. In summer, refreshing beverage. Ceiling fans in second-floor rooms. Down comforters. Free loan of bicycles.

Arundel Meadows Inn   207/985-3770
Route 1, Arundel, ME
Mailing address: P.O. Box 1129, Kennebunk, ME 04043

Hosts: Murray R. Yaeger and Mark Bachelder
Location: On 3½ acres next to the Kennebunk River. Three minutes to Kennebunk center, 10 to Kennebunk Beach and Kennebunkport; 11 miles from Ogunquit.

Open: Year round.
Rates: Doubles $75–$90; with fireplace $90–$95. Suites $100–$125. Additional guest (up to two) $20. Less Columbus Day–Memorial Day except for holiday weekends.
♥ ✤ ✖ ⊬

> From Massachusetts: *"Delightful . . . filled with the most fascinating variety of art . . . warm, friendly innkeepers. . . . Never had same menu twice. Superb . . . attractively presented."*

Mark's afternoon tea with homemade sweets is another highlight. Before becoming an innkeeper, Mark studied with Madeleine Kamman and cooked for her as well as at other Boston area restaurants. He was also an administrator at Boston's Parker House and Copley Plaza hotels.

Television performers, network producers, and magazine editors all come here to visit their former prof. Murray is a professor emeritus of Boston University's College of Communications and president of a presentational skills consulting firm. His own paintings and his collection of art objects are throughout the antiques-filled inn.

The 1830 farmhouse, just about rebuilt before its 1986 B&B opening, was featured on FNN television. The most recent addition is a large suite that can be converted to a conference room for twelve.

In residence: Hildie, "a schnauzer who 'knows' she's a person."
Bed and bath: Seven air-conditioned rooms, three with working fireplaces. All private baths. Most with queen beds. Two have private entrances. One suite with queen-bedded room and a room with two twin beds. One suite with king bed, sitting room.
Breakfast: 8–10. Eggs Benedict, quiche, fresh vegetable tart, seafood crepes, or amaretto French toast. Juices, fruit compote (homegrown berries). Homemade muffins, coffee cakes, croissants. In dining room overlooking patio.
Plus: Fireplaced living room. French doors leading to patio. Mark's perennial gardens. Cable TV in several bedrooms.

The Ocean View   207/967-2750
72 Beach Avenue, Kennebunk Beach, ME 04043

Hosts: Bob, Carole, "and, in order of appearance, Mike, Rob, and Chris" Arena
Location: Directly on Kennebunk Beach, one mile from center of Kennebunkport. In a neighborhood of private homes.

Open: April–December.
Rates: Mid-June through mid-September, $110 double, $130–$155 suite. Before June, $85–$90 double, $110 suite. After September, $90–$105 double, $120 suite.
✖

"We live in a tourist area. Carole had years of inn experience while managing the White Barn Inn in Kennebunkport, so opening our own place seemed natural. For a long time, this property, built in the 1800s, was all we dreamed about."

Since they opened in 1985, the Arenas have made—and are still making—many changes. Carole has become full-time innkeeper. Bob is still employed in human resources. If you peruse the before-and-after pictures, you'll see how they changed the original guest house, decorating with a light, airy, "beachy" feeling. Due credit is given to the sons, all athletes, for making the whole project possible. The big reward comes in the form of enthusiastic guests (many returnees) who call this "bed on the beach." Some say the location gives them a feeling of being on a boat. One from Connecticut wrote: "The atmosphere is wonderful inside and out. An ocean lover's paradise."

Foreign language spoken: A little French.
Bed and bath: Nine oceanfront carpeted rooms. All private baths; some tub and shower, some shower only. In main house, queen, double, or twin beds. Next door, in Ocean View Too (where you might have breakfast in bed), four suites with queen bed, sitting area, color cable TV, wet bar/refrigerator and small individual terrace.
Breakfast: 8–10. In main house oceanfront breakfast room. Fresh fruit. Croissants. Granola. Yogurts. Biscuits with honey, French toast, blueberry pancakes, or waffles. Continental breakfast delivered to Ocean View Too rooms.
Plus: Main house—fireplaced living room. TV room, porch, yard. Fresh fruit, coffee, tea, soft drinks always available. Garden flowers. Day trip itineraries.

Bufflehead Cove   207/967-3879
P.O. Box 499, Kennebunkport, ME 04046

Hosts: Harriet and James Gott
Location: On five acres of woods and an orchard perched at the edge of the tidal Kennebunk River—with its sea gulls, geese, blue herons, and egrets. In view of Kennebunkport.
Open: Year round except February–April. Two-night minimum on weekends.

Rates: $75 room with hand-painted mural. $80 queen with river view, $90 queen (studio) with private entrance and patio, $95 queen with balcony. $130 suite (for three). $10 extra person.
♥ ⁂ ⚥

Ecstatic guests wrote: *"Bufflehead Cove is the serenity and beauty that one seeks to feel in Maine . . . a spot that you can place inside you and reclaim once you return to your own chaos. . . . From the dock we paddled upstream as adventurous as Lewis and Clark. . . . The house, decorated with flair and attention to detail, enlivens one's curiosity and sense of intrigue, yet makes you feel as if at a favorite aunt's. . . . Harriet is an intelligent, affable ray of sunshine . . . cooks the most amazing breakfast and serves it with such style . . . tells you the best secret picnic spots, hidden coves, perfect beaches . . . gives you a sense of the whole area in an insightful, colorful way."*

(Please turn page.)

Harriet, "an ongoing college student," and her husband, Jim, a commercial fisherman, are Maine natives who love to share the former sea captain's house on the cove "where even the gulls find shelter during an ocean storm." Their own sabbatical took place in 1991, when all three Gotts lived in a small fishing village on the Pacific coast of Mexico for almost four months.

In residence: Erin, 17. Whump, the cat.
Foreign language spoken: Nonfluent Spanish.
Bed and bath: Three rooms have queen bed (one with private balcony). One has double bed. Suite has a queen-bedded room plus a room with twin bed. All with private baths. All but studio (private entrance and view of apple orchard and woods) have river view.
Breakfast: 8:30. A typical example—freshly squeezed orange juice, fruit plate, asparagus-cheese strata, bread stuffed with sausage and spices, home-made cranberry muffins. Served in the dining room or on the porch. If requested, continental breakfast served in room.
Plus: Some rooms have ceiling fans. Tea or mulled cider by fireside in spacious beamed living room. Wraparound veranda (good for sunbathing). Private dock on tidal river.

The Captain Lord Mansion

207/967-3141
800/522-3141
fax 207/967-3172

Pleasant and Green Streets, P.O. Box 800, Kennebunkport, ME 04046-0800

Hosts: Bev Davis and husband, Rick Litchfield
Location: Set back from road with huge lawn in front. Across from Kennebunk River. Three blocks from shops and restaurants.
Open: Year round. Two-night minimum on all weekends.
Rates: Vary according to season, weekday, weekend, fireplace (or not), size (third-floor rooms are about 16 feet square, others 25 feet square), and river view. January–April, midweek $75 or $125 (fireplaced $175 weekends). May–December, $125–$195; hideaway $225. Discover, MC, VISA.
♥ ✤

Countless "best" awards. Magazine picture perfect for many major publications. An elegant 1812 Federal mansion, on the National Register, that has period wallpapers, fine antiques, and many personal touches. A luxurious, welcoming creation by innkeepers, almost a legend in their own time, who personally did everything—sanding, plastering, and carpentering—from the first day of ownership in 1978 until 1983, "when they could afford to hire a painting crew!"

Bev was a McDonald's advertising manager and Rick an account manager at an advertising agency. Today they live just down the street from the inn and they have a staff. Five days a week, Rick greets guests and shares the history of the mansion. Bev dovetails behind-the-scenes work with her antiques and crafts shop (here) and mothering of two daughters.

In residence: Aggie, their Maine coon cat, might escort you to your room.

Bed and bath: Sixteen rooms. All private baths; all with showers, some with tubs only. Eleven rooms have working fireplaces. All have four-poster beds (many are queen), sitting area. Hideaway with whirlpool tub, candlelit breakfast.
Breakfast: 8:30 and 9:30. Coffee earlier. Blueberry or apple cinnamon pancakes, French toast, ham quiche, or cheese strata. Fruit, muffins, yogurt, muesli cereal, eggs. Family style in air-conditioned country kitchen.
Plus: Beach parking passes, towels, mats, umbrellas. Afternoon tea and sweets. Maps galore. Fragrance soap. Window fans. Lawn chairs. Chocolates. Cookies.

The Chetwynd House Inn

207/967-2235
800/833-3354

Chestnut Street, Box 130,
Kennebunkport, ME 04046-0130

Host: Susan Knowles Chetwynd
Location: Within walking distance of everything. Across street from whale watch excursion departures.
Open: Year round. Two-night minimum on weekends.

Rates: Per room. June 15–January 1, $99–$110 private bath, $84 semiprivate. Rest of year, excluding holidays, $89–$99 private bath, $69 semiprivate.
♥ ❖ ◆ ✈ ⚊

"Breakfast is festive! The conversation seems to cover literature, movies made from books, art, fascination with the ocean—and always New England. After breakfast some guests sit around on the porch and enjoy the river breezes—the geraniums and impatiens too. They scribble recipes on index cards; they exchange addresses and business cards and routes to destinations. President Bush waves when he drives by. In winter, especially after guests take walks along the ocean, high tea by candlelight—the more Victorian the better—is great fun."

Susan lives in a tall-windowed blue-shuttered home, built around 1840 for a sea captain. Its wide pine floorboards are graced with antique and traditional furnishings with lots of blue, Susan's favorite color. Since coming here from Connecticut in 1971, the former English teacher has become quite knowledgeable about the historic town.

Foreign languages spoken: Some French and Italian.
Bed and bath: Four carpeted rooms. One with king bed, private shower bath, TV, air conditioning. One with two double beds, private full bath, TV, air conditioning. Two queen-bedded (four-poster) rooms share a shower bath.
Breakfast: A hallmark. At 9. (Coffee earlier.) Fresh fruits, blueberry muffins, egg dishes, fillet of sole or haddock, crabmeat souffle, quiches, oyster stew, Belgian waffles. "A different vegetable every day for non-egg eaters."
Plus: Bedroom fans. Living room/library. Fruit bowl or basket. Tea or hot chocolate. On-site parking.

---

*O*ne out of five guests leaves with
the dream of opening a B&B.

The Inn at Harbor Head   207/967-5564

RR 2, Box 1180, Pier Road, Kennebunkport, ME 04046-9793

Hosts: Joan and David Sutter
Location: Quiet. In Cape Porpoise. On the harbor, with private dock. Set back from a picturesque winding road, 2½ miles from Kennebunkport.
Open: Year round. Advance reservations recommended. Two-night minimum on summer and fall weekends.

Rates: January–May 15, $95–$120. May 16–June 16, $120–$160. June 17–December, $130–$175. Extra person $25. MC, VISA.
♥ ❖ ◆ ✕ ✄

> Guests wrote: *"A piece of paradise . . . an uncovered treasure . . . hosts who have an extraordinary ability to make guests feel welcome . . . lovely linens, antiques . . . unreal baths . . . exquisite view. . . . Breakfast is an experience."*

This is a peaceful waterfront showplace on an intimate scale. The Sutters have turned their 1898 home, their residence for almost 25 years, into a designer's dream. Audiences everywhere gasp when I show slides of Joan's murals and trompe l'oeil effects, the floral arrangements, the harbor setting. In a Bloomingdale's cooking demonstration, shoppers marveled as Joan and David simultaneously stuffed French toast, garnished with violets, and chatted. Here, the gulls swoop. The bell buoy beckons.

In residence: One quiet, attentive English cocker spaniel.
Bed and bath: Five imaginative rooms, all with private bath. On first floor, water-view room with queen bed, shower bath, French doors, and private deck; one with king brass bed, bath with Jacuzzi. Upstairs, queen-bedded room, shower bath. Suite with four-poster queen-bedded room plus room with twin bed, shower bath, water views. Most popular suite—king bed, sitting area, large bath with Jacuzzi and bidet, cathedral ceiling, skylight, "unparalleled view."
Breakfast: At 9. Freshly squeezed juice in stemmed glasses. Fruit. Perhaps a vegetable medley or Belgian waffles with amaretto-flavored whipped cream. At table set with flowers, linen, and silver in dining room with wood stove.
Plus: Classical music always. Ceiling fans. Down pillows and comforters. Phone jacks. Special occasions acknowledged. Beverages, cheese and crackers. Hammock. Library, games, puzzles. Beach passes, towels, chairs.

The Inn on South Street   207/967-5151

P.O. Box 478A, South Street, Kennebunkport, ME 04046

Hosts: Eva and Jacques Downs
Location: On a quiet tree-lined street in the historic village area, within easy walking distance of shops, restaurants, and beaches.
Open: February–December. Two-night minimum most of the time.
Rates: Double occupancy. First-floor fireplaced room, $105 summer and holidays, $95 fall, $125 winter and spring. Second- and third-floor rooms, $105 summer and holidays, $95 fall, $85 winter and spring. Suite $175, $155 fall, $145 winter and spring (includes served full breakfast). Less for three or more nights. AMEX.
♥ ❖ ◆ ✄

Guests wrote: *"A gem . . . that special something you long to come back to . . . exquisite traditional furnishings . . . gracious hosts."*

"Gracious" also applies to the 19th-century Greek Revival house, which became a beautifully decorated and impeccably maintained B&B when the children were in college. That's when so many of the Downses' interests and talents came together. There are creative window treatments, an Oriental influence in the living room, attractive gardens, and cuisine that is "presented." Plus a room arrangement that provides much privacy.

Jack, an extraordinary bread baker, is a professor of American history at the University of New England; he is also an expert on the early American trade with China. Before becoming full-time innkeeper—"with just four rooms so that we can carry out our personal style"—Eva was an occupational therapist and child care administrator.

Foreign languages spoken: Fluent Spanish and German; some Russian.
Bed and bath: Three spacious rooms, one per floor, plus an apartment/suite. On first floor, queen four-poster canopied bed, a single daybed, shower bath, working fireplace, small refrigerator. On second, queen brass bed, full bath, small refrigerator. On third, queen bed, a twin sleigh bed, full bath. First-floor apartment/suite (perfect for honeymooners or a family) has private entrance, kitchen, room with queen four-poster bed and wood-burning stove, living room with double sofa bed, full bath with Jacuzzi.
Breakfast: Intentionally special. 8:30–9; 9–10 in winter. Jack's incredible breads. Souffle omelets with fruit sauces, filled German pancake, or blintzes. Juice. Fruit. Homemade jams. Served in country kitchen, sometimes in garden.
Plus: Coffee at 7:30. Afternoon beverage. Living room with fireplace, Franklin stove, balcony. Fresh flowers. Limo service arranged from airport. Use of refrigerator. Secluded garden. Fans. No TV. "Valet jogging."

Maine Stay Inn and Cottages

207/967-2117
800/950-2117

Maine Street, P.O. Box 500A,
Kennebunkport, ME 04046-1800

Hosts: Lindsay and Carol Copeland
Location: On a main street in a residential historic district. On two acres of lawn. Five-minute walk to Dock Square.
Open: Year round. Two-night minimum on most weekends.
Rates: Inn rooms and one-bedroom cottages $120–$130. Suites, fireplace cottage, and two-bedroom cottages $145–$180. Late October–mid-June $85–$120; $95–$150. "Romance renewal" package, November–June, includes dinner at fine restaurant. Discount for stay of seven or more nights. AMEX, MC, VISA.
♥ ♨ ❖ ◆ ✗

It's romantic. It's historic. And families are comfortable here too. It's all according to the plan that evolved when Lindsay, who was in bank marketing for 17 years, and Carol, who was in strategic planning and product management, decided to make a living "in a hands-on way, in a small year-round

(Please turn page.)

town that has a diversity of culture." Since moving from Seattle three years ago, when their daughters were two and five, the Copelands have redecorated most of the inn with a Victorian flavor, using Laura Ashley and Waverly wallcoverings, wicker, and brass and iron headboards. During breakfast and at tea, Lindsay and Carol are often asked about restaurants—including some that are kid-friendly—and about beaches, rainy day hints, and what it's like to be an innkeeper. "We love it!" (Guests can tell.)

Built in square block Italianate style around 1860, the inn is on the National Register of Historic Places. The main house has had many additions—including bay windows, porches, a cupola, and a suspended flying staircase.

In residence: "A neighbor's playful black Lab is practically a member of the family." Occasionally Sara, age eight, and Lizzie, age five, visit. (The family lives in another Kennebunkport property.)
Foreign language spoken: Carol speaks a little German.
Bed and bath: In main house, six rooms. Four corner rooms with queen bed, private bath; one with private deck and entrance. First-floor suite has queen bed, fireplaced parlor with double sofa bed. Second-floor suite has queen canopy bed, parlor with double sofa bed. Ten cottages, one with fireplace, all with kitchenettes; nine are one-bedroom, one is two-bedroom. Plus queen-bedded cottage without kitchenette but with sitting room and fireplace. In cottage, option of breakfast brought to you in a basket.
Breakfast: 8–9:30. Sumptuous. Varies daily. Entree repertoire includes Serbian eggs, apple bread pudding, apple or blueberry blintzes, French toast. Fruit. Muffins, breads, or coffee cakes. Homemade granola. Yogurt. Hot beverages. In dining room set with lace cloths, china, and mugs—or on wraparound porch.
Plus: Beach passes. Activity book in each room. Table fans. In each room color cable TV (hidden in armoires in main inn). Setups. Afternoon tea, coffee, lemonade, or cider with homemade cookies or brownies. Swing set. Access to nearby private pool ($2 per person).

Old Fort Inn

207/967-5353
800/828-3678
fax 207/967-4547

P.O. Box M, Old Fort Avenue
Kennebunkport, ME 04046-1688

Hosts: Sheila and David Aldrich
Location: On three acres in an area of large summer estates. One block from the ocean in a secluded setting with tall pine, oak, and birch trees.
Open: Mid-April through mid-December. Two-day minimum July–Labor Day and Memorial and Columbus Day weekends. Two-day minimum mid-September through mid-October.

Rates: Double occupancy. June–December $98 queen to $225 for three-room suite. Off-season $89–$165 (excludes Memorial Day weekend). $15 third person. Spring and November midweek package rates. AMEX, MC, VISA.
♥ ♦ ✖

When the Aldriches created an intimate inn and mini-resort—with freshwater heated pool, tennis court, and shuffleboard—they converted an 1880s barn to a lodge with a massive brick fireplace, exposed beams, and weathered pine wall boards. A turn-of-the-century brick and stone carriage house now has antiques-furnished guest rooms, each with electric heat, wall-to-wall carpeting, color TV, a refrigerator, and a direct dial phone.

This has been home to the Aldriches since 1980, when David left the oil industry and Sheila, a former flight attendant, brought antiques-shop experience. She decorated with country pieces, Laura Ashley papers and prints, and stenciling. David oversees construction and maintenance—and spends time in the antiques shop, where he's always ready to discuss tennis or skiing, or maybe the restoration of antique cars.

In residence: Shana, 14. A large gray fluffy female cat called Samantha.
Bed and bath: Twelve large rooms, each with a private bath. Most with canopied or four-poster bed—king, queen, two doubles, or two twins.
Breakfast: 8:30–10. "Deluxe buffet." Juice, fresh fruit, cereals, yogurt, home-baked fruit bread, croissants, butter and jams, brewed coffee, tea, cocoa.
Plus: Cookies. Chocolates. One hour of free tennis daily. Bedroom window fans. Babysitting. Laundry facilities. Bicycles for rent. No pipe or cigar smoking in the guest rooms.

The Welby Inn   207/967-4655
P.O. Box 774, Ocean Avenue, Kennebunkport, ME 04046-0774

Hosts: David Knox and Betsy Rogers-Knox
Location: In a quiet residential neighborhood, a five-minute walk to town (Dock Square) or hosts' favorite little beach.
Open: May–October plus weekends in April, November, and, December.

Reservations preferred. Two-day minimum in July and August.
Rates: Double occupancy. June 22–October, $80–$90. Rest of year, $60–$85. Singles $5 less, third person $15. AMEX, MC, VISA.
✂

Betsy's touch is everywhere, starting with the sign on the lawn and on into the kitchen with its hundreds of hand-painted counter tiles. She is a published botanical illustrator who has enhanced every room with an original illustration.

David's touch is everywhere too. An Air Force captain before he was a Vail, Colorado, high school teacher, he learned everything about the building trade by doing. The gambrel-roofed captain's house, built in 1900, had been a guest house for 38 years when the Knoxes bought it in 1985. And all because they followed up on a *Down East* magazine ad that they saw during their fifth Maine vacation!

(Marathoners) Betsy and David grew up in New England, but Betsy's grandparents come from Welby, England. (Hence the name of the inn.) The extension of this blend can be seen in the Laura Ashley wall prints, old New

(Please turn page.)

England beds, English wardrobes, and old quilts. Recent additions include an awning-covered patio, built with reproduction cobblestone and tucked among mature shrubbery. And the inn is now fronted by a traditional "dry" (without mortar) New England stone wall.

In residence: Daughter Jessica Ann, 13.
Bed and bath: Seven rooms, all private baths. On second floor, four with double beds, one with queen (full bath). Two third-floor skylit rooms; one with king bed, one with queen bed. Cot available.
Breakfast: 8:30. (Coffee at 7:30.) Homemade breads and muffins, an egg dish, and a variety of fruit. Juice, coffee, tea, milk; toast and cold cereal. In country-style dining room or enclosed sun room. Continental breakfast in bed upon request (9–10).
Plus: Evening beverage. Mints on the pillow. Flowers in rooms. Fireplaced living room. Guest pantry. Yard. Small gallery with paintings and tiles for sale.

Gundalow Inn   207/439-4040
6 Water Street, Kittery, ME 03904-1641

Hosts: Cevia and George Rosol
Location: On the town green and the banks of the Piscataqua River. Fantastic cycling country. Ten-minute walk across bridge to Portsmouth, New Hampshire (80 restaurants, Strawbery Banke, arts festival, concerts); 15-minute scenic drive to ocean beaches; 20 minutes to University of New Hampshire.
Open: Year round.
Rates: Double occupancy. Mid-May through mid-October, $95 double, $85 single. Off-season, $20 less. $15 additional person. MC, VISA.
♥ ✲ ✖ ✄

Very much the feeling of Grandmother's house, this 1889 brick Italianate Victorian was "rediscovered" when Cevia, a former editor/writer/antiquarian bookseller, and George, an electrical engineer, created the inn two years ago. There's a story for everything, including the hidden good-morning staircase, the builder's self-portrait with handlebar mustache, the inn's name (gundalows are workboats), and the innkeeper's award for having "the most books worth reading." If you're visiting locals, they are invited for breakfast. If you're a guest when the innkeepers host their choral group after a concert, you are invited to the party.

Foreign languages spoken: Some French, Slovak.
Bed and bath: Six rooms, private full baths. Queen-bedded room on first floor. On second, two double-bedded rooms, river views; another one with two extra-long pineapple twin beds. On third, one with queen bed, one with two twins, skylit river views, claw-foot tubs, hand-held showers. Rollaway available.
Breakfast: An event. Usually 8–9:30, Sunday 8:30–10. Freshly squeezed juice. Maybe peach yogurt soup. Exotic homemade scones. Egg dish, meat, or maybe George's smoked salmon, garnished with fresh fruit or herbs. Served on patio or in breakfast room with fireplace and river view.

Plus: Completely sprinklered. Piano. Ceiling fans. Individual thermostats. Beverages. Phone jacks. Perennial and herb garden. Rockers on porch overlooking river.

> From Connecticut: *"A special place . . . thought of every detail . . . met us at the car with an umbrella."* From Virginia: *"Fresh flowers, extra-large pillows and towels, blueberry scones to die for."* From Wisconsin: *"We went to bed—like on Christmas eve—barely able to wait to see what was for breakfast. Delightful fascinating hosts who have wonderful style in fixing up an old house."*

The Gazebo
207/646-3733

P.O. Box 668, Route 1, Ogunquit, ME 03907-0668

Host: Tony Fontes
Location: On Route 1, one mile north of Ogunquit village center. Ten-minute walk to beach. At trolley stop—to shops, restaurants, Perkins Cove.

Open: Year round except for the month of January. Two-night minimum, June 15–October 15.
Rates: Per room. $90–$100.
♥ ✼ ✄

Every day Tony hears, "What are we having for breakfast tomorrow?" It's a big feature here in the 150-year-old Greek Revival house that Tony gutted and rebuilt five years ago when he decided to leave his job as supervisor of an airlines complaint department. Perhaps you've heard Gene Burns on Boston's WRKO talk about The Gazebo. Or maybe you know some honeymooners who have been here. Or have seen the recipe for ham and egg croquettes with tomato and basil sauce in *Gourmet* magazine. Some weekends there are popular packages that include cooking demonstrations with the acclaimed Arrows Restaurant.

The latticed gazebo, a landmark on the trolley stop, has hanging geraniums in each of its eight archways. Window treatments—balloon shades, jabots, and swags—are often a source of comments from guests, who say that the inn feels like Grandmother's place. In the summer the pool surrounded by gardens is a peaceful place for predinner (bring your own) drinks. "And winter guests love the quiet pace of off-season."

Bed and bath: Nine air-conditioned rooms, all with private baths. One room with two twin beds, one suite with queen bed. A double bed in all other rooms. All antique beds. Upstairs rooms have sun deck.
Breakfast: 8:30–10. Maybe stuffed French toast with apricot-orange sauce, homemade turkey sausage, poached pear with raspberry sauce, eggs Benedict, homemade apple-walnut muffins. Served on china and crystal in fireplaced dining room overlooking the in-ground swimming pool.

---

*I*f *you have met one B&B host, you haven't met them all.*

The Morning Dove   207/646-3891

P.O. Box 1940, 30 Bourne Lane, Ogunquit, ME 03907-1940

Hosts: Peter and Eeta Sachon
Location: Off Shore Road. Away from major traffic. With lovely gardens. Short walk to trolley, beaches, shops, galleries, restaurants, harbor, and Ogunquit Playhouse.
Open: February–October. Two-day minimum preferred. Three-day weekend minimum on holidays and third June weekend through Labor Day weekend.

Rates: Late June–Labor Day: $100 private bath, $75 shared bath, $105 (the favorite) Grandma's attic room. Labor Day through mid-October: $90/$70/$95. February 11 through mid-May: $80/$60/$85. May 17–June 20: $85/$65/$90. Weekly stays, 10 percent less.
♥

More than an Ogunquit Christmas-by-the-Sea award winner, this B&B created two new careers for the hostess. Eeta had experience with people (as a flight attendant), art (as an art major in college), and antiques (her mother owned an antiques shop). In 1982 she and Peter, a commercial pilot, bought the "modernized" 1860 farmhouse. They added arched and bay windows and a Palladian one too. Peter became official architect, landscaper, and gardener. Eeta decorated with light colors, original paintings, and quilts, using an antique—a spinning wheel, a cradle or rocking horse, a collection of old toys—as a focal point in each room. And she became a professional interior designer who has decorated rooms for the Old York Historical Society show houses.

In residence: "Sultan, our boxer who thinks he's human, often visits."
Bed and bath: Six air-conditioned rooms on three floors; some with refrigerator. Third-floor room, a favorite, has king bed, private shower bath. Three queen-bedded rooms have private bath. Two rooms—one with double bed, other with two twins/king—share bath across the hall (robes provided). First-floor room has a queen and a twin bed, private bath.
Breakfast: 8:30–10. Muffins, croissants, bagels, Danish, fruit, juice, and freshly ground coffee. Served on bone china and linens on sun porch or in common room.
Plus: Suggestions for a romantic picnic site, a champagne breakfast, and wonderful sunsets. Welcoming beverage. Games, books, magazines. Huge covered porch. Garden. Chocolates in room.

> From Massachusetts: *"A treat. . . . Wonderful house. . . . Friendly, charming spot."* From New Jersey: *"On a scale of 1 to 10, it's 11!"*

Unless otherwise stated, rates in this book are per room for two and include breakfast in addition to all the amenities in "Plus." As for taxes and gratuities, please see page xii.

The Pine Hill Inn   207/361-1004

14 Pine Hill South, P.O. Box 2336, Ogunquit, ME 03907

Hosts: Charles and Diana Schmidt
Location: Secluded, "with just the sound of birds." Five-minute walk to Perkins Cove, restaurants, shops, beginning of cliff walk. Three-mile trolley ride to sandy beach; 10 minutes to Kittery outlets.

Open: Mid-May through October.
Rates: $60–$70 double, $50–$60 single. MC, VISA.
♥ ❖ ✈ ✂

Eight years in coming—to Maine and to innkeeping! This Victorian house, converted to a B&B about seven years earlier, was the dream place that in 1991 inspired the Schmidts to take early retirement. Wicker chairs, love seat, ottomans, and tables are in the common room surrounded by tongue-and-groove pine walls and ceilings. In Ohio Charles and Diana were self-employed in their own network-marketing business.

Bed and bath: Four rooms plus two-bedroom cottage; all private baths, individual heat control, ceiling fans. One double-bedded room has bath across the hall (robes provided). Two rooms with two twin beds. One room with queen bed plus two twins. In cottage, a double and two twin trundles.
Breakfast: Usually 8–10. Freshly squeezed orange juice, fruit cup, homemade granola, yogurt. Homemade muffins, breads or pastries, jams and jellies. Served in common room or on screened porch.
Plus: Beverage. Down pillows. Forgotten items.

> From Massachusetts: *"Diana has an eye for detail . . . fresh flowers . . . gorgeous (50-foot) screened porch that runs length of house . . . felt pampered."*

Bed & Breakfast of Maine Host #302

Portland, ME

Location: In town. On a quiet street with well-maintained historic mansions and town houses.
Reservations: Available year round through Bed & Breakfast of Maine,

page 41. Two-night minimum on weekends.
Rates: Per room. $95 double, $105 king, $125 suite. Less in off-season.
♥ ❖ ❖ ✈

All in one—the feeling of an art gallery, a museum, and a small sophisticated hotel, with fine antiques, collectibles, and enough decorating ideas and fascinating combinations to inspire many guests. There are extraordinary signed hand-done designs on the walls, marbleized floors, faux finishes, and a white wall too (filled with art). Before opening this landmark 1884 stucco Italianate in 1989, the hosts had experience in Scottish imports, antiques, and interior design.

Bed and bath: Six rooms on second and third floors. All private baths; some full, some tub or shower only. King, queen, double, or twin beds. Phone and small TV (sort of hidden) in each room.
Breakfast: 8–9. Fresh fruit, juice, blueberry pancakes or quiche, hot breads, hot beverages. Served in dining room.
Plus: Fireplaced parlor plus upstairs guest sitting room.

(Please turn page.)

From Massachusetts: *"One of the most outstanding B&Bs in the country. Splendid art, elegant furnishings, superb breakfasts, charming and well-informed host and hostess, outstanding downtown location. We would give it a five-star rating."*

West End Inn   207/772-1377
146 Pine Street, Portland, ME 04102-3541

Hosts: Tom and Hilary Jacobs
Location: Residential. In historic Western Promenade area. Within walking distance of restaurants, art galleries, shops, Old Port.
Open: Year round.

Rates: Memorial Day weekend–Columbus Day weekend, $90 double, $80 single. Off-season, $10 less. AMEX, MC, VISA.
♥ ⬛ ⁂ ◆ ✈ ⊁

The gracious restored brick town house, built in 1871, is the home of transplanted New Yorkers—a nurse and a banker. Their interests in sailing, art, auctions, and the coast brought them in 1990 to Portland, "where there are lighthouses, parks, and beaches—spectacular and unexpected." Hilary, a New Zealander, brought walking sticks (borrow one, if you wish) and paintings to remind her of her native country.

Bed and bath: Four carpeted rooms, all private modern baths. Three rooms on second floor, all with full baths; two are attached, one is across the hall. One third-floor room, shower bath. King, queen, or twin beds. Rollaway available.
Breakfast: Flexible hours. Blueberry pancakes with Maine maple syrup. Home-baked muffins and breads. Dining-room table set with china, silver, and fine linen.
Plus: Ceiling fans. Phone jacks in some rooms. Tea and freshly baked cookies. Fresh fruit and flowers. Mineral water. Transportation to/from airport.

From Massachusetts: *"The best."*

Crown 'n' Anchor Inn   207/282-3829
121 North Street, P.O. Box 228, Saco, ME 04072-0228

Hosts: John Barclay, Jim and Martha Forester
Location: On two acres of landscaped lawns in historic district. One mile from I-95, exit 5. Five-minute walk to museum, library, Thornton Academy. Two miles to Saco Beach,

10 to Kennebunkport, 18 to Ogunquit.
Open: Year round.
Rates: Double occupancy. $55–$75. Third person $10. MC, VISA.
♥ ⁂ ◆ ⊁

Townspeople applauded all through 1991 as Jim, a retired (Louisiana) professor, and John, a book jobber and retired banker, restored the elegant Federal/Greek Revival house that had been vacant for four years. Meanwhile,

Martha, a retired university librarian, was innkeeper at the well-received (smaller) B&B in Newcastle that they had all opened in 1988. By the time you read this, the antiques from Newcastle—ranging from Victorian rococo to primitives—will have been placed in the columned Saco mansion, in the double parlor with 18-inch-thick brick walls and an enormous marble-based gold leaf mirror, and in the earlier-built ell with its lower ceilings, gunstock corners, and hand-hewn beams. The grounds, too, are of particular interest. The property, on the National Register, was once owned by Dr. George Lincoln Goodale, the botany professor who was responsible for acquiring the Harvard University glass flower exhibits made by the Blaschka family of Germany.

> Guests will tell you that there's more. From New Jersey: *"Three people who complement each other and provide the key ingredient to create an ambiance."* From Minnesota: *"Saw them drive an anxious guest to the airport."* From Illinois: *"Comfortable . . . well-appointed . . . delicious breakfast sustained us till dinner. . . . There was a family emergency. The innkeepers managed to help the state police find us at our next unscheduled stop."*

Foreign language spoken: Some French.
Bed and bath: Six second-floor rooms, most with sitting areas, all with private baths. Three with working fireplaces. Antique twin or double beds. Rollaway available.
Breakfast: 7–10. "Country gourmet." Freshly squeezed orange juice, fresh fruit, home-baked bread, meat and egg dishes, tea, Louisiana dark roast coffee. By candlelight in formal dining room on Royal Doulton china.
Plus: "Books that have followed us home." TV. VCR. Beverages. Fans. Special occasions acknowledged. Guest refrigerator. Dinner, by advance reservation only. Small pets welcomed by prior arrangement only.

Academy Street Inn   207/384-5633
15 Academy Street, South Berwick, ME 03908-1506

Hosts: Thomas and Edith Boogusch
Location: Overlooking the town square. Ten miles from York Beach, Portsmouth, outlet shopping.

Open: Year round.
Rates: $45, double occupancy. $10 each additional person.

♥ ✚ ⬛ ✤ ✈ ✂

The Boogusches love this small town. "We're away from the hustle and bustle." They love their house. "Over a six-year period, we restored and decorated elegantly." And guests can tell that B&B as a family venture is another good match.

Once a restaurant in addition to being a Berwick Academy headmaster's house, the Victorian colonial has Austrian chandeliers, three carved oak fireplaces, paneled wainscoting in the dining room—and the pièce de résistance, a 65-foot screened wraparound porch.

> Guests wrote: *"A beautiful, comfortable, friendly place. . . . We were in town for a 50th reunion. Staying at that grand home was the highlight for us . . . lovely rooms . . . privacy . . . great cook . . . great people."*

(Please turn page.)

In residence: Jeremy, during college vacations. Shawn, 16; Andrew, 8; Kelsey, 4. One friendly golden retriever, Honey.

Bed and bath: Two very large second-floor rooms, one with a queen bed and one with a double and a twin bed, share a full hall bath. Rollaway and crib available.

Breakfast: 7–10. Choice of bacon or sausage with eggs, waffles, blueberry pancakes, or French toast. Fresh fruit. Juices. Coffee cakes and muffins. In formal dining room; in plant room; "at the kitchen bar, watching us cook"; or on the deck.

Plus: Fresh flowers from gardens that, too, are being revitalized. Piano. Room phone and TV by request. Window fans. Robes. Laundry. Kitchen privileges. Guest refrigerator.

Harbour Cottage Inn   207/244-5738

Clark Point and Dirigo Roads, P.O. Box 258, Southwest Harbor, ME 04679-0258

Hosts: Ann and Mike Pedreschi
Location: Across the road from harbor and lobster wharfs. Two-minute walk from oceanarium and town dock.
Open: Year round.

Rates: Double occupancy. $50–$85 twin, $55–$90 queen, $60–$95 king, $85–$125 suite, depending on season. Single $5 less. AMEX, MC, VISA.
♥ ❖ ✈

From Alabama: *"Decorated with some absolute treasures from Ann's family in England. . . . Most luxurious B&B bath I've seen."* From New Jersey: *"Fabulous gourmet breakfasts and lively, kind personalities of the young couple."* From New York: *"A gem. Pass it along."*

As Ann, a ceramicist and former motel manager, says, "Mike traveled from Poughkeepsie, New York, to Mt. Desert Island in 1989 and fell in love with the area, and within six months we were here, undoing four apartments in the 1870 structure, installing a sprinkler system, and furnishing with some antiques, including a German piano."

In residence: One cat "not allowed in inn." Bert, a very old dog "allowed on the front deck and in the back office."

Bed and bath: Eight rooms on three floors, private baths (with hair dryers and heat lamps). First-floor canopied king bed, steam shower with seat. On second floor, queen and king beds with whirlpool steam shower or seated steam bath. On third floor, twin beds or king; suite with queen bed, sitting room with daybed, bath with double whirlpool.

Breakfast: 7:30–10. While you eat continental buffet—home-baked breads and muffins, fresh fruit salad, juice—chef's special (served at individual tables) announced. Could be blueberry pancakes, waffles with homemade raspberry or blueberry sauce plus cream, banana delight, French toast, quiche Lorraine. (Please request special diet accommodation before breakfast.) Coffee, decaf, tea.

Plus: Ceiling fans/individual thermostats (except ground-floor king room). Tea or coffee at 5:30 with homemade nibbles. Fresh flowers in season. Thick bath sheets. Turndown service. TV with VCR. In winter, dinner packages by advance arrangement.

Harbour Woods

207/244-5388

P.O. Box 1214, Southwest Harbor, ME 04679

Hosts: Margaret Eden and James Paviglionite
Location: Across from the harbor, within walking distance of the village and Wendell Gilley Museum (wooden carved birds). Next door to town-owned ice skating pond.
Open: Year round. Three-night minimum during holidays and on holiday weekends.

Rates: Double occupancy. August, $85 harbor view, $95 garden view, $105 queen four-poster. July $10 less. September–October $60–$95, November–April 14 $50–$70, April 15–June $55–$75. Singles $5 less.
♥ ☚ ⁂ ✖ ⌇

The multifaceted innkeepers—everything from sailing to being an EMT—were in real estate (Margaret) and managed a plant (Jim) in Connecticut and Illinois before they came here for a summer cottage business. In 1990 they opened their dream, a renovated 1800s farmhouse (in the front room only the moldings could be salvaged) with comfortable furnishings and interesting window treatments. Flexible hosts, they will direct you to the best view on the island or lend you a cooler, and they get a big kick out of seeing interesting guests entertain one another.

In residence: Charlie, a friendly cocker spaniel, "not allowed to entertain guests as much as he would like to."
Bed and bath: Three second-floor queen-bedded (one four-poster) rooms, private baths. Two with harbor views. Two with individual thermostats.
Breakfast: 8–9 (coffee at 7). A picture. Garnished. Oatmeal pancakes with sauteed apples or lemon with raspberry sauce, noodle kugel, grilled citrus salad/melon salad/banana crunch with yogurt, granola, omelets, herb baked eggs, puffy cheese-and-egg bake, filled or cinnamon French toast. Fresh flowers and background music. In fireplaced dining room. By candlelight on foggy mornings.
Plus: Beverages. Beach towels. TV in parlor. Fresh flowers. Mints. Special occasions acknowledged (extra charge).

> From Canada: *"High standards. They managed to convert us to B&B stays."* From North Carolina: *"Beautifully decorated . . . a delicious multicourse breakfast."* From another Maine innkeeper: *"Truly a memorable experience."*

KEY TO SYMBOLS
♥ Lots of honeymooners come here.
☚ Families with children are very welcome. (Please see page xiii.)
☚ "Please emphasize that we are a private home, not an inn."
⁂ Groups or private parties sometimes book the entire B&B.
♦ Travel agents' commission paid. (Please see page xii.)
✖ Sorry, no guests' pets are allowed.
⌇ No smoking inside *or* no smoking at all, even on porches.

The Island House

207/244-5180

Box 1006, Clark Point Road, Southwest Harbor, ME 04679-1006

Host: Ann Gill
Location: Across the street from the harbor. Ten-minute walk from the village center. Five minutes' walk to lobster docks, Oceanarium, and Coast Guard station. Five minutes' drive to Acadia National Park and the open ocean; 15 miles from Bar Harbor.

Open: April through December. Two-night minimum in July and August.
Rates: June–October, $45 single, $55 double. April, May, November, and December, $40 single, $55 double. $20 cot. Loft apartment $95 for two; $115 for three; $135 four.
♥ ♯ ⛵ ❄ ♦ ✄

From Maine: *"We are professional craftspeople who first stayed at Island House when we were there for a show. We are about to return for our seventh year. Ann is a warm, gracious hostess who makes her guests feel very much at home. . . . Always ready to recommend a favorite restaurant. . . . Rooms are very clean, bright, and comfortable, and the breakfasts are excellent."*

Mount Desert Island's first summer hotel grew to four stories before being separated in 1912 into two houses, one of which is The Island House, home to the Gill family for 22 years. Old photos, a page from an old register, and an advertising poster illustrate the changes. Today the house has much of the original pine woodwork, a kitchen (the gathering place in cool months) with wood stove, and furnishings that reflect Ann's childhood years in Southeast Asia. Often Ann is happy to assist with outing plans, and she also enjoys playing the piano and cello.

Foreign language spoken: Some French.
Bed and bath: Four second-floor rooms share a full bath on the second and a shower bath on the first floor. One room has two twin beds, one a double bed and decorative fireplace. One cozy room with sloped ceiling has two twin beds. One spacious queen-bedded room. Cot available. Loft efficiency apartment sleeps up to four (who eat breakfast in main house).
Breakfast: Usually 7:30–8:30. Full. Perhaps eggs Florentine and cheese/sausage souffle, blueberry coffee cake or warm muffins. Juices, fruits, dry cereal, toast, coffee, teas.
Plus: Welcoming beverage. Piano. Porch glider. Large garden with picnic table. Fresh flowers.

Many B&Bs that allow smoking restrict it to certain rooms and/or public areas. Although some of those B&Bs that have the ✄ symbol allow smoking on the porch and/or patio, others do not allow smoking anywhere on the property.

Island Watch

207/244-7229

P.O. Box 1359, Freeman Ridge Road, Southwest Harbor, ME 04679

Host: Maxine M. Clark
Location: Quiet. High atop Freeman Ridge, overlooking harbors of Southwest Harbor and Mount Desert. Five-minute walk by graveled road through woods to the village, 15-minute walk by paved town road. Within walking distance of Seal Cove's narrow graveled Acadia National Park Road with scenic winding trails.
Open: March–November. Two-night minimum.
Rates: Double occupancy. $55–$65 depending on length of stay. $15 third person in room.
♥ ❉ ♦ ⅋

The grandmother of four (ranging from age 13 to 24) likes to hike, motorcycle, snowmobile, sail, sew, and cook. Maxine, a professional Realtor, spent her early years on an island; and as a teenager, when her father was a lighthouse keeper, she lived in Bass Harbor Lighthouse.

With its white walls and clear, uncluttered space, the family-built (1967) house uses the great outdoors as its primary decor. The floor-to-ceiling windows give the feeling of living above the treetops. (The songbirds love the area too.) And the sunrise was a treat right from here! There are plenty of comfortable chairs in front of the enormous fieldstone fireplace, which was built with stones from the family farm site. Likely to be around are native-born friends who offer sailboat rides, tell fish stories, and help with maps.

In residence: Sonsie, a black poodle, seldom with guests.
Bed and bath: Six rooms, all with private bath (one with tub, rest with showers). Two handicapped-accessible rooms (suites) each have a double and a single bed. King, queen, or double beds plus cot available.
Breakfast: 7:30–9:30. French toast, pancakes, waffles, or bacon and eggs. Homemade breads. Coffee, juice, and cereal. Maxine cooks in a marvelous arrangement that allows her simultaneously to work in the kitchen, socialize with guests, and point out the Bluenose ferry rounding the tip of the island.
Plus: One deck for sunning, one for shade; both for stargazing. Barbecue. Will meet guests at Bar Harbor airport. Storage space for bikes, skis, camping equipment, snowmobiles.

Penury Hall

207/244-7102

Box 68, Main Street, Southwest Harbor, ME 04679

Hosts: Toby and Gretchen Strong
Location: In the village, "just 2¾ miles from Echo Lake and Acadia Mountain Trail."
Open: Year round except March 15–April 15. Two-night minimum June–September.
Rates: June–September $45 single, $55 double. October and May $40 single, $50 double. November–April $30 single, $40 double.
🐾 ⅋

Turn the old bell on one of the etched-windowed double doors—and you will be warmly greeted by horn-rimmed Toby and, very likely, those two felines, who may assist in escorting you to your room.

(Please turn page.)

A 1981 trip to Cape Breton and Nova Scotia inspired the Strongs to become one of the first "quiet side" B&Bs. In summer their porch is blossom-filled by the Tremont Town Manager, Gretchen. Toby's diverse professional experiences include newspaper editing, innkeeping, his own software company, and, most recently, the duties of acting Chamber of Commerce director.

Since moving here in 1978 with their two teenage sons, the Strongs have been restoring the house, which was built in sections at different times. The oldest part dates back to 1830. It is comfortably furnished. "And don't forget to mention the forest green living-room walls with pure white trim." (Everybody does.)

In residence: Two cats, Patches and Trepid, who have been "brought up with guests." One son during college vacations.
Bed and bath: Three second-floor rooms. One with twin beds, two with double beds. Two shared baths, one with shower and one with tub.
Breakfast: 7:30–9. Juice, fresh fruit, maybe eggs Benedict, blueberry pancakes, omelet, date-walnut French toast, assorted eggs with muffins, homemade jams and jellies, pure maple syrup. Prepared and served by Toby, who usually joins guests.
Plus: Tea. Sauna. Laundry. Kitchen privileges in winter. Use of canoe, windsurfer, 21-foot day sailer. Very helpful printed information about the area.

Two Seasons   207/244-9627

Box 829, Southwest Harbor, ME 04679-0829   winter **919/855-5622**
Winter address: 14 Brandy Court, Greensboro, NC 27409

Host: Dorothy Lazareth
Location: On the harbor side of Main Street. Within walking distance of town center.
Open: June 15–October 15. Two-

night minimum in July and August.
Rates: Per room. $60 shared bath. $70 private bath.
✹

One morning the block letters in the wall-mounted printer's tray read, "We love 2 seasons." The message changes according to the whim of guests, who, Dorothy says, "seem to be interested in everything."

The hostess had visited relatives in the area for many years. Six years ago, upon early retirement from teaching on Long Island, she thought of "this beautiful place, the sunsets, and the harbor."

Built for a doctor (hence the two entrances and the caduceus in the shutters) in the 1940s, and at one time a motel annex, the square colonial received the Lazareth touch—casual, clean comfort, good beds, some wicker, imaginative use of wallpaper and borders, and some whimsy too. (Ask to see room 2A.) Dorothy, an ardent winter golfer, planted flower gardens and provided lawn chairs for harbor viewing. "People seem to gather in my kitchen. They often express surprise at all there is to do and see in the second most visited national park—and they wish they could stay longer. Of course there's always talk about restaurants, and sometimes, yachts. (The Hinckley Boat Yard is in town.)"

Foreign languages spoken: French and German.
Bed and bath: Four second-floor rooms, two with private bath, each with one double or two twin beds. (Maximum of two persons per room.) Two rooms face the harbor, two the street. All shower baths with hand-held showers.
Breakfast: 8–9. Juices, fresh fruit, cereals, home-baked breads and muffins, hot beverages. Served on screened/glassed porch overlooking harbor.
Plus: Fireplaced living room. TV. VCR. Front porch. Ice. Use of refrigerator.

Broad Bay Inn and Gallery   207/832-6668
P.O. Box 607, 1014 Main Street, Waldoboro, ME 04572

Host: Libby Hopkins
Location: In residential village neighborhood, a half mile off U.S. Route 1. Short drive to ferries for Monhegan Island, Islesboro, and Vinal Haven. Close to Audubon wildlife sanctuary, Damariscotta Lake, Medomak River, Camden.
Open: Year round. Two-night mini-

mum on July and August weekends.
Rates: Per room. May–October, $70 Victorian double. $75 Canopy Room. $60 and $45, second- and third-floor rooms. Other months, 20 percent less. Thanksgiving and Christmas packages. MC, VISA.
♥ ◢ ⁂ ◆ ✈

> Guests send accolades: *"Our favorite (of all stayed in throughout the country). . . . Breakfasts are hearty, subtle, and delicious. . . . Furnished with elegance of a kind that doesn't get in the way of comfort . . . a woman of great kindness and extraordinary thoughtfulness. . . . One feels both comfort and a sense of occasion. . . . Charm, charm, charm all the way."*

Waldoboro reminds Libby of North Carolina summer stock days, when she ran art shows at the theater and met one Jim Hopkins, a designer/actor/puppeteer/singer. Three decades later, having been artists with Princeton University, the Educational Testing Service, and the *Wall Street Journal*, the Hopkinses settled here, opened an art gallery, established workshops with renowned instructors, and became professional caterers as well as community leaders—with the reopened Waldo Theatre, the library and schools, the Lions Club, and much more. Guests remember sleigh rides, a wedding in the garden, the decor, the food—and the hosts.

Foreign language spoken: Some French.
Bed and bath: Five rooms, three shared shower baths. First-floor double-bedded room shares hosts' bath. Two second-floor baths are shared by second-floor double-bedded room, one room with canopied four-poster double (floor-to-ceiling windows overlooking garden), one with two twin beds, and a third-floor room (reached by steep stairs) that has one twin bed.
Breakfast: 8–9. Special diets may be accommodated by advance notice. Menu at host's whim. Maybe croissants, blueberry muffins, homemade breads; frittata, Parmesan baked eggs, ham, bacon, sausage, pancakes, crepes, baked apples, fresh fruit ambrosia. Served on English china on starched

(Please turn page.)

hand-embroidered white tablecloths, in dining room or by kitchen wood stove.

Plus: Sun deck. Screened porch overlooking garden. Hammock. Evening beverage. Fresh flowers and fruit. VCR; musical film tapes. Art and theater library. Robes. Fans. English soap, potpourri. TV, games, piano.

Le Vatout
218 Kaler's Corner Street, Waldoboro, ME 04572-6003

207/832-4552

Host: Donald Slagel
Location: On Route 32 south (has water views all the way to Pemaquid Point). Half mile from Route 1. Near the Old German Meeting House (1779).
Open: Year round. Advance reservations required November through April.

Rates: $40 single, shared bath. $50 double with shared bath, $65 private bath. $10 third person. No charge for babes in arms or use of portacrib.

♥ ♨ ♨ ♣ ♦ ✈

> From Austria: "... and above all the landlord himself radiates charm and made us really feel at home ('gemütlich')." From New York: "Superb recommendations for restaurants and a bicycle route." From Massachusetts: "Homey comfort combined with taste ... gourmet-delicious and healthful breakfast. Most enchanting, however, were the gardens with walks and benches. The breakfast room overlooks this beautiful splendor and made one never want to get up and leave."

Before returning here in 1986, this popular host lived in many places from Maine to Mexico as musician, teacher, composer, conductor, author, actor, singer, artist/sculptor. He filled his pre-Civil War expanded Cape house with family pieces and much art. Overlooking the gardens, which have attracted garden clubs from Maine to Massachusetts, is the barn-turned-gallery complete with antique Palladian windows.

In residence: CioCioSan, "a friendly cat who comes in only to eat in the summer." Four named bantams; one was famous for a short time in 1991.
Foreign languages spoken: "Vestigial German, Spanish, French."
Bed and bath: Five rooms. On first floor, room with queen bed, a twin bed, private bath. On second floor, two double-bedded rooms and one room with twin beds share two and one-half shower baths. Available June through September is one large second-floor room with private entrance, one double bed, two twin beds, private shower bath; minimum three-day stay.
Breakfast: 7:30–9. Perhaps gougere, fruit cobbler, asparagus on toast, quiche—"something not found in a restaurant." Freshly brewed coffee/tea, orange juice and/or fruit, homemade breads, muffins, jams/jellies, cereals.

---

*T*hink *of bed and breakfast as a people-to-people concept.*

The Barn Bed and Breakfast   207/832-5781

2987 Friendship Road, South Waldoboro, ME 04572

Host: Helen Power
Location: "The only humanly inhabited barn along this country road." Not far from a barn depicted in one of Andrew Wyeth's paintings. Six miles from Waldoboro (and Morse's sauerkraut); three from Friendship, where one of the original sloops departs for summer morning and afternoon cruises.
Open: May 15–October 15. Advance reservations appreciated.
Rates: $45 double, $35 single. $10 cot.
♥ ♦ ➤ ✳ ✈

Pages and pages! Guests' letters written to me from all over the world extol everything from the wildflowers at the doorstep to the tasteful decor, from the sense of humor to discussions about poetry, health care systems, cycling routes. From Canada: "I learned a lot from Helen about Maine, but even more importantly, about enjoying life fully, wherever I happen to be. Bravo Helen!"

First built across the road about 1793, the barn has been moved, divided, added to, and finally reconstructed into a well-insulated architectural gem. Helen, too, loves this place, and the fields and open sky, "the blue smile of the firmament." In 11 years of hosting, this grandmother, a potter, has had the pleasure of seeing the growing children of many repeat visitors.

In residence: A 15-year-old shy cat, Heimie, has "a Spanish past" and lives in the unreconstructed end of the barn.
Foreign languages spoken: "Some French and German."
Bed and bath: Three rooms share one full bath and an upstairs skylit living room. One large room with double bed; one medium-sized room with two twin beds. One small room, Helen's favorite (comfortable but "you cannot swing a cat in it"), with single bed. Cot available.
Breakfast: Usually at 8. Fruit (maybe blackberries picked that morning in the lane) or juice. "Blintzes are my specialty. Give me a bit of warning." Bacon and eggs, crepes, or omelets; homemade blueberry, rice, or kasha muffins served in old-fashioned cast iron muffin pans. Served on her own blue-and-brown pottery in brick-floored kitchen.
Plus: Flowers from Helen's garden. Wood stoves for heat. Plenty of books. Comfortable outdoor chairs. Horseshoes.

From Minnesota: *"A delight to the senses . . . exquisitely set table . . . a gift."*

Maine Back Roads Bed & Breakfast

Tatnic Road, Wells, ME   **207/676-9460**
Mailing address: RD 1, Box 530A, South Berwick, ME 03908-9602

Hosts: Joseph Hardy and Alice Schleiderer
Location: Rural. Five miles inland from Route 1. Six miles from beaches. On 100 acres of woods and a few fields. Within half hour of Kennebunkport, Ogunquit, York.
Open: Year round.
Rates: $37 single, $48 double. $18 extra adult, $10 child.
♦ ➤ ✂

(Please turn page.)

"We press our own cider in the fall, cut our wood in winter, and have large organic gardens in summer. We are much like the farm family that takes in a traveler for a night's lodging. There's nothing commercial about our B&B."

Over a five-year period Alice and Joseph designed and built their post-and-beam solar house with four levels, following the natural contours of the south-facing slope, using timber from their own land. It is cool in the summer and warm in the winter; but they do have four wood stoves, including an antique cookstove in the kitchen. The house has wonderful natural light, wood floors and ceilings, and black granite masonry walls in dining and living rooms.

Joseph, an educator and native Mainer, formerly ran historical tours of rural Maine that was and is—everything from shipbuilding sites to marshes and glacial boulders. Alice, originally from California, has her own private counseling practice.

In residence: Daughter, Hesper Dawn, 12. Her pride and joy, Half-Bar-Three, quarter horse. Peabody, a friendly cat "who is bossy with Max, a calm Husky mix."
Foreign language spoken: "Stumbling" French.
Bed and bath: A double bed and a twin bed in a very private large second-floor room lined with windows, surrounded by trees. Full bath shared with hosts. Crib available.
Breakfast: 7–9 at time set according to guests' schedule. Fruit, eggs or pancakes with real maple syrup and homemade preserves, cereals including homemade granola. Homemade muffins, biscuits or cinnamon rolls. All without additives.
Plus: Private entrance and deck. Welcoming tea. Fresh flowers. Babysitting possibilities. From here, trails for hiking and cross-country skiing.

Tatnic B&B   207/676-2209
Tatnic Road, Wells, ME
Mailing address: Box 518A, South Berwick, ME 03908-9607

Hosts: Tin and Jane Smith
Location: Secluded. On 63 acres at the end of a five-mile uphill road off of Route l. Six miles to Ogunquit's beaches; 15 to Kennebunkport and to Durham, New Hampshire.

Open: Year round.
Rates: $30 single, $45 double. $10 each daybed. Children's special— $55 for one family in a room. MC, VISA.

This warm, inviting environment is enhanced by two people who haven't changed their outlook since building their passive-solar, almost maintenance-free home "with the help of all our friends" in 1978–80. It heats with about 3½ cords of wood in the winter. Insulation and cross-ventilation keep it cool "like a cave" in summer.

Tin, in addition to being a talented builder-by-doing and gardener (130 fruit trees plus crops), is a board member of the Maine Organic Farmers and Gardeners and works with a local land trust. Jane loves teaching, creating, and quilt making. Since being featured in *Family Circle* for her ingenious patterns and "Quilt-in-One-Day" presentations (inquire about some held in Ogunquit), she travels nationwide to give workshops.

As in an expanded New England farmhouse, a solar addition was built in 1986 for Tin's mother, Marie-Louise Smith, who plants hundreds of flowers each year. "And out by the road" are 1,500 different vegetable and flower varieties grown by a successful market gardener.

In residence: A tabby named Sam. "Ben and Jake are our Percheron workhorses, who help farm, gather wood, and give us cart rides."
Foreign language spoken: Marie-Louise speaks Danish.
Bed and bath: Two "treetop" rooms—reached via open curved oak staircase from two-storied living room—share first-floor full bath. One room with extra-long queen bed and space for three cots; one with two twin beds.
Breakfast: Usually 8–9. Fruit; corn pancakes with real maple syrup; home-made blueberry muffins; granola or eggs. Tatnic's honey. Cheerios available for kids. Served in dining area by fireplace and windowed walls that overlook beautiful gardens (and hummingbirds, too, when we were there).
Plus: Tree swing. Fans. Outdoor furniture (and maybe mosquitoes too). Ideas for a floor plan with well-designed built-ins. Kitchen facilities for dinner preparations. Evening swim at Ell Pond, seven miles away. Quilt-making session (nominal fee) by advance arrangement.

The Sunset House   207/963-7156

Route 186, HCR 60, Box 62, West Gouldsboro, ME 04607

Hosts: Carl and Kathy Johnson
Location: On the Schoodic Penin-sula near Flander's Bay. Bordered by Jones Pond. Six miles from Winter Harbor; an hour "down east" of Bar Harbor.
Open: Year round. Two-night mini-mum, July–October weekends.

Rates: Double occupancy. Novem-ber–April 15, $49; April 16 through June and September 16 through Oc-tober, $55; July–September 15, $65. Singles $10 less. Extra person $10. Six-day or longer stays, seventh night free. MC, VISA.
♥ ♯ 🐾 ⁂ ✗ ✄

From Massachusetts: *"The view was breathtaking, the sea air invigorating, Carl's feast for my husband's birthday—memorable. A lovely home. Highly recommended for a place to get away and renew yourself."*

The Johnsons, active community members, came from Cape Cod in 1989 to this aptly named Victorian B&B that "has only been modernized by heat, electricity, and running water. The decor changes while we make painting and papering ongoing projects." Right here there are mesmerizing sunsets and moonlit nights on the water. There's swimming, fishing, canoeing. A millstream with babbling water running to the bay. And Carl, an executive chef at a large seasonal hotel, who uses locally grown products.

In residence: Mason, 13, and Matthew, 11. Tammy and Maggie, "official greeters," are toy apricot poodles. Smokey and Slash are mother/daughter cats.
Foreign language spoken: Some German.

(Please turn page.)

Bed and bath: Seven rooms on second and third floors. One room overlooks pond; four have ocean view. On each floor, two shared full baths. Double or twin beds. Daybed and crib available.
Breakfast: 7–9. Specialties include sour-cream cinnamon-raisin French toast, yeast-raised sourdough waffles, omelets. Special diets accommodated.
Plus: Tea or coffee with homemade goat milk cheeses and pastries or breads. Wood stove in parlor. Robes. Beach towels. Volleyball. Badminton. Wrap-around second-floor deck. In winter, dinners (extra charge).

Hannah's Loft Bed & Breakfast   207/363-7244

162 Chases Pond Road, York, ME 03909-5716

Hosts: Hannah and Dan Rothermel
Location: Wooded. Surrounded by sound of birds, miles of country roads. Five minutes from historic downtown York and four public beaches.
Open: April–October.

Rates: Double occupancy $65. Two or more nights, $60/night. Singles, $10 less weekdays. Extra person $15. Five percent donated to Maine Children's Cancer Program.
♥ ♦ ✦ ✗ ✂

Five years ago the Rothermels were thinking of moving and decided that this is just where they wanted to be—with B&B guests. They built a breakfast/common room—it connects their reproduction Cape house to the gambrel-roofed garage and new guest rooms above—with a blue ceramic tile floor and gray-stained barnboard walls. It's Hannah's favorite room, "where the magic happens," decorated with friends' photographs, a local potter's ware, mugs hung on antique nails, and stitchery.

Dan, an author/writer, teaches seventh-grade English. Hannah is a hospice volunteer, at-home mother, runner, and biker.

In residence: In hosts' quarters, Molly, 12; Robyn, 10; Will, 8. One kitty.
Bed and bath: Two private-entrance "treetop" rooms, each with skylight. One with queen, one with twins/king option share a large deck. Private en-suite shower baths with heat lamps. Built-in desks. Individual thermostats. Rollaway and crib available.
Breakfast: Flexible hours. Early coffee. Then omelets, Texas French toast, fruited pancakes or waffles, quiche. Fresh fruits, breads, muffins, biscuits.
Plus: Beverages and homemade goodies. Nuts and candies. Babysitting. Down quilts. Flannel sheets. Fresh flowers. Use of refrigerator, microwave, freezer.

From New York: *"Our favorite relaxation spot . . . cozy and charming, wonderful homemade breads . . . peaceful privacy, early coffee and newspaper; special diets accommodated; huge fluffy bath towels; easy conversation . . . romantic . . . felt pampered."* From New Jersey: *"Best vacation ever. I'd be back tomorrow if I could find a job and they could put up with me. I did not want to leave."*

B&Bs offer the ultimate concierge service.

Hutchins House   207/363-3058

209 Organug Road, York, ME 03909

Hosts: Linda Hutchins and daughter Liz Barrett.
Location: On a hill overlooking the river and the country's oldest pile-driven drawbridge. Surrounded by lawns, gardens, and large oak trees. "Twenty-minute walk upriver through a wooded park, passing by boats and shorebirds to York Harbor Beach." Within walking distance of downtown.

Open: Year round. Two-night minimum on weekends July–August.
Rates: (Include continental breakfast; hot entree $5 extra.) Double occupancy. June weekends, holiday weekends, and July–October, $75 shared bath, $85 private. Saturdays, $4 one-night surcharge. Off-season $65–$69. $25 third person. $130 suite. Picnic baskets, $5.50/person.

♥ 🏠 ⁂ 🐾 ✂

> From Massachusetts: "*Spacious rooms—with a view! A lovely home with loving people.*"

"I raised six kids in this 17-room turn-of-the-century house, and I am so very happy to have a reason to stay here and keep it beautiful! Guests are welcome to use the Jacuzzi or borrow a canoe or rowboat."

Linda is a registered nurse, a massage therapist, an avid gardener, and an adventure traveler who spends almost two winter months a year traveling all over the world while her daughter and partner Liz Barrett runs the B&B. Often, breakfasts here have a Caribbean flavor, a holdover from Linda's days as owner and operator of a charter boat in the Virgin Islands.

In residence: "O.J. Ole! is our large orange coon cat."
Foreign language spoken: College French.
Bed and bath: Four large tall-ceilinged rooms overlooking the river. Two with air conditioning and private full baths. Two second-floor queen-bedded rooms. On third floor, one queen and one room with two twin beds. Rollaway available.
Breakfast: 8–9:30. Homemade breads, fresh fruit, juice, and coffee. Hot entrees—blueberry pancakes, eggs Benedict, or Western omelets. Served on flower-filled river-view deck with awning or on wicker-furnished sun porch.
Plus: Guest refrigerator. Down comforters. Mints on pillow. Bikes for rent.

Scotland Bridge Inn   207/363-4432

1 Scotland Bridge Road, York, ME 03909

Hosts: Sylvia and Dick Jansen
Location: About 800 feet from the river. In rural area known as "Scotland in York." Five-minute drive to center of town.
Open: Year round. Two-night minimum on weekends June–October.

Rates: $65 double, shared bath, $85 private. $20 extra person $5 less per night for four-day or longer stays. MC, VISA; service charge for credit cards.

♥ ⁂ 🐾 ✂

Lace in the windows. A canopied bed. A horse-buggy seat upholstered with flowered black fabric. They are part of the transformation of this large

(Please turn page.)

2½-storied 1835 farmhouse, perhaps the first B&B in York when Sylvia, mother of five grown children, opened in 1983. She serves afternoon tea in the 27-foot-long fireplaced living room—or in your bedroom. The large yard has a chip and putting green. (Dick, a retired sea captain, is an avid golfer.) And some guests bring a canoe or skiff to launch—just 800 feet from the house.

In residence: Liberty, a 12-year-old female English cocker.
Bed and bath: Four second-floor rooms. One room with four-poster twin beds and two double-bedded rooms (one canopied) share a pine-paneled full bath. (Kimonos provided.) A two-room suite with private shower bath, double bed plus trundle bed. Rollaway available.
Breakfast: 8:30–9. Blueberry pancakes with bacon, eggs Benedict or omelets with sausage, codfish cakes and eggs, or French toast with blueberry sauce. Juice, fresh fruit, coffee, tea. In dining room with sterling silver and linen napkins.
Plus: Ceiling and window fans. Phone jack. Down quilts. Beach towels. Mints. Guest refrigerator. English herb and perennial gardens. Front porch.

> From Connecticut: *"Early 19th-century decor, lovely and comfortable rooms, delicious gourmet breakfasts . . . off the beaten path but close to attractions . . . a hostess who makes us feel at home."*

The Wild Rose of York B&B   207/363-2532
78 Long Sands Road, York, ME 03909

Hosts: Fran and Frank Sullivan
Location: One mile from the ocean. On a hill in a quiet area near center of the historic village. Just down the road from a game preserve with trails for hiking or cross-country skiing.
Open: Year round except for some times in the winter. Two-day minimum on summer and holiday weekends.
Rates: June–October 15, $50 single, $60 double. Rest of year, $45 single; $55 double one night, $50 two consecutive nights. Extra person $20; child age 11–15 $10; 1–10 $5. Year round, seventh night free.
✹ ✂

Captain Rufus Donnell built this columned colonial mansion in 1814 for his bride. In 1985 Fran and Frank, authors of *Budget Dining and Lodging in New England,* moved here from Massachusetts "for the fun of meeting new people, making them comfortable, and helping them to appreciate an area." Fran is still a nurse/counselor who works with older persons. In addition, she is an artist and quilter who offers summer art "get-togethers." Frank, a biology professor at Salem (Massachusetts) State College, often suggests tide pool areas and York's mile-long cliff walk. Winter brings cross-country skiing and hot soup by the fire.

Foreign languages spoken: French and some German understood.
Bed and bath: Three rooms, all private baths. One first-floor room with a queen and a single bed, unattached private shower bath. On second floor, one room with double four-poster and working fireplace, full bath. One with a double bed and enclosed sun porch with single bed and room for a cot, full bath. Cot available.

Breakfast: 8–9. Fruit-filled crepes, apple nut waffles, peach pancakes, Belgian waffles, Dutch puff (popover with apples). Juice, fruit, coffee or tea. Served in dining room fashioned after a tavern, or on large front porch.
Plus: Welcoming beverage. Two large common rooms, fireplaced living room. Piano (spontaneous concerts and sing-alongs encouraged). Library/TV/game room. Window fans. Wraparound partially screened porch. Hibachis. Umbrella tables. Huge yard with swing, lawn darts, bocci ball.

Canterbury House   207/363-3505
432 York Street, P.O. Box 881, York Harbor, ME 03911-0881

Hosts: James T. Pappas and James (Jim) S. Hager
Location: Overlooking York Harbor. Within walking distance of soft sand Harbor Beach. Near restaurants, outlets, deep-sea fishing, antiques shops.
Open: Year round. Two-night minimum on holiday weekends and all weekends in season.

Rates: $69 double, shared bath; $85 private. $10 less with continental breakfast. $20 extra person. Weekly rates and weekend packages. MC, VISA.

♥ ♥ ❖ ♦ ✈ ⊁

R&R accompanied by classical music is the order of the day in this century-old Victorian restored by James, a retired travel agent turned drapery designer, and Jim, a justice of the peace who works in real estate. They feature theme weekends for most holidays and dinner parties for up to 20. Weddings, too, are held here.

In residence: Butchy, a cat not allowed in guest quarters.
Foreign languages spoken: Greek, French, and German.
Bed and bath: Seven rooms, some with harbor view, on second and third floors. One with private bath, double bed, sofa bed. Other baths shared (robes provided) by three rooms. Two doubles, a twin, or a double bed and a twin bed in each room.
Breakfast: 8–10. Fresh orange juice, fruit salad, fresh hot muffins. Full includes Belgian waffles, French toast, or casserole. At separate tables set with china, crystal, sterling silver, linens.
Plus: Tea time at 4, munchies and beverages at 5. Down comforters. Turndown service. Mints on pillow. Fresh flowers and fruit. Beach towels and chairs. Guest refrigerator. Transportation to/from airport, bus, and train station.

> Innkeeping may be America's most envied profession. As one host mused, "Where else can you get a job where, every day, someone tells you how wonderful you are?"

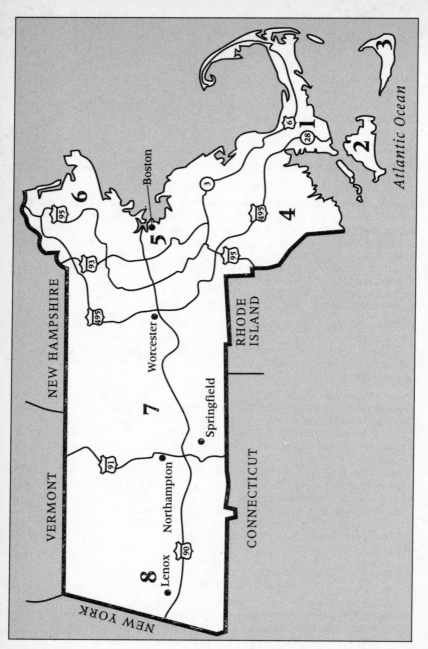

The numbers on this map indicate the areas for which there are detailed sections.

MASSACHUSETTS

Massachusetts
_____ Reservation Services _____

Many B&Bs throughout the state are represented by:

Pineapple Hospitality, Inc.
P.O. Box F821, New Bedford, MA 02742-0821

Phone: 508/990-1696 or 800/698-1696 (MA); 800/743-1696 (USA). Monday–Friday 9–5.

Fax: 508/997-8488.

Listings: 150+. Located throughout all six New England states; about half are in Massachusetts. They are in big and small cities and towns, villages, and farmlands—and even on a boat (summer only, including a half-day charter). Most are hosted private residences; many inns and a few unhosted apartments. Directory ($6.95 plus $1.00 shipping/handling) is a booklet with descriptions, rates, some sketches.

Rates: $40–$60 single, $50–$125 double. Some weekly rates available. Deposit of one night's lodging required plus a $5 processing charge. (A total of $10 for reservations made less than 48 hours in advance.) "Our New England Experience" processing fee is $29 (includes postage and handling). MC, VISA. ◆

In addition to matching overnight guests with the "right hosts," Pineapple Hospitality features "Our New England Experience" (see below). One of the state's oldest B&B reservation services, it is owned and run by Rob Mooz, a historic preservationist who has worked on several revitalization programs. Many of his hosts have been with the service since it began in 1981.

Plus: "Our New England Experience" (three weeks' advance notice required) is a personalized service offering a suggested itinerary together with bookings (total of at least four nights) for overnight lodging in homes throughout the six-state area. It is a package complete with hints and tips.

Other Massachusetts Services:
Although other Massachusetts-based services concentrate on one area, several have hosts in neighboring regions. Those services, going east to west, are:

Cape Cod, Martha's Vineyard, and Nantucket
Bed & Breakfast Cape Cod. Please see page 112.
House Guests, Cape Cod and the Islands. Please see page 112.
Orleans Bed & Breakfast Associates. Please see page 113.

Southern Massachusetts
Be Our Guest, Bed & Breakfast, Ltd. Please see page 179.

Boston and Just a Little West

AAA Accommodations. Please see page 187.

A Bed & Breakfast Above the Rest. Please see page 187.

A Bed & Breakfast Agency of Boston, Inc. Please see page 188.

Bed and Breakfast Associates Bay Colony, Ltd. Please see page 188.

Bed & Breakfast, Cambridge & Greater Boston/Minuteman Country. Please see page 189.

Boston Bed and Breakfast, Inc./Boston Reservations. Please see page 190.

Greater Boston Hospitality. Please see page 190.

Host Homes of Boston. Please see page 191.

University Bed & Breakfast, Ltd. Please see page 192.

North of Boston

Bed & Breakfast Folks (northwest). Please see page 206.

Bed and Breakfast Marblehead & North Shore/Boston & Cape Cod. Please see page 206.

Central Massachusetts

Folkstone/Central Massachusetts Bed & Breakfast Reservation Service. Please see page 220.

Berkshires

Berkshire Bed & Breakfast Homes. Please see page 232.

KEY TO SYMBOLS

♥ Lots of honeymooners come here.

⚓ Families with children are very welcome. (Please see page xiii.)

⚑ "Please emphasize that we are a private home, not an inn."

♣ Groups or private parties sometimes book the entire B&B.

♦ Travel agents' commission paid. (Please see page xii.)

✖ Sorry, no guests' pets are allowed.

✖ No smoking inside *or* no smoking at all, even on porches.

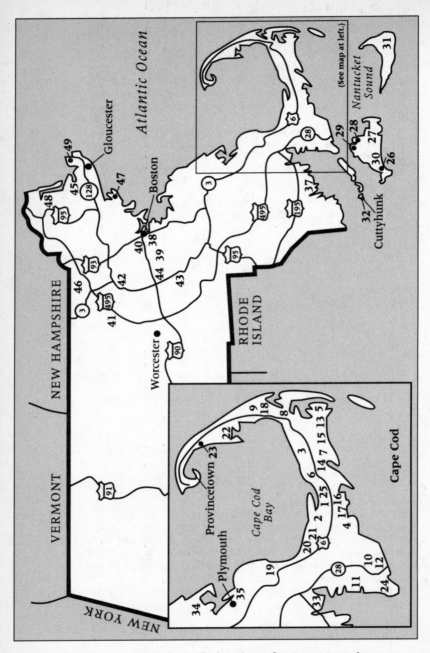

The numbers on this map indicate the locations of eastern Massachusetts B&Bs described in detail in this chapter.

Cape Cod, Martha's Vineyard, and Nantucket; Southeastern Massachusetts; Boston; Just a Little West; North of Boston

In this book, areas of Massachusetts are arranged roughly from east to west. Please see page 219 for Central Massachusetts, Connecticut River Valley, and Berkshires.

Cape Cod, Martha's Vineyard, and Nantucket Reservation Services

Bed & Breakfast Cape Cod

P.O. Box 341, West Hyannisport, MA 02672-0341

Phone: 508/775-2772. Year round. Best time to call is 8:30–5. Mail requests answered by return mail.

Fax: 508/775-2884.

Listings: 85. Located mostly on Cape Cod and the islands of Martha's Vineyard and Nantucket. A few are in metropolitan Boston, in the north shore area including Gloucester, and in south shore communities including Scituate. All are hosted residences or inns.

Reservations: "For midsummer visits, we suggest several months' advance notice; otherwise two weeks is recommended." Two-night minimum stay in season and on weekends.

Rates: $40–$60 single, $50–$185 double. $5 surcharge for one-night stay, when available. $5 nonrefundable booking charge. Deposit required is 25 percent of total charge. Deposit less $20 is refunded if cancellation is received one week prior to arrival. AMEX, MC, VISA for deposit; balance to be paid in cash or traveler's check. Five percent surcharge for balance payment by credit card. ◆

Guests booked through this service receive extensive information before arrival, "ensuring that guests know what to expect, leaving room for no surprises." Available accommodations—all inspected annually—range from modest to luxurious and include houses built in the seventeenth century as well as contemporary beachfront properties with many amenities.

Plus: Studios, carriage houses, or apartments available for weekly rental.

House Guests, Cape Cod and the Islands

Box 1881, Orleans, MA 02653

Phone: 508/896-7053 (information). 800/666-HOST (or 4678) reservations only. Live 9–9 daily except January. Answering machine all other times.

Listings: 100. Half are hosted private homes; half are inns. Located in every Cape Cod town plus Edgartown, Vineyard Haven, and Oak Bluffs on Martha's Vineyard and on Nantucket. Directory ($3) is a 50-page booklet including descriptions and rates.

Reservations: Two weeks' advance notice suggested. Two-night minimum Memorial Day–Columbus Day, three nights on all three-day (holiday) weekends.

Rates: $35–$68 single. $40–$250 double. $15 one-night surcharge at some locations. Some weekly rates and senior citizen discounts. $15 booking fee. Fifty percent deposit required; full prepayment for one-night stays. Ten days' advance notice required for refund of deposit less 10 percent service charge (minimum $12) on private home reservations. If less than 10 days, deposit refunded, less processing fee, only if accommodations can be rebooked over entire reserved period. Inns and guest houses have individual cancellation policies. AMEX, MC, VISA. ◆

Charles DiCesare and Richard Griffin are B&B innkeepers in addition to being the owners of the Cape's original bed and breakfast reservation service. Previously, Charles, a Swiss-trained hotelier, had a career in London and Saint Moritz. Richard managed a large professional association. On the Cape, they take pride in their efficient and recognized service.

Plus: Guided tours of the Cape arranged. Several hosts provide pickup and return service to airport and train and bus stations. Short-term (over seven days) arrangements available for unhosted cottages and housekeeping units.

Orleans Bed & Breakfast Associates

P.O. Box 1312, Orleans, MA 02653-1312

Phone: 508/255-3824 or 800/541-6226. Daily, 8–8, year round except holidays. Live answering service at all other times.

Listings: 75. Mostly nonsmoking private one- to three-bedroom host homes; a few small country inns and select unhosted cottages. Located in the area known as the Outer or Lower Cape, "from the elbow to the wrist of the arm that juts out to sea," including only the towns of Harwich, Chatham, Brewster, Orleans, Eastham, Wellfleet, and Truro. Annual directory available.

Reservations: Ten days' advance notice preferred. Day-before reservations accepted if arrangements can be made. Two-night minimum stay.

Rates: $60–$140 per room. Deposit of two nights' rate required, plus a $10 nonrefundable reservation handling fee. For cancellations, notification is required 10 days prior to scheduled arrival date; deposit is then refunded, less a $20 service charge. For less than 10 days' cancellation notice, deposit is refunded if accommodation can be rebooked. Discover, MC, VISA.

"I just called yesterday and today the confirmation arrived in the mail," exclaimed a friend who had booked wedding guests through this service. How was the match? "She listened carefully and placed us perfectly," said the father of the groom.

Mary Chapman is more than a reservation service owner. She hosts in her own home, and she knows her hosts. She is keenly aware of travel trends and provides for them within the B&B context. She and her hosts are active in their communities. This is a service that is based on the people-to-people concept, a system of sharing. Rare and refreshing.

Other services with some B&Bs on Cape Cod:
A Bed & Breakfast Above the Rest, page 187.
Bed and Breakfast Marblehead & North Shore/Boston & Cape Cod, page 206.
Be Our Guest, Bed & Breakfast, Ltd., page 179.
Bed and Breakfast Associates Bay Colony Ltd., page 188.
Host Homes of Boston, page 191.

All the B&Bs with this ✒ symbol want you to know that they are a private home set up for paying guests and that they are not an inn. Although definitions vary, these private home B&Bs tend to have one to three guest rooms. For the owners, people who enjoy meeting people, B&B is usually a part-time occupation.

_____ Cape Cod B&Bs _____

Many Cape Cod hosts report that guests come to see all of Cape Cod in a weekend. "Please remind them in your book that Cape Cod is 90 miles long." The following B&Bs are in alphabetical order according to the towns and villages where they are located. B&Bs on the islands of Martha's Vineyard and Nantucket are on pages 161–178.

Ashley Manor   508/362-8044
P.O. Box 856, 3660 Olde King's Highway (Route 6A), Barnstable, MA 02630

Hosts: Donald and Fay Bain
Location: On two acres of parklike grounds, set back from Route 6A, up a sweeping driveway behind huge privet and boxwood hedges. Within walking distance of harbor, beach, village, whale watch excursions.
Open: Year round. Reservations recommended. Two-night minimum on weekends, more on some holidays.
Rates: Double occupancy. $100 double-bedded room. $125 with working fireplace. $145–$165 suites. $155 cottage. Third person in suite or cottage 25 percent extra. AMEX, MC, VISA.
♥ ❖ ◆ ✄

> From Connecticut: _"Absolutely charming . . . a constant supply of logs . . . each breakfast more delicious than the first . . . special coffee . . . delightful innkeepers who make guests feel at home."_

The whole scene is just what Fay, a former advertising executive, and Donald, a lawyer, were ready for when their children were grown. Six years ago they left Manhattan and came with their antiques, Oriental rugs, grand piano, and comfortable sofas to a "special property originally built in 1699" that has seven fireplaces, wide floor boards, the original steep stairway, and Cape Cod blown glass windows.

The secret passageway that now connects two suites was probably used as a hiding place for Tories during the Revolutionary War. Restored in 1964, the house has been an inn since 1985. Outside there's a gazebo and a 44-foot brick terrace facing two acres of manicured lawns, the inn's new tennis court, and age-old plantings including cherry and pear trees.

Foreign language spoken: French.
Bed and bath: Six spacious rooms, private baths. Five with working fireplace. Downstairs suite with queen canopied bed. Two second-floor suites; one with king canopied bed, one with queen pencil-post bed. Two double-bedded rooms. The Garden Cottage, a separate building, has queen bed, sitting area, kitchenette, fireplace, bath.
Breakfast: 8:30–9:30. Freshly squeezed orange juice, coffee, teas, homemade breads and muffins, cereals incuding homemade granola. French toast with bacon, quiche, omelets, Swedish pancakes. Served on terrace or by candlelight in fireplaced formal dining room.
Plus: Complimentary wines. Fresh fruit. Candies. Flowers. Fine linens. Free loan of bicycles. Hammock. Croquet.

Bacon Barn Inn

3400 Main Street, P.O. Box 621
Barnstable, MA 02630

508/362-5518
(617/508 area) **800/696-5518**

Hosts: Mary and Robert Giuffreda
Location: Within walking distance of village, restaurants, beach, harbor, and whale watch boats.
Open: Year round. Two-night minimum, May 15–October 31.

Rates: Double occupancy, tax included. $90 May 15–October; $80 November–May 14. $15 additional person. Winter weekend packages include dinner at Barnstable Tavern.
♥ ❖ ◆ ✗ ✃

"Outstanding" say many guests about this unique B&B, which was converted from an 1820s barn (once the home of the Cape Cod Art Association) to a private home by another innkeeper. In 1989 it fulfilled Mary's dream of living on the Cape "with just a few B&B rooms." The ambiance is "country" all the way from the entrance, up the (open) staircase that came from an old Cape courthouse, to the 28-foot-ceilinged Great (common) Room with a working fireplace and original pegs and beams. An antique cow weathervane tops the cupola.

Often, guests who talk about a relaxing vacation and island day trips take Mary's advice: Plan to explore the Cape *or* to stay at least a night on Martha's Vineyard or Nantucket. Mary, a collector of antique glass and linens (they are for sale), was a raw material planner with Polaroid Corporation. Bob, the weekend host who is still a contractor in the Boston area, collects steins and early 1800s lamps. And how is the dream working? "Perfectly," says Mary, who adds that guests are delighted to hear that she has no plans to expand.

Bed and bath: Three second-floor rooms. All private baths. To left of stairway, room with king/twins option, full bath. To the right, one king/twins room and one with queen bed, each with glass-enclosed shower in bath. Rollaway available.
Breakfast: 8–9:30. (Newspaper and coffee waiting for early risers.) Stuffed French toast is a specialty. Muffins, scones, or breads. Fruit. Juice. Coffee or tea. Served May–October in enclosed wicker-furnished porch at tables set for two; November–April by Great Room fireplace.
Plus: Individual thermostats. Phone jacks in rooms. Bar with refrigerator. Champagne for honeymooners. TV in Great Room. Window fans. Flannel sheets. Beach towels. Mints on pillow. Croquet. Volleyball. Badminton.

Beechwood

2839 Main Street, Barnstable, MA 02630

508/362-6618

Hosts: Anne and Bob Livermore
Location: On Old King's Highway in the Barnstable Village historic district. Half mile to village, harbor, beach, historic sites, whale watching boats.
Open: Year round. Two-night minimum on holiday weekends.

Rates: Double occupancy. First floor, $135 queen-bedded room, $125 double. Second floor, $100 except room with king and single ($135). Third floor, $95. Third person $20. Less November–April, excluding holidays. AMEX, MC, VISA.
♥ ❖ ◆ ✗

As seen in a National Trust for Historic Preservation calendar, this Victorian is a wonderful example of fanciful Queen Anne style—from the lighting fixtures to antique furnishings to hand-cut exterior shingles painted yellow, gold, and jade green.

In 1987 the Livermores—a Connecticut innkeeper and an engineering sales manager—realized their dream by buying the restored step-back-in-time Beechwood. Here, they both enjoy sailing and "real Cape" walks.

In residence: One cat restricted to hosts' quarters.
Bed and bath: Six rooms. All private baths; some full, some shower only. Two first-floor rooms, each with working fireplace—one with double, one with queen canopied bed. Second floor: one room with double bed, stained glass windows, view of harbor and bay; one with two doubles; one with a king and a single bed. Third floor has air-conditioned room with double brass bed, panoramic view of bay. Rollaway available.
Breakfast: 8:30–9:30. (Flexible for early ferry.) Fresh juice, seasonal fruit, freshly baked breads and muffins, omelets, quiche, French toast, crepes or waffles, and breakfast meats. Prepared by both hosts and served in fireplaced dining room on tables for two with flowers and small oil lamps; classical music.
Plus: In summer, lemonade on wraparound veranda furnished with wicker, hammock, rocking chairs; other seasons, tea with sweets. Bedroom fans. Beech-shaded lawn chairs. Croquet. Badminton.

Charles Hinckley House   508/362-9924
Old King's Highway (Route 6A) and Scudder Lane
P.O. Box 723, Barnstable, MA 02630

Hosts: Les and Miya Patrick
Location: High on a hill, a short distance from Route 6 exit 6. A five-minute walk down a lane to Cape Cod Bay.
Open: Year round. Reservations recommended. Two-night minimum on weekends. Three-night minimum on holidays.
Rates: Double occupancy. $115 double bed, $129 or $139 queen. $149 suite.
♥ ❖ ♦ ✄ ⚋

From Kentucky: *"Charming and filled with much rich history, but Les and Miya make it come alive. They're quite a team!"*

The "team" consists of a caterer/landscape gardener married to a contractor/renovator/designer. Ten years ago, inspired by the inn restoration they had done for someone else, they purchased this unoccupied hip-roofed Federal colonial built by shipwright Charles Hinckley in 1809.

Featured in both *Country Living* and *Country Home*, the house has an oft-photographed hip-high wildflower garden that lines the granite steps to the front door. Floors are a pumpkin pine. Country furniture is painted or refinished. Enormous flower arrangements—gladioli, cosmos, lilies, or daisies, in baskets or vases—are replenished daily in season. The paint colors

(Please turn page.)

(often mixed by the Patricks themselves) and fabrics all blend and say "country" in the warmest sense.

In residence: Zydako, a mild-mannered Great Dane.
Bed and bath: Four rooms, all with working fireplaces and private baths, all antique beds. One double with tub-only bath. Three queens (two are four-posters) with shower (no tub) bath.
Breakfast: 9–9:30. Coffee, tea, or espresso, fresh orange juice, homemade pastries, fresh fruit plate garnished with flowers; crepes, omelets, or French toast. In dining room by the fireplace.
Plus: Beverages. Chocolates. Fresh fruit. Special occasions acknowledged (let Les and Miya know). Will meet guests at the airport. With advance arrangements, dinner served to overnight guests (only).

The Thomas Huckins House   508/362-6379
2701 Main Street, Route 6A, Barnstable, MA 02630

Hosts: Burt and Eleanor Eddy
Location: In historic district. Fifteen minutes from Cape Cod Canal. A short walk to a saltwater inlet overlooking the 10 miles of Sandy Neck Beach dunes. Five minutes to whale watch departure area.

Open: Year round. Two-night minimum on weekends, May through October.
Rates: Per room. $80–$100. $15 per extra person beyond two in room or suite. MC, VISA.
♥ ♟ ♨ ✗ ✈

North Dakota, the only state that is missing from the guest list, where are you? Many foreign travelers, too, are fascinated with this house, which the Huckins family occupied from 1705 to 1956. *Early American Life* featured the l8th-century hinges, latches (no doorknobs), paneling, flooring, three cooking fireplaces—one with beehive oven—and nine-over-nine window panes. "Guests also ask about the paint colors."

Burt, a furniture maker who sometimes carves birds, and Eleanor, an historian, have traveled extensively with their antiques business. When they bought this historic house in 1979, they took it apart (structurally) and put it back together again. In 1984, with the restoration done and the children grown, the Eddys welcomed their first B&B guests.

In residence: Barney, a collie. O'Malley, an Irish setter, a semipermanent resident while son is abroad. One outside cat. "All pets, kept from the guest areas, are not a problem unless a guest has severe allergies."
Bed and bath: Three large rooms, each with modern private bath. First-floor room has canopied double bed, full bath, working fireplace. On second floor, one double-bedded room, private staircase, sitting area, bath with oversized shower and seat. One room with queen canopied bed, fireplace, large shower bath; a room with double bed can be added to make a suite (good arrangement for families).
Breakfast: 8–10. Fresh fruit, juice, bacon, sausage, eggs any style, French toast with New England maple syrup or banana pancakes, Cape Cod cranberry muffins, maybe Swedish coffee cake. Homemade jams and jellies. Served in keeping room, opposite a 10-foot walk-in fireplace.

Plus: Tour of the house. Parlor with fireplace and TV. Patio. Portable telephone. Fresh flowers from "old-fashioned" perennial garden. (Many guests leave with cuttings.) Croquet.

A guest wrote: *"Not only is the house charming, but so are the proprietors!"*

Honeysuckle Hill

508/362-8418
591 Main Street, Route 6A   (617/508 area) **800/696-1397**
Old King's Highway   (USA) **800/441-8418**
West Barnstable, MA 02668-1128

Host: Barbara Rosenthal
Location: In National Historic District with sheep, meadows, cranberry bogs, and salt marshes. Five-minute drive to Sandy Neck Beach.
Open: Year round. Two-night minimum on summer weekends.

Rates: Double occupancy. Summer and fall $90–$105. Off-season $72–$105. $20 third person in room. AMEX, Discover, MC, VISA.
♥ ♣ ♦

Guests wrote: *"A treasure trove of historical information . . . saw places we might have missed . . . our own cozy retreat with a fire in the fireplace, homemade cookies by the bedside, sherry on the hall table, lovely decorating touches."*

Pampering is intentional at Honeysuckle Hill. From "the best B&Bs in England" the Rosenthals borrowed ideas that include everything from needle and thread to feather beds (which everyone wants to buy!). Their weathered-shingled farmhouse—restored by former owners, a well-known Cape family of weavers—"is at least 175 years old." A recent addition is a cathedral-ceilinged Great Room with huge windows overlooking gardens and lily pond.

In St. Louis, Missouri, Bob was a business executive (and hockey referee). Barbara taught art. Both are active in historic groups and produce videos of old Cape Cod.

In residence: Two dogs: "Chloe, a Cavalier King Charles spaniel, loves to check guests in. Annie strikes glamour poses and hopes you won't mention her pedigree (none)."
Foreign languages spoken: A little French and Italian.
Bed and bath: Three air-conditioned rooms, private full baths. Two first-floor queen-bedded rooms, one with working fireplace. On second floor, very private room with king bed.
Breakfast: 8:30–10. Juices, fruit, hot breads and muffins, cinnamon rolls. Souffles (recipe from Rosenthals' Salmon River rafting trip), blueberry pancakes, or French toast. Served on whimsical china.
Plus: Afternoon tea; homemade cakes, cookies, or scones. Wide-screen TV, VCR, tape library. Mountain and 10-speed bicycles, car bike rack. Beach towels, chairs, umbrellas, pails. Binoculars. Bird books. Inn-to-inn bicycling arrangements.

House Guests Cape Cod Host #91115

Brewster, MA

Location: Peaceful. On spacious grounds between two ponds. Two miles to bike trail. A mile from mid-Cape highway, four to Orleans.
Reservations: March–December through House Guests, Cape Cod and the Islands, page 112. Two-night minimum.
Rates: $70 queen room. Fall weekends, $100 for two nights. $25 third person in nearby single room.

♥ ⚕ 🐾 ✕ ⚬

Drive along the unpaved "cartway" and around the carriage barn to the rear of this old farmhouse, a 200-year-old Cape with 19th-century addition. Walk across an expanse of lawn to the front of the house, which faces a lake. And then it's through an old-fashioned porch (where breakfast is served) into the antiques-furnished house, home of a Cape resident who will direct you to a new park area with walking paths and to bike paths, whale watching, fishing charters, and shopping. She provides maps of nearby towns and a list of various recommended restaurants. "And many guests use our canoe or kayak to paddle over to another lake, the largest on Cape Cod, and enjoy a swim."

In residence: "Two well-behaved cats."
Bed and bath: On second floor, one room with queen bed, private shower bath. Across the hall, a room with a single bed for another member of traveling party.
Breakfast: Fruit, homemade muffins, hot beverages. Served on large screened porch overlooking the water.
Plus: Badminton, croquet, large yard. Games for children.

From Vermont: *"A wonderful spot. Delightful hostess. An undiscovered treasure."*

Isaiah Clark House & Rose Cottage

1187 Main Street (6A), Box 169
Brewster, MA 02631-0001

508/896-2223
fax 508/896-7054

Host: Charles DiCesare
Location: On historic Old King's Highway, two minutes from the general store. On five acres of gardens, fruit trees, and wild berry patches.
Open: Year round. Two-night minimum Memorial Day–Columbus Day. Advance reservations required.

Rates: May 24–October 7, $85–$110 in inn, $65–$85 in cottage. October 8–May 23, $65–$90 inn, $52–$64 cottage. Honeymoon package available. AMEX, MC, VISA.

♥ ⚕ ❉ ♦ 🐾

From Connecticut: *"The house is furnished in a quiet understated style, inviting us to put our feet up. Charles, the trained and world-traveled hotelier, intuitively knows when to join the conversation, to discuss choice of English teas, or, if you know enough to ask him, how it was when he presided over the Hilton opening in London."*

Exposed beams, stenciling, colonial colors, and antiques are throughout this beautifully restored rambling sea captain's house, which is deceptively small from the outside. Since opening as a B&B in 1986, it has won the Brewster Garden Club's Outstanding Landscape Design award. There are two new rooms that "you can't tell" have been added. And the neighboring Rose Cottage, a modernized 1850s farmhouse with Cape/country decor, is popular too.

As host Charles brings to B&B 200 years of family experience in the hospitality business. In addition, he runs a reservation service (page 112)— and enjoys history, opera, jazz, skiing, and swimming.

In residence: Two cats; Grigio, a Persian, and Miss Olga, "kept in private quarters but available for pictures."
Foreign languages spoken: French, Italian, some German.
Bed and bath: Twelve rooms (including five in the Rose Cottage). In main inn—seven air-conditioned rooms, private full baths. Two first-floor rooms, each with queen bed and fireplace. Second-floor rooms include one fireplaced room with king bed, one beamed skylit room with double high-poster bed, one room with twin pineapple beds. In Rose Cottage, one room with private bath, semiprivate for others; queen, double, or twin beds.
Breakfast: 8–10 (coffee earlier). Homegrown fruits and herbs. Homemade muffins. Smoked Nova Scotia salmon, broiled ham, frittata, cheddar omelet, raspberry or blueberry pancakes. In dining room or on deck overlooking pond.
Plus: Welcoming refreshments. Robes. Turned-down beds. Bedtime cookies and milk. Fireplaced parlor. Upstairs parlor with TV, VCR, stereo, library. Bicycles. Beach chairs and towels. Complimentary transportation to/from airport, train, bus, private beach. "Narrated" tour of house. In summer, iced tea and lemonade 3–5 p.m.

Copper Beech Inn   508/771-5488

497 Main Street, Centerville, MA 02632

Hosts: Joyce and Clark Diehl
Location: On a tree-shaded street, in the historic district. A half mile to warm-water Craigville Beach. Five-minute drive to Hyannis and island ferries.
Open: Year round. Reservations required. Two-night minimum Memorial Day weekend–mid-October.

Rates: Double occupancy. Memorial Day weekend–October, $80 double, $85 king. Off-season, $70 double, $75 king. Suite for three $120. Accept AMEX, MC, VISA for deposit only. Weekly rates available.
♥ ❃ ✈

The original graceful stairway and wrought iron latches are part of the appeal of this three-quarter-Cape-style house built by Captain Hillman Crosby in 1830, opened as a B&B in 1985, and now listed on the National Register of Historic Places. For 30 years the Diehls had vacationed and visited in all areas of the Cape. Through their own hard work and with the help of a contractor

(Please turn page.)

who had been a caretaker of the property for the past 25 years, the character of this old-fashioned home has been retained. A mix of antiques and furnishings creates the warmth of a home away from home for guests.

Clark is a former field executive for a major corporation. Joyce raised four children. Through their reservation service, Bed & Breakfast Cape Cod (page 112), the Diehls have even more contact with B&B travelers—as well as with other hosts who appreciate Cape Cod.

Bed and bath: Three air-conditioned rooms with private baths. On first floor—room with king bed, private bath with shower, Oriental carpets. Another room with double bed, full bath, and a quilt made by the hosts' artist/designer daughter. Second-floor suite has a pencil-post king bed, bath with shower, and adjoining room with twin bed.
Breakfast: 8–10. Fresh fruit, pastries, and house specialties including berry bowl with whipped cream, pancakes, eggs with breakfast meats. Served family style in the dining room in summer; in the kitchen next to a 100-year-old cookstove in winter.
Plus: Refreshments in family living room or parlor. Bicycles. Beach mats. Outdoor heated shower. Lounge chairs in yard overlooking pond. Wicker-furnished porch. By prior arrangement, will meet guests at Hyannis airport, bus, or train.

From Kansas: *"A beautiful home and a warm heart."*

The Inn at Fernbrook

508/775-4334
481 Main Street, Centerville, MA 02632-2918   fax 508/778-4455

Hosts: Brian Gallo and Sal DiFlorio
Location: Quiet. Residential. Set back from the road. Half a mile to Craigville Beach.
Open: Year round. Two-night minimum on weekends.

Rates: Per room. $115; with sitting room, $125; with fireplace, $135. Two-room suite with fireplace, $185 one couple, $250 two couples. Cottage, $105. AMEX, MC, VISA.
♥ ❖ ♦ ✈

Cecil B. DeMille and Gloria Swanson slept here. Frederick Law Olmsted, landscape architect for Boston's Emerald Necklace and New York's Central Park, landscaped the grounds. In the 1930s the coinventor of technicolor, Dr. Herbert Kalmus, owned the property. Built in 1881 as a summer/retirement house by Howard Marston of Boston's Parker House fame, the Queen Anne mansion was restored in the 1980s by Brian (now the chef) and Sal (now a masseur), former Omni Dunfey hoteliers. Throughout, the walls, woodwork, and window coverings are light-colored, a backdrop for Victorian antiques. The Cardinal Spellman room has a 17-foot pyramid-shaped ceiling, stained glass windows, and a private entrance. Oriental rugs are on the oak, cherry, and maple floors. And then there are those grounds, with a heart-shaped rose garden, a lake, fish ponds, a bench in just the right place, a secluded arbor.

Foreign language spoken: Italian. "Spanish and French understood."
Bed and bath: Six rooms—no two share a wall—on first and second floors. All private full baths; all but one are attached. Some rooms have sitting room,

working fireplace, and/or sun deck. Choice of king, queen, or double bed. (Some are canopied.) At end of pebble path, a cottage with double-bedded room, private shower bath, wraparound porch.

Breakfast: Weekdays at 9, weekends at 8:30 and 9:30. Varied menu. Perhaps Dutch babies with sausage and orange marmalade or eggs Linden with bacon. Freshly ground hazelnut Columbian coffee. Juice. Fruit. Home-baked breads or muffins.

Plus: Decanter of cream sherry in each room. Individual thermostats in some rooms. Ceiling and window fans. Beach towels. Fans. Guest refrigerator. Down comforters. "One singing parlor canary."

> From Rhode Island: *"The food, service, and decor make it a very special inn. . . . What makes it unsurpassed, however, are the people. . . . Their meticulous care, sincere warmth, and good humor are the reasons we'll return."*

Bed & Breakfast Cape Cod Host #12

Chatham, MA

Location: Residential. About a mile from the village and its restaurants, shops, scenic lighthouse, fishing pier, windmill, and, in summer, bandstand concerts.

Reservations: Available year round through Bed & Breakfast Cape Cod, page 112.

Rates: $65 for two, $15 third person. For up to four guests, $105 for two adjoining rooms, each with a double and a twin bed.

🧍 🏠 ✈ ⌦

> From Massachusetts: *"Charming folks, perfect for kids, a homey welcoming atmosphere."*

Built twelve years ago by the host, a former college professor, with the help of sons, this is a reproduction bow-roofed house with a fireplaced living room, lots of exposed wood, wide board floors, and skylights. Now the host is a management consultant and auditor. His wife, a nurse, comments: "When our [nine] children were young, we moved to a New Hampshire farm for a few years. As vacationers, when we camped at Nickerson State Park, Chatham became our favorite town. Even now, we join the tourists and walk along the main street every night. Morning walks are usually by the ocean; it's such a mystery, always with something new to see. Guests often ask: Where to swim? Where to eat? And do we ever get bored in the winter? (No.) We love sharing this wonderful area with bed and breakfast travelers."

Bed and bath: On first floor, room with queen bed, private full bath. On second floor, two adjoining rooms, each with a double bed and a twin bed, share a full bath.

Breakfast: 8–9:30. Juice, muffins, baked goods, cereal, beverage. Served in dining room or on deck.

Plus: Shells collected by hostess are "for the taking" by young guests. A menu collection from area restaurants.

Cyrus Kent House Inn

63 Cross Street, Chatham, MA 02633-2425

508/945-9104
800/338-5368

Host: Richard Morris
Location: In center of historic district. On a corner lot (of Kent Street), just off Main Street. Within walking distance of beaches, golf, shops, and restaurants.
Open: March–December. Two-night minimum on June–October weekends, three nights on major holidays.
Rates: Per room, single or double occupancy. Memorial Day–October, $85–$145. Off-season, $78–$110. Lower in winter. $20 third person. AMEX, MC, VISA.
♥ ♦ ✈

From personnel director to restorer extraordinaire. In 1984 Dick left Aetna Insurance in Hartford and tackled the spacious rooms with marble fireplaces and 13-foot ceilings of the then boarded-up white Victorian. One year later renovations were completed, and many English antiques were moved in. Along came a restoration award, which is hung in the front hall. And every day there are exclamations about those refinished wide board floors (which had been covered with five coats of paint), elaborate plaster moldings, and fine antiques.

More yet: Following the redoing of another B&B in town, Dick put his skills and talents into Chatham's Cranberry Inn. Through all this, the Cyrus Kent House remains his home and primary high-season activity. As Dick muses, "As host, every day I have the chance to talk about all this area has to offer. It's quite different from the office environment where I spent 17 years."

Bed and bath: Eight rooms with private bath, telephone, and color cable TV. Two first-floor queen-bedded rooms, full baths. On second floor, queen bed with full bath; double-bedded rooms (one shares deck with one queen room) with shower bath; double-bedded room with cathedral ceiling, skylights, full bath. Carriage house second-floor suite (very private) has a double bed, beamed and fireplaced living room, cathedral ceiling, shower bath.
Breakfast: 8–10:30. Juice, fruit, homemade muffins and breads, coffee, tea. Buffet style, eaten in fireplaced dining room or on front porch.
Plus: Fireplaced living room. Landscaped grounds. Garden flowers.

The Four Chimneys Inn

508/385-6317

Route 6A, 946 Main Street, Dennis, MA 02638

Hosts: Christina Jervant and Diane Robinson
Location: Residential. Across the street from Scargo Lake. Within walking distance of a bayside beach, Dennis village, Cape Cod Playhouse and Cinema, Cape Cod Museum of Fine Arts, fine restaurants, antiques shops. One mile to biweekly antiques auction. Within two miles of bicycle trails, golf courses, tennis courts.
Open: May through October.
Rates: July–Labor Day $45–$65 shared bath, $75–$90 private. September–June $40–$50 shared bath, $55–$70 private. $15 per night third person in room. AMEX, Discover, MC, VISA.
♥ ⁂ ♦ ✈

From Massachusetts: *"A renaissance lady indeed. . . . It is an uncommonly real and welcoming threshold to cross over."*

Canadians, too, have found the "friendly, spotless, cozy inn," thanks to a guest who wrote a newspaper article about his "Cape Cod secret."

The 1881 Victorian had been a bakery in the 1970s. It had "charm and potential" when purchased in 1984 by Chris, then a banker, and Diane, a hospital administrator and occupational therapist. They have pictures to help tell the story of 180 pounds of joint compound, New Hampshire antiques dealers who took them under their wing, and supportive friends. In addition to all the inside "touches" there's a marvelous perennial garden with 60 varieties of flowers, 700 bulbs, and a brick patio with wisteria arbor. Chris has learned to quilt; Diane has learned chair caning and bird carving and "could be passionate about golf and bird-watching." Both take pleasure in seeing guests "unwind, relax, and have fun."

Foreign language spoken: Swedish.
Bed and bath: Nine rooms—seven big, two small—on three floors. Seven have private baths. Rooms have a queen bed, a queen and a single, a double, or a double and a twin. Features include fireplaces, a skylight, views of lake and/or gardens.
Breakfast: Generally 8–9:30. Juice, coffee, tea, homemade muffins and breads, fruit, cereal. At large dining room, on the porch, or, if you wish, in your room.
Plus: Fireplaced living room. Quiet library. TV, VCR, and stereo. Seating under wisteria arbor. Bedroom fans. Use of refrigerator. Free use of canoe on Scargo Lake. Dinners arranged for groups. Will meet guests at airport or bus.

Isaiah Hall B&B Inn
152 Whig Street, Dennis, MA 02638

508/385-9928
800/736-0160

Hosts: Marie and Dick Brophy
Location: In a quiet year-round residential area on the historic bay side. A half mile from the beach and one-third mile from the village and Route 6A. About 15 minutes from Hyannis.
Open: March–October 19. Two-day minimum June 15–Labor Day and on holidays.
Rates: Vary according to size of room and bed and amenities such as fireplace or balcony. June 15–Labor Day, double $68–$94 private bath, $52 shared; single $58–$83 private, $46 shared. Off-season, double $65–$89 private, $50 shared; single $55–$79 private, $44 shared. $12 extra person. AMEX, MC, VISA.
♥ ❖ ♦ ✈

Inside and out, "the real Cape" was all there one weekend in May, when we took a short prebreakfast bicycle ride to the accompaniment of bird songs—to the endless beach, where quahogs were being harvested; past sand dunes; and back to the 1857 Greek Revival farmhouse (and renovated carriage house). Last year photographer Norm Darwish captured the simplicity of a room with canopied bed, hooked rug, and single daffodil in bedside vase for *Innsider* magazine.

(Please turn page.)

Since the Brophys came here in 1983, they have made major changes but retained the ambiance of another era with beams and antique rockers, white curtains, and wicker. In the kitchen and dining room there is some artwork done by former owner Dorothy Gripp, whose work can be seen in museums all over the country.

Marie, a B&B consultant, was a school counselor and then a high-tech compensation analyst. Dick hosts when he is at home from his job as a high-tech personnel manager.

In residence: "Clyde, our 16-year-old black cat, minds his own business."
Bed and bath: Ten rooms with queen, double, or a queen (or double) and a single bed. Nine rooms with private baths, one with working fireplace. Five rooms (two on first floor) in main house; five (two on first floor, four with balconies) in attached barn/carriage house. Extra bed available.
Breakfast: 8:30–10. At 8 by request. Cereals. Fruit, English muffins, home-made breads and muffins, jams, jellies, raisins. Juice, coffees, teas. Served from a 19th-century buffet in the antiques-filled dining room made for camaraderie.
Plus: Guests' parlor with Victorian coal stove. Great Room in converted carriage house. Table games. TV. Porch rockers. Terry robes. Forgotten items. Clock radios. Desk fans. Ironing boards. Large yard with badminton/volley-ball/croquet. Lawn chairs. Use of refrigerator.

> From a flood of letters: *"Charming . . . lovely grounds . . . great innkeepers who know the area . . . felt at home . . . felt fortunate to stay there."*

The Rose Petal B&B   508/398-8470

P.O. Box 974, 152 Sea Street, Dennis Port, MA 02639-2405

Hosts: Dan and Gayle Kelly
Location: Within walking distance of village center and Nantucket Sound beaches. Seven miles east of Hyannis.
Open: Year round. Please make advance arrangements for young children.

Rates: Per room. Mid-June through mid-September $55. Rest of the year $40–$50. Extra person $15. Family rates available.
♥ ❖ ◆

Such excitement is generated when Dan bakes a wedding cake and the bridal party stays here! In May there are guests who eat "commencement cake" after university ceremonies in Boston. Dan, who trained at the Culinary Institute of America, bakes for a local bakery/restaurant as well as for the B&B. Both he and Gayle, a substitute teacher in winter, have experience in university (Princeton and Rutgers) food service administration. Their house, built for early Dennis Port settlers, was a summer retreat for a church when they bought it and expanded their talents to include everything from tiling to plastering, from landscaping to stenciling. They have furnished with family pieces and colonial reproductions.

Foreign language spoken: Gayle speaks "rusty" French.

Bed and bath: Four second-floor rooms; one queen or two twin beds in each. Three rooms share carpeted second-floor shower bath. Fourth room shares first-floor full bath (restored footed tub) with hosts. One twin-bedded room has private staircase from kitchen and private entrance from deck. Rollaway twin bed available.

Breakfast: Usually 7:30–9:30. Freshly ground coffee, specialty teas, cereal, granola, fruit, juice, jams, cranberry butter. Homemade muffins, croissants, strudels, coffee cake, Danish. Eggs Benedict, waffles, or French toast with toppings. Buffet style in dining room.

Plus: Beverages. Complimentary homemade pastries "to go" for excursions. Window fans. Guest parlor with TV, piano, regional magazines, daily newspaper. Simmering potpourri. Sun porch. Guest refrigerator. Gas grill, utensils, condiments. Beach towels and mats. Collection of restaurant reviews.

> From Massachusetts: *"Comfortable and meticulously clean. Friendly, thoughtful hosts who anticipate what every guest needs."* From Canada: *"Breakfast itself is worth a stay."*

The Nauset House Inn   508/255-2195

143 Beach Road, P.O. Box 774 East Orleans, MA 02643-0774

Hosts: Diane and Al Johnson; Cindy and John Vessella
Location: Residential. On two acres, a half-mile walk to Nauset Beach. Three-minute drive to town center.
Open: April–October. Two-night minimum on weekends.

Rates: Per room. $65–$75 shared bath. $95 private bath. $105 cottage or honeymoon suite. $55 single. MC, VISA.
♥ ✂ ⅙

> From Pennsylvania: *"More important than the serenity and beauty of the greenhouse; the perfect attention to detail; . . . the ideal location within walking distance of the beach and away from town, are the innkeepers, who have an uncanny ability to know which guests will like what and also to know when guests want solitude and when they want conversation."*

This inn is the answer to those who want a home-away-from-home ambiance—with a hint of fantasy (the conservatory)—yet not a *very* small B&B. It is owned and operated by two generations who garden (flowers arranged in every room); go whale watching; explore the area (great hand-drawn annotated map provided); go to auctions and hand-paint furniture; make dinner and theater reservations; cook (whimsical sketches in cookbook); experience spontaneous bagel-making and guest chef sessions; and, everywhere, display arts and crafts including their own stained glass, quilts, pottery, and stenciling. Camellias and a weeping cherry tree grow in the 1910 conservatory (from Connecticut) that was added to the 1810 Cape-style dormered farmhouse. The family's 10-year dream was discovered by *Country Living* in 1983, shortly after Al left his executive position at Beechcraft Airplanes and just after Cindy graduated college.

In residence: In hosts' quarters, Nicholas, born December 1989. Winny, a bearded collie, "a real lover." Roo, a cairn terrier, "equally loving."

(Please turn page.)

Bed and bath: Fourteen rooms. Eight with private shower baths; three rooms with private tub and shower bath. Three first-floor rooms share one bath; three upstairs rooms share one bath. Queen, double, twins, and one single available. One cottage with queen bed, sitting room. Honeymoon suite (reached by separate staircase) with double bed, private balcony.
Breakfast: 8–9:30. Always muffins and omelet-of-the-day. French toast and sticky buns are specialties. Served family style in fireplaced, brick-floored publike beamed breakfast room that opens onto a terrace.
Plus: Wine and cranberry juice with hors d'oeuvres at 5:30. Fireplaced common room. Bedroom table fans. Guest refrigerator. Beach towels. Herb and perennial gardens. Picnic table.

The Parsonage Inn   508/255-8217
202 Main Street, P.O. Box 1051, East Orleans, MA 02643-1501

Hosts: Ian and Elizabeth Browne
Location: In the village, opposite farm stand, on the road (1.3 miles) to Nauset Beach on the Atlantic Ocean. Within walking distance of fine restaurants and shops. Two miles from Route 6.
Open: Year round. Two-night minimum on June–September weekends and holidays.

Rates: Double occupancy. June–September, $75–$90 queen beds, $65–$75 double beds. $10 additional person. $15 less December–March; $10 less April–May and October–November. MC, VISA.
♥ ❖ ♦ ✈ ⊱

Sit by the fire or on the patio and listen to Chopin, Mozart, or Liszt played by Elizabeth, a piano teacher who grew up in Kenya and lived in England—all before going to Chicago, where she taught 40 students and met Ian, an English-born accountant and medical group executive director. When they decided to purchase an inn, they remembered their first inn experience right here in Orleans.

A year ago they bought this B&B, a full Cape house, a parsonage in the 1880s, built c. 1770. Despite all the remodeling over the years, the house retains the feeling of history, of old Cape Cod. Today its uncluttered, fresh, crisp look is embellished with country antiques and some art from Africa, England, and California.

Foreign languages spoken: "A little French and a smattering of Swahili."
Bed and bath: Seven rooms; two on first floor, five on second. All private baths. One room with canopied queen, TV. Two rooms with queen plus a single bed. In studio apartment—private entrance, queen plus futon bed, TV, kitchen; breakfast is optional with more than two-day stay in apartment.
Breakfast: 8–9:30. Fresh fruit. Scones with Devonshire-type cream, fruit breads, muffins, yogurt and granola, juices, Colombian coffee, teas. Served in dining room, on patio at umbrella tables, or in your room.
Plus: Air conditioning in two rooms. Window fans. Hors d'oeuvres 6–7 p.m. Turndown service. Fresh flowers. Robes. Guest refrigerator.

The Red Geranium

East Orleans, MA

Location: Residential. On a rural main street. On landscaped grounds with gardens and reflecting pond. One and a half miles to Nauset Beach, two miles to bayside beach. Short walking distance to shops and fine dining.

Reservations: January–November through Orleans Bed & Breakfast Associates, page 113. Two-night minimum stay.
Rates: $70 per room. $90 guest wing.
♥ ◖ ⁂ ✈ ⊱

For many guests a stay here is the highlight of a Cape visit. The charming English-style (larger) Cape furnished with family heirlooms, collectibles, and original oil paintings is the home of Peggy, a painter (and craftsperson with a sense of whimsy) who always wanted to be an innkeeper, and her husband, Marcus, a restorer of antiques. When they settled here in the late 1970s, they made authentic restorations, wallpapering and stenciling in the New England tradition.

With each changing season Peggy changes decor in the colonial dining room. Special occasions, including yours, are celebrated. Everywhere, in many ways, there's a strong sense of old-fashioned caring in this warm and friendly B&B.

Bed and bath: Double or twin beds in airy second-floor rooms furnished comfortably with period antiques. Large full semiprivate bath. Plus a spacious guest wing with queen- bedded room, private bath, living room, full kitchen. Guests who book this wing are welcome to join others for breakfast in the main house.
Breakfast: 8–9:30. "Lavish and imaginative" with fruits, juices, cereals, homemade breads and muffins, coffee, brewed tea.
Plus: Private guest entrance. Fan/air conditioner and TV in each bedroom. Second-floor sitting room with desk, games, and refrigerator. Hot water for tea or coffee. Tour of house.

The Over Look Inn

508/255-1886

P.O. Box 771, County Road (Rte. 6), Eastham, MA 02642   800/356-1121

Hosts: Nan and Ian Aitchison and son Mark
Location: Set way back from the road, across from entrance to main Cape Cod National Seashore visitors' area. Bike paths (and bicycles) are right here. Three miles to Orleans and fine restaurants.

Open: Year round. Reservations required.
Rates: Per room. $110 July–August. $65–$110 off-season. Packages available. AMEX, MC, VISA.
♥ ⁂ ◆ ✈

From England, New Jersey, Massachusetts: *"This is one popular inn—and for good reason . . . like being in an elegant Victorian world . . . a lovely tranquil retreat. . . . Meals are a treat to the palate, appealingly presented. . . . Interesting*

(Please turn page.)

*family. . . . Recommendations for fun beaches, historic sites, good places to eat . . .
everything arranged for guest's comfort."*

For 20 years the Scottish ("our accents give us away") couple had a summer
home in the area. When they thought about living here year round, Nan,
director of development at a Toronto girls' school, and Ian, a chartered
surveyor, bought this Queen Anne Victorian house, which had been a lodging
establishment for about 60 years. Following a two-year restoration done by
their college-age sons, the inn opened in 1985 with brass beds, down
comforters, antiques, reproductions, African and Eskimo art, and Ian's collection of Churchill's works. In 1988 the Aitchisons built an addition with
large bedrooms, more baths, and a "Hemingway Billiard Room" decorated
with Victorian antiques. Business and international groups meet here. Wedding parties love it. Son Mark, who is writing his first novel (set in Costa Rica),
publishes the inn's newsletter. Artist son Clive's painting and sculpture studio
is in the 18th-century barn.

In residence: Sandie, an outdoor Lab/shepherd mix. Winnie, a basset
hound.
Bed and bath: On second and third floors, 10 rooms (5 are air conditioned)
with ceiling fans. All private baths (some with shower, no tub); most are en
suite (terry robes for hall bath). Queen (mostly), double, or twin beds.
Breakfast: 8–10. Scottish fare. Maybe kedgeree made of finnan haddie, rice,
onions, chopped eggs, and raisins sauteed in butter and served with a dab of
mango chutney. Served in the Edward Hopper dining room.
Plus: Afternoon tea, hot scones. Five common rooms, including Winston
Churchill library with books and Victorian card table. Four fireplaces. Expansive lawn. Porches. A New Year's celebration that has become an inn
tradition.

The Penny House Inn   508/255-6632
4885 County Road, Eastham, MA
Mailing Address: P.O. Box 238, North Eastham, MA 02651-0238

Hosts: Bill and Margaret Keith
Location: On 1½ acres of lawn. In
the Cape Cod National Seashore
area, midway between Hyannis and
Provincetown. Minutes to bike trails
and Massachusetts Audubon Society
sanctuary.
Open: Year round. Two-night mini-

mum on holiday weekends. Advance
reservations required.
Rates: Double occupancy. Late
June–early September $95 (second-
floor rooms) to $110 (with working
fireplace). Off-season $60–$90.
AMEX, Diners, Discover, MC, VISA.
♥ ❖ ♦ ✈

The 1751 captain's house with bow roof and wide-planked floors reflects the
shipbuilding techniques of the year it was built. Newer rooms added in the
1980s are also furnished with country antiques and collectibles. Just completed—a large fireplaced gathering room with beamed ceiling and wide
board floor. Planned for the time this book is published—a sizable brick patio
behind the main house.

In 1987 the Keiths, world travelers, found this "right place," as Margaret calls it, when Bill retired as a General Motors engineer. They decorated with paintings from Australia, Margaret's homeland, and with porcelain and some Chinese artworks. It's right for travelers, too, people who often exchange travel experiences as well as conversations about food, sailing, the outdoors, and cycling from inn to inn.

In residence: Beau, a Maltese terrier.
Bed and bath: Eleven rooms (five are air conditioned) on two floors. One with private entrance and balcony. All private baths. King (one with working fireplace), queen, double, or twin beds. Some rooms with cathedral or bow-roof ceiling.
Breakfast: 8–10. French toast, eggs in toast cups, or waffles served with bacon, sausage, or ham. Fresh fruit. Juice. Cereals. Homemade muffins. Served in 1751 dining room that has 200-year-old beams.
Plus: Afternoon tea. Fireplaced living room. Bedroom window or ceiling fans.

The Whalewalk Inn

220 Bridge Road, Eastham, MA 02642-3215

508/255-0617
fax 508/240-3374

Hosts: Dick and Carolyn Smith
Location: Residential. On three acres of lawn and meadowland. Ten-minute walk to beaches; 10-minute drive to National Seashore; 100 yards from bike path. Less than a mile to galleries, shops, restaurants.
Open: April 1–December 15. Two-night minimum June–September weekends; three night minimum on Memorial Day, July 4, Columbus Day weekends.
Rates: $90 guest house twin beds or main inn first-floor queen. $105 main inn upstairs rooms. $135 cottage double bed or main inn king. $150 guest house or barn suites. April–May 21 and October 12–December 15, $15 less.
♥ ❖ ◆ ✈

From Massachusetts: *"Perfect. . . . Absolutely gorgeous . . . simply elegant . . . gracious hosts . . . I even asked for a recipe."*

"We're here just because, upon departure in 1989, we told the innkeepers that we were thinking of doing this some day. For that purpose, Richard, a former Boston advertising executive, had taken a year off to visit inns. . . . By the time your book is published, I will have left my advertising career for full-time innkeeping."

The main house, a Greek Revival built for a whaling captain, became a farm before being converted to an inn in 1953. The saltbox honeymoon cottage was a chicken coop. Major renovations were done in the 1980s. The Smiths have decorated with country antiques from the United States, France, England, and Denmark. Rooms are light and airy with soft colors—peach, rose, or blue. Carolyn has made all the silk and dried flower arrangements. Devotees abound. First-timers feel like discoverers.

Bed and bath: Twelve rooms, private baths. Main inn first floor—queen bed; king bed, full bath with oversized tub, private entrance. On second floor—twin, double, or queen beds. Two barn suites (one has private deck), each

(Please turn page.)

with king/twin bed, living room, kitchen, full bath. Two guest house suites (room with two twins can be added to either), each with queen bed, kitchen, living room, working fireplace, full bath; one has a loft with twin beds. In cottage—double bed, full bath, kitchen/dining area, private patio, working fireplace. Rollaway available.

Breakfast: Usually 8:30–9:30. Grand Marnier French toast, blueberry pancakes, strawberry shortcake, apple walnut raisin crepes with ice cream, homemade breads, fresh fruits. Served in garden patio or in sun-porch breakfast room.

Plus: Hors d'oeuvres by the fire during BYOB cocktail hours. Individual thermostats in some rooms. Ceiling or window fans in each room. Down comforters. Fresh flowers. Mints on pillow. Guest refrigerator. Bikes. Beach towels. Irons. Access to computer and fax.

Bed & Breakfast Cape Cod Host #10

Falmouth, MA

Location: Peaceful. On an ocean inlet that is ideal for swimming, fishing, clam digging, windsurfing. Fifteen-minute walk to Martha's Vineyard ferry landing in Woods Hole.

Reservations: Year round through Bed & Breakfast Cape Cod, page 112.
Rates: Double occupancy. $85 per room.
🛏 ✶

A private beach. Ocean views from rooms. And your own private entrance.

"Little Jewel," named by the current owners, began in 1960 as a traditional ranch. Now it has wings, guest wings, on each end. Throughout, everywhere you look, there are antiques: a Victorian doll carriage, a cradle used as a magazine rack, Sandwich glass shards, a birdcage with dolls, French hats, china birds among bath crystals, decoys, gravy boats with freshly picked yellow roses. And potpourri, lots of lace, monogrammed and ironed sheets, geranium boxes, and many mirrors that reflect the nearby ocean.

"Guests come with great plans and, often, don't go anywhere! They sit, ponder, talk, look, and visit. Occasionally they might join us for clams on the half shell after we've been clamming. For us, this is a storybook come to life," says the hostess, who wrote real estate ads. Her husband, who has also been in real estate, was in the Connecticut State Police.

Bed and bath: Those two ocean-view rooms—one with double bed, sitting area, skylights; one with double bed, working fireplace. Each has a private entrance, private full bath, air conditioning, small refrigerator.

Breakfast: 8–10. Juice, fruit, baked goods, beverages. Served in dining room, "always set with silver, crystal, and candles and often photographed," or on deck.

Plus: Warm-water outside shower. Fireworks over the water on weekends from June through early July.

---

*H*ospitality *is the keynote of B&B.*

Capt. Tom Lawrence House   508/540-1445

75 Locust Street, Falmouth, MA 02540-2658

Host: Barbara Sabo-Feller
Location: Set back 100 feet from road that leads to Woods Hole. Within walking distance of restaurants, shops, bus and train stations, ferry shuttle. One block to bike path and bird sanctuary. Half mile to town beach with warm-water swimming.

Open: Year round except January. Two-night minimum June–October weekends. Reservations preferred.
Rates: Double occupancy. June–October $79–$99. Singles $10 less. $20 additional person. Off-season, 15 percent less. MC, VISA.
♥ ⁂ ✘

> From England: *"We were so impressed with the quality of the rooms, the breakfast, and the charming hospitality of the owner that we adjusted our itinerary to visit again the following week."*

Barbara moved to New England from Europe 15 years ago. After years of thinking about B&B while she was an office manager in Boston, she opened here in 1985—with much encouragement and background information shared by Dudley Hallett, the town historian. I heard him get pretty excited about the restoration of this 1861 sea captain's house.

Barbara made decisions about the wallpapers (including the paper for the curved hall wall), the colors, the arrangement of hand-carved antique furniture from Germany and the Steinway baby grand piano. At breakfast she serves specialties and, often, (unbelievably good) bread made with organic grain that is purchased in 50-pound sacks and ground right here in her own kitchen.

Foreign language spoken: German.
Bed and bath: Six spacious first- and second-floor corner rooms with private shower baths. Laura Ashley or Ralph Lauren linens. King or queen beds; some are four-posters, three are canopied.
Breakfast: Full at 9, earlier if requested. Menu varies daily. Fresh fruit, an egg dish, quiche, crepes, pancakes or Belgian waffles with strawberry sauce, freshly whipped cream.
Plus: Ceiling fans in all bedrooms and common room. Large deck overlooking back yard. Fireplaced sitting room. Will meet guests at bus station. Ferry tickets, sightseeing, dining assistance.

Mostly Hall Bed & Breakfast Inn   508/548-3786
                                     800/682-0565

27 Main Street, Falmouth, MA 02540-2652

Hosts: Caroline and Jim Lloyd
Location: In the historic district, across from the village green. Set back from the road on over an acre of lawn, trees, and shrubs. One mile to town beaches. Around the corner from the bike path to Woods Hole. Two blocks from bus and train stations.

Open: Year round except for January and first two weeks of February. Two-night minimum preferred May–October and weekends.
Rates: May–October, $85 single, $105 double. Off-season, $60 single, $80 double. Honeymoon and other special packages available.
♥ ✘ ⚰

(Please turn page.)

From Florida: *"Have stayed in B&B inns around the world. None have compared . . . great food . . . elegantly decorated rooms . . . two people who genuinely enjoy what they do. This feeling is passed on to their guests."*

Unmistakably grand and gracious, even romantic, with 13-foot ceilings, Oriental rugs, antiques, dramatic floral wallpaper, and a cupola sitting room. Named decades ago by an owner's youngster when he first saw the inside of the new family home. A B&B since 1980, it's a four-storied residence that was originally built in 1849 by a sea captain for his New Orleans bride.

The Lloyds, avid travelers (and cyclists) who have been to other New England states, Hawaii, Australia, New Zealand, Egypt, Yucatan, and Kenya, changed careers eight years ago. In Boston Caroline had been a department store buyer and planning director; Jim was a computer corporate executive.

Foreign language spoken: Some German.
Bed and bath: Six spacious corner rooms, each with private en-suite shower bath and queen four-poster canopied bed.
Breakfast: Full at 9, continental earlier by arrangement. Guava or cranberry blend juice, fresh fruit, homemade sweet breads or muffins (peach poppyseed). Entree might be Mexicali eggs, stuffed French toast, or cheese blintzes with warm blueberry sauce. Special diets accommodated—with advance notice, please. Served on the covered porch that wraps around all four sides or in living room.
Plus: Central air conditioning plus ceiling fans in most rooms. Sherry, iced tea, or lemonade. Library/game area. Piano. Gazebo with swing. Croquet. Badminton. Complimentary bicycles.

Peacock's "Inn on the Sound"   508/457-9666
313 Grand Avenue, P.O. Box 201, Falmouth, MA 02540-0201

Hosts: Phyllis and Bud Peacock
Location: On a bluff along an ocean-front drive 1.5 miles from the village, flanked by deluxe condos on one side, a private home on the other; 100 yards from steps that lead down to a quiet beach. Ten-minute walk along seawall to harbor and Martha's Vineyard ferry.

Open: Year round. Two-night minimum stay.
Rates: Double occupancy. $75–$115 June–September. $65–$95 off-season. $20–$30 third person. Singles $20 less. Midweek, week-long, honeymoon, and holiday package rates available. AMEX, MC, VISA.
♥ ♦ ✈

"I've been in love with this house since the day I saw it," says Bud, who together with Phyllis created Falmouth's Palmer House Inn—which was also a boardinghouse before becoming a B&B. "Here, in 1989, we installed huge picture windows so that you can lie in bed and (from most rooms) see Martha's Vineyard. This house, built in the 1880s, has had eight additions. A large stone fireplace is in the living room, which features our million-dollar view. Wainscoting is throughout. We decorated simply in country style with light colors, lots of wicker, and antiques."

The inn's newsletter includes some of the Peacocks' almost-famous recipes. A decade ago, before innkeeping, Bud (who has produced some local public-access TV programs) worked in the computer world. Phyllis is a registered nurse. They are a great source for the best Portuguese food, the "in" place for lobster, the viewing spot for swans along the bike path.

In residence: In hosts' quarters—Lana, age 12, and Joy, age 14.
Bed and bath: Ten rooms, each with queen bed. Five have an additional twin or daybed. Two have a working fireplace. All private baths; all with shower, four with tub also.
Breakfast: Buffet 8–10:30, with juice, fresh fruit, homemade muffins, breads, coffee cake, pastries, coffee, tea. 8:30 and 9 seatings for hot entree— banana-stuffed French toast with blueberry compote, creamed eggs with leeks, or pina colada pancakes. Fruit butters. In air-conditioned dining room set with flowers and china. Eat on the porch, if you'd like.
Plus: Air-conditioned dining room. Front porch. Ceiling and window fans in all rooms. Cable TV and VCR with large assortment of tapes in living room. Library. Lemonade or hot spiced cider. Guest refrigerator. Beach towels. Will meet bus in Falmouth.

The Village Green Inn   508/548-5621
40 West Main Street, Falmouth, MA 02540-2678

Hosts: Linda and Don Long
Location: On the village green, surrounded by homes and churches dating to early 1700s. Minutes' walk to shops and restaurants, bus station, ferry shuttle. Bicycle distance to beaches and Woods Hole.
Open: April–December. Two-night

minimum on holidays. Reservations recommended.
Rates: Double occupancy. Memorial Day–Columbus Day $85, suite $100. $10 less single. $20 third person. Off-season packages.
♥ ❖ ✈ ✦

> From England: *"Whilst on holiday, touring New England, we stayed at a number of B&Bs. . . . Village Green Inn was the top . . . tastefully decorated . . . goodbye hugs a delightful surprise . . . mints in the room . . . lemonade on the veranda . . . breakfasts were the best anywhere. . . . Truly a relaxing place."*

Many letters about the Village Green Inn give long dissertations about the Longs. Don is one of the few Cape Cod innkeepers who is a native. He is also a skilled craftsman and builder. Linda is decorator, emphasizing attention to detail—swags and drapes in the living room, an unusual Victorian rocking chair, Grandfather's high chair in the dining room—and many plants. The hosts are both (early) retired educators who "feel challenged to find new ways to pamper guests, wonderful people—and we learn a lot about history, geography, and various careers." They moved in 1985 from East Falmouth to the 1804 Federal-style family house that was made into a Victorian in the late 1800s.

(Please turn page.)

Bed and bath: Four large rooms (two on first floor) plus a two-room suite with a queen bed and a twin daybed. Two rooms with working fireplace. All with private baths, ceiling fans, and queen beds (two are four-posters).
Breakfast: 8–9. Fresh fruit dishes include hot spiced fruit and tangy ambrosia. Wide variety of special entrees. Homemade rolls, breads, and muffins. Freshly ground coffee, assorted teas. Served in the dining room or on large wicker-furnished porch overlooking the green.
Plus: Complimentary seasonal beverages. Magazines. Books. Games. Puzzles. Extra pillows. Chocolate treats. Will meet guests at bus station or ferry. "Breakfast bags" for early departures.

The Elms   508/540-7232
495 West Falmouth Highway, West Falmouth, MA 02574-0895

Hosts: Betty and Joe Mazzucchelli
Location: On shore route (28A), within walking distance of Chapoquoit Beach. Half hour from departure point (Barnstable harbor) of whale watch trips. Ten minutes to Woods Hole and four public golf courses.
Open: Year round. Reservations required. Two-night minimum on weekends, June–October. Three nights on long holiday weekends.
Rates: Double occupancy. June 15–Columbus Day $65 shared bath, $85 private. Off-season $55 shared bath, $65 private.
♥ ✈

Betty was literally born into the business. Her mother had a B&B in Ireland. Still, it was a trip to Europe that spurred the Mazzucchellis to start their own in this country. Perhaps it is no coincidence that many Europeans find their way to The Elms. Those who have written to me from England and France rave about how much at home they felt and about the food, the food, and the food. They also appreciated local suggestions, including a secluded nature walk that leads to a breathtaking view of the ocean.

Betty, formerly a nurse in Boston, and Joe live in a Victorian house that was built in 1739 and added on to in 1850. "It has nooks, unexpected closets, and an alcove that only an old-house sleuth could explain." A large fireplace with crane is in the huge living room. A gazebo and flower and herb gardens are part of the beautifully landscaped grounds.

In residence: Annie, a Lhasa apso.
Bed and bath: Nine rooms, seven with private baths. Two first-floor rooms, one with twin beds and one with a double. Five second-floor rooms have private baths; two share a full bath. Some double four-posters, twin brass beds, two queen; all are antiques.
Breakfast: 8–9:15. Fresh fruits. Juice. Eggs Benedict, bananas Foster served on French toast, or crepes; homemade codfish cakes, Irish bread, blueberry and cranberry muffins. In plant-filled solarium that overlooks deck.
Plus: Sherry. Living room with TV. Deck and lawn furniture. Ironed eyelet-trimmed percale sheets. Will meet guests at Falmouth bus. Bicycles on a first-come basis. Winter "Stressless Weekends" with gourmet dinners.

Sjöholm Inn Bed & Breakfast   508/540-5706

17 Chase Road, West Falmouth, MA 02574-0430

Host: Barbara Eck
Location: In a quiet country area, on 2½ acres, one mile to Chapoquoit Beach. Minutes to Falmouth and Woods Hole.
Open: Year round except for several weeks in winter.
Rates: June 14–September 22, single $40–$50; carriage house $55; main house double $68 shared bath, $80–$85 private. November 1–April 15, single $40; double $50 shared bath, $65 private. Rest of year, single $40; double $60 shared bath, $70 private. $15 extra person in room. Senior citizens and stays over five days, 10 percent discount.
♥ ❄ ✈

"This is a very relaxed place with very few rules. Guests sit on the porch in their swimsuits. Cycling groups come here. Road racers know they get an early, light, special breakfast. Board sailors know how close we are to their favorite beach. Families feel comfortable. And we have a couple of rooms that are favorites for romantics. Some guests come all scheduled. Others let each day unfold, sleep until noon, or read."

Seven years ago Barbara, a nurse and counselor, came here from Boston with her three teenagers (now grown). "The name of this inn, built 140 years ago as a farmhouse, was appealing because I am Swedish on my father's side. It's quiet here. We go to sleep hearing the crickets and wake up hearing the birds."

In residence: The official welcomer is Amber, a female golden retriever. Oliver is a German short-hair pointer.
Bed and bath: Ten rooms in winter, 15 mid-May through mid-October. Bed sizes vary from a single twin to queen size. Some rooms sleep three or four. Private baths for four ground-floor rooms of carriage house and one upstairs in the inn. Five upstairs rooms in the inn share three shower baths. Five unheated (portable heaters available) sail loft rooms and one four-person room (off the porch) share two baths.
Breakfast: All-you-can-eat buffet. Homemade quick breads, muffins, eggs, quiches, homemade jams, fruit. Homemade granola. Swedish dishes include rosettes, a deep-fried sugared pastry. Swedish pancakes are the Sunday special.
Plus: Intentionally, no clocks, TVs, or radios in rooms. Outdoor hot/cold water shower, also available for beachgoers late on day of checkout. Line-dried linens. Big screened porch with extensive library and games. Cable TV, stereo, books, magazines. Picnic tables. Lawn chairs. Large grass lot for spontaneous ball games. Use of refrigerators, outdoor clotheslines. Beach permits ($3/day).

Unless otherwise stated, rates in this book are per room for two and include breakfast in addition to all the amenities in "Plus." As for taxes and gratuities, please see page xii.

Seawinds

Falmouth Heights, MA

Location: Residential. On Vineyard Sound, two houses from the beach. Very close to bike paths, antiquing, fine dining. Ten-minute walk to Martha's Vineyard ferry.

Reservations: Year round through Be Our Guest, Bed & Breakfast, Ltd., page 179.
Rates: $40 single, $60 double.
🏨 🖼 ✈ ⚕

The hosts, a young couple, moved from a large converted carriage house to this antique Cape-style house so that they could be near the water. The location is sought by many—including an ambassador who arrived in a limousine and an extended Japanese family who expressed appreciation for staying in an American home. The hostess, employed with a health insurance agency, and her husband find that there have been so many requests for their pumpkin roll recipe that a great recipe swap is flourishing.

Bed and bath: Three second-floor rooms—one with a single bed, two with a double bed—share a full bath and a half bath.
Breakfast: Juice, fresh fruit, homemade breads and muffins, hot beverages. Served in dining room.
Plus: Outdoor shower for swimmers. Fresh flowers.

Victorian Inn at Harwich   508/432-8335

P.O. Box 340, 102 Parallel Street, Harwich, MA 02645-0340

Hosts: Betty and Charlie Schneiderhan
Location: On a quiet street in the village. Within walking distance of bike trail, historic landmarks, restaurants, tennis court, band concerts. Minutes from beaches.
Open: May–October. Two-night

minimum on weekends; three-night on holiday weekends. Advance reservations required.
Rates: $80 double occupancy. $90 single weekend night, other than holiday weekend. MC, VISA.
✈ ⚕

> From Wisconsin: *"It's difficult to gauge whether the charm of another era that glows through each room or the lively coffee visits with Charles and Betty were the highlight."* From New York: *"Delicious breakfast . . . great tips on restaurants and sightseeing . . . classical music in the parlor . . . made my Cape vacation the best ever."*

When Charlie knew he was retiring early from his position as a Mobil Oil Corporation marketing executive, the Schneiderhans considered innkeeping in other states, but they settled on the village where they had spent many summers. Now Charlie is on the Board of Selectmen and Betty is active with the Harwich Conservation Trust.

The 1866 Victorian had been completely redone as a B&B when they bought it in 1985. Dark pine floors are covered with Oriental rugs. Furnishings are period antiques and reproductions. Afternoon tea—indoors or out—has become a hallmark.

Foreign languages spoken: Spanish and French.
Bed and bath: Five second-floor rooms (each with a sink and vanity) accessible via interior and exterior stairways. One has queen brass bed, private full hall bath. One queen canopied bed, private full hall bath. One room with twin beds, air conditioning, adjoining private full bath. Two air-conditioned rooms, one with a double Shaker bed and one with a queen four-poster, share a full bath. (Other rooms have oscillating fans.)
Breakfast: 8–9. Fruit juices. Fruit salad. Muffins, Danish pastries, biscuits, cinnamon bread, or sour cream coffee cake. Cereals. Bagels and cream cheese. Freshly perked coffee, brewed tea, decaf. Served in fireplaced "Country English" tearoom.
Plus: Two parlors. Turned-down beds. Bathrobes. Special soaps. Full tea and picnic lunch by reservation. Lawn chairs under shade trees.

Cape Cod Sunny Pines B&B Inn   508/432-9628

77 Main Street, P.O. Box 667   800/356-9658
West Harwich, MA 02671-0667   (outside MA, for reservations only)

Hosts: Eileen and Jack Connell
Location: On two acres. A 15-minute walk to warm-water Nantucket Sound beaches. Near Dennis Port, theater, restaurants, tennis, biking and hiking trails.
Open: April 1–January 15. Two-night minimum for advance reservations.
Rates: $75 single. $75–$95 (according to size of room) double. $25 extra bed. AMEX, MC, VISA.
♥ ❖ ◆

> Guests wrote: *"Delightful . . . spotlessly clean . . . enormous breakfasts . . . cozy bedrooms."*

"Irish hospitality in a Victorian ambiance" is the theme of this welcoming B&B, inspired by Eileen's aunt who has a B&B in Ireland's County Kerry. From the comfortable furnishings to the endless breakfasts, from Jack's declaration that he's too young to be a grandfather (four times) to the porch Jacuzzi, this is a B&B that appeals to all ages, "even folks who treat us like Mom and Dad, making it a point to tell us where they're going and when they'll be home."

The turn-of-the-century house, built for a Baptist minister by Caleb Chase of Chase and Sanborn coffee fame, has been a guest house since 1945. The Connells have decorated with lots of lace, family photographs, and figurine collections. Eileen is a psychiatric nurse. For 20 years Jack, an oceanographer with the Woods Hole Oceanographic Institute, sailed the world researching the ocean floor.

Bed and bath: Six rooms (one on first floor, rest on second). Each with sitting area, air conditioning, color TV, private bath (two with shower and tub, rest with shower only), and small refrigerator. King, queen, double, twins, and extra beds. Plus two honeymoon cottages (set in woods), each with king bed, air conditioning, shower bath, color TV, refrigerator.

(Please turn page.)

Breakfast: 9–?. "Irish gourmet" by candlelight with Irish music. Homemade Irish soda bread and muffins. Seafood or vegetable-and-cheese omelets, "surprise" French toast, or silver dollar buttermilk pancakes. Tipsey (mixed grilled meats). Juices, tea, coffee. In summer, fresh fruit bowl and granola. In winter, Irish oatmeal with cranberry raisin conserve and heavy cream or milk.
Plus: If you are Jack's size, a pair of dress pants that came in handy when one guest, here for a wedding, found he'd left his own at home. In-ground 16-by-32-foot swimming pool. Jacuzzi on the wraparound porch. Bedroom fans. The Claddagh Tavern (separate entrance) has a very European feeling with lincrusta (wallcovering), antique plates, and coppersmithed bar. Romantic celebrations acknowledged.

The Tern Inn   508/432-3714
91 Chase Street, West Harwich, MA 02671-1612

Hosts: Bill and Jane Myers
Location: In a residential area on two acres of pine and oak trees, lawn, and gardens. A 10-minute walk to Nantucket Sound beach.
Open: April–November 1. Two-night minimum June 15–September 15.

Rates: Double occupancy. June 15–September 15, double or twin bed $70, suite $125. $50 single. $15 additional person in room. No charge for cot or crib. Off-season, $65.

♥ ⚔ 🏠 ⚜ ♦ ✈

Such enthusiasm! After Bill, a graduate of Cornell's School of Hotel Administration, retired early from the food service profession, he and Jane, parents of five grown children, realized their dream of living on the Cape (as innkeepers) with an old home as a backdrop for their antiques. More than a decade later, they are still ecstatic about this "stimulating and absorbing lifestyle—with conversations about history, house styles, geology, ecology, shopping, the family. . . . It's wonderful!"

Their Cape Cod house—"the real article"—was built as a summer home about two hundred years ago. Through the years it has expanded to about four times its original size. In addition to the Myerses' antiques, there are traditionally styled pieces made by Bill, a banjo player who visits nursing homes and plays in parades.

In residence: Kizzy, a setter, "the formal greeter."
Bed and bath: Five rooms, all private baths. First-floor suite, "popular with families with children," has a room with queen bed and a room with two twin beds. On second floor, three rooms with antique double or twin beds. Cot and crib available.
Breakfast: 8–9. Varies. Fruits and juice, freshly baked goods, sunflower bread French toast or Belgian waffles with maple syrup, egg dishes. In dining room overlooking gardens and bird feeders.
Plus: Two spacious common rooms. Afternoon cranberry juice. In-ground pool. Beach towels. Bedroom floor fans. Robes. Babysitting. Basketball court. Guest refrigerator. Brick grill. Complimentary wine or champagne on special occasions. Jane's recipes for egg crisp and blueberry muffins. Will pick up guests at Hyannis airport.

Dunscroft by the Sea Inn

24 Pilgrim Road, Harwichport, MA 02646-2304

508/432-0810
800/432-4345

Hosts: Alyce and Wally Cunningham
Location: A few steps to private mile-long beach. (Water view from some inn rooms during winter.) In a lovely quiet residential area. Within walking distance of village.
Open: Year round.
Rates: Double occupancy. Mid-June through mid-October, $105–$115 queen or king; suites $115–$125 for two; $25 extra person; $145 cottage. Off-season, $85 queen, $95 king, $85/$95 suite, $120 cottage. Under age 12, no charge. Romance packages available. AMEX, MC, VISA.
♥ ❖ ◆ ✗ ✁

> From Massachusetts: *"Relaxing, clean, homey, nicely decorated."* From Wisconsin: *"Delightful retreat, far enough from the madding crowd, yet within walking distance of enough amenities in the event you tire of silence ... unassuming yet comfortable ... lovely ample breakfast ... friendly hostess with grace."*

One guest with a "Piano Sam" license plate gave a spontaneous postbreakfast performance. Others come to this weathered-shingled Colonial—an inn for 41 years—for a honeymoon, for business, or as vacationers.

True to plan, when Alyce and Wally bought the inn in 1987, they were married here. In Connecticut Wally had had considerable experience in management for public utilities and Alyce was a high school teacher of English. As owners of a Cape motel where they offered a continental breakfast, they were inspired to become innkeepers. For six months during the Gulf War, Wally served in the Merchant Marine. Currently Alyce is president of the Harwich Accommodations Association.

Foreign language spoken: Some French.
Bed and bath: Eight rooms plus one cottage with king bed and fireplace. Three first-floor rooms (two with private entrances) with twin/king option and private shower bath. On second floor, king- or queen-bedded corner rooms (two with canopied beds); adjoining private full or shower baths.
Breakfast: 8:30–10. Full. Juice, fresh fruit, three or four homemade breads, custards, cottage pudding, fried apples, muffins, cheese molds, cereal, coffee, tea. Egg dishes with breakfast meats. Buffet style in dining room.
Plus: Air conditioning in some rooms. Complimentary sherry. Candy kisses. Wicker-furnished sun porch. Brick terrace, shaded lawn, umbrella tables. Guest refrigerator.

Harbor Walk

6 Freeman Street, Harwichport, MA 02646-1902

508/432-1675

Hosts: Marilyn and Preston Barry
Location: One house in off of Route 28, right behind the house known for miles around for its roses. Five-minute walk to sandy beach, restaurants, and shops.
Open: April–November. Two-night minimum June–September.
Rates: Double occupancy. $40–$45 shared bath. $50–$60 private bath. $15 extra bed. Seventh night free.
♥ ♨ ❖ ◆

(Please turn page.)

"Our guests make every year a new experience. We love it! B&B is just as I imagined it would be when I was a physical therapist in Philadelphia and noticing, every day, a wallpaper scene of Wychmere Harbor. Why not live near the real thing? We're golfers. And we wanted to be closer to our kids. So when Preston retired as a school administrator, we opened here, just across the road from the harbor, in 1978. Although this is a Queen Anne house, it's a summer place, with floors painted navy blue. Walls are stenciled. Log cabin quilts give the color to the pencil-post lace-canopied beds. Breakfast is the time when everyone talks about their first-ever trip to an island, antiquing, shopping, the homes of the rich and famous, restaurants plain and fancy, and whale watching—which, we found out, is like seeing magic."

In residence: Otto, a large, gentle black short-haired dog.
Bed and bath: Six rooms. On first and second floors. Four have private full baths (one is tub only); of these, three have queen canopy beds (one on first floor has private sitting area); one has twin/king bed option. King-bedded room and one with two twin beds share a full bath. Rollaway available.
Breakfast: 8–10. Two fruit juices, fresh fruit platter or compote, home-baked goods (many requests for kuchen recipe), homemade granola, strawberry yogurt, cheese platter, coffee, tea. On the porch in summer, family style in dining room in spring and fall.
Plus: Turndown service. Flannel sheets. Beach towels. Fresh flowers. Guest refrigerator. Will meet bus from Boston in Barnstable (15-minute drive).

From California: *"Harbor Walk has Cape Cod panache, in a great location. . . . Rooms are comfortable and airy . . . wonderful breakfasts. . . . The invisible art of making one feel at home."*

The Inn on Bank Street   508/432-3206

88 Bank Street, Harwichport, MA 02646

Hosts: Janet and Arky Silverio
Location: In a residential area in center of town. Five- minute walk to ocean. Ten miles from ferry to Martha's Vineyard and Nantucket.
Open: Mid-April through November. Two-night minimum in July and August and on holidays.
Rates: Double occupancy. July–August, $75–$80. Fall and spring, $65. Singles $5 less. $12 cot. MC, VISA.
♥ ✿ ◆ ✈

"We started to think about retiring on Cape Cod; we saw this 45-year-old Cape. How could we justify a place of this size for just two people? Why not retire early and move to the Cape now? After nine years here, Arky has become a town historian of sorts. This lifestyle gives us great satisfaction and pleasure."

They came from Connecticut, where Janet was a teacher. Arky was an executive in industry, often working in Canada and Italy. Here they appreciate their proximity to a bicycle trail and opportunities to walk and to sight the great blue heron in winter and black-bellied plover during the fall migration. The Cape Cod Board of Realtors appreciates the Silverios. For their part in enhancing the neighborhood with wild and cultivated flowers on the property, the innkeepers received a plaque.

Foreign languages spoken: Italian and Spanish.

Bed and bath: Six first-floor rooms with private en-suite shower baths (one also has a tub). Two large rooms have original wide pine floors. King, queen, double, twins, and extra bed available.

Breakfast: 8–9:30, earlier for ferry departure. Juice, granola, homemade bread, mile-high corn muffins, fresh fruit. Maybe French toast made from Portuguese bread with maple syrup. Leisurely; served on enclosed sun porch, in patio, or in the garden.

Plus: Living room and library with TV, fireplace, piano, books, magazines and games. Outdoor tables and chairs, grill, hot and cold shower. Late-afternoon or evening beverage. Flowers and champagne for special occasions. Will meet guests at Hyannis airport or bus.

> From New York: *"Great beach and wonderful restaurant within walking distance. . . . Gourmet cooking. . . . Spotless inn. . . . Warm, helpful hosts."*

The Inn on Sea Street   508/775-8030

358 Sea Street, Hyannis, MA 02601-4586

Hosts: Lois M. Nelson and J. B. Whitehead

Location: In a quiet residential beach neighborhood, 10 minutes from Route 6, within walking distance of everything, including the beach, Kennedy Compound and Memorial, island ferries, bike rentals, restaurants.

Open: April–November.

Rates: Canopied beds $60 and $70 shared bath, $85 private bath. Other rooms $85 double, $95 triple; garden barn room $90. Singles $5 less. $15 additional guest. AMEX, MC, VISA.
♥ ❀ ✈ ⌇

"Last year we stayed because you were convenient to the ferry. This year we want to spend more time at your B&B."

No one is more surprised and delighted with that kind of call than Lois, a former director of airline in-flight services whose job was phased out. That was just about the time that this Greek Revival house, the one she had admired for 18 years, came on the market. Thus was born, in 1983, the first B&B in Hyannis. There are antique Persian carpets throughout, a crystal chandelier in the foyer, a huge photograph of Grandfather over the mantel— all intentionally lovely "but not stuffily elegant." By the time you read this book, the house across the street will be an annex with canopied beds. Adirondack chairs will be on the wraparound porch, and the acre of backyard will be accessible to guests. When J. B., an antique-car buff and a pilot with Continental Airlines, is home, you might see him driving a Model A truck with the inn's logo.

Bed and bath: In the main inn, five rooms. On first floor, double-bedded room, private bath. Two second-floor rooms (one has a canopied bed) share a bath across the hall. Third second-floor room is separated from its private bath by the former maid's back stairway. Down a flagstone path through the yard is barn room with queen canopied bed, TV, private full bath. Across the street—five rooms, canopied beds, private baths.

(Please turn page.)

Breakfast: 8–9:30. Fresh fruit. Homemade baked goods. Served in dining room on tables set with sterling silver, china, linen, and fresh flowers.
Plus: Window fans. One guest room is air conditioned. TV in guest sitting area. Beach towels. Use of refrigerator. Complimentary package of inn recipes. Fresh flowers. Restaurant review book (where guests have chosen to insert compliments about the inn!). Will meet guests at Hyannis airport or bus or train station.

The Simmons Homestead Inn

508/778-4999
800/637-1649

288 Scudder Avenue
Hyannis Port, MA 02647-0578

(outside eastern Massachusetts)

Hosts: Bill and Peggy Putman
Location: "Up the street from Kennedy compound." Walking distance to beaches. A mile to harbor, shops, restaurants.
Open: Year round. Two-night minimum on summer weekends and holidays.

Rates: Double occupancy. $110 twins, $120–$125 queen, $130–$140 king. $20 extra person. Singles $10 less. $75–$120 off-season. Seventh night free. AMEX, MC, VISA.
♥ ❖ ♦ ✈

As Bill says, "When Dinah Shore was here last year on a cookbook tour, she took over for breakfast. Usually, though, I'm the cook for what is a very social occasion. And to think I never cooked before 1988 when I bought this beautiful inn! Restored by the previous owner, it's an 1820 Cape farmhouse with an 1845 Greek Revival addition. Most rooms are traditional with wicker, antiques, four-posters (some canopied), wide board floors, and Oriental rugs. Two are more modern. In the upstairs hall you'll find hoods from my old race car along with Paul Newman's. There are comfortable sofas in the 32-by-16-foot living room. Many huge needlepoint hangings that everyone comments on. And annotated maps for the area, for the Kennedy homes, Nantucket, Plymouth, driving tours, along with tailor-made day trips for guests, wonderful people!"

In residence: "Samantha, our dog, tells guests that this is her house, but she'll share."
Bed and bath: Ten rooms on first and second floors. All private baths; some shower only, some tub and shower. Rooms with king bed (some canopied, one with a private deck, two with working fireplaces), queen, or twin beds. Rollaway available.
Breakfast: 7:30–9:30. Fresh fruits, juices, coffee, and teas. Maybe French toast with homemade cinnamon bread and sausage; blueberry pancakes with bacon. In gracious dining room.
Plus: Fireplaces. Individual thermostats and ceiling fans in all but two rooms. Wine and cheese at 6 p.m. Fresh flowers. Beach towels. Down comforters. Guest refrigerator. Will meet guests at Hyannis bus station or airport.

Academy Place Bed & Breakfast 508/255-3181

8 Academy Place, P.O. Box 1407, Orleans, MA 02653-1407

Hosts: Sandy and Charles Terrell
Location: On the village green, at the edge of Orleans's shopping district. At Route 28 and Main Street. Ten minutes from the National Seashore, 2½ miles to Skaket (charter fishing boats) and Nauset beaches.
Open: Memorial Day weekend to Columbus Day weekend.

Rates: $50 double or twin beds, shared bath. $60 queen or $70 king bed, private bath. $15 extra bed in room. Off-season (after Labor Day) 10 percent less. MC, VISA.

"Charles grew up in this authentic 1752 Cape Cod house when his parents ran it as a guest house (1955–75). We exposed beams, painted and papered with colonial colors, and opened as a B&B in 1989. Period furnishings include spool beds, spinning wheels, and a fainting couch. During much of the summer season, Charles commutes from Washington, D.C., where he is the national water quality specialist for the Soil Conservation Service."

When the Terrells were year-round Massachusetts residents, Charles was a college biology professor; Sandy, a registered nurse. Their fascinating house history (a copy is in each room) is complete with sketches and notes about the size of Cape houses—"small, to minimize heat loss." As hosts they offer personalized day trip suggestions including National Seashore programs, restaurants, and whale watches. "Guests come with different expectations. One told us that the only thing we were missing was a cat. The next day someone said, 'I hope you don't have cats; I'm allergic to them.'"

Bed and bath: Five rooms. Two first-floor queen-bedded rooms overlook the village green; each has nonworking fireplace, private shower bath. Up steep, narrow steps to second floor with skylit guests' lounge, one king-bedded room with private shower bath. One room with two twin beds shares a full bath with double-bedded room. Rollaway available.
Breakfast: Usually 7–9:30. Buttermilk bran muffins, chocolate and other homemade breads, or blueberry coffee cake. Freshly brewed coffee or tea. Fruits and juices. By candlelight in beamed dining room.
Plus: Sunken garden with picnic table and barbecue behind house. TV in upstairs lounge. Hot or iced tea. Guest refrigerator. Table fans.

> From Georgia: *"Comfortable . . . immaculate. . . . Sandy introduced us to beach plum jelly, which we loved . . . plenty of books and magazines to enjoy on the porch rockers, in the garden, or in the upstairs reading room . . . perfect location . . . welcoming, warm and cheerful."*

Can't find a listing for the community you are going to? Check with a reservation service described at the beginning of this chapter. Through the service, you may be placed (matched) with a welcoming B&B that is near your destination.

Morgan's Way Bed & Breakfast   508/255-0831

Nine Morgan's Way, Orleans, MA 02653-3522

Hosts: Page McMahan and Will Joy
Location: Rural and peaceful. On four acres of landscaped grounds, one mile from Orleans center.
Open: Year round. Two-night minimum stay.

Rates: Double occupancy. $90 May–October. $75 November–April. $15 additional person in room. Singles $10 less.
◀ ❖ ♦ ✖ ✂

This architect-designed Cape contemporary has cathedral ceilings, plenty of windows—many arched and half-circled—and a spacious downstairs living room with comfortable seating, porcelains, and original Cape art. An oak spiral staircase leads to an upstairs living room with TV/VCR, wood-burning stove, library, small refrigerator, and a large window seat overlooking a multilevel flower-filled deck and large swimming pool. Beyond the extensive gardens—perennials, annuals, a kitchen garden, and a cut flower garden—are acres of woods and wetlands, a bird-watcher's paradise.

Page, the gardener, sings with several groups, has a strong interest in nutrition, fitness, health and human services, ecosystems, and the arts. Will, an outdoorsman, is president of an engineering and surveying firm and is active in the community. They love sharing their property and Cape Cod.

In residence: Kitty-man is "an entertaining Himalayan." Blitzen is "a shy gray long-haired cat."
Bed and bath: Two rooms. On first floor, one with queen bed, private shower bath, cable TV; connects to pool and deck area. On second floor, queen-bedded room with private full bath overlooks pool and gardens. Rollaway available.
Breakfast: 7:30–9. Varies. Fruit dish could be simmered plums with cream or honey walnut baked apples. Pancakes with maple syrup and sausages or Grand Marnier French toast with maple syrup and bacon. Carrot/pineapple bread or apple oat-bran muffins. Hot beverages. Yogurt, fruit, cereals, Egg-Beaters always available. All garnished with fresh fruit, herbs, and edible flowers.
Plus: Bedroom floor fans. Pool (20 by 40 feet). Beach towels. Guest refrigerator. Mints on pillow. Map of back roads to Provincetown. Complimentary champagne for special occasions.

From New Jersey: *"Pleasant, friendly, and very helpful. . . . Breakfasts were 'oralgasmic.' I am a professional taster by trade. . . . Bedroom tastefully decorated. . . . I regret not having the opportunity to stay there more often."*

------

*B*ed and breakfast gives a sense of place.

Bed & Breakfast of Sagamore Beach

One Hawes Road, Box 205   508/888-1559
Sagamore Beach, MA 02562   fax 508/888-1859

Host: John F. Carafoli
Location: Peaceful. On a hill with view of Cape Cod Bay, all the way to Provincetown. On grounds with lawn and vegetable, herb, and flower gardens. Minutes on foot to a sandy beach where you can walk for miles. Two miles from Sagamore Bridge ro-

tary. Four miles to Sandwich center via Sagamore Bridge.
Open: Year round. Reservations required. All answering machine messages returned promptly.
Rates: $85 per room.
♥ 🏠 ✳ ✂

"With that smile, you oughta be on television." How often I have said that to John. And it just might be—as soon as his book, the first ever on food styling, is released. His clients include many major food companies, newspapers, magazines, and advertising agencies. A former art director for several publishing companies, he is also food editor for *New Choices* magazine. "Last weekend, while a New York couple was here—he proposed to her Saturday night—I was testing recipes for a microwave cookbook. So they sampled chocolate and upside-down peach cakes and a cranberry orange coffee roll—and then got to take them all with them. For a quasi-Mexican menu I might make corn muffins, omelets with fresh herbs on a bed of tortilla with fresh salsa, served with cinnamon coffee—all on Fiesta ware with a bright-colored table cloth."

What was a heatless century-old beach house on stilts when John purchased it 20 years ago has been rebuilt and featured in *Better Homes and Gardens* and *Bon Appétit*. Everywhere there's the Carafoli treatment, with much use of fabric and color. Eclectic furnishings include the bedspread Grandmother brought from Italy. In the fireplaced living room there's a rug John bought in Morocco and a huge painting of Carmen Miranda "from my days as a fine artist." French doors lead to a wicker-furnished, flower-bedecked porch, where former guests had their wedding complete with a string quartet.

Bed and bath: Three second-floor rooms, each with an antique double bed (one is a four-poster, one is brass, third is mission oak), share one full bath plus, in summer, the big hot-water shower room under the deck.
Breakfast: Usually 8–9. "Healthy food!" Perhaps baked French toast made with two eggs plus three egg whites, pancakes with fresh fruit, or raspberry muffins. Presented on oak pedestal dining room table or on porch with view of water.
Plus: Fresh flowers. Welcoming beverage. Down comforters and flannel sheets in winter.

---

*B*reakfast is where the magic happens.

Captain Ezra Nye House

152 Main Street, Sandwich, MA 02563-2283

508/888-6142
800/388-2278

Hosts: Harry and Elaine Dickson
Location: In the center of the village. Within walking distance of Sandwich Glass Museum, Heritage Plantation, Thornton Burgess and Yesteryear's Doll museums. Less than a mile to beach.
Open: Year round. Two-night minimum on holiday, summer, and fall weekends.

Rates: Double occupancy. May–October, private bath $75 queen or double bed, $80 king; shared bath $70 double bed, $65 three-quarter beds. Off-season, private bath $65 queen or double, $80 king; shared bath $50 double, $55 three-quarter beds.
♥ ❖ ♦

From Canada: *"A treasure. Antiques and artwork . . . warm hospitality."* From New York: *"Just right. A sense of history, the Cape, and a short drive to the island ferry."* From Massachusetts: *"Offered more than the comforts of home . . . genuine caring."*

Harry and Elaine, world travelers, came here on their honeymoon in 1986 when Harry retired from 10 years as an engineer with GTE (preceded by 25 in the Air Force); they were starting what might have been a coast-to-coast search for a B&B site. "This 1829 sea captain's house on a main street in a small town, near the ocean and surrounded by greenery, gives the feeling of a private home. It is just what we were looking for. There's so much to do right here that you can leave your car for a few days and just walk."

They furnished with fine antiques, including four-posters, a sleigh bed, and a pineapple bed. Some of Harry's family pieces, a collection of Chinese export china, and Elaine's paintings (her studio is in the barn) have found a home here too. If you take a tour of the house, you'll see the first owner's name chalked under a roof beam, and the name and date of a subsequent owner etched by diamond on a window pane. Praise has appeared in *Glamour, Innsider,* and *Cape Cod Life* magazines.

Bed and bath: Six second-floor rooms. Private baths for room with king/twins option, working fireplace, shower bath; queen-bedded rooms with shower baths; canopied wicker double bed with claw-footed tub bath. A shower bath is shared by a double-bedded room and a room with two three-quarter beds.
Breakfast: 8–10. Sample menu—cranberry juice, fresh pineapple, shirred eggs with cheese and parsley, homemade beer bread, cranberry nut bread, preserves, coffee and tea.
Plus: Fireplaced living room with piano. Games. Books. TV with VCR. Large deck. Beach towels. Will meet guests at Sandwich train or bus.

Wedding guests love to stay at a B&B. One innkeeper tells of the bride who asked to have relatives booked on different floors. "Be forewarned, my aunts haven't spoken for 15 years."

Isaiah Jones Homestead

508/888-9115
800/526-1625

165 Main Street, Sandwich, MA 02563-2283

Hosts: Kathy and Steve Catania
Location: In center of historic Sandwich, within walking distance of museums, restaurants, shops, and public tennis courts.
Open: Year round except Christmas eve and day. Two-night minimum on weekends and holidays.

Rates: Double occupancy. June–October, $89, $95 (in fall with fireplace), $119 (room with whirlpool). Off-season, $65, $75, $95, $110. Singles $10 less. AMEX, Discover, MC, VISA.
♥ ♦ ✖ ✄

> From Texas: "'Perfect' describes it perfectly . . . a definite elegance about it." From Hawaii: "The best place we stayed. . . . Antiques-filled rooms that would be considered suites in other inns." From Massachusetts: "Attended to our every need and some we didn't even know we had."

From the day the Catanias opened in 1987, guests have been rebooking "on the spot." They book rooms with 12-foot ceilings and fine Victorian antiques. They book the room with the whirlpool pictured in *National Geographic Traveler*. In addition, guests book for the hospitality, a family tradition. Kathy is the former training director for dining room personnel of a family-owned business that now includes four restaurants, Sandwich's historic Daniel Webster Inn (Steve is general manager), and the John Carver Inn in Plymouth.

In residence: Bethany, 13, and Michael, 10.
Bed and bath: Four carpeted queen-bedded rooms, each with a sitting area. On first floor, two rooms, each with a high four-poster, private full bath. On second floor, one room furnished with white wicker; one with half-canopied bed, oversized whirlpool tub, and separate shower. (In the barn, awaiting restoration, is a copper tub from one of the first indoor Sandwich bathrooms.)
Breakfast: Usually at 9. Three freshly baked items daily. House specialty is corn bread. Fresh fruit, yogurt and Mueslix, five kinds of juices. House blend of coffee and teas. Served by candlelight in gathering room.
Plus: Nighttime cookies, afternoon tea, hot cider or lemonade. Hair dryers. Beach towels. Fans, if needed. Toiletries you may have forgotten.

Ocean Front

508/888-4798

273 Phillips Road, Sandwich, MA
Mailing address: Box 346, Sagamore Beach, MA 02562-0346

Host: Mary A. Blanchard
Location: On Cape Cod Bay with private beach, two miles from Sagamore Bridge rotary. Within walking distance of path along the Cape Cod Canal.

Open: April 15–October 31. Reservations required.
Rates: $55 double bed, $75 king bed, $95 suite.
♥ 🛏 ❀ ♦ ✖ ✄

"'Well, Mary, what are you going to do with your big beautiful home?' my friends asked. And that's how I got the idea of B&B. I can't believe it, Bernice,

(Please turn page.)

yesterday someone called from Hong Kong with your book in hand! Guests come from Sicily, Rome, and Australia. We have great conversations."

Mary used to have a restaurant in a small town outside of Boston. She bought this Cape Cod weathered-shingled house in 1975 and over a 10-year period did extensive remodeling to take advantage of the views. Wicker furnishings add to the summery feeling. For a fun year-round accent, there is a Christmas tree in the living room. "Currently I am renting a six-foot Pinocchio from my 10-year-old grandson."

Foreign language spoken: Italian.
Bed and bath: Three rooms, all private baths. The suite that encompasses an entire floor has a double and a twin bed, full bath, and sliding glass doors that lead onto a large oceanfront balcony. On lower level, one room with king bed, shower bath; one room with double bed, shower bath. Rollaway available.
Breakfast: 8–10. Juice, fresh fruit, muffins, toast, and Mary's own cinnamon bread, coffee. Served in dining room overlooking the ocean.
Plus: Beverage. Living room with wood stove, TV, organ. Babysitting. Use of refrigerator. Huge decks. Outdoor furniture.

> From Massachusetts: *"The panoramic view is spectacular (an understatement)— with the open Atlantic ocean, ocean liners and many ships and sailboats entering and leaving the Cape Cod Canal . . . to the right, sand dunes of Sandy Neck Beach, to the left the White Cliffs of Plymouth. . . . Low tide is a special treat with its huge sandbars for walking. . . . In the morning, beautifully set table, delicious home-baked goods. . . . Immaculately maintained . . . Mary Blanchard is a very rare person—warm, kind, and compassionate. . . . Our cup runneth over."*

The Summer House   508/888-4991
158 Main Street, Sandwich, MA 02563-2232

Hosts: David and Kay Merrell
Location: In the historic district. Walking distance to restaurants, museums, shops, pond, and gristmill. One mile to Heritage Plantation and beach.
Open: Year round. Two-night minimum on holiday weekends.

Rates: Double occupancy. $60 shared bath. $75 fireplace and private bath. Singles $10 less. $15 rollaway. October 16–May 24, $10 less. AMEX, Discover, MC, VISA.
♥ ❊ ◆ ✄ ⅙

> From California: *"We planned to stay for one night and extended to three. . . . Charming and creative decor. . . . Exquisite quilts. . . . We stayed in B&Bs throughout New England. The Summer House breakfasts were the loveliest. . . . A jewel . . . a labor of love. . . . As for Dave and Kay, I wish we were neighbors."* From New Jersey: *"I love everything about Summer House . . . black-and-white checkerboard dining room floor . . . four-poster beds . . . the front porch with its glorious climbing rose just invites you to 'sit a spell.'"*

Conclusion: Summer House guests are ecstatic. The Greek Revival house, built in 1835, features original wavy handmade window glass, detailed moldings, latch hardware, and seven fireplaces. For 10 years, while David, a senior scientist, and Kay, an executive secretary, were working for a Los Angeles aerospace firm, they planned on becoming innkeepers. "All that time we collected antiques, Kay made quilts, and in 1988 we took early retirement and here we are!"

Bed and bath: Five rooms. First-floor room has queen four-poster, working fireplace, private attached shower bath. On second floor, queen-bedded room shares full bath with antique twin four-poster pineapple beds. Another queen-bedded room shares a shower bath with two twins/king four-posters. Rollaway available.

Breakfast: 8–9:30. Entree may be quiche, stuffed French toast, strata, eggs Benedict, crepes, or pancakes; garnished with garden vegetables and herbs. Freshly ground coffee. English or herbal tea. Fruit juices. Fresh fruit. Two freshly baked items. Served in plant-filled dining room at tables for two set with floor-length cloths, Victorian butter servers, pressed glass plates and cups and saucers.

Plus: Afternoon iced or hot tea (brewed in antique silver pots) with baked goods; served in garden, on sun porch, or in guests' room. Beach towels. Hammocks in à secluded garden, "a haven." Umbrella table. Enclosed sun porch. Window fans. Transportation to/from Sagamore Circle bus or Sandwich train depot. Hints from Dave about scenic jogging routes. Printed Sandwich Walking Guide (coordinated by Dave). Champagne for special occasions.

The Village Inn at Sandwich

508/833-0363
800-922-9989

4 Jarves Street, Sandwich, MA 02563

Hosts: Patricia and Winfried Platz
Location: In center of village on quiet side street. Next door to Corpus Christi Church. Minutes' walk to beach, restaurants, and museums.
Open: April–December.
Rates: Double occupancy. June 15–

October 31, $85 queen bed with private bath, $70 twin beds with shared bath. Off-season, $70 private bath, $60 shared; $10 extra for fireplaced rooms. AMEX, MC, VISA.
♥ ⁂ ♦ ✗ ✂

Guests take pictures of the sign hanging inside the fence, which consists of 289 spindles hand-turned by Winfried. And then they comment on the furnishings in this 1837 Federal style house, restored/rebuilt by Winfried and Patricia four years ago. The common room, with dark floral wallpaper, white-painted woodwork, and raspberry swags, has authentic Victorian pieces. To match the breakfast room's Victorian chairs, the innkeeper/woodworker made tables. He made all the four-poster beds, and for every room a hand-rubbed armoire, each hand-painted with a floral motif. Wide board floors are natural or painted. "Just last week a Canadian couple left with directions, paint brand names, and a list of tools necessary for whitewashing a piece. And yes, I am happy to talk with visitors in my workshop located behind the house in what was the old town barn."

In Connecticut Winfried, a German-born engineer, designed medical equipment. Patricia, "a New Englander who is *real* Italian," worked in the

(Please turn page.)

reservations department of American Airlines. They chose Cape Cod's oldest town to replicate the best of the B&Bs they have enjoyed during extensive European and American travels.

In residence: "The world's sweetest dog," Tiger, a cockapoo.
Foreign language spoken: German.
Bed and bath: Eight rooms. First- and second-floor rooms (two have working fireplaces) have queen beds, private shower baths. On third floor, two rooms, each with two twin beds, share a shower bath.
Breakfast: 8:30 and 9:30. French toast, bananas Foster, or eggs du village. Fresh fruit. Homemade biscuits and muffins. Served in breakfast room at tables set with roses.
Plus: Ceiling fans. Wet bar with ice maker and refrigerator off common room. Mints on pillow. Turndown service. Down comforters. Rockers and a swing on wraparound porch bordered by roses on the south side. A before-and-after (restoration) album.

Wingscorton Farm Inn   508/888-0534

11 Wing Boulevard, East Sandwich, MA 02537-1104

Hosts: Sheila Weyers and Dick Loring
Location: Across from the Great Marsh and Bird Sanctuary. Five miles from Sandwich village. A five-minute walk down a lane to private bayside beach.
Open: Year round.

Rates: House suite $95 single, $115 double. Carriage house $150 for two, $240 for four. $5 crib (for child six months or younger) or rollaway. $45 additional person. November 1–May 25, $95 house suite, $115 carriage house. AMEX, MC, VISA.
♥ ♯ ❉ ◆

Restoration, with the aid of a meticulous Cape craftsman, has resulted in a gracious home on a real working farm (not just a name). "It's rather amazing to see how guests unwind as soon as they see the animals, gardens, and manicured lawns," observes Sheila, who has resort experience in California and Vermont.

There are chickens, goats, ducks, sheep, and horses. Dick, the farmer/innkeeper, says, "Many guests leave with some attachment to one animal. Next week we're having a wedding here, and the bride has insisted on having Charlie, the goose, attend! . . . Even on the Fourth of July, you don't know anyone else is on the Cape. This lifestyle is, for me, a switch from aquaculture to agriculture. I was with a Cape corporation involved in breeding and raising clams for almost three decades. In 1980 I bought this large 1758 farmhouse, once part of the Underground Railway, that had been in the Wing family for six generations."

In residence: Two well-behaved, people-loving dogs.
Bed and bath: Features vary and include canopied beds, four-poster, sitting room (one with balcony, one with Jacuzzi). Three main house rooms, each with a queen bed and private full bath; two have adjoining singles available only as suites. Cottage has two bedrooms with two twins/king in each room plus a double sleep sofa in living room. Carriage house suite has a queen bed,

queen-sized sleep sofa, fireplaced living room, kitchen, sunning deck. Roll-away and crib available.

Breakfast: At 9. Five-course farm meal. (10–10:30, continental.) Fruit, fresh eggs and breakfast meats, cold or hot cereal, homemade jams and jellies, home-baked breads and cakes (chocolate too), coffee, tea. Served in fire-placed dining room.

Plus: Beverages. Gather your own eggs. Maybe observe a delivery in the barn. Fresh flowers. Paneled library with fireplace flanked by wing chairs. Bedroom window fans. Croquet. TV and VCR.

> From California: *"Fun and relaxing. . . . Breakfasts were outstandingly delicious. . . . Our three-year-old daughter was enthralled."*

Bed & Breakfast in Truro   508/349-6610

Castle Road, Box 431, Truro, MA 02666-0431

Host: Tonie Strauss
Location: On a winding picturesque Cape road. Between ocean and bay, next door to the Truro Castle Hill Center for the Arts, in a quiet, rather sparsely settled residential area.
Open: May–October. Two-night minimum. Reservations required.
Rates: $75 per room.
♥ ⛵ ✈

Tonie's flair means that the house is comfortable and she welcomes you graciously, but there's nothing formal about the 200-year-old captain's house set among lilac bushes, apple trees, and rolling lawns. Tonie is an abstract colorist who paints in oil. She is happy to show you her studio as well as tell you the history of the house.

"Most guests are seeking a quiet time. They come here because Truro leaves the hectic pace and fast-food concessions behind. They usually leave by 10, enjoy the Cape, come back to get ready for dinner, and retire early."

In residence: Tonie breeds wirehaired dachshunds and has two champion females, Lucy and Sophie, and a toy Pekinese named Lolly.
Foreign languages spoken: French and German.
Bed and bath: Two rooms share one guest bath. Private guest entrance and up a captain's staircase to one room with twin beds and another with a double bed. Furnished eclectically with antiques and "Cape decor." (No food in rooms, please.)
Breakfast: 8–9:30. A specialty such as fruit soup. Fresh fruit and juices, muffins, yogurts, cheese, coffee. Served in a stylish European manner—"no plastic ever"—on the covered porch or indoors at a wonderful big table.
Plus: Bedroom fans. Comforters. Duvets. Flowers. "Mints, of course." Hammock under the apple trees. Landscaped grounds.

> From Massachusetts: *"I cannot imagine ever going anywhere else . . . tasteful furnishings . . . European-style hospitality. . . . Mrs. Strauss is charming, her food excellent, and the quiet and privacy of the setting would be restorative for anyone."*

Parker House   508/349-3358

P.O. Box 1111, Truro, MA 02666-1111

Host: Stephen Williams
Location: In the center of this tiny beautiful town. Two miles from Cape Cod National Seashore ocean or bay beaches. Ten minutes' drive to Provincetown (north) or Wellfleet (south). Between the Cobb Memo-

rial Library and the Blacksmith Shop restaurant.
Open: Year round. Two-night minimum on summer weekends.
Rates: $50 single, $55 double, $65 triple. $5 less in winter.

The classic full-Cape house is filled with history, ancestors' portraits, books, period furniture, and wide painted floors.

"My great-grandmother bought this place for $4,500 in 1920. I have been restoring it over a 10-year period, and it's getting there! For the last 2 years I have been carrying on the B&B tradition established in the 1980s by my mother, Jane Parker, a world traveler and writer."

Stephen, official B&B host/baker, is the town's building commissioner and agent to the board of health. "Guests enjoy a secluded walk, the clean beaches, and the history of the area. Some find that the house offers the perfect opportunity to just think or to curl up and read."

In residence: "One gray cat, a shy female hunter, permanently grounded after getting hit by a car."
Bed and bath: Two second-floor rooms, each with (new) sink, share a full bath with claw-foot tub under a skylight and a shower. A (reinforced) four-poster double and a day couch/single bed in each room.
Breakfast: 7:30–10:30 "to the soft chimes of a ship's clock." Homemade muffins and coffee cakes. Breads for toast. Jams. Cereals. Juice and fresh fruit. Coffee or tea. In dining room by bay window or on screened porch. Can last for hours.
Plus: Line-dried sheets. Private off-street parking. Recipe for orange coffee cake.

KEY TO SYMBOLS
♥ Lots of honeymooners come here.
⚓ Families with children are very welcome. (Please see page xiii.)
🏠 "Please emphasize that we are a private home, not an inn."
⚶ Groups or private parties sometimes book the entire B&B.
♦ Travel agents' commission paid. (Please see page xii.)
✖ Sorry, no guests' pets are allowed.
✁ No smoking inside *or* no smoking at all, even on porches.

House Guests Cape Cod Host #91181

North Truro, MA

Location: On five acres within the National Seashore boundaries. Set on a hill with view of ocean ¾ mile away. Within minutes' walk of the Cape Cod Light and the Highland Golf Course.

Reservations: Year round through House Guests, Cape Cod and the Islands, page 112. Two-night minimum.

Rates: $75 twin beds; $75 double bed, working fireplace; $30 third person in room. $110 double-bedded room and adjacent parlor plus private bath (if twin-bedded room is not booked).

The National Park Service considers this 1760 vintage full-Cape house to be the least altered of the antique homes in the park. The owners—a retired biologist who serves on the conservation commission and his wife, who has restored several houses and is in the construction business—came for their first Cape vacation 10 years ago. "We were living in a 19th-century house in New Jersey but had not seen such a collection of wonderful old structures as the Cape has. Within four days we bought this structurally sound 12-room L-shaped gem from descendants of the original owners. We put in central heat, redecorated, furnished with family pieces, many antiques, some reproductions—and kept all the handmade doors and latches and wide pine floors. The layout is perfect for B&B—allowing for visiting and plenty of privacy."

The hostess is building a studio for oil painting and refinishing antiques. Her husband is an ardent surf fisherman and gardener. Word of their warm hospitality brings many relatives and friends of former guests.

Bed and bath: On first floor, one room with double bed and working fireplace, plus a room with single bed for person traveling in same party. On second floor, one room with two twin beds. One shared first-floor guest bath with tub and shower.

Breakfast: Usually 8–9. Juice, cold or hot cereal, homemade muffins made with wild blueberries from property, or hosts' own organically grown raspberries or strawberries. Pancakes or French toast, eggs any style, bacon or ham. Special diets accommodated.

Plus: Screened porch. Two guest parlors; one with color TV, VCR, woodburning Vermont cast iron stove.

"Guests arrive as strangers, leave as friends."

The Marlborough
508/548-6218

320 Woods Hole Road, Falmouth, MA
Mailing address: Box 238, Woods Hole, MA 02543-0238

Host: Patricia Morris
Location: On a secluded wooded half acre. On the main road in a residential section, 1.5 miles from the center of town and from a private beach with parking. Two and one-half miles to Falmouth. One mile to bus terminal for New York or Boston.
Open: Year round. Two-night minimum on some weekends. Teatime hospitality reception, 3–5. "Late arrival arrangements can be made; sorry, early arrivals cannot be accommodated."
Rates: Double occupancy. June 15–October 15 $85–$105. January–March $65–$75. Other times $75–$85, $20 trundle twin. $15 cot. $10 portacrib. Singles $5 less. In winter, package antiques and arts weekends. AMEX, Diners, Discover, MC, VISA.
♥ ♯ ❖ ♦ ✄

> From Arizona: *"A little bit of heaven . . . done in such good taste. . . . Even the rope of the yard swing was intertwined with flowers . . . omelets with herbs from the garden, as was the nasturtium on top—with a candle. She remembered it was my 70th birthday. 'She' is Pat Morris, a charming lady."*

It's an authentic full-Cape reproduction decorated with Pat's style—with antiques, collectibles, and fabric-covered walls, all done by an innkeeper who has been known to take a skiing sabbatical. She also has an antiques shop right here. And an almost-famous story about her start as an innkeeper: A teacher and an architectural and interior designer in California, Pat vacationed here in 1980 and envisioned how it could be done over. "As I was warming up my rented car to leave, the owner tapped on my window and said, 'Did you know this place is for sale, Mrs. Morris?' I made an offer, he accepted, and two days later I owned the Marlborough. Within a month I became an innkeeper with a full house of guests. I have loved every moment (well, almost) of it since."

In residence: November–March, one cat, "Thomas-of-the-Many-Toes."
Foreign languages spoken: "Je parle francais un petit peu, but staff members may speak several languages."
Bed and bath: Five air-conditioned rooms with adjoining (except one down the hall) private shower bath (one with tub also). Rooms—on first and second floors—have either a double or a queen bed; one has an additional twin trundle bed. Room sizes vary from large to cozy gabled.
Breakfast: 8:30–10. Buffet from a repertoire of 37 extraordinary entrees, a dozen home-baked breads. Served in the garden; in the fireplaced parlor at tables set with lovely linen, china, and flowers; or in bed.
Plus: Pool 9–3 for all ages; 3–5 adults only. Midafternoon wine and cheese. Bottle of champagne for honeymooners. Terry robes. Heated towel bars. Croquet, hammock, picnic facilities. English paddle tennis court. Formal gardens. Reservations required for proper English afternoon tea (elaborate menu) in winter by the fire. Off-street parking.

Woods Hole Passage   508/548-9575

186 Woods Hole Road, Falmouth, MA 02540

Host: Cristina Mozo
Location: Peaceful. On Woods Hole Road, midway between (two miles to) Woods Hole and Falmouth.
Open: Year round.

Rates: Double occupancy. Mid-June–late September $80–$85. Off-season $60–$75, senior citizens 10 percent less. Singles $10 less.
✈ ⅄

Contentment. For guests and the innkeeper too. On grounds with mature trees, a little fish pond, and berry bushes. The main structure is an 1875 carriage house that was converted to a private residence in 1952. When in 1991 Cristina, a graphics designer, realized her dream of working at home, she bought this two-year-old B&B and converted the attached barn by raising the roof, matching the angle and molding—it looks like it was built that way originally—and furnishing with lace curtains, collectibles, and restored pieces. A piano is in the comfortably furnished large living room with raspberry sherbet-painted walls and a wonderful huge multipaned window overlooking the grounds. Throughout, all art is original.

As Cristina says, "This is the perfect place to do pencil drawing (my old passion!), to take long walks on the beach, to garden, and to paint." Many of her guests are associated with the Woods Hole Oceanographic Institute. And, of course, the island ferry dock is minutes away.

In residence: Camilla, 13-year-old daughter. Lady, "a very sweet dog." Fluff, Mud, and Nina, "quiet and polite cats."
Foreign language spoken: Spanish.
Bed and bath: Five large rooms. All private shower baths with seats. In main house, room with antique double bed. In barn, two rooms on first floor, two on second (with cathedral ceilings). Queen beds; two rooms have a twin bed also. Crib available.
Breakfast: 8:30–10. Quiches. Home-baked breads, souffle, French toast, fresh fruit. Juices, tea, coffee. Buffet style. Eat in living room, on patio, or at picnic table on grounds.
Plus: Two rooms with ceiling fans; portable air conditioner available. Plenty of reading material. Fresh flowers. Mints on pillow.

Bed & Breakfast Cape Cod Host #71

Yarmouth Port, MA

Location: On a residential side street, a marked "scenic way" in this picturesque village. Four blocks to freshwater lake; half a mile to bay beaches. Within walking distance of fine restaurants and shops. Ten-minute drive to Hyannis and the Martha's Vineyard and Nantucket ferries.

Reservations: Available (mostly) year round through Bed & Breakfast Cape Cod, page 112.
Rates: Queen bed $80, year-round rate. Other rooms $65 in season; $55 October 12–May 25. Single in twin-bedded room, $48 year round. Third person $15.
♯ ♠ ✈

(Please turn page.)

Maybe you, too, will join those who comment on this traditionally furnished Cape house, built in 1800, which "looks like a painting." Among its fans are many B&B guests who leave with the feeling that they have a Cape Cod home to come back to. And for the past two years, hundreds have viewed it during a fall house tour held to raise restoration funds for the West Barnstable courthouse.

The impeccable restoration was done by the friendly and knowledgeable hosts, a former senior citizens' services director and her husband, who worked in the industrial sales field. "After all those family vacations on the Cape, these retirement years—combined with our guests from all over the world—are a dream come true," say the former Connecticut residents, who now work in retailing and at a conference center.

In residence: One small dog.
Bed and bath: Three air-conditioned rooms, each with private full bath. One first-floor room with queen bed, full bath. On second floor—room with two twin beds, full bath; one with a double bed and a single bed.
Breakfast: 8:30–9:30. Juice, fresh fruit, baked apple or homemade muffins or breads. Served in fireplaced dining room.
Plus: Screened porch. TV in parlor. Grill on grounds. Three working fireplaces.

From Florida: *"Exquisite service out of the ordinary."*

Liberty Hill Inn   508/362-3976
77 Main Street, Yarmouth Port, MA 02675-1709

Hosts: Beth and Jack Flanagan
Location: On Old King's Highway (Route 6A), set back on a little hill (site of Revolutionary War rallying point) with views of Barnstable Harbor. Across the road from a conservation area. Within walking distance of fine restaurants, antiques, and crafts shops. Ten-minute drive to Hyannis.
Open: Year round. Two-night minimum on holiday weekends.

Rates: Per room, double occupancy. Memorial Day–Columbus Day, $90, double-bed, $110, $125 bridal suite. Off-season, $75 per room, $125 bridal suite. $20 extra person. Singles $70; off-season, $55 and $60. Five-night honeymoon package $575. Off-season one-night getaway package $99 includes dinner for two. AMEX, MC, VISA.
♥ ◆ ✈

From New Jersey: *"I had the pleasure of experiencing a B&B, a kind of establishment I had heard and read about. The service at Liberty Hill was extra special, the rooms well-kept and beautifully furnished with lovely antiques and quilts, the food very satisfying, and the atmosphere very homey and friendly. We felt truly welcome."*

Although Beth and Jack had experience restoring three houses, when it came time for a "retirement occupation" in 1987, they bought an 1825 shipowner's Greek Revival house that had been completely redecorated as a B&B. In the New York/New Jersey area Jack had been an auditor and in real estate. (He is a Cape broker.) Beth was an actress and worked in international college admissions. Their list of very local suggestions includes everything from an old-time soda fountain to historic houses to a chapel popular for weddings to nature trails. Yarmouth Port, Liberty Hill Inn, and The Wedgewood Inn (below) were featured in a 1992 *Colonial Homes* magazine.

Bed and bath: Five large rooms with private baths. One first-floor room, three steps up from driveway, with two twin beds and oversized stall shower bath with seat. On second floor, three rooms with sitting areas; two rooms with queen beds and stall shower baths, one air-conditioned room with a four-poster double bed and full bath. Third-floor air-conditioned bridal suite has a king bed, nonworking fireplace, and full bath. Rollaway available.
Breakfast: 8–10. Includes recipes tested for Beth's B&B book. Fruit, apple strudel, quiche, French toast, home-baked breads, hunks of cheese, fresh fruit, juice, coffee, tea, and decaf. Served in dining room on separate tables set with lace.
Plus: Cocktail hour. Tea and cookies on holiday weekends. Veranda chairs. Croquet lawn. Terraced garden. Cable TV in common room. Library includes area restaurant menus and maps. Dinners by arrangement.

The Wedgewood Inn 508/362-5157
83 Main Street, Yarmouth Port, MA 02675

Hosts: Milt and Gerrie Graham
Location: On Route 6A, in the historic district. On two landscaped acres with patios and gardens. An eight-minute drive to island ferries.
Open: Year round. Advance reservations recommended.

Rates: Per room. $125 double with working fireplace, $105 or $115 without. $135 suite, $145 with sitting room. $10 rollaway. November 1–June 1, except holidays, 15 percent less. AMEX, Diners, MC, VISA.
♥ ❖ ♦ ✈

"Send me *there!*" said the Boston television interviewer as I was commenting on the slides of B&Bs being shown for Valentine's Day suggestions. (Book early here.) The touch of elegance in the area's first architect-designed house—built in 1812—attracts some famous-name guests, but as innkeepers, the Grahams find much satisfaction in hosting first-time B&B guests (and many returnees too). "Frequently we answer questions about art galleries, historic houses, antiques shops, and restaurants. One of our favorite suggestions is a somewhat-hidden tiny old church."

Milt, a former professional football player (who now does some sculling and mountain climbing) was with the FBI for 20 years. Gerrie taught school in Darien, Connecticut. In 1986, when they saw this inn with working fireplaces, spacious rooms, and wide board floors, the "what next" decision was made. Every guest room has upholstered wing chairs, an antique or handmade bed (many are pencil post), and a handmade quilt—all enhanced by fresh flowers, a late-afternoon tea tray, and fresh fruit.

In residence: Sasha, a Shih Tzu dog, "enjoys guests from a distance." Three cats—Tom, Sam, and Sheba.

(Please turn page.)

Bed and bath: Six rooms; no two have adjoining walls. All private baths; most have hand-held showers. First-floor suites have queen-size fishnet-canopied bed, private screened porch and sitting area, working fireplace, full bath. On second floor—one queen-bedded room with working fireplace; one room with a double and a twin day bed. Entire third floor (suite) with private exterior entrance accessed by narrow staircase; queen bed and, in the sitting room, a single bed. Rollaway available.

Breakfast: 8–9:30. French toast, scrambled eggs on puff pastry, or maybe Belgian waffles. Homemade and English muffins. Cereal. Yogurt. Served on tables for two set with china and flowers in dining room with handcrafted Windsor chairs.

Plus: Air conditioners for guest rooms. Patio and lawn seating.

Martha's Vineyard
_____ Reservation Services _____

The following reservation services represent B&Bs on Martha's Vineyard:
Bed & Breakfast Cape Cod, page 112.
House Guests, Cape Cod and the Islands, page 112.
Pineapple Hospitality, page 106.

Many B&Bs that allow smoking restrict it to certain rooms and/or public areas. Although some of those B&Bs that have the ✁ symbol allow smoking on the porch and/or patio, others do not allow smoking anywhere on the property.

——— Martha's Vineyard B&Bs ———

Breakfast at Tiasquam   508/645-3685
RR 1, Box 296, off Middle Road, Chilmark, MA 02535-9705

Host: Ron Crowe
Location: At the top of a hill, surrounded by farms, ponds, woodlands, rolling pastures, and scenic roads. Four miles from Menemsha and Lucy Vincent Beach. (Note: Transportation is necessary. See "Plus" below.)
Open: Year round. Two-night minimum for Saturday night stays in summer and fall.
Rates: Double occupancy. June 7–September 7, $100–$175. April 12–June 6 and September 8–October 31, $90–$150. November–April 11, $70–$115. Children under 2, free. Ages 2–12, $25; two or more, $20 each.
♥ ♯ ✻ ✖ ✂

> From New Hampshire: *"Your book could say a great deal more about Ron Crowe and his gorgeous home and hospitality and you still wouldn't overdo it."*

Two years after Ron, a Massachusetts native, "discovered" the Vineyard during a bicycling vacation with his son, he found this site and left his 19-year position as director of Bowdoin College's dining service. He built the house in seven months, during the 1987 winter of record island snow.

One guest dubbed this B&B "the perfect place." Others have been inspired to write poems. "The perfect place" is unique for many reasons. It was built to be a B&B. It has an enormous bow roof, 20 skylights, many sliding doors, and a two-storied greenhouse atrium. Even with all the public space, there's the feeling of home and privacy. Outstanding craftspeople handcrafted much of the furniture, a graceful spiral staircase, the pottery sinks, 32 paneled cherry doors, and cabinets and woodwork. The bonus, of course, is ebullient Ron, the convivial host and cook.

Bed and bath: Eight quiet carpeted rooms; many with skylights, two with private baths. Two handicapped-accessible first-floor rooms, one queen-bedded and one with one twin bed, share a full bath. On second floor, two rooms duplicate first-floor bed and bath arrangement. The master room has queen bed, cathedral ceiling, ceiling fan, wood stove, two skylights, private full bath with two-person Jacuzzi. Another room has a queen bed, private full bath, four skylights. Two-room suite has a room with two double beds, one with queen bed plus a single futon, connecting doors, private deck, private full bath (or shared bath if two rooms are used individually). Rollaway for children.
Breakfast: 7–9:30. "Practically anything you want." Fresh corn (in season), blueberry pancakes with Vermont maple syrup, cinnamon raisin French toast, fresh fish when available. Served at kitchen counter, at dining table, or on the outside deck.
Plus: Two outdoor hot/cold showers. Plenty of deck space. Lucy Vincent Beach passes. Beach towels. Ron has one rental car which includes pickup service at airport or ferry.

The Arbor

508/627-8137

222 Upper Main Street, P.O. Box 1228, Edgartown, MA 02539

Host: Peggy Hall
Location: Six-minute walk into town, 10 minutes to harbor. On the bicycle path. Shuttle bus to downtown Edgartown, South Beach, Oak Bluffs, Vineyard Haven (in season) stops at front door.

Open: May–October. Three-day minimum July–August; Two-day May–June and September–October.
Rates: Double occupancy. June–September $80–$125. Off-season $55–$90. MC, VISA.

♥ ❖ ♦ ✈

The weathered-shingled house, built in 1880, was moved from the adjoining island of Chappaquiddick in 1910 and added on to through the years. Since Peggy took it over in 1979, she has been in a position to share her love affair with the island and its hideaways. Rooms are decorated with painted walls, stenciling, shutters, ball fringe curtains, vintage furniture, and, in the living room, chintz-covered sofas. "When English guests say it looks like an English country cottage, I feel I succeeded."

It's all because she played an experimental game that asked what you wanted to be doing in 10 years. Why wait? she thought. "The children were grown, so the time was right. After training real estate brokers for 20 years, I can say that work has never been so much fun. . . . I like to tell about the two guests, high-powered New York advertising people, who, upon arrival, walked and talked as though they were in a contest to finish first. By the time they left, they were strolling casually. I told them they would probably be picked up for loitering when they returned to Manhattan. . . . We get a great mix of people—young, retirees, singles, couples, lots of Europeans. . . ."

Bed and bath: Ten rooms, eight with private baths (four shower only, four are full). Six are queen-bedded rooms. One has a pair of twin beds. One cozy single room. Two double-bedded rooms share a full bath. Designer linens. Comforters.
Breakfast: 8–10. Juice, homemade corn and other breads or muffins, tea or coffee. Buffet style with linens, cloth napkins, silver service. Eat in dining room, outside at umbrella tables, or in the courtyard.
Plus: Living room with vaulted ceiling fan. Fireplaced beamed dining room. Enclosed outdoor hot/cold shower. Hammock for two suspended from trees. Setups (ice, glasses, mix) 5–7 p.m. Bicycle rack.

> Guests wrote: *"Caring hostess who knows her island! Joyful and restful visit. A super place either to be alone or for finding a group of people to be with . . . cozy . . . like home."*

"It's been a great season—filled every night," said the happy but tired innkeeper. As I began to calculate $60 times seven nights times. . . my husband quipped, "Forget it, that's 600 sheets."

Meeting House Inn

40 Meeting House Way, P.O. Box 2420
Edgartown, MA 02539-2420

508/627-8626
800/654-2649

Hosts: Jerry and Maria MacKenty
Location: On 58 acres of open and wooded land. On a country road. Two miles (five-minute drive) from South Beach, town center, shops, galleries, and restaurants. About a 15-minute drive to boat terminal.
Open: Year round. Two-night minimum on Memorial, July 4th, Labor Day, and Columbus Day weekends.
Rates: Double occupancy. Memorial Day through Columbus Day, queen bed $80 or $85. Double bed $75. Off-season, $15 less. Singles 10 percent less. $15 third person. MC, VISA.
♥ ⬛ ❀ ✗ ✄

From New York: "*I cannot imagine a more relaxing vacation. . . . Not a detail was forgotten. . . . As we enjoyed the best breakfast we've ever had at a B&B—served on lovely china—Jerry helped us plan our day . . . even referred to a barometer, telling us which beach would be the least windy . . . beach towels and blankets a big plus . . . arrived home from beach to a relaxing hot tub and view of the many acres of wheatfields. The grounds are beautiful! Jerry was happy to answer questions about the house . . . ideal location. . . . And the price is right.*"

Home it is, a 1750s center entrance colonial farmhouse, in Jerry's family for over 50 years. The living and dining rooms are furnished with antiques, Oriental rugs, and comfortable chairs. Guest rooms are attractive and functional.

Jerry, who returned to the island in 1976 after being a stockbroker in New York and Connecticut, and Maria, a nurse, began hosting three years ago—"to share our home, a peaceful atmosphere, and this island filled with history, country roads, bike paths. And year round, they love our hot-tub greenhouse spa."

In residence: In hosts' separate wing, one-year-old James, "already an official assistant." In the summer, Bill and Susan, college students. Sandy is a friendly golden Labrador. Cats, Dundie and Libbie, live outside in the summer.
Bed and bath: Four second-floor rooms, each with queen or double bed, semiprivate full baths. Rollaway and portacrib available.
Breakfast: 8–9:30. Waffles (Jerry's favorite), eggs, pancakes, or French toast with bacon or sausage. Fruit, homemade coffee cake, juice, coffee and tea. Served in fireplaced dining room.
Plus: Fireplaced living room. Library. Late-afternoon cheese and crackers. Guest refrigerator. Window fans. Picnic cooler. Babysitting arranged.

---

*I*s B&B like a hotel?
How many times have you hugged the doorman?

The Shiverick Inn
508/627-3797

P.O. Box 640, Edgartown, MA 02539-0640

Hosts: Claire and Juan del Real
Location: In the center of town; five-minute walk to the waterfront.
Open: Year round.
Rates: Double occupancy. June 1–October 13, $150–$200, suite $230–$265. May 4–May 31 and October 14–November 4, $95–$150, suite $160–$195. November 5–May 3, $75–$125, suite $140–$165. AMEX, MC, VISA.

Intentionally grand—with crystal chandeliers, brocades, gilt mirrors, Oriental rugs, and ancestral portraits—this 19th-century Victorian with mansard roof and cupola was built in 1840, during the height of the whaling era, by Dr. Clement Shiverick, the town's physician. Family members opened the house as an inn in 1984. It was completely restored to its elegant style in 1988 when Juan, a lawyer and general counsel of the Department of Health and Human Services, and Claire, press secretary for Senator Strom Thurmond, decided to change careers and lifestyle. Throughout, there are 18th- and 19th-century English and American antiques. Wraparound terraces off the library overlook a formal garden. And the garden/breakfast room is filled with mementoes of the innkeepers' days as Reagan administration appointees.

In residence: Cognac, a chocolate Labrador.
Foreign language spoken: Spanish.
Bed and bath: Ten rooms with queen beds (some canopied). Most with working fireplace, all with private full bath. Cot available.
Breakfast: 8–10. Served in garden room off enclosed garden. Hosts join guests.
Plus: All rooms but two are air conditioned. Private phone in suite. Guest refrigerator. Turndown service.

The Oak House
508/693-4187

Corner Seaview and Pequot Avenues, P.O. Box 299 BNE
Oak Bluffs, MA 02557-0299

Host: Elizabeth Convery-Luce
Location: Across from an ocean promenade and a (safe) surf beach. Walk to the ferry, shuttle bus, restaurants, shops, Victorian cottages. Four blocks to bike path.
Open: Mid-May–mid-October. On weekends, three-night minimum in season; two nights, off-season.
Rates: Late June–mid-September, $145–$160 with water view, $110–$135 without. Suite $220 quad occupancy. Spring, 30 percent less; fall, 20 percent less. MC, VISA.
♥ ✣ ♦ ✈

> From California: *"A glimpse of 19th-century grandeur and all the comfort a house could give. Charming!"*

"Peace, quiet, and the romantic atmosphere are the reasons many of our guests come. At 4 p.m. homemade Victorian tea (lemonade in summer) with home-baked cookies, pastries, and breads is served on the open and wicker-

(Please turn page.)

furnished glass-enclosed porches. This house was built in 1872 from a two-storied design by Boston architect Samuel Freeman Pratt, known for his Newport, Rhode Island, mansions. When it was purchased and enlarged four years later by Massachusetts Governor William Claflin, they preserved the Queen Anne-style roof with its many angles by jacking up the second floor and putting in a new second floor. On the first floor, oak is everywhere—furnishings, ceilings, walls, and floors. Some bathroom ceilings are tin. Sinks are marble. Guest rooms are uncluttered and include brass and mahogany beds. The entire house was renovated and redecorated in 1989."

Betsi, daytime innkeeper—and daughter of the owner, a past president of the island's preservation society—was trained in pastry making at Le Cordon Bleu in Paris. She and her husband are fourth-generation island residents.

Bed and Bath: Ten rooms including two suites with ocean-view balcony. All private shower baths. Nine rooms with queen bed; one with king/twins option. One suite with queen bed, sitting room with queen pull-out couch and daybed; the other has a queen and a king bed.
Breakfast: 8:30–10. Continental buffet includes Betsi's breakfast breads or pastries; breakfast is served in antiques-filled paneled dining room, but it may be taken to the sun porch overlooking the ocean or outside onto the veranda.
Plus: Individual thermostats and ceiling fans in each room. Two rooms are air conditioned. TV in three rooms. Baby grand piano and TV in living room. Porch rockers and swing. Beach towels and chairs. Guest refrigerator.

Captain Dexter House   508/693-6564
100 Main Street, P.O. Box 2457, Vineyard Haven, MA 02568

Hosts: Lucky and Pat Noll
Location: One block from ferry dock. In historic residential district that abuts shops, restaurants, beach.
Open: Year round. Three-day minimum on high season weekends.
Rates: Depends on room size and furnishings. May 15–September 30, $95–$145; suite with fireplace $145. October–May 14, $55–$75; suite with fireplace $115. AMEX, MC, VISA.
✖ ✁

More than a piece of history has changed hands here. When Washingtonians bought the 1843 captain's house in 1988, they acquired all the furnishings of the previous owner, a consultant on 18th-century house restoration and decorating. So the first inn to be part of the Island Historical Society's annual house tour still has the fine antique Sheraton and Chippendale pieces and Oriental rugs.

Romance plays a part in the current history of the inn. The Nolls were New Yorkers (in the restaurant industry and modeling) who vacationed at the inn and married on the island. In 1989, after taking an innkeeping seminar with the Washington owners, they became partners and full-time innkeepers.

Bed and bath: Eight rooms. All private baths; some full, some shower only or tub only. Two rooms each with a canopied queen four-poster and fireplace. The suite has a queen canopied bed and living room with queen-sized sleep sofa. Other rooms have a king, a double, or twin beds. Cot available. (November–April, ocean views from several rooms.)

Breakfast: 8:30–10. Homemade fresh fruit breads and muffins. Freshly squeezed orange juice, coffee, teas. Served in elegant dining room.

Plus: Fireplace in living room. Afternoon lemonade or sherry. Bedroom ceiling fans. Garden with tables and chairs. Locked garage for bicycles. Off-street parking.

Guests wrote: *"Personable hosts . . . perfect innkeepers . . . attentive but discreet . . . everything was wonderful."*

Lothrop Merry House   508/693-1646

Owen Park, Box 1939, Vineyard Haven, MA 02568

Hosts: John and Mary Clarke (April–December). "In winter, inn-sitters who are delighted to be here."

Location: A quiet spot with harbor view and private beach. A block from ferry dock. Short bus or bicycle ride to public beaches. Across from town park (with summer band concerts some Sunday nights).

Open: Year round.

Rates: Double occupancy. $88 for room with double and single bed, shared bath; $98 for double or double and single with harbor view, shared bath; $145 double, working fireplace, private bath; $155 queen, working fireplace, private bath. Mid-October through early April, about $10–$20 less per room. $15 extra person. $6 child under seven or crib. Summer sails: per person; $50 for three daylight hours, $50 for evening sail, $300 overnight to Cuttyhunk or Nantucket. MC, VISA.

♥ ♨ ❀ ✈ ⌘

From Connecticut: *"A little piece of heaven. . . . The view from my cozy room was of the front lawn stretching down to the harbor full of sailboats. Flowers everywhere. . . . Peace and contentment sustained me all winter. . . . The charm and beauty is surpassed only by John and Mary."*

As Mary says, "We enjoy our somewhat unusual lifestyle, combining innkeeping with sailing. We live aboard our 54-foot ketch, which John captains on day sails here in the summer and on weekly winter charters in the Caribbean."

The Clarkes, a social worker and a teacher, have worked in Afghanistan, Greece, and Japan. Before becoming islanders in 1980, the parents of four grown children ran a New Hampshire ski lodge. Here they have an antiques-filled 1790s shingled house that was moved to its perfect site in 1815 by forty oxen. It is "settled," with uneven floors, a reception room that doubles as a common room in the winter, and fresh cheerful decor. Adirondack chairs are on the terrace overlooking the lawn and harbor beyond. Guests may use the canoe, Sunfish, and small private beach.

Bed and bath: Seven rooms, five with harbor views, four with private baths. On first floor, off of sitting area, one with canopied queen bed, working fireplace, private shower bath; one room with double bed, working fireplace, private full bath. Also on ground floor, one room ("perfect for families with

(Please turn page.)

children") with a double and a single bed, access to patio. Upstairs, with outside stairway, three rooms; two with a double and a single bed, one with a double. All three share a bath with tub, hand-held shower. In summer there is also an enclosed outside hot/cold shower plus changing room. Rollaway and crib available.

Breakfast: Orange juice, homemade sweet bread (recipes shared), coffee, teas, cocoa. Outside on patio, or in reception room (in winter or in inclement weather) with trays guests may take to their rooms.

Plus: Beach chairs. Garden flowers in summer; dried bouquets in winter. Babysitting. Conference room for about 12.

Phil and Ilse Fleischman   508/693-5562

Box 1951, Drews Cove (off Northern Pines Road)
Vineyard Haven, MA 02568

Hosts: Phil and Ilse Fleischman
Location: Two miles from Vineyard Haven center on Lake Tashmoo, a beautiful 1½-mile-long saltwater lake open to Vineyard Sound.

Open: Year round. Advance reservations required.
Rates: Per room. June 15–September 14, $95. Off-season $75.
♥ ✈

> From California: *"Magical. Through quiet woods to a clearing . . . flower-filled patios . . . a warm welcome usually reserved for old friends. . . . The house blends Ilse's European flair with Philip's down-to-earth practicality . . . charming room (more like a studio apartment) with all the comforts of home and a private balcony overlooking sparkling blue water."*

After 17 years of living in the German country-style house they designed and built in Edgartown, the Fleischmans moved to this "forever" spot—where "the total traffic consists of ducks, geese, seagulls, hawks, swans, and, this spring, a new family of otters."

Phil, an architect who has been a yacht captain and boat builder, designed this traditional New England house with cedar shingles and trim, French doors, red brick paths, and European details. He built it with Ilse, a kindergarten teacher in her native Germany and also in Greece, and now a travel agent here. Their informal style of hosting provides for opportunities to visit on the porch or in the garden—or even by the boathouse, where Phil is currently restoring some boats, including one that is over 100 years old.

In residence: "G.T., our friendly gray cat, can be easily encouraged to sit in your lap."
Foreign language spoken: German.
Bed and bath: Overlooking the lake, two rooms, each with private entrance and shower bath. King bed in Balcony Room; queen in cathedral-ceilinged Patio Room.
Breakfast: Full breakfast provided in refrigerator of guest rooms. Help-yourself arrangement.
Plus: Deep-water pier (guests' boats are welcome) used for swimming. Horseshoes and bocci. Use of grill. Ample parking.

Thorncroft Inn

508/693-3333
800/332-1236
fax 508/693-5419

P.O. Box 1022, 278 Main Street
Vineyard Haven, MA 02568

Hosts: Karl and Lynn Buder
Location: On 3½ acres with big old trees in a residential neighborhood. A half mile beyond the edge of the village. One mile from ferry landing.
Open: Year round. Three-night min-imum on major holiday weekends.
Rates: Double occupancy. June 14–September 15, $129–$299. Off-season, $99–$249. AMEX, MC, VISA.
♥ ◆ ✈ ⊁

"It's the type of place where we find ourselves falling in love all over again." Since that comment from a guest appeared in my first B&B book, the Buders have continued to embellish the house, which was built in 1918 for the son of an industrialist. At first Karl, with his father, restored everything and helped install new baths. Now there are Jacuzzis and hot tubs. To add rooms (and keep the same noncommercial feeling), they bought nearby property. Lynn selected turn-of-the-century lamps, colonial pieces, and beds that include four-posters, brass beds, and high-back Victorians too. Now there is air conditioning throughout and each guest room has a telephone. "By popular demand," dinner is served here. And some guests return with colleagues for meetings and for the hospitality of these friendly hosts. The Buders share their knowledge "of the wonders of Martha's Vineyard—and career transitions." Ten years ago Karl, who has a master's degree in public administration, was a probation officer and marathon runner. Lynn commuted on weekends from her executive position with a Connecticut insurance company.

In residence: In innkeepers' quarters, sons Alex, age six, and Hans, age five.
Foreign language spoken: French.
Bed and bath: Thirteen rooms with queen (some canopied) or a double bed. Some with working fireplace and/or a balcony. All with private bath; some full, others shower only. Two two-room suites can accommodate children; both have two-person Jacuzzi, one has a private 300-gallon hot tub.
Breakfast: (Continental for early ferry departures.) Announced by a breakfast bell when the French doors are opened at 8:15 and 9:30. Buttermilk pancakes and bacon, blueberry or strawberry honey sauces, almond French toast, quiche, croissant sandwiches, baked goods or granola. Classical music played.
Plus: Gazebo/deck with four-person hot tub. Color cable TV in some rooms. Screened porch. Wicker-furnished sun room. Victorian reading parlor. Lawn furniture. Extra bath for post-checkout refresher.

One out of five guests leaves with the dream of opening a B&B.

The Tuckerman House   508/693-0417

45 William Street, P.O. Box 194, Vineyard Haven, MA 02568-0194

Hosts: Joe and Carolyn Mahoney
Location: Seven-minute walk from ferry. In historic district in a neighborhood of sea captains' houses. Three miles from gingerbread cottages.
Open: Year round. Two-night minimum on weekends April–October; three-night minimum on Memorial, July 4th, Labor Day, and Columbus Day weekends.
Rates: Double occupancy. June 15–September 15 king $160–$180; queen $150–$170; double $130–$150, $120–$160 with sitting room, $110 back of house. Off-season $80–$160. AMEX, MC, VISA.
♥ ⬛ ♦ ✗ ✂

The Greek Revival house was built in 1836 as a wedding gift from mariner Thomas Tuckerman for his bride. Shortly after the Mahoneys bought it as a one-year-old B&B in 1988, they hosted a small winter wedding by the fireplace.

"We had vacationed here since 1976 and find that many travelers are surprised to learn how big the island is, how laid back and idyllic it is, and at the same time, how many activities it offers. We give them a map, explain the differences of the six towns, and highlight places including our own favorite spots."

The Mahoneys, former Bostonians, furnished with antiques. In the winter Carolyn teaches. Joe, a certified financial planner, does consulting.

Bed and bath: Five antiques-furnished rooms, all private modern baths. King-bedded first-floor room has private entrance. On second floor, room with queen four-poster canopy bed with two wing chairs. One with double four-poster, seven windows. Another double-bedded room with Victorian rocker. In rear, private entrance to room with quarter-canopy double bed, shower bath.
Breakfast: 8:30–10. Choice of juices and cereals. Fruit. Homemade granola and muffins. Coffee. Herbal tea. Preserves. In the summer, served on veranda; in the winter, in dining room.
Plus: All air-conditioned rooms (except queen). Tea in winter by fireplace; lemonade in summer on veranda. Cable TV in living room. Guest refrigerator. Guest phone room. Off-street parking.

The Bayberry   508/693-1984

Old Courthouse Road, P.O. Box 654, West Tisbury, MA 02568-0654

Host: Rosalie Powell
Location: Down a country lane where there are birds, woods, meadows, horses. Ten minutes to beaches. Five miles from ferry landing.
Open: Year round (except maybe January or February). Two-day minimum on many weekends.
Rates: Double occupancy. June–September, $98 twin beds or queen canopy, semiprivate bath; $130 double canopy, private bath; $135 king, private bath. Off-season $75–$95. AMEX, MC, VISA.
♥ ⬛ ❄ ✗ ✂

From Massachusetts: *"Rosalie Powell, a native who is a descendant of Governor Thomas Mayhew, founder of the Vineyard and Nantucket, extends herself to her guests in every way possible—from the quaint rooms, to fresh flowers bursting everywhere, to passes to wonderful beaches and tennis courts, to providing sherry and mints, to a gourmet breakfast . . . but most importantly, you feel welcomed and appreciated!"*

Others call The Bayberry "the perfect honeymoon spot." They comment on the "warm and tranquil environment" in this rambling, weathered-shingled Cape Cod-style house built (surprise) just 20 years ago on land settled by Rosalie's family in 1642. A B&B since the hostess took early retirement 11 years ago from the University of Massachusetts Extension Service, it is filled with family heirlooms and restored antiques. There's an open country kitchen (watch Dutch aebleskivers being made); a beamed ceiling with hanging baskets; pottery; quilts; hooked rugs (Rosalie offers workshops here); and lacy pillows (made by Rosalie). The bobwhite calls. The meadow is filled with daisies. Horses graze. The hearth beckons. Joie de vivre.

Bed and bath: Five rooms. On first floor, two rooms share a hall full bath; one has an arched canopied queen bed, the other has two pineapple-post twin beds. On second floor, two rooms with king beds (one wicker, one high Victorian) and private shower baths; one with canopied double bed, private full bath.
Breakfast: Usually 8:30. (Coffeepot on for early risers.) A favorite entree— Dreamboats, named by a guest and almost always photographed before eaten. Or Belgian waffles with fresh blueberry sauce and bacon, sausage, or ham. Fruit or juice. Homemade muffins and jams. Served with linens and china at fireside tables overlooking gardens or on flower-filled patio.
Plus: Outside hot/cold shower big enough for two. Depending on guests' plans, afternoon tea, wine, hors d'oeuvres. Bedroom fans. Grand piano. Library of books on antiques. Croquet. Occasional seafood chowder or barbecues. Champagne for honeymooners. Hints for beaches with shells and fossils. Aromas: "Heavenly today. I am making beach plum jelly from the plums I picked yesterday on the sand dunes at Lobsterville."

__ Nantucket Reservation Services __

The following reservation services represent B&Bs on Nantucket:
A Bed & Breakfast Agency of Boston, Inc., page 188.
A Bed & Breakfast Above the Rest, page 187.
Bed & Breakfast Cape Cod, page 112.
House Guests, Cape Cod and the Islands, page 112.
Pineapple Hospitality, page 106.

KEY TO SYMBOLS
♥ Lots of honeymooners come here.
♯ Families with children are very welcome. (Please see page xiii.)
🐚 "Please emphasize that we are a private home, not an inn."
♣ Groups or private parties sometimes book the entire B&B.
♦ Travel agents' commission paid. (Please see page xii.)
✠ Sorry, no guests' pets are allowed.
✌ No smoking inside *or* no smoking at all, even on porches.

Nantucket B&Bs

Nantucket's unique characteristics have always been appreciated by its residents. Since others have discovered the island, it has become increasingly popular.

B&B guests are likely to find little need for a car. Advance reservations for autos (carried by the Steamship Authority only) are essential and are often made months before the summer season. The ferry ride from Hyannis and Woods Hole is 2¼ hours. The Steamship Authority (phone 508/540-2022) services the island from Hyannis and Woods Hole. Hy-Line (508/778-2600) sails from Hyannis spring through fall. Bicycles (extra charge) are allowed on ferries.

Centerboard Guest House

508/228-9696
fax 508/228-1957

8 Chester Street, P.O. Box 456
Nantucket, MA 02554-0456

Hosts: Marcia Wasserman and Reggie Reid
Location: On edge of historic district, a few blocks from cobblestoned shopping area.
Open: Year round. Two-night minimum on weekends. (Reserve early for August and Christmas Stroll.)

Rates: Double occupancy. Peak season (Memorial Day–Columbus Day) $225 suite, $150 studio, $135 other rooms. Rest of the year $125–$150 suite, $100–$125 studio, $85–$110 other rooms. $25 additional person in room. AMEX, MC, VISA.
♥ 🛏 ❄ ♦ 🐾

"People call and ask for our unnamed suite by the name of a famous performer who honeymooned there! And now, five years after our opening, we find that 'oldtimers' share all their island 'bests' with first-time guests. We're small. We're both home and a romantic place. We offer privacy and opportunities to mingle. Our linens are spectacular. All the quilts are antiques. There are Tiffany and electrified oil lamps, Oriental rugs, and painted murals. The floors, except for the century-old parquet floor in the suite, are pickled. Bouquets of fresh flowers are everywhere. We repaint almost every year. And I am amazed at the details guests notice—even when we change the color of mugs. They bike, walk, have wine on the porch, watch the fish being weighed after a tournament. They relax—and return to this wonderful place."

Reggie, who started coming to the island 20 years ago, has been in residence since the day Marcia, a former New York artist and interior designer (who now lives a couple of blocks from the inn) transformed and opened this Victorian house.

Bed and bath: Six rooms, all private baths. One two-room suite with fireplace, queen canopied bed, queen sofa bed, Jacuzzi in full bath. Other rooms have queen bed, queen with twin sofa bed, or one or two double beds. Studio has two double beds, one platform twin bed, kitchen, private exterior entrance. Crib available.
Breakfast: 8:30–9:30. Fresh fruit. Homemade muffins and breads. Granola. Cereals. Coffees and teas. Served in dining room at tables with cloths and fresh flowers.

(Please turn page.)

Plus: Ceiling fans in every guest and public room. Each room has individual thermostat, private telephone, and a refrigerator with fresh fruit, cheese, and sodas. Champagne for honeymooners. Living room with window seat. Down comforters. Plush beach towels.

The Century House   508/228-0530
10 Cliff Road, Box 603, Nantucket, MA 02554-0603

Hosts: Jean Heron and (husband) Gerry Connick
Location: In quiet section of the historic district, at the top of the hill, surrounded by sea captains' mansions. Three blocks from town center. Ten minutes to beach. Five-minute walk from steamship landing.
Open: Spring through Christmas Stroll weekend in December. Three-night minimum on weekends, late June–late September; shorter stays accommodated when posssible.
Rates: Depends on room size. Late June–late September and holidays, $80–$100 single, private bath; $95–$100 double, shared bath; $95–$145 double, private bath. Off-season, $55 single, private bath; $65–$75 double, shared bath; $75–$125 double, private bath. Group rates available. AMEX, MC, VISA.
♥ ♨ ◆ ✕ ✄

> From New York: *"Warm and inviting . . .wonderful wraparound porch . . . outrageous breakfasts . . . could choose to make conversation or to sit alone and think."* From Pennsylvania: *"Terrific combination of friendliness and service."* From Massachusetts: *"Originally booked for the location but we return for the innkeepers."*

Exuberance—for Nantucket, for the inn, for life! Two former high-tech executives, Gerry (who was trained as an architect) and Jean, answered a "needs work" real estate ad in 1984 and proceeded to "plan an inn with special appeal for people with stressful careers. It works! Guests enjoy the tranquillity of the island, the fireplace, the *New York Times* in peace on a Sunday." The exterior of Nantucket's oldest continuous (since 1833) guest house, decorated "in simple Nantucket country with Laura Ashley highlights," is a backdrop for some scenes on the television series "Wings." And it's home to many artists who come to the island for opening nights or private shows.

Foreign languages spoken: Several, according to staffing.
Bed and bath: Fourteen rooms on three floors. Most have private shower baths (three also have tubs). The two third-floor double-bedded rooms that share a bath have sinks in the rooms "and the best harbor views." Other rooms have double, twin/king, or queen beds. Some are four-posters or canopied; many are draped. Six rooms have nonworking fireplaces. Some have separate entrances. Cot available.
Breakfast: 8:30–10. Bach music indicates it's time for fresh fruit, juice, English muffins, coffee cakes, granola and cereals, bagels with cream cheese, hot beverages. Eat in pine kitchen or on the veranda or patio.
Plus: BYOB cocktail hour with setups and munchies provided. Afternoon tea or soda. Ceiling fans in most rooms, portable fans available. Beach towels. Guests' refrigerator.

Cliff Lodge   508/228-9480

9 Cliff Road, Nantucket, MA 02554-4025

Host: Gerrie Miller
Location: Five blocks from village center and ferry dock. Set on a hill overlooking town and harbor. Residential area with many large homes dating back to whaling times.
Open: Year round.

Rates: Mid-June–late September, Christmas Stroll, and Memorial and Columbus Day weekends $60 single, $100–$150 double. Spring and fall plus Thanksgiving and Christmas, $50 single, $75–$120 double.
♥ ✈

> From New Jersey: *"After seeing Cliff Lodge in a* USA Today *article, I called. . . . Gerrie Miller enthusiastically explained . . . described . . . and promised it would be a special Valentine gift. It was all Ms. Miller boasted about and more. Beautifully decorated . . . very clean . . . wonderful aromas from the kitchen made us wish it was morning already. . . . The main parlor, with fireplace, antique furnishings, and wonderful selection of books and magazines gave one the nostalgic warmth of a Charles Dickens novel. Breakfast and afternoon tea were served in this room . . . conversation among the guests included similar comments from everyone about this lodge. . . . The first evening at dinner my (now) husband proposed to me. . . . For a very different, yet comfortable getaway, this is the perfect place and perfect setting, with very personal attention from an innkeeper who truly loves her job and makes everyone feel so welcome."*

The 1770s captain's house has been a guest house for over 50 years. When purchased by the current owner in 1986, it was completely done over—with a light and airy feeling, spatter-painted floors, white eyelet bedding, Laura Ashley wallpaper, and rag rugs and dhurries.

Four years ago Gerrie, an interior designer, visited her daughter on the island, and within a matter of weeks, "by accident" (as she says), became the inn's contented—and "perfect" (as guests say)—innkeeper. She suggests the best places to see the sun rise or set, a cemetery "that *is* Nantucket history, the library that is very special, and tips about the famous Nantucket restaurants."

Bed and bath: Twelve rooms (on three floors), each with adjoining private bath, cable TV, phone. Twin, double, queen, and king beds available. Some rooms have views of harbor. Third-floor rooms have air conditioning.
Breakfast: 8–10. Buffet. Homemade bread, biscuits, scones, apple crisp, 14 varieties of muffins, bagels, cream cheese, homemade granola, fresh fruit. In fireplaced breakfast room with door leading to garden patio. Trays for carrying to your room, if you wish.
Plus: In summer, afternoon iced tea with tarts, cakes, cookies, and snacks. Color cable TV. Outside shower. Beach towels. Widow's walk with panoramic view of harbor is accessible to guests. Four common rooms. Pantry with refrigerator and ice maker. Games. Croquet. Parking lot.

---

*In this book, areas of Massachusetts
are arranged roughly from east to west.*

Corner House

508/228-1530

49 Center Street, Box 1828, Nantucket, MA 02554-1828

Hosts: Sandy and John Knox-Johnston

Location: Residential. In old historic district. Around the corner from village center, on a quiet side street. Few minutes' walk from Steamboat Wharf.

Open: Year round except two January/February weeks. Mid-June through mid-September, four-night minimum including Saturday, three nights during the week. (Inquire about shorter periods, often available.) Other times, two-night minimum. (Maximum group size is two couples traveling together.)

Rates: Double occupancy. Late June–mid-September and Christmas Stroll, $75–$135. Mid-May–late June, mid-September–late October, Thanksgiving week, and 12 days of Christmas, $65–$115. Winter excluding Thanksgiving and Christmas, $55–$90. Singles $5 less. MC, VISA. ♥ ✈

Gourmet magazine and Swedish and German publications are among many that have raved about everything from the muffins to the decor and hospitality at this B&B, which now has all private baths, skylights, a welcoming hearth, afternoon tea, and English perennial gardens. Filled with family antiques, original art, botanical prints, Oriental rugs, antique brass and pewter, and big bouquets of dried flowers, the house built in 1723 is as the hostess hoped it would be: "quintessential Nantucket, without the decorated look." It features knowledgeable concierge service—"better than the Ritz," according to one well-traveled Irish businessman—for everything from sailing lessons to historical walking tours.

It all started in 1980 when Sandy, a designer and restorer of 18th- and 19th-century buildings, was asked to "do up" a former five-room boarding house for selling. "I loved it so I kept it!" she says. British-born John, whom she met in Nantucket, brought country house and rose growing (and Lloyd's of London) experience to the Corner House, "our home, lifestyle, and joy."

In residence: Summer staff includes young women from England, Scotland, and/or New Zealand.

Foreign languages spoken: Some French and a little German.

Bed and bath: Fifteen rooms. All private adjoining baths; some full, some shower without tub. In *main* house—eight rooms on three floors. Some with nonworking fireplace, sitting area, canopied or four-poster bed. King, queen, and twin beds available. In *reproduction* house nearby—four rooms, each with queen canopied bed, refrigerator, small TV. Plus, in the Rose Cottage—penthouse suite and two queen-bedded rooms (with TV).

Breakfast: 8:15–9:45. Homemade muffins, coffee cakes, and granola. Juices, coffee, cocoa, teas. Cold cereal. Served buffet style in keeping room.

Plus: Two fireplaced sitting rooms. Screened porch with wicker and flowers, overlooking the garden terrace. Cable TV. Library with games, puzzles, books, current magazines. Afternoon tea with homemade baked goods. Down pillows and comforters. Beach towels. Window fans. Bike racks.

Seven Sea Street

508/228-3577

7 Sea Street, Nantucket, MA 02554-3545   fax 508/228-8700

Hosts: Matthew and Mary Parker
Location: On a quiet shady side street in historic district. Two-minute walk to Harbor Beach and Steamship Wharf, five to Main Street.
Open: Year round. Two-night minimum on April–October weekends, three nights on holiday weekends.
Rates: Double occupancy. January–late May $95 room, $125 suite. Late May–late June and early fall $125/$165. Late June–late July $145/$185. Late July–Labor Day and Christmas Stroll weekend $165/$210. Mid-October through December $95/$125. Columbus Day–late June, discounts for week-long stays or Sunday–Thursday three-day stays. $15 rollaway or crib. AMEX, MC, VISA.
♥ ♦ ✈ ⊁

> From Massachusetts: *"The charm and beauty of the island is matched and exceeded by this inn."*

As Matt says, "In cool weather, guests walk on the beach, use our Jacuzzi, play cribbage, and read by the fire. This year-round inn with a widow's walk, canopied beds, braided rugs, and local art is the realization of my childhood dream." Built just five years ago, it's an early American-style post-and-beam colonial with Scandinavian features (lots of natural wood). It opened in 1987, the year the Parkers—who are still in their twenties—were married.

Matt grew up in Rhode Island, vacationed on Nantucket, earned a B.S. in management engineering, and then joined his father in developing Nantucket real estate and designing Seven Sea Street. He met Mary when she was selling advertising for a publication that has become a quarterly magazine, *Nantucket Journal*, published by the Parkers. Seven Sea Street has been Matt's project from groundbreaking to working with the crew to assembling all the reproduction furnishings. Now, as coinnkeeper, he finds that guests enjoy cultural activities, art galleries, restaurants—and the suggestion of a secluded beach with moorland views.

Foreign language spoken: French.
Bed and bath: Eight rooms plus two two-room suites, each with queen fishnet-canopied bed, cable TV, sink in room. All private baths with tiled bath floors and two-seat shower stalls. Rollaway and cribs available.
Breakfast: 8–10. Home-baked muffins. Granola. Fresh fruit salad. Juice, coffee, tea, milk. Buffet style in fireplaced breakfast room. Or served in bed, if you'd like.
Plus: Panoramic harbor views from widow's walk. Two common rooms with wood stoves, without TV. Individual thermostats. Window fans. Private phone and desk in some rooms. Guest refrigerators. Beach towels. Wall-mounted hair dryers. Mints on pillows. Babysitting arranged.

---

*T*o tip or not? *(Please turn to page xii.)*

Stumble Inne

508/228-4482

109 Orange Street, Nantucket, MA 02554

Hosts: The Condon family—Mary Kay and Mal and daughter Carol
Location: Residential. Ten-minute walk to Main Street and historic downtown.
Open: Year round. Two-night minimum late June to mid-September weekends. Three-night minimum July 4, Memorial Day, Labor Day, Columbus Day weekends.
Rates: Vary according to amenities and bath arrangements. Before mid-May and after third week in October, $35–$65. Daffodil weekend, mid-May–late June, and mid-September–late October, $45 (shared bath) to $130 (two-room suite, sleeps four). High season rates, including Memorial Day and Columbus Day, $75–$125 ($195 for suite). Two-room suites in Spring Cottage $110–$175. Inquire about Thanksgiving and Christmas Stroll rates. $20 extra adult. $10 child with adult. MC, VISA.

♥ ❖ ♦ ✖

> From Massachusetts: *"Wonderful people who make you feel like part of the family. . . . Rooms are relaxing and homelike with fresh flowers, fragrant soaps, charming antiques. On cool afternoons there's hot coffee with cinammon."*

It's a real family venture that was always in the parents' minds during many years of Nantucket vacations. In 1985 the Condons bought the Stumble Inne, a 1704 house later rebuilt in the Greek Revival style, and the Starbuck House, an early 19th-century Quaker-style house. Mal, a technical specialist in the paper industry, became the "technical expert." (One guest, a 60-year-old groom, wrote, "Mal even helped me fix my bike.") Carol, a year-round island resident, now hosts Spring Cottage, the latest addition, located just across the street. Added help comes from son Malcolm and his wife, Carolyn. When Mary Kay isn't rearranging new finds—lace, pictures, antique quilts—in the Laura Ashley-styled rooms, some with "undulating random width floors," she's probably suggesting bike routes and dining spots or making her famous muffins (a *Gourmet* magazine-requested recipe).

Bed and bath: Fifteen rooms, on first and second floors. In Stumble Inne, seven double or queen-bedded rooms, all with TV, small refrigerator; most with private bath. In Starbuck House, six double-bedded rooms, each with private bath, ceiling fan; one with sun deck, one is a family suite. In Spring Cottage, two-room suites, all private baths, air conditioning.
Breakfast: 8:30 and 9:30 (at 9 in off-season). Fresh fruit and juices. Homemade breads and muffins. Freshly made granola, coffee with cinnamon, and teas. By hearth. (Served in your room in Spring Cottage.)
Plus: Parlor with TV and VCR. Spacious backyards with lawn furniture. Bike racks. Babysitting referrals. Champagne for special occasions. Air conditioning in Spring Cottage.

> From Connecticut: *"A genuine feeling of warmth and friendliness. . . . Beautifully decorated. . . . Clock radio, candy, flowers . . . every amenity you can think of."*

The place to stay has become the reason to go.

Southeastern Massachusetts
—————— Reservation Services ——————

Be Our Guest, Bed & Breakfast, Ltd.
P.O. Box 1333, Plymouth, MA 02362-1333

Phone: 617/837-9867. Monday–Sunday 9–9. Answering service at other times.

Listings: 25. Located in Plymouth area (commuting distance to Boston), including other nearby seacoast towns—Hanover, Kingston, Marshfield, Duxbury, and Scituate—and on Cape Cod in Falmouth and Sandwich. All hosted private residences; several homes are over 200 years old. Directory brochure: $1.

Reservations: Last-minute calls accommodated, if space available.

Rates: $40–$60 single, $50–$75 double. In adults' room—$7 for children age 12 and under, $15 per teenager. Weekly rates available. $25 deposit required. $10 service charge for cancellations; if less than seven days' notice, $25 deposit is retained. If less than 24 hours' notice, rate for one night is charged. AMEX, MC, VISA. ♦

Two couples, Diane and David Gillis and Mary and Jaime Gill, have all had jobs working with the public. When selecting hosts for their 10-year-old agency, they stress cleanliness, congeniality, and knowledge of the area, with an eye to the type of atmosphere they themselves would enjoy staying in.

Plus: All hosts have tourist brochures and restaurant menus. One host enjoys taking guests for tours of Plymouth. Short-term (one-month) hosted housing available.

Other services with some B&Bs in Southeastern Massachusetts:
Bed & Breakfast/Inns of New England, page 257.
Bed and Breakfast Associates Bay Colony, Ltd., page 188.
Host Homes of Boston, page 191.
Pineapple Hospitality, page 106.

KEY TO SYMBOLS
♥ Lots of honeymooners come here.
♣ Families with children are very welcome. (Please see page xiii.)
♠ "Please emphasize that we are a private home, not an inn."
♣ Groups or private parties sometimes book the entire B&B.
♦ Travel agents' commission paid. (Please see page xii.)
✻ Sorry, no guests' pets are allowed.
✁ No smoking inside *or* no smoking at all, even on porches.

__ Southeastern Massachusetts B&Bs __

Allen House Inn   508/996-9292
Box 27, Cuttyhunk Island, MA 02173

Hosts: Nina Brodeur and Margo Solod
Location: Quiet. A small, hilly island with a winter population of 30 and with gorgeous beaches; trails through tall grass and along rocks; a general store; a couple of gift shops; a full-service marina; and seven pay (no private) phones. From New Bedford (an hour south of Boston), an hour's ferry ride or 15-minute seaplane ride.

Open: Memorial Day–Columbus Day. Two-night minimum on weekends.
Rates: July–August, $85 double, $65 single. May–June and September–October, $75 double, $55 single. Midweek, Monday–Thursday, three nights for price of two. $20 third person; under age three free. MC, VISA.
♥ ♫ ✳ ✈

Breakfast companions said, "Our best vacation ever. Yesterday we walked around the perimeter of the entire island (hiking boots recommended). This place is a step back in time with easygoing people who respect your privacy. There's no pressure, no must-see-and-do list, no traffic, not even a streetlight." (But you can, they say, read by moonlight when conditions are right.)

I, too, found time to think here at an inn that is an exception to my definition of a B&B. Allen House, built in the early 1900s and "intentionally not Laura Ashley," serves three meals a day to the public. It is the only place to stay on this one-mile-by-two-mile island (two-thirds is undeveloped) that has 1.3 miles of paved road.

Ten years ago Margo arrived "for a hammering job" from Boston, where she had been lighting director for the Boston Shakespeare Company. Now, as co-innkeeper, she's in the kitchen, dreaming up fantastic seafood dishes. You are more likely to meet Nina, her sister and coinnkeeper, who had some Hilton front desk experience and was a World's Fair folklife coordinator before the two young women bought the inn in 1985. For a romantic twist, we can report that Nina married the island's only commuter. She and her husband are the proud parents of Matt, born May 1, 1991.

In residence: Two outdoor dogs—Jesse, "who gives great island tours," and Bubba.
Bed and bath: Twelve rooms with mix-and-match furnishings on first and second floors. Six in the main building (with public dining room) share two baths. Six in next-door house share two shower baths. Twin beds, a double, and some rooms with additional twin or daybed. Rollaway and crib available.
Breakfast: 7:30–10:30. Muffins and breads, fruit, juice, and coffee. In guests' lounge. Full breakfast (nominal charge) in dining room.
Plus: Turndown service. Mints on pillows. Transportation to/from ferry or seaplane. Picnic baskets ($4/person). TV in guest lounge. Seafood dinners and sinful desserts are specialties. Charter fishing trips arranged.

Edgewater   508/997-5512

2 Oxford Street, Fairhaven, MA 02719-3310

Host: Kathy Reed
Location: On the water, facing New Bedford harbor. In a quiet residential neighborhood, five minutes from I-195. Short drive to Martha's Vineyard and Cuttyhunk ferries; within 45 minutes of Plymouth, Massachu-setts, and Newport, Rhode Island; 75 minutes from Boston.
Open: Year round.
Rates: $50–$70 single, $55–$75 double. Each extra person $10. AMEX, MC, VISA.

♥ 🏠 ❄ ♦ 🐾

> From Texas: *"A tub with a view! Large bright breezy rooms by the water. Restful."*

The idea of living in an historic home had always appealed to Kathy, a college professor. This one was built in the 1760s by Elnathan Eldridge as his store and home when he was involved in shipbuilding and the East Indies trade. Kathy's home—since 1983—has a colonial section that reflects that era with stenciling and simple furnishings. The Victorian part is more formal, and the sunken living room with big windows offers spectacular water views.

Fairhaven is a town of architectural gems. The high school has Tiffany windows, Italian marble floors, and intricately carved plaster ceilings. The town hall was dedicated by Mark Twain. Just across the bridge, within walking distance if you are energetic, is New Bedford, the largest fishing port on the east coast, with its Whaling Museum, cobblestone streets, and manageable historic trail.

Bed and bath: Five rooms, all with private baths. Some with fireplace and/or water views. Three double-bedded rooms (one has a canopied bed). Plus two suites, each with sitting room; one with twin beds, the other with a queen bed. One suite has private entrance, kitchenette.
Breakfast: 7–9:30. Homemade muffins, toasted Portuguese sweet bread, coffee, tea, juice, jams; butter shaped as daisies, swans, roses. Served with china and linens in the formal dining room, which overlooks the harbor.
Plus: Spacious lawns bordering water. Upper deck for sunbathing or watching the sunset.

> From Massachusetts: *"Rooms are decorated to soothe rather than astonish. . . . Perfect setting. . . . Home is out of a fairy tale. . . . Our daughters made us promise that we would visit in the winter and enjoy the fireplace and the view of water edged by snow."*

Little Inn

Marshfield, MA

Location: On a quiet scenic road, less than a mile to marina and five-mile-long beach. Twenty minutes to Plymouth, 40 to Boston.
Reservations: Year round through Be Our Guest, Bed & Breakfast, Ltd., page 179. Two-day minimum for Columbus Day and Thanksgiving weekends.
Rates: $40 single, $60 double.

♥ 🚭 🏠 ❄ ♦ 🍴

(Please turn page.)

The gracious 200-year-old white Federal colonial has brick sides, clapboard front and back, and mature plantings. Inside there are original moldings, wide pine floors, six working fireplaces, Oriental rugs, and antique furnishings.

Within their first year of ownership, the hosts, a chemist and a former marketing representative, began B&B in time to have advance bookings for an unforgettable holiday weekend. When, in the middle of the night, the hostess went into labor, they left B&B guests sleeping and went to the hospital. The baby came quickly and the new father rushed home to serve breakfast.

Less eventful visits have followed, with guests from around the world who appreciate suggestions for fine dining and for sights on land and at sea, in the city or in the country.

In residence: In hosts' quarters—three children, ages five, four, and two. Two rabbits and one cat live outside.
Bed and bath: Three rooms. First-floor room has queen bed, private full bath, white wicker furnishings. On second floor, one room with antique double brass bed, stenciling, and fireplace and another with two twin mahogany sleigh beds share a full bath that has a Jacuzzi.
Breakfast: Usually at 8. Orange juice in champagne flutes, fruit, homemade breads, quiche or egg-sausage casserole, coffee, tea. Served in fireplaced dining room.

Pilgrims Place   508/747-0340
264 Court Street, Plymouth, MA 02360-4038

Hosts: Kathleen Herlihy and Gilbert Fox
Location: On main road (Route 3A), one block from ocean. One mile north of town center, 35 miles south of Boston.

Open: April–November. Reservations preferred.
Rates: $58 shared bath. $65 private bath. $6 third person.
♥ ♣ ♠ ❉ ✈

Step through the double entry to be greeted in the hall with grandfather clock, winding staircase, and window seat. On a clear day you can see the tip of Cape Cod from the upper floors of this shingled Federal-design house built in 1904 for the president of the world's largest rope company, for 124 years the largest employer in town.

Kathleen says, "B&B is really my fourth career. I started as a chemist, brought up a family in New Jersey, and became a counselor. Now, back in my native state with a view of the lighthouse I knew from childhood summers, I am a psychotherapist, B&B host, and grandmother to six. Sharing this (traditionally furnished) home and seeing the interaction—as I have since 1987—makes me think that we could avoid wars with such communication." As cohost, Gilbert, a semiretired salesman, also enjoys sharing local lore with "wonderful people, B&B travelers"—including many returnees.

Bed and bath: Three rooms. Double-bedded room with modern shower bath on second floor. On third floor, old-fashioned tub bath shared by two rooms, each with two twin beds. Rollaway and crib available.

Breakfast: 8–9. Juice, fruit, homemade muffins, cereals, coffee, tea, milk. Served in formal dining room.
Plus: Gazebo. Backyard. Rocking chairs on front porch. Bedroom window fans. Guest refrigerator.

Remembrance   508/746-5160
265 Sandwich Street, Plymouth, MA 02360-2182

Host: Beverly Bainbridge
Location: Residential. One mile from historic Plymouth, Plimoth Plantation, and Route 3; a little more to beach. Five-minute walk to ocean (walking area) or local bus stop (to Boston). Near Jordan Hospital. Twenty-minute drive to Cape Cod, one hour to Boston.

Open: Year round.
Rates: $55 single, $60 double. Twin-bedded room $12 in conjunction with another room, $45 as a single. $5 floor mattress or sleeping bag for child.
♯ ♠ ⁂ ⚐ ⚖

> From Connecticut: *"Definitely a spread-the-good-word place!"* From Arizona: *"Charmed by her beautiful house as well as her tasteful decorating style."* From Mississippi: *"[While] I served as surgeon general to the Society of Mayflower Descendants . . . stayed in other enjoyable places, but we enjoyed this one far more than others."* From Georgia: *"Picturesque . . . immaculate . . . well-stocked library . . . breakfasts enticing to the palate and eye. . . . My sons decided to call her 'Aunt Bev' . . . she took them on walks, taught them how to make shortbread . . . a treasure."* From England: *"Met me at bus station, showed me around Plymouth . . . felt very much at home . . . fine colonial-style home."*

Beverly has experience as mother to two, art teacher, department store display designer, herb lady and open hearth cook at Plimoth Plantation, picture framer, and now as a calligrapher working at home. Her handmade gifts have sold in museum gift shops. Her sense of display, color, and style—with wicker, antiques, original art, and plants and flowers—is everywhere in the 1920s center chimney cedar-shingled Cape-style house.

In residence: Tyler, a "gentlemanly old sheltie." Two cats, Pandora and Morgan.
Bed and bath: Three second-floor rooms with sloping ceiling share one full bath and a downstairs half bath. Two with an antique brass double bed, air conditioning. One with a twin bed. Child-size floor mattress and lined sleeping bag available.
Breakfast: At guests' convenience. Fruit salad. Homemade muffins. Heart-shaped waffles with raspberry sauce and whipped cream, eggs Benedict, French toast or pancakes with maple syrup. Cereals. Freshly ground gourmet coffee. Teas. Served at Victorian ice cream table in greenhouse overlooking gardens bounded by old dry-stone wall; in winter, in the kitchen. Special diets accommodated.
Plus: Piano, VCR and films, music, books, magazines, toys, beach towels, afternoon or evening teatime with shortbread or cookies, special occasion treats.

Gilbert's Bed & Breakfast   508/252-6416
30 Spring Street, Rehoboth, MA 02769-2408

Hosts: Jeanne and Pete Gilbert
Location: On a 100-acre tree farm in a rural town, 35 minutes from Great Woods Center for the Performing Arts, 20 minutes from shopping outlets and Providence. Near clambakes and hay and sleigh rides.
Open: Year round. Advance reservations, even last-minute ones, required. (Please do not arrive at door unannounced.)
Rates: $32 single, $50 double ($45 if two or more nights). Additional person over age five, $10; $5 if younger. Two horse stalls ($10 each includes shavings and water).

Guests who are just here overnight often wish they could stay to enjoy all (see "Plus" below) that the Gilberts have to offer—far beyond the basics of B&B.

Remembering a trip to Vermont, Jeanne knew that she would like to host in her in-laws' 13-room farmhouse. Ever since the "some day" idea began in 1984, guests have written to me.

> From Massachusetts: *"Rooms were private, quiet, and cozy. Jeanne took a lot of time showing our daughters around the horses, took them for rides in the pony cart, and found books and games for them to play with. We returned home rested, relaxed and well cared for. And the prices are quite reasonable."* From Ohio: *"Overwhelmed with the home-style breakfast each morning."* From New York: *"Greeted us with lemonade, and within a half hour we were helping Jeanne walk her Shetland ponies to another field."* From Michigan: *"Reminded me of B&Bs in Ireland."*

Jeanne, a local newspaper reporter and photographer, is an avid equestrian who teaches riding. Pete, named Massachusetts Tree Farmer of the Year, is a pipe organ repairman, and he plays bluegrass music on banjo and bass.

In residence: Son John, 13. Screech, a cockatiel; four registered Shetland ponies, four horses, roosters, and several hens.
Bed and bath: Three second-floor rooms tucked into the eaves share a full bath. Two rooms have a double bed, one has two twin beds. Cot and crib available.
Breakfast: Menu varies. Eggs, bacon, blueberry pancakes, sausage, homemade muffins, fresh fruit, juice, coffee or tea. In country kitchen.
Plus: Horses welcome! In-ground pool. Guest sitting room that also is storage area for saddles and bridles. Popcorn. Mints. Fresh wildflowers. Bedroom fans. Wood stove. Babysitting. Piano, 95-year-old reed organ, pipe organ. Hiking and bridle paths. Cross-country ski trails. Cabin (12 feet square) in the woods for cookouts, campfires, and listening to the great horned owl.

Perryville Inn

157 Perryville Road, Rehoboth, MA 02769 (from Boston) **508/252-9239**
800/439-9239

Hosts: Betsy and Tom Charnecki
Location: Quiet. In rural community seven miles east of Providence. Within an hour of Boston, Plymouth, Newport. Twenty minutes from Great Woods Center for the Performing Arts. Across the street from an 18-hole golf course open to the public. Near antiques shops.

Open: Year round. Two-night minimum on summer and fall weekends. Reservations not required but please call first.
Rates: Double occupancy. $50 semiprivate bath, $65–$85 private bath. $10 extra person in room. AMEX, MC, VISA.
♥ ♨ ✻ ♦ ✖ ⚲

Brass, oak, and canopied beds. (Locally) refinished and reupholstered antiques. Locally handmade quilts. A huge wonderful kitchen. Immaculate housekeeping combined with comfortable country charm and family hospitality. It has been discovered by wedding guests, lots of first-time B&B travelers, and many business people. For their impressions (and fascinating reading), check out the Secret Drawer Society diaries in the night tables.

You can hardly imagine the abandoned farmhouse that the Charneckis bought in 1984. That was the year Tom returned here to his childhood hometown, ending a countrywide search for a B&B location that would provide a desired small-community lifestyle. In Colorado Tom was a bank president and Betsy a nurse. Their Massachusetts home, now on the National Register of Historic Places, consists of two top floors built in the 1820s and a bottom floor built in 1897! The third floor, reached by a private staircase, was originally used for hired hands. "Still is," says Betsy, a four-time marathon runner, referring to the family's quarters. And both hosts are active with the local historical society.

In residence: Sara, 19 (during college vacations); Tim, 17; and Tina, 11. Ann, Betsy's mother, is "resident quilter." Two cats, Horsefeathers and Junior.
Bed and bath: Five rooms on two floors. Three rooms with private, two with semiprivate baths. Queen, double, or twin beds. One room has both a queen and a double bed. Cot and crib available.
Breakfast: Usually 8–10. Freshly squeezed orange juice, seasonal fruit, croissants, homemade bread, muffins or sticky buns. Served in dining room or, weather permitting, on screened porch.
Plus: First-floor sitting room with piano. Second-floor sitting/game room. Four acres of wooded grounds with trout stream (fishing allowed). Access to additional 30 acres with ponds and old mill site. Tandem bicycle. Within minutes, clambakes, hay and sleigh rides, and even champagne (after landing) hot-air balloon rides, all by arrangement. Bedroom fans. Babysitting sometimes available.

If you've been to one B&B, you haven't been to them all.

Salt Marsh Farm Bed & Breakfast

322 Smith Neck Road, South Dartmouth, MA 02748-1402 **508/992-0980**

Hosts: Sally and Larry Brownell
Location: Serene. Three miles from scenic Padanaram harbor. Fifteen minutes from I-195, New Bedford's historic district and waterfront, and Martha's Vineyard and Cuttyhunk ferries. Within walking distance of extra-large cones of locally famous ice cream sold from art deco bottle- shaped stand featured in *New York Times*.
Open: Year round. Two-night minimum on Columbus Day weekend and May–September weekends.
Rates: Tax included. $65–$80 per room. Varies according to season. MC, VISA.

Whatever your definition of "real New England" might be, it fits this B&B. A stone wall in front. A freshly decorated 200-year-old weathered-shingled Federal house on 90 acres with chickens, an old-fashioned flower garden, fruits, and vegetables; trails through a nature preserve with a pine grove, salt meadows, and tidal marshes. Cozy bedrooms. "Hardly a straight line in the house." Working fireplaces in the living and dining rooms. Enough family antiques to arouse your curiosity for hours. A visiting octogenarian mother (Sally's) who arranges spectacular bouquets. And much more—including an apron-wearing hostess who greeted us with clothes basket in hand. "I love to listen to the foghorn and gulls while hanging out the sheets." And an enthusiastic, knowledgeable, sharing host, the gardener, who is active with historical organizations and the New Bedford Whaling Museum.

Before the Brownells, area natives and parents of four grown children, returned to the family homestead in 1987, they lived in the Philadelphia area, where Larry was a banker and fund-raiser. Sally was a librarian who established a secretarial business. "We hosted so many out-of-town visitors that B&B here just seems natural." The neighbors, corporations, wedding parties, and vacationers from all over the world are grateful.

In residence: Two cats. Lady Jane is long-haired; George's hair is short.
Bed and bath: Two rooms, each with private bath, hall, and stairway. One room has two twin four-poster beds, bath with large old-fashioned tub. The second room is really a choice: a room with one double bed or one with two twin four-poster beds; full bath for either one.
Breakfast: Full 8–9, continental after 9. Earlier by request. Prizewinning blueberry muffins. Farm-fresh eggs (maybe Portuguese or herb omelets or French toast with special sauce). Heart-shaped waffles for honeymooners. Fruit; in season, homegrown cantaloupe. Special diets accommodated.
Plus: Afternoon sherry, tea, or lemonade. Flannel sheets. Electric blankets. Forgotten items. Beach towels. Use of three-speed and tandem bikes (for marvelous country roads). Lots of books and sightseeing information.

Innkeeping may be America's most envied profession. As one host mused, "Where else can you get a job where, every day, someone tells you how wonderful you are?"

__ Boston Area Reservation Services __

AAA Accommodations

2218 Massachusetts Avenue, Cambridge, MA 02140-1204

Phone: 617/491-6107 or 800/232-9989, 8 a.m.–10 p.m. daily.

Fax: 617/868-2848.

Listings: About 100. Mostly private residences. Some inns and some un-hosted residences. Most are in Boston (including the waterfront) and Cambridge; others are in Arlington, Brookline, Lexington, Medford, Newton, and Somerville.

Rates: $50–$70 single, $60–$95 double. For cancellations received at least 10 days before arrival date, refunds made less a $10 processing fee; for less than 10 days, refund made less the sum equal to one night's stay for each room booked. AMEX, MC, VISA. ♦

Since Ellen Riley and Tony Femmino restored a historic house that has become an acclaimed B&B in Cambridge, they have had requests for many more accommodations than they could provide. The result is this reservation service, based in their B&B, A Cambridge House Bed & Breakfast (page 201).

Plus: Car rentals, tours, "and whatever else the traveler wants. We'll get it done!"

A Bed & Breakfast Above the Rest

50 Boatswains Way, Suite 105, Boston, MA 02150-4036

Phone: 617/884-7748 or 800/677-2262 Monday–Friday, 8–5; Saturday and Sunday, 10–4. Answering machine at other times.

Fax: 617/884-1544.

Listings: 120. Located primarily in Boston (Back Bay, Beacon Hill, Copley Square, South End, Faneuil Hall, and waterfront), Brookline, and Cambridge. Some on Cape Cod and Nantucket. Most have private baths and air conditioning. All are near public transportation. Free booklet of detailed listings available.

Rates: $50–$70 single, $70–$110 double. $10 one-night surcharge. Weekly rates available. Twenty-five percent of total required as deposit. $10 service charge for cancellations up until 72 hours before reservations; after that, deposit is retained. AMEX, MC, VISA. ♦

Colleen Hartford's hosts live in Beacon Hill brownstones, in Victorian town-houses, in National Register historic homes and mansions, and in well-maintained apartments. As professionals and active community members they are prepared to assist with information on dining, transportation, cultural events, and activities.

A Bed & Breakfast Agency of Boston, Inc.

47 Commercial Wharf, Boston, MA 02110-3801

Phone: 617/720-3540 or 800/CITYBNB (or 248-9262), 9 a.m.–9 p.m. daily.

Fax: 617/523-5761.

Listings: 145. Most are located in downtown Boston—on the historic water-front and in Faneuil Hall/North End areas of the Freedom Trail, Back Bay, Beacon Hill, Copley Square, and the South End. All are private air-conditioned residences near public rapid transportation. Most are hosted B&Bs, but in addition there are a wide variety of unhosted studios and one- and two-bedroom condominiums.

Rates: $60–$85 single, $70–$110 double. Weekly rates available. Nonrefund-able deposit of 30 percent of entire cost of booking required. MC, VISA. ◆

Ferne Mintz, an experienced host (whose lively beagle, Fanny, is still on many guests' Christmas card lists), features placements with "hosts who put you in close touch with the city." Before starting the reservation service, Ferne did public relations, advertising, and special events.

Plus: Car rentals and tours arranged. Short-term (one week to six months) hosted and unhosted downtown housing available.

Bed and Breakfast Associates Bay Colony, Ltd.

P.O. Box 57166, Babson Park, Boston, MA 02157-0166

Phone: 617/449-5302 or 800/347-5088. Monday–Friday, 9:30–5:30. In win-ter, 10–12:30 and 1:30–5. Answering machine at other times. Closed Christ-mas week.

Fax: 617/449-5958.

Listings: 150, mostly historic properties—hosted private residences and some small inns. Many are in downtown Boston. Others are in the Greater Boston area (35 communities)—as far west as Boylston (near Worcester), north to Gloucester, and south to Brewster on Cape Cod. Directory ($5 plus $1 postage) is a detailed booklet including descriptions and rates.

Reservations: Most hosts require a two-day minimum stay, May–October. "We try to accommodate last-minute callers (for one or more nights) but prefer a week's notice." Available through travel agents, but service prefers direct contact with guests.

Rates: $50–$90 single, $60–$110 double. Family and weekly rates available. Some homes offer the seventh night free. $10 surcharge for one-night stay. Thirty percent of total is required as a deposit. Full advance payment required on one-night stays and on special event weekends. Deposit minus $25 processing fee refunded on cancellations received at least 14 days prior to arrival. AMEX, MC, VISA. ◆

Arline Kardasis and Marilyn Mitchell focus on minute details that even the experienced traveler may not think of. Hosts, many of whom have been with

Bay Colony since it started in 1981, often speak of the professional, personal, and efficient service that the agency performs. While maintaining high standards, they offer wide variety—"unforgettable luxury as well as basic comfort and convenience at a modest rate. For our guests, bed and breakfast is a preference, not simply an alternative."

Plus: For short-term stays (one week to several months), there are house-sharing opportunities as well as unhosted apartments.

Bed & Breakfast Cambridge & Greater Boston/ Minuteman Country

P.O. Box 665, Cambridge, MA 02140

Phone: 617/576-1492 or 800/888-0178. Monday–Friday, 10–6; Saturday, 10–3.

Fax: 617/576-1430.

Listings: 65. Mostly hosted private residences. A few unhosted furnished apartments. Although most are in Boston, Cambridge, Lexington, and Bedford, there are some in Arlington, Belmont, Brookline, Concord, Needham, Newton, Somerville, and Waltham. "For many that are located near good public transportation, you may not need a car." Generous continental breakfasts include fruit and cereal as well as juice, rolls and/or baked goods, hot beverages.

Reservations: Advance notice always preferred, but they will do their best to accommodate last-minute requests. Two-night minimum, with occasional one-night bookings (usually for last-minute) possible.

Rates: $45–$90 single, $60–$105 double. Senior citizens (over 65), 10 percent less. $10 one-night surcharge. Weekly rates depend on length of stay, location, and season. Confirmed reservations require 30 percent nonrefundable deposit. AMEX, MC, VISA for deposit only.

"A personalized service with each home unique and wonderful, with attention given to individual needs." Pamela and Tally Carruthers have been making careful, appropriate matches of host and traveler since 1987. They accommodate tourists in the historic Boston/Cambridge/Lexington area, visitors to area universities, and business travelers who work along Route 95/128. In addition, the agency works with high-technology companies that need short- and long-term housing for business consultants and visiting executives.

Plus: Air conditioning available in most homes. Unhosted apartments and houses available for up to three months.

Think of bed and breakfast as a people-to-people concept.

Boston Bed and Breakfast, Inc./Boston Reservations

643 Beacon Street, Suite 23, Waban, MA 02168-1545

Phone: 617/332-4199. Monday–Friday, 9–5.

Listings: Most are in Boston (Beacon Hill, Back Bay, and the South End); included are hosted private residences as well as some inns, private clubs, and fully furnished unhosted apartments. Hosted residences are available in Cambridge, Brookline, and Newton. All are within walking distance of public transportation; most are within walking distance of major hotels.

Reservations: At least a few days' notice required.

Rates: At hosted private homes, $60/$70 single, $70/$80 double. At un-hosted residences, club facilities, and small inns, $60–$120. One-night surcharge $5. Full amount is due as deposit. If stay is longer than 20 nights, billing is done weekly. Deposit less $15 processing fee is refunded if cancellation notice is received at least three business days before arrival date; otherwise, in addition to fee, one night's deposit is retained. AMEX, MC, VISA.

Liz Moncreiff and Cynthia Spinner have offered accommodations since 1980, when they started their business at the request of the Continuing Education Department of the Harvard Medical School. Now, in addition to booking reservations for professionals attending courses, conferences and seminars, they accommodate the general public as well.

Plus: Short-term (up to three months) hosted and unhosted housing available.

Greater Boston Hospitality

P.O. Box 1142, Brookline, MA 02146

Phone: 617/277-5430. Monday–Friday, 8–5:30; Saturday, 8:30–1. Answering machine at other times.

Listings: 100. Mostly hosted private residences. Some inns and unhosted private residences. Located mostly in and around Boston—in the city and in Brookline, Newton, Needham, Cambridge, Somerville, Lexington, Arlington; and north in Danvers, Lowell, Marblehead, Gloucester, and Swampscott. Free directory describes homes and includes rates.

Reservations: Advance notice preferred. Sometimes, last-minute reservations accommodated. Two-night minimum stay preferred.

Rates: $40–$145 single, $45–$145 double. $10 one-night surcharge. Family and weekly (seventh night free) rates. $50 nonrefundable deposit required. For cancellations made at least 10 days before arrival date, refund minus deposit made. Credit cards accepted at inns only. ◆

Lauren Simonelli offers a broad range of homes but tries to select hosts who are close to major hospitals, schools, and tourist attractions. Most hosts have been on her roster for two years. "Amenities differ. Most hosts are native Bostonians; all are congenial hosts who make that extra effort for the comfort and convenience of guests."

Plus: Walking tours of historic Boston. Dining in exclusive private city clubs may also be arranged with advance notice. Short-term (two weeks) hosted and unhosted housing available.

Host Homes of Boston

P.O. Box 117, Waban Branch, Boston, MA 02168-0001

Phone: 617/244-1308. Monday–Friday, 9–noon and 1:30–4:30. Reduced live hours November–March. Answering machine at other times. (Prompt response.) Closed December 23–January 2.

Fax: 617/244-5156.

Listings: 52. Located in Boston area plus some on Cape Cod and the north shore. They are in Boston (Beacon Hill and Back Bay), Brookline, Newton, and Cambridge; and in Lexington, Marblehead, Milton, Wellesley, Westwood, Weymouth, and on Cape Cod in Sandwich and Waquoit. Mostly hosted private residences. A few inns and one city club. Free booklet directory; SASE appreciated.

Reservations: At least two weeks' advance notice advised. Two-night minimum stay required with the exception of reservations made within two days of arrival; $10 one-night surcharge for those last-minute bookings.

Rates: $48–$85 single, $57–$125 double. $15 extra adult or child (infants excepted). Winter weekly rates available. Deposit of one night's lodging required; half of total required for short-term housing. Balance of payment (or cancellation) is due at least 72 hours before arrival, or seven days before arrival if stay is five or more days. For cancellations received by that time, all monies, less $20 service fee per room, refunded. AMEX (for deposit only), MC, VISA.

Marcia Whittington has carefully selected hosts who live in city brownstones or in close-to-Boston (older Victorian and colonial) homes where guests can leave their car and use public transportation. Some "country feeling" homes are within a half hour's drive of downtown Boston. Marcia has lived in Boston more than 30 years and knows the territory. Since 1982 she has managed all B&B inspections and reservations, giving personalized attention to both hosts and guests. It's a spirit and style that is appreciated by visitors from all over the world.

Plus: Highlighted road and subway maps with reservation confirmations. Relocation assistance for short-term hosted housing (over 10 days) arranged.

The tradition of paying to stay in a private home—with breakfast included in the overnight lodging rate—was revived in time to save wonderful old houses, schools, churches, and barns all over country from the wrecking ball or commercial development.

University Bed & Breakfast, Ltd.

12 Churchill Street, Brookline, MA 02146

Phone: 617/738-1424

Listings: 50. Most are private residences; some are inns. They are located in the metropolitan Boston area—in downtown Boston, Brookline, Cambridge, Jamaica Plain, Lexington, Newton, and Somerville. Most offer the ambiance of the countryside and convenience to the city and are accessible to public transportation or within walking distance of universities and other meeting places.

Reservations: A minimum of two days' notice is preferred.

Rates: $45–$70 single, $60–$100 double. $10 one-night surcharge. Prepayment required. If cancellation is received at least 14 days before expected arrival date, refund less $20 processing fee is made. MC, VISA. ♦

Ruth Shapiro and Sarah Yules accommodate visiting professionals and accompanying spouses and/or traveling companions who come to the Boston area for academic or other reasons. They also accommodate relatives and friends of area students.

KEY TO SYMBOLS
♥ Lots of honeymooners come here.
⋆ Families with children are very welcome. (Please see page xiii.)
⬛ "Please emphasize that we are a private home, not an inn."
⬥ Groups or private parties sometimes book the entire B&B.
♦ Travel agents' commission paid. (Please see page xii.)
✕ Sorry, no guests' pets are allowed.
✂ No smoking inside *or* no smoking at all, even on porches.

_____ Boston Area B&Bs _____

B&Bs are in all downtown Boston neighborhoods—including Back Bay, Beacon Hill, and the waterfront—in brownstones and penthouses, high-rise buildings and converted warehouses. Many are in restored Victorians in the South End, the fashionable place to live before the tidal flats of the Back Bay were filled in the 1800s. Scene of many changes, the South End in its latest renaissance is the city's most culturally diverse neighborhood, complete with a full array of shops and restaurants, and abuts the expanded Hynes Convention Center and Copley Place shops.

For many, the convenience of being in the city is primary. The Greater Boston area, however, is compact; several hosts in "outlying" (mostly suburban) areas are actually closer to downtown Boston than many who live in the city. If you have time to commute, many of these B&Bs are less expensive than in-town locations. Traffic and parking in the city can be time-consuming and frustrating. The public transportation system, relatively simple and color coded, has convenient routes. Its schedules are not as dependable as those Europeans are used to; even so, the "T" is recommended.

Beacon Hill Bed & Breakfast   617/523-7376
27 Brimmer Street, Boston, MA 02108

Host: Susan Butterworth
Location: Overlooking Charles River. On quiet street in historic downtown residential neighborhood. Within walking distance of everything, including restaurants, Hynes Convention Center, Freedom Trail, subway system, and Cheers.
Open: Year round. Two-night mini-

mum stay (one-night bookings at last minute only). Three-night minimum on holiday weekends.
Rates: Per room, double or single occupancy. $100–$120 second-floor rooms, $95–$115 third floor. $20 rollaway or sofa bed. Ten percent less on stays over seven nights.
♥ ❖ ◆ ✈ ✂

> From Ohio: *"An elegant, well-appointed six-story home . . . superb creative breakfasts."* From Alabama: *"Delightful. Personable, knowledgeable, talented, and interesting hostess who contributed a significant part to making our visit to Boston so enjoyable."*

Built in 1869 with elegant details, this very large and beautiful brick row house has marble fireplaces, high ceilings, and deep moldings. The French touches reflect this San Francisco-born hostess's many years of living in France. A professional caterer, Susan trained at La Varenne in Paris and has taught French in several New England schools.

Foreign language spoken: French.
Bed and bath: Three air-conditioned rooms, all private baths. On third floor two spacious rooms with fireplace, full bath. One with river view has a queen bed and a double sofa bed; one that overlooks Beacon Hill has a double bed and queen sofa bed. On second floor, queen-bedded room, shower bath.

(Please turn page.)

Breakfast: 8:30–9 weekdays, 9–9:30 weekends. Extremely popular home-made granola. Muffins or coffee cake. Eggs or French toast, fruit, and "good strong" coffee. Under crystal chandelier from Loire chateau. In large dining room overlooking the Charles River.
Plus: Elevator for luggage. Nearby parking garage, $10 per 24-hour day.

Bed and Breakfast Associates Bay Colony Host #M128

Boston, MA

Location: "You can walk to any-where in town (including Faneuil Hall Marketplace, theater, restau-rants, Freedom Trail sites), but we are minutes from three different sub-way lines."

Reservations: Year round through Bed and Breakfast Associates Bay Colony, page 188.
Rates: $90 for suite. Cot, $10 for children (only).
♥ 🐕 ✈ ⊁

"A couple of years ago we moved from nearby Back Bay to this well-built c. 1835 townhouse that is authentic with lovely features—six fireplaces, original floors and moldings. For B&B, we designated the original parlor floor, the one with the prettiest fireplaces, and furnished with English antiques. The bed-stead is 150 years old, about the same age as the house."

The hostess, a writer who participates as a guide for special tours of Beacon Hill homes, has lived in the Boston area all her life. Her husband is an interior designer. His special, helpful takeaway map for guests highlights points of interest in the city.

In residence: Three school-aged children. Three cats and a dog.
Foreign languages spoken: French and Spanish.
Bed and bath: Entire air-conditioned second floor with double-bedded room, sitting room, dressing area, full bath, small refrigerator.
Breakfast: Usually 7–9. Homemade muffins, fresh fruit, juice, coffee. Served on tray in room.
Plus: A warm welcome with beverage at dining room table, an orientation map, and, if you'd like, an explanation of subway system.

From Ohio: *"A great way to experience Boston."* From Wisconsin: *" 'Excellent' says it all . . . wonderful hospitality . . . delicious breakfasts."* From Florida: *"Helpful suggestions and recommendations."*

Coach House

Boston, MA

Location: Quiet street in historic dis-trict. Within walking distance of city's information center, historic sites, fine dining, theater, shopping, convention center.

Reservations: Available through Host Homes of Boston, page 191. Two-night minimum.
Rates: $85 single, $100 double.
🐕 ✈ ⊁

"When we moved from Montreal for business reasons 15 years ago, we looked for a family home that was downtown in an American city. By the time those business reasons were no longer relevant, we had come to appreciate Boston, a top-drawer city that has a unique quality of life, flavor, and history, all here within a few blocks. A few years ago we started to share all of this with guests, interesting people from all over the world."

The hosts, world travelers who have lived in several countries, reside in a converted 1870s coach house that once held 12 coaches, with staff living on the upper floors. When it was made into a private home, the ground-floor living room was designed for musical presentations. Now it is decorated with antiques and an eye for color and detail. The host is in the air pollution control field. His wife is a marketing consultant and former builder.

In residence: One 12-year-old son. "Four lovable and interesting Siamese cats—mother, father, son, and daughter."
Foreign language spoken: French.
Bed and bath: Two air-conditioned rooms; TV in each. Second-floor room has twin bed, private en-suite shower bath. Third-floor room has double bed, private en-suite full bath.
Breakfast: 7:15–8:30. Fresh fruit, cereals, juice, baked goods with jams and jellies. Freshly ground coffee. Tea. Served in dining room.

Greater Boston Hospitality Host #29

Boston, MA

Location: In historic district, within walking distance of theaters, fine dining, historic sites.
Reservations: Year round through

Greater Boston Hospitality, page 190.
Rates: $80 single, $85 double.
♥ ◢ ✕ ✁

For an experience in elegance and a sense of old Boston, this B&B is the home of a host who provides a flexible breakfast arrangement (in your own apartment area)—appreciated by honeymooners who are looking for privacy as well as by tourists who seek suggestions and information. The 1790 townhouse is furnished with an outstanding collection of European antiques. Off of the living room, there's a roof deck with flowers, blue spruce, and an interesting view of the city.

Bed and bath: The entire second floor is for you, with double-bedded room, living room with daybed, dining room, modern kitchen, full bath.
Breakfast: Served 8–9:30; or, if you prefer, help yourself from stocked kitchen. Fresh fruit, muffins, croissants, jams, jellies, butter, coffee, tea.

B&Bs offer the ultimate concierge service.

Pineapple Hospitality Host #MA153

Charlestown, MA

Location: In historic district, one block from the Freedom Trail. A 15-minute walk or 10-minute bus ride to Faneuil Hall Marketplace.
Reservations: Year round through Pineapple Hospitality, page 106.

Rates: Suite $60 single, $70 double. Double room $55 single, $65 double.
✗ ⅄

> From Florida: *"Ironically, we were most concerned about staying in the city, but this turned out to be the most charming of all the New England B&Bs we stayed at. . . . One of the high points of our vacation was the evening we sat on the deck atop our hosts' townhouse. There we overlooked Boston harbor and the masts of the* USS Constitution *while we enjoyed refreshments and chatted with our hosts."*

"Before moving here about 10 years ago, we lived in the suburbs. Here, I still have a garden, but it's more private. I walk to work in Boston. And we are in a perfect place (with the perfect arrangement) for B&B."

The hostess first came to America as an exchange student in 1956. Shortly after returning to the United States in 1965, she met her husband, an engineer who was born of Polish parents in India and brought up in Afghanistan. They made some exciting changes while restoring their lovely home, an 1846 brick townhouse. It has been appreciated by a well-known film actress, international travelers, marathon runners, interns-to-be (it's within 15 minutes' walk of Massachusetts General Hospital), and professional innkeepers too.

Foreign languages spoken: French, Polish, and Turkish.
Bed and bath: A second-floor suite has a room with a double bed, adjoining sitting room, and private full bath. On third floor, room with an antique brass double bed and private shower bath, plus, off hall, a library with TV.
Breakfast: Weekdays, at guests' convenience; self-service after 8. Continental with freshly squeezed orange juice and homemade cake, croissants, or Irish bread. Weekends, you may have orange yogurt or puffed baked pancakes with fruit in season. With classical music.
Plus: Use of deck. Storage for bicycles. A shared love of the city.

The Emma James House

47 Ocean Street, Boston, MA 02124-3624

617/288-8867
617/282-5350

Hosts: Vicki and Bob Rugo, Moo Bishop, and husband Michael Stella live in homes directly across the street.
Location: In a neighborhood of Victorian houses, on Ashmont Hill, at the southern edge of the city. Five-minute walk from subway station (15-minute ride to downtown Boston). Ten-minute drive from Interstate 93. Close to Kennedy Library and Bayside Expo Center (subway accessible) and World Trade Center. Within an hour's drive of Plimoth Plantation and the Cape Cod Canal.
Open: Year round.
Rates: Double occupancy. $50 or $60 shared bath. $70 private bath. Singles $10 less. Weekly rates available.
♯ ✣ ◆ ✗ ⅄

From Missouri: *"A HUGE lovely Victorian mansion in the middle of a forest of Victorian homes for blocks in every direction. . . . Lots of sitting areas with bay windows; lace curtains; carved wood; a front porch where I enjoyed the morning newspaper."* From New Jersey: *"It is as close to the feeling of coming home I have experienced while on the road."*

"I designed a hallway just like this a few weeks ago!" exclaimed the California set designer upon seeing the expansive 25-foot-long entrance of this 1894 house.

Stained glass, wainscoting, spindles, and built-in benches are among the well-preserved features of the "retired retirement home" purchased in 1986 by the host couples, longtime neighborhood residents. When they redid "just about every surface," they discovered a magnificent parquet floor under linoleum. Now the grand hall has a 20-foot Oriental rug. "Guests often comment that this reminds them of their grandparents' house: big, old, comfortable—and rather special," says Vicki, who does public relations for an architectural and planning firm. Moo designs children's clothes. Bob, a former city planner, is a real estate broker. Michael specializes in renovating older structures. Boston information and restoration tips abound here.

Bed and bath: Six second-floor rooms entered from a large central hall. Two large queen-bedded rooms (one has a single bed also) with adjoining private full baths. Other rooms that have a queen, two twins, or a double share two baths with showers. Inflatable single mattresses available for children.
Breakfast: Help yourself to juices, fresh fruit, cold cereals, toaster waffles, coffees, teas. From local bakery—freshly baked scones, muffins, and breads.
Plus: Kitchen for guests' snacks, take-out meals. Bedroom window fans. Clock radios. Candy. Plenty of on-street, some off-street, parking. Space for miniconferences, family groups.

Bed and Breakfast Associates Bay Colony Host #M314

Boston, MA

Location: On a quiet residential street in historic South End. Five minutes from Back Bay Amtrak/subway station, Copley Square, Hynes Convention Center. Within 15 minutes' walk (no car needed here) of Faneuil Hall Marketplace, Beacon Hill, and the waterfront.

Reservations: Year round through Bed and Breakfast Associates Bay Colony, page 188.
Rates: Double occupancy. May–October, $110. Rest of year, $90. Weekly and monthly rates available.
♥ ✣ ✖ ✄

From California: *"Marvelous. . . . Delicious breakfasts at a beautifully set table."* From Michigan: *"We would recommend this B&B to anyone, especially first-time visitors to Boston . . . helpful hosts . . . cranberry and walnut muffins . . . wonderful restoration."*

A very popular B&B. An 1863 red brick row-style townhouse, restored in 1980 and fully renovated and refurbished a couple of years ago so that each

(Please turn page.)

guest room has a new bath. And decor that fulfills the expectations of many who anticipate a decorated, inviting B&B with floral drapes, period furnishings, marble mantels, color-coordinated linens, and Oriental rugs.

For an orientation to the city, the hosts, a city administrator and an artist, utilize a large framed map of Boston. Many guests follow their custom-designed day trip suggestions to nearby historic communities that can be reached by public transportation.

In residence: Sylvester, the cat, "official greeter who loves attention."
Foreign language spoken: A little French.
Bed and bath: Five rooms, all with brass queen beds, private shower baths with granite floors. On second floor, two rooms with hidden kitchenettes. On third floor, two more rooms with kitchenettes. Plus the fourth-floor penthouse the hosts call "room with a view," which has exposed brick wall, an antique armoire, adjacent hall skylit bath.
Breakfast: Usually 8:30. Family style. Depending on hosts' schedules, they either serve breakfast or provide juice, cereal, muffins, coffee, and tea.
Plus: Phone, air conditioning, and ceiling fan in each room. Fresh flowers. Nearby parking garage ($15–$17 for 24 hours).

The Terrace Townehouse   617/350-6520
60 Chandler Street, Boston, MA 02116

Hosts: Gloria and Bob Belknap
Location: In a row of South End Victorian houses, minutes from convention center. Two blocks from Copley Place, home of Neiman Marcus. Half block from Amtrak/subway station. The ethnically diverse neighborhood is always changing and currently includes longtime residents, families, and young professionals.
Open: Year round. Reservations required. Two-night minimum during the summer and on fall weekends.
Rates: Per room. May 1–November 30, $115 and $140. December 1–April 30, $105 and $130.
♥ ✈ ⊬

Romantic. Elegant. Luxurious. Private. And just when Gloria has every last accessory in place, she finds another fine antique and there's a change! New Yorkers love to come here and walk to restaurants, museums, the theater. When a horse-drawn carriage arrived to take a bride to a Back Bay church, the neighbors gathered to wish her well. Executives appreciate the private phones. And honeymooners, too, enjoy the "fantasy rooms" that have been created with marble mantels, an antique Waterford chandelier, a mirrored armoire, shuttered windows, and fresh flowers.

The 1870 townhouse, found in 1986 when a daughter came to Boston to go to college, ended the Belknaps' five-year search for a neighborhood location in a cosmopolitan city. In California Gloria was a successful caterer. Here she became a house restorer who selects Pierre Deux fabrics and goes to auctions. And she serves afternoon tea in the library with its collection of more than 1,000 volumes. Guests leave with the ultimate compliment: "Thank you for having us."

In residence: Two cats "who tell us they don't go into guests' rooms."
Foreign languages spoken: Some Spanish and French.
Bed and bath: Four rooms on first two floors. All private shower baths. Beds are king, canopied queen, or double.
Breakfast: 8:30. Freshly squeezed orange juice, fresh fruit and yogurt, "just out of the oven" scones, coffee or tea. Served in your room on antique china with crystal and silver.
Plus: Air-conditioned bedrooms. Bathrobes. Down pillows and comforters. Common room, the library, is available until 7 p.m. Three parking lots within a two-block radius.

Heath House
Brookline, MA

Location: On an acre of land in the Chestnut Hill neighborhood. Minutes' walk to Pine Manor College. One mile to Boston College. Ten-minute drive to Boston University and downtown Boston. Ten-minute walk to Chestnut Hill trolley stop with 15-minute ride to Boston.
Reservations: Year round through Host Homes of Boston, page 191. Two-night minimum.
Rates: Per room. $68 private bath, $61 shared.

Just five miles from downtown Boston—with no other house in sight until the leaves fall—is this picture-book colonial, custom built in 1948 with the feeling of a wonderful older home. It is white with black shutters and has large windows and a great sense of space. Furnished traditionally, it is a haven for tourists, parents of college students, and some business travelers too.

As the host, a professional in patent law, says, "This location is wonderful for those who want to tour the city and take day trips. If you are 'home' at dinner time, it is just minutes to many recommended restaurants." At home, guests may relax in the living room or on the terrace, which looks out on expansive lawn, mature plantings, and trees.

Bed and bath: Two spacious second-floor rooms with private or shared full bath, TV. One with queen bed, air conditioning; one with twin beds.
Breakfast: Usually 7–9. Juices, fresh fruit, cold cereals. Toast, English muffins, or croissants. Perhaps yogurts. Coffee and tea.

Guests wrote: *"Enjoyed the hospitality, breakfast, and the beautiful home."*

Can't find a listing for the community you are going to? Check with a reservation service described at the beginning of this chapter. Through the service, you may be placed (matched) with a welcoming B&B that is near your destination.

A Bed & Breakfast in Cambridge   617/868-7082
1657 Cambridge Street, Cambridge, MA 02138-4316   800/287-7082

Host: Doane Perry
Location: Two blocks from Harvard Yard. In the historic district. Within walking distance of museums, theaters, restaurants, bookstores. Across the street from public park, health club (with three indoor pools), and library. Five-minute walk to subway; eight-minute ride to Boston. City bus that stops at door takes you to many sites, including Boston's Museum of Science.

Open: Year round. Two-night minimum on weekends or during special events.
Rates: Double occupancy. $40–$70 winter, $55–$90 summer. (Plus $5 for use of air conditioner.) Singles $5 less. Off-street parking, $5. MC, VISA.

A warm family environment in a wonderful location is embellished by suggestions for cultural events, a restaurant menu book (with guests' additions), and a library with tourist literature, historical information, and poetry too. And then there's the Perrys' experience as world travelers on five continents. "Now the world comes to us," they say. Because of their experience as educators—currently Doane is a sales and marketing manager with Digital Equipment Corporation—the Perrys find that often their knowledge of area school systems is valuable to guests who are relocating.

The 1897 Colonial Revival house is comfortably furnished with antiques, Oriental rugs, original paintings, overstuffed chairs, and Grandmother's cane rockers.

In residence: Curt, seven, assistant innkeeper.
Foreign languages spoken: French, German, Greek, Swahili.
Bed and bath: Two bright and sunny third-floor rooms share a large full bath. Each has lace half-canopied double bed, phone jack and desk, TV. Trundle beds available.
Breakfast: Usually 7:30–9. Home-baked specialties. Blueberry pancakes. Cranberry bread. Homemade granola, jams and preserves. Served on table set with linen and silver pieces. In large common room or on porch surrounded by trees.
Plus: Off-street parking. Air conditioning in common rooms and in each bedroom. Afternoon tea or sherry. Window fans. Down comforters and pillows. Flannel sheets. Mints on pillow. Sachet made from homegrown herbs. Guidebooks loaned.

People are funny.
From Cape Cod: "One guest said the house needed a cat. The next day another lady said, 'I hope you don't have cats. I'm allergic to them.'"

A Cambridge House Bed & Breakfast

617/491-6300
800/232-9989
fax 617/868-2848

2218 Massachusetts Avenue
Cambridge MA 02140-1204

Hosts: Ellen Riley and Tony Femmino
Location: On a main street with a smorgasbord of residences, businesses, and fine restaurants. Bus stop at front door for service to Harvard Square. Five-minute walk to subway stop that is one stop from Harvard Square; from there, a 10-minute sub-way ride to downtown Boston.
Open: Year round. Reservations required.
Rates: May–November, $79–$119 single, $89–$149 double. Rest of the year, $59–$89 single, $69–$119 double. AMEX, MC, VISA.
♥ ❖ ◆ ✖ ⊁

"It happens all the time. People realize that we're here. They are curious. They ring the bell, request a tour, and then book family or business associates."

The Hartwell and Richardson-designed house, built in 1892 and on the National Register of Historic Places, has been a featured B&B on BBC in Europe and on "Evening Magazine" in Boston. Completely redone in 1986, it has hundreds of yards of fabric on windows, on walls, in entryways. Chinese vases are on pedestals. There are Oriental rugs and, throughout, antiques. Of the six fireplaces in the house, the tall intricately carved one in the den is the most outstanding. And then there's the showplace carriage house created from a shell.

Ellen, former membership director of the Boston Chamber of Commerce, and Tony, former investment property broker, are realtors.

In residence: Joyce Kerrigan, assistant innkeeper.
Foreign language spoken: Italian.
Bed and bath: Twelve air-conditioned, carpeted rooms. Seven in main house (some with working fireplaces) on second and third floors; five in carriage house (only place where smoking is allowed) on first and second floors. Some baths with tub and shower. Some rooms have private half baths; some share baths. Several rooms have canopied four-poster beds. Bed sizes include queen, double, and twins.
Breakfast: 7:30–9 weekdays, 8–10 weekends. Elaborate and beautiful. Fresh fruit. Freshly squeezed juice. Belgian waffles, crepes, omelets, or frittata. Served in dining room under crystal chandelier.
Plus: Evening white wine or sherry. Afternoon coffee, tea, or mulled cider with freshly baked pastries. Background classical music. Cable color TV with remote control in each guest room.

According to guests (many are preservationists and/or house restorers), there ought to be a medal for the meticulous work—everything from research to labor—done by B&B owners. Indeed, many have won preservation awards.

_____ Just a Little West B&Bs _____

Deerhorn Farm Bed & Breakfast 508/456-3370
2 Brown Road, Harvard, MA 01451-1901

Hosts: Frank and Emilie Coolidge
Location: Idyllic. In apple country. A dressage center with indoor and outdoor riding rings (shows held quarterly). On 120 acres with pond. Five minutes from I-495 and Routes 111 and 117. Three miles to winery (tours offered) and Fruitlands Museum, 15 to Worcester Art Museum or Concord, 36 to Boston.

Open: Year round.
Rates: Shared bath, $65 single, $75 double. Private bath, $15 more. $100 suite for one or two, $10 extra person. No charge for crib. Corporate rates and senior citizen discounts available. MC, VISA.
♥ ⚘ 🏠 ⁂ ◆ 🐾 ✂

> From Pennsylvania: *"Authentic . . . a working King's Grant farm with dressage horses and some black Angus . . . breakfasts are a dream . . . hosts who are there for company, if wanted. I'm sure everyone 'wants' if one is their guests. . . . Sensational suite . . . all with those heavenly views."* From Massachusetts: *"Beautifully restored . . . serene . . . rolling hills . . . stone fences . . . trails . . . cattle grazing . . . I didn't want to leave."*

At the end of a long maple tree-lined driveway you arrive at the barn-red colonial house that began as a saltbox around 1690. Inside there's a rare feeling of space and light, thanks to walls that were knocked down years ago. Heating and plumbing were added in the 1950s, when the Coolidges became the fourth owners. Today there is much more, all shared by Emilie, a former nursery school teacher who is farm manager/horse trainer and breeder/gardener and cook, and Frank, a financial consultant/"official farm putterer." Emilie rides. Frank sails. They both enjoy skiing. And they are active volunteers with museums and with historic and affordable housing organizations. In the early 1970s they ran a Harvard/urban summer program here on the farm.

In residence: "Ban is our 23-year-old Cambodian son. Kiki, the cat, comes in to be patted. Plato is a laid-back golden retriever." Horses, cattle, chickens.
Foreign language spoken: Cambodian.
Bed and bath: Three rooms. First-floor room with working beehive fireplace, two antique four-poster twin beds, sometimes shares shower bath (hand grips in shower) with second-floor air-conditioned loft room that has skylight over four-poster double bed. First-floor air-conditioned suite has room with double bed (plus double futon available) and beehive fireplace, desk, and private phone; cathedral-ceilinged living room with fireplace/stove, cable TV, French doors to terrace overlooking gardens, pasture, and pond; full kitchen with washer/dryer; private entrance to driveway.
Breakfast: 7–9 weekdays, until 10 weekends. On request, blueberry pancakes. Homemade breads, muffins, sweet buns, and granola. Farm-fresh eggs. Orange juice. Fruit in season. Served in dining room by huge fireplace.
Plus: Individual thermostats. Sherry; champagne for honeymooners. Fresh fruit and flowers. Trout fishing.

The John David House at Lexington Green

1963 Massachusetts Avenue
Lexington, MA 02173

617/861-7376
fax 617/863-9977

Host: Rosalie Tavilla
Location: Residential. In historic district, steps from the Battle Green and famous Minuteman Statue. Five miles from Concord, 10 west of Boston. Minutes from Route 128/95.
Open: Year round. Two-night minimum June–October.

Rates: Double occupancy, $75–$95. $150 master suite. Singles $5 less. $10 third person. Weekly rates available. MC, VISA.
♥ ❀ ♦ ✖ ✄

When Rosalie learned in 1989 that this gracious formal turn-of-the-century colonial house was for sale, she "just knew" that it would make a wonderful B&B. Once the Tavilla family, longtime Lexington residents, became the new owners, they installed thermopane windows and central air conditioning and refurbished with Victorian wallpapers. Weddings take place in the large foyer, which features dramatic twin staircases. Concerts are held in the fireplaced parlor. Many executives appreciate this home away from home. History buffs and tourists love the location. "On weekends, especially, breakfast can last for up to two hours," observes Rosalie, formerly a travel coordinator and activities director in Boca Raton, Florida.

Foreign language spoken: Italian.
Bed and bath: Four second-floor rooms, all with private full baths. Master suite has king brass bed, wicker queen sleeper plus rollaway available, 10-by-13-foot bath with deep tub and tiled corner shower, sitting room with working fireplace. One room with two twin four-poster beds, two with queen beds.
Breakfast: 8:30. Homemade poppyseed bread and muffins. Fruits, yogurt, cheeses. Cold cereals. Often, eggs, French toast, pancakes, or waffles. Special blend of coffee.
Plus: Grand piano. Organ. Ceiling fans in all rooms. Desks in master suite and one other room. Phones and jacks in all rooms. Fruit or homemade cookies. Beverages. In summer, ice cream or sherbet on porch. Feather beds and down quilts. Flannel sheets. Turndown service. Mints on pillow. Hair dryers. Robes. Guest refrigerator. Fresh flowers. Porch rockers. Yard. Workout equipment. Access to computer and fax machine.

Brock's Bed & Breakfast

617/444-6573

60 Stevens Road, Needham, MA 02192-3314

Hosts: Anne and Frank Brock
Location: In a quiet residential neighborhood, half a mile from Route 128, two miles from the Massachusetts Turnpike (I-90). To Boston, nine driving miles, one-half mile to commuter train, or three miles to subway station with parking. Four miles to Wellesley College, 15 minutes to Boston College, 35 minutes to Cambridge.
Open: Year round.
Rates: $50 single, $55 double. $20 rollaway. $5 surcharge for one-night booking.
♥ 🏠 ❀ ✖ ✄

(Please turn page.)

From Wisconsin: *"They don't charge enough!"* From Texas: *"A soothing backdrop to the fast pace of Boston . . . breakfasts made to order with healthy doses of friendliness."* From New York: *"The only place we'll stay in Boston area . . . my husband stayed there rather than the upscale hotel his expense account would have covered."* From New Jersey: *"Your books have guided our way to many wonderful B&Bs, but our favorite is the Brocks . . . hot and delicious breakfasts that meet needs of our limiting diets."* From Connecticut: *"The feeling of coming home."*

Those are just a few excerpts from a huge stack of letters written to me. What started with area colleges in 1984 has become "a wonderful people business" for the Brocks.

Their house, the first by Royal Barry Wills, was built in 1922 when Wills was an architecture student at MIT. It was built Cape style with nooks and crannies, lots of built-ins, and high ceilings. The flagstone walk, landscaping, and Williamsburg decor has all been done by the Brocks, second owners of the house as of 1966. Guests have much privacy; since becoming a B&B, the hosts have established their own quarters on the lower level.

Before retirement Anne worked in the medical field and Frank in human resources.

Bed and bath: Three rooms, each with cross-ventilation, share a full bath and a half bath. One on first floor with double four-poster. On second floor, one with two twin beds; one with queen bed.
Breakfast: 6–9. Juices, fresh fruit cup, cereals, homemade muffins. Eggs with bacon or sausage; 24-hour French toast (marinated in eggs, cream, orange juice, vanilla, and sugar); pancakes; or Brocks' crepes. Hot beverages. Served in the dining room.
Plus: Bedroom air conditioning, when necessary. Ceiling fans. Electric blankets. Portable TV by request. Rear sun deck. Good neighborhood for walking and jogging. Guest den with books and TV.

Sage and Thyme   617/332-0695
P.O. Box 91, Newtonville, MA 02160-2244

Hosts: Edgar and Hertha Klugman
Location: On a hill in a lovely quiet residential neighborhood. One and a half miles from I-90, the Massachusetts Turnpike. Six miles from downtown Boston. Within walking distance of restaurants and Boston College's Newton campus. Close to "Heartbreak Hill" of Boston Marathon.

Open: Year round. Two-night minimum preferred. Reservations requested; will accommodate last-minute guests when possible.
Rates: $49 single, $59 double. $20 for third person in double room. No charge for children under five. $10 surcharge per room for one-night stay.
♥ ♨ ⊞ ❄ ✗ ⊬

From New York: *"Their home is your home . . . they are happy to share it with you . . . seem able to ascertain your needs . . . accommodate your dietary requirements (ours were not easy), provide excellent directions whether you are driving or using public transportation, respect your privacy."* From Canada: *"We would have loved to stay longer."* From Rhode Island: *"Articulate and interesting, not overbearing, but very natural."* From England: *"A lovely, quiet environmment, within easy reach of Boston, comfortable accommodation . . . marvelous people, so friendly and helpful. They made our stay in Boston memorable."*

Guests from all over the world have written about Ed, a professor at Wheelock College in Boston, and Hertha, who has taught on the college level as well. The eclectic decor of their center entrance colonial reflects some of their own travel and living in other countries. Their activities reflect their concern for our total environment.

In residence: "Takara, our five-year-old granddaughter, is a part-time resident. And a new young cat in need of a home is in process of being selected."

Foreign languages: German. Plus some French, Italian, and Persian.

Bed and bath: First-floor room with two twin beds, adjacent half bath, overlooking yard and garden. Second-floor room with double bed, sofa, full guest bath (shared if both guest rooms occupied). Crib and cot available.

Breakfast: Usually 7–9. Juice and fresh fruit cup. Thereafter, menu varies. Freshly made bread or muffins, croissants, toast, pancakes or waffles, hot or cold cereals, hot beverage. "Requests cheerfully accommodated." Can be quick or leisurely.

Plus: Bedroom air conditioners, fans, electric blankets. Evening beverages. Portable black/white TVs. Screened porch. Yard. Off-street parking.

KEY TO SYMBOLS
♥ Lots of honeymooners come here.
⚓ Families with children are very welcome. (Please see page xiii.)
🚤 "Please emphasize that we are a private home, not an inn."
♣ Groups or private parties sometimes book the entire B&B.
♦ Travel agents' commission paid. (Please see page xii.)
✗ Sorry, no guests' pets are allowed.
✄ No smoking inside *or* no smoking at all, even on porches.

North of Boston
Reservation Services

Bed & Breakfast Folks

48 Springs Road, Bedford, MA 01730

Phone: 617/275-9025. Answering machine messages responded to the same day—until 11 p.m.

Listings: 25 and growing. Mostly hosted private residences north and north-west of Boston and Cambridge. Within 30–60 minutes' drive of Boston and Cambridge and convenient to southern New Hampshire. Communities represented include Acton, Bedford, Billerica, Burlington, Chelmsford, Concord, Groton, Lexington, Lowell, Pepperell, Reading, Stow, Tyngsboro, and Westford.

Reservations: Advance notice is requested. Last-minute calls accommodated, when possible.

Rates: $40–$50 single. $50–$75 double. $10 crib or extra bed in room. Deposit equal to one night's lodging required. Full refund, less $10 handling charge, if cancellation is received at least 48 hours prior to arrival.

Phyllis Phillips lists hosts who enjoy sharing their New England homes with tourists and business travelers, and with newcomers who are relocating. Her agency fills a very special need in an historic area that is also known for its rural character (tap maple syrup or feed animals), high-technology firms, and the Lowell National Historic Park. Listings include locations where you can swim in a private pond, relax in a hot tub, or enjoy water views.

Plus: Monthly hosted housing available.

Bed and Breakfast Marblehead & North Shore/ Boston & Cape Cod

P.O. Box 35, Newtonville, MA 02160

Phone: 617/964-1606 or (outside Massachusetts, for reservations only) 800/832-2632. Monday–Friday, 9–5 and 7–9 p.m. Saturday, 9–12 noon, Sunday, 1–9 p.m.

Listings: 110. Many are within 30 minutes of Boston and Logan Airport—in oceanside towns and historic homes, convenient to colleges, universities and business areas. Many are north of Boston, including the shore communities of Gloucester, Marblehead, Manchester, Newburyport, Rockport, and Salem. Others are in Cambridge; west of Boston in Newton, Concord, and Sturbridge; and in Brewster, Chatham, and Provincetown on Cape Cod. "Plus some elegant B&Bs in Maine, New Hampshire, and Vermont; some close to ski areas."

Reservations: Advance notice preferred; last-minute bookings may be possible. Two-night minimum on weekends and in summer, during fall foliage, during special events such as Haunted Happenings in Salem, and on holidays.

Rates: $45–$75 single. $55–140 double. Family, weekly, and long-term rates available. Deposit of 25 percent required. $15 booking fee (but $10 for one-night reservations) waived for members who pay an annual fee of $25 (unlimited bookings and free directory of listings). If cancellation is received at least two weeks before expected arrival, refund less $15 per room per night is made; $15 booking fee is nonrefundable. MC and VISA accepted for late bookings and to secure reservation.

Accommodations for both tourist and business traveler "ranging from the reasonable to the regal" are in private residences and inns that are inspected annually by Suzanne Ross and Sheryl Felleman, two professionals who have always had people-oriented careers. "We know our hosts and their wonderful and unique homes and inns. After we place guests according to their needs, the result seems to be a mutually unforgettable experience: The stay is a memorable visit for guests, a highlight for hosts too."

Plus: Many hosts provide complimentary transportation to and from train or bus stations and Logan Airport. Some offer private tours. And they acknowledge special occasions.

North of Boston B&Bs

George Fuller House   508/768-7766
148 Main Street, Route 133, Essex, MA 01929-1304

Hosts: Cynthia and Robert Cameron
Location: On the main causeway, with views of marsh from yard and garden area. Within walking distance of antiques shops (there are 50 in town) and lobster-in-the-rough and other seafood restaurants. Ten-minute drive to Crane's Beach, whale watch excursions, deep-sea fishing. Thirty miles north of Boston, three from Route 128.

Open: Year round. Two-night minimum on holiday weekends.
Rates: Double occupancy. June–November $70 double bed; $83 king, queen, or twins; $103 suite. $10 additional person. Off-season, $10 less. Midweek sailing packages; sails are $40/hour, three-hour minimum. AMEX, Discover, MC, VISA.
♥ ❖ ◆ ✈

> From California: *"Super . . . could even watch TV from the tub . . . lots of character with modernized plumbing. We'll be back for sailing lessons, history, hospitality, and Cindy's breakfast crepes."* From Illinois: *"Beautiful home . . . treated me like family. . . . Returned with my husband and he was thrilled."* From Washington: *"Excellent breakfast was beautifully presented."*

"A cookbook is in the works," says Cindy, the Essex-born hostess, a registered nurse. She and Bob fulfilled their lifelong dream when they restored the 1830 shipbuilder's Federal house four years ago. Aunt Blanch, age 90, contributed braided rugs, antiques, and those glorious handmade quilts that set the tone and color scheme for each attractive room. All the caning was done by Cindy's mother, age 84. For years Bob has operated a sailing school. Here he also offers day trips on his 30-foot sailboat. Then there are antiques weekends with guest experts. And, year round, romantic escapes (fireplaces are especially popular in winter), visiting relatives, and business travelers too.

In residence: Sarah, Cindy's mother. Mittens, a double-pawed calico cat "who meanders around evaluating guests."
Bed and bath: Four large rooms and one suite. All with air conditioning, TV, private baths, phones and jacks. On first floor—cathedral-ceilinged room with partial-canopy queen bed, shower bath, Palladian window overlooking marsh. One room with double bed, full bath across the hall. On second floor—two rooms with king/twins option, one with working fireplace. Suite has queen canopy bed, working fireplace, shower bath, sitting room with daybed, private exterior entrance. Rollaway available.
Breakfast: 7:30–9:30. Pina colada pancakes, Belgian waffles with yogurt and orange sauce, or French toast with brandied lemon butter. Juice, fruit, home-baked breads. In dining room or guests' room.
Plus: Individual thermostats. Fresh flowers. Babysitting. Late-afternoon tea, coffee, or hot cider with homemade cookies. Robes. Fireplaced living and dining rooms with Indian shutters.

Sherman-Berry House

508/459-4760
fax available; phone first

163 Dartmouth Street
Lowell, MA 01851-2425

Hosts: Susan Scott and husband David Strohmeyer
Location: In a residential neighborhood of a city known for its 19th-century cotton mills. Minutes' drive to National and State Historic Parks headquarters and guided tours, canal and open-air trolley rides. Close to New England Quilt Museum and Merrimack Repertory Theater. Less than two miles from I-495; 26 miles north of Boston.
Open: Year round except for Christmas.
Rates: $45 single. $50 double. $5 surcharge for one-night stays. Family rates available.
♥ ♨ ❀ ♦ ✗ ⅍

> Guests wrote: *"The breakfasts were extravaganzas with many delightful Victorian touches. . . . Our three-year-old daughter felt welcome and especially enjoyed the player piano. For any antiques lover, this is a must-see. . . . The Sherman-Berry spirit is relaxed, happy, and adventurous . . . an unforgettable experience . . . ability to be hosts and friends at the same time . . . 19th-century books . . . collections of dance programs . . . suggestions for museums . . . where to find the best ice cream in town."*

After 25 years in Alaska, David was transferred to Wang Laboratories' corporate headquarters to manage a marketing group. Because of Susan's and David's interest in historic preservation and Victoriana, Lowell was a natural choice. (The country's first planned industrial city has retained miles of canals, part of an extraordinary park system that is just being discovered by many Bostonians.)

Susan and David bought "a mostly restored grand old house—but not a mansion," toured New England in search of appropriate furnishings, and commissioned a spectacular stained glass window that has a story of its own. Susan, a therapist in Alaska and now an enthusiastic B&B hostess, was the prime mover behind a neighborhood drive to create an historic district, and now she serves on the Lowell Historic Board. There's more—worth a special trip!

Bed and bath: Two second-floor rooms. One with a double bed; the other has two twins. Victorian Murphy bed and crib available. Shared full bath (hand-held shower).
Breakfast: 7–9. Could be Alaskan reindeer sausage and eggs with garden-grown herbs; eggs Benedict; a Lowell Mill Girls' Breakfast menu with ham, baked beans, and apple pie. Susan cooks on weekdays, David on weekends.
Plus: Susan's award-winning walking tour. Moxie, a Lowell-developed drink. Use of tandem bicycle. Stereopticon viewer. Access to computer, copier, fax. Extensive library on restoration and Victoriana. Fresh flowers. Babysitting by prior arrangement.

Looking for a B&B with a crib? Find a description with the ♥ symbol and then check under the "bed and bath" section.

Harborside House   617/631-1032

23 Gregory Street, Marblehead, MA 01945-3241

Host: Susan Livingston
Location: In historic district of this town, which is four square miles in all. Thirty minutes north of Logan Airport, downtown Boston, I-95. Minutes' walk along winding streets, past old-fashioned doorways and interesting gardens, to historic sites, shops, restaurants, beach.

Open: Year round.
Rates: April–January $60 single, $70 double. Off-season $50 single, $65 double. $5 one-night surcharge. Weekly rates available.

From this cozy mid-19th-century house, built by a ship's carpenter, there are views of hundreds of sailboats in the famous harbor. In 1985 Susan, mother of two grown children, made her home into a B&B. It is a welcoming place that blends her interests—sewing (she's a professional dressmaker), baking (recipes shared), arranging homegrown flowers, and history (she's a former historic house guide). And for good measure there's a list of "the best everything—from antiques shops to tour of chocolate maker"—in Susan's opinion. "When guests discover the hidden charms of this historic village/yachting center, they spend more time exploring here."

Susan's major avocational interest is competitive Masters swimming; she's among the country's top 10 in her age group.

In residence: Kahlua, a friendly cat, often under the breakfast table but never under guests' rooms.
Foreign language spoken: "Un petit peu de francais."
Bed and bath: Up steep stairs to two second-floor rooms—each with desk, clock radio, TV—that share a full bath. Harbor-view room with two antique twin beds tucked under the eaves. One room with double bed, garden view.
Breakfast: Usually 7–9. Juice. Fresh fruit in season. Homemade applesauce; warm home-baked raisin bran, blueberry, or cranberry muffins; banana, muesli, or cranberry bread. Cereals. Yogurt. Coffee and teas. On covered porch or in dining room with harbor view.
Plus: Third-story deck. Fireplaced living room. Flagstone patio. Secluded yard. Beverages. Mineral water. Flannel sheets. Toiletries. Specialty chocolates. Discounts at some restaurants.

> From California: *"Tastefully decorated . . . clean . . . warm and friendly . . . congenial atmosphere."*

All the B&Bs with the ⬛ symbol want you to know that they are a private home set up for paying guests and that they are not an inn. Although definitions vary, these private home B&Bs tend to have one to three guest rooms. For the owners, people who enjoy meeting people, B&B is usually a part-time occupation.

Spray Cliff on the Ocean

508/744-8924
800/626-1530
fax 508/744-8924

25 Spray Avenue, Marblehead, MA
Mailing address: c/o Salem Inn, 7 Summer Street
Salem, MA 01970-3315

Hosts: Diane and Dick Pabich
Location: In a residential neighborhood, 2½ miles outside of town, 15 miles north of Boston. Steps away from sandy Preston Beach, atop a 20-foot seawall "with views that extend forever."
Open: Year round. Two-night minimum June–October weekends. Reservations strongly suggested along with estimated arrival time, please, so someone will be available to greet you.
Rates: Per room. Varies according to street-side or ocean-view location. May–October $95–$130, anniversary suite $200. Off-season $85–$125, suite $175. $10 third person in room. AMEX, Carte Blanche, Diners, Discover, MC, VISA.
♥ ❖ ♦ ✈

"Last week we hosted a public television crew while they were filming a special on Doris Day. They interviewed John Updike, a Doris Day fan, from our seaside patio with the surf crashing in the background. Next week we'll have a retreat for an academic dean on our deck. Honeymooners love this place. And landlocked people from other parts of the country never want to leave the patio!"

Once the scene of many fashionable weddings and graduation parties, the 18-room Tudor mansion, built in 1919 as a summer home, became an inn in 1940. It was a rooming house "in shambles" when the Pabiches bought it 16 years ago. After they repaired it for their own home, Dick, a software manager for Raytheon, and Diane, a real estate developer, opened a 23-room inn in nearby Salem. As their children went off to college (two have just opened a restaurant in Salem), "opening our waterside home as a B&B was a natural extension of our inn activity."

In residence: Daffodill is the family's chocolate Labrador retriever.
Bed and bath: Seven spacious rooms; five with ocean views, all with private baths. First-floor street-side room has two queen beds, shower bath, working fireplace. On second floor, one room with king bed, shower bath; a two-room suite with king bed, working fireplace, private oceanfront deck, sitting room with cable TV, full bath. Two queen-bedded rooms (one with working fireplace), full baths. On third floor, two king-bedded rooms with shower baths. All rooms are furnished with antiques, wicker, flowered chintz curtains.
Breakfast: 8–10. Buffet style in the oceanfront breakfast room. Baked goods, fresh fruit, juice, coffee and tea.
Plus: Brick patio with that mesmerizing view. Refrigerator and toaster available. Fireplace in breakfast/sitting room overlooking Massachusetts Bay. Gardens. Fruit bowl. Aperitifs. (No cigars or pipes, please.)

---

*T*he place to stay has become the reason to go.

Ten Mugford Street

617/639-0343

10 Mugford Street, Marblehead, MA 01945-3449   617/631-5642

Hosts: Liz and Mike Mentuck
Location: In historic Old Town section, one block from town landing on harbor. On a bus line from Boston (30 minutes). Eighteen miles north of Boston. Near antiques shops, historic sites, restaurants—everything.
Open: Year round.

Rates: In hosts' residence $60 single, $65 double. Suites $85 couple, $95 family (two bedrooms and a bath), $110 two couples, $525 weekly rate in season. Special rates for groups, e.g., wedding guests or family reunions, that book entire B&B.
♠ 🐕 ❊ ✗

"Six years ago we bought the perfect house for B&B." That may sum things up for the first B&B in a four-square-mile charming town that needed lodging facilities. This "19th-century beauty" was a home for elderly women, originally donated to the Marblehead Female Humane Society by a local family. It was restored by the Mentucks and decorated in grandmother's-house style—comfortable and fresh-looking with books and antiques. In 1988 the Mentucks, lifelong Marblehead residents, also gutted and rebuilt a three-story Federal-style house (that began as a 1700s carriage house) across the street. Furnishings in this all-suite property (popular with families and with business and weekly guests) are "typically New England." In both locations a casual, friendly atmosphere prevails—a tone set by a very enthusiastic hostess. Mike owns a marina, and sells floats and docks.

Bed and bath: In the main house—four second-floor rooms with double or twin beds share three baths. Across the street—four two-room suites with king or queen bed. Each has refrigerator and, overlooking the garden, a balcony. Two suites have shower bath; two have kitchenette, cathedral ceiling, skylight, full bath.
Breakfast: 7:30–10:30. Fruit, muffins, cereal, coffee, tea, juice. Buffet in dining rooms (no smoking allowed)—at one large round table at Ten Mugford and at several smaller tables across the street.
Plus: Night parking provided. Make-yourself tea or coffee. Yard and garden. At main house, use of refrigerator; setups provided; private guest entrance. Kitchen available to visitors in guest house.

The Windsor House

508/462-3778

38 Federal Street, Newburyport, MA 01950

Hosts: Judith and John Harris
Location: Within walking distance of the harbor and shops. Across from historic Old South Church. Just off Route 1A. Five-minute drive to the ocean, Parker River Wildlife Refuge, and the magnificent grounds of Maudsley State Park on the Merrimack River.
Open: Year round. Two-day minimum on weekends and holidays.

Rates: Tax and service charge included. Double occupancy $75–$90 shared bath, $125 private. Singles $62–$70 shared bath, $90 private. $25 trundle bed (or third person in room). No charge for crib. Special rates for business travelers. Discover, MC, VISA.
♥ ♠ ❊ ♦ ✂

The warmth in this recently refurbished inn radiates from the blend of old New England, the feeling of an English country house, and the influence of Cornwall, England. Built in 1786 by Aaron Pardee as a wedding present for his bride, the former mansion/chandlery is a three-storied brick building that combines colonial, Georgian, and Federal styles of architecture.

Judith created the inn in 1978 with her late husband. A couple of years ago, at a B&B in Tintagel, England, while studying Megalithic Cornwall, she met John, a retired senior communications officer of the Royal Navy who lived in a lovely cottage not far from King Arthur's Castle. "We courted on the high cliffs of North Cornwall and were married in 1990. Now, together, we delight in sharing the traditions of merry old England with our guests."

In residence: Two cats, Sir Thomas More, now 19 years old, and Trelawny, age 1. "Lilabet is our 15-year-old toy guard poodle."
Foreign languages spoken: A little French, less German.
Bed and bath: Six large rooms. Three with private full bath. One shared full bath for other three rooms. Some rooms have four-posters or sleigh beds, single as well as double, king, or queen beds. One first-floor room, particularly good for older people and for those traveling with children and/or pets, has a private street entrance, beamed ceiling with fan, private bath. Three trundle beds and a crib available.
Breakfast: 8–9. Fruit. Traditional cooked English breakfast including eggs, turkey ham, tomatoes, mushrooms, beans. Bread and muffins and their own brew of coffee. Watch preparations and chat with innkeepers (occasionally in Cornish dress) in huge country kitchen.
Plus: Afternoon tea. Tour that may include attic where the original chandlery hoist wheel is located. Common room with TV. Formal dining room. Court-yard, patio, and English garden. Alarm clocks, window fans, candy, lots of books. Gift shop with Windsor House coffee and Cornish crafts, including tartans, Celtic pewter crosses, and brooches from Penzance. November–May, evening meals featuring English regional cooking.

Inn on Cove Hill   508/546-2701
37 Mount Pleasant Street, Rockport, MA 01966-1727

Hosts: Marjorie and John Pratt
Location: One block from village, harbor, and shops. Bus servicing Cape Ann goes by the inn. One mile to train to Boston.
Open: April–October. Two-night minimum in July and August and on holiday weekends.

Rates: Double occupancy. April–early June (excluding Memorial Day), $44 shared bath, $53–$75 private bath. Late June–October, $46 shared bath, $60–$95 private bath.
♥ ✖ ⅄

They took a trip around the world and stayed in many B&Bs. John, a civil engineer specializing in soils and foundations, and Marjorie, a registered nurse in public health and home care, found that the idea of "being together, sharing a business in a lovely location" had strong appeal.

(Please turn page.)

Now, 14 years later, the Pratts have completely restored the classic square, three-story, 200-year-old Federal-style home, the very inn where they spent their own honeymoon. What they offer all guests is a friendly atmosphere and the option of privacy. Their attention to architectural detail can be seen in the wood-shingled roof, pumpkin pine floorboards, H and L hinges, dentil molding, and a spiral staircase with 13 steps symbolizing the original 13 colonies. Furnishings are some fine family antiques, some reproductions, and original paintings. One guest from England wrote, "Beautifully decorated room . . . a lovely restful atmosphere. Muffins lived up to their reputation, and the tea was the best so far in the USA."

In residence: In the nearby family residence, nine-year-old daughter Michelle, "apprentice innkeeper."
Bed and bath: Eleven rooms on three floors. Nine with private bath. Two first-floor rooms, one with private entrance. Third floor reached via a steep narrow stairway or outside metal spiral staircase. Rooms have queen bed (some canopied), queen and trundle, a double bed, or a double and a twin; some are four-posters or cannonball.
Breakfast: 8–9:30. Continental with one of seven varieties of muffins. Served around the pump garden (weather permitting), in living room, or on individual trays in guest rooms.
Plus: Bedroom fans. Fresh summer flowers. Tour of house, complete with legendary saga of how the mansion was built with pirates' gold. Third-floor porch with view of harbor. Hot spiced cider in fall. A suggestion for an ocean walk "that never gets crowded." Will meet guests at train station. Parking.

Old Farm Inn   508/546-3237
291 Granite Street, Route 127, Rockport, MA 01966-1028

Hosts: The Balzarini family— grandma Mabel; son Bill and his wife, Susan; and grown daughter Mandy.
Location: Quiet country setting on the northernmost tip of Cape Ann. On five acres of lawns, meadows, trees, and gardens. Surrounded by Halibut Point State Park and Reservation, one of my family's favorite ocean viewpoints (with tidal pools). Five-minute drive to center of Rockport.
Open: April–December. Two-night minimum on weekends, three nights on most holiday weekends.
Rates: $78–$98 in season. $65–$88 off-season. AMEX, MC, VISA.
♥ ♨ ◆ ✖ ✄

As Susan says, "The inn has always had an inviting sit-on-the-floor-in-front-of-the-fireplace kind of feeling. Restoration of the 1799 farmhouse is not museum quality or especially authentic, but it's what we like! I came from Pennsylvania and married a native Rockporter and into the hospitality business 23 years ago. For many years Old Farm Inn, established by Bill and his parents in 1964, had a restaurant; but now it's a B&B where we have impromptu corn-popping sessions, hot cider by the fire, or maybe a glass of sherry while watching a sunset. Because of our location, many guests enjoy the ocean at Halibut Point or Folly Cove. It's amazing how many people dream about this lifestyle."

Bed and bath: Nine rooms, all with TV and private baths. Four barn rooms on two levels; one king-bedded room with kitchenette, three with a queen and twin bed each. In main inn, on first floor, one two-room suite with queen bed, two twin daybeds in sitting room, full bath. Upstairs, two cozy double-bedded rooms with shower baths; one has private sitting room. "Especially romantic" room with queen canopied bed, antique love seat, shower bath. Plus cottage with two units. Rollaway and crib available.

Breakfast: 8:30–9:30. Fresh fruit, juice, cereal, homemade muffins, bread, coffee cake, yogurt, coffee, herbal teas, hot chocolate, Sanka. On some quiet days, surprise French toast, eggs, or pancakes. Served buffet style on black iron stove in sun room, where floor-to-ceiling windows on two sides overlook gardens.

Plus: Fireplaced living room with beamed ceiling. Bikes for guests' use in this beautiful and interesting area. Fans—some window, some ceiling—in all rooms. Library nook. Basketball hoop in parking lot. Air conditioning by request.

Pleasant Street Inn

17 Pleasant Street, Rockport, MA 01966-2152

508/546-3915
800/541-3915

Hosts: Lynne and Roger Norris
Location: Residential. Two blocks from the center of town with its shops, beaches, galleries, restaurants. Set back and up from the street, over-looking church-steepled profile of the village with Sandy Bay beyond.
Open: Year round. Two-night mini-mum on Memorial Day, July 4, Labor Day, and Columbus Day week-ends.
Rates: Vary according to room size and location. Double occupancy. July and August $75, $80, $85, $90, $95. September–December $65–$85. January–June $63–$83. Singles $3 less. Discover, MC, VISA.
♥ ⊶ ❖ ◆ ✖

> From Massachusetts: *"Just right. He's in the business (a remodeling contractor) and did the beautiful work on the huge Victorian . . . wonderful moldings and woodwork . . . polished floors . . . traditional and simple furnishings. . . . And they know how to host too."*

The Norrises, longtime Rockport residents, were looking for a larger house. Eight years ago they found one, "an ark a bit big, so we decided to share it. We have met Russians traveling with an international people-to-people program, members of the Swedish girls' basketball team, and many who come for whale watching and return to this charming area time and time again."

It's a Shingle Style 1893 Victorian with huge front lawn. One guest room has a tin ceiling. Another has a spiral staircase leading to its own turret with sofa. Some have a window seat and/or a bay window. And there's the popular front veranda with overview of town.

In residence: Son Curt and daughter Brett, in their teens. Toddy, Lynne's mother. Duke, "our Labrador, who craves attention."
Bed and bath: Eight rooms, all with private baths, on three floors. (Steep stairs to third floor.) One room with whirlpool tub, color TV, refrigerator,

(Please turn page.)

private entrance. Queen or double bed; some rooms with twin beds also. Rollaway available.

Breakfast: 8:30–10. Juice. Fruit. Homemade baked goods. Cereals. Coffee and tea. In dining room or on veranda.

Plus: Window fans. Some rooms with ceiling fans and/or individual thermostats. Beverages. Babysitting. Guest refrigerator. Garden flowers. TV in guest living room. Off-street parking.

Rocky Shores Inn
65 Eden Road, Rockport, MA 01966

508/546-2823
800/348-4003

Hosts: Renate and Gunter Kostka

Location: Quiet. Fifteen-minute picturesque walk to center of town; shops, galleries, restaurants, beaches. Thirty miles from Boston, 20 to Marblehead and Newburyport.

Open: April 1–November 1.

Rates: Per room. Ocean-view rooms $83 spring, $97 summer, $87 fall. Other rooms $5 less. AMEX, MC, VISA.
♥ ♨ ◆ ✈

> From New York: *"Quiet . . . relaxing . . . clean and cheerful rooms . . . from some you can see the sun rise over the twin lighthouses."* From Canada: *"One of the prettiest locations on Cape Ann . . . warm, friendly people."* From Massachusetts: *"Classical music in the parlor . . . delightful solarium and porch looking out onto the islands."*

When the Kostkas changed careers in 1980, they bought this substantial shingled mansion that had become an established inn. It was built by a wealthy Texan at the turn of the century with lots of woodwork and cross-ventilation, spacious rooms, and an ocean view that features the twin lighthouses (which you can visit) on Thachers Island. First-time guests feel as if they have discovered this inn; it is on a bumpy road—part of a fantastic bicycle loop—that has wonderful properties. For others, Rocky Shores has become, as a New York family wrote, "a tradition for what is now four generations." It's a comfortable place with some simple furnishings, some lovely antiques, many plants, and a wicker-furnished solarium/library.

In residence: Grown children, Christine and Stephen. "Momma, our black Persian cat, has a beautiful disposition."

Foreign language spoken: German.

Bed and bath: Ten rooms on three floors, all private full baths; nine have shower and tub. One room with private exterior entrance; one with private porch; many with ocean views. Double or queen bed; two with twin-sized bed also. Rollaway available.

Breakfast: 8–10. Homemade muffins, boiled eggs, fresh fruit, cereals, juices, jams, breads, coffee and tea. Served in dining room.

Plus: Air conditioning in the one third-floor room, formerly used for billiards. Fans for other rooms. TV in each room. Beverages. Sweets. Apples. Fresh flowers. Mints on pillow. Covered and open porch areas with umbrella table.

Seacrest Manor

508/546-2211

131 Marmion Way, Rockport, MA 01966-1988

Hosts: Leighton T. Saville and Dwight B. MacCormack Jr.
Location: About 300 yards from the ocean, overlooking spectacular rocky coastline. On two acres of gardens and woodland. On scenic (seasonal) trolley route. One mile from center of Rockport, off Route 127A.

Open: April through November. Three-day minimum on holidays, two-day on weekends. Reservations required.
Rates: April–November, $78–$102 double depending on bath arrangement. $6 less for singles.
♥ ✈

Leighton and Dwight host in an English style intended as "concierge-type guest assistance." Hence the attention to turned-down beds, tea at four, shined gentlemen's shoes (when left outside door at night), and peace and quiet in a beautiful setting. In an English guest's words, "Seacrest Manor must be heaven—came for one, stayed for seven!"

The part-Georgian, part-Federal house, built in 1911 and an inn since the 1940s, was for many years the summer home of Arthur Park of Boston's Durgin-Park restaurant family. In 1973 the two current hosts took it over when Dwight, an ordained Congregational minister, was looking for an alternative career. (He had lived in England for a few months and was on the faculty of three area colleges.) Leighton's family home is three doors away. (He retired from his NBC executive position in 1985.)

Furnishings, a mixture of contemporary and antique, include a dramatic living room floor-to-ceiling mirror that came from the old Philadelphia Opera House. The inn is surrounded by prizewinning gardens. And then there's that endless ocean view from the big second-story deck.

In residence: Tansy, an 11-year-old black Lab mixture, really does greet guests with a paw-shake.
Foreign language spoken: Some French.
Bed and bath: Eight rooms, all carpeted. Six with private bath; one two-room suite with shared bath. Two rooms on the first floor, all others on the second. Queen beds or twins/king option.
Breakfast: 7:30–9:30. A different specialty each day. Fresh fruit cup, juices, spiced Irish oatmeal with chopped dates, dry cereals, bacon and eggs, toast and sometimes muffins. Coffee, English tea, chocolate. All prepared and served "by Lillian Baker, a local lady who has been with us for all 19 years." At tables set with fine china and linens.
Plus: Mints on pillow with quote from Shakespeare. Huge living room with books, magazines, English publications. Bedroom oscillating fans. Hammock between trees. Library. Complimentary newspapers Monday–Saturday. Beach towels. Bicycles ($5 for half day). No cigar or pipe smoking indoors.

---

*I*n this book, areas of Massachusetts
are arranged roughly from east to west.

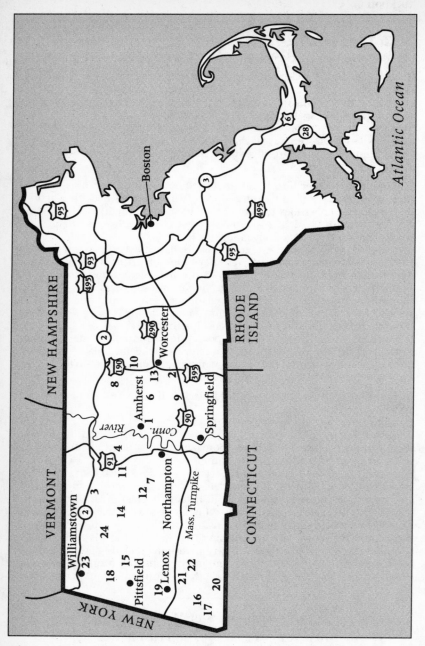

The numbers on this map indicate the locations of western Massachusetts B&Bs described in detail in this chapter.

Central Massachusetts, Connecticut River Valley, and Berkshires

Please see page 108 for Cape Cod, Martha's Vineyard, and Nantucket; Southeastern Massachusetts; Boston; Just a Little West; North of Boston.

Central Massachusetts and Connecticut River Valley
_____ Reservation Services _____

Folkstone/Central Massachusetts Bed & Breakfast Reservation Service

Darlington Road, Dudley, MA 01571-9703

Phone: 508/943-7118 or 800/762-2751. (Machine messages returned promptly.)

Listings: 15. Most are hosted private residences. A few inns. Several are in the Worcester/Sturbridge area of Central Massachusetts. They range from in-town to mountainside locations, from colonial to Victorian, from remodeled farmhouse to "elegant modern."

Reservations: Most hosts appreciate at least 24 hours' notice. Some long-term housing available; host on premises.

Rates: $45–$60 single, $55–$75 double. $3 surcharge for one-night stay. Monthly and weekly rates available. Cost of first night's lodging is required as a deposit. Deposits (less $15 service fee) are refundable if cancellation is made at least seven days in advance. AMEX, MC, VISA.

Priscilla Van de Workeen (featured in _GBH_ magazine) traveled all over the world as deputy director of the Harkness Fellowships. A couple of years ago, she and her husband moved from Manhattan to his grandmother's Central Massachusetts farmhouse, which they transformed (rebuilt). Then, utilizing her considerable experience as both B&B traveler and host, Priscilla took on this personalized reservation service. (She gives much credit to her mother, who at age 72 opened and ran a successful B&B in the 1980s.) She has continued to add new listings, all interesting homes and hosts.

Other services with some B&Bs in Central Massachusetts and the Connecticut River Valley:
Bed & Breakfast/Inns of New England, page 257.
Berkshire Bed & Breakfast Homes, page 232.
Pineapple Hospitality, page 106.

KEY TO SYMBOLS
♥ Lots of honeymooners come here.
♣ Families with children are very welcome. (Please see page xiii.)
♠ "Please emphasize that we are a private home, not an inn."
♣ Groups or private parties sometimes book the entire B&B.
♦ Travel agents' commission paid. (Please see page xii.)
✕ Sorry, no guests' pets are allowed.
✖ No smoking inside _or_ no smoking at all, even on porches.

Central Massachusetts and ___ Connecticut River Valley B&Bs ___

Allen House Inn   413/253-5000

599 Main Street, Amherst, MA 01002-2409

Host: Alan and Ann Zsieminski and Cathy Learn
Location: In town, on three acres. Across the street from the Emily Dickinson House. Within walking distance of Amherst College; Hampshire College; University of Massachusetts; galleries, museums, shops, restaurants.
Open: Year round. Two-night minimum on weekends, May–October.
Rates: Tax included. Vary according to season and length of stay. $45–$85 single. $55–$95 double.

♥ ✈ ✄

The hand-carved cherry mantels of this Queen Anne Stick Style house are pictured in the Metropolitan Museum of Art catalog. Some of the wallpapers were designed by William Morris and Walter Crane. The antiques have been collected through the years by Alan; he "has a perfect eye for spotting Aesthetic Period pieces," according to his brother, Jonas, who has helped to research the "Oscar Wilde period." Other family members, museum staffers, and guests have also exchanged information with Alan, a biochemist who lived in the house as a student before he bought it "with the desire to make an 18-room Victorian into other than student housing." Built in 1886, it still has original woodwork. All of Alan's restoration work is recorded in an album. And students still come to research the history.

Many overnight guests come for one of the five colleges in the area, for literary safaris—focusing, perhaps, on Emily Dickinson or Robert Frost—or for nearby Deerfield Village.

Bed and bath: Three large rooms, all private baths. One room with a double bed, two rooms with a double and one twin bed. Rollaway available.
Breakfast: At guests' convenience. Perhaps eggs Benedict, Swedish pancakes, stuffed French toast, or Southwestern-style eggs. In formal dining room.
Plus: Bedroom ceiling fans. Beverages. Goose-down comforters and pillows. Innkeeping seminars.

Capt. Samuel Eddy House B&B Inn

609 Oxford Street South   508/832-3149
Auburn, MA 01501   508/832-5282

Hosts: Carilyn and Jack O'Toole
Location: On an herb farm. Three
miles to Worcester, 16 to Sturbridge
Village, 45 to Boston.
Open: Year round. Advance reservations required.

Rates: $50 single. $65 double. $85
suite. $20 third person. Long-term
rates available. MC, VISA.
♥ ⚑ ❄ ◆ ✈ ✂

> From Oregon: *"We toured the area from here during our 10-day stay. The hosts
> made us feel as if we were members of the family. . . . Unique old house provides
> warm and friendly atmosphere with excellent bedroom and bath facilities. . . . The
> food deserves special mention."*

It is all just as Carilyn dreamed when she saw the 1985 newspaper ad that
read, "1750 Colonial. 3 acres. Fireplaces and lots of potential. Good location."

The story, recently featured in *Country* magazine, continues with the
O'Tooles, parents of five grown children, transplanting an herb garden (26
truckloads) and restoring for almost three years. Now guests sleep in the
Rosemary, Spearmint, or Thyme chamber. They comment on the collectibles—dolls, lamps, wreaths, wicker, and folk art—displayed everywhere.
Although Jack sells real estate, innkeeping is the O'Tooles' main focus. There
are murder mystery weekends and storytelling sessions, along with the
gardens, fruit trees, and spring maple sugaring. And there's a Carilyn-
designed smokehouse where she uses hickory, apple, peach, and pear twigs
to flavor foods. Today's big news: The family is creating a sister inn in nearby
Millbury on 149 acres with views and three rebuilt houses, two Victorian and
one colonial. Inquire about planned festivals.

In residence: All outside—geese named Bernard, Samuel, Mat, and Jessy;
one cat named Sabrina.
Foreign language spoken: French.
Bed and bath: Six second-floor rooms with ceiling fans. All with private
baths (one is full, rest are shower without tub). One two-room suite with a
king bed plus daybed, shower bath. One room with twins/king option. Three
queen-bedded rooms. Rollaway available.
Breakfast: 7:30–10. All natural ingredients. Repertoire includes stuffed
French toast with raspberries and cream, ham-and-cheese souffle, eggs in a
basket. Cooked on open hearth in winter. Served in sun room, dining room,
or guest's room by Carilyn (and staff) wearing long white antique dresses.
Plus: Air conditioning in some guest rooms. Two parlors. Fireplaces. Books.
Music. Games. TV. Turned-down beds. Afternoon tea with cookies and cakes.
"Goblets and lots of ice." In-ground outdoor pool. Huge yard. Walking trails.
Picnicking at Eddy Pond. Dinners by arrangement.

Amarcord 1797 House
(days) **413/625-2697**
Charlemont Road, Box 23   (evenings and weekends) **413/625-2975**
Buckland, MA 01338

Host: Janet Turley
Location: Rural. West of Greenfield, 5 miles from nearest village; 17 miles from historic Deerfield. About 30 minutes to University of Massachusetts, Smith College, Williams College, Deerfield Academy, Stoneleigh-Burham, Eaglebrook, Amherst. Minutes to Shelburne Falls' Bridge of Flowers and to Berkshire East and Cummington Farms ski areas.
Open: Year round.
Rates: $60 single, $75 double.
♥ ⊯ ⁂ ✈ ⊱

"Even New Englanders are surprised at how 'terribly New England' it is here. The church bells chime three times a day. Two couples have bought or built within a few blocks. Many guests come for academic-related reasons. And we've become known as a romantic getaway and honeymoon spot!"

Janet, a kindergarten teacher, lives in a large two-story 1797 colonial. Mary Lyon, the founder of Mount Holyoke College, used the house for the Winter School for Young Ladies in 1829–31. Today the neighborhood is one of 18th- and early 19th-century homes together with a traditional spired white New England church, a historical society, and some properties with horses and sheep.

Since Janet moved here (with her teenagers, now adults), she has designed two new baths, a kitchen, and an addition. Earlier, she had experience redoing an abandoned seven-bedroom house that was without any bathroom, heat, electricity, or kitchen. As a result of all she has learned, she now consults on remodeling, decorating, and B&B.

Guests wrote: *"She makes you feel warm, welcome and very full."*

In residence: Janet's mother, who has her own apartment in the house, is a big hit with guests. (So are her hand-stitched items and English garden.)
Bed and bath: Three second-floor rooms. Private full bath for double-bedded (one brass, one four-poster) rooms; private shower (no tub) bath for room with a double and a twin bed.
Breakfast: 8–9:30. Served in 18th-century fireplaced dining room or on large screened porch. Juice, fresh fruit, beverage. Stuffed croissants, sausage/apple ring or sauteed ham strips, French toast with local syrup and bacon, or mushroom egg casserole with baked tomatoes.
Plus: Beverages. Sometimes a guided tour of area. Lots of suggestions—including auctions. Big screened porch with wicker furniture and plants, overlooking old cemetery and abandoned orchard. Bedroom fans.

---

*I*s B&B like a hotel?
How many times have you hugged the doorman?

The Tea House

413/772-2675

Main Street, Deerfield, MA 01342-0367

Hosts: Natasha and Jonathan Lowe
Location: Along a mile-long street in Old Deerfield Village, an historic district with 12 museum houses and Deerfield Academy. Surrounded by farmland and rolling hills. Twenty minutes from Amherst and Northampton.

Open: Year round. Two-night minimum on weekends.
Rates: Per room including tax. $95 with fireplace, $85 without. AMEX, $5 surcharge per night.
♥ ⁂ ✗ ⅄

"My husband went to school in Deerfield, fell in love with the village, and bought this 1840s house in 1975 when he was 18. When we restored it as a B&B in 1989, we kept all the floorboards and fireplaces, altering little. The fabrics and furnishings—with lots of chintz and flowers—give the feel of a country house in my native England. I love to cook (what some call 'outrageously inventive breakfasts') and to meet people who consider this a home away from home. Many find it so relaxing here that they don't do as much sightseeing as they had intended."

Natasha writes children's stories. Jonathan works in real estate.

In residence: Thomas, a golden retriever "who loves everybody and, sometimes, tries to sneak into guests' cars when they are leaving."
Bed and bath: Two second-floor rooms, each with own staircase, have own entrance to their shared full bath. One room, overlooking street, has antique queen mahogany bed, cathedral ceiling, working fireplace. The other, overlooking garden, has queen antique pine bed. Cot available.
Breakfast: "At guests' convenience." Maybe chocolate walnut butter bread French toast or raspberry walnut pancakes served with local maple syrup. Always homemade granola, seasonal homemade fruit compote, and yogurt. Served in fireplaced dining room.
Plus: Bedroom ceiling fans. Individual thermostats. Afternoon tea with homemade shortbread (grandmother's recipe) or lemon curd. Down comforters. Bathrobes. Turndown service with chocolate on pillows. Fresh flowers. Fireplaced living room. Stereo. Books. Backgammon, chess, and checkers.

Greenview

508/448-5861

P.O. Box 422, Groton, MA 01450-0456

Hosts: Ruth and Norm Johnson
Location: In apple country, within walking distance of an orchard. Just off Route 119 amidst country views in a town noted for its architecture, schools, and picture-book New England setting. About an hour's drive northwest from Boston.
Open: April 15–December 15. Reservations required.
Rates: $30 single, $50 double.
🖐 ✗

"Twenty years in this house, 33 years in this town, 9 years doing B&B, and many memorable guests!"

The hosts, parents of four grown children, experienced B&B in England, Scotland, and Wales. Then they tried it in Vermont before deciding that it was the thing for them to do in their own home.

They have been in the restaurant business, and for quite a while Norm has been a general contractor/builder of single-family homes. Their beautifully landscaped contemporary Cape is close to the Groton School and Lawrence Academy and within 30 minutes of two national historic parks, Minute Man (in Lexington and Concord) and Lowell. The feeling of congeniality here is mutual. One guest, an 85-year-old world traveler, commented, "Your home is a castle of perfect comfort."

In residence: Izzy, a tricolored male cat "who usually greets guests at breakfast."

Bed and bath: Three rooms. On second floor, one with twin beds and one with a double bed share a bath. Small room downstairs has a single bed suitable for a child.

Breakfast: At 8. Orange or tomato juice, cold cereal, cheese omelets, English muffins, milk, coffee or tea. Served in the greenhouse area, in the dining room, or on the porch overlooking the pool.

Plus: 5–6 p.m. is usually hospitality hour. Air conditioning throughout the house. In-ground swimming pool during summer.

Folkstone/Central Massachusetts Bed & Breakfast Host #037

Hardwick, MA

Location: Quiet. Two miles from town center. With not another house in view. Half hour west of Worcester, 45 minutes east of Northampton. Twenty minutes via back roads to Brimfield, 10 to Quabbin Reservoir. Within 10 miles of many restaurants and antiques shops.

Reservations: Available through Folkstone/Central Massachusetts Bed & Breakfast, page 220.

Rates: $55 single, $60 double.

Stone walls. Gardens. Gnarled old apple trees. Lawns. Corn, clover, and alfalfa fields. Berry bushes, grapevines, apple and pear trees. In the summer, cows across the street. And a driveway lined with maple trees "that must have lived at least a thousand years." That begins to describe the setting for this 1800s farmhouse, which was rebuilt after lightning struck it a decade ago. Now everyone gathers in the combination living room/dining room/kitchen. Decor is "intentionally simple country without clutter," but there are examples of the host's talents—grapevine wreaths, dried herbs, and some knitted items—as well as old pictures and artwork done by family members. And for the latest: "My newest interest is hatboxes," said the hostess, who would be happy to share her expertise, "maybe with the help of a glue gun."

Now that the family is grown and gone (but you can be sure they are here for the Hardwick Fair, the country's oldest agricultural fair, in August), business travelers, fishermen, antiquers, bird-watchers, and cyclists are among those who are discovering this B&B.

(Please turn page.)

Bed and bath: Three second-floor rooms—one with a double high bed (step provided), one with a double bed and a skylight, and one with two twins—share a tub bath (plus use of first-floor shower).
Breakfast: 7:30–9:30. Menu at whim of host. Fresh orange juice. Fruit. Eggs with Canadian bacon or sausage, French toast made with French bread, or blueberry pancakes. Homemade muffins and breads—maybe shredded wheat or raisin cinnamon—and home fries.

The Knoll   413/584-8164
230 North Main Street, Florence, MA 01060-1221

Hosts: Lee and Ed Lesko
Location: Set far back from the road on a knoll overlooking 17 acres of farmland and forest. Three miles from Smith College, 9 from Amherst, 15 from Mount Holyoke, 12 from Deerfield. Five-minute walk to beautiful public park.

Open: Year round. Reservations preferred.
Rates: $40 single, $45 double, $50 twins.
🛥 ✖ ⅍

We overlapped with the Leskos' first B&B guests. The other couple had come from Princeton to look for a house, and they had just succeeded. It was spring and the two-story-high Michigan redbud blossoms peeking in our room were magnificent. The strawberry beds, later to be pick-your-own, had just been set out. For the evening activity, we had our choice of contra dancing or a Rudolph Serkin concert.

Time has brought a few changes. The strawberry beds have been discontinued. Ed, a former Air Force pilot, is retired from his window and door sales. Many more B&B guests have discovered the Leskos, Ed a Northampton native and Lee originally from Biloxi, Mississippi. Their spacious 12-room English Tudor is furnished with many Oriental rugs. In the corner of their large living room is a striking (in every sense of the word) seven-foot-high grandfather clock made in Germany around 1900. Traditional furnishings are in the guests' (formerly the children's) rooms. Housekeeping is impeccable.

Bed and bath: Three second-floor bedrooms share two tub baths. One room with twin beds, the others with double beds. Cot available.
Breakfast: At 8. Lee will usually join you for coffee after you have had your cereal, fresh fruit, their homegrown raspberries, strawberries, fresh farm eggs any style, bacon, toast, muffins or coffee cake, homemade jam.
Plus: Large screened porch. Tour of the house and grounds, if you'd like. Paths for jogging or walking. Over an acre of lawn. Walk to Look Park for its beautifully landscaped grounds, plenty of running and roaming space, playground, picnic grounds, tennis courts, and pool.

Harrington Farm Country Inn   508/464-5600

178 Westminster Road, Princeton, MA 01541   800/736-3276 (FARM)

Hosts: John Bomba and Victoria Morgan
Location: Quiet. Surrounded by thousands of acres of reservation land. On the western slope of Wachusett Mountain; 45 miles west of Boston, ten north of Worcester. Short walk to Wachusett Audubon Sanctuary. Cross-country skiing from front door.
Open: Year round.
Rates: Double occupancy. $57.50–67.50 shared bath, $75 private. $100 suite. $15 third person in room. MC, VISA.
♥ ❁ ♦ ✂

"A lot of guests oversleep because it's so quiet here! After breakfast, some just sit on the porch or lawn and read. Others go antiquing or go to Boston or to Old Sturbridge Village, or they hike (using our map), bird-watch, cycle, jog, or ski."

Vicki, a horticulturist, and John, a Culinary Institute of America graduate who has been chef in gourmet restaurants from coast to coast, liked the idea of working in their home town, a resort at the turn of the century. In 1987 they bought the Harrington property (the oldest part is a 1762 saltbox), which had been a working farm and, for a century, a summer lodging place. Rejuvenation took place. Rooms were stenciled. Extensive herb, vegetable, and flower gardens were planted. And by the time you read this, the solar greenhouse should be completed with enough greens and herbs to sell to Boston restaurants. Meanwhile, *Worcester Magazine* "best" awards have been received in the "romantic" and "restaurant" categories. Once again, Princeton has become a destination.

In residence: Three cats. "Mika, a Siamese; Bill loves guests; Willey, black with white bib and socks."
Foreign languages spoken: "Vicki speaks enough German to get by. French, Dutch, and/or Spanish depending on staff."
Bed and bath: Seven second-floor rooms, some over dining area, all with views of gardens, lawn, or pond. One suite with queen bed, sitting room, and private full bath. One room with extra-long double bed, private full bath. Five rooms—with extra-long double or an extra-long double plus a twin bed—share three baths.
Breakfast: 8–9:30. "Visiting time with innkeepers." Fresh fruit. Eggs any style. Wisconsin bacon. "Seasonal muffins." Hot or cold cereal. "Fabulous coffee."
Plus: Two acres of lawn. TV in third-floor common room. Gazebo. Down comforters. Flannel sheets. Fresh flowers in common areas. Discount coupons for Wachusett Mountain ski area. Beverages. Dinner seatings, Wednesday–Sunday 5–8:30 p.m.; entrees $16–$18.

Deer Meadow Farm   413/436-7129

Bragg Road, Warren, MA
Mailing address: RFD 1, Box 21B, Bragg Road, West Brookfield, MA 01585-9705

Hosts: Carol and Edward Perron
Location: Quiet. On 22 acres in fruit-growing country, 10 miles northwest of Old Sturbridge Village. Midway between Routes 9 and 20. Within 10 minutes' drive of restaurants and shopping.

Open: May–October.
Rates: $35 single. $45 double. $10 rollaway.

From Texas: *"A find . . . tucked into the hills on an exquisite country road . . . so pretty . . . within easy access of Sturbridge and Brimfield . . . cheery, bright house . . . helpful, thoughtful, sharing hosts."* From Pennsylvania: *"Stayed there while en route to Maine with our four children . . . an authentic colonial retreat in the unspoiled countryside."*

As Carol says, "For Old Sturbridge Village visitors, our c. 1780 twin chimney colonial is an extension of their day at the village—with the addition of modern conveniences." The guests' second-floor sitting room has original wide board paneling, Indian windows, exposed beams, and wing chairs. There are four working fireplaces, including one with a large cast iron hog kettle crafted into it. Some guests are interested in the post-and-beam construction. And then there are those berries—three acres of blueberries planted in 1976 (now part of a pick-your-own operation) and, more recently, red raspberries, a great source of supply for some restaurants and bakeries.

After military tours, the Perrons returned in 1976 to this area, where Ed grew up. In 1985, with their own four children grown and gone, they started B&B.

In residence: Cricket, a kitty who stays outdoors in the summer.
Bed and bath: Entire second floor—with views of open meadows and distant woods—is for guests. Two large rooms, each with two twin beds, share a full bath. Adjacent sitting room. Rollaway available.
Breakfast: 7–9. Fresh morning buckle, muffins, and compote, with home-grown berries. Cold cereals, juice, coffee, tea, milk. In dining room with small baby grand piano.
Plus: Their own nature trail. Pick your own (free) quart of berries (red raspberries in July, blueberries in July and August). TV in guests' sitting room. Afternoon tea or soft drinks.

From Bernice's mailbag: "And then there was the classmate from 1935, whom I hadn't seen in 50 years, who read about us in your book. He's been here twice."

The Rose Cottage   508/835-4034

24 Worcester Street, Routes 12 and 140, West Boylston, MA 01583-1413

Hosts: Michael and Loretta Kittredge

Location: On landscaped grounds overlooking Wachusett Reservoir. Forty-five minutes west of Boston in a country setting at the junction of Routes 12 and 140. Ten minutes to Worcester, Mount Wachusett ski area (snowmaking), and winery (tours and picnic area). Forty minutes to Sturbridge Village.

Open: Year round. Two-night minimum on holiday, college graduation, and college parents' weekends. Reservations required.

Rates: $65 double. $10 extra person in room.

♥ 🏠 ⁂ ⊀

Loretta, a West Boylston native, changes the seasonal decor in this antiques-filled 1850 classic Gothic revival cottage. She makes the wreaths and silk flower baskets (and provides lunch and/or dinner for weddings or business groups). Mike is an engineer who, together with his son, entered a new business inspired by a B&B guest's conversation. In 1984 the Kittredges moved to this big house—"very much a home rather than an inn"—and for six years Loretta had an antiques shop in the barn. The B&B has lots of gingerbread and tall windows, wide board floors, white marble fireplaces, electrified gas fixtures, lavender glass doorknobs, and "the comfortable kind of Victorian furnishings—all enjoyed by guests from 27 countries and 40 states."

Bed and bath: Five rooms. Private full bath for first-floor room with iron and brass double bed. Upstairs, three doubles and one room with twin beds share two baths.

Breakfast: Usually 7:30–10. "We're into gourmet meals, and we also accommodate special diets." Quiche, French toast made with cream and cinnamon (at Christmas, with eggnog!), or omelets. Skim milk, low-cholesterol foods, and sugar substitutes used too. Fruit or fresh flower garnish. Served in candlelit dining room.

Plus: A welcoming beverage. Fruit bowl. Candy. Fresh herbs year round. Fans in bedrooms. Toiletries you may have forgotten. Three wicker-furnished porches. Large yard with umbrella tables and swings. "A gazebo is in the works." Air-conditioned and fireplaced dining/conference room.

Sunnyside Farm   413/665-3113

11 River Road, Whately, MA
Mailing address: P.O. Box 486, South Deerfield, MA 01373

Hosts: Mary Lou and Dick Green

Location: In a farming community, next door to Nourse Strawberry Farms. Five miles south of Deerfield, 15 minutes from Northampton and Amherst, near many colleges and private schools. Along a wonderful cycling route that is flat, very rural, very much old New England.

Open: Year round. Reservations required.

Rates: $35–$40 single, $60 double, $70 twins.

♥ 🏠 ✗ ⊀

(Please turn page.)

If you've never had grandparents who lived in a big yellow farmhouse with a red barn complete with big letters that spell out its name, here's the place, and it's well maintained and loved. The 14-room home, previously owned by Mary Lou's grandparents, has been handed down through the years. "This is one of the reasons I want to stay here and hand it down to our children and grandchildren. I spent summers here as a child and have wonderful memories. . . . We have been living here since 1972, when we moved up from Northampton with our four children. (Two have been married on the grounds.) Although the house is basically the same as when my grandparents remodeled it in 1920, we have done much redecorating.

"My husband, a former comptroller at Amherst College, visits with guests in the evening when I am working as head nurse in the emergency department of Northampton's Cooley Dickinson Hospital. Breakfasts are a fun time for me. In season, guests not only wake up to the aroma from one of the largest strawberry (and raspberry) farms in the Northeast, but some join me in picking before breakfast."

In residence: Dick hopes to quit smoking some day.
Bed and bath: Three rooms, all with cross-ventilation (and window fans), share two baths (one full, one shower only). Two large rooms with twin beds. One room with a double bed. Cot available.
Breakfast: 8:30–9:30. Seasonal fruits, homemade muffins and jams, eggs, bacon or sausage, or a cheese strata. Please indicate special diets in advance. Served in country kitchen or dining room.

> From New York City: *"It's very peaceful, pretty, and comfortable. The children loved the sense of freedom that they lack living in the city. The breakfasts are wonderful too, but our favorite thing about Sunnyside is the hospitality of Mary and Dick Green."*

Twin Maples   413/268-7925
106 South Street, Williamsburg, MA 01096

Hosts: Eleanor and Martin Hebert
Location: Two miles from village, surrounded by fields, garden, stone walls—and mountain view. Seven miles from Northampton; 9 miles to I-91 interchange and 25 miles to Springfield.

Open: Year round. Two-night stays preferred.
Rates: $45 single, $50 double. $5 surcharge for one-night stay. $15 cot (child only) or crib.

What started out to be a sometime-maybe activity has almost become the headquarters—or at least a model—of B&B in the area. For many years Eleanor was a librarian in town. Now she not only hosts but is very involved with the expanded B&B scene in the Hampshire Hills as well as the Berkshires. Martin, an engineer, shares the role of host.

Since the Heberts arrived in 1962, they have restored the wonderful 200-year-old farmhouse inside and out. There are exposed beams in the dining room; the kitchen has a large fireplace with Dutch oven; the antique and reproduction furniture is colonial in style. Ribboned vases and flowers are color coordinated. We are among the guests who have found everything, including hospitality, "just perfect." Or, as guests from New York wrote, "Like the candy on the pillow . . . 'mint!'"

In residence: Daughter Jennifer, in her twenties. Two dogs; Toby, a miniature sheltie, and Tasha, a dalmatian.

Bed and bath: Three rooms in a guest wing share a full updated bath. One room with restored iron and brass double bed, nonworking fireplace. Another room with twin iron and brass beds, nonworking fireplace. Third room has restored double brass bed. Cot and crib available.

Breakfast: 7:30–9 on weekdays, until 10 on weekends. "We cater to vegetarians." Juice, fresh fruit; buttermilk pancakes (with or without blueberries), sausage, homemade sweet breads; coffee, tea, and milk; homemade maple syrup. Served on table set with flowers, linens, and handcrafted pottery, in dining room or on screened porch.

Plus: Flannel sheets and electric blankets in winter. Guests' sitting room with TV and games. Wood stove in huge country kitchen. Screened porch. Picnic table. Bedroom fans.

Folkstone/Central Massachusetts Bed & Breakfast Host #609

Worcester, MA

Location: In historic district of Victorian homes. Ten-minute walk to downtown. Near Mechanics Hall, Clark University, Worcester Art Museum, American Antiquarian Society, and the Centrum.

Reservations: Year round through Folkstone/Central Massachusetts Bed & Breakfast, page 220. Two-night minimum on October weekends.

Rates: $60 single, $65 double. Second room $40 single, $50 double. ✈

The hostess is an interior designer, antiques collector, and writer who enjoys cooking and travel. In 1980 she purchased and restored this 1887 Queen Anne cottage, filling it with her collections of art and decorative objects. She is a wonderful resource for information about the area's historic houses, restaurants, and cultural activities. And right here, in the summer, there's a deck with spa surrounded by gardens.

In residence: Lily, a tiger cat. Ashby, a small black dog.

Bed and bath: A second-floor room with two twin beds, private shower bath down the hall. Second room with double bed available for members of the same party.

Breakfast: 8–9:30. Fresh orange juice, French toast or eggs, sausage, bacon, muffins or croissants. Cereals. Served in formal dining room.

Plus: Fireplaced parlors. Air conditioning in bedrooms. Afternoon or evening tea or wine.

___ Berkshires Reservation Services ___

Berkshire Bed & Breakfast Homes
P.O. Box 211, Williamsburg, MA 01096

Phone: 413/268-7244. Monday–Friday, 9–6; Saturday, 10–12 noon. Year round.

Listings: 90. Located in Massachusetts—North and South County Berkshires (many near Tanglewood and Williams College), Pioneer Valley and Hampshire Hills (close to the five-college area), greater Springfield (some near Civic Center and Big E), and Sturbridge. Also in northern Connecticut, southern Vermont, and eastern New York state. Mostly hosted private residences, some inns, plus unhosted private residences. Free (partial) list includes rates.

Reservations: Two weeks' advance notice is recommended. In the Berkshires, two-night minimum stays are often required on weekends or holidays and during the Tanglewood season.

Rates: $30–$145 single, $45–$150 double. $8 booking fee. For some locations, $5, $10, or $15 surcharge for one-night stays. Twenty percent deposit required. Deposit minus $15 processing fee refunded if cancellation is received at least two weeks prior to arrival date. "For less than two weeks' notice, no refund unless our office or your host can rebook your reserved room; full refund if room is rebooked." AMEX, MC, VISA. ♦

Attention to detail is a hallmark of this highly regarded service. For six years it has been owned and run by Eleanor Hebert, an experienced B&B host who was, for many years, a professional librarian. She is aware of the importance of meeting the needs and expectations of hosts and guests. She knows what needs to be done and does it—well.

Plus: Short-term (several weeks) hosted and unhosted housing also available.

Other services with some B&Bs in the Berkshires:
The American Country Collection, page 335.
Bed & Breakfast/Inns of New England, page 257.
Covered Bridge, page 4.
Pineapple Hospitality, page 106.

KEY TO SYMBOLS
♥ Lots of honeymooners come here.
⚶ Families with children are very welcome. (Please see page xiii.)
☛ "Please emphasize that we are a private home, not an inn."
⚓ Groups or private parties sometimes book the entire B&B.
♦ Travel agents' commission paid. (Please see page xii.)
⚵ Sorry, no guests' pets are allowed.
⚮ No smoking inside *or* no smoking at all, even on porches.

Berkshires B&Bs

Cumworth Farm

413/634-5529

Route 112, Box 110, Cummington, MA 01026

Hosts: Ed and Mary McColgan
Location: On a scenic rural road with mountain views, 3.4 miles from town center. Hiking trails nearby; 45 minutes to Tanglewood, Williamstown, Amherst; 30 to Northampton. Near Hickory Hill and Cummington Farm for cross-country skiing.

Open: Year round. Reservations preferred.
Rates: $60 double. $40 single. $10 one-time charge for a cot.
🏃 🛏 ⁂ ✈ ✄

> From Mississsipi: *"Like finding a buried treasure."* From New Hampshire: *"From good conversation we were lured to the fields. . . . Lost ourselves in rows upon rows of raspberries . . . walked two miles on the property."* From Connecticut: *"Out-of-this-world pancakes. Went at maple syrup time with our children for a pancake breakfast and tour of sugar house. . . . Besides the warmth of the McColgans, our family has enjoyed cross-country skiing at uncrowded places they suggested, and hiking during foliage. It's a very special place, coupling the best of outdoor living with a warm home environment."*

We too have experienced the traditional European-like B&B. You'll get tips about restaurants, a great cycling route, and a fun Tuesday night auction. You can read by the parlor stove, have tea by the kitchen stove, and get to know multifaceted hosts—who, for good reason, have a lengthy roster of fans.

As a youngster Ed worked on potato, dairy, and tobacco farms. As an adult, he has experience as college history professor, Massachusetts Bicentennial director, state legislator, and Department of Public Health executive. Parents of seven grown children, Ed and Mary have both been Northampton city councilors. Since buying this 200-year-old farmhouse in 1979, they have had many animals, held a barn roofing (completed in one weekend), and established a big vegetable garden. Mary still works as a congregate housing coordinator.

Now they concentrate on maple sugaring, using wood to boil sap that is collected from 4,000 taps. (Lots of people come to see—and taste—in early spring.) From the 1,000 blueberry and 2,500 raspberry bushes, there's plenty of jam and jelly for the newest enterprise, gift packs of Massachusetts-grown products.

In residence: Neil, a Border collie. Barn cats and sheep.
Bed and bath: Six second-floor rooms, each with either a double bed or two twins. Four rooms share a full bath. Two rooms share a tub bath. Three have ceiling fans. Cot available.
Breakfast: 7–9. Pancakes with homegrown berries and the McColgans' syrup. Also cereal, fruit, and muffins. Served around the claw-footed oak

(Please turn page.)

table in the beamed kitchen with restaurant stove and dozens of hanging baskets.
Plus: A new hot tub in the yard, with views of rolling hills, mountains, fields, and gardens. Beverages. Patio with lounge chairs. Dinner by advance arrangement.

The Dalton House   413/684-3854
955 Main Street, Dalton, MA 01226-2100

Hosts: Gary and Bernice Turetsky
Location: On the main street of a small town that is the home of the company that makes all the paper for U.S. currency. Close to Tanglewood and to cross-country and downhill skiing at Jiminy Peak and Brodie Mountain.
Open: Year round. Two-night minimum in July and August.

Rates: Double occupancy. Varies according to room size. $78–$100 summer, $58–$85 fall, $48–$65 winter/spring. Suites $65–$100. $10 extra person. Ten percent discount for five-night stays Monday–Thursday.
♥ ❖ ✈

"We were doing B&B before we knew what a B&B was. Through 16 years we have made many changes. We have torn down walls that we put up!"

The meandering place—main house with wing and converted carriage house—is complete with fireplaced common room; a 20-by-40-foot swimming pool; a deck with colorful striped awning; and the newest addition, a large breakfast room that has skylights, lots of plants, and a Shaker ambiance with Windsor chairs.

When the Turetskys came here from Freehold, New Jersey, in 1971, it was the flower business in a quaint town that attracted them. Then there was a gas shortage that resulted in changed customer habits. A visit to innkeeper friends in Vermont provided the inspiration to think differently about their four-season Massachusetts location and their 1810 colonial home. Now the three daughters are grown and gone. The flower shop was sold and moved in 1990. Guests, including campers' parents, speak of "visiting" with Bernice and Gary at "my place in the Berkshires."

In residence: "Occasionally, Pumpkin, our 13-year-old senior citizen cat, gets to visit his fans."
Bed and bath: Nine carpeted rooms plus two suites with very large rooms and sitting areas. All with private shower baths. Choice of two twin beds or a double bed. One suite has double beds, the other has a twin and a double bed. Cots available.
Breakfast: Continental buffet. Hot and cold cereals. Blueberry, cranberry nut, and banana muffins. Toast-your-own English muffins and bagels. Fresh fruit in season. Juice, coffee, hot chocolate, teas.
Plus: Air conditioning and individual heat control in bedrooms. Large sitting room with fireplace, old beams, loft, piano. Patio. Picnic area in the woods.

From California: *"We have stayed in quite a few B&Bs over the years, and the Dalton House is one of the most comfortable that we've stayed in. . . . Bernice shared lots of interesting facts about the area and Crane Company." From New York: "Wonderful hosts . . . very, very pleasant rooms."*

Elling's Guest House B&B   413/528-4103
RD 3, Box 6, Great Barrington, MA 01230

Hosts: Josephine and Raymond Elling
Location: On five acres of lawns, gardens, and wooded areas. One mile west of town on Route 23, 300 feet from the main road. Twenty minutes to Tanglewood. Minutes to Butternut Basin and Catamount ski areas, and to small river beach.

Open: Year round. Two-night minimum weekends June–August. Reservations required.
Rates: June–October and holidays, $85. November–May, $75. Singles $15 less Monday–Thursday.
♥ 🏡 ❄ 🐾 ✄

> From Seattle: *"What a thrill to return to your former home and find it more beautiful than when you left!"* From Rhode Island: *"Peaceful surroundings . . . warm, comfy feeling. . . . There's nothing like waking up to Jo's freshly baked muffins or scones."*

This B&B is almost a legend. "When our summer-only address turned out to be a nonpaying guest house, we decided that running a B&B would be the thing to do. Now, almost 20 years later, we still have wonderful guests!"

The Ellings, local historical society members, restored the white frame house that was built in 1746 for a woolen-mill owner. "Among family pieces is our pride—an 1820 tall clock that strikes each hour." Ray is a do-it-yourself buff. Jo gardens, hooks rugs, and makes wreaths. They will suggest anywhere in the Berkshires as a favorite place, "but we are partial to the small back roads. If you get lost, you'll enjoy it anyway."

Foreign language spoken: Some Italian.
Bed and bath: Four cozy rooms with air conditioning; private guests' entrance and parlor. King/twins option, queen, or double beds available. All private baths; two with tub and shower, two with shower only.
Breakfast: 8:30–10. "Full continental." Fresh fruit, hot muffins or biscuits with homemade jam, juice, and a bottomless pot of coffee or tea. In lovely dining room. In summer, eat on the wicker-furnished porch or on lawns.
Plus: Garden swing suspended from an old maple. Adirondack lawn chairs. Fireplaced common room with TV, games, cards. Badminton, horseshoes. Guest refrigerator. An invitation to see the original cooking fireplace in the Ellings' part of the house.

---

*A*ccording to many hosts:
"Guests come with plans and discover the joys of lawn sitting."

Littlejohn Manor   413/528-2882

1 Newsboy Monument Lane, Great Barrington, MA 01230

Hosts: Herbert Littlejohn, Jr., and Paul DuFour
Location: On spacious grounds with views of hills and cornfields. One mile west of downtown. Across lane from the Newsboy Monument. Within a mile of tennis, golf, and swimming; five miles to Butternut Ski Basin or Catamount; 20 minutes to Tanglewood.
Open: Year round. Two-night mini-

mum on summer weekends and in foliage and ski seasons. Three-night minimum on holiday weekends.
Rates: Double occupancy. Memorial Day weekend–October, $65–$80. November–May, $60–$75. Midweek $5 less except in July, August, October, and on holiday weekends. Singles $5 less.
♥ ⚓ ✗

Hundreds of repeat guests have come to these innkeepers, whose experience includes 15 years as owners of a Maine summer resort, 20 years as Harvard University food service administrators, and considerable international travel. Here they prepare breakfasts that are almost famous. They invite guests to take garden tours and to taste, touch, and smell many of the over one hundred herbs and edible flowers.

Drying herbs are in the colonial-style dining room, which features a chandelier, "a whimsical concoction of Viennese and Baccarat crystal, cleverly brought together by the head designer for Tiffany." The house, a combination of American Shingle and Greek Revival architecture, is furnished with early American and Victorian pieces, European and Oriental accents, and dried arrangements.

Herb is active with the Great Barrington Historical Society. Paul is president emeritus of the Berkshire Concert Choir, president of the Berkshire Bach Society, a notary public, and a justice of the peace.

In residence: Maine coon cats, Maid Marion and Robin Hood.
Foreign languages spoken: Minimal German and French.
Bed and bath: Four second-floor carpeted rooms share two full baths. Two double-bedded rooms. One with two twin beds. One with working fireplace has twins/king bed option.
Breakfast: 8:30–9:15. Memorable. Eggs with ham, bangers, sauteed mushrooms, grilled tomato, potato. Garnished with flowers. English muffins. Homemade marmalades and jams. Coffees and teas.
Plus: Air conditioner in every room of house. Chocolate on the pillow. Tea at 4 p.m. if arranged by noon—perhaps with marigold or lemon thyme and lemon balm scones. Fireplaced living room with color cable TV. Bus pickup to rental car.

B*reakfast is where the magic happens.*

Round Hill Farm Non-Smokers' B&B

17 Round Hill Road, Great Barrington, MA 01230-1557   413/528-3366

Hosts: Thomas and Margaret Whitfield
Location: A working farm on a dirt road, 2.6 miles northwest of town, with 20-mile views of the Berkshire Hills. On 300 acres with fields, woods, trails, and trout stream. Walking, jogging, bicycling, cross-country skiing nearby. Eleven miles to Tanglewood.
Open: Year round. Two-night minimum in July and August. During Tanglewood season, in farmhouse, two-night minimum; in dairy barn, three-night minimum in studio and four-night minimum in apartment. Advance reservations required.
Rates: Per room. *Farmhouse* (shared baths): $75–$85. *Barn:* studio $115 weekdays, $125 weekends; apartment $125 weekdays, $150 weekends. Singles, $10 less. AMEX, MC, VISA.

♥ ⌂ ♦ ✈ ✂

"There's something magical about the space on this hilltop. Guests unwind before they reach the bell at the top of the farmhouse steps." And the *Architectural Digest* kind of transformation of the 19th-century dairy barn hayloft, "the Uttermost Barn" (with an extraordinary 1990 handmade "Shaker wall" of cabinets) has added to the list of guests who appreciate the Whitfields' joy in sharing their "nonsmokers' haven." Round Hill is filled with antiques, books (seven libraries), Laura Ashley, and comfort.

Tom, a tidewater Virginian and inspired cook and gardener, left a suburban pediatric practice in 1973 to establish a model rural children's clinic in this area. Now his office is in the wing of the house. Peggy, born in Great Barrington, brings many skills to her roles as farm manager, equestrian, and writer. Together, the parents of a grown family do the beds and "breakfast parties."

In residence: Two Welsh corgis—Bittersweet and her daughter, Capybara; not allowed in B&B. Kittery, an outdoor cat. Horses. (Cows are on the adjoining farm.)
Foreign language spoken: French.
Bed and bath: Eight rooms. *In house*—five rooms (three available March–November only) share three baths. Queen, double, or twin beds; most are oversize. *In air-conditioned barn*—two second-floor luxury suites with private baths and ceiling fans. One is apartment with queen bed, living room, dining area, kitchen, deck, and full bath with laundry facilities. Studio has seven-foot queen bed, queen-sized sofa bed, claw-foot tub with European shower. (Plus a double-bedded room available with a barn suite.)
Breakfast: Time, place, and menu chosen night before. Fruits; juice; cold or hot cereals; eggs any style; breads, pastry, muffins; teas, coffees, milk.
Plus: Private farmhouse guest entrance. Formal parlor. Wicker-furnished wraparound porches. Hammock. Swimming holes in trout stream. Terry robes. Privacy locks. And horses are welcome!

Seekonk Pines

413/528-4192
(for reservations only) **800/292-4192**

142 Seekonk Cross Road
Great Barrington, MA 01230

Hosts: Linda and Christian Best
Location: Just off Route 23, bordered with pine trees. Two miles west of town and Route 7. Fifteen minutes to three state forests. Eight miles to Stockbridge, 5 to Butternut Basin and Catamount ski areas, 16 to Tanglewood.
Open: Year round. Depending on room, two- or three-day minimum July, August, and October weekends; two-night minimum in June and September.
Rates: November–May $65–$80. June/September–October $70–$90. July–August $75–$95. Singles $25 less (weekdays, shared bath). $20 extra adult, $15 extra child, $10 crib, $5 cot (if not extra person). Ten percent less for stays of over one week, five percent if five or more nights.

They met while playing the lead roles in *Damn Yankees*. Now Linda and Chris give programs of show music in the area—and unscheduled performances at the inn. In addition to their perennial gardens, an attraction for passersby, they grow black raspberries, strawberries, rhubarb, and squash for jams and jellies—sold to guests only, by popular demand. Guests often ask about the stenciling in the house, the handmade quilts, the dollhouse that Linda and her daughter decorated, or Linda's watercolors. Auction acquisitions emerge in a reconditioned state from Chris's barn workshop. All these projects are part of "the continuing creative process" started 13 years ago when the Bests converted the expanded 1830s house to an inn. It's an environment that, as a recent innkeeper guest wrote, "radiates charm and taste—truly what an inn should be."

In residence: Grown daughter, Jill. Ivory, "a lively white shepherd/yellow Lab mix."
Foreign language spoken: German.
Bed and bath: Six rooms on first and second floors. One with queen and double, ceiling fan, sitting area, private full bath. One with queen and trundle, private shower bath. Queen with private shower bath. Queen and twin, private full bath. Room with twins/king option shares the shower in its full bath with room that has double bed, private half bath. Rollaway and crib available.
Breakfast: In season, 8–8:45; off-season 8–8:30. Heart-healthy menus; whole grains used. Homegrown fruit, yogurt, granola; maybe corn pudding, oatmeal souffle, pancakes, or stuffed French toast; hot cereal. Special diets accommodated.
Plus: In-ground swimming pool. Cross-country trails from the door. Fireplaced common room with piano, chess, puzzles. Wildflower meadow, extensive lawn area, picnic table. Portable fans. Bicycles may be borrowed. Guest pantry with refrigerator and hot water dispenser. After skiing, hot mulled cider.

Some executives who book a meeting at an inn return on a weekend for a getaway. Some on a getaway return with colleagues for a meeting.

The Turning Point Inn

413/528-4777

RD 2, Box 140, Great Barrington, MA 01230-9808

Hosts: Irving, Shirley, and (daughter) Jamie Yost

Location: On 11 acres with nature trails. Close to the Appalachian Trail. Fifteen minutes from Tanglewood. On a well-traveled road, just down the road from lake swimming and Butternut Basin.

Open: Year round. Two- or three-day minimum for summer, fall, and holiday weekends; sometimes, one-nights are available.

Rates: Weekends $55 single; $75 double; $75 twin, shared bath; $95 king (or twin), private bath. Weekdays $5 less. $5 crib. $10 cot, under age 12; $15 if over 12. Cottage $185 for four; optional breakfast, $5 per person. Seventh night free. MC, VISA.

♥ ⚓ ❀ ✈ ✄

"Is this really zucchini bread? It's unbelievable. And so is this (baked) fruit!" exclaimed everyone who came to meet the Yosts during a bed and breakfast promotion in New York. And so it goes with all the whole-grain and sugarless creations served in the inviting home that was "a mess" when Irv, an architect, and Shirley, a teacher, bought it 15 years ago. During conversion of the old tavern/inn, they discovered a beehive oven and two Rumford fireplaces. Plans for a vegetarian restaurant were changed to B&B, and the New Jerseyites, warm innkeepers with contagious enthusiasm, became year-round Berkshire residents in 1982.

The couple mentioned in my first B&B book as having been here for their 50th anniversary have returned annually for the last nine years. ("The husband was a member of a Witness for Peace group captured by the Nicaraguan Contras. . . . They are a magnificent couple!") Honeymooners come; some send their parents. And now two generations are running the inn.

In residence: Alana, 12-year-old granddaughter.

Bed and bath: Seven cozy second-floor rooms, attractively furnished with "19th- and 20th-century furniture." One room with private bath and twin/king bed option. One single room, four double-bedded rooms, and a twin-bedded room share three full baths. Cribs and cots available. Two-bedroom cottage (with or without breakfast provided) has living room, kitchen, and sun porch.

Breakfast: Usually at 8:30 and 9:30. Bountiful. Served in dining/common room. Maybe Irv's own blend of whole-grain hot cereal; bran and whole wheat pancakes; eggs with veggies; or Shirley's hot baked fruit, Jamie's bran muffins, or zucchini and date bread. Tofu and tofu salad too. Special diets accommodated.

Plus: Fresh fruit always available. Fireplaces in three common rooms. Piano. Babysitting. Library. TV and stereo. Refrigerator. Laundry facilities. Picnic tables. Hammocks.

Innkeepers are sharers. One recalls the guest who arrived for a wedding only to find he'd left his dress pants at home. The innkeeper wore the same size. The guest appeared at the wedding properly dressed in borrowed pants.

Baldwin Hill Farm Bed & Breakfast

Baldwin Hill Road, Egremont   413/528-4092
Mailing address: Box 125, RD 3, Great Barrington, MA 01230-0125

Hosts: Richard and Priscilla Burdsall
Location: Spectacular. On a hilltop with 360-degree view of hills and valleys. Surrounded by 500 acres with gardens, hiking, and (ungroomed) cross-country ski trails. Five miles west of Great Barrington; 25 minutes to Tanglewood.

Open: Year round. Two-night stays preferred on weekends.
Rates: Double occupancy. June 15– Labor Day weekend, October, and holiday weekends $75–$85 shared bath, $95 private. Rest of year $10 less. MC, VISA.
♥ ✉ ❖ ◆ ✗ ⚞

Surprise! Many guests who come with a list of planned activities spend much of their time right here. Views of rolling hills are everywhere—from the bay windows and screened porch of the white clapboard Victorian farmhouse, from the heated in-ground swimming pool surrounded by orchards, and on the trails too. They are part of what drew the Burdsalls back to the farm where they lived in their early years of marriage and where Richard was born and raised. He has experience as a farmer (who sometimes takes guests on a tour of the huge red barn complex and its carriages, sleighs, tools, and old farm machinery), as a banker, and as a teacher. (Inquire about literature seminars here in November and April.) "And many guests ask about wildlife, conservation, and the town history."

Richard and Priscilla did most of the restoration work before opening as a B&B in 1990. All the furnishings are family pieces: antiques, paintings, Orientals. The fieldstone fireplace, Victorian woodwork, and spacious porch—all in such a spectacular setting—draw interested comments.

In residence: Harriet, an English springer spaniel. "Our repeat guests ask for her first!"
Foreign language spoken: "A bit of French."
Bed and bath: Four second-floor rooms. One double-bedded room has private bath with full-sized shower. Three rooms—one with two twin beds and sink/vanity, one with king/twins option and sink/vanity, and one with a double bed—all share a full bath and a half bath.
Breakfast: Usually 7:30–9:30. Fruit from the orchard. Blackberry or apple pancakes; buckwheat cakes; white or whole wheat French toast; fresh farm eggs. Juices. Hot or cold cereal. Homemade muffins. Bacon, sausage, or creamed dried beef. Served in dining room under antique Tiffany chandelier.
Plus: Welcoming beverage. Two living rooms, one with fieldstone fireplace. Down comforters. Color TV, VCR, piano, books. Wicker-furnished porch. Spacious lawns. Beach towels. Picnic table. Fresh flowers.

"I'll just sleep in the morning," said one college-age son, until the next day when he smelled the muffins.

Bread & Roses 413/528-1099

Route 71, Corner Baldwin Hill Road, Egremont
Mailing address: Star Route 65, Box 50, Great Barrington, MA 01230-0050

Hosts: Elliot and Julie Lowell
Location: On three acres with gardens, bubbling brook, and small pond.
Open: Year round. Three-night minimum on summer weekends.

Rates: Per room. July–October $95. November–June $75. Extra bed in room $15.
♥ ❖ ♦

> From Connecticut: *"We spent our wedding night at a lovely old farmhouse run by a charming couple who presented us with an unexpected gift and cooked us a delicious breakfast. Please consider them for your next book."*

Put simply, Julie says, "We love people, and I got tired of computers (as a data processing manager) as a way of life. I did the renovation, not a slavish restoration, as a wonderful home to enjoy. Many people come here just to relax. And lots of cyclists stay with us."

Just looking at the bridge that arches over the brook is enough to make guests unwind. Inside, the focal point is the large brick fireplace, a divider between the living and dining rooms. To the 1802 farmhouse, once used as a school, the Lowells added lots of new plumbing and a wraparound porch.

Julie is active with the League of Women Voters. Elliot was a lawyer in Long Island; he now practices law here.

In residence: "Artemis is a friendly tiger cat. Dinah is a skittish one."
Foreign languages spoken: French. Some Spanish and German.
Bed and bath: Five air-conditioned second-floor rooms, all with private baths. Accessible by stairs or inclinator. One room with double bed, shower bath. Another with double bed, full bath. One with a double and a twin, shower bath. A room with two twin beds, shower bath. Queen-bedded room with full bath. Rollaway available.
Breakfast: 8:30–10 with Mozart accompaniment. Freshly squeezed orange juice, fresh fruit, homemade breads and rolls. Entree could be French toast Grand Marnier, spinach souffle with mushrooms, huevos rancheros, crustless quiche. Special diets accommodated. Served in dining room or on porch.
Plus: Phones in rooms. Tea. Steinway piano. Bathrobes. Screened porch. Plenty of books. Telephones in rooms.

KEY TO SYMBOLS
♥ Lots of honeymooners come here.
✤ Families with children are very welcome. (Please see page xiii.)
✦ "Please emphasize that we are a private home, not an inn."
❖ Groups or private parties sometimes book the entire B&B.
♦ Travel agents' commission paid. (Please see page xii.)
✖ Sorry, no guests' pets are allowed.
✌ No smoking inside *or* no smoking at all, even on porches.

Townry Farm

413/443-9285

Greylock Road, Lanesborough, MA 01237-0155

Hosts: Barbara and Cliff Feakes
Location: Rural. Just off Route 7 between Pittsfield and Williamstown, on a well maintained road. At the base of Mount Greylock State Reservation, which surrounds the highest peak in Massachusetts. Three miles to Brodie Mountain, four to Jiminy Peak; close to cross-country ski areas. Twenty minutes to Tanglewood.
Open: Year round except Thanksgiving and Christmas Day. Two-day minimum on weekends during Tanglewood season.
Rates: $40 single, $45 double. $15 third person in room.

> From Massachusetts: *"Delightful hosts . . . immaculate rooms . . . comfortable, homey, peaceful . . . perfected muffins loaded with plump, juicy berries. . . . Tell guests to bring a cooler if they want to buy lamb."*

It may seem like a long way from the women's apparel business to a working farm, but as Barb and Cliff say, "Everyone wants to move to the Berkshires and live our lifestyle." Since coming here 20 years ago, the Feakeses have established a breeding sheep flock, currently with 100 Dorset and crossbred ewes plus varying numbers of growing lambs. In starting B&B as the children grew older and left, Barb drew on hotel experience that began when she was 15 years old. There's more! The thriving baking business includes Cliff's fudge and a mail order arrangement. And this B&B is the source of the ultimate networking anecdote: One daughter, now a restaurant owner, got her first fabulous job through a B&B guest. For their own vacations Cliff, the official shearer, and Barb usually hike and travel by train in Switzerland, sometimes in a group where they are the only Americans. They return to welcome many Europeans on the farm.

In residence: Two Labradors, one yellow and one black.
Foreign language spoken: Some French.
Bed and bath: Three first-floor rooms (with 18-inch-wide floorboards) share one full bath. One room has a double bed, the other two have both a double and a single bed.
Breakfast: It's work time on the farm. The dining room table is set with lace tablecloth and fine china and a self-serve continental breakfast with Barbara's own breads—blueberry crunch, cranberry, peach, or maybe Irish soda.
Plus: Guest den with color TV. Coffee/tea always available. Bedroom fans. Tour of farm. Bread-making demonstrations. A suggestion for "the bargain of the century, the Clark Art Institute in Williamstown." In nearby state reservation—hiking trails, blueberry picking, hunting in legal season, and cross-country skiing.

Unless otherwise stated, rates in this book are per room for two and include breakfast in addition to all the amenities in "Plus." As for taxes and gratuities, please see page xii.

Brook Farm Inn
413/637-3013
15 Hawthorne Street, Lenox, MA 01240

Hosts: Bob and Betty Jacob
Location: In a quiet glen with gardens. Three-tenths of a mile from Lenox center.
Open: Year round. Reservations required during Tanglewood season. Three-day minimum, July and August weekends; two-day minimum, October weekends.

Rates: Vary according to amenities. Double occupancy. July–September 6, $95–$155; September 7–30 and November–June, $55–$95; October, $85–$120. Holiday weekends $85–$100. Weekday and weekly rates available. $20 extra person in room. MC, VISA.
♥ ⁂ ✈ ✄

When we visited during a National Trust for Historic Preservation conference, we heard how experienced innkeepers had suggested to the Jacobs that "poetry won't work." Half a dozen years later, Bob and Betty (grandparents of nine now) often hear about the impact—"total relaxation"—of their Saturday afternoon poetry readings, the specialty of the inn.

Honored Tanglewood performers stay here. And so do poets (as guests of the innkeepers), honeymooners, and many who haven't thought about poetry since school days. They enjoy the ambiance of the century-old home filled with artworks, framed old posters, and turn-of-the-century programs. Among the antiques is a podium that holds the "poem of the day" and a table with a jigsaw puzzle. Regularly, Bob, a former sales executive, reads poetry in area nursing homes. And it's all because he and Betty, who was a member of the English faculty of the University of Hartford, attended an innkeeping seminar and found their new career in 1986.

Bed and bath: Twelve rooms, some with beams, skylights, canopied beds. All private baths (some shower only without tub). One first-floor room with two twin beds and working fireplace. Six second-floor rooms; five with queen beds, one with a double bed; four have working fireplaces. Five air-conditioned rooms on third floor; two with two twin beds, two with double beds, and one queen-bedded room with two twin beds.
Breakfast: 8–10. Buffet. Fruits, freshly squeezed orange juice, homemade granola, yogurt, cold cereals, homemade muffins, sticky buns, bagels, cream cheese. Served in breakfast room overlooking grounds. Music played.
Plus: Sherry on arrival. Heated outdoor swimming pool. Tea with homemade scones. English soaps. Bedroom window fans. Picnic tables. Shaded seating in garden. Poetry tapes for use during a scenic mountain drive. Over 1,500 books; if you start one, borrow it till finished.

From New York: *"Cordial, warm, friendly hosts. Beautifully furnished. Made me feel as if I stepped back in time. Great location. It's a must!"*

---

*A*ccording to many hosts:
"Guests come with plans and discover the joys of hammock sitting."

The Gables Inn   413/637-3416

103 Walker Street (Route 183), Lenox, MA 01240

Hosts: Mary and Frank Newton
Location: In the village center, one mile from Tanglewood.
Open: Year round. Three-night minimum in July and August. Two-night minimum in October and on holiday weekends.

Rates: Vary according to room size, amenities, time of year, weekday or weekend. Double occupancy, $60–$140. Suite (summer only) $175. $20 additional person.
♥ ♣ ✗

"Young man, I see you have kept the Whartons' red damask wallpaper," said the 82-year-old Lenox resident while visiting with Frank Newton in the former home of Edith Wharton, the Pulitzer Prize-winning writer.

For their eighth house restoration (six were Manhattan brownstones done while they lived in them), the Newtons, both former bankers, took on this elegant Queen Anne-style Berkshire Cottage built in the Gilded Age of 1885. In addition to hanging fresh red damask wallpaper, they restored the eight-sided library (which had become a restaurant with bar) and added a tennis court and a greenhouse with solar-heated 40-foot pool (I loved the prebreakfast swim) and Jacuzzi. Most recent additions are two 500-square-foot suites: "The Teddy Wharton Suite is very masculine with leather furniture; Edith Wharton Suite is feminine and flowery." The Presidents' Room is complete with a collection that delights history buffs. The Show Business guest room has signed photos (plenty of nostalgia) and an extensive library. Throughout, there are period furnishings and examples of Mary Newton's painting, pierced lampshades, and quilting.

Innkeeping also allows Frank to do other things that he likes to do: write and produce shows and recordings; play piano; lecture on restoration and period style; and, as president of the Lenox Chamber of Commerce, create even more area cultural events. More than one of his Manhattan friends has been drawn to this lifestyle.

In residence: Son Andrew is 17. "'Cat' is a quiet friendly pet."
Foreign language spoken: Spanish.
Bed and bath: Sixteen air-conditioned rooms on three floors, all with private baths. Six have working fireplaces. Some have canopied beds. Rollaway available.
Breakfast: 8–10. Fruit, juice, homemade bread and pastry, coffee, tea. Cereal in the summer. In dining room at tables for 2, 4, or 20.
Plus: Afternoon or evening wine. Lounge chairs in quiet garden.

---

*One out of five guests leaves with
the dream of opening a B&B.*

Garden Gables Inn   413/637-0193

141 Main Street, P.O. Box 52, Lenox, MA 01240

Hosts: Mario and Lynn Mekinda

Location: In historic district of village. Set back from the main road on five wooded acres with gardens, fruit trees, and huge old pines and maples. One mile from Tanglewood.

Open: Year round. Three-night minimum on weekends July–August; two-night minimum weekends June and September–October.

Rates: Double occupancy. Late June–Labor Day and late September–October—weekends $90 (double bed, smaller room) to $160 (king four-poster, whirlpool bath, porch), most rooms $130–$140; weekdays $75–$110. Mid-September and winter months—weekends $70–$110, weekdays $65–$100. MC, VISA.

♥ ⁂ ✈

It's home. It has white clapboards and green shutters. The gabled part with low ceilings was built in 1780. Subsequent additions were made to the private estate, which was an inn for 35 years before the Mekindas bought it in 1988.

"A tinkerer," Mario says he is. Every old-house owner would appreciate a Mario-in-residence. The results of his efforts include fresh, inviting rooms, tile baths, a homelike atmosphere. There are books, fireplaces, comfortable sofas, a piano, English antiques, Dutch and English 18th-century watercolors, and early American furniture. On the spacious grounds, there's a picket fence, gardens, that long in-ground pool with umbrella tables on the deck, and many trees.

In Canada Mario was a professional engineer. Lynn worked in public relations. Here Lynn writes and is active with the historical society; Mario is active with several arts organizations. Five years and many returnees later, they know they made the right career change.

In residence: Two teenagers, Emma and Jonathan. Also, two nameless 12-year-old turtles.

Foreign languages spoken: French and German.

Bed and bath: Twelve cozy rooms on first and second floors. King bed (one is canopied, Jacuzzi bath), queen, double, or twins. All private baths. Rollaway available.

Breakfast: 8–10. Buffet. Homemade bran and blueberry muffins, cantaloupe and native berries, farm-fresh eggs, healthy cereals, cheese-filled crumb cakes, yogurts, croissants. Served in dining room overlooking gardens and pool.

Plus: Individual thermostats. Bedroom window fans. Some rooms with desk and phone jack. Guest refrigerator. Late-afternoon wine or tea. Down comforters. Flannel sheets. Beach towels. Games. Radio/tape deck. Fresh flowers. Mints on pillow.

---

*H*ospitality is the keynote of B&B.

Rookwood Inn   413/637-9750

19 Old Stockbridge Road, P.O. Box 1717, Lenox, MA 01240

Hosts: Tom and Betsy Sherman
Location: On a quiet road, half a block from town center, dining, shopping. A mile from Tanglewood. Twenty minutes to five major ski areas, golf, hiking.
Open: Year round. Three-night minimum on summer weekends.
Rates: Double occupancy. June 30– Labor Day: Thursday–Monday $90– $175; Tuesday–Wednesday $75–$110.
September and June: Friday and Saturday $60–$120; Sunday–Thursday $55–$110. Late September–October: Friday and Saturday $90–$160; Sunday–Thursday $65–$110. November–May: Friday–Saturday $60– $110; Sunday–Thursday $65–$85. Holidays $80–$130. Singles $10 less. AMEX.

♥ ♨ ❀ ♦ ✕ ✂

Here it is, the answer to those who have said that Rookwood—"the place run by the wonderful couple who have made fantastic changes"—belongs in this book.

Those changes, a complete restoration done with dedication, were done to the oldest building (the back part, at least) in town. Now it's the kind of place where guests relax enough to ask "What day is it?" The 1886 summer "cottage," built onto an 1820 colonial structure, is decorated with Oriental rugs, antiques the Shermans bought in England, "comfortable-not-high-Victorian" American pieces, and period wallcoverings.

Betsy, a nurse, always wanted to become an innkeeper. Shortly after she and Tom, an investment advisor with a major stock brokerage firm, moved from Boston to the Berkshires, they bought the classic inn. They renamed it after an eclectic kind of Victorian pottery and made many renovations, including giving their "painted lady" an historically accurate coat of exterior paint. Today, Tom says, "We both enjoy this great place, which is home for our family and our guests."

In residence: Brooks, five, and Hannah, three.
Foreign language spoken: "A small amount of Spanish."
Bed and bath: Fifteen air-conditioned rooms on second and third floors. Ceiling fans and individual thermostats. Some rooms with working fireplace and/or private balcony. All private baths. Queen, double, and twin beds available. Some four-posters, some canopied. Rollaway and crib available.
Breakfast: 8–9:30 or 10. Buffet of homemade muffins, eggs, cereal, fresh fruit, cheese, juice, yogurt, coffee, and milk. In fireplaced dining room at individual tables.
Plus: Verandas with striped awnings. Screened porch. Lawn for lounging or picnicking. Fireplaced living room. Late-afternoon tea with cookies or cakes; lemonade in the summer. Down comforters. Formal gardens. Transportation to and from bus stop.

Walker House   413/637-1271

74 Walker Street, Lenox, MA 01240-2718

Hosts: Peggy and Richard Houdek
Location: On a main street. Set on three gorgeous acres. Within walking distance of shops and restaurants. Buses from New York and Boston stop a block away. Within one mile of cross-country skiing. Within 25 minutes of Brodie, Jiminy Peak, and Butternut mountains.
Open: Year round. Three-night minimum on July, August, and all holiday weekends.

Rates: Late June–Labor Day $95 or $140 weekends (Thursday–Sunday), $70–$90 Monday–Wednesday. Early September $70–$90 Friday and Saturday, $50–$70 Sunday–Thursday. Late September–October $95 small room, $125 larger, $135 with fireplace. November–late June $70–$90 weekends, $50–$70 Sunday–Thursday.
♥ ✲ ⅄

They were a successful arts-oriented couple living in a Spanish-style house on a southern California hill and looking for adventure. Once the Houdeks decided on the Berkshires, they set out to establish a B&B that would give them the feeling of having some friends visit for a few days. And it has been that way—"an ongoing open house"—since 1980. It is the sought-after change from when Peggy was managing editor of *Peforming Arts* magazine. Dick was director of public affairs at the California Institute of the Arts, a *Los Angeles Times* contributing critic, and a Long Beach Opera consultant. Now his observations—everything from town meetings to spelling bees—appear in a weekly Berkshires newspaper column.

The art- and antiques-furnished 1804 house, once the house of the headmaster of the Lenox School (disbanded in the early 1970s), is one of the last remaining examples of Federal architecture in Lenox. Each spacious guest room is quite different and, always, subject to change. "Whenever we have a request, we feature good films, operas, plays, concerts, and TV shows on a 100-inch (7 by 5.5 feet) screen in the Library Video Theatre." (Curtains to come someday.)

In residence: Six friendly but unobtrusive cats.
Foreign languages spoken: French and Spanish.
Bed and bath: Eight rooms, each with private bath (two are shower only) and radio. Bed sizes include one or two doubles, two twins, or queen. Five rooms have working fireplaces; one also has a private veranda.
Breakfast: 8–10. Juice, fresh fruit (baked in winter), several kinds of muffins and biscuits, cold cereals, beverages. Served around large oak dining room tables (displacing huge seated stuffed animals) or on wide plant-filled veranda overlooking acreage.
Plus: Tea at 4. Parlor grand piano for professional performance; for an impromptu one by guest; or, occasionally, for accompanying Peggy, a trained singer. Old-time radio cassette library. Guest refrigerator. Large lawn for picnics. Ten bicycles. English soaps. Special winter theme weekends.

Staveleigh House   413/229-2129

South Main Street, Route 7, Sheffield, MA 01257-0608

Hosts: Dorothy Marosy and Marion Whitman
Location: Set back from the road. Next to the town green in National Historic District of village that has a wildlife preserve, 30 antiques shops, and state's oldest covered bridge. Tanglewood, museums, hiking, and skiing all within 30 minutes; Housatonic River canoeing one mile away.

Open: Year round. Two-night minimum weekends July–October. Three-night minimum on holiday weekends.
Rates: June–October and holiday weekends, $85 queen bed, private bath. $75 twins/king or double bed. Singles $5 less. Off-season, queen room is $10 less, others $5 less.
♥ ❖ ✈

> From Connecticut: *"Marion and Dorothy know how to make you feel at home but like a guest . . . know the best scenic roads to walk or bike, where to shop for antiques or fabrics. . . . The rooms are all charming and decorated with so many handmade items."* From Pennsylvania: *"We are antiques dealers who have used your book numerous times . . . this is the best bed and breakfast in your book . . . two active, intelligent, and talented women who convey the joy of life to their guests . . . possess that rare ability of balancing socialization and privacy. . . . Fruit is served artistically, i.e. nectarine wedges encircle mint leaves, sliced cantaloupe is adorned with dew-wet violets. The main course might be a new recipe recommended by a former guest."*

Many Staveleigh House devotees return for crafts workshops such as rug hooking, quilting, or cross-stitching.

Since arriving in 1983 from New Jersey—where Dorothy was a teacher and Marion worked in business—the innkeepers have become well versed in the history of the 1821 house (originally a parsonage), which they have completely redone. For accents they have decorated with Marion's quilts and samplers and Dorothy's hooked rugs and needlepoint.

In residence: Two cats, Tiffy, a gorgeous Himalayan, and Lucy, a sociable domestic shorthair.
Bed and bath: Five rooms. On first floor, room with twins/king option and one with a double bed, each with private entrance, share a full bath. Upstairs, a twin-bedded room with view of the green and one with antique double brass bed share a full bath. Private full bath for room with queen bed, wicker furnishings.
Breakfast: 8–9. Maybe crepes or puffed apple pancakes, meat, juice, fresh fruit, homemade muffins and breads, coffee, tea. In dining room (by candlelight on cloudy days).
Plus: Afternoon tea. Potpourri from perennial and herb gardens. Books and games in library. Deck and garden furniture. Sherry. Murder mystery weekends.

---

*T*hink of bed and breakfast as a people-to-people concept.

Historic Merrell Tavern Inn   413/243-1794

Route 102, Main Street, South Lee, MA 01260-0318

Hosts: Charles and Faith Reynolds
Location: On main street in small village. One mile from Norman Rockwell's Stockbridge, three miles from I-90 Lee exit. Five miles to Tanglewood. Ten minutes to ski areas (with snowmaking).
Open: Year round. Two- or three-night minimum July–August weekends.
Rates: $65–$75 per room. $20 more for fireplaced room; $30–$50 more on summer and fall weekends. $15 third person. MC, VISA.
♥ ♠ ✿ ✈

> From Connecticut: *"Captures the feeling of the 19th century while more than satisfying the expectations of 20th-century travelers by anticipating all of their needs."*

Authenticity, charm, and old-fashioned hospitality are evident from the moment you sign in at the only surviving circular colonial bar in America. The grandfather clock in the central hallway dates from the late 1700s, when the building was constructed. Authentic colors, researched by Faith and Charles, are a background for their period Hepplewhite and Sheraton furniture collected over 25 years. The inn is on the National Register of Historic Places and is under historic covenant with the Society for the Preservation of New England Antiquities.

Once a stagecoach stop, over time the inn has seen changes that include guest rooms made from an elegant front parlor and a third-floor ballroom. The original keeping room with cooking fireplace and beehive oven has been made into a guest parlor. The work of the innkeepers, two former Rochester, New York, teachers, was recognized when they received the 1982 Massachusetts Historical Society Preservation Award.

In residence: A cat named Patches. Brandy is a golden retriever.
Bed and bath: Ten air-conditioned rooms on three floors. All with private shower baths (one has tub) and wing chairs or Chippendale sofas. Four rooms have fireplaces. Bed sizes are queen, double, twins, or double and twins; most are canopied. Cribs and cots available.
Breakfast: 8:30–10. Juice, hot beverage. Cereal, ham or cheese omelets, or sausage with French toast or blueberry pancakes. Served in original fireplaced Tavern Room with 1817 birdcage bar.
Plus: Grounds with old stone walls, English garden, two acres of lawns to banks of Housatonic River. Guest refrigerator.

Looking for a B&B with a crib? Find a description with the ♠ symbol and then check under the "bed and bath" section.

The Golden Goose   413/243-3008

Box 336, Main Road, Tyringham, MA 01264-0336

Hosts: Lilja and Joseph Rizzo
Location: Quiet. In the town center, "protected from—though so near to—all the Berkshires have to offer." Just across from steep and beautiful Tyringham Cobble (for hiking) and Hop Brook (with trout fishing). Six miles from Stockbridge; eight from Lenox.
Open: Year round. Two-night minimum July–August weekends; three-night minimum on holidays.

Rates: Double occupancy. June–November, $70 semiprivate bath; $80 and $85 double bed, private bath; $95 twin beds, private bath; $110 studio. December–May, $10 less. January–March, two-night stays 10 percent less, 15 percent less for studio. $5 single-night surcharge. AMEX.
♥ ❖ 🐾

"Now that we have completed work on our music room, we'd love to encourage guests to bring instruments for after-breakfast music sessions."

The Rizzos' warm welcome begins with the front-porch flags on the 200-year-old white colonial farmhouse: "Swedish (for me); the state flag; the 13-star American flag; and the Italian for New York-born Joe, who left his engineering management position for innkeeping/groundskeeping and, when time permits, some cello study. I am a Californian whose checkered career includes public relations, multimedia production, and Victorian antique furniture in Manhattan. (My struggles with violin continue with frustration and joy.)"

Since the Rizzos opened nine years ago, wide plank floors have been refinished. Beveled-glass French doors now lead to the deck. Antiques are everywhere. The hosts' suggestions include restaurants, a music-stand craftsperson, and a spectacular cycling route.

Guests wrote: *"A bit of the old country. . . . Casual. . . . Authenticity, charm, warmth. . . . A little spot of Eden along the Appalachian Trail."*

In residence: Bubula, "our sometimes-entertaining cat."
Bed and bath: Six second-floor rooms (up a steep, narrow staircase). One large room with two twins/king bed, small sitting area, private full bath; "we call it the minisuite." Five double-bedded rooms; three have private full baths, two share a full bath. An extra shower bath available at foot of stairs. In studio apartment, queen bed, double sleep sofa, kitchen, private entrance and bath.
Breakfast: 8–9:30. "Sometimes extended 'til noon!" Homemade biscuits, cranberry or banana bread, homemade jams, marmalade, and applesauce. Fresh fruit. Cereals. Juice, teas, and coffee.
Plus: Hot or cold apple cider, tea, or wine with hors d'oeuvres. Two fireplaced common rooms. Bedroom table fans. Guest refrigerator in barn. Barbecue. Croquet, volleyball, and badminton sets. Swimming pond nearby. Guests' pets allowed December–May only.

B&Bs offer the ultimate concierge service.

The American Country Collection Host #029
Williamstown, MA

Location: A 600-acre dairy farm; three-state view from upper part of farm. On a secondary state road. Two miles from Williamstown center. One hour to Tanglewood, 15 minutes to Brodie and Jiminy Peak ski areas.

Reservations: Year round through The American Country Collection, page 335. Two-night minimum on summer weekends and in foliage season.
Rates: $45 per room. $5 portacrib.
✖ ⅙

"We're two of the few natives," the hostess will tell you. Her husband, born in this house, has seen many changes in the dairying business, especially since the boyhood days when he milked six cows before going to school. Still a family operation, with three grown sons and one grandson helping, it is also a tree farm. (Cut Christmas trees are sold right here.) And for something really different, you might walk the 17-bluebird-house trail.

Both host and hostess are community volunteers extraordinaire, putting much effort into issues of land development, conservation, and preservation. They have refinished several antiques for their comfortable, cheery, and welcoming home away from home.

In residence: A friendly golden Labrador. Barn cats.
Bed and bath: Two cozy second-floor paneled rooms share a full bath plus a downstairs half bath. One has double bed, the other has two twin beds. Portacrib only, not a full-size crib, available.
Breakfast: 8–9. Orange juice, fresh fruit, homemade muffins and breads, homemade jellies and jams. Coffee, tea, real cream. Served on antique china in dining room or on wicker- and plant-filled front porch.
Plus: Garden flowers. Tea, lemonade. Bedroom window fans. Piano in den. Books. Magazines. Color TV in living room. Tour of farm. Swimming and fishing in a man-made pond. Make-your-own cross-country ski trails through open fields and wooded areas.

Steep Acres Farm B&B   413/458-3774
520 White Oaks Road, Williamstown, MA 01267-2227

Hosts: Mary and Marvin Gangemi
Location: High on a hill with panoramic views of New York, Vermont, and Massachusetts. Two miles from Clark Art Museum and Williamstown Summer Theatre. Adjacent to the Appalachian and Long trails.

Forty minutes to Tanglewood. Many downhill ski areas within a 20-mile radius.
Open: Year round.
Rates: $40 single, $60 double. $20 cot or crib.
♥ ⊶ ✖ ⅙

"Our guests love the pond. They explore the 50 wonderful acres. The apple, cherry, peach, pear, and nut trees are flourishing. We no longer have cows or sheep and I don't churn butter any more, but there are turkeys, chickens, ducks, and pigs. And the bountiful gardens get a boost from the greenhouse.

(Please turn page.)

And yes, B&B is a grand fit because we have the room and have found that every guest has been wonderful."

The Gangemis bought this great site with house and three barns after they sold the summer camp where their six kids were first campers and then staff. Son Daniel, a professional landscaper, the only grown child who lives on the property, helps to keep things going. Marvin, the beekeeper, is a teacher. Mary, the creative chef, is a nurse.

In residence: Two dogs plus. (They breed Labrador retrievers.)
Bed and bath: Four rooms with antique beds share two full baths and a half bath. Two double-bedded rooms, one with single bed, one with two twins.
Breakfast: Full. Varies. "Today's menu started with a half pineapple (per person), sliced bananas, and strawberry garnish. Oatmeal blackberry pancakes are this year's hit. Sometimes I make a Mexican egg dish or breakfast puffs." Plus homemade muffins and breads. Eat by the fireplace in dining room in winter or on the screened porch with its tri-state view in summer.
Plus: Ceiling fans on porch and in upstairs hall. Use of canoe, rowboat, and raft with diving board on the pond. Five kilometers of hiking and cross-country ski trails.

Windfields Farm   413/684-3786
154 Windsor Bush Road, Windsor, MA
Mailing address: RR 1, Box 170, Cummington, MA 01026-9301

Hosts: Carolyn and Arnold Westwood
Location: On dirt road. From West Cummington off Route 9, two miles uphill (winter guests should have snow tires!). Twenty miles west of Pittsfield; 25 miles east to Northampton. Six miles to Notchview (cross-country skiing); 40 minutes to Tanglewood.

Open: May–February. Two-night minimum on most weekends. Reservations required.
Rates: $45 single, $60 double. $15 cot. Special winter weekends, $250 for two couples includes two nights, two breakfasts, and your own kitchen.
♥ 🖊 ❀ ✖ ✂

Just thinking about this B&B makes me feel good all over. The interesting house is a haven, way up and away, with scenic surroundings—but in true B&B style, the hosts make the difference.

Arnold, retired as a Unitarian Universalist minister, now edits the town (pop. 600) newsletter and founded the town land trust. With the help of his youngest (then college-age) son, he built most of the solar addition, the Westwoods' part of the residence. The maple syrup—500 taps, sugarhouse, and mail order—is Carolyn's responsibility. Vegetables from her organic garden win prizes at regional fairs, as do her flowers, bread, pies, syrup ("first prize in 1991 after trying since 1975!"), and jam. Their 200-acre homestead borders an Audubon sanctuary, part of which was donated by the Westwoods, hosts who are concerned with conservation, building community spirit, and ending the arms race.

Carolyn refers to "living in a sculpture," a summer retreat—"a mess" purchased in 1962—that became, after 10 years of family work, a year-round "joyous house." The active/passive solar addition retains parts of the original c. 1815 cottage. The connecting (c. 1830) farmhouse is now reserved for guests, who have their own private entrance and living and dining rooms. Furnishings include many family antiques, carved pieces done by both Arnold's and Carolyn's mothers, and paintings done by artists the Westwoods know.

In residence: On the Westwood settlement—"Hui, an Irish golden, and Pushamet, a four-way mix, are often within call of the megaphone to act as B&B guide dogs."

Bed and bath: Two spacious corner bedrooms, "your castle as long as you're here." One with 1818 canopied double bed that belonged to Carolyn's great-great-great-grandmother. Queen walnut bed in other. Shared full bath with old-time barber's sink and claw-foot tub with shower.

Breakfast: 7:30–9. "Announced to strains of Mozart and Bach." Homegrown organic produce, berries, eggs. Pancakes, yogurt, maybe Irish oatmeal topped with granola, natural-grain homemade muffins or popovers, Windfields' low-sugar jams. Served in guests' dining room.

Plus: Bedroom fans. Cross-country skiing and hiking trails (with blueberries for picking). Spring-fed swimming pond with sandy beach. A short walk to waterfall in the state forest. Beverages. Piano, hi-fi, fireplace, extensive library. Sun-dried towels.

From New York: *"The world's most effective therapy for urban stress."*

KEY TO SYMBOLS
- ♥ Lots of honeymooners come here.
- ⚕ Families with children are very welcome. (Please see page xiii.)
- ⬤ "Please emphasize that we are a private home, not an inn."
- ♣ Groups or private parties sometimes book the entire B&B.
- ◆ Travel agents' commission paid. (Please see page xii.)
- ✗ Sorry, no guests' pets are allowed.
- ⌇ No smoking inside *or* no smoking at all, even on porches.

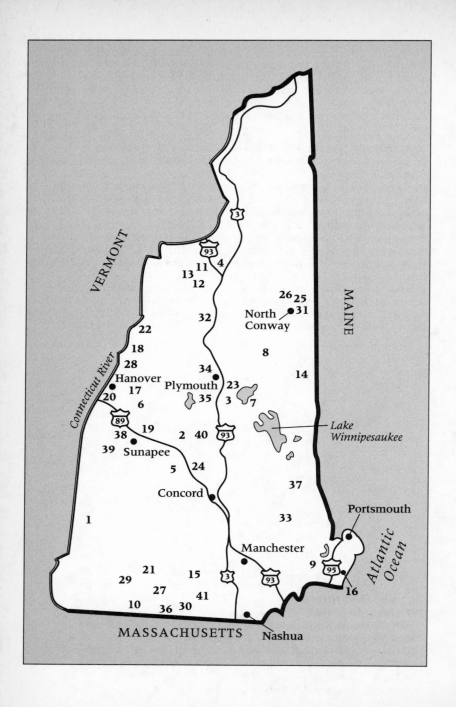

VERMONT

3

93

4

11
13
12

32

26 25
31
North
Conway

8

22

18
28

34
Hanover
Plymouth   23
17   35
20   6   3
89   7
19
38   2   40   93
39   Sunapee

5   24

Concord

1

21
29
27
10   36   30   15   41

MAINE

14

Lake
Winnipesaukee

37

33

Manchester

9

Portsmouth

95

16

Atlantic
Ocean

Connecticut River

3   93

MASSACHUSETTS   Nashua

NEW HAMPSHIRE

KEY TO SYMBOLS
♥ Lots of honeymooners come here.
♣ Families with children are very welcome. (Please see page xiii.)
♦ "Please emphasize that we are a private home, not an inn."
♣ Groups or private parties sometimes book the entire B&B.
♦ Travel agents' commission paid. (Please see page xii.)
✗ Sorry, no guests' pets are allowed.
✗ No smoking inside *or* no smoking at all, even on porches.

New Hampshire
_____ Reservation Services _____

Bed & Breakfast/Inns of New England
P.O. Box 6351, Hamden, CT 06517

Phone: 603/279-8348, daily 9 a.m.–8 p.m.

Listings: 100+ B&Bs and inns. Located throughout the state (and New England) in and around cities and towns. Included are hosted private residences and small inns—restored colonials, farms, and lakefront and mountain-view homes. Directory ($1).

Reservations: Two-day minimum on holiday weekends. Available through travel agents. Short-term (one month plus) hosted housing available.

Rates: $35–$65 single. $45–$85 double. Weekly rates available. Deposit required is first night's rate plus tax or 50 percent of multinight reservation. If cancellation is received seven days before expected arrival, refund made, less $15 service fee. ◆

Ernie Taddei, an experienced innkeeper, has a growing list of hosts who believe in "the friendly way to travel." When he became owner/director of this personalized New Hampshire–oriented reservation service in 1990, he added listings in the five other New England states. Some hosts offer cross-country skiing, tennis courts, and swimming pools on the premises.

Other reservation services with some B&Bs in New Hampshire:
Pineapple Hospitality, page 106.

From the country: "Rural living is great. Did I tell you about the night the cows came? A farmer neighbor up the road had left a gate unlatched. About 10 p.m. I had 22 Holsteins and one bull milling around the back yard, peering in the windows, mooing and munching! The guests loved it. (The garden didn't.)"

New Hampshire B&Bs

Darby Brook Farm   603/835-6624

Hill Road, Alstead, NH 03602

Host: Howard C. Weeks
Location: Rural. On a town road, 2
miles from the village. Six miles west
of Connecticut River valley, 15 miles
north of Keene.

Open: May–October.
Rates: $25 per person.

Authentic. A classic 18th-century Georgian house. Discovered by relatives
and friends of area residents who sometimes say that it is a bit like being in a
museum. Every room except the kitchen has raised paneling. Moldings are
beveled. There's stenciling. And beams. Other than plumbing and electricity
and one kitchen window, everything is original. Where the wide floorboards
(mostly painted) have been scuffed by boots, knots are exposed. The 19th-
century furnishings were put in place when Howard's parents bought this
house in 1929. A few newer pieces were made by Howard, who was a
furniture designer in New York. Since 1980 he has become a farmer, with
sheep and chickens, a vegetable garden, apple orchard, berry bushes, and
some maple trees (for syrup). He takes his produce to the Keene farmers'
market. He directs guests to antiques shops, scenic roads, and the local lake.
In the winter he is a cabinetmaker and lives in the house next door.

In residence: Queenie, the dog. Barney, the cat.
Bed and bath: Three rooms share one large full bath. One with two twin
four-poster beds, working fireplace. One with half-canopied double bed,
working fireplace. One room with a twin four-poster. Rollaway and crib
available.
Breakfast: "Anything you wish." Cereal, fruit juice, bacon and eggs, muffins,
toast, coffee. Howard joins guests.
Plus: Fireplaced living and dining rooms, a treat in the fall. Tea or soft drinks.
Beverages. Down comforters. Fresh flowers.

The English House   603/735-5987

P.O. Box 162, Main Street, Andover, NH 03216-0162

Hosts: Ken and Gillian Smith
Location: In village center with Ragged Mountains behind, Mount
Kearsage view in front. Next to Proctor Academy. Within 15 minutes of
King Ridge, Ragged Mountain, Norsk
Cross-Country Ski Center; 20 minutes to Mount Sunapee. Near fishing,
golf, water sports.

Open: Year round, except late
March. Reservations advised. Two-
night minimum on foliage, holiday,
and special school weekends.
Rates: $50 single. $75 double. $20
extra person. MC, VISA.

> From Connecticut: *"A successful combination of old-world innkeeping with attention to detail and warm American hospitality . . . privacy in (well-insulated) rooms . . . beautifully renovated dwelling. . . . Breakfast is sumptuous."*

What was a big old unoccupied and neglected house has gone through a metamorphosis, thanks to Ken, a retired British army officer, and Gillian, a needlecrafter (featured in *Quilt* magazine) who enjoys her adjacent carriage house studio. The maple, birch, and oak woodwork is no longer black. Now there are Oriental and other area rugs, rocking chairs, plants everywhere, and traditional prints, all giving the feeling—embellished by afternoon tea—of an English country house.

Foreign languages spoken: Simple French and German.
Bed and bath: Seven rooms, each with private shower bath. One on first floor with two twin beds. On second floor, three with queen and one with two twins. Two large third-floor rooms, each with a queen and a twin bed. Rollaways available.
Breakfast: Usually 8:30, earlier by request. All homemade. Breads, rolls, muffins, jams, jellies, marmalades, yogurt, granola. Entree repertoire includes whole-meal pancakes with homemade sausage patties, honey pecan sauce; elaborate omelets; or kedgeree with smoked fish and rice. Fresh fruit.
Plus: Rear deck accessible from guest sitting room. Heated ski storage and waxing area. No cigars or pipes, please.

Glynn House *"Victorian" Inn*

603/968-3775
800/637-9599
fax 603/968-9338

43 Highland Street, P.O. Box 819
Ashland, NH 03217-0819

Hosts: Betsy and Karol Paterman
Location: Residential; two-minute walk from the village. In the Golden Pond area; two-minute drive to Squam Lake swimming; within 30 minutes of Waterville, Loon, and Tenney mountains. One mile from I-93. Ten minutes to Plymouth State College and Holderness School.
Open: Year round.
Rates: $75 double occupancy. $10 less Monday–Thursday. $10 third person. MC, VISA.
♥ ❖ ♦ ✗

From the turret to the oak foyer, from the square piano (bought at auction from an area historical society) to ornately patterned wallpaper, Victoriana is the theme at this B&B restored and opened in 1989. The hosts, former restauranteurs, are auction buffs and know which auctioneer specializes in furniture, Depression glass, or porcelain. They have this week's auction schedule (and a story about last week's find)—as well as books and magazines about antiques. They'll direct you to fine restaurants and the rolling waters of the Basin, their favorite scenic spot. Karol, the chef/plumber/electrician/gardener, enjoys his role as full-time host. Betsy is regional sales manager for a food company.

In residence: In hosts' quarters, Gracie, age nine; Christopher, age three. One cat, Frisky.
Foreign languages spoken: Polish and Russian.

(Please turn page.)

Bed and bath: Four second-floor rooms, all with new private baths. Bridal suite with queen canopied bed, Jacuzzi/shower bath. Room with double bed, fireplace, shower bath. One room with double bed, air conditioner, tub and shower bath. One room with queen and a single bed, air conditioner, desk, phone jack, cable TV.
Breakfast: Usually at 9 (coffee and tea an hour earlier). Whim-of-chef menu. Belgian waffles, thick French toast, or eggs Benedict. Maybe muffins or apple strudel.
Plus: Beverage. Fruit basket. Fresh flowers. Mints and souvenir photo of room on pillow.

The Bells   603/869-2647

Strawberry Hill Street, P.O. Box 276, Bethlehem, NH 03574-0276

Hosts: Bill and Louise Sims
Location: On a quiet village street. Surrounded by stone walks and perennial gardens. One-half block off Route 302. Walk to golf, tennis, cross-country skiing, antiques shops, restaurants; 15-minute drive to Cannon Mountain and Bretton Woods ski areas, Mount Washington, and Franconia Notch State Park.
Open: Year round. Two-night minimum during foliage weekends and holidays.
Rates: Double occupancy. $60–$80. $15 extra person. AMEX, MC, VISA.
♥ ❖ ♦ ✈

National Geographic Traveler magazine featured it on a cover. Many guests, including my son, have declared this B&B "perfect." Recent guests concur.

> From Canada: *"Feels as though you stepped into a time machine . . . a period where charm and hospitality reign supreme . . . an antique music box in the living room; everywhere, objects of interest . . . delicious breakfast, artistically arranged . . . warm, humorous, helpful hosts."*

The Victorian summer cottage, which includes bells hanging from the pagoda-shaped roof, was built in 1892. It has been unoccupied for 10 years when the Sims bought it in 1985. Bill, a contract engineer, is responsible for much of the revitalization. Furnishings include lifetime collections and family heirlooms, comfortable furniture, and some whimsy too. Louise is a painter, quilter, and former grants writer who also worked in public relations and marketing in New York and Tennessee.

Bed and bath: Four suites, private baths. Two on second floor, each with full bath, sitting room; one with twin beds, one with queen. Honeymoon cupola treetop suite—third-floor bath with footed tub, open stairway to treetop double bedroom. Summer guest house with twin beds, shower bath, screened porch.
Breakfast: 7–9. Could be corn fritters, sausage and wild rice casserole, or blueberry oatmeal pancakes. Fruit bowl, juice, homemade breads. Special diets accommodated.
Plus: All bedrooms have TV, radio, ceiling fan, and individual heat control. Afternoon refreshments. Wraparound veranda with hammock, original rockers. Refrigerator space. Hose for washing cars.

Mountain Lake Inn

603/938-2136
800/662-6005

P.O. Box 443, Route 114, Bradford, NH 03221

Hosts: Carol and Phil Fullerton
Location: On 165 acres of lawns, woods, trails, streams, waterfalls. Within 15 minutes of Pat's Peak, Sunapee, King Ridge. Near Indian Museum and antiquarian bookstores.
Open: Year round, except April and part of November. Two- night mini-

mum on holiday weekends and in fall.
Rates: Double occupancy, $85. $25 third person. $70 single. $110 family room based on quad occupancy. Discover, MC, VISA.
♥ ♯ ✿ ♦ ✕

A good old-fashioned inn with pine-paneled living room and a screened front porch facing the lake. A four-room "hotel" when built in 1764. And changed several times since Carol, a caterer, and Phil, a stockbroker, came from Boston in 1987. The parents of five grown sons boil maple syrup in the spring. They have the waterfront location (a private swimming beach) they wanted. Their tree work has resulted in snowshoe trails (snowshoes provided). They offer cooking-on-wood-stove, innkeeping-seminar, and family-reunion weekends as well as hike and bike tours. They also offer, as one guest wrote, "a wonderful sense of peace."

In residence: Cameron, 22; Andrew, 24; and Greg, 28. Parker, "our friendly English springer spaniel, a real inn dog." Two cats, Pepper and Casey.
Bed and bath: Nine second-floor rooms, all private baths (some shower without tub). King, queen, or double beds. Family room has two twin beds plus a queen sofa bed. Rollaway and crib available.
Breakfast: 8–9:30. Juice, fresh fruit, homemade muffins and coffee cake. A different hot entree every morning.
Plus: Tea, wine, hot cider. Babysitting. Canoe, horseshoes, badminton, croquet. Fishing. An 80-year-old pool table. Option of dinner ($15 per person).

From Massachusetts: *"It's like going home for a visit with family."*

The "Inn" on Canaan Street

603/523-7310

RD 1, Box 92, Canaan Street, Canaan, NH 03741-9761

Hosts: Lee and Louise Kremzner
Location: On lake. At the foot of Mount Cardigan on 14 acres. 2½ miles up hill. Five minutes off Route 4; 25 minutes from Dartmouth College.
Open: Year round. Reservations required.

Rates: $65–$75 single. $75 double, shared bath; $75–$85 private. $150 two bedrooms as a suite with private bath. $15 cot.
♥ ✿ ✕ ⚞

Guests are always asking, "How did you ever find this lovely place?" Located on a 1788 street that is in the National Register, it's the home of a Columbia professor emeritus and his wife, a former nutritionist/consumer publicist (two

(Please turn page.)

terrific people who gave a wonderful cooking demonstration in my first Bloomingdale's Meet-the-Hosts program). Since the Kremzners restored the "Federal but country-style house" nine years ago, they have met many "Cardigan School parents, folks from Dartmouth, and big-city people who come to catch their breath, to enjoy the views and the lake. We love pampering them, sharing this area, laughing at ourselves, solving the world's problems, and relaxing over a fun breakfast."

In residence: Son, Stuart, assists. Labradors Snickers and Ginger are "our lovable wigglebottoms."
Foreign language spoken: A little French.
Bed and bath: Five second-floor rooms. Private baths; one has shower only, rest are full. One double bed. One canopied queen, working fireplace. King/twin option. Two rooms can be a suite. Cot available.
Breakfast: 8–9:30. Juice, fruit, toast. Homemade sweet breads, muffins or popovers. Blueberry pancakes, yogurt, granola. Prepared by Louise, "the muffin lady," who has a collection of over 800 cookbooks. Served in Garden Room that opens onto porch.
Plus: Swimming. Cross-country skiing right here. Sherry. Tea. Fruit. Library, games, movies. Ping-Pong, badminton. Dinner during inclement weather and with theme weekends (antiques, auction, gardening, cooking, reading series).

Watch Hill Bed and Breakfast   603/253-4334

Old Meredith Road, P.O. Box 1605, Center Harbor, NH 03226

Host: Barbara Lauterbach
Location: On the same road as post office and a farm. (Ask about the night the cows came.) Five-minute walk to village and beach. Just off Route 25, on the northernmost end of Lake Winnipesaukee.

Open: Year round.
Rates: $60 double occupancy. Singles $5 less. $15 rollaway. After three nights, $5 less per night.
🐾 ❅ ⊁

> From Georgia: *"Of course the syrup was from New Hampshire, but how many B&Bs make their own sausage?"* From Massachusetts: *"Wonderful host . . . marvelous Staffordshire dog collection . . . comfortable, roomy, and clean accommodations . . . terrific view of the lake and mountains beyond."*

Barbara, too, is enthusiastic—about the view of the lake, where the S.S. *Mount Washington* appears "precisely at 9:40 a.m."; about "the ancient locust trees of mammoth proportions" and about how her interests dovetailed into her 1989 B&B opening. A 1772 Cape with Victorian additions, the house is furnished with many English and American antiques, dog prints, and Staffordshires. (The hostess was a breeder of champion bullmastiffs.) Barbara is a world-trained chef and food consultant, a former Ohio cooking school director, a spokesperson for King Arthur flour, a local historic district commission officer, and a New Hampshire League of Craftsmen board member. She enjoys meeting guests who talk about "getting centered in Center Harbor."

In residence: Martin, an Amazon parrot with limited vocabulary. Two cats—"super friendly" Frank and Moxie, an orange Morris.
Foreign languages spoken: Fluent French. Some German.
Bed and bath: Four second-floor rooms; two have slanted ceilings. Two shared hall baths—one full, one shower only. King, queen, or two twin beds. Rollaway available.
Breakfast: Usually 7:30–9:30. Belgian waffles, maple French toast, sausage, "muffin du jour," eggs, home fries, mulled cider applesauce, homemade jams and jellies. In paneled room with fresh flowers, sterling silver, and linens or on screened porch with that lake view.
Plus: Beverages. Fruit bowl. Beach towels. Horseshoes. Bocci balls. Window fans. Off-season cooking weekends. For sale—jams (tomato a specialty) and corn relish.

The Farmhouse—Bed & Breakfast

P.O. Box 14, Page Hill Road   **603/323-8707**
Chocorua Village, NH 03817-0014

Hosts: John and Kathie Dyrenforth
Location: On seven acres of meadows, gardens, and orchards; 15 minutes south of Conway. Short walk from Trailways bus stop in the small White Mountains village.

Open: May through October. Two-night minimum on holiday weekends.
Rates: $50 single, $60 double. Seventh night free.

♥ ❄ ✈

"When the former owner sent six sons to World War II, she found she had lots of time and space for guests. Twelve years ago, we found her sign in the woodshed, put it up, and it worked!" Many guests tell Kathie (a former teacher) and John (who still teaches) that this B&B feels like Grandmother's house with its "some antiques, some old-fashioned" furnishings. Around 1860 the original part of the house, a blacksmith shop, was moved to this site by a young man for his bride. As Kathie says, "this young bride worked her magic."

In residence: Fourteen-year-old David and eight-year-old Tom, "who will tell you about a nearby swimming hole or hiking trails."
Bed and bath: Three cozy second-floor corner rooms share two hall baths (one with shower, one with tub). Two double-bedded rooms; one with two twin beds.
Breakfast: 8–9. (Gather eggs or pick your own fruit, if you'd like.) The Dyrenforths' own maple syrup for pancakes. Homemade muffins and breads. Heart-healthy foods by request.
Plus: Tea and cookies. Plant-filled screened porch. Window fans. Use of refrigerator.

***H**ospitality is the keynote of bed and breakfast.*

The Curtis Field House   603/929-0082
735 Exeter Road, Hampton, NH 03842

Host: Mary Houston
Location: Route 101C. On five wooded acres, on Exeter line. Three miles to Exeter Academy, 7 to ocean, 10 to Portsmouth.

Open: May–November. No check-ins after 8 p.m. please.
Rates: Per room. $65 including tax. MC, VISA.
✈

In 1638 Mary's ancestors were Exeter's first settlers. Her father, "a master craftsman by hobby," built this Royal Barry Wills Cape with wide floorboards 38 years ago. Often, during the 1980s restoration, carpenters commented on the attention to detail. Now the house has antiques, reproductions, and hooked, braided, and Oriental rugs. The gardens, too, receive loving care.

Mary, a retired decorator, opened the house as a B&B in 1988. Her own extensive travels include trips to China and Japan and, still, an annual ski trip to Europe. And she describes cooking as "pure enjoyment."

Bed and bath: Three rooms, all with air conditioners and window fans. On first floor, room with double four-poster shares shower bath with hosts. On second, room with two canopied twin beds, private full bath; room with queen-sized bed, shower bath.
Breakfast: 7:30–9. Omelet, bacon or ham and eggs, strata, or French toast. Fresh fruits, yogurt, Swiss familia cereal, juice, coffee, tea, coffee cake. In dining room or on sun deck.
Plus: Piano. Down comforters. Ping-Pong. Croquet. Badminton. Flower and vegetable gardens. Smoking on enclosed porch only.

Hannah Davis House   603/585-3344
186 Depot Road, Route 119, Fitzwilliam, NH 03447-9625

Hosts: Kaye and Mike Terpstra
Location: In the historic district, on a scenic route (119). Twelve miles south of Keene; 28 miles east of Brattleboro, Vermont.
Open: Year round.

Rates: Double occupancy. $55 double bed, $65 queen bed, $80 carriage loft. $20 third person in room, $10 fourth person. Singles $5 less.
♥ 🏠 ⁂ ♦ ✗ ⅍

Everything. It's all here, a few steps from the common in a small New England town with spired church: a c. 1820 Federal house with its original kitchen/hearth room, added baths with brass and porcelain fixtures, demolished and restored you-name-it, all embellished with antique furnishings and linens, country quilts and braided rugs. It is the home, a B&B since 1990, of an engineer and a social worker who owned and operated a small Brookline, New Hampshire, grocery store until they began work on this house three years ago. Kaye and Mike welcome you with cider or coffee and a treat. They turn down your bed and leave homemade cookies. They love the smell of fresh-popped popcorn. These two sharers—of cooking tips, carpentry lessons, antiquing hints, local history, a secluded waterfall, a covered bridge—give B&B mentoring credit to a neighbor at The Amos Parker House, where you are invited to see extraordinary gardens.

In residence: "Sadie, a shy red setter/black Lab. Toby, a gregarious collie/shepherd mix. Triscuit, an aloof tiger cat."
Bed and bath: Five rooms. All private full baths. First-floor suite, private entrance, extra-long twins/king option, sitting room with double-size sleep sofa, fireplace. On second floor, one queen canopied four-poster; one queen plus a twin bed, working fireplace; one double-bedded room. In carriage shed, queen bed in cathedral-ceilinged loft with double-size sleep sofa in sitting room below.
Breakfast: "The main event." Usually 8–10, tea and coffee earlier. Fresh fruit. Juices. Homemade granola, chunky applesauce, sour cream/poppyseed or blueberry bread. Elaborate entrees such as stuffed French toast with cheesy Dijon sauce.
Plus: Sitting room with stereo and piano, "but everyone ends up in the kitchen or on its long screened porch." Lots of pillows. Down comforters. Forgotten items.

Blanche's B&B   603/823-7061
351 Easton Valley Road, Franconia, NH 03580

Hosts: John Vail and Brenda Shannon
Location: Set in a meadow along a country road. Backyard is Kinsman Ridge, part of Appalachian Trail. Near working farms. Five miles from I-93 and Franconia village.
Open: Year round. Two-night minimum during foliage season and on major holiday and folk event weekends.
Rates: Double occupancy. $60 shared bath. $75–$85 private bath. $35–$45 single. $20 third person in room.
❀ ♦ ✖ ⅟

From Vermont: *"Brenda and John, with their warmth and friendship, are probably the primary attraction. . . . I have reviewed inns for* Ski *magazine and other publications . . . there is something special, very special about Blanche's."*
From Massachusetts: *"Decorated in an artistic, homey, inviting style, all fitting together beautifully . . . breakfast alone is worth going for."*

"One particular British B&B inspired us to leave our Boston area jobs. Using parts salvaged from other old houses, we have restored the unadorned farmhouse to a glory it probably never had. John does carpentry here. I am a decorative painter who makes colorful floorcloths and hand-painted furniture. Our most recent addition: scheduled storytelling and folk music events. Guests gather round the living room wood stove for an intimate concert."

In residence: Blanche, a black dog, "a respected member of the family, who greets guests, gives a house tour, and poses for photos."
Bed and bath: Five rooms with Brenda's hand-painted and stenciled walls. Private shower bath for first-floor room with hand-carved four-poster double bed. On second floor, four rooms—a single, a double-bedded room, a room with a canopied double and one twin, and a queen-bedded room—share one full and one half bath.

(Please turn page.)

Breakfast: Usually 8–9. Maybe Dutch pancakes with sauteed apples or blueberry compote, or cheese souffles with homemade sausage and honey nut rolls. Served at separate tables in dining room.
Plus: Sitting room. Yard. Games. Books. Sheets of 100 percent cotton. Pickup arranged at Franconia bus station. Dinner for groups by reservation only.

The Bungay Jar
                                                603/823-7775
Easton Valley Road, Easton, NH   **603/444-2919**
Mailing address: P.O. Box 15, Franconia, NH 03580

Hosts: Lee Strimbeck and Kate Kerivan
Location: Franconia range of the White Mountains. Tucked back from the road on eight wooded acres with hiking paths to a stream. Six miles south of Franconia. Ten minutes to I-93, Sugar Hill, Cannon Mountain, Lost River; 30 to Loon, Bretton Woods.

Open: Year round. Two-night minimum during foliage season and holiday weekends.
Rates: $50 single (not available during foliage season); $60–$65 double with shared bath; $75–$95 private. Slightly higher holidays and foliage season. $20 third person. AMEX, MC, VISA.
♥ ✷ ✖ ✄

From Ohio: *"Even surpassed your glowing recommendation . . . picturesque . . . most charming proprietors we have met in our extensive travels in this country and on the continent."*

A treat. Built from an 18th-century post-and-beam barn, it is filled with antiques and collectibles (some for sale): Benny Goodman's porcelain tub, old marble sinks and stained glass windows, some confessional doors, English pub panels . . . all arranged by Kate, the landscape architect, who has become innkeeper/gardener (the herb and perennial gardens are spectacular) and chef (who uses a commercial stove) and craftswoman (wreaths, dried flowers). Guests have full access to the two-storied fireplaced living room (former hayloft), a sauna, a small library, and multiple decks that offer mesmerizing mountain views. Both Lee, a patent attorney, and Kate are experienced hikers and skiers.

In residence: Kyle, age six. "Lila, our standard poodle; Checkers, the cat."
Bed and bath: Six rooms, four private baths. First floor—room with two twin beds shares a bath with double-bedded room. Second floor—Victorian queen bed with private balcony, bath with six-foot tub; king canopied bed plus daybed, full bath, interior reading balcony. Third floor—Stargazer suite with four skylights, king bed, tub bath; another skylit room with double bed, shower bath, French doors to private balcony. Plus a "private primitive (soon to be changed) house in the woods that sleeps two or more."
Breakfast: 8:30–9:30. Full. Blueberry pancakes with local maple syrup. Popovers. Local smoked meats and salmon. Fresh fruit. In dining room or on porch overlooking gardens and mountains.
Plus: No TV. 3–5 p.m. tea or cider with homemade snacks. Coffee or tea anytime. Freshly cut flowers in season. CD player. Games.

The Hilltop Inn
603/823-5695

Route 117, P.O. Box 9, Sugar Hill, NH 03585

Hosts: Mike and Meri Hern
Location: In this tiny village with cheese store, post office (open three hours a day), and an historical museum. Ten minutes from Franconia Notch.
Open: Year round. Two-night minimum during fall foliage and holiday weekends.

Rates: Double occupancy. $60–$80 double, $75–$100 queen, $85–$110 suite. Pets $10. Additional person $15–$20. Singles $10 less. AMEX, Discover, MC, VISA.
♥ ✽

"Yesterday I helped the postmistress round up her chickens. Today I'm hanging French silk wallpaper in the dining room. Guests (and their pets— one even came with a llama) are surrounded by homey Victoriana, handmade quilts, lots of lace—and outside, perennial gardens and hummingbirds. Our barn reminds me of the antiques shop I had on Cape Cod. Nearby there's a lovers' lane—really!—with benches placed for sunset views."

Brooklyn-born Meri discovered Sugar Hill when she visited a college friend twenty years ago. ("I never left.") She and Mike, an electrical engineer, are also caterers. In the last seven years, they have made many changes in the 1895 inn.

In residence: Casey, a 15-year-old Irish setter. Boop, a 10-year-old black Labrador mix. Lucy and Elphie, sister cats.
Bed and bath: Six second-floor rooms, private full baths. Double beds in smaller rooms; queen beds in others. Rollaway and crib available.
Breakfast: 8:30–9:30. Hearty buffet. Cinnamon French toast, souffles, farm eggs; local berries and maple syrup. Homemade jams and muffins. In dining room or on deck or porches.
Plus: Ceiling fans. TV with VCR (250 movies) in sitting room. Flannel sheets. Teas or local cider with snacks. Porch swings and rockers. Transportation to/from Franconia bus stop. Option of dinner.

Sugar Hill Inn
603/823-5621

Route 117, Franconia, NH 03580

Hosts: Barbara and Jim Quinn
Location: On 16 acres—half rolling lawns with flowers, half wooded— with spectacular mountain views. "Our only neighbor is a goldsmith's studio/shop." Four miles from Franconia Notch.

Open: Year round except April and mid-November to December 27.
Rates: $65–$85 single, $90–$125 double.
♥ ✽ ◆ ✗ ⚄

"So many of our guests began to say that this was the quintessential country inn that I looked quintessential up in the dictionary! 'The purest essence of a country inn' is just what we have tried to create ever since we ended our 8-year search in 1986. Jim spent 28 years in the grocery business in Rhode

(Please turn page.)

Island. Here, he is delighted with his role as chef. *Bon Appétit* and *Yankee* magazines have published some of his recipes."

Barbara has stenciled most of the rooms (some have small-print wallcoverings) and furnished them with antique or period reproductions. The dining room, recently refurbished and now called the Rockwell Dining Room, has Rockwell prints, an old spinning wheel—and lots of light, thanks to windows on three sides, complete with those mountain views. For a better look, use the telescope on the porch. You might focus on the tram going up Cannon Mountain.

Bed and bath: Ten second-floor rooms, all private baths. Queen, double, or twin beds; most have full baths, two have shower without tub. Six two-room cottages, May–October, each set up for two with rollaway available.
Breakfast: 8–9. Full country menu. Could be juice, pumpkin raisin muffins, egg/cheese/cream souffle, breakfast meats, hot beverages.
Plus: Afternoon tea. Piano in fireplaced living room. Four working fireplaces. Wicker-furnished wraparound porch. Dinners (menu announced on chalkboard in morning) for overnight guests only; make reservations at breakfast.

Freedom House   603/539-4815

P.O. Box 478, 1 Maple Street, Freedom, NH 03836-0478

Hosts: Bob and Marjorie Daly
Location: By the millpond in a quiet country village. Half hour south of the Conways' shopping outlets and ski slopes. Half hour to Wolfeboro.
Open: Year round. Two-night minimum, September 15–October 15.

Rates: $40 single, $60 double. $10 cot or crib for child in same room. MC, VISA.
🛏 ❄ ✕ ⚹

A genuine Old Home Week and Fireman's Parade is held every August is this friendly New Hampshire village. Within walking distance of a lake, country store, church, town hall, and library, is this B&B. It's a white Victorian house with bay windows, gray shutters, and an American flag. The comfortable Victorian/country decor includes straw hats made by a local friend and Marjorie's own handmade quilts.

Since 1985, when the Dalys left their resort management positions, the world has come to their doorstep. And now Bob, retired from the U.S. Coast Guard, serves in the state legislature.

In residence: Muffin is a friendly and declawed house cat who helps show guests to their rooms.
Bed and bath: Six rooms. On second floor, four rooms share two baths across the hall, one with tub, one with shower. Two rooms each with two twin beds; two double-bedded rooms. On third floor, one room has double bed and antique crib for infant; one room is a single. Cot available.
Breakfast: 7–9. Homemade muffins, pancakes with Freedom's own maple syrup, French toast, farm-fresh eggs, bacon, ham, and sausage. Served in breakfast room (with ceiling fan).
Plus: Welcoming beverage. Portable fans in guest rooms.

Greenfield Bed & Breakfast Inn   603/547-6327

Town Center, Forest Road, Route 31 North, P.O. Box 400
Greenfield, NH 03047-0400

Hosts: Barbara and Vic Mangini
Location: On main road in center of small town, next to the library. On three acres of lawn. Three minutes from Greenfield State Park, 15 from Peterborough, Crotched and Temple mountains, 90 from Boston.

Open: Year round. (No phone calls or arrivals after 9:30 p.m.)
Rates: Per room, double occupancy. $65 private bath, $45–$55 shared (with one other room) bath. $20 each additional person. MC, VISA.
♥ ♔ ❖ ♦ ✈

Sign equals lifestyle. The "for sale" sign on the big beautiful white Victorian, built in 1817, was too much to resist just about the time the Manginis, parents of six grown children, were about to retire to their nearby farm. They insulated. They decorated with plenty of white wicker, Laura Ashley linens, antiques, dolls, wallpapers, crystal, and laces. Twenty minutes after their B&B sign went up in 1986, the first guests—honeymooners—arrived. That couple has returned annually. And, as you'll see (mementoes), Bob and Dolores Hope have come.

Vic, who has spent 30 years in advertising and marketing, has found that corporate executives, too, enjoy the ambiance here—so much so that the inn now has a new glass-walled deck house, with mountain views of course, "built for rocking-chair strategy meetings."

Bed and bath: Eight rooms. Large first-floor room has two twin beds, TV, private full bath. On second floor are king, double, or twin beds; most have private shower baths, one a tub bath. Two rooms share a full bath. One twin-bedded and one double-bedded room form a suite with private hallway. Rollaways available. (Infants must have own portable crib and high chair.)
Breakfast: 7:30–9:30. Egg casseroles, strata (meatless or with sausage), ham, chicken. Barbara's home-baked muffins, one kind known as "miracle muffin." Bagels. Cereals. Fresh fruit. Buffet style in the garden room.
Plus: Air conditioning, phone service, and TV in some rooms. Sherry in crystal decanters in all rooms. Bedroom ceiling fans. Games. Books. Rockers on veranda. Mountain-view sun deck. Fireplaced living room with TV. A sleep-six suite with kitchenette. "Everything is for sale except the inn and Vic."

The Inn at Elmwood Corners   603/929-0443
252 Winnacunnet Road, Hampton, NH 03842   800/253-5691

Hosts: John and Mary Hornberger
Location: In residential area, on main street, 1½ miles from Hampton Beach. Walk to village theaters, antiques shops, restaurants. Kennel nearby.

Open: Year round.
Rates: June–October, $55 single, $65 double, $90 studio. November–May, $40 single, $50 double, $75 studio. $10 extra person. MC, VISA.
♥ ♔ ❖ ♦

(Please turn page.)

"It is fun to see so many returnees, but the most amazing thing is the number who tell us that we are living their dream of a lifestyle."

John had experience as a restauranteur. Mary, a computer analyst, enjoys creating a casual country feeling. They spent a year on restoring and opened the century-old former sea captain's house in 1988—with braided rugs, stenciled walls, and quilts. Some rooms have exposed beams. One wall of the library/sitting room is filled with books. (Take the paperback home with you.) Groups, including those who come for quilting workshops held here, may arrange for dinner.

In residence: "Assistants" Keith, nine, and Kevin, five.
Bed and bath: Seven rooms. Five second-floor rooms, each with queen or double bed, share two shower baths and one half bath. Two studio suites on the third floor include queen beds, private shower baths, air conditioning, and kitchenettes. Rollaway beds and crib available.
Breakfast: 8–10. May include eggs Benedict, cheddar-and-chive omelet, French toast, pancakes, or huevos rancheros. Home fries, juice, fresh fruit. Plum/oatmeal or banana nut bread. In dining room or on porch.
Plus: Wraparound porch. Large yard. Terry robes for rooms with semiprivate bath. Nighttime homemade cookies. Library. Games.

> From Massachusetts: *"Charming rooms . . . great breakfast . . . welcoming family."*

Moose Mountain Lodge   603/643-3529
P.O. Box 272, Etna, NH 03750-0272

Hosts: Kay and Peter Shumway
Location: One mile *up* a winding dirt road (winter shuttle provided) to a view of Connecticut River valley below, Green Mountains beyond. Eight miles from the Dartmouth College campus and Connecticut River in Hanover. The Appalachian Trail crosses lodge property and continues over Moose Mountain.
Open: June 1–October 20 and De-cember 26–March 21. Reservations required.
Rates: $55 per person. $32 under age 12. (B&B usually not offered in winter, when $75–$90 per person includes two or three meals, respectively, here "on the top of the world.") Ten percent discount for three or more nights. MC, VISA.
♥ ♨ ❖ ◆ ✕ ✁

One of a kind. Recommended to REI, the sporting goods store, for its first New England ski trip. "The place, the people, the food—all more than we could have hoped for. And what a setting!" they reported.

For 17 years devotees—including canoeing inn-to-inn registrants—have been returning to the Shumways, easygoing folks who have time to listen. "We love to share this tranquil place, to introduce people to the beauty of our trails and the Beaver Pond with its wonderful animal and bird life."

Their rustic building, built as a ski lodge in 1938, has a massive stone fireplace, pine walls, and couches and four-poster beds made of logs. Last year

Peter, the vegetable gardener/song leader/former wholesale lumber business-man, took tap-dancing lessons to celebrate his 60th birthday. Kay, chef extraordinaire, has produced the *Moose Mountain Lodge Cookbook*. And she spins the wool of the goats (a fairly recent addition). The Shumways' guests come looking for peace and quiet and relaxation—and find it.

In residence: Tulla, a grey weimaraner, the perfect guide for walks. Two Angora goats, Tom and Billy. One pig named Sylvia Pigeoli. Two sheep.
Foreign languages spoken: French, some Spanish and Swedish.
Bed and bath: Twelve rooms, all with views, share five full baths. Queen, double, double and twin, or two twins; one room has a double and two bunks.
Breakfast: Huge. Leisurely. 8–9. Could include homemade granola, fresh farm eggs, turkey sausage, black bean hash, hot cereals, or pancakes with Shumways' own maple syrup.
Plus: No TV. Player piano. Huge porch with 100-mile panoramic view. Hiking, cross-country skiing, and snowshoeing trails start at the front door. Option of lunch and dinner (extra charge).

White Goose Inn   603/353-4812
Route 10, P.O. Box 17, Orford, NH 03777

Hosts: Manfred and Karin Wolf
Location: Fifteen miles north of Hanover, across the bridge from Fairlee, Vermont, on the outskirts of an unusual town that is essentially a street of elegant Bulfinch mansions.
Open: Year round. Advance reservations required. Two-day minimum on weekends, May–October.

Rates: Per room, double occupancy. $75 twin beds, shared bath, or double bed, private bath. $85 queen bed, private bath. Plus $15 for air conditioning. $15 third person in room. MC, VISA.
✖️ 🍴

This beautiful brick inn, built in 1833 and often called "the house with the tree growing through the porch roof," is filled with style and elegance, simplicity and friendliness. Guests usually ask for "the story," one that begins in 1983 when Karin, who was working in retailing, and Manfred, a Firestone production supervisor, stayed in inns while looking for an old New England property as a second residence. When they walked into what had become an apartment house and saw the potential of beamed rooms, wide-planked floors, and many fireplaces, they knew that they had found new careers as well as a new location. In 1987 *Country Living* featured the rooms furnished with family heirlooms from Germany, auction and antiques shop finds, and Karin's pierced lampshades and other country crafts.

In 1988, a few feet from the inn with its fireplaced living room, the Wolfs added a gambrel-roofed air-conditioned Cape house, "Gosling House," complete with a common room, a dining room, and a deck overlooking circular flower gardens with sun dial.

In residence: Three sheep called Alex, Wooley, and Emily. Three schnauzers called Schnecke, Max, and Purzel.

(Please turn page.)

Foreign language spoken: German.
Bed and bath: Fifteen rooms. Five in Gosling House. Most with private shower bath, two with old-fashioned tub (only). Two rooms share one bath. Bed sizes include queen, double, and twins; some four-poster beds. Six rooms have nonworking fireplaces.
Breakfast: 8–9:30. Waffles, eggs, or French toast. Fresh fruit in season. Homemade muffins. By candlelight.

Wonderwell   603/763-5065
Philbrick Hill, West Springfield, NH 03284

Hosts: Susan and Samuel Alexander
Location: High on a hill with rolling fields, woods, mountain views. Six minutes to I-89. Twenty minutes south of Dartmouth College, 20 to six ski areas including King Ridge and Mount Sunapee. Five minutes to Eastman Golf Links. Near antiquing and the country's longest covered bridge (recently restored).

Open: May 1 until weekend before Thanksgiving plus December 26–March 31.
Rates: Double occupancy: $120 one night, $210 two consecutive nights, $296 three consecutive nights. Singles $80 per night.
♥ ❖ ✈

Some guests call it grand. Or elegant. Or luxurious. Or their private estate for as long as they're here. It's perfect for musicales or wedding receptions—which are held occasionally in the huge beamed two-storied Great Room with twin fieldstone fireplaces, a balcony around four sides, a grand piano, and Oriental rugs. Guests read (or lounge) under skylights, in front of fireplaces, or in the "secret garden."

Built in 1911 as a summer residence and named for the well that functioned through the 1913 drought, the mansion has evolved as the setting for a new lifestyle for the Alexanders. They have decorated with antiques, insulated for sound, and added to the original building. When they lived in Washington, D.C., Sam was a worldwide business traveler.

In residence: Jon, 16; David, 14; Susie, 13. One dog and one cat.
Bed and bath: Eight rooms (some suites) on second and third floors. All private baths; some full, some shower or tub only, one with Jacuzzi. Queen, double, or twin beds. One room with working fireplace. Rollaway available.
Breakfast: 8:15–9:45. In ski season, 6:45–9. Entree might be walnut waffles with strawberry cream. Eggs with bacon, ham, or sausage. Juice. Fruit. Cereals. Homemade rolls or muffins.
Plus: Complimentary wine and hors d'oeuvres. Air conditioning in some bedrooms; ceiling fans in all. Bedroom TV jacks. Badminton. Croquet. Ping-Pong. Fireplaced terrace.

-----

*I*s B&B like a hotel?
How many times have you hugged the doorman?

Stonecrest Farm Bed & Breakfast 802/295-2600

119 Christian Street, Wilder, VT
Mailing address: P.O. Box 1163, Hanover, NH 03766-1163

Host: Gail Sanderson
Location: On two country acres with classic red barns. Near I-91 and I-89, 3.7 miles south of Dartmouth College, 13.5 east of Woodstock, Vermont.
Open: Year round. Two-night minimum on Dartmouth's graduation weekend and September 15 through October.
Rates: Per room. $95–$110. $110 graduation weekend. MC, VISA.
🛥 ⚹ ✈

> From New York: *"Down comforters. Floor-to-ceiling bookcases. Antiques. Gail Sanderson could make anyone feel as if they had just discovered Shangri-La."*

Following years of world travel and academic administration, the Sandersons moved to this stately 1810 house. It has much stonework, a curved oak staircase, and a beamed living room with French doors that lead to a terrace; it made a marvelous setting for a six-page *Family Circle* feature.

Since Gail redecorated and opened as a B&B, she has also become a practicing lawyer. She sings with choral groups and enjoys hiking. She often suggests the Saint-Gaudens Historic Site with its lovely gardens; the tour of the sculptor's studio includes the showing of a film produced by Gail's son, Paul.

In residence: Tessa, an affectionate collie. McDougel is a Border terrier.
Foreign language spoken: "Very limited German."
Bed and bath: Five rooms. First floor—queen bed, private full bath. Second floor—on west end, room with queen bed and one with twin beds share bath that has cedar shower stall; on east end, room with a canopied four-poster double bed and room with twin beds share a full bath. All but queen beds are antiques.
Breakfast: Usually 7:30–9. Could be freshly squeezed orange juice, fresh strawberries with rhubarb sauce, homemade lemon yogurt muffins, local honey spread. Served in beamed dining room with individual bouquets at each place, or on the terrace.
Plus: Baby grand piano. Bedroom ceiling fans. Wood stove in living room. Flower-filled terrace. Books. Board games.

The Harrisville Squires' Inn Bed & Breakfast

Keene Road, Box 19, Harrisville, NH 03450-0019 603/827-3925

Hosts: Doug and Pat McCarthy
Location: Peaceful. On 50 acres. One-half mile from idyllic 19th-century textile village, a National Historic Landmark, with weaving center and supply shop. Twelve miles from Crotched and Temple mountains.
Open: Year round. Two-day minimum on some holiday weekends.
Rates: Shared bath, $45 single, $55 double. Private bath, $55 single, $60 double. $5 more in foliage season. $15 third person. Tour planning, including maps and reservations, $30. MC, VISA.
♥ ⚹ ✈

(Please turn page.)

Guests wrote: *Comfortable, charmingly decorated, reasonably priced. Delicious breakfast. . . . A warm, friendly couple who go 'the second mile' to make your stay a more memorable one.*

The century-old caretakers' quarters, once part of a working farm, are now the home of Monadnock Bicycle Touring. Doug plans custom-designed day or overnight routes, both on- and off-road, through covered bridges and small villages. Guests also come to this B&B for getaways, reunions, and small weddings (Pat is a justice of the peace). Others cross-country ski or hike on the trails right here.

With the help of their three adult sons, the McCarthys completed their third house restoration in 1985. Located in one of the most photographed towns in New England, it is decorated in country style with hats, wreaths, and potpourri.

Before hosting, Pat was an interpreter for the deaf and a Hilton Hotel restaurant manager. Doug was a special needs teacher for the deaf in the Boston area. Both know American Sign Language.

In residence: Sable, a barn cat. Candy, the dog. Four ducks. Two geese.
Bed and bath: Five large rooms. First-floor wheelchair-accessible room has double four-poster bed, private full bath. On second floor three rooms sharing full skylit bath have king, double, or twin beds; one room has two twins/king bed, sitting area, private full bath. Two rollaways.
Breakfast: Served 7:30–9. Buffet after 9. Fruit dish; homemade breads, muffins, and coffee cakes; hosts' own maple syrup. In dining room or in country kitchen by fire.
Plus: Tea with cakes, breads, and cookies. Swimming in nearby pond. Gift shop in the largest barn left in town.

Haverhill Inn   603/989-5961
Dartmouth College Highway, Haverhill, NH 03765-0095

Hosts: Stephen Campbell and Anne Baird
Location: On main route NH 10, with a wonderful view of Connecticut River valley and Vermont hills. Half a mile south of the double common. Half hour north of Dartmouth College. Within an hour's drive of five major ski areas. Antiquing in town.
Open: June through February.
Rates: $85 double occupancy, tax included.
♥ ⁂ ✈

There's a sense of place in this gracious 1810 Federal house turned inn. In the living room you'll see antique maps on the walls, area history books, and two volumes on the history of the house. There are wide board floors, painted-grain interior doors, solid panel interior (Indian) window shutters, an enormous kitchen hearth with bake-oven, and the warmth of antique furnishings. And for architecture buffs there's a detailed description of the forty Haverhill buildings, including the inn, that are part of a National Historic District.

Steve and Anne are among the the friendly and helpful innkeepers who participate in an acclaimed inn-to-inn canoeing program. Both professionals at Dartmouth College, they are members of community groups that sing mostly classical music "one evening a week, when we alternate as innkeepers."

In residence: Two dogs.
Foreign languages spoken: Steve knows some Spanish; Anne, some German.
Bed and bath: Four large rooms, each with working fireplace and private bath. First-floor room has canopied twin beds. Upstairs are one double, one queen, and one pair of double beds. Two full baths, two with showers only.
Breakfast: 8–9. Always a full meal. Fresh bakery, locally smoked bacon, freshly brewed coffee.
Plus: Afternoon tea. A decanter of sherry on the hall desk. Other meals prepared for inn-to-inn canoeing participants. Cross-country ski trails at the door.

The Inn on Golden Pond   603/968-7269
P.O. Box 680, Holderness, NH 03245-0680

Hosts: Bill and Bonnie Webb
Location: On 55 wooded acres with trails. Across the street from Squam Lake, setting for the film *On Golden Pond*. Twenty minutes to White Mountain National Forest, 15 to Ten-ney Mountain. Four miles from I-93. Near many maple sugaring shacks.
Open: Year round.
Rates: $90 double. Suite $120–$140. $25 third person. MC, VISA.
♥ ♦ ✕ ⚹

If you have seen the film, your expectations of a fairly undeveloped area will be fulfilled. And if you're looking for a family-run inn where you get to know the innkeepers and other guests (and where there's still a respect for privacy), this is the place. It's immaculate and comfortable (not lavish) and in a location that appeals to outdoor-oriented travelers.

Since Becky and her brother, Ricky, arrived from Korea five years ago, they too have taken to the world of innkeeping—a career that is a perfect match for Bill and Bonnie, who left their jobs in guidebook publishing and data processing when they moved from California in 1984. Their country home, built in 1879, is surrounded by stone walls, antique split rail fences, flowers, bushes, and shade trees.

In residence: Ricky, age 10, and Becky, age 9.
Bed and bath: Nine rooms (two are suites) on second and third floors. All private baths (some full, some tub or shower only). King, queen, or double beds; one room with a queen and a twin bed.
Breakfast: 8:30–9:30. Cooked by Bonnie. Apple pancakes or eggs and bacon. Homemade bread and muffins. Fresh fruit. At individual tables. Usually a very social time. Innkeeper/waiter Bill joins guests for coffee.
Plus: Turndown service; homemade mint on the pillow. Fireplaced living room. Picnic tables. Lawn games. A 60-foot screened porch. Ice and glasses. Swimming (small fee) at town beach just around the corner.

Windyledge Bed & Breakfast 603/746-4054

Hatfield Road, RFD 3, Hopkinton, NH 03329

Hosts: Dick and Susan Vogt
Location: Fifteen minutes west of Concord. On an old country road. Less than two miles from Routes 202 and 9. Four miles from I-89, 10 from I-93. Five minutes to New England College, 10 to Saint Paul's School.
Open: Year round.

Rates: Double $55 shared bath, $75 private. Single $10 less. Rollaway $15. No charge for crib. Monday–Thursday, 10 percent less for senior citizens, business travelers, and families. MC, VISA.
♥ ♯ ♠ ❄ ♦ ✂

From New York: *"My children called Windyledge a fairyland because everything was so perfect—just as you wished your home and life to be, but never is. The experience was truly relaxing yet invigorating. The Vogts are unusually thoughtful, interesting, and sharing people . . . gourmet breakfasts with homemade jams and freshly squeezed orange juice. I especially enjoyed strolling the gardens and taking in the great view of the surrounding hills. Our children loved feeding the horse, collecting eggs, and visiting a nearby dairy farm."*

Perfect by design. With handmade quilts, Oriental rugs, a beamed sitting room adjoining the open kitchen, a swimming pool, and lots of amenities. All planned by the Vogts, a Digital Equipment Corporation manager and a dental receptionist, about the time their youngest was getting ready to leave for college. That's when they rearranged/rebuilt their 1970's all-electric colonial house (which is heated primarily with two wood stoves)—even though a local official had asked, "Who in the world would want to go out to Hatfield Road, anyway?" Since 1990 lots of delighted guests have come to Hopkinton!

In residence: On the property: Margot, 20-year-old horse; two barn cats; a dozen chickens.
Bed and bath: Three second-floor rooms, all with desks and phone jacks. One with queen pencil-post bed, adjoining private shower bath. Two rooms—one with handmade Victorian double bed, one with twins/king bed with handmade pine headboard—share a double-sinked hall tub-and-shower bath. Rollaway and crib available.
Breakfast: Flexible schedule and menu. Maybe Belgian waffles or sour cream souffle with raspberry sauce. Muffins and sweet breads. On deck, in sun room, or in dining room at table set with linen, silverware, china, antique pressed glass, and fresh flowers.
Plus: Ceiling fans. Individual thermostats. Snacks. Guest refrigerator. Flannel sheets. Turndown service. Bedside candy. Pool towels. Video film library. Piano. When you leave, a gift of muffins and jar of jam.

---

*O*ne out of five guests leaves with
the dream of opening a B&B.

The Forest, A Country Inn   603/356-9772
P.O. Box 37, Route 16A, Intervale, NH 03845-0037   **800/448-3534**

Hosts: Ken and Rae Wyman
Location: On 25 wooded acres on a quiet country road. Between North Conway and Jackson, near Mount Washington.
Open: Year round.
Rates: Double occupancy. May 1–June 30, $56–$70 in inn, $78 cottage. July 1–September 19, $62–$78 inn, $78–$80 cottage; weekends $8 higher. September 20–October 19 (foliage), $82–$98 inn, $98–$102 cottage. October 20–December 31, $60–$80 inn, $90–$100 cottage. Thanksgiving weekend includes three nights and holiday dinner, $202–$252 inn, $252–$266 cottage. January–April, $64–$85 inn, $80–$105 cottage. Ski weekend packages available. Singles $10 less. AMEX, MC, VISA.
♥ ⋔ ⁂ ✁

Twice, *Bon Appétit* has featured the Wymans' afternoon tea. Their century-old inn is also known as a place for relaxation, for its inn-to-inn cycling and cross-country ski programs, and for its innkeepers, who are active mountain climbers, skiers, and cyclists.

In 1986 Ken was a vice president of a Boston area life insurance company and Rae managed a dentists' office. They created a casual atmosphere in the mansard-roofed inn with Victorian and colonial antiques and a quilt collection. They installed a solar-heated outdoor swimming pool. And by the time you read this, there will be a nature trail through the forest and campfires will be burning in the new firepit in the picnic area.

Bed and bath: Thirteen rooms (some are suites) plus stone cottage. On second and third floors rooms have double or twin beds, private or shared baths. One king-bedded room with private bath. One with a double and a twin bed, shared bath. Two units in cottage, each with queen bed, private entrance and bath; one with fireplace, screened porch. Rollaway available.
Breakfast: 8–9. Eggs, rum raisin or amaretto French toast, spiced Belgian waffles, apple or blueberry pancakes, homemade yeast and sweet breads, muffins and donuts, fruits.
Plus: Ceiling fans. Hot beverages with sweet bread or homemade donuts. Candy. Fruit. Guest refrigerator. Fireplaced common room. Glassed/screened porch with wood stove. Afternoon tea during foliage season. Option of Saturday dinner in ski season.

From New York: *"Ken and Rae contribute to that magic formula which makes the inn a special place."*

---

*B*ed and breakfast gives a sense of place.

Wildflowers Guest House   603/356-2224

Route 16, P.O. Box 802, Intervale, NH 03845-0802

Hosts: Eileen Davies and Dean Franke
Location: On the main road, fronted by award-winning gardens. Minutes to shops, outlets, and restaurants. One and a half miles north of North Conway village and Saco River.
Open: May–October.
Rates: Double occupancy. May 1–

July 15, $60 private bath, $50–$55 shared. July 16–September 25 and October 16–31, $80 private, $60–$68 shared. September 26–October 15, $92 private bath, $72–$80 shared. Single rate (when available) $40. $15 extra person. MC, VISA.

This traffic stopper fulfilled the name Eileen and Dean gave to it when in 1978 they left the corporate world and bought their "jewel in the rough." As Eileen says, "'Wildflowers' seemed to have the right aura for this house, built in 1878 with wonderful woodwork, six fireplaces, and six-foot windows." It was several years before Dean (an avid fisherman too) discovered his horticultural talent. Today the front gardens are a photographer's delight with about 75 varieties of perennials. From the first floor with its 11-foot ceilings, a U-shaped staircase leads to a square hallway and corner guest rooms, many with dramatic, colorful wallpaper. Furnishings include Oriental rugs, a working Victrola, marble-topped bureaus, and Dean's paintings of familiar local scenes. "We have stayed small so that we can spend time with our guests—often sharing information about waterfalls and ponds, restaurants and cycling routes."

In residence: Three cats who spend the entire summer outside.
Foreign language spoken: "Enough French to relay area information and directions."
Bed and bath: Six carpeted bedrooms. Private shower baths for two second-floor double-bedded rooms. Semiprivate shower baths for other rooms on second and third floors, each with a double or a double and a twin bed. Rollaway available.
Breakfast: 7:30–9:15. Juice, sour cream coffee cake, seasonal fruit, hot beverages. In plant- and flower-filled fireplaced dining room.
Plus: Individual thermostats. Window fans. Transportation to and from center of North Conway.

> From New York: *"A storybook house . . . absolutely immaculate . . . a superb B&B."* From Massachusetts: *"Easy to converse with. . . . House is not very large . . . intimate . . . Eileen has a definite knack for baking."*

According to guests (many are preservationists and/or house restorers), there ought to be a medal for the meticulous work—everything from research to labor—done by B&B owners. Indeed, many have won preservation awards.

Ellis River House

603/383-9339
800/233-8309

P.O. Box 656, Route 16, Jackson, NH 03846-0656

Hosts: Barry and Barbara Lubao
Location: Set back from the road, overlooking the river. Ten minutes to Attitash, Wildcat, Black Mountain, Tuckerman's Ravine. On Ellis River Trail to Jackson Cross-Country Ski Foundation.
Open: Year round.
Rates: Vary according to season and whether it's midweek or weekend.

Highest in September and October. Per person, double occupancy, $25–$60. $15 under 12 in parents' room. Single rates depend on availability. Suite (sleeps six) $95–$350; cottage (sleeps four) $85–$225; rates vary according to number of people and date. AMEX, MC, VISA.

♥ ♦♦ ❖ ♦ ✂

The farm and the farmhouse continue to change. Barry was chief engineer for the Sheraton Hotels when the family came here seven years ago. Now he tends award-winning organic gardens and a small vineyard. There are chickens (gather your own breakfast eggs), geese, ducks, rabbits, a pig, and, "best of friends," a pony and a cow. In addition to the atrium with Jacuzzi spa (where hot mulled cider is enjoyed in winter), there's a sun deck that also has river and mountain views. A new cottage down by the river is ideal for honeymooners and families—and even pets too.

Decor is farmhouse style, with many crafts made by Barbara. Enthusiasm is Olympic style—for the area, for the rubber duck race, for river swimming and fishing (trout), for skiing champions and beginners, and for a wide variety of guests.

In residence: Barry (Jay), age 17, and Jennifer, age 11.
Foreign language spoken: Polish.
Bed and bath: Five rooms, a suite, and a cottage. Three on second floor share two baths with claw-foot tubs; one room with queen bed, one with queen and a twin, one with double bed. Third-floor room with two double beds and another with a double and a twin share a full bath. Suite has queen bed, four twins, private balcony, shower bath. Cottage with spiral staircase has queen bed plus queen sofa bed, full bath. Rollaways available.
Breakfast: 8–9:30. Juices, fruit, homemade tea breads; Barry's cinnamon, oatmeal raisin, and beer breads. Hot and cold cereals. Farm-fresh eggs, sausage, bacon, French toast or pancakes.
Plus: Popcorn and hot toddies by the fire. VCR. Wraparound screened porch. Piano. Playground. Horseshoes. Croquet. Volleyball. Terry robes. Five-course dinner ($22.50) by reservation only. Pets allowed in cottage only.

Innkeeping may be America's most envied profession. As one host mused, "Where else can you get a job where, every day, someone tells you how wonderful you are?"

Paisley and Parsley

603/383-0859
800/248-0829

Box 572, Jackson, NH 03846-0572

Hosts: Beatrice and Charles Stone
Location: High on a country road, Route 16B, with an "exclusive view" of Mount Washington. Surrounded by birch trees and herb and perennial gardens. Within walking distance of village. Near five major ski areas.
Open: Year round except May–late June. Two-day minimum on July 4, Labor Day, and Thanksgiving week- ends and from September 20 to October 15.
Rates: Double occupancy. September 15–October 15, $85 double, $95 queen, $115 king. June 15–September 15 and January 2–February 28, $20 less. March 1–May 5, $30 less. Singles $15 less. $15 additional guest. $10 children up to age 10. MC, VISA.
♥ ❀ ◆ ✈ ⊁

This new contemporary Cape house, filled with antiques, textiles, folk art, and books, is the home of Bea, who was a school librarian in New Jersey; Chuck, an environmental planner in New York; and Bridget, their full-sized doll. They vacationed here, loved the area, "retired," built the house (after searching for a "right" old house), and began hosting corporate transferees. As a next step, B&B was a natural. One guest took photographs and measurements and had a similar house built. Many, even those who come for outdoor activities, "just relax." They remember the food, the pampering, the privacy, the views, the hammock—and the hosts.

Foreign language spoken: A little French.
Bed and bath: Three rooms, all private baths. Handicapped-accessible first-floor room has twins/king bed, two-person whirlpool, ceiling fan. On second floor—one room with queen canopied bed; one with two double beds, sitting area with TV and VCR. Rollaway available.
Breakfast: 7:30–9. Special. Crepes, omelet with feta cheese and herbs, shellfish quiche, poached pears. Served on English bone china in dining room by full-length windows or on deck. Special diets accommodated.
Plus: Welcoming beverage. Beach towels. Terry robes. Croquet. Fruit basket. Flowers. Terrace. Shortbread recipe. Picnic baskets.

> From New Hampshire: *"An exceptional job of blending old New England charm with the luxury of contemporary style and comfort. . . . A breakfast that held us through a good long hike."*

Benjamin Prescott Inn

603/532-6637

Route 124 East, Jaffrey, NH 03452-1810

Hosts: Jan and Barry Miller
Location: Overlooking a working dairy farm on Route 124, 2.3 miles east of town center. Near Cathedral of the Pines, Mount Monadnock, Sharon Art Center.
Open: Year round. Two-night mini- mum on summer and fall weekends.
Rates: $50–$75 single. $60–$130 double. $15 cot. Ten percent senior citizen discount. Weekly/monthly rates available. AMEX, MC, VISA.
♥ ❀ ◆ ✈

TLC in the form of nightly homemade chocolate truffles in a basket. Fresh berries in the fruit breads. And, if you'd like, advice (often sought) about innkeeping; but most guests come for a getaway, mountain views, antiquing, hiking, or local colleges.

After Barry, an avocational wood-carver, had spent 26 years in the corporate hotel world, the Millers moved in 1988 from Michigan to this 1853 Greek Revival house, once owned by Vannevar Bush, inventor of the computer. They created a warm, inviting ambiance with country antiques and decorated some rooms with Jan's stenciling and needlepoint. Each spring they tap the 300-year-old maple trees. Each day, guests are grateful that the Millers are doing what they do.

Bed and bath: Nine rooms; all private baths. On second floor, king, queen, double, or twin beds; rollaway available. Third-floor suite has king four-poster canopied bed, cathedral ceiling, skylight, private balcony with fantastic countryside views, wet bar.
Breakfast: 8–9:30. Juices, fruit breads, coffee, teas. Jan's creations include cinnamon sourdough French toast, Dutch apple pancakes, and egg croquettes.
Plus: Ceiling fans. Portable telephone available. Down comforters. Local restaurant menus. Transportation to and from Jaffrey airport.

The Galway House   603/532-8083
247 Old Peterborough Road, Jaffrey, NH 03452

Hosts: Joe and Marie Manning
Location: On a quiet woodland road, 10 minutes from the villages of Jaffrey and Peterborough. In foliage and skiing country. Near Cathedral in the Pines, Mount Monadnock, and beaches.

Open: September–June. Two-night minimum, September and October.
Rates: $40 single, $50 double. $10 per extra person.
🛉 🛆 ❄ ✈

> Guests wrote: *"House is lovely—an unspoiled rural delight with nearby wooded paths for an early-morning wander.... Breakfast was a treat in the bay-windowed dining room where we watched the birds.... The Mannings have a rare sixth sense that makes one feel that she 'belongs.' ... Best place I have ever been for a good night's sleep. Rooms large and pleasant.... On maps they showed us back roads for bicycling and trails for hiking that were less crowded during peak fall season. We plan on returning this winter to cross-country ski on the trails leaving from their backyard."*

The Mannings have hosted guests from as close as the next town (while the guests' house was being readied) and from as far away as mainland China. Their oversized Cape house was built in 1974 on a 1760s road (paved just a few years ago). Joe is semiretired. He and Marie think that the people-to-people concept of B&B makes it a great way to travel.

(Please turn page.)

Bed and bath: Two large second-floor rooms share a bath. One has a double bed and two twin beds, the other a double and a single bed. Cot and two cribs available.
Breakfast: 7–9. A full country breakfast including juice, hot and cold cereal, pancakes or eggs, homemade muffins, and hot beverages.
Plus: Afternoon tea. Will meet guests at Logan Airport (Boston) or the Fitzwilliam bus for an extra fee. Babysitting available. TV. Sun deck.

Lilac Hill Acres Bed & Breakfast 603/532-7278
5 Ingalls Road, Jaffrey, NH 03452

Hosts: Frank, Ellen, and Jacqulyn McNeill
Location: Two miles from historic Jaffrey center. Overlooking Gilmore Pond. Surrounded by Mondadnock, Pack Monadnock, and Temple mountains.
Open: Year round except Thanks-giving, Christmas, New Year's. Reservations required. Two-night mini-mum, October weekends.
Rates: $50 single, $60 double, $70 private bath. $25 extra person in room.
♥ ⌂ ✣ ✈ ✄

"When we looked up the hill and saw this marvelous old 1740 white farmhouse, we knew we had found a new family homestead and lifestyle. There's always family around. My father, a plasterer who worked on Boston's Music Hall/Wang Center (and his father did the original ornate work there) loves having a farm."

Now Jackie, a flight attendant, is at the farm occasionally. At Christmas-time, all the grandchildren and their parents fill the house. (But the thousands of decorations—inside and out—are up at least through the month of Janu-ary.) Frank, now retired, has an enormous (and expanding) garden with vegetables and many berries that keep Ellen busy in the wonderful open country kitchen. All the McNeills visit with guests in the comfortably fur-nished common rooms that are filled with antiques, Oriental rugs, and a glowing fire. There's an apple orchard, a stocked spring-fed pond that you can swim in, and open hay fields. As the McNeills notice, "Guests feel very relaxed here." (We did, after a day of cross-country skiing.) "They sit on the porch. They read." And when in Boston, some travelers from other parts of the country drive up just to visit and catch up.

In residence: Bengie, a dog, and four or five cats. And, some years, many farm animals.
Bed and bath: Four second-floor rooms. Private shower bath "and a superior view" for room with king bed. Two baths—one with tub and shower, one shower only—shared by three rooms, which have either a king or two twin beds.
Breakfast: 8:30–9:30. Full country. The record length is four hours!
Plus: Fireplaced living room. Tea or hot mulled cider. Ceiling fans in bed-rooms.

Old Gould Farm B&B　　　　　603/532-6996

40 Prescott Road, P.O. Box 27, Jaffrey, NH 03452-0027

Host: Margaret Gould
Location: About 2½ miles from Jaffrey center on 80 acres. Terrific view of Mount Monadnock. Near Windblown cross-country trails and Temple and Crotched Mountain ski areas. A mile to Cathedral of the Pines. Within 15 minutes of Peterborough Players, Sharon Arts Center, Monadnock trails.
Open: Year round. Advance reservations required.
Rates: Per room, $50 tax included.
🏠 🧳 🛫 ⚭

The sleighs are gone and so is the ice house, but guests are welcome at this marvelous farmhouse furnished with antiques accumulated over several generations. When Margaret retired in the summer of 1982 from her Pennsylvania kindergarten position, she came right back to the homestead that has been in the family since the 1770s. There's crisp white paint. The floors are refinished, and the antique rugs are everywhere. Margaret brings her enthusiasm to hosting a traditional B&B—with guests pretty much taking in the area during the day, rather than treating the home as an inn.

In residence: Pushkin, "my golden retriever who thinks he is a butler."
Bed and bath: Two second-floor rooms share one full hall bath. One room with two twin beds, one with a double bed. (A third room with two twin beds is available for families or friends willing to share the bath.)
Breakfast: 7–9. Full and simple. Juices, fruits, toast, muffins, eggs, cereals, jams, jellies. In dining room or on porch overlooking Mount Monadnock.
Plus: Bedroom fans. Fireplaced living room. TV. Front porch. The property has accessible woods, fields, hiking possibilities, and a rough trail around the pond.

Loch Lyme Lodge　　　　　603/795-2141
　　　　　　　　　　　　　　　　　800/423-2141

RFD 278, Lyme, NH 03768

Hosts: Paul and Judy Barker
Location: On Route 10, one mile north of the village. On a spring-fed lake surrounded by hills. Eleven miles from Dartmouth College, four miles from Dartmouth Skiway.
Open: Mid-September to Memorial Day. Closed Thanksgiving and Christmas days. Three-night minimum on Columbus holiday weekend.
Rates: $25 per person, $7 age 7 and under, $14 ages 8–15. One-time charge of $5 for crib.
🏠 🧳 ❄ 🛫 ⚭

> From New Jersey: *"Accommodations with a relaxed, old-fashioned flair. . . . Huge and delicious breakfasts. . . . We enjoyed cross-country skiing on the frozen lake. And the children had fun sledding."* From Connecticut: *" . . . entered the ambiance of a Grandma Moses farmhouse after a brisk fall walk."*

"Immediately after Labor Day we close the cabins, move from the barn (the location of our summer apartment) into the main Lodge, move all the tables and chairs out of the dining rooms (which become our living room and piano

(Please turn page.)

room), and reopen as a bed and breakfast. We enjoy all seasons, but fall and winter give us more time to spend with guests."

By 1923 the 1784 farmhouse had become part of a boys' camp and a lodging place for campers' parents and tourists too. Eventually Judy's parents ran it as a resort. When Judy and Paul left their teaching careers in 1977, they took over and added B&B in their home.

In residence: Jon Paul, age 10. Joshua, age 5. Three cats—Willie (20 years old), Beefer, and Princess.
Foreign languages spoken: Paul speaks Spanish, Judy a little French.
Bed and bath: Four second-floor rooms share two full baths, one upstairs, one downstairs. One room with king bed, one with double bed. Two have twin beds. Cot available.
Breakfast: Usually 8–9; flexible. Full country breakfast served family style on the sun porch. Busy bird feeder in view.
Plus: Fireplaced living room. Beverages. Woodlands, fields, and lake shore on 125 acres. Informal cross-country lessons and tours. Babysitting possible.

Thatcher Hill Inn   603/876-3361
Thatcher Hill Road, Marlborough, NH 03455-2539

Hosts: Marge and Cal Gage
Location: On a quiet road at top of hill. Surrounded by 60 acres of meadows and woodlands. Five miles to Mount Monadnock.
Open: Year round, but not every day in March, April, November, or December. Two-night minimum mid-September through October and all holiday weekends. Advanced reservations preferred.
Rates: Double occupancy. $68 double or twin beds. $78 king or queen. $88 queen with fireplace. $176 three-room/two-bath suite with fireplace. Singles $5 less. MC, VISA.
♥ ✿ ✖ ⌇

I couldn't decide on a favorite wide pine-floored room. Each one is "perfect" yet very livable. The sound from Cal's music boxes is a treat. Marge's decor includes braided stair rugs, her own quilts, wonderful paint colors, and small-print wallpapers.

Having owned the property since 1977, the Gages decided, upon Cal's retirement as a Chicago advertising executive, to have the 1794 house completely restored as a B&B. Now they also book wedding receptions and other special events in their gorgeous 98-year-old five-story red barn surrounded by meadows. Equestrians, antiquers, parents visiting college students, skiers, guests with special needs, world travelers—all have written to extol the hospitality and charm here.

In residence: "Our two 'corporate' cats have private cellar quarters."
Bed and bath: Seven large rooms, all private baths. Wheelchair-accessible first-floor room with two twin beds, full bath. Second-floor rooms have two twin beds, a double (one with private porch), a queen (one room with working fireplace), or a king bed; baths with claw-foot tubs, hand-held showers, and heated towel bars.

Breakfast: 8–9, Sundays 8:30–9:30. Buffet. Juices, fresh fruit. Homemade breads and muffins. Hot entrees include oatmeal with apples and wild blueberry pancakes. In fireplaced breakfast room.
Plus: Fireplaces. Games. Books. Puzzles. Snowshoes. Cross-country skiing on grounds. Private telephone room. Refrigerator privileges.

The Inn at New Ipswich   603/878-3711
P.O. Box 208, Porter Hill Road, New Ipswich, NH 03071-0208

Hosts: Ginny and Steve Bankuti
Location: Up the hill from the village center, on a peaceful road. Abutting an old cemetery. Near antiquing; 15 minutes to Mount Monadnock trails.
Open: Year round. Advance reservations preferred. Two-night minimum during foliage season and on holiday weekends.
Rates: $45 single, $60 double. $10 cot for child. $95 suite. $5 use of guest room fireplace. MC, VISA.
✹ ⅙

> From Rhode Island: *"Rooms are spotless and comfortable. . . . Great location for running, cross-country skiing, hiking."* From New Jersey (echoed by many): *"Warm, hospitable, delightful people. The breakfast alone is worth a visit."*

"B&B was our justification for buying (and redecorating) this splendid 1790 farmhouse with its fireplaces and wide plank floors. Steve, who grew up on a farm in Hungary, now has chickens. He continues to enlarge the garden—and to send guests home with zucchini. Innkeeping is so different from our days of rushing off to the office and the garage and towing business. The world comes to us—even bridal parties and, last Christmas, a South African family who joined us for a sleigh ride."

In residence: "Star is our gentle, affectionate yellow Labrador."
Foreign language spoken: Steve speaks Hungarian.
Bed and bath: Five rooms. First-floor room with two twin beds, working fireplace, private shower bath. Three second-floor queen-bedded rooms, private shower baths (one has tub and shower). Suite has double-bedded room, adjoining room with two twin beds (room for cot too), shower bath.
Breakfast: 8:30–9. (Continental thereafter.) Fresh fruit, juices, oven puffed pancakes, bacon or sausages, fresh eggs, home-baked muffins and breads. In season, homegrown berries and rhubarb. Special diets accommodated.
Plus: Welcoming refreshments. TV in living room. Quiet second-floor sitting room. Books. Games. Screened porch. Front porch rockers. Lawn chairs. Horseshoes.

---

*T*hink of bed and breakfast as a people-to-people concept.

The Buttonwood Inn

(in NH) **603/356-2625**
(in U.S. & Canada) **800/258-2625**
fax **603/356-3140**

P.O. Box 1817, Mount Surprise Road
North Conway, NH 03860-1817

Hosts: Hugh, Ann, and (son) Walter Begley
Location: Secluded. At top of hill on five acres of woods and spacious lawns. Two miles from Route 16 and village.
Open: Year round. Two-night minimum preferred on winter and holiday weekends.
Rates: Per person, double occupancy. April 1–June 20 and October 25–December 23, $20 shared bath, $35 private bath. $10 more June 21– September 12. $15 more September 13–October 24. $25–$35 midweek January–March. $30–$40 Christmas week and March weekends. $78–$98 January and February weekends includes two nights and breakfasts, Saturday dinner. Singles, $15 extra. $18 third person in room. Ski, family, and sailboat charter (on Casco Bay in Maine) packages available. AMEX, MC, VISA.
♥ ⚓ ❄ ♦ ✈

From Massachusetts: *"The entire atmosphere is simply one of warmth and hospitality."*

That atmosphere was captured for a British television feature on New England. It's all part of the fun for the Begleys, sports-oriented hosts who "have a ball teaching skiing to local schoolchildren."

After working with innkeepers while booking tours for a New Jersey bus company, Ann, together with Hugh, a school equipment salesman, opened this B&B in 1984. A waterfall in the newly done living room was their introduction to country plumbing—and calm plumbers. ("If that don't beat all.") Their 20-room added-on-to 1820s Cape farmhouse has wide board floors, country antiques, print wallpapers. There's a 40-foot swimming pool. "The real hit is Penny, who will walk, hike, or cross-country ski with any guest who will take her—and just about everyone does."

In residence: Penny, a retriever and Lab mix dog; Icis, a cat. Five grown children and five grandchildren "are always coming and going."
Bed and bath: Nine second-floor rooms, some dormered, three with private (mostly shower) baths. Three shared baths (two shower, one full). Two queen-bedded rooms have sinks. Others have a double, two twins, or a double and a twin bed. Cot available.
Breakfast: Usually 8–9:30. Full country breakfast featuring a popular low-cholesterol menu or thick French toast stuffed with preserves and fruit. At tables set with linen and fresh flowers. Sometimes hosts are assisted by granddaughter Marisa, age eight.
Plus: Dryer. Guest refrigerator. Two TV rooms. Game room with open fireplace. Horseshoes, badminton, croquet. Ski season Saturday dinner ($15 per person); summer barbecues for groups. Hiking and 60 km of groomed cross-country trails from the door.

Nereledge Inn

603/356-2831

River Road, P.O. Box 547, North Conway, NH 03860-0547

Hosts: Valerie and Dave Halpin
Location: Just off Route 16, on the road to Echo Lake State Park and Cathedral Ledge; 100 yards from Saco River. Within walking distance of village.
Open: Year round. Two-night minimum most weekends, including holidays, except April/early May and November/early December.
Rates: Per couple. $60–$80. $45–$65 singles when available (seldom on weekends). $15 extra adult. Children $1 for each year of age up to 12. AMEX, MC, VISA.
♥ ♠ ♣ ✗ ✂

> From Pennsylvania, Connecticut, Massachusetts, Indiana: *"Warmth and hospitality that makes everyone feel like they just walked into their childhood home . . . comfortable and attractive . . . hearty and delicious breakfast. . . . Dry sense of humor. . . . Advice about hiking trails."*

From all over the country letters have extolled every aspect of this old-fashioned inn built in 1787. Ten years ago Valerie, a classical music lover and beginning skier (and, in Florida, a teacher and commodity broker), established the B&B style she knows from her native England. Here she met Dave, expert skier, professional landscaper, and former Hawaii resort manager (and now deputy fire chief). And the letters go on: "My daughter wanted to stay forever. . . . Walls lined with photos of climbers . . . extras like second pillows and alarm clocks. . . . Accommodated our low-fat diet. . . . However, their cribbage board and cards favor female players over male ones."

In residence: Loki, "a large photogenic dog."
Bed and bath: Nine rooms on second and third floors. Private shower baths for queen-bedded room and one with two double beds. Private full bath in second-floor wing, queen bed, sitting room. On each floor, three rooms—with queen, double, or twin beds—share a full hall bath and a half bath. Crib and rollaway available.
Breakfast: 7:30–9:30. Juices. Eggs, French toast, pancakes, omelet (a meal in itself). Home fries. Homemade muffin or toast. Apple crumble and vanilla ice cream. In room with wide plank floors and wood stove.
Plus: Welcoming beverage. Two sitting rooms; one with wide plank floors, large wood stove, mountain views. Window fans. Sprinkler system. Some rooms with individual thermostats. Bicycle shed. Ski-waxing area. Guest refrigerator. Option of packed lunch. Babysitting arranged. Fridays and Saturdays, small beamed pub (former carriage house) open about 5–11 with English beer on draught and wine, piano, games.

Looking for a B&B with a crib? Find a description with the ♠ symbol and then check under the "bed and bath" section.

The Wilderness Inn   603/745-3890

Route 3 and Courtney Road, RFD 1, Box 69
North Woodstock, NH 03262-9709

Hosts: Michael and Rosanna Yarnell
Location: Residential with river in back yard. At Routes 3 and 112, facing a spired church and Loon Mountain's south peak. Three miles to Loon Mountain, 8 to Cannon, 20 to Bretton Woods and Waterville Valley.

Open: Year round. Two-night minimum during foliage and on holidays.
Rates: Per room. $40–$60 shared bath, $50–$75 private bath. $60–$85 suites and cottage. $10–$15 additional person. Winter and spring midweek discount.

♥ ♨ ♣ ♦ ✗

> From Massachusetts: *"An aura of warmth radiates from both the sitting room hearth and the Yarnells' quiet loving care. . . . Gourmet meals . . . a little piece of paradise."*

The shingled cottage-style house, built by a lumber baron in 1912, has mahogany-trimmed living and dining rooms and, in guest rooms, examples of the Yarnells' stained glass work. Michael, a Cornell-trained hotelier who teaches downhill skiing at Cannon Mountain and plays the violin, was with the Los Angeles Biltmore. Rosanna, a French teacher of Italian and Indian parentage, was born and raised in Ethiopia. Summers, students from France help, learn English, "and teach our guests French!"

In residence: Charles Orion, age three; Pia Camille is a year old. "Our cat, Madiera, the concierge."
Foreign languages spoken: French, Italian, Bengali, Amharic.
Bed and bath: Six rooms on two floors. Two double-bedded rooms share a full bath. One queen-bedded room, private shower bath. One room with two double beds, private shower bath. Two suites, each with a queen bed, two twin beds, and private full bath. Plus the queen-bedded cottage with beamed ceiling, built by Michael, which overlooks river. Crib available.
Breakfast: 7–10. Fresh fruit compote, juice, homemade breads, teas, hot milk with freshly ground coffee. Entrees include cranberry-walnut or apple pancakes, crepes with homemade applesauce, French toast. In warm weather, served on long enclosed porch. Option of continental breakfast in bed.
Plus: Tea, wine, or mulled cider with snacks. Fruit basket. Back yard (river) swimming hole. Dinners ($10–$20) and babysitting by arrangement.

Meadow Farm   603/942-8619

Jenness Pond Road, Northwood, NH 03261-9406

Hosts: Doug and Janet Briggs
Location: Quiet. Lake frontage, 50 acres of field and woods. Five-minute drive from Route 4; 25 minutes east of Concord and west of University of New Hampshire; 45 minutes to Gunstock ski area. Near Shaker Village in Canterbury, and antiquing.

Open: Year round. Reservations preferred.
Rates: $45 single, $60–$65 double. $10 third person. Children under three free. Family and weekly rates available. AMEX.

♨ ⛵

From New York: *"Refreshing and relaxing. An exciting trip back in time in a very old home, yet with modern comforts and a great breakfast. . . . Interesting people to be with."*

Pretty as a picture. Authentic. And it keeps getting even better. The 1770 center chimney colonial with old beams, four fireplaces, and original paneling has been restored, stenciled and painted over a period of 14 years by the Briggses. The latest addition: a screened porch, furnished with handmade twig furniture, overlooking the meadows and perennial gardens. And there are fruit trees and raspberry bushes for preserve making. And the lake for swimming (private beach and dock), fishing, and canoeing (canoe provided). And a pony for children to ride. When they aren't hosting or skiing or gardening, Janet is director of the University Program of Horsemanship and Doug manufactures and markets equipment for agricultural research.

In residence: Two dogs, Rainee, a friendly female Doberman, and Nifty, a Jack Russell terrier with lots of personality.
Bed and bath: Three antiques-filled rooms. First-floor single room shares shower bath with hosts. On second floor two double-bedded rooms share a full bath. Cot available.
Breakfast: 7:30–9. Homemade breads, muffins, and preserves. Specialties such as bismarcks, German pancakes, Belgian waffles with New Hampshire maple syrup. Served in keeping room with fireplace and bake-oven or on screened porch.
Plus: Window fans. Marked cross-country trails.

From Massachusetts: *"Interesting hosts. Marvelous home. We loved it."*

Pineapple Hospitality Host #NH621
Northwood, NH

Location: Peaceful. In the woods, without another house in sight. Two miles from Route 4, "New Hampshire's antique alley." Forty minutes from Portsmouth and Concord.

Reservations: Available year round through Pineapple Hospitality, page 106.
Rates: $65 per room.
♥ ⚕ ✽ ✕ ✁

A house restorer. An historian. A farmer with a huge vegetable garden, ducks, chickens, and geese. An artist who makes lamps from old china and hand-paints shades. A furniture maker who builds reproductions that "you can hardly tell." A chef who loves to cook. The host wears all these hats and more.

Until five years ago his pre-Revolutionary Cape-style house, a camp getaway for a symphony musician, was without plumbing or heat. The host rebuilt it, all on one floor, saving what he could. He put a central chimney where it was originally, built a brand-new kitchen, put new wide board floors in the living/dining room (which was made from three rooms), and installed a big black stove, the kind everyone gathers around. And he settled in his native New England, his favorite place, "where people now come to visit me." This after "almost becoming a doctor, studying to be a portrait painter, living in Paris for eight years, living on several continents, and in between, having

(Please turn page.)

a career in advertising." The house is filled with pewter and polished brass, old china, and family heirlooms. Two of the three porches are screened. Guests can cross-country ski or walk (two minutes) through the woods to the pond. And occasionally, you may see a fox hunt go through the property.

In residence: One dog and one cat, not allowed in bedrooms.
Bed and bath: Two first-floor rooms share a shower bath. Each room has a canopied and curtained queen bed and a working fireplace.
Breakfast: Usually 8:30. Homemade sausage, home-smoked ham, or cheese-and-mushroom omelet; granola, homemade bread, jams, jellies.

Crab Apple Inn   603/536-4476
RR 4, Box 1955 (Route 25), Plymouth, NH 03264

Hosts: Carolyn and Bill Crenson
Location: Beside a brook at the foot of Tenney Mountain, on Route 25; 4 miles west of Plymouth, gateway to the White Mountains; 40 miles north of Concord.
Open: Year round. Two-night minimum in October, on all holiday weekends, and on selected "parents weekends."
Rates: $70–$85 double occupancy. $20 extra person in room. AMEX, MC, VISA.
♥ ❖ 🐾

The 1835 brick house of Federal design is a beauty inside and out, complete with white picket fence, fan window over the entrance, and French doors leading to the patio. There's an antique wood stove in the common room, wide pine floors, and period furnishings. The Crensons embellish all this with fresh flowers, sherry-filled decanters, handmade quilts, and lace-trimmed sheets.

They had thought about hosting for a long time while Bill was an educational administrator and Carolyn a medical director for developmentally disabled adults. To complete their style of "B&B in the English tradition," they offer croquet and afternoon tea. And their brochure is a keeper, the kind that you want to put on your coffee table.

In residence: Two Lhasa apsos not allowed in guest areas.
Bed and bath: Four rooms on second and third floors, all with private full baths. Some with fireplaces. One room with queen canopy bed. Suite with queen sleigh bed and adjoining sitting room convertible to bedroom. Other rooms have a queen bed or a double and a twin. Cot available.
Breakfast: 8–9. Juice, fresh fruit, herbed cheese omelet or pancakes with ham or sausage, Crab Apple's "famous" muffins (featured in *Bon Appétit* magazine and cookbook), English jams, teas, coffee. Served in the common room or on brick patio.
Plus: Bedroom air conditioners. Hall ceiling fans. Library. Down comforters. Beverages. Candies. Fruit. Beautifully landscaped yard with English garden and wooded path through pine grove. Use of snowshoes.

Six Chimneys
603/744-2029

HC 58, Route 3A, North Shore Road, East Hebron, NH 03232-9701

Hosts: Peter and Lee Fortescue
Location: Across the road from (hidden) Newfound Lake; Mount Cardigan on the horizon. A few miles south of Plymouth. Minutes from Tenney Mountain.
Open: May–February. Two-day minimum on holiday weekends.

Rates: $55–$60 double, private bath; $50 shared. $40 single. $15 third person in room. Weekly and family rates available. MC, VISA.
♥ ❖ ◆

"Records of the old stagecoach stop show they sold a glass of rum for 10 cents. And a bed here could be rented for the same price. With all the changes this 1791 house has seen, we really feel good when someone from New Mexico leaves with the comment that they (at last) have seen the authentic New England they were looking for. Our changes include redecoration, more baths, a fireplace, and wood stoves. Our furnishings include braided and Oriental rugs and reflect the places we have lived in all over the world."

The Fortescues came here in 1971. Peter is a retired Air Force colonel who now works in the post office. Lee, a former teacher, has terrific off-the-beaten-path day trip suggestions. Their summer visitors are offered the treat of a private sandy beach and picnic facilities just a mile away.

In residence: Abigale, a friendly Border collie-spaniel "who likes to hike with guests," allowed in kitchen only.
Bed and bath: Six second-floor rooms, private shower baths (sometimes shared by families). Some large rooms, some cozy with sloped ceilings. Twins (option for king in some rooms), double, queen. Cot available.
Breakfast: 7–9. Varies daily. Entree could be pancakes or one of six kinds of French toast with bacon and sausage, local maple syrup. Fruit, orange juice, homemade muffins. Cereals. Eggs from resident hens. Served in dining room set with silver and china.
Plus: Four common rooms. Gorgeous gardens. Window fans. Ice and glasses provided. Turned-down beds. Dinner ($10–$15 each) on winter weekends by special arrangement. Cards, puzzles, croquet, horseshoes.

From New Jersey: *"A sheer delight. It's like being a guest in a lovely home. Beautiful antiques and fine food."*

Grassy Pond House
603/899-5166
603/899-5167

Rindge, NH 03461-9520

Hosts: Carmen Linares and Robert Multer
Location: Secluded. On 150 acres of woods and fields on an unspoiled lake. Minutes' walk to groomed cross-country trails and Cathedral of the Pines. Three miles from junction of U.S. Route 202 and N.H. 119.

Open: Year round. Reservations required. Two-night minimum October 5–20.
Rates: Tax included. $45 single. Double $55 shared bath, $65 private bath.
♥ ⬛ ❖ ✈ ✂

(Please turn page.)

"We're in the boonies, a place where city folks come just to hide away. Others come for weddings, for area schools, or for the outdoors. We are a traditional (small) B&B, with a layout that allows guests to have their own wing with pocket doors to our older part of the house."

There's a story for each antique, quilt, or mantel in the 1831 farmhouse, which has been carefully restored by Carmen, a management consultant-trainer who knits and weaves, and Bob, a chemical engineer. Here, on the site of Rindge's first sawmill, where the dam is now maintained by beavers, the hosts have taken on the roles of builders, gardeners, and historians. A couple of years ago they added porches that look out over the pond to Cathedral of the Pines. The latest creation "for a joyful summer" is a screened, wicker-furnished octagonal gazebo with a cupola—located between the house and the pond and surrounded by perennials.

In residence: One or two cats.
Foreign languages spoken: Spanish "and a trace of Japanese."
Bed and bath: Three first-floor rooms, private entrance. Room with two twin beds shares adjoining bath with double-bedded room. One room with double bed, private full bath.
Breakfast: Usually 8–9. In dining room overlooking pond. Carmen and Bob join you for juice, baked apple or poached pear, buckwheat pancakes, French toast or pecan waffles, breakfast meats and local maple syrup, Columbian coffee, decaf, or tea.
Plus: Beverages. Fruit. Thermostat in each room. Fans. Wool blankets. Terry robes. Audiocassette player, games, piano, books, magazines in fireplaced common room. Extensive gardens.

The Tokfarm   **603/899-6646**
P.O. Box 1124, Rindge, NH 03461

Host: Mrs. W. B. Nottingham
Location: On a 1,400-foot-high hill, on a country lane off Route 119, just beyond Massachusetts border. Five miles from Rindge village and Cathedral of the Pines, 12 from Fitzwilliam. Mount Monadnock is almost in the backyard. Near antiques shops and Franklin Pierce College.

Open: April–November. Reservations preferred. (Best time to call is early morning or evening.) Two-day minimum during foliage season.
Rates: $25 single, $35–$40 twin or double, $45 king ($50 with extra bed).
🛍 ✖️ ⚜️

"The most noise here is the chirping of birds in the morning and/or the wind in the trees when it's windy." It's a 150-year-old farmhouse that over the years became a 23-room inn on the Boston-to-Keene stagecoach road. Bought by the Nottinghams as a summer place many years ago, it is now a much smaller, very casual, comfortable B&B as well as an active 100-acre tree farm (with a cut-your-own arrangement around Thanksgiving time). The tri-state viewing site is a great vantage point for watching sunsets or, on moonlit nights, fireflies.

Mrs. Nottingham, a land preservationist who was born in Holland and educated in Canada, received an MBA from Cornell in the days when "Cornell's program was the only one that took girls." For 10 years she and her MIT professor husband ran a ski lodge in Stowe, Vermont. At times she can be talked into showing slides and home movies of the exotic and not-so-exotic places she has been to.

In residence: One cat who is mostly outdoors.
Foreign languages spoken: German, Dutch, French, and Spanish.
Bed and bath: Six rooms (never all booked at one time) on first and second floors. Each floor has one shared full bath. King, double, twin-sized beds available. Private guest entrance.
Breakfast: At 8. Continental. Juice, muffins, toast, rolls, tea, coffee, milk.
Plus: Living room with Franklin fireplace. TV. Two spring-fed ponds for cool swimming. Hiking trails. Wild blueberry picking in summer. Trout fishing in private (stocked) pond.

Province Inn 603/664-2457

Box 309, Province Road, Bow Lake, Strafford, NH 03884

Hosts: Steve and Corky Garboski
Location: Pastoral setting on a cove of a quiet lake with beavers and herons; 120 wooded acres with trails and waterfall. Near summer theater, weekend dancing and sing-alongs, restaurants, country stores, antiqu-ing. Half hour to Portsmouth or University of New Hampshire.
Open: Year round. Two-night minimum on Columbus Day weekend.
Rates: $68 per room. $12 cot. $7 crib. $5 one-night surcharge.

♥ ⚐ ⚑ ❖ ◆ ✗ ✁

The setting may be perfect for a country wedding, but this personalized B&B comes complete with a justice of the peace, the hostess. Corky is also an airline stewardess and an ice skating instructor. Steve, a former Olympic class bicyclist, is an airline pilot. The Garboskis combined all their interests and expanded their skills in 1984 when they bought and restored their 18th-century center chimney colonial, furnishing the living room with Victorian furniture and swags, the den in casual style. The extensive facilities here (see "Plus" below) make it almost a miniresort—without crowds.

In residence: In hosts' wing of house, daughter Bethany, seven. Two dogs who lead guests to the waterfall. Thai Kitty, a Siamese cat, has been known to sleep at the foot of a guest's bed or knock on the window to be let in.
Bed and bath: Four second-floor rooms share two full baths plus a half bath. Three double-bedded rooms, one with twin beds. Two rooms have nonwork-ing fireplaces. Crib or cot provided for one child in room with parents; maximum of three persons per room.
Breakfast: Usually 8:30–9. Full country meal with eggs or pancakes, bacon, fruit, muffins. In fireplaced keeping room.
Plus: Enclosed heated swimming pool. Lighted tennis courts. Use of canoes and bicycles, a solar/electric-powered sailboat, and windsurfers/paddle-boards. Cross-country skiing on 40 miles of groomed trails. Snacks. Fruit. Guest refrigerator. Barbecue. Babysitting possibility.

Haus Edelweiss Bed & Breakfast   603/763-2100
Maple Street, P.O. Box 609, Sunapee, NH 03782   800/248-0713
                                                        fax 603/763-5232

Hosts: Alan and Lillian Norton-McGonnigal
Location: At Sunapee harbor, 500 feet from the public boat landing. On a residential street. Five minutes to Sunapee ski area.
Open: Year round. Two-day minimum on holiday weekends.

Rates: $30 single. $45–$55 double, $55 with private half bath. $15 third person. Ten percent less for students, active duty military, or stay of more than three days; 15 percent less for more than seven days.
♣ ❖

Breakfast and hospitality. They are the big draw in this "Grandmother's house" Victorian decorated with comfortable furnishings and lots of plants and flowers. Alan, retired from the Air Force, and Lillian, who was a manufacturer's buyer, moved here from Cape Cod in 1986. Each evening they feature light snacks. Bavarian gluhwein (hot mulled wine), served by the living room wood stove, is a winter favorite.

In residence: Cats that love to visit with guests who book the double room.
Foreign language spoken: German.
Bed and bath: Six rooms with cross-ventilation. Private bath for third-floor double-bedded room. On second floor, one single and four doubles (three with daybeds also, one with private half bath) share two full baths.
Breakfast: Usually 7–9. All prepared by Alan. Big choice. Eggs with home fries and toast, French toast, or cold cereal with toast (Irish oatmeal in winter); all with bacon or sausage. Yankee—fish cakes, baked beans, scrambled eggs, corn bread. Bavarian—cheeses, soft-boiled eggs, German hard rolls; or German apple pancakes with whipped cream. Or continental. Juice or fruit. In dining room, on the porch, or in bed!
Plus: Extra pillows. Flowers. Mints. Fans.

The Inn at Coit Mountain   (in NH) 603/863-3583
HCR 63, Box 3, Newport, NH 03773   800/367-2364

Hosts: Dick and Judi Tatem
Location: Two miles north of Newport on Route 10 with mountain and river views. Seven miles west of Sunapee. Cross-country skiing at the door.
Open: Year round.
Rates: Singles, $70 double or queen bed, $85 queen with fireplace, $100

king with fireplace. For two, $85 double or queen bed, $100 queen with fireplace, $115 king with fireplace. Two-room suite $135 single, $150 double. MC, VISA.
♥ ♣ ❖ ♦

From Massachusetts: *"It's a lovely place. And don't forget to mention the light with wide shade directly over one bathtub. The lady of the house used to read there."*

From the outside, it's the quintessential New Hampshire inn. Inside, the 1790 Georgian features spacious and inviting rooms. But the real magnet is the turn-of-the-century addition, a 35-foot, two-storied library with Palladian window, lots of books, and huge stone fireplace. "Often, guests who come with a long list of things to do settle in there and really relax."

In 1878 the developer of Coney Island and the Long Island Railroad bought the house as a wedding present for his daughter. It has been home to the Tatems since 1985, when a B&B trip to England influenced their move from rural northeastern Connecticut. A former artist's studio is now Dick's art gallery and custom frame shop. Chef Judi is a professional retouch artist.

In residence: Dan, 17, and Melissa, 16. Becky, a red setter. Rascal, an old orange tabby. Spooky, a black Lab born on Halloween. A pony, two horses, and a family of English game hens, including a rooster.

Bed and bath: Six rooms, two with working fireplaces, on three floors. A first-floor room has a double and a twin bed, shared shower bath. Rooms on second and third floors have a king bed, a queen bed, or a double bed and a queen-sized sofa bed. A bath with footed deep tub, no shower, for each two rooms. One king-bedded suite has fireplace and an extra room with a double bed and queen-size sofa bed. One suite has queen bed, working fireplace, adjoining room with queen bed, private bath. Rollaways and crib available.

Breakfast: Usually 7:30–9. Freshly squeezed orange juice, fruits, bacon and eggs, breads and muffins, plus a specialty such as sherried creamed eggs and mushrooms on toast or pecan waffles with honey butter.

Plus: Turned-down beds. Refrigerator in each room. Grand piano. Two-storied porch. Large yard and garden. Babysitting available. Dinner ($18) by prior arrangement.

The Atwood Inn

Route 3A, RFD 2
West Franklin, NH 03235-9361

603/934-3666
800/732-5117
fax 603/934-6949

Hosts: Phil and Irene Fournier
Location: Wooded acreage with river. Twenty miles north of Concord. Within 30 minutes of Gunstock, Sunapee, and Loon mountains; 20 minutes to five lakes, including Winnipesaukee. Ten minutes to Tilton School or Proctor Academy.

Open: Year round. Two-night minimum in October and on holiday weekends.
Rates: $55 single, $70 double. $75 suite. $20 per extra person in room. $10 more for fireplaced rooms. AMEX, Diners, MC, VISA.
♥ ❖ ◆ ✈

> From Massachusetts: *"Thoughtfully decorated . . . kind, helpful hospitality . . . everything from good beds and toiletries to books and candy . . . surpassed expectations that Bed & Breakfast in New England set for us."*

Candles in each window welcome you to the 1830 Federal brick building, which was restored by the previous owners with great attention to authenticity and colonial colors and wallpapers. Six fireplaces, wide board floors, and

(Please turn page.)

Indian shutters form the backdrop for comfortable chairs, many antique four-poster beds, an eclectic collection of artwork, and antique bric-a-brac.

Phil, an insurance adjuster, and Irene, a former educational administrator and college instructor who now has an antiques booth in a cooperative shop, took early retirement in 1986. Ever since then they have been receiving rave reviews for their breakfasts; for their hints about restaurants and scenic routes; and for, as one guest said, "pampering guests to life."

In residence: Mini, a miniature schnauzer.
Foreign languages spoken: French and Greek.
Bed and bath: Seven rooms on three floors. All private shower baths. Second-floor suite has full bath and a double-bedded room plus a room with one twin bed. Four double-bedded rooms with working fireplace. One room with a double and twin beds; one with a queen and twin beds.
Breakfast: 7:30–9. Pancakes, French toast, quiche, or omelets. Fresh fruit, juice, breakfast meats, muffins, breads. Served by fireplace or on patio.
Plus: Snacks and beverages always available. Cable TV. Popcorn. Games. Bedroom window fans. Bicycle and ski storage. Patio (with bug zapper). Umbrella table amidst gardens.

Stepping Stones   603/654-9048
RFD 1, Box 208, Bennington Battle Trail, Wilton Center, NH 03086-9751

Host: D. Ann Carlsmith
Location: Quiet country setting in Monadnock hills. Facing a reservoir. Two minutes from a picture-book village. Six miles to Temple Mountain; 20 miles west of Nashua, 60 north of Boston.

Open: Year round. Reservations recommended.
Rates: Double occupancy. $50 private bath, $45 shared bath. $35 single, shared bath. No charge for infant in crib. Seventh night free.
♥ 🏡 ⁂ ✄

> From Massachusetts: *"It's a magical older home, peaceful yet inspiring, friendly yet private, comfortable yet beautiful to behold. . . . Many exquisite works of artists and artisans. . . . People travel great distances just to wander the winding paths of the spectacular perennial gardens. . . . A guest is reminded that some people and some places are still extra special."*

Many long glowing letters have arrived to praise the garden designer who spends winters weaving (rugs, throws, pillows) on her many looms. Perhaps you have come for chamber music concerts, weaving lessons, antiquing, theater, or to rest in the quiet country. When you tear yourself away, Ann can direct you to a 30-foot waterfall or to a back road lined with farms. People from all over the world—"people whom I never would have met otherwise"—have found this haven.

In residence: Mehitabel, a long-haired cat; some kittens; one dog; all kept out of bedrooms. Bantams and ducklings in the yard.
Bed and bath: Three second-floor bedrooms. One with two twin beds shares full hall bath with room that has an extra-long double bed plus a crib. Queen-bedded room has a private shower bath.

Breakfast: By 10. Belgian waffles or French toast with maple syrup or homemade preserves, sausages, omelets, croissants, homemade muffins and sweet breads, seasonal fruit and orange juice. In solar breakfast room that has plants, pottery, wood stove, and view of garden.

Plus: Beverages and ginger cookies. An opportunity to visit gardens and to observe weaving. Down comforters. Window fans. Guest refrigerator. Color TV, stereo, books and magazines in fireplaced living room.

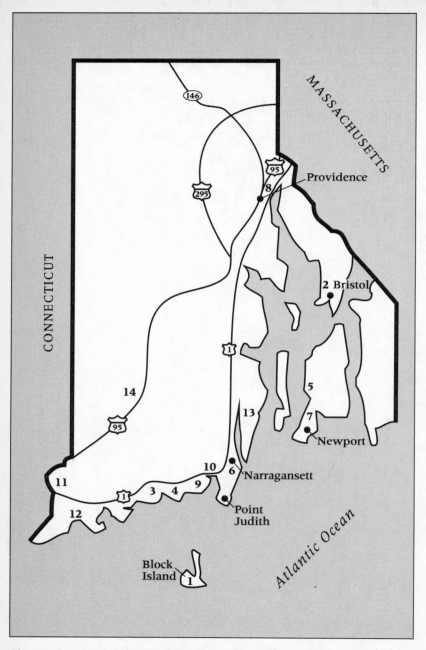

The numbers on this map indicate the locations of B&Bs described in detail in this chapter.

RHODE ISLAND

KEY TO SYMBOLS
♥ Lots of honeymooners come here.
⚘ Families with children are very welcome. (Please see page xiii.)
⚑ "Please emphasize that we are a private home, not an inn."
♣ Groups or private parties sometimes book the entire B&B.
◆ Travel agents' commission paid. (Please see page xii.)
✖ Sorry, no guests' pets are allowed.
✄ No smoking inside *or* no smoking at all, even on porches.

Rhode Island
_____ Reservation Services _____

Anna's Victorian Connection

5 Fowler Avenue, Newport, RI 02840-1820

Phone: 401/849-2489. 24-hour live answering service. Reservations made daily: May, June, September, and October, 9 a.m–9 p.m.; July and August, 8 a.m.–10 p.m.; November–April, 12 noon–8 p.m.

Listings: 120. Some inns, apartments, houses. Mostly private residences within 15 minutes of downtown Newport. A few are in other parts of Rhode Island and over the Massachusetts border in North Attleboro and New Bedford.

Reservations: Advance notice preferred. Some available through travel agents.

Rates: $25–$150 single. $50–$200 double. One night's lodging rate required as a deposit. Balance due upon arrival. Refunds of 90 percent for cancellations made two weeks or more before scheduled arrival date. AMEX, Diners, Enroute, MC, VISA. ♦

Susan White, a school guidance counselor, and Susan Mailey, a nurse (who, 20 years ago, started Newport's first cooperative day care center), teach a how-to-run-a-B&B course. As hosts who found a need for a service, they established Anna's with a handful of listings. Now they "make careful matches" in a wide variety of annually inspected properties—a house on the harbor, a Cape Cod-style home, an antebellum Ocean Drive mansion, neighborhood Victorian houses, and historic inns.

Bed & Breakfast, Newport Ltd.

33 Russell Avenue, Newport, RI 02840-1723

Phone: 401/846-5408, 9 a.m.–8 p.m. daily.

Fax: 401/846-1828.

Listings: 60+ private residences. Most are in Newport, but several are in nearby Middletown ("five minutes down the street from Newport"), Portsmouth, and Jamestown. Just added—South County, which includes Narragansett and Wickford.

Reservations: Two weeks' advance notice suggested.

Rates: $65–$85 shared bath, $75–$125 private bath. Some with family and weekly rates. One night's lodging rate is a required deposit. (Balance due in cash or travelers' checks upon arrival.) For cancellations made more than a week before scheduled arrival, deposit refunded less $15 service charge. If cancellation made within seven days of scheduled arrival date, refund less $15 service charge made if filled by another reservation. AMEX, MC, VISA.

As owner/hostess of Bluestone, page 317, Cindy Roberts found that she was booking so many Newport area residents with her overflow that she established this attentive service. "We inspect and interview. We are concerned about cleanliness and friendliness. Every one of my listings is special—whether right in town within walking distance to everything or in quiet residential sections with extensive gardens." The homes range from modest to luxurious, from urban to rural, from waterfront to hilltop. Many are historic; some are contemporary. Free directory of sample listings available.

Plus: Dinner reservations, floral arrangements, champagne . . . "whatever you wish."

Bed & Breakfast of Rhode Island

P.O. Box 3291, Newport, RI 02840-0993

Phone: 401/849-1298 Newport County; 401/941-0444 Providence and Massachusetts; 401/782-3666 Narragansett; Monday–Friday 9–5, Saturday 9–12.
Listings: 120. Most are hosted private residences; some inns.

Reservations: Two-night minimum on summer weekends in resort areas.

Rates: $38–$225 single. $50–$225 double. Weekly and monthly rates available. Required deposit is one night's lodging rate plus one-half of each additional night. If cancellation is received at least two weeks before reservation date, refund is given minus $15 processing fee. No refunds within two weeks of scheduled arrival date. AMEX, MC, VISA usually accepted for last-minute reservations only.

Although Barbara and Rodney Wakefield have a roster that is concentrated in and around Newport, Providence, and Narragansett, many other Rhode Island communities are represented. In addition, a few are just over the Massachusetts border.
  Rodney has considerable travel experience—as director of health care systems for a major corporation. Now he and Barbara visit and inspect each home, and each is "hosted by interesting, friendly and hospitable people." And they offer tours, discounts to attractions, concerts, theme packages, and assistance with special events.

Other reservation services with B&Bs in Rhode Island:
  Bed & Breakfast/Inns of New England, page 257.
  Covered Bridge, page 4.
  Pineapple Hospitality, page 106.

Rhode Island B&Bs

The Barrington Inn   401/466-5510

P.O. Box 397, Beach and Ocean Avenue, Block Island, RI 02807

Hosts: Joan and Howard Ballard
Location: On a knoll overlooking Great Salt Pond. Three-quarters of a mile from ferry, one-half mile from airport. Five-minute walk to beach.
Open: April–November. Advance reservations necessary for summer weekends. Two-night minimum July, August, and weekends; three nights on holiday weekends spring through fall.

Rates: Per room. Summer $85, $115, $125, $130, or $140. About $20–$40 less September, October, May (except Memorial Day weekend), and early June. 40 to 50 percent less April and November. $20 per night for third adult in room. MC, VISA.
♥ ✳ ✈ ✄

Even though Howard's family had vacationed on the island since the turn of the century, he never had any idea—not even a dream—that he would be doing what he is. When the Ballards lived in Michigan, Joan was mother to four and a secretary. It's a long story, but it ends (or begins really) with the purchase of what was a family summer home. "We were sort of thrown into this. Howard, a former shipyard manager, has always repaired everything we own. Now he has his own home maintenance business, he handles all the repairs at the inn, and our family is grown. The vacation atmosphere is very different from working in an office. I love it!"

Furnishings include wicker and antiques—all in keeping with a big old farmhouse, "but we're constantly making changes and redecorating." A picture of the original 1886 house is in the living room. Other photographs—of tall ships, sunsets, and old island scenes—are Howard's work. On the grounds there's an old apple orchard favored by many colorful birds.

Bed and bath: Six rooms of various sizes on three levels. All with private shower baths and ceiling fans. On second floor, double or queen bed, sliding glass doors to private deck, water views. On third floor, two rooms with a double and a single bed and sitting area; and one room has a queen, a single, and wonderful water views.
Breakfast: 8–9:30. Fresh fruit, juices, cereal, homemade muffins, coffee, tea, milk, and hot chocolate. Served by Joan and Howard in dining room and/or on deck.
Plus: Late-afternoon or evening beverages. Well water. Two living rooms, one with color TV, VCR, games. Deck with water view and sunsets. Outside shower. Off-street parking. Off-season, will meet guests at ferry or airport.

From New York: *"Quiet . . . within walking distance of beach, harbor, and restaurants. . . . Tasteful renovations. Comfortable rooms. Delightful in off-season."*

The Sea Breeze   401/466-2275

Spring Street, P.O. Box 141, Block Island, RI 02807-0141

Hosts: The Newhouse family with Lisa Stiepock
Location: On the crest of a hill overlooking a two-acre meadow and ponds, with broad view of the ocean and coastline. Five-minute walk to restaurants, shops, and ferry landing.

Open: Year round. Two-night minimum; three nights on holiday weekends Memorial Day–Columbus Day.
Rates: Double occupancy. $80–$100 shared bath; $130–$150 private bath. MC, VISA.
♥ ❀ ✈ ✄

"The gardens are just as we planned—with several hundred varieties of perennials, roses, and flowering shrubs. They make the perfect spot for small weddings. And the five original cottages are now four, completely renovated with the feel of seaside cottages."

Mary Newhouse, a Manhattan artist, and her physician husband listened when one of their daughters suggested B&B for the compound of five very tired houses purchased in 1979. Together, the family, known for their decorating service and the Sea Breeze Gallery (now located in an old harbor-area building) planned and redid. Rooms were enlarged and filled with English chintzes, country antiques, and contemporary art. And now two of the rooms are open year round.

In residence: Daughter Lisa's "quiet and gentle" Australian shepherd, Blue.
Foreign languages spoken: German, French, some Spanish and Italian, depending on family members in residence.
Bed and bath: Ten rooms on first and second floors. All shower baths; five are private. Double or twin beds; six rooms have ocean views; four have private porches.
Breakfast: 8:30–9:30. Viennese coffee, English tea. Freshly baked croissants or muffins, homemade preserves, fruit, juice. Served on trays in the sitting room or in baskets brought directly to rooms with private baths. May be taken to rooms or onto porch or lawns.
Plus: Sitting room. Sitting and writing area on the second floor. Guest refrigerator, sink, and glasses provided.

The Sheffield House   401/466-2494

P.O. Box C-2, High Street, Block Island, RI 02807   **fax 401/466-5067**

Hosts: Steve and Claire McQueeny
Location: In historic district, one block from ferry landing. Two blocks from beach.
Open: Year round. In season, two-night minimum on weekends.
Rates: Double occupancy. Memorial Day weekend through September and Columbus Day weekend, $80–$100 shared bath; $110–$125 private. Rest of year, $40–$80. Senior citizen and midweek discount (except in August), 10 percent less. AMEX, MC, VISA.
♥ ❀ ♦ ✈

(Please turn page.)

"Aunt Claire," as one guest dubbed the enthusiastic hostess, has a very big family these days. When the McQueenys started B&B it was a casual second home, with Claire spending winters as a florist in Connecticut. In 1987 they became permanent residents. ("How lucky we feel.") Their family pieces and antiques add to the home-away-from-home atmosphere of the summer cottage built in 1888 for a Providence doctor.

"The wraparound front porch has been rebuilt complete with gingerbread. Steve, now chairman of the planning board, continues with his worldwide brokerage firm. As gardener, he added zillions of daffodils (that bloomed for six weeks). The perennial gardens are flourishing. Through my flower business, I design wedding arrangements. Our oldest daughter, also a permanent resident, is in her sixth season with a gift shop. Lots of guests are returning, but we still see new faces every year. And please remind your readers that the Nature Conservancy just declared Block Island 'one of the Ten Great Places in the Western Hemisphere.'"

In residence: "Heather is our aging calico cat who sunbathes on her back. Maggie, our 'black golden' retriever, gets lots of attention." (Neither allowed inside.)

Bed and bath: Seven rooms on first and second floors. Double or twin beds; five private baths, one with tub.

Breakfast: Juices, coffee, herbal tea, fruit, homemade muffins. Buffet style in country kitchen that has a bottle collection from all over the world.

Plus: Beverages. Fans and heat in bedrooms. Will meet guests at airport or ferry. Books and games. Refrigerator, ice and glasses. Grill. Picnic table. Porch rocking chairs. Bike rack. Sometimes, an island tour. One downstairs room becomes a library in winter.

From Maryland: *"Personal, helpful, charming . . . it's great!"*

The White House   401/466-2653

Spring Street, Block Island, RI 02807-0447

Hosts: Joseph V. and Violette M. Connolly

Location: On top of rolling lawns overlooking the ocean. About a three-minute walk to town and beaches.

Open: Year round. Three-night mini-

mum on Memorial Day, July 4, Labor Day weekends.

Rates: $120 for Captain's Quarters, $100 for Oriental, $75 for Louis Philippe. Weekly rate. Off-season, 50 percent less. AMEX, MC, VISA.

♥ ⛵ ✈

The hosts bring a strong sense of community to their B&B involvement. Joseph, a *Block Island Times* columnist, is a former president of the Block Island Residents' Association. Violette is president of Block Island Gardeners and founder/chairman of the Block Island House & Garden Tours that benefit the Historical Society.

The Connollys' varied interests and experiences certainly make for lively conversation. When they started B&B in 1985, Joseph said that if he liked the guests, he would invite them for a drink. Violette reports, "So far, no one has gone dry." Joseph was brought up in a publishing family, was a World

War II navy pilot, studied drums with Gene Krupa, and is still very much into big band jazz. Now retired, he was chairman of Synthetic Oil Corporation of America. Violette had a long association with the Brooklyn Botanic Garden, has been media consultant to the Association of Junior Leagues of America, and worked on special assignments for NBC.

Their seven-bedroom house has seen many changes since being built almost 200 years ago. From the late 1800s until World War I it was a successful B&B. The wide board floors in the west wing are century-old planks found in the hayloft.

In residence: Two dogs, one cat.

Restrictions: No smoking in bedrooms. The Connollys are "old-fashioned about guests' marital status. Joseph says he's not square; he's a cube." Sorry, no pets.

Bed and bath: Two B&B rooms; shared full bath. In summer, Captain's Quarters (canopied four-poster double bed) and Oriental Room (two twin beds). Both with French doors to an ocean-facing balcony. In winter, single beds in Presidents' room (with documents and autographs) and Louis Philippe Room (collections pertaining to royalty).

Breakfast: At 8:30. Juices, cereals, bacon and eggs, muffins, fresh fruits, French toast. Hosts join you at oval table facing the ocean.

Plus: Separate guests' entrance and living/TV room. Fireplace in 60-foot-long Tavern room. Garden flowers. House furnished with French provincial antiques and collections. Possibility of island tours. Japanese garden. Occasionally, dinner in winter. Will meet guests at airport or ferry.

Anna's Victorian Connection Host #103

Bristol, RI

Location: On about an acre of land on a side street in a town with big old homes. One block from movie theater and coffee shop; 25 minutes to Providence or Newport.

Reservations: Available year round through Anna's Victorian Connection, page 300. Two-night minimum on holidays.

Rates: $65 single, $75 double.
🛏 ✂

Hometown USA. A town of 15,000 known for its Fourth of July celebration, which begins in early June and culminates in a week of free concerts before the parade seen by 250,000 people. And within two blocks, first-run movies for 99 cents, a well-patronized coffee shop with sidewalk chairs (gotta see what's going on in town), six churches, a synagogue, and a YMCA. Word has it that some Newporters come here for an evening getaway.

The host, a retired navy man, observes that New York City folks come here for the peace and quiet of a real New England town. His enthusiastic wife also loves to share. "They lie out on the grass or in our hammocks. They throw a beach ball around. And they borrow one of our bicycles for the 15-mile-long path that goes from here along an old railroad bed to East Providence. And

(Please turn page.)

on July 4, B&B guests are welcome to join our endless family buffet, which follows the parade and precedes the carnival."

Grandparents of four, the well-traveled hosts—Tahiti, Australia, New Zealand, Soviet Union, Africa—have "some old, some new, some collectibles, and some world-wide furnishings" in their 14-room 1845 Victorian house.

Bed and bath: Two first-floor rooms in guest area, each with antique sleigh double bed (step stool provided to reach one), share a full and a half bath. **Breakfast**: 8:30–10. Ever-changing repertoire. Fruit compote. Maybe stuffed French toast. "Something different" such as Portuguese sausage. Fresh Portuguese bread from the neighborhood bakery. Served in dining room, or at umbrella table on large deck. **Plus**: Beverages. The yard. Suggestion for neighborhood walking route.

Pineapple Hospitality Host #RI225

Bristol, RI

Location: On Route 114, a main road. In a residential area, a mile from downtown; 13 miles from Providence and Sakonnet Winery. Minutes to neck of Bristol harbor. Across from 500-acre bay-front Colt State Park; 10 minutes to 33-acre bayside Blithewood Gardens and Arboretum.

Reservations: Available year round through Pineapple Hospitality, page 106. Two-day minimum preferred on weekends and holidays. **Rates**: Per room. $75 four-poster, fireplace. $70 twins, fireplace. $130 suite. $60 twins or double four-poster. $45 double.
♥ 🛄 ❄ ✂

"A living museum rather than a Newport mansion," say many of the guests who stay where George Washington and Thomas Jefferson once had dinner. This is the oldest known three-story wooden structure. It's a saltbox with three floors and an attic, 17th-century marbleizing, an entrance hall that was probably used for dancing, and a Jacobean staircase. Not until the hosts bought it—in 1983, when they were looking for an historic house—did they realize its special significance. Now listed on the National Register of Historic Places, it is hosted by a lawyer and his wife, an Englishwoman who remembers the style of B&B practiced by her relatives and neighbors. She considers cooking an art form. She has a special appreciation for textiles. And she is volunteer coordinator at the Herreshoff Marine Museum (America's Cup). Both hosts make restaurant reservations, suggest lots of local museums, and, yes, share the history of the impressive house filled with traditional pieces, antiques, crystal, watercolors—and a feeling of home.

In residence: Two cats who go into guests' rooms by request only (happens often). One short-haired dog with his own fan club of guests. **Foreign language spoken**: A little French. Nearby daughter-in-law visits with guests who speak French, Italian, and Spanish. **Bed and bath**: On second and third floors, seven rooms, comfortable but "intentionally not overly furnished or decorated." Three shared baths; two full, one with tub only.

Breakfast: Usually 8–9:30. Large platter of fruit, homemade creme fraiche. Chocolate popovers or "invented on the spot" homemade muffins. Main dish could be German pancakes, frittatas, or "hangtown fry" (a gold rush dish: omelet with onions and oysters).

Plus: Welcoming refreshments. Lots of books and reading areas. Large keeping room with original kettle cranes in fireplace.

Inn the Meadow

401/789-1473

1045 Shannock Road, Charlestown, RI 02813

Hosts: Yolanda and Michael Day

Location: Quiet. On five acres of meadow and woods.

Open: Year round. Two-night minimum on Memorial, July 4, and Labor Day weekends. Eight miles south of Wakefield; 20 minutes' drive to Block Island ferry, 10 minutes to beaches, 40 minutes to Newport.

Rates: $40 single, $45 double, $50 queen. $60 three twins or king and one twin. October 15–Memorial Day, 20 percent less. B&B and Valentine's Day dinner, $60 for two. Discover, MC, VISA.
♣ ♦ ✈ ⅙

The comfortable contemporary garrison colonial, built on a former horse farm, is surrounded by open meadows and woods and, sometimes, visits by deer. "The closest we'll come to having horses (everyone asks us) is our two wooden 'lawn cows,'" says Yolanda, an adult education instructor in business math/accounting. The old horse stalls are now used by Michael, a chemist, for his stained glass studio.

Since 1989, when the Days moved here (having lived in Rhode Island for 15 years), they have been hosts "mostly to beachgoers and Newport tourists, but we also remember the week of singing and sword fighting by *Man of La Mancha* cast members."

In residence: Three short-haired cats, "Lewis, all girl; Clark, all male; Snowball, old girl."

Foreign language spoken: German.

Bed and bath: Four carpeted second-floor rooms share a second-floor full bath and a first-floor shower bath. Two queen-bedded rooms, one with private deck and garden view. One room with double bed. One with two twins/king plus a twin.

Breakfast: Usually 8–9:30. Homemade granola, muffins, bagels. French toast or eggs. Fruit. Yogurt. Juice. Coffee. In guest dining room with hat collection.

Plus: Afternoon tea or soda. Fireplaced living room. Down comforters. Forgotten items basket. Piano. Picnic basket, $4 per person. Backyard stargazing.

If you have met one B&B host, you haven't met them all.

One Willow by the Sea   401/364-0802

1 Willow Road, Charlestown, RI 02813-4160

Host: Denise Dillon Fuge
Location: On a quiet road. Bordered by a large meadow and wilderness area. Seven-minute drive to sandy beach; 5 miles to wildlife refuges, 4 to Theatre-By-The-Sea, 10 to University of Rhode Island, 25 to Mystic and Newport, 11 to Block Island ferry.

Open: Year round. Two-day minimum on national holidays and on University of Rhode Island and Brown University graduations.
Rates: April 15–November 1, $55 double, $50 single. Off-season, $10 less.
♥ ☛ ❖ ♦ ✂

A flexible hostess. A comfortable kick-off-your-shoes-and-relax split-level house furnished with "good" antiques and comfortable sofas and lots of books (read by a family who left very rested) and flowers. A deck where you can "hear the sea and smell the sea breezes."

Denise spent 31 years in New York City, where she created and edited a medical journal for Memorial Sloan-Kettering Cancer Center. As a teenager in London during World War II, she was inspired by the suffragists. In the 1980s she was president of the New York City NOW chapter. She also helped create the National Women's Health Network. Denise has experience in publishing, speaking, and lobbying—and, since coming here, as a library trustee and literacy volunteer. For winter beach walks, she "borrows a dog." Next? Inquire about owl prowls, murder mystery, or bird migration theme weekends.

In residence: Lizzie, "a 10-year-old Russian blue ex-Manhattanite cat." Minou, a young Siamese, "takes role of discreet morning greeter seriously."
Foreign languages spoken: "Slightly fractured French; some understanding of Danish-Norwegian/Swedish."
Bed and bath: Three rooms plus family room. Main floor, two queen-bedded rooms sharing a full bath. Lower level, room with two twin beds, adjacent shower bath. Family area with double bed, space for two cots and a crib.
Breakfast: 6:30–10. Cantaloupe with ginger, vanilla yogurt, fresh fruit, bagels, blueberry muffins, and "my son's killer croissants from the best deli in town." Juices. Gourmet coffee and tea. Upon request, French crepes; Irish oatmeal; English scrambled eggs with sausages, ham, or bacon. On sun deck or in dining room on glass-topped table with fine china.
Plus: Thick bath sheets. Sun-dried sheets. Terry robes. Extra pillows. Window fans. Bedside radio. Boat trailer parking. Champagne for special occasions. Will meet train or plane. Wood stove in winter. Dinner and theater reservations. Discount beach passes and bridge tokens.

---

*I*s B&B like a hotel?
How many times have you hugged the doorman?

Fairfield-By-The-Sea

401/789-4717

527 Green Hill Beach Road, Green Hill, RI 02879-5703

Host: Jeanne Ayers Lewis
Location: Between Westerly and Wakefield, in a secluded country setting, ¾ mile from ocean beach, 2 miles from Theatre-By-The-Sea, 10 from University of Rhode Island. Twenty miles east of Mystic; 25 west of Newport. Near Block Island ferry and Yawgoo ski area.

Open: Year round. Two-night minimum on weekends, three nights on most holiday weekends.
Rates: Per room. $55 May through October. Less, off-season. Cot $10 child under six, $12 anyone six and over.
♥ 🏠 ❄ ✈ ⚭

Zest, here art thou! A blueberry-soup cooking expert, as seen in Bloomingdale's. An entrepreneur with a small mail-order business selling her truffles and bouquets of chocolate roses. A poet, avid gardener, and grandmother who has explored "every inch of this accessible and culturally rich state." A creative home economist who has been a nationwide consumer consultant and has edited national publications. A retired teacher, considered the B&B mentor of the state, who gives many workshops on food, crafts, stitchery, use of phyllo leaves, bread making.

The contemporary country home on 3½ acres was what Jeanne's husband always wanted to design and build. And at last he did. It is a lovely place—one of our havens on a B&B-to-B&B cycling trip—filled with art, maps, family pictures, quilts, silhouettes, painted rocks, and books. "Stress reduction" is a theme, especially in winter. Guests sit by the fire, bird-watch, read, walk on the beach, enjoy breakfast conversations—and return.

In residence: Murphy, a friendly terrier. "And Harrington, a life-sized soft sculpture butler."
Bed and bath: Two rooms "in the treetops" reached by a living-room spiral staircase. One with twin/king option, one with double share a full bath and a half bath.
Breakfast: 8–10 but flexible. Continental with fresh fruit and homemade breads. Eat in dining room or on an open deck.
Plus: An answering machine with message that makes you smile. Wonderful hot/cold outdoor shower. Picnic area. Fans. Option of seafood feasts if prepared cooperatively. "Mine is an equal opportunity kitchen."

B&Bs offer the ultimate concierge service.

Lindsey's Guest House
401/846-9386

6 James Street, Middletown, RI 02840

Hosts: Anne and Dave Lindsey
Location: In residential area. Ten-minute walk to Second Beach, restaurants, Norman Bird Sanctuary, Sachuest Point Wildlife Refuge. Two miles to Newport's harbor, shops, entertainment; 1½ to Bellevue Avenue mansions, Tennis Hall of Fame, Cliff Walk.
Open: Year round. Two-night minimum July and August.

Rates: Double occupancy. July and August, $60 weekends, $10 one-night stay surcharge; $50 weekdays. May, June, September, October, $5 less. $10 less November–April. $20 extra person. $10 under age 12 (with two adults). MC, VISA.
♥ ⌂ ♣ ♦ ✂

Over 30 years as bed and breakfast hosts—and still going strong. Away from the hubbub is the Lindseys', a split-level house where conversation runs the gamut—from family to Newport attractions, from hints about bargain hours at good restaurants to Elderhostel, from gardening to shell collecting.

"This last year we had the opportunity to share our home with couples from China and East Germany, and a family from Russia. The more people we meet, the more we realize how much we as humans are alike."

Dave traveled the world over in his days with the navy. He and Anne have 7 grown children and 13 grandchildren.

Bed and bath: Three rooms. One on street level with double bed, private entrance, private bath (handicapped accessible, 27-inch access). Queen-bedded room and one room with two twin beds share a full bath. Rollaway and crib available.
Breakfast: Usually 8–10. Juice, cereal, fruit in season, English muffins, bagels and cream cheese, homemade jams and coffee cake, coffee, tea, and milk. In dining room at table set with linens, candles, and color-scheme-of-the-month flowers.
Plus: Ceiling fans in guest rooms and dining room. Off-street parking. Wraparound deck. Large yard. Swing.

From Missouri: *"Almost from the time we arrived, we felt as if we had known them a long time. A homey, relaxing atmosphere with clean, comfortable rooms."*

Polly's Place
401/847-2160

349 Valley Road, Middletown, RI 02840

Host: Polly Canning
Location: On the Newport line, a mile from Newport harbor. On Route 214, set back from the road. Fronted by split rail fence and rosebushes. In back, large backyard and brook.

Open: Year round. Two-night minimum July and August weekends.
Rates: Memorial Day–September 30, $75 and $80. Off-season, $50–$65.
♥ ⌂ ♣ ♦ ✈ ✂

As a Newport Realtor and B&B hostess, Polly has met many America's Cup crew members. Her own extensive travels have taken her as far as Australia, where she visited some guests who have stayed in her comfortably furnished extended Cape house.

"Sometimes guests linger in the kitchen or on the deck. They enjoy sitting on the Adirondack chairs in the yard, under the weeping willow by the brook. I love to bake and to garden and to suggest cycling routes, picnic spots, or concerts. It's a good feeling to see people who arrive as strangers leave as friends."

Bed and bath: Four rooms. Two first-floor rooms, one with a double, one with two twin beds, share a shower bath. On second floor, two large rooms, each with king bed, share a full bath.
Breakfast: 8–9:30. Juices, fruit salad, yogurt, cereal, breads, homemade muffins and jams, coffee, tea. In dining room or on deck overlooking yard.
Plus: Egg crate foam on all beds. Bedroom ceiling fans. Down comforters. Fresh flowers. Thick towels. Sometimes, in season, take-home veggies from the garden. Living room with brick fireplace and grandfather clock.

From Philadelphia: *"Gracious hostess. Clean, comfortable, beautiful surroundings. Very quiet and relaxing."*

Ilverthorpe Cottage   401/789-2392
41 Robinson Street, Narragansett, RI 02882

Hosts: Chris and John Webb; Jill Raggio
Location: On a residential street in historic district. Three blocks to shops, restaurants, The Victorian Towers. Five-minute walk to beach.

Open: May–November. Two-night minimum on summer weekends.
Rates: Per room. $65–$70 shared bath, $70–$75 private.
♥ 🏠 ✿

From Massachusetts: *"A most gracious breakfast. Every bit of of the house artistically beautiful . . . all wonderful."*

Those artistic touches change as Chris, a first-grade teacher, finishes a new (gorgeous) basket or is inspired to redecorate a wall or even an entire room—with stenciling or small-print wallpaper, dried or fresh flower arrangements, messages written in calligraphy, or lace heart pillows. From the flower, vegetable, and herb gardens come garnishes and flavorings for the breakfast, one of the features shown on an NBC television news segment. Teenaged daughter Jill, who has grown up as "assistant innkeeper," often greets guests and helps with the morning meal.

Bed and bath: Four second-floor rooms. Two have private baths: one room with king bed, the other with canopied four-poster double bed. Room with twin beds and five windows shares a full bath with adjoining double-bedded room. Cot available.
Breakfast: "Meant to spoil each and every guest." At 8:30. Maybe breakfast pizza, cheese souffles, pocket omelets, baked eggs, blintzes. Fresh fruit, juices,

(Please turn page.)

coffee, and regular, herbal, or English tea. Homemade breads; could be fruit flan, French egg puff, poppy seed bread. In the dining room or on the veranda.
Plus: Wraparound porch; screened half accessible through living-room French doors. Wine. Foyer ceiling fan. Will meet guests at the Greene airport, Kingston train station, or bus stop. Bus to Newport passes by the street. Babysitting. Off-street parking. Use of refrigerator, dishes, and glassware. Outdoor children's gym set. Games for adults and children.

Mon Rêve   401/783-2846
41 Gibson Avenue, Narragansett, RI 02882

Host: Eva Doran   **Rates**: $55 double or twin bedroom.
Location: One mile to town beach. $80 suite.
Ocean is three blocks away.   ♥ ♨
Open: Year round. Two-day mini-
mum stay on weekends.

> Guests wrote: *"Memorable. . . . Beautiful Victorian decor . . . delicious breakfasts served with warmth and with care to epicurean detail. . . . It's like being with family. . . . Helpful advice about the area . . . charming conversations. . . . Exceeded my expectations. I left relaxed and smiling."*

For all those reasons, guests return—sometimes with extended family—to this home built in the 1890s for a New York financier and later owned by sculptress and artist Florence Kane. It's now on the National Register of Historic Places and filled with Victorian furnishings.

The Dorans, longtime residents, were among the first to host B&B guests when the Narragansett Chamber of Commerce began encouraging the arrangement in private homes. Since the last edition of this book, Eva, a lecturer and writer who has taught French at three Rhode Island colleges and universities, has acquired a "good working fluency in Spanish." Her husband, Jim, a retired sea captain, enjoys boating, fishing, "and those two antique cars he is working on."

In residence: Jim smokes a pipe.
Foreign languages spoken: French, Italian, Spanish.
Bed and bath: Four rooms on second and third floors, each with its own private hall and private full bath. Double beds are antiques. One suite with double bed and a twin bed, two double-bedded rooms, and one with two twins.
Breakfast: 9 and 10. Hearty and varied, "some dish you're apt not to have at home, with homemade breads, blueberries from nearby woods, and Mon Rêve's raspberries." First course is a fruit dish. Entrees alternate a variety of egg dishes, a wide range of pancakes/crepes/waffles. Fresh-brewed coffee, decaf, tea (including herbal). Orange juice. Fresh-baked breads or muffins. Served in enclosed plant-filled sun porch.
Plus: Fans in bedrooms. Picnic table and grill. Free use of bicycles. Half-price tokens for Newport Bridge.

Murphy's B&B   401/789-1824

43 South Pier Road, Narragansett, RI 02882

Hosts: Martha and Kevin Murphy
Location: In a residential neighborhood, one block from the ocean and a small boat launch site with fishing pier. Ten-minute walk to beach.
Open: Daily May–October; weekends rest of year. Two-night minimum on weekends, three nights on holiday weekends.
Rates: $60 single, $65–$80 double. $10 more, holiday weekends. Discount for one week or longer.

♥ ⊯ ❄ ✖ ⌇

> From Connecticut: *"As we approached Murphy's, I just knew I would love it. The grounds were well kept and lovely."* From New York: *"Martha Murphy's warm hospitality is exceeded only by her culinary expertise, served with charm in beautiful surroundings."* From Colorado: *"The room was lovely. Everything was spotless. Martha was friendly yet gave us the privacy we needed."*

As you approach the fuchsia door, you pass the steps and columned porch filled with fuchsia-colored geraniums. Built in 1894 as a summer residence, it's a comfortable Victorian restored with care by Martha, a teacher and writer, and Kevin, a commercial fisherman and artist. It has oak parquet floors, a massive stone fireplace, Waterford crystal sconces, and antique furnishings; but this B&B's latest claim to fame is *The Bed & Breakfast Cookbook*, which features hundreds of recipes—submitted from B&Bs all over the country—that Martha tested (and guests critiqued). Kevin's scrimshaw pieces, some of which have been exhibited at Mystic Seaport, are etched on cured swordfish swords that have the look of ivory.

In residence: "Some guests never see our two sweet dogs who live in fenced-in backyard."
Foreign languages spoken: Very little French and German.
Bed and bath: Two third-floor rooms with no common wall. Large private full baths. Queen-bedded room (and its bath) have an ocean view. One room with two twin beds convertible to king.
Breakfast: Full 8:30–9:30; continental, 9:30–10:30. Repertoire from "The Book." Fresh fruit in season, pastries, pancakes, French toast or waffles, juices, freshly ground coffee. Murphys' own herbs, vegetables, and raspberries. Served at table with linen, silver, fresh flowers.
Plus: Afternoon tea (recipes from "The Book"). Beverages. Fireplaced living room. Third-floor sitting area with lots of sightseeing information. Color TV in each bedroom. Much reading material in guest rooms. Cafe tables on porch. Cookbooks, antique silver, and Kevin's scrimshaw for sale.

"I'll just sleep in the morning," said one college-age son, until the next day when he smelled the muffins.

The Old Clerk House   401/783-8008
49 Narragansett Avenue, Narragansett, RI 02882-3386

Host: Patricia Watkins
Location: One block from Narragansett beach and mile-long sea wall walk. In residential pier section. Six miles to Block Island ferry. Fine restaurants, shops, cinema within four-block radius.

Open: Year round.
Rates: May 1–October 15, $65 single, $75 double. Off-season, $15 less. $20 third person in room. $10 one-night weekend surcharge.
♥ ✖ ✄

The yard is "very English," with a white picket fence and lots of flowers, particularly roses. The c. 1890 house, once the home of a succession of town clerks, was completely redone over a period of three years by Pat, a former technical reference specialist with an international development organization. Here she is a computer consultant and Friends of Oceanography board member who shares her lovely home with beachgoers and Block Island visitors—and with business guests, who feel comfortable enough to spread out their work on the oak dining-room table. The living room has leather sofa and chairs. Guests ask about the clocks, the copper collection, and sons' photos (one is a literary novelist). For someplace different, Pat will suggest "a delightful nearby village huddled around a cove" and "an historic house nestled in a woody hollow with millstream."

In residence: Four cats. "Max, the car inspector, is black and short-haired. Persian Miss Moppet is chief inspector of guests and their luggage, if given the opportunity; Pansy, her daughter, was born April Fool's Day, 1990." Tigger, a flame-point Himalayan.
Foreign languages spoken: French and "rusty" German.
Bed and bath: Two air-conditioned second-floor rooms, private full baths. Front room with cannonball double bed and rollaway with back board. "Romantic" room with dormer windows, twins/king bed.
Breakfast: 7:30–9:30. Special. From menu with cranberry or freshly squeezed orange juice. Fruit. Cereal. Banana bran, apple walnut, apricot almond, or walnut cream cheese muffins. English toast with butter, homemade jams. Crepes with orange sauce, mushroom and cheese omelet, French toast, Belgian waffle, or blueberry pancakes.
Plus: Refreshment tray. Acknowledgment of celebrations. Patio with chaises, gas barbecue, picnic table with umbrella. Screened porch. Color TV. Video library. Record and CD player; classical to pop music. Games. Transportation from bus (three blocks away) or from Kingston train station. Half-price beach passes.

Newport is just 20 minutes away from Narragansett, a community that has long been known for its beaches. Now, as one host said, "In Narragansett there are people beaches, radio beaches, quiet beaches, surfing beaches;" and hosts can direct you accordingly.

The Richards   401/789-7746
144 Gibson Avenue, Narragansett, RI 02882

Hosts: Steven and Nancy Richards
Location: On a quiet, private, dead-end road. One mile from center of town. One-quarter mile from ocean; one mile to beach.
Open: Year round. Two-night mini-mum on weekends. Three-night minimum on holiday weekends.
Rates: Double occupancy. $75 private bath, $65 shared bath.

> From New York: *"The history is fascinating. We loved the quiet, the privacy, the spectacular breakfasts, the furnishings, the wonderful large bathroom, and the log-burning fireplace . . . a perfect honeymoon retreat."*

The gabled 1884 stone house, dubbed "Nancy's dream" from the day she first saw it, has become a destination for many guests. A circular gravel driveway leads to an entrance topped by a copper cupola. The only other house in sight is the former caretaker's house of what was a 20-acre estate. Inside there's a grand 40-foot-long entrance hall and 11 fireplaces.

Since purchasing the house (that process is part of the interesting history), the Richardses have decorated with Oriental rugs and antiques. And they have established a gem of a shade garden with bench. "Still, after 14 years of hosting (including 10 in a Narragansett Cape-style house), we are constantly amazed and delighted with guests. Last week a musician, thinking no one was home, sang while she went up and down the steps. It was fun to hear such a great voice in our home."

Steven, weekend co-chef and former director of a state legislature program, is in real estate sales and development.

In residence: Daughters, Victoria, 20, and Kristina, 19, both college students. Two cats; not allowed in guest areas.
Bed and bath: Four large second-floor rooms, all with working fireplaces. One room has king and one has queen canopy bed, each with private bath (tub, hand-held shower). One double-bedded room shares a bath with a room that has two twin-sized antique sleigh beds. Cots available.
Breakfast: 8:30. Fresh fruit. Repertoire may include eggs Florentine, baked apple pancakes, seafood strudel, Steven's johnnycakes, cheese blintzes. Homemade (raspberry) muffins or bread. Freshly ground coffees. In formal dining room under crystal chandelier.
Plus: Working fireplaces everywhere. Library. Down comforters. Patio. Badminton. Guest refrigerator. Sherry. Newport Bridge tokens.

From Narragansett, Watch Hill is only a half hour's drive. The fishing village of Galilee is just down the road. Block Island, reached by the ferry that leaves from Point Judith (10-minute drive), is a popular day trip. The University of Rhode Island is a 15-minute drive. Musical theater and restaurants make the list, too. Cycling in this pocket of Rhode Island is scenic and pretty flat.

Stone Lea   401/783-9546

40 Newton Avenue, Narragansett, RI 02882-1368

Hosts: Carol and Ernest Cormier
Location: On two oceanfront acres. Residential neighborhood. Five-minute drive to beach, 10 minutes to Block Island ferry.
Open: Year round. Two-night minimum on weekends, Memorial Day–Labor Day.
Rates: Double occupancy, tax included. Memorial Day, June and September weekends, July, and August, $85–$95 queen bed, ocean view. $105 two twins, oceanfront. $125 queen and two twins, oceanfront. $95 double, attached bath. $115 suite with queen and two twins, attached bath. Off-season, $60–$100. $25 third person.
♥ ⬛ ❖ ✗ ⚒

Drive up to the porte cochere of this stone and shingled mansion built in 1884 by McKim, Mead and White, the same architectural firm that designed the Rhode Island state house, the Towers in Narragansett, and the Boston Public Library. Enter the grand central hall with its magnificent staircase and English sideboard. Sit on the patio and watch the surf against the rocky shore.

"Stone Lea was a B&B when we fell in love with it five years ago," says Carol, craftswoman and B&B chef. "Since, we sold our company and became full-time hosts. We meet many guests who arrive with plans to do everything. They take nature walks, watch the sunset over the water—and leave, slowed down and unstressed."

Cohost Ernie, "an antique and classic car lover," is volunteer administrator for a nonprofit educational corporation that offers apprenticeships in the metalworking industry.

In residence: Brandy, a seven-year-old black dachshund "who thinks guests have come to see him."
Foreign language spoken: French.
Bed and bath: Eight rooms, varied in size and decor, on second and third floors. Some rooms oceanfront; others, ocean view. All private full baths (one has shower, no tub); some attached, some in hall. Queen, double, or twin beds.
Breakfast: 8–9:45. Fresh fruit. Juice. Homemade coffee cakes, breads, muffins or sticky buns. Puffed apple pancakes, French toast, or quiche. At tables for four in fireplaced dining room.
Plus: Piano and pool table in living room. Chaises in sun room with floor-to-ceiling windows. Croquet. Expansive lawn. Fruit. Fresh flowers. TV in living room. Special occasions acknowledged.

> From New York: *"Location reminds me of estates in Ireland . . . appointed with the greatest of care. . . . Clocks chiming at different intervals were delightful . . . indescribable breakfast. . . . Used binoculars to view the bay from the picture window. . . . We are still not over having to leave after one heavenly week in Nirvana!"*

Bluestone   401/846-5408
33 Russell Street, Newport, RI 02840-1723

Hosts: Cindy and Roger Roberts
Location: In a quiet residential area, a half mile from downtown Newport.
Open: Year round. Two-night minimum on weekends, three-night minimum on holiday weekends.

Rates: March 15–November 15, $75 and $95. November 15–March 15, $55 and $65.
🛏 🛫 ✄

Country Almanac magazine photographed the country store decor in this 1905 country Victorian, which was owned by one family until the Robertses bought it in 1983. "It is just the right place for our collections of country antiques and refinished furniture." Natural woodwork is throughout. The focal point is an old Newport store tobacco case filled with Bennington pottery.

When the Robertses lived in Massachusetts, Cindy was in restaurant and hotel management work. Roger is a retired electrical lineman. "We are Newport natives who moved back here with the idea of having a rooming house. When friends sent us our first (unplanned) B&B guests, we were hooked!" Soon Cindy found herself placing so many overflow guests with selected private home B&Bs that she established a reservation service (described on page 300).

In residence: Tootsie is a cat who was discovered one freezing January night outside the emergency room of the local hospital. One dog, Ms. Wrinkles, a Shar Pei. Grandchildren, ages 5–23, are occasional visitors.
Bed and bath: Two air-conditioned rooms. One large room with double bed, private shower bath. One with queen bed, private full bath.
Breakfast: 8–9:30 a.m. Entree might be strawberry waffles with fresh whipped cream, strata, or Monte Cristo French toast. Served in dining room surrounded by stoneware, samplers, baskets, plants, and quilts.
Plus: Beverages. Porch. Yard. Bicycle and surfboard storage. Will meet guests at the Newport bus. Guest refrigerator for beverages only.

From Rhode Island: *"Cindy's thumb is green. And she's a marvelous cook. The experience of being there and with them is the BEST."*

Cliffside Inn   401/847-1811
2 Seaview Avenue, Newport, RI 02840   800/845-1811

Host: Annette King
Location: In a quiet residential area, one block from main entrance to Cliff Walk. Six blocks from the mansions on Bellevue Avenue; 15 minutes' walk from the waterfront, 5 from First Beach.
Open: Year round. Two-night minimum required May–October weekends, requested for other weekends.

Rates: May–October $115 queen bed, shower bath; $135 (several rooms); $145 suite with two double beds, daybed, full bath; $155 queen bed, extra large bath; $185 suite with Jacuzzi or king with whirlpool bath. Rest of year, $20–$30 less. AMEX, Diners, MC, VISA.
❤ ❄ ♦ 🛫 ✄

(Please turn page.)

What became known as "one of Newport's best-kept secrets," thanks to a reader of this book, has been embellished in the last couple of years. The gracious Victorian, built in 1880 by the governor of Maryland as a high-ceilinged, bay-windowed summer cottage, is decorated with wonderful fabrics, wallpapers, and art that give a sense of home. Period furnishings include a gilded ballroom mirror in the entrance hall.

Annette King, an experienced, flexible, and joyful innkeeper, came to Cliffside from North Carolina, where she had established an inn-sitting service and given seminars to others who wanted to be substitute innkeepers. As innkeeper here, she added (and decorated to perfection) some rooms; inaugurated lots of amenities, including hors d'oeuvres from 5:30 to 6; made the breakfast a feature (a cookbook is in process); and began to accommodate corporate meetings. All this with warm hospitality hailed by many as "exceptional."

Bed and bath: 12 rooms on three floors. All private baths; some with whirlpool, some with shower only. One room with king bed, cathedral ceiling, four skylights, French doors to whirlpool bath and shower. One suite with two double beds and a sitting room with daybed. One suite with queen bed, media center, Jacuzzi. One room with two twin beds. Many with queen, one canopied.

Breakfast: Enormous repertoire. Freshly squeezed orange juice, fruit dish, egg, meat, homemade muffins, "and sometimes heavenly pancakes!"

Plus: Individual thermostats. Air conditioning in three rooms, ceiling or window fans in others. Mulled cider in winter, iced tea and lemonade in summer. "Wonderful front porch." Bicycle storage. Beach towels. Off-street parking.

1855 Marshall Slocum House

29 Kay Street, Newport, RI 02840-2735

401/841-5120
401/846-3787

Host: Joan Wilson
Location: Canopied by a copper beech on a street of Victorian homes. Five-minute walk to waterfront, shops, beaches, and harbor.
Open: Year round. Reservations pre-ferred. Two-night minimum on summer weekends.
Rates: Per room. $70 shared bath. $90 private half bath. AMEX.
✻ ✈

"Yes, this really is my home, but it has turned out to be home away from home for sailors, students, writers, artists, croquet players, musicians, and lots of international visitors . . . every one with an interesting tale to tell, and many return every year. . . . I've tried to take breakfast to state of the art. Guests have shared their expertise, bread baking specifically, and I share my recipes, some of which are painted on the kitchen wall tiles."

Before buying this restored Victorian in 1985, Joan managed an orange grove in Florida. And then there was a short interlude as a travel agent. Her friendly house is furnished with family heirlooms, antiques, and collectibles.

In residence: One cat, Buttons, "who graciously accepts a friendly pat from kitty lovers."

Bed and bath: Five large rooms, one skylit, on two floors; two with private half bath. Three shared full guest baths, one with claw-foot tub, shower, sink set in antique server. Queen, double, or twin beds.
Breakfast: 8–10. (Coffee earlier.) Perhaps Belgian waffles with fresh strawberries or peach French toast. Plus homemade bread, fruit, juice, cereal. Served in dining room or on back deck overlooking large shaded backyard.
Plus: Afternoon refreshments. Off-street parking. Bedrooms have ceiling or window fans. Down comforters and pillows. Library. Front porch rockers. Parlor with TV, VCR. Dinner and picnics (extra charge) by request.

> From South Africa: *"An ideal base during my visit, which was in connection with a book I was writing on a South African contestant in the BOC Challenge singlehanded race around the world . . . [located] in an attractive and quiet part of town . . . tastefully furbished and well run. . . . Joan Wilson is a most friendly and knowledgeable person . . . breakfast a full and tasty meal."*

Elm Tree Cottage

401/849-1610
800/882-3ELM

336 Gibbs Avenue, Newport, RI 02840

Hosts: Thomas and Priscilla Malone
Location: On an acre of land in a residential area, 1½ blocks from the ocean and Cliff Walk. Within 15-minute walk of restaurants. One mile from mansions.
Open: Year round. Two-night minimum on weekends, three nights on holiday weekends.

Rates: Double occupancy. Memorial Day through October, weekdays $115–$175, weekends $150–$200. Off-season, weekdays $75–$125, weekends $100–$150. MC, VISA.
♥ ❀ ✈ ⅙

A true story that sounds a bit like fantasy. Two personable Long Island stained glass artists/designers (for religious, commercial, and residential buildings) fell in love with Newport and innkeeping. In 1989, when they were substitute innkeepers for one week, they took time for a bicycle ride and found this 1882 shingled-style summer "cottage" surrounded by weeds and in need of everything. A year later, having used their talents, skills, and advanced degrees in interior design, fine arts, and woodworking, they furnished with fine antiques from auctions and estate sales. Soon after its opening this elegant B&B, with a marvelous open-style floor plan, was discovered by wedding parties. The spacious (enormous) and gracious (welcoming) living room—with grand piano and Oriental rugs—overlooks Easton Pond and First Beach. The hosts' eye for color, design, and texture is apparent everywhere—in linens and fabrics in English and French country styling, in the window treatments and Louis XV French beds. Here the cuisine, too, is a fine art.

In residence: In hosts' quarters, three daughters—Keely, 10; Briana, 7; Erin, 5.
Bed and bath: Five second-floor rooms with private baths. One room, 39 by 20 feet, with canopied king bed, working fireplace, winter water views. Queen beds in three rooms, two with working fireplace. Room with two twins/king, working fireplace, private bath across the hall. Rollaway available.

(Please turn page.)

Breakfast: 9–10. Intentionally special. Fruit. Homemade breads and/or muffins and granola. Perhaps fruit-stuffed crepes, French bread/toast with amaretto syrup, sausage in puff pastry, or fresh fruit in wine custard. Served at candlelit dining-room tables set with flowers, lace, and china.

Plus: Air conditioning in some bedrooms. Late-afternoon beverage. Mints. Floor fans. Amenities basket. No TV. BYOB bar. Off-street parking.

> From New York: *"Rooms are romantic and exquisitely done. Tom and Priscilla made our vacation perfect."* Another from New York: *"Best business trip in ten years. . . . Can't wait to return to the beautiful home for a vacation."*

Flag Quarters   401/849-4543

54 Malbone Road, Newport, RI 02840-1746

Hosts: Joan and Rich Hulse
Location: On a corner in a residential neighborhood. Within a 15-minute walk of shops, restaurants, and harbor.
Open: Year round. Two-day minimum, June–September weekends.

Rates: Double occupancy. January–March $65–$75. April $75. May–June and October 15–December $85. July–October 15, $95. AMEX, Diners, MC, VISA.
♥ ⬛ ◆ ✖ ✂

One guest called the breakfast "culinary artistry." Another wrote, "The Vanderbilts can have their mansions. We can't wait to return here." Others comment on the "romantic" rooms, which are decorator-finished with drapes, wall-to-wall carpeting, some antiques, some reproductions.

Rich, a navy captain and carrier pilot, teaches at the Naval War College. Joan, a native Newporter who has taught English in four states, observes, "Our first-time weekend guests find they can't 'do all of Newport.' We assist with the high spots and save some of the out-of-the-way places for veterans. Ever since our stays in European B&Bs, I wanted to run my own. Three years ago we found this 1880 former gardener's house, perfect for private suites and a landscaped yard. Our discoveries continue; we have just uncovered cobblestones that we think were part of a stable."

In residence: Teenage daughter Jessica. Chewbaca is part poodle, part terrier.

Foreign language spoken: "Minimal German."

Bed and bath: Two third-floor suites with tall slanted ceilings, private exterior entrance (as well as an interior former servants' staircase), double bed, scented lace or embroidered linens, satin quilt, private shower bath, living-room area.

Breakfast: 8:30–9. In a Victorian basket with lace and Wedgwood china; left at your door with bell announcement. Juice, fruits in silver compote, baked goods; entree might be broccoli quiche or eggs in pastry shell with bacon; coffee or tea.

Plus: Air conditioning. Individual thermostat. Ceiling fans. Color TV with movie channel. Private phone. Small refrigerator. Microwave. Perrier on silver tray with crystal glasses. Mints. Forgotten-items basket. At Christmas, a welcoming candle light in every window. Off-street parking.

Hydrangea House Inn

401/846-4435

16 Bellevue Avenue, Newport, RI 02840-3206

Hosts: Grant Edmondson and Dennis Blair
Location: On top of Newport's historic hill, with brick sidewalks, gas lighting, old trees, and shops. Across from Viking Hotel. Five-minute walk to harbor, 10 minutes to first mansion on Bellevue Avenue and to the beach.

Open: Year round. Two-day minimum June, July, August, all weekends, and three-day holidays.
Rates: May through October, $115 double, $125 queen. $155 two double beds. Off-season, $75 double, $85 queen. Deposit required. MC, VISA.
♥ ❖ ◆ ✂

A transformation by Newport antiques dealers. In an 1876 building that was, in 1988, shops, apartments, and offices, is a gracious B&B—"not a mansion"—created by Dennis, a former customer service administrator, and Grant, a former construction company owner who is currently president of the Newport Historic Inns Association.

Now the first floor is a contemporary fine arts gallery, the breakfast room for overnight guests. Antiques, sculpture, paintings, and fine fabrics are throughout. In the rear, a 500-square-foot veranda overlooks hydrangea and perennial flower gardens. It's all as Grant and Dennis imagined during their long property search.

In residence: Two cats, Chester and Miss Kitty.
Bed and bath: Six carpeted second- and third-floor rooms. All private baths; some full, some shower only. Queen or double beds. One room has two double beds.
Breakfast: 8:30–10:30. Homemade everything. Freshly squeezed juice. Fruit salad. Granola. Seasoned egg entree or raspberry pancakes. English muffins and breads. "Our own blend of coffee." In gallery or on veranda.
Plus: Air-conditioned bedrooms. Down comforters. Turndown service. Fresh flowers. Mints on pillow. Guest refrigerator. Amenities basket. Picnic baskets ($12). Off-street parking. Tour bus, city bus, and airport shuttle leave from the door.

From France: *"Un charmant petit nid."*

The Melville House

401/847-0640

39 Clarke Street, Newport, RI 02840-3023

Hosts: Rita and Sam Rogers
Location: On a quiet street of restored colonial homes. One block from harbor. Around corner from shops and restaurants. Short walk to Touro Synagogue and Trinity Church.
Open: March–December. Two-day minimum weekend stay; three days on major holiday weekends.

Rates: May–September, $85–$95 private bath; $75–$85 shared bath. October, $15 less. November, December, and March, $45–$55 private bath; $40–$50 shared bath. Twelfth weekend (by one party) is free. AMEX, MC, VISA.
♥ ❖ ◆

(Please turn page.)

A bed and breakfast that could win a "friendliest B&B award" is featured in a Newport video and, often, in the press. This is an unpretentious restored 1750 house with oak pieces, braided rugs, lace curtains, and, in a hutch, a collection of early small home appliances accumulated during Sam's years as a design engineer of modern versions.

Rita and Sam greet international guests with a flag of their country. Total to date: 54. One New Yorker, a student of architecture and historic preservation, wrote about "climbing into the rafters and down into the original basement. And for our anniversary celebration, our lovely room was decorated with balloons!" Others have commented on "a comfortable, cozy mini-museum with its antiques and paintings . . . hints for hidden shops . . . spotless . . . a rich, warm experience."

From the hosts' point of view: "In six years, we have sewn women into formal dresses for weddings; provided tuxedo studs; tied bow ties; rescued lost tourists in Newport; dried wet clothing in our dryer; and chauffeured people to their destination. After years of living in Milwaukee and New Jersey and traveling to B&Bs, we're glad to be back in New England, having even more fun than we thought."

In residence: "Our cat, Roco, is afraid of strangers and is seldom in the guests' area."

Bed and bath: Seven rooms. A first-floor double-bedded room, private shower bath. On second floor, four rooms each with a double bed, private shower bath; a large shower bath shared by one double-bedded room and one with two twin beds, nonworking fireplace.

Breakfast: 8–10. Rita's own granola cereal served with yogurt. Sam's home-baked bread. Homemade muffins and preserves. Coffee, teas, milk, hot chocolate. Buffet style at pub tables.

Plus: Fireplaced living room. Complimentary sherry, 5–6. Fresh fruit. Large window fans. Two bikes for guests' use. Games. Books. Picnic table in garden. Restaurant menus. Off-street parking.

Queen Anne Inn   401/846-5676

16 Clarke Street, Newport, RI 02840-3024

Host: Peg McCabe

Location: In the historic district, on a street that is one block long, just two blocks from the waterfront.

Open: At least April through early November. Two-night minimum on weekends, except three nights on holiday weekends. Phone reservations, to clarify room selection, necessary.

Rates: Per room. $70–$90 Memorial Day–Columbus Day. Other times, $55–$75. Varies with location, size of room, shared or private bath. AMEX, MC, VISA.

♥ ❖ ✈

Flash! At press time, Peg was thinking of semi-retirement. The ultimate concierge lives here. Peg is known for her instant orientation for guests. And her spontaneous acknowledgment of special occasions. One guest's description: "A B&B where breakfast is 'happy hour in the morning.'"

It's an immaculate Victorian townhouse decorated just as Peg envisioned when she lived across the street. Since opening a decade ago, she has continued to make changes—while keeping the uncluttered light and airy look. This attractive, "not intended to be luxurious" B&B has wallpaper on some ceilings, lovely lamps, lace curtains, and many touches including old crocheted pieces that have been framed by one of Peg's daughters. There's an armoire in one room, a four-poster and Oriental rug in another, and, in season, cut flowers arranged in the common rooms. And then there's the small inviting garden. All at an inn created by a "people person," a former librarian and a restaurant devotee, who came from New York in the 1970s.

Foreign language spoken: "The most rudimentary French."
Bed and bath: Eight rooms and one suite. Four private hall baths. Three semiprivate baths.
Breakfast: 8:30–10:30. Continental. Fruit, juice, Portuguese sweet bread and selection of breakfast biscuits, coffee and tea. In reception room or in outdoor garden.
Plus: Off-street parking. Bedroom fans. Porch. TV. Guest phone.

Stella Maris Inn   401/849-2862

91 Washington Street, Newport, RI 02840-1531

Hosts: Dorothy and Edwin Madden
Location: In the historic, quiet Point section, across from a small park overlooking the bay. On about an acre of land with beech and sycamore trees. Within 10 minutes' walk of harbor.

Open: Year round.
Rates: Per room. November–April, $75 room with garden view, $85 room with water view. May–October, $125 garden view, $150 water view.
♥ ❖ ◆ ✗ ✗

It's a big beautiful French Victorian mansion built as a summer residence in 1861 with Connecticut fieldstone and 13-foot ceilings throughout. A convent for about 60 years—and unoccupied most of the late 1980s—the structure was purchased and renovated completely by the Maddens, including one son who is an architect and another who restores old houses. Before opening here in 1990, Dorothy and Ed had a smaller B&B in Newport and one on Cape Cod before that.

Dorothy, an antiques dealer when the six grown children were younger, has decorated with Victorian antiques, many upholstered pieces, fine art, and French lace. Here she combines her loves of "people and cooking." Ed, an orthopedic surgeon, cohosts in evenings and on weekends.

Bed and bath: Eight large rooms on second and third floors; all with private baths, some shower only. All queen beds except two with two twin beds. Four rooms with working fireplaces. Rollaway available.
Breakfast: 8–9:30. Juices, fresh fruit, cereals, homemade breads and muffins, coffee, tea, milk. In formal dining room by the fireplace or on porch overlooking the bay.
Plus: Wraparound porch overlooking gardens. Fireplaced living room. TV. Late-afternoon wine or tea. Ceiling fans in guest rooms. Off-street parking.

The Victorian Ladies   401/849-9960

63 Memorial Boulevard, Newport, RI 02840

Hosts: Donald and Hélène O'Neill
Location: On a main street, 10 minutes' walk up the hill from the harbor. Five minutes to mansions. Three blocks to public beach.
Open: Year round, except January.

Two-night minimum on weekends, three nights on holiday weekends.
Rates: Double occupancy. Memorial Day–Columbus Day, $145. Off-season, $85. MC, VISA.
♥ ✶

"The O'Neills just know. They know how to welcome people. Hélène serves a huge breakfast, and to honeymooners, heart-shaped cakes. She and Don gutted their place and did everything with flair, with yards of fabric draped and pouffed on windows, with wallpaper borders, lots of pinks and blues, and reproduction period furniture. Please tell your readers about them." So reported an established and acclaimed fellow innkeeper.

California can take credit for this inn, which is now three separate houses connected by a latticed and flower-filled brick courtyard. In 1986, after purchasing the property in need of renovation, the O'Neills stayed in their first B&B in California. "On the return flight we decided to open an inn." Six years later, they know they made the right decision. "Our guests are wonderful. We know some returnees so well that it is difficult to charge them!"

Helene is a former banker. Donald, the renovator extraordinaire, has lived in Newport all his life.

In residence: Wiley, "our loving golden retriever."
Bed and bath: Eleven rooms; all full private baths. On first, second, and third floors. Queen, double, or twin beds; some canopied. Five rooms in main building, four in carriage house, two in cottage.
Breakfast: 8–9:30. Menu changes daily. Sampler: fresh fruit with yogurt; homemade hash with poached eggs; pumpkin bread with spread of cream cheese, nuts, raisins, and honey. Orange juice. Coffee or tea. In dining room or at umbrella table in courtyard.
Plus: Air conditioning and TV in guest rooms; private phone in some. Down comforters. Old-fashioned swing. Off-street parking. Their own cookbook (for sale).

Bed & Breakfast of Rhode Island Host #122

Providence, RI

Location: Quiet residential area on street of historic homes. Near Brown University. Five-minute walk to area restaurants and shops. Five-minute bus ride to center of city.
Reservations: Available late August–

early June through Bed & Breakfast of Rhode Island, page 301.
Rates: $60 single. $70 double. $15 rollaway.
🐚 ✶

"Our office is wallpapered in maps. Visitors enjoy showing us where they came from and where they are going."

They come from all over the world, from London, Japan, New Jersey, and the west coast. They come for Brown University, the Rhode Island School of Design, historic house tours, interviews, or performances (sometimes their own). The bonus is the opportunity to stay with the caring voice teacher/music director and sculptor/consultant who live in a gracious 1882 Victorian furnished with comfortable antiques and reproductions.

In residence: Three cats: Pippa, a female calico; her brother Nehi (short for Nehemiah); and Sam, a stray Persian-tiger.
Foreign languages spoken: French and some Italian.
Bed and bath: Two second-floor rooms, each with two twin beds, desk, private full bath. One has a sitting area, TV, bath with double sink. The other bath has a claw-footed tub, hand-held shower. Rollaway available.
Breakfast: 8–9. Juice, cereal, eggs, sausage or ham, homemade muffins, hot beverages. Special diets accommodated. Served in large formal dining room with many plants and flowers, silver service, lace cloth.
Plus: Bedroom fans. Library/TV room filled with books. Music/living room (when lessons not being given) with grand piano. Off-street parking. Guests' deck overlooking secluded backyard.

From England: *"Delightful hosts, excellent breakfast, homey atmosphere. Could not be bettered altogether. We were treated like relatives."*

Admiral Dewey Inn

668 Matunuck Beach Road
South Kingstown (Matunuck), RI 02879-7021

401/783-2090
800/457-2090

Hosts: Joan and Hardy LeBel
Location: In a small beach village, one straight mile from Route 1, 75 yards to the surf. Ten miles to University of Rhode Island and Kingstown train station; half mile to Theatre-By-The-Sea; 20 miles to Mystic, Connecticut, and to Newport; 4 to Block Island ferry.

Open: Year round. Two-night minimum on weekends, May–November.
Rates: Double occupancy. May–November, $80–$120. December–April, $40–$60. Single, 15 percent less. $20 rollaway. AMEX, Discover, MC, VISA.
♥ ❖ ◆ ✈ ✂

If you arrive on the wraparound porch and tell the LeBels that you drove beyond the inn to the dead end point, turned around, and found the (lovely oval) sign facing the wrong way, the innkeepers will respond that the local landscaper put it that way "because it's right architecturally, and besides," he said, "they'll see it on the way back."

That sign is in front of a Victorian showcase, a former beach boardinghouse, a plumbingless wreck in 1987. Saved from demolition by Joan and Hardy, who had the 137-ton house moved onto a new foundation, it has indoor baths, claw-footed tables, brass and tall-headboard beds, overstuffed living-room chairs, Victorian wallpaper, and lace curtains.

(Please turn page.)

Joan, an antiques dealer and Realtor who has taught in Hawaii, Japan, and Europe, furnished the inn with fine old pieces. She and Hardy, a retired Air Force staffer who flies a seaplane, have four years' worth of rebuilding experience to share. And they have a pictorial history album.

In residence: "Brat and Cat, twin black fluffy litter mates." One smoker, Joan.
Foreign languages spoken: Polish and French.
Bed and bath: Ten rooms, each furnished in a different period; most with ocean view. Eight with private shower bath. Two share a full bath. Queen, double, or twin beds. Rollaway available.
Breakfast: 8:30–11. Buffet on 1840s table. Fresh fruit, juices, homemade breads and muffins, English muffins or bagels, coffee and tea.
Plus: Fruit, beverages, munchies always available. Outside shower. Beach towels. Amenities basket. Down comforters. Acknowledgment of special occasions. Pickup at Amtrak station or Westerly airport. Porch rockers. Off-street parking.

From New York: *"Perfect . . . location . . . decor . . . breakfasts, hosts."*

The Gardner House   401/789-1250
629 Main Street, Wakefield, RI 02879-4012

Hosts: Nan and Will Gardner
Location: On two acres along what was known as Old Post Road. Bordered by stone walls, rhododendron, and woodlands. Two miles to beach, Block Island ferry, summer theater, fishing villages. Five minutes to University of Rhode Island, 20 to Newport, 40 to Mystic Seaport. Near wildlife sanctuary and fine restaurants.

Open: Year round. Two-night minimum on summer weekends and during holidays.
Rates: Tax included. $60 twin, $70 double, $80 suite. Deposit required for one-night stay.
♥ ⬛ ✗ ✄

"A happy house," said one guest. Nan speaks of "this gem of a history-filled 1818 Federal house that has been our home since 1986, when our own family (there are eight grandchildren now) was weaned. It is the perfect place for sharing 'whatsis?' and 'whatsats?'—collections of yesteryear, everything from bird cages to rocking horses—gathered over 42 years."

Next to people, Nan, a former antiques shop owner, specializes in designing rugs and teaching rug braiding. Will, retired from the telephone company, is "full-time pool cleaner, handyman, and internationally known chef." Both love their gardens, woodlands, and hosting. Nearly every guest—from 22 countries and 45 states—is in their photo album.

Bed and bath: Three rooms (with stool for climbing into the highest antique bed). All private baths. On second floor, one room with antique cannonball bed, adjoining room-sized full bath. One room with antique double bed, full bath, adjoining room with twin bed. Third-floor room has two twin beds, tub bath.

Breakfast: 8–9. Menu varies daily. Fruits with lime ice. Homemade muffins. Rhode Island Johnny cakes with Rhode Island maple syrup, eggs, bacon, ham, sausage. "Best coffee around." Served by candlelight.
Plus: In-ground pool (with a necessary set of rules). Porch. Garden. Down comforters.

Grandview Bed & Breakfast   401/596-6384

212 Shore Road
Westerly, RI 02891

(outside RI) **800/441-6384**
fax: call to activate

Host: Patricia Grande
Location: High on a hill, overlooking Block Island Sound and Winnapaug Pond. Within walking distance of golf courses and tennis courts. Five miles from downtown historic district and Watch Hill.
Open: Year round. Advance reservations required. Two-night minimum on July, August, and holiday weekends.
Rates: Memorial Day–Labor Day, $60–90 double; rest of year, $45–$75. Singles $7 less. Families in more than one room and senior citizens and returning guests, 10 percent less. $15 extra person. AMEX, MC, VISA.
♥ ♨ 🏠 ❀ ◆

Guests write to me about "the perfect hostess in the perfect spot . . . good food . . . comfortable and spotlessly clean rooms . . . a brilliant choice for our family reunion." Among those who have returned to have their wedding here, one couple issued a hint sheet (everything from Newport to villages, from walks to restaurants) for friends. Birding groups use the inn as a base. Retreat groups have been known to break into song before each discussion or art session.

The inn consists of a main house that, legend says, was moved from Connecticut by barge and a wing built in 1910. Pat, library trustees' board member, former teacher, and former Chamber of Commerce president, and her husband, a radio station owner who covers major international sports events such as Wimbledon, fell in love with the too-big-for-two house with wraparound stone porch and ocean view. Thus, in 1986, innkeeping became Pat's third career.

In residence: Nike, a black Labrador retriever, an outdoor dog, "sulks on summer Sunday afternoons when guests leave."
Bed and bath: Twelve rooms with a double or two twin beds. Private shower bath for two annex rooms; one has two twin beds, one has a double bed. Other rooms, with shower or full bath shared by two or—in one case—three rooms, are on first floor of annex or third floor of main house. Some with porch and/or water view. Rollaway available.
Breakfast: 8–9:30. Fresh fruit pies, strawberry shortcake, blueberry cobbler or hot cranberry apple crisp with whipped cream. Freshly baked muffins, bagels, English muffins, jams, fruit, yogurt, cereals, juices, coffee, tea. Buffet on sun porch or open wraparound porch.
Plus: Welcoming beverage. Fruit. Living room with fieldstone fireplace. Family room in wing with player piano, cable TV, games. Lounge chairs on spacious grounds. Babysitting with notice. Outside shower. Fax available.

From New York: *"To me, it is a place to relax and be surrounded by (new) friends. To my son, it is a place to explore inside and out. To him, it is a wonder."*

Woody Hill B&B   401/322-0452

330 Woody Hill Road, Westerly, RI 02891-5901

Host: Ellen L. Madison
Location: Just off busy Route 1, but really in the country. Two miles from ocean beaches. Minutes from Mystic Seaport and Newport.
Open: Year round. Two nights pre-ferred for summer and holiday weekends.
Rates: $70 for two. $10 additional person in room. One night free for a week's stay. Off-season, slightly less.

♥ ♯ ♛ ✻ ✈ ✂

Some come for a romantic getaway, a quiet retreat, or a nearby family reunion. David and I were guests during a marvelous cycling/swimming vacation.

Through 11 years of hosting, Ellen has continued to change the gambrel-roofed colonial reproduction that many can "hardly tell"—with its wide floorboards, fireplaces made with old bricks, and quilt collection. She also designed and did much of the finishing work for the 1986 addition, which features nooks and crannies. One guest room, The Library, has four walls of books, shuttered windows, and window seats. Summer guests enjoy the latest addition, a 40-foot in-ground pool. Winter guests may be treated to fireplace cooking weekends where you do as little or as much as you wish.

Ellen, a high school English teacher who earned her Ph.D. recently, is very involved with Connecticut's program for mentoring with new teachers. She has "starred" in a how-to B&B videotape. And her guests continue to write about the "warm, comfortable, and serene house." One from New York reminisced, "Breakfast in the bright country dining room pleases eye and palate as Ellen, a gastronomical intellectual, serves her unique creations."

In residence: Three cats. "Treasure cozies up to anyone and molds himself to that person. Lady's aloof and skittish, although less than usual because of her total deafness. Tomasina is frustrated in dealing with the other two."
Bed and bath: Three large rooms on two floors. Double sofa bed in The Library; private full bath. Full bath shared by double-bedded room and, at opposite end of hall, another corner room with a double and a ¾ bed.
Breakfast: 8–9. Full. Huge repertoire from hundreds of cookbooks. Maybe strawberry nut or blueberry ginger muffins, seasonal fruit with interesting sauces, pear waffles and waffles, or apple crisp; "anything but eggs!"
Plus: The pool. Yard with flower and herb gardens, privacy, "and sometimes mosquitoes." Porch swing. Fireplaced living room. Pump organ.

> From Massachusetts: *"Our eight-year-old daughter fell in love with the darling antique dolls tucked under the eaves and took delight in the mischievous cat. . . . Suggestions for restaurants and sightseeing were 'right on.' We've already booked again."*

If you have been to one B&B, you haven't been to them all.

Rockbound

Haversham, RI

Location: Rural. At the end of a narrow country road, minutes from Westerly, with view of saltwater pond and ocean beyond. Ten minutes by car, bike, or rowboat to beaches (private one available off-season). Within 15 minutes of restaurants, Theatre-By-The-Sea; 25 to Mystic, Connecticut; 45 to Newport.

Reservations: Available year round through Covered Bridge, page 4. Two-night minimum on weekends and holidays.
Rates: Main house, $95 per room. Cottage, $100 for two; breakfast is extra.
♥ ⚔ ♠

Here she is, the artist/gardener/gourmet cook from my first B&B book who lived in a passive-solar contemporary home with wood stove, walls of books, antiques, pretty linens, flowers, and lots of windows. An architectural designer now, she has remodeled her grandfather's summer residence, an Arts and Crafts-style farmhouse, by making the first floor one long flowing spectacular space. A huge fieldstone fireplace defines areas. The floor is Mexican tile. Glass doors are on the kitchen cabinets. Everywhere there are windows with water views, "quadrillions of books," the hostess's paintings, and antiques—Queen Anne, Chippendale, and Sheraton. And examples of trompe l'oeil and faux finishes. Outside, a wisteria-covered pergola is built over the wicker-furnished brick terrace that "everyone uses."

The hostess, a columnist who covers art, theater, music, food, and travel, invites guests to feel at home and to enjoy the surroundings and the privacy.

Bed and bath: Two second-floor rooms; private baths. (Plus a summer cottage.) One room, treehouse-like, with four-poster double bed, claw-foot tub bath (no shower), antique spinet desk, love seat, high ceiling, porch overlooking pond and ocean. One larger room with two double beds, shower bath, lots of windows, armoire, wing chairs. Private cottage has three bedrooms, fieldstone fireplace, full kitchen, laundry.
Breakfast: 7:30–9:30. Fresh fruit, cheese and/or yogurt, homemade muffins, coffee, tea, juice. Served on china and silver in dining room or on terrace overlooking water.
Plus: Down comforters. Use of entire house. TV. Hammock. Rowboat. Perennial gardens. Setups. Option of private dinner by prior arrangement.

Anna's Victorian Connection Host #105

Saunderstown, RI

Location: Peaceful. On six waterfront acres with spectacular view of Narragansett Bay. High on a cliff at the end of a rural road. Ten minutes to Newport, Wickford, beaches; 20 to Theatre-By-The-Sea.
Reservations: Available year round

through Anna's Victorian Connection, page 300. Two-night minimum on weekends and holidays.
Rates: $65–$85 single, $75–$95 double. Off-season, $5 less.
♥ ♠ ✈

(Please turn page.)

Arrive by boat, if you wish. Look over Narragansett Bay from the wraparound stone porch—built with cedar limbs from the yard—atop this 50-foot cliff. Or take in the view from the terrace benches in the woods on the way down to the water.

This place to stay has become the reason to go. "Many who come to 'rush off to Newport' return here, sit by the water, use the cabana, and have a picnic," says the hostess, a well-traveled (former airline stewardess) Realtor who "loves to walk the mile-long Narragansett Beach."

Her one-of-a-kind country house with a huge quarry stone living room fireplace was built over a quarry in 1910 by a Philadelphia lawyer. Since, beams were put in first-floor ceilings and the living room has been paneled in walnut. The hostess, a resident for 10 years, has furnished with traditional country pieces, many oil paintings, and Oriental rugs. And on the hillside heather, planted by Scottish builders of the Jamestown Bridge, blooms.

In residence: Fetch, the dog.
Bed and bath: Two second-floor rooms with water views. Each with two twins or one king, antique furnishings. One with private full bath, one with shared shower bath.
Breakfast: 8–10. Juice, fruit, muffins and breads, gourmet coffees and teas. Served on veranda or in dining/living room area overlooking the water.
Plus: Complimentary sherry hour. Private beach. Use of mooring, and cabana with refrigerator and bathroom.

Anna's Victorian Connection Host #104

Wyoming, RI

Location: On three acres, with house set back from road. On residential/rural two-lane Route 138E, the main road to nearby University of Rhode Island (10 minutes) and Newport (35 minutes). Fifteen minutes northeast of Westerly, 25 to Block Island ferry, less than a mile from I-95.

Reservations: Available year round through Anna's Victorian Connection, page 300. Two-night minimum on holidays.
Rates: $55 double occupancy. Single, 10 percent less. November–April 15, 20 percent less. Extra person, $15 cot includes big breakfast.
🐾 ✗ ⚡

The "ordinary shingled farmhouse" (from the outside) has a fascinating interior. The wood ceiling, hand-hewn beams, and granite walls of the living room indicate changes since the house began as a blacksmith shop on a plantation in 1732. The forge was replaced by the large stone fireplace, built by an American Indian stonemason. Today the property has two homes, a barn, and a swimming pool. One of the three acres is grass. There are 40 fruit trees, grapevines, berry bushes, and a flower garden.

The chief cook and bottle washer (and old-house renovator) has had considerable experience as a hotel manager, accountant, and furniture manufacturer. His wife, a former nun, teaches psychiatric nursing at the Community College of Rhode Island.

Bed and bath: Three rooms. On first floor, one queen-bedded room and one with two twin four-poster beds; both are carpeted; each has a sink. They share a huge bath that has shower with bench seat. On second floor, room with a double and a king bed, sink in room, private shower bath.

Breakfast: 8–10. Select from menu night before. Juice. Cereal. Waffles, pancakes or eggs, bacon or sausage. Coffee and tea. In dining room.

Plus: Fireplaced living room. Porch, sun room. A 29-foot (diameter) circular pool.

The Way Stop   401/539-7233

161 New London Turnpike, Wyoming, RI 02898

Hosts: Billie and Bill Stetson
Location: Idyllic. On 50 rural acres with fields and pond. Two miles east of I-95, 30 miles from Providence and from Mystic, Connecticut; 12 to University of Rhode Island. Half hour to Newport, 20 minutes to beaches.

Open: At least May–November.
Rates: Double occupancy $53.50 tax included. Additional person $25. Crib $12.
♦♦ ♦ ♦

An experience awaits. All possible because the hosts share their 1757 center chimney farmhouse (post-and-beam construction); their canoe (swim in the pond too); the berry bushes ("come and pick"); and "the symphony of frogs calling from the lily pads, the crickets and whippoorwills." And there are lounge chairs and a grill and picnic table on the two-level patio that overlooks the herb garden.

Furnished with 46 years of "accumulated and inherited antiques and eclectic stuff," this is the place along the old toll road where stagecoaches changed horses. (The deed still reads, "Not allowed to charge tolls.") The doll-like "mouse house" built under the stairwell has children's toys old and new, all touchable, all captivating. The ell, a 1930s addition, was built with beams and boards from a house of the same era.

Bill, a ceramic engineer, has consulted all over the country. Billie, a museum volunteer, has a strong interest in fiber arts.

Bed and bath: On second floor, via a narrow staircase, two large rooms share a full bath. One room with queen-sized antique spool bed, a daybed, crib. One with two twin beds, a crib, adjoining sitting room with additional single bed possible.

Breakfast: 8–9. Fresh fruit, juice, muffins, bagels. "And if the spirit moves, never when it's hot, Bill will cook on our old iron cookstove." Served in keeping room, in glass-enclosed porch overlooking pond, or on patio.

Plus: Late-afternoon beverage. Down comforters. Flannel sheets. Amenities basket. Transportation from local airport and train station.

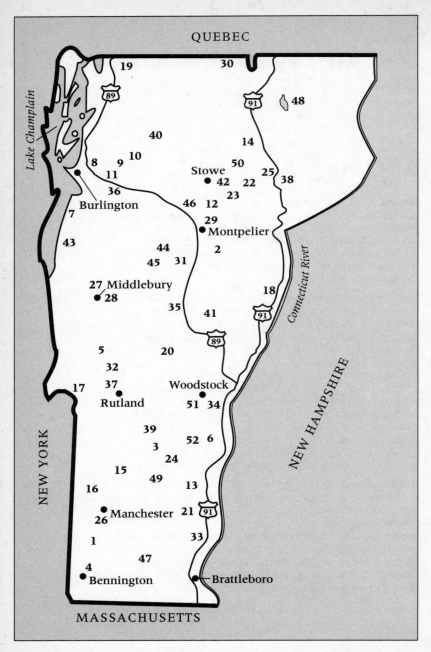

The numbers on this map indicate the locations of B&Bs described in detail in this chapter.

VERMONT

KEY TO SYMBOLS
♥ Lots of honeymooners come here.
♣ Families with children are very welcome. (Please see page xiii.)
♠ "Please emphasize that we are a private home, not an inn."
✿ Groups or private parties sometimes book the entire B&B.
♦ Travel agents' commission paid. (Please see page xii.)
✖ Sorry, no guests' pets are allowed.
✂ No smoking inside *or* no smoking at all, even on porches.

___ Vermont Reservation Services ___

The American Country Collection
The Willows, 4 Greenwood Lane, Delmar, NY 12054-1606

Phone: 518/439-7001, Monday–Friday 10–1, 2–5. Closed December 24–January 3.

Listings: 100. Mostly hosted private residences; a few unhosted. Many inns. Several are on the National Register of Historic Places. Most New England listings are in Vermont and in the Berkshires of western Massachusetts. A few are in the Connecticut River Valley sections of Massachusetts. In New York state, most are in the Albany/Saratoga, Hudson Valley, Catskill, central Leatherstocking, Lake George, and northern Adirondack regions. Directory ($4.95).

Reservations: Two weeks in advance preferred. Last-minute accepted when possible. Two- to three-day minimum stay at some locations in season.

Rates: $30–$70 single, $40–$185 double. Some weekly rates. Senior citizen discounts midweek (excluding foliage season and Saratoga in August) and off-season. Deposit required is equal to one night's lodging or half of total stay, whichever is higher. If cancellation made no less than 14 days prior to scheduled arrival, deposit refunded if room can be filled. For August–October bookings, refunds made only if notice received 30 days prior to arrival. Two percent fee for credit cards, AMEX, VISA, MC. ◆

Arthur Copeland's hosts are attentive to guests' needs but aware of their desire for privacy. They present homemade foods, know their area, and often help guests to plan an itinerary.

Plus: "Ski 'n B&B," romance, and theater packages available. Pickup at transportation points provided by some hosts. Short- and long-term (up to several months) hosted and unhosted housing booked for relocation and business purposes.

Other reservation services with some B&Bs in Vermont:
  Bed & Breakfast/Inns of New England, page 257.
  Pineapple Hospitality, page 106.

Six weeks *after* one B&B opened, a neighbor inquired: "I need lodging for visiting relatives. When are you going to open?" This was the same neighbor who, during a zoning hearing, had expressed great concern about traffic and noise that a B&B would create!

Vermont B&Bs

Hill Farm Inn
RR 2, Box 2015, Arlington, VT 05250

802/375-2269
800/882-2545

Hosts: Joanne and George Hardy
Location: At the foot of Mount Equinox, surrounded by 50 acres of lawns, gardens, and farmlands. Between Bennington and Manchester, one-half mile off Route 7A.
Open: Year round. Two-night minimum for Saturday bookings during summer, fall foliage, and winter ski seasons.
Rates: $60 shared bath, $75 private bath. $90 suite. Discount for children under 12; age 2 and under free unless crib ($5) is required. AMEX, Discover, MC, VISA.
🛏 ❀ ◆

This is home—to the Hardys (since 1983), the first owners since 1775 not to be named Hill; to·hikers; to couples who have been married by George; to Irish setter lovers; and to farm lovers. There is a piano in the living room and a wraparound porch with rockers, but the kitchen is the real heart of this unpretentious, immaculate inn. Joanne, who grew up on a farm, makes all those jams and cooks with the garden's bounty. She's a teacher of early childhood education and a former school committee chairman. When the Hardys lived in Indiana and Ohio, George was a minister and social worker. Here he's on the local rescue squad. He and Joanne (and Patches, too) are among the many reasons that there is such a feeling of contentment here.

The main (Federal) building was in part moved up the road by 40 yoke of oxen in 1840. The Cape guest house dates back to 1790. Guests find apples and a detailed "things to do" booklet in their room. They enjoy the take-home jam. And, at Christmas, a filled stocking.

In residence: Patches, the offspring of an English setter and a traveling hound dog, "the first to welcome guests and the last to say goodbye,"—not allowed in guest areas.
Bed and bath: Eleven rooms plus two suites (with skylight, ceiling fan, porch). On first and second floors of main inn and guest house. Eight private baths; rest are semiprivate baths. King, queen, double, or twin beds available.
Breakfast: 7:30–9:30. Cooked to order for each guest, according to your menu selection. Juices (tomato is homemade), cereals (including homemade granola), eggs, homemade muffins, French toast or blueberry pancakes.
Plus: Afternoon snacks. Fireplaced dining and living rooms. Bedroom fans. Board games. Books. Puzzles. Croquet. Badminton. Fishing in the Battenkill River, which winds through the farm. Herb and perennial gardens. Dinner ($15) for overnight guests only, by advance reservation. Will meet guests at Manchester or Arlington bus.

Looking for a B&B with a crib? Find a description with the 🛏 symbol and then check under the "bed and bath" section.

Woodruff House

802/476-7745

13 East Street, Barre, VT 05641-3806   (to leave message) **802/479-9381**

Hosts: Robert, Terry, and (teenage daughter) Katie Somaini
Location: Near center of the city, on a quiet old-fashioned park. Halfway between Boston and Montreal. Near the state capital, Montpelier; the largest granite quarries in the world; and Sugarbush and Stowe ski areas.
Open: Year round.
Rates: $45 single, $65 double.
🐾 🪽 ⅙

> From Connecticut: *"So-o-o Victorian. The house was built for opulent living—so was Robert . . . breakfast in the dining room surrounded by gleaming silver, tea before bed in the upstairs drawing room, feather pillows, the finest all-cotton percale sheets, perfectly white towels . . . Robert, wonderfully gregarious and artistic, Terry friendly and dry, both terribly funny. Go! You will be wrapped in fun and happiness and warmth."*

One thing led to another, and in 1987 Robert, a native Vermonter and interior consultant, and Terry, a CPA, bought "a quality furniture and decorating business. Our own home, an 1883 Victorian, is filled with an eclectic, ever-changing collection of antiques. After eleven years of hosting, we have many rich and precious memories."

Bed and bath: Two rooms with private baths and porches. Cozy first-floor room, queen bed, shower bath. Large second-floor room—two twin-size beds with king headboard, sitting room, full bath with hand-held shower.
Breakfast: At 8 weekdays, 9 on weekends. In one of two dining rooms. Menu varies from simple to fancy. French toast, fruit, ham or bacon, juice, coffee or tea.
Plus: Fireplaced living room. TV upstairs. A large wood-burning furnace. Dessert often served in the evening.

The Leslie Place

802/259-2903

Box 62, Belmont, VT 05730

Host: Mary K. Gorman
Location: On undeveloped (west) side of Okemo Mountain. On a quiet dirt road, minutes from a paved one, with meadows, mountain views, and, in summer, cows. Fifteen minutes to Weston Priory and Okemo ski area; 30 to Killington ski area; 25 miles from Route 91.
Open: Year round. Advance reservations recommended. Two-night minimum for foliage and ski season weekends. Three nights for national holiday weekends.
Rates: Suite, according to group size, $27–$35 per person post-Easter through mid-September and November through early December; $30–$40 per person mid-September through October and early December through Easter. Singles $50, $45 off-season. Doubles $65, $55 off-season. $10 each additional guest. MC, VISA
🐾 ❄️ 🪽 ⅙

> *Oh, for the opportunity when fleeting weekends can stretch to more abundant weekdays for Re-creation.*
> *The Leslie Place is my farmhouse for all seasons.*

(Please turn page.)

So concludes a warm, enthusiastic poem enclosed in one guest's letter I received. Others spoke of the privacy, the tranquillity, the friendly and helpful hostess, the old-fashioned flower gardens. From New York: " . . . charming, spacious, uncluttered, yet Old World styled. . . . It's tempting to never leave the house."

It was different when Mary moved in 17 years ago. She explains, "The land was farmed, but the house had been empty for 16 years. No bathrooms, water, heat, or electricity! I was young and determined, I guess. Although my family had doubts, I didn't as I milked cows next door and restored this house. Everything was done by the Gorman Method, mixed with tears, laughter, frustration, and pleasure. I furnished with a rescued schoolhouse piano, hooked rugs, some of my own oil paintings, and a Kalamazoo cookstove. Now I sell firewood in the fall, make maple sugar in the spring, and, year round, share my home with guests, each one a wonderful surprise."

Bed and bath: Four rooms. One room with queen and one twin bed, private shower bath. Separate entrance to large two-storied suite (great for groups and families) with three bedrooms. On first floor of suite—kitchen, living room with piano, full bath. On second floor—a half bath, one room with two twin beds, one double, and one room with a double and two twin beds.
Breakfast: Until 9:30. Menu varies daily. French toast, pancakes, or apple crisp. Homemade muffins or breads, maple syrup, and granola. Cereals. Juice. Coffee.
Plus: Phone in suite kitchen and in (fourth) room with private bath. Barbecue and picnic table. Books. Games. TV and fans available.

The American Country Collection Host #041

Bennington, VT

Location: On Main Street. One mile from town center, five to Bennington College. Within walking distance of shops and services. Thirty minutes south of Manchester and Arlington. Two miles to Appalachian Trail.
Reservations: Available year round through The American Country Collection, page 335.

Rates: (All plus 10 percent gratuity.) $70–$80 Memorial Day–September 15. $80–$90 September 16–October 25. $60–$68 rest of year. Singles $10 less. $10 extra person. Champagne/restaurant dinner package available.
♥ ❀ ✗ ✁

The front brick walk leads to comfortable surroundings with classical and jazz music playing in the background. Collectibles and antiques—most acquired at area auctions and sales—are everywhere in this 1860 country home. It's just the way the host imagined it when he saw the *New York Times* ad in 1988. That was the year he, a political science major (in his twenties then), decided it was time to change careers—from retail manager to "manager of everything": the wood stove, the three common rooms, braided and hooked rugs on wide board floors, claw-footed tubs, and the cuisine (a new department now mastered). Photography is his main hobby. And he volunteers with the court system and children's youth services.

Bed and bath: Six rooms on three floors. First-floor antique double sleigh bed with private full bath. On second floor a queen, a double, or two doubles share two full and a half bath. Third-floor suite with a queen and a double, private full bath. Rollaway available.
Breakfast: 8–9:30. Pancakes, French toast, bacon, sausage, cheese omelets, or Belgian buttermilk waffles with blueberries. Vermont maple syrup. Juice. Fresh fruit cup. Homemade granola.
Plus: Welcoming beverage. Ceiling fans in many rooms. Herbal teas and coffees. Games, puzzles, TV, books.

> Guests wrote: *"Absolutely charming . . . the best waffles ever eaten. . . . Of the six inns we stayed in during our visit to New England, we found this one the most enjoyable."*

Old Mill Inn   802/247-8002
Stone Mill Dam Road, Brandon, VT 05733

Hosts: Annemarie and Karl Schreiber
Location: Quiet. Ten acres with brook, woods, meadows, farmland. Near swimming hole and Blueberry Hill Cross-Country Ski Center. One mile from village. Twenty minutes to Killington, 45 to Shelburne Museum. Public golf course borders property.

Open: Year round. Two-night minimum September 15–October 15, three nights December 24–January 3.
Rates: Per room, double occupancy. $75 weekdays, $85 weekends. $95 September 10–October 10 and December 20–February 28. Singles $20 less. $20 extra person in room.
♥ ⚲ ⌂ ❊ ⚡ ✄

> From Massachusetts: *"Hospitality that makes for intriguing conversation, diet-defying dining, and a desire for lifelong friendship. . . . Decor represents the finest collection of country-style antiques outside of a museum! . . .I caught a very nice rainbow trout on the property while others were making friends with Ben and a couple of curious goats. . . . "* From California: *"The unanimous first choice of all my tour participants . . . warm, enchanting atmosphere."*

"Paradise" is the way some others have summed up this 1786 colonial, a former dairy farm, the Schreibers' B&B for five years. They came here after 25 years in Los Angeles, where they were in the automobile business and Annemarie did interior design work. Here she has a painting studio (early American folk art). Karl is an accomplished woodworker. In summer they have barbecues; in August, a pig roast. Year round, they have ecstatic, articulate guests who write glowing comments to me.

In residence: Ben, a golden retriever. Some horses, goats, chickens, ducks, pigs, and cats.
Foreign language spoken: German.
Bed and bath: Six rooms, all with private baths, antique beds, handmade quilts, and sitting rooms. One has a working wood stove. First-floor triple
(Please turn page.)

(one double and one twin bed) with full bath. Three double-bedded rooms with en-suite shower baths. On second floor—one room with three single beds, one with a double and a twin bed. Rollaway and crib available.
Breakfast: 8–10. French toast, eggs Benedict, German apple pancakes, farm-fresh eggs and sausage, or strata. Homemade muffins and jams (farm-grown berries). Juice, fruit, hot beverage.
Plus: Fully air conditioned. Individual thermostats. Wine and cheese hour. Beamed living room, ceiling fan, wood stove. Bathrobes. Down comforters. Flannel sheets. Beach towels. Mints on pillow. Champagne for special occasions. Option of dinner, $15 per person.

Mill Brook B&B   802/484-7283

Route 44, P.O. Box 410, Brownsville, VT 05037-0410

Host: Kay Carriere
Location: Across. from Mount Ascutney in a rural village "with famous summer baked bean suppers." Ten miles from I-91, 14 south of Woodstock, 30 to Dartmouth College. Brook runs next to the property. Walk to covered bridge.
Open: Year round. Two-night minimum preferred on weekends, including Christmas and holidays.
Rates: Double occupancy. Vary according to day of week, season, and holidays. Year round, pay for three nights, stay for four. $40–$52 double bed, $50–$67 one double plus one twin bed, $52–$63 two double beds, $55–$65 queen, $65–$77 king. Private bath $10 more. Singles $5–$10 less. $13 per extra person in room. $10 one-night surcharge on weekends, holidays, and foliage season. Discounts for senior citizens, families, extended weekends. MC, VISA.
♥ ♨ ❖ ♦

"We are a farmhouse—not a mansion—with a down-home feeling. We have a wood-burning stove, board games, croquet and horseshoes, a hammock, picnic tables, and grill. Sheets are line-dried year round. Cloth napkins are used, even for tea. You can go anywhere and have a Sara Lee cake, but not here. We have back roads for walking or mountain cycling. You can feed a horse and cow. (Map and apples provided.) There's a mountain to climb and a brook to fish or swim in. Need a thermos, backpack, fishing pole? It's yours for the borrowing."

Kay, a food writer/cookbook author, was a college hospitality instructor and hotel salesperson in New Jersey. Her husband, a retired contractor, has a farm "two miles uphill, with apples, raspberries, and vegetables that find their way into jellies, pies, and omelets."

In residence: Son Mike is a chef. "Neither the Philadelphia street cat rescued by my daughter nor our black Lab is allowed inside."
Foreign languages spoken: A little Spanish, Italian, and French.
Bed and bath: Eight rooms. On first floor, private baths for rooms with a double and a single bed. One room with two queen beds and a single bed share hall bath. Up narrow steep staircase to king-bedded room, ceiling fan, private bath. Double-bedded room, private bath. Room with a double plus a single bed shares bath with room that has two doubles.

Breakfast: Usually 8–9. Or "fixed to go." Varies daily. Hot cereal, fruit, juice; meat dish, egg dish, or pancakes; coffee cake or home-baked bread. Buffet style.
Plus: Playpen. Babysitting. Two sitting rooms. TV. Tea room with microwave and refrigerator. Afternoon tea with cake in summer. Hot soup in ski season. Ten percent discount at five area restaurants.

Green Meadows
802/425-3059

Box 1300, Mt. Philo Road, Charlotte, VT 05445-9721

Host: Mary Louise Smith
Location: In a small valley surrounded by meadows and woods. Five miles to Shelburne Museum or Charlotte–Essex ferry. Between Burlington and Middlebury with view of Green Mountains.

Open: Year round.
Rates: Private bath $70 single, $75 double. Other rooms $50 single, $55 double. $10 futon. $5 crib.
♥ 🏡 ✾ ♦ 🐾 ✄

Mary Louise Smith, a retired teacher from Colorado, fits into the category of the "one out of five guests inspired to start a B&B." While she was house hunting in the area, a B&B stay prompted her to think about B&B in the big house she was looking for. What she found was a restored 1864 Victorian, just perfect for her 19th-century antique oak furniture. She has papered with small prints. White curtains are in all the windows. Floors are wide board pine, some fir, and even the bathrooms have wooden floors.

"It's a warm, comfortable nonintrusive atmosphere. Most people leave after breakfast and come back after dinner. I am surprised and delighted with inquiries and guests who come from all over the world."

In residence: Maud, the basset, and Ned, the Great Dane.
Bed and bath: Four rooms. On second floor, a large room with double bed, private bath with Jacuzzi. One room with two twin beds and one with a double bed share a shower bath. A large attic bedroom has one queen and one twin bed, shared bath downstairs. Cot and crib available.
Breakfast: 7–9. Served in the dining room, which overlooks the Vermont countryside. Bacon, French toast, juices, beverage, fruit, and warm Vermont maple syrup. (Breakfast is the best "visiting time" here.)
Plus: Air conditioning in master and attic bedrooms. Grand piano. Wicker-furnished screened porch.

The American Country Collection Host #073

Colchester, VT

Location: A quiet country road. On 10 acres of woods, pasture, and gardens. Ten minutes to downtown Burlington, five to Lake Champlain.
Reservations: Year round through

The American Country Collection, page 335.
Rates: $50 single, $70 double; $85 private bath.
🐾 ✄

(Please turn page.)

It was a riding school for girls at the turn of the century. Although each subsequent owner has made changes, the restoration was done seven years ago by the hostess together with her husband, who is in the construction business. The Victorian house, a set for many television spots, has bay windows, pillars, and porch rockers; it is decorated inside with subtle colors, wallpaper, many oak and wicker pieces, and handmade quilts and braided rugs.

In New Jersey the hosts had collected antiques. Since coming to Vermont, they have opened an antiques shop. And they make time for sheep farming, gardening, and sailing. "B&B came naturally—as a way for us to share this wonderful old house. The entire front area, including a private entrance, is exclusively for guests. People are so appreciative that B&B has made us love our home and this lifestyle even more!"

In residence: Fifteen scene-stealing sheep, each with a name. Remus, "a large, gentle malamute." Two mostly outdoor cats.
Bed and bath: Three second-floor rooms, each with double bed. One with private shower bath. Two share a full bath.
Breakfast: Usually 8–9. Juice. Grapefruit. Locally baked goods. Cold cereal. Beverages. Served in dining room or on front porch.
Plus: Fireplaced living room, TV, VCR, and stereo. Guest refrigerator. Mints. Fresh flowers. Suggestions for nontouristy restaurants.

Eaton House   802/899-2354

Box 139, Browns Trace, Jericho, VT 05465-9803

Hosts: Sue and Dave Eaton
Location: On a quiet main road, in a pastoral setting with mountain views. Three miles off I-89. Twenty minutes from Burlington, 10 to Essex; 45 minutes to Shelburne Museum and major downhill ski areas; 20 to Bolton Valley.
Open: Year round. Eaton family plans vary for Thanksgiving, Christmas, and Easter. Two-night minimum in foliage season. Business travelers welcomed for short- or long-term stays.
Rates: $70 double with private bath. With shared bath, $50 double, $30 single. Weekly rates available. Additional persons $7 ages 3–12, $10 over 12. $5 one-time crib fee.
♥ 🛏 ❖ ♦ 🛇 ✂

Guests' letters continually arrive here, all raving about their "experience" (the real reason the Eatons host) at a "beautiful home with charming hosts and fabulous breakfasts."

The Eatons' reproduction saltbox, once on an Old House tour, was designed by one of their sons, Kent (who now lives here with his family), when he was an architecture student. The artwork of another son can be seen throughout the very personalized house, which has a cozy country feeling, wide board floors, open fireplaces in old brick, and colonial colors. Sue is quilter and gardener.

When the Eatons had four growing children, they lived on a Maine poultry farm with 20,000 layers. Sue was a practicing nurse. Here, they began hosting in 1981. They are active in recycling and in the Beyond War movement.

Recently they purchased an old house that serves as Dave's insurance office and their in-town apartment.

In residence: In private quarters, Kent and Becki, and Jessica, age 11, and Liz, age 8.

Bed and bath: Three cozy second-floor rooms. Queen-bedded room with adjoining private full bath (two sinks). Room with two twins/king and doubled-bedded room share shower bath.

Breakfast: 7–9. Dutch babies (oven pancakes) with fruit, hot maple syrup, and bacon or sausage on the side. Or frittata or waffles, or casserole. Juice, homemade muffins, fruit cup, coffee and tea. Served by fireplace with view of Adirondack Mountains.

Plus: Study/library with books and TV. Grand piano and pump organ.

Homeplace Bed and Breakfast   802/899-4694

RR 2, Box 367, Jericho, VT 05465

Hosts: Hans and Mariot Huessy
Location: Very quiet. "Way in the woods, down a half-mile-long driveway." One and one-half miles off Route 15, 15 miles to Burlington, half hour to Shelburne Museum, ¾ hour to Stowe and Mount Mansfield.

Near University of Vermont and Ben & Jerry's ice cream factory.
Open: Year round. Reservations appreciated.
Rates: $40 single, $50 double.
♥ 🏠 ✿ ◆ ✖ ⚕

An 82-line poem written by a couple from Ohio comments on everything from "appointments fit for bride and groom" to "A flock of sheep with bells and bleat. They seemed to say, 'We're glad to meet.'"

Spring is the season for sugaring and newborn lambs here. When the Huessys built this wonderful modern country home on 100 acres of woodland in 1968, they furnished it with lovely antiques from Mariot's American family and Hans's European family. Hans is "slightly retired" from his teaching position at the University of Vermont Medical School. Mariot, mother to 11 (all grown now), is caretaker of the farm.

In residence: Two friendly dogs—a golden retriever and an Australian shepherd. One cat. Horses, donkeys, sheep, chickens, pigs, and ducks.

Foreign language spoken: German.

Bed and bath: In a separate wing, four ground-floor rooms share two full baths. One room has two antique twin beds; another has twin beds made by a local craftsperson. The third room has a double bed, a twin, and a crib. One room with double bed. Crib and cot available.

Breakfast: 7–10. Juice, fresh fruit, "homegrown" eggs, Vermont smoked bacon, homemade muffins or breads, and freshly ground coffee. By wood stove or in dining room.

Plus: Fireplaced living room with flagstone floor, Oriental rugs, floor-to-ceiling windows, bookcases. Fans. Trails in acres of woods for hiking and cross-country skiing. Pond for swimming (at your own risk). Babysitting, with advance notice. Their own wool, fleeces, and maple syrup for sale.

Sinclair Towers Bed & Breakfast Inn

RD 2, Box 35 (Route 15)   (Vermont) **802/899-2234**
Underhill, VT 05489-9318   (USA/Canada) **800/433-4658**

Hosts: Al and Betty Royce
Location: Four-minute walk to village green. Five miles to Underhill State Park (Mount Mansfield trails); 13 to Smugglers Notch (return via Ben & Jerry's ice cream plant); 14 west of Burlington. "One mile to excellent restaurant."

Open: Year round. Two-day minimum on holiday weekends.
Rates: $55 double or queen. $60 or $65 queen plus twin. $65 king. Ten percent less for entire inn. MC, VISA.
♥ ❖ ✈ ⅄

Pampering equals fantasy. Sheets are ironed. Some dishes, silver, and scarves are antiques. When beds are turned down, towels are changed again. The flower gardens with bird feeders are spectacular.

The Queen Anne Victorian is a purple-painted traffic stopper. "Orchid sounds better," says Betty, a University of Vermont professor emeritus (School of Education). She and Al, a retired builder, lived here for almost 15 years before opening as a B&B in 1989. Their restoration project involved storing and reassembling all the moldings, woodwork (in nine types of wood), newel posts, and medallions. There are towers and turrets, leaded and stained glass, and octagonal bedrooms. The stairway valance was carved with a fretsaw run with power generated by a windmill.

Betty is a native Vermonter. She and Al have lived in New York state and the Virgin Islands. From 1944 to 1955 they ran a full-service Rutland area inn. Now they meet guests who delight in mailing letters in the Underhill rural mailbox. Many write to me about "delightful hosts . . . superb decor, accommodations, and food . . . a special place, the most oustanding B&B encountered in coast-to-coast stays."

Bed and bath: Six air-conditioned mountain-view rooms, all private baths en suite. Handicapped-accessible first-floor room with a queen and a single bed, seat-and-two-level-shower bath. On second floor, two rooms with a queen and a single bed; one with full bath, one with shower only. Room with queen bed, full bath. King-bedded room and room with a double and a single bed, each with shower bath. Rollaway available.
Breakfast: Continental at 7:30 and 9, full at 8:30. Coffee available earlier. (Special diets accommodated.) Waffles or blueberry pancakes with Vermont maple syrup; omelet; or French toast. Orange juice. Fresh fruit. Bread basket includes bagels and/or English muffins. Cold or hot cereals. Served in dining room, under silver chandelier.
Plus: Fireplaced living room. TV with VCR. Cheese and crackers or fruit. Candy. Guest refrigerator. Gas grill. Lawn chairs and table.

According to guests (many are preservationists and/or house restorers), there ought to be a medal for the meticulous work—everything from research to labor—done by B&B owners. Indeed, many have won preservation awards.

Partridge Hill Bed & Breakfast   802/878-4741
P.O. Box 52, 102 Partridge Hill, Williston, VT 05495-0052

Hosts: Roger and Sally Bryant
Location: Up a dirt road to 900 feet above sea level for a panorama of the Green Mountains. Eight miles east of Burlington, 30 minutes from Shelburne Museum, one-half mile from Route 2 in Williston village.

Open: Year round.
Rates: Tax included. $65 double, $35 single. (UVM parents are encouraged to invite their child to breakfast at no charge.)
🛏 ✈ ⚬

"The view." The Bryants, too, marvel at it. When Roger became head athletic trainer (he still is) at the University of Vermont in 1965, they built a contemporary chalet. Now the parents of four grown children and grandparents of nine enjoy sharing the sun that pours in from the east through those big glass windows.

Bed and bath: Off of guests' common room are one queen-bedded room and one room with king bed, vanity, and sink; these share the only guest bath (tub and shower). In addition, for families, there is a suite of two small rooms, one with two twin beds, one with a double bed.
Breakfast: Usually at 8. Freshly squeezed orange juice. Fresh fruit. French toast, waffles, or pancakes with Vermont maple syrup. "Surprise" muffins. Homemade strawberry jam (a hit). Vermont Cabot cheeses, Vermont ham and bacon made without preservatives. Hot cereals and eggs. Served in fireplaced dining room or on the deck overlooking the view. "Guests usually have plans and are on their way by 10."
Plus: Large fireplaced common room with TV. Fresh flowers. Electric blankets.

> Guests wrote: *"The essence of a B&B, with marvelous hosts and immaculate accommodations.... Read late into the night in front of a blazing fire with freshly baked brownies and coffee.... We were part of a warm and gracious extended family."*

Yankees' Northview Bed & Breakfast
Lightening Ridge Road, Calais, VT   802/454-7191
Mailing address: RD 2, Box 1000, Plainfield, VT 05667-9802

Hosts: Joani and Glenn Yankee
Location: Off a rural country road, eight miles north of Montpelier in an historic, picturesque town. On a hill, surrounded by stone walls and white fences, with meadows and mountain views. Five minutes to swimming, boating, horseback riding, summer theater.

Open: Year round. Reservations required.
Rates: $35–$45 single. $40–$50 double. Less for stays that are longer than three nights. Cot $15 adult, $10 child; under age five, free.
🛏 ❄ ⚬

(Please turn page.)

From Texas: *"Just what I always pictured New England to be—stenciled walls, tab curtains, antiques, dried herbs, theorem paintings, French toast with Vermont maple syrup, freshly picked blueberries in muffins, and a friendly host and hostess. . . . I loved the countryside and quiet. . . . We have stayed in much more expensive B&Bs, and I still rate Northview my favorite."*

Other guests, who cross-country skied from the door, wrote about getting engaged on "Huggers' Hill." A New Mexico family that stayed for 10 days took time to borrow the Yankees' big deep boots so they could tromp around on the quaking bog a five-minute walk from the house. Glenn, a school superintendent, and Joani, a teacher who lists windsurfing among her interests, sometimes join visitors in the unusual bog nature preserve, which has carnivorous plants, orchids, and other rare flowers.

In residence: "Beaver is a friendly, comical cat. Bruinie is a placid one."
Bed and bath: Three antiques-filled rooms share a second-floor full bath and a first-floor half bath. One corner room has a double canopied rope bed. A double bed in another corner room. One room with two twin beds. Cot available.
Breakfast: 6–9 (7:15 on school days). Beautifully served in the country kitchen by the potbellied stove, in the stenciled dining room, or on the garden patio. Juice. Fruit. Homemade coffee bread and muffins, eggs, breakfast meats, homemade jams, Dutch babies—a type of souffle, recipe sent by a guest.
Plus: Beverages. Beamed living room. Fresh flowers. Mints. Picnic area with table and fireplace. Yard games.

Chester House

802/875-2205

Main Street, P.O. Box 708, Chester, VT 05143

Hosts: Irene and Norm Wright
Location: Across from the village green in this lovely village.
Open: Year round. Two-night minimum on major holiday and foliage season weekends.

Rates: Double occupancy. $75 king, $65 queen, $55 double, $50 twins. $10–$15 third person.
♥ ❖ ◆ ✈

"B&B fulfills the idea that came to us in 1986 while I was working as a Mobil employee relations manager in Saudi Arabia. [Before that, Norm was at corporate headquarters in Manhattan.] When I retired early, we moved to Vermont, 12 miles from where I was born, where we still have family. Irene is from Algona, Iowa, an area that has provided some small-world stories around our breakfast table."

They looked at several places before buying this c. 1780 colonial, now restored and furnished with Oriental rugs and early American antiques.

In residence: One "extremely friendly" husky/collie mixed-breed named Kiela, "not allowed in guest areas."

Bed and bath: Four rooms, all private baths. On first floor, room with canopied double bed. On second floor, king-bedded room with sitting area; room with canopied queen bed and large Jacuzzi; another with twin beds.
Breakfast: 7:30–9. Varies. Could be waffles with fried apples or scrambled eggs with home fries. Always fresh coffee, tea, juice, fruit dish, homemade breads and muffins. In dining room with two-tiered brass chandelier, wainscoting, and French print wallpaper.
Plus: Individual thermostats. Fans. TV in guest living room. Gathering room with fireplace. Down comforters. Flannel sheets. Turndown service. Front porch rockers. Fresh flowers.

Greenleaf Inn   802/875-3171
P.O. Box 188, Chester, VT 05143-0188

Hosts: Liz and Dan Duffield
Location: Just off Main Street. Surrounded by spacious lawn, old apple trees, and in back a babbling brook. Within 30 minutes of Magic, Okemo, and Bromley ski areas; 45 to Ascutney and Stratton. Walking distance to restaurants. Close to three cross-country ski centers.

Open: Year round except April. Advance reservations preferred.
Rates: Double occupancy. $70 dormer room. $80 others. $25 rollaway. $10 less for singles. "Rent an inn" (10 people) $330. Midweek ski package available. MC, VISA.
♥ ❖ ✈

The Duffields, parents of a grown family, looked at 50 inns before returning, in 1986, to Dan's "unchanged childhood summer territory." He had retired as colonel from the Marine Corps and worked for a defense contractor when he and Liz decided to work together. To their "dream" Liz brings diverse experiences. She was "a navy officer way back." After marrying Dan, she cooked and entertained all over the world, did newspaper reporting, and became a full-time antiques dealer. Family heirlooms and some of Liz's paintings are in the 1850 Victorian home that the Duffields restored.

In residence: "Our three cats are restricted to first floor, except when Tippy, the people cat, escapes to sleep behind the upstairs hanging quilt."
Bed and bath: Five second-floor rooms, each with private full bath. Two four-poster twin beds in large corner room. Queen beds in four rooms include one in large room with old harpsichord, one in dormer room with large bath across hall, one high four-poster with footstool. Rollaway available.
Breakfast: 7–9. Vermont bacon and sausage, scrambled eggs, pancakes. Cinnamon oatmeal in winter. Homemade muffins and breads. On Sundays casserole of sausage, egg, and cheese. Juice and hot beverages.
Plus: Iced mint tea or hot spiced tea and cookies. Morning papers. Bedroom window fans. Storage space for skis and bicycles. Fireplaced living room and den. Games. Books. Magazines. Small art gallery. For groups, option of dinner ($15) in winter.

> Guests wrote: *"The best innkeepers we have found. . . . We appreciated the closet and drawer space. . . . Tastefully furnished. . . . Offers peace and quiet. . . . Spotless. . . . A breakfast that will get anyone out of bed."*

Craftsbury Bed & Breakfast on Wylie Hill

Craftsbury Common, VT 05827-9602 **802/586-2206**

Host: Margaret Ramsdell
Location: Rural and peaceful. About a mile from Craftsbury Common, two from Craftsbury Sports Center (whose groomed cross-country ski trails pass through fields of this B&B). High up, with views, sunrises, sunsets, rainbows, "startlingly beautiful moonrise seen through slats of our barn." Near miles of back roads (good for mountain bikes) and lakes. Thirty miles from Stowe. One mile from Sterling College.
Open: Year round. Reservations preferred.
Rates: $35 single room, $55–$65 double. $5–$10 crib or cot.
♥ 👪 🏠 ❄ ✈ ✂

From Washington, D.C.: *"I was very fortunate to stay a considerable time. Each morning was a miniconference on the humanities."* From New York: *"Warm, caring hostess . . . comfortable rooms . . . breakfasts are out of this world."* From Connecticut: *"Our six-year-old says that he likes the apple pancakes and he likes Maggie."* From Maine: *"Relaxed atmosphere . . . feel right at home."*

The hostess, too, enjoys her 1860s farmhouse. "I feel so peacefully in tune with my surroundings. It is a joy to share this with guests. . . . When the family was young, we had a summer residential riding camp here. A few years ago the timing was perfect to convert to B&B."

In residence: Michelle, a "mostly Morgan" horse. Dusty, a barn cat who wishes she could live inside. Willoughby, a golden retriever.
Foreign language spoken: French.
Bed and bath: In separate wing, four rooms on the ground level. Two shared guest shower baths. Three rooms with a double bed, one with twin beds. Cot and crib available.
Breakfast: Usually not before 8. Juice, fruit, cinnamon apple pancakes or French toast with hot applesauce. Or cinnamon-apple coffee cake and omelets with Vermont cheddar. Homemade corn bread. Vermont maple syrup and Craftsbury honey are staples. Served in dining room (off the country kitchen with wood stove) on table set with hand-thrown pottery, silver, and fresh flowers. Winter birds at feeder outside window.
Plus: Guest living room with wood stove, no television. Flannel sheets. Individual thermostats. Dinner for cyclists or groups by special arrangement. Babysitting arranged. Grill.

Quail's Nest B&B Inn

802/293-5099

P.O. Box 221, Main Street, Danby, VT 05739-0221

Hosts: Anharad and Chip Edson
Location: In a quiet Vermont village, surrounded by the Green Mountains. Between Manchester and Rutland, just off Route 7.
Open: Year round.
Rates: $35 single with shared bath, $40 private. $50 double with shared bath, $65 private. $10 third person. MC, VISA.
👪 ❄ ✈

Anharad (a Welsh name meaning "country flower") and Chip worked in the restaurant business and wanted to try their own related activity. Their parents are artists, and Chip has been an art teacher. Anharad was also in real estate in New Jersey. Eight years ago the young couple came to Vermont to work on the 1835 house, which has a brief history of being the town's post office. They painted the outside colonial blue with white trim. For the inside they chose "original artwork and yesteryear pieces and fixtures that we love."

They love Vermont and B&B too. "We encourage people to curl up by the fireplace or to see the waterfalls and explore the woods. If they want excitement, we steer them to the ski areas or the country auctions or the alpine slide. And we often recommend a restaurant where mom and pop do home cooking."

In residence: In hosts' quarters, a growing family—Aubrey is five; Chelsea, three. "Pumpkin is a golden Lab retriever. Daisy, our cat, is Pumpkin's good friend."

Bed and bath: Five second-floor rooms, all with handmade quilts. Each room has a double bed; two have a twin bed also. Three rooms have a private shower bath. Two rooms share a full bath.

Breakfast: Usually 8–9. Served family style at large dining room table. Cheese baked eggs, apple muffins, fresh fruit or apple puff pancakes, banana bread, homegrown raspberries. Juice, coffee, tea, milk, and assorted cereals.

Plus: Beverages and home-baked goodies. Deck and two front porches. Guest refrigerator.

> From New York: *"A delight to the senses . . . wholesome breakfasts . . . cozy, clean rooms with antique quilts . . . adorable girls, fat Labrador, a cat add to the family 'home' atmosphere."* From New Jersey: *"A peaceful, gentle place to reflect and unwind . . . full of country atmosphere . . . enjoyed it so much we gave my brother and his wife a gift certificate to spend their 25th anniversary there."*

Dovetail Inn   802/867-5747

P.O. Box 976, Main Street, Route 30, Dorset, VT 05251-0976

Hosts: Jean and Jim Kingston
Location: Across from the village green (on the main road) in historic district "free of architectural intrusions," according to the National Park Service. Within walking distance of summer theater and fine restaurants. Within 30 minutes of Bromley, Magic, and Stratton mountains. Six miles north of Manchester and designer outlets.

Open: Year round except for late fall and early spring. Two-night minimum most weekends.
Rates: Double occupancy. $60–$80 smallest rooms, $65–$90 average room. $80–$125 with fireplace and wet bar. $15 extra person. No charge for crib. MC, VISA.
♥ ❖ ✈

What's it like to live in such a pretty village year round? It offers the strong sense of community that the Kingstons hoped for when they moved here from Connecticut with their teenagers in 1984. They are active members of the local historical society (museum is next door to the inn). Jim, an engineer

(Please turn page.)

and woodworker, has served as a town lister. Now he is a freelance building inspector and property manager and serves on the regional planning commission. Jean wears aprons (really!) and is the inn's official gardener/seamstress/baker.

The inn, consisting of two buildings that served as the annex and tearoom of the Dorset Inn (located across the street), is warm and comfortable with country decor. When local residents drop in (often), they usually join guests for coffee.

In residence: Alice, "our regal Irish setter/golden retriever mix."
Bed and bath: Eleven rooms (10 are air conditioned) on first and second floors, each with private bath (one with shower only, others are full baths). King, queen (one with fireplace and wet bar), double, or twin beds. Cot and crib available.
Breakfast: 8–9:30. Fruit. Juices. Yeast breads, muffins, or coffee cakes. Locally made jams and jellies. Plenty of coffee and tea. Served by the fireplace in the keeping room during cool months, by the pool in summer.
Plus: Ceiling fans. Free use of pool (unguarded). Afternoon tea and sweets, 4–5. Sitting room with cable TV. Games. Second-floor library nook with cushioned window seat.

The Little Lodge at Dorset   802/867-4040
Route 30, Box 673, Dorset, VT 05251

Hosts: Allan and Nancy Norris
Location: Set back from road on a hillside, one block from the village green. A pretty pond in front and mountain view beyond. Across the street from the oldest nine-hole golf course in the country and adjacent to hiking and cross-country trails. Close to craft and antiques shops and summer theater; 15 minutes to Bromley, 30 to Stratton and Magic Mountain; six miles to Manchester. "Excellent biking terrain."
Open: Usually year round. Reservations preferred. Two-day minimum in foliage season and busy weekend times.
Rates: $80–$90 for two. $30 extra person. Discount for extended stays. AMEX, Discover (preferably for deposits only).
♥ 🏠 ❖ ♦ 🐾 ✂

Just five guest rooms, but so much space for relaxation: an antiques-filled living room with stenciled wallpaper and wood stove; a five-sided sun porch screened in summer, glassed in winter; a unique barnboard den; and all that lawn. The original part of the inn, c. 1810–20, was moved here in the 1930s from Hebron, New York. Subsequent additions resulted in an unusual and interesting arrangement of windows, staircases, and halls. The country decor includes stenciling and quilts done by Nancy and crocheted bedspreads done by Allan's sister.

Since the Norrises moved here from Baltimore, Maryland, in 1981, they have traveled (between seasons) in 12 countries including Kenya, Egypt, China, Yugoslavia, and India.

In residence: A very friendly dog.
Foreign languages spoken: Some Spanish and French.

Bed and bath: Five rooms on first and second floors. All with private baths (some full, some shower only). Twin beds/king option in each room. One room with private exterior entrance is accessible to the handicapped but cannot accommodate a wheelchair. Cot and crib available.

Breakfast: 8–9:30. Juice, cereals, unusual toasted homemade breads, muffins (many made from recipes exchanged with guests), and beverage. Served in dining room furnished with antiques.

Plus: Tea, coffee, and hot chocolate always available. Late-afternoon cheese and crackers. Turned-down beds. Mints on your pillow. Refrigerator and (BYOB) wet bar. Dartboard, games, books, puzzles, mini pool game. Terrace. Bike and ski storage. Skating on the pond.

> From New York: *"Charming . . . friendly . . . perfect hosts who anticipate every need a guest could have."*

Maplewood Inn

Route 22A South, RR 1, Box 4460
Fair Haven, VT 05743-9721

802/265-8039
800/253-7729

Hosts: Cindy and Doug Baird
Location: Pastoral with mountain views. Forty minutes west (Route 4) of Killington and Pico ski areas. One mile south of historic village center. Minutes to Lakes Bomoseen and Saint Catherine.
Open: Year round.

Rates: Per room. $65–$70 shared bath. $70 double with private patio. $95 suite. $20 third person. Ten percent discount for five nights or more. Continental breakfast rate, $5 less. AMEX, MC, VISA.
♥ ❖ ♦ ✄

Sunsets from the front porch, the fresh traditional decor, and the many amenities all get high marks from guests who enjoy the hospitality at this B&B. It was the Maplewood Dairy homestead from 1880 until 1979. Six years ago Cindy bought the three-part Greek Revival house and red barn and restored and redecorated inside and out.

On Long Island Cindy had her own restaurant/cafe. Doug, a native Vermonter, "is a treasure trove of information—for cycling routes, hidden waterfalls, and fishing coves."

Bed and bath: Five rooms (four are air conditioned) including two suites with private baths. (One suite has private steep stairway.) First-floor room has double four-poster, private shower bath. One room with queen four-poster and private half bath shares full bath with room with double brass and enamel bed. Suite has queen bed with bedsteps, living room with double sleep sofa, rollaway. Other suite has room with a double and a twin bed, living room.

Breakfast: 8:30. For full, entree may be quiche, Belgian waffles, or French toast. Continental—juice, fruit, homemade breads or muffins, coffee, tea.

Plus: Coffee, tea, hot chocolate. Complimentary sherry in rooms. Cheese platter. Candies. Fireplaced room with cable TV and stereo. Gathering room for reading and board games. Stereoptic viewer and slides. Toiletries. Extra towels. Croquet. Shops in barn with country antiques, crafts, and home brewing supplies.

Silver Maple Lodge

802/333-4326
800/666-1946

RR 1, Box 8, South Main Street, Fairlee, VT 05045

Hosts: Sharon and Scott Wright
Location: On Main Street, one mile south of town center. Next door to Leda's Pizza Restaurant (popular with local residents and tourists). Opposite open farmland with barn. Views of White Mountains to the east and Green Mountains to the west; 17 miles from Dartmouth College.
Open: Year round.

Rates: In inn (no smoking)—shared bath $38 single, $44 double; private bath $48–$50 single, $50–$58 double. Cottages (smoking and pets allowed)—$50–$56 single, $56–$62 double. Ten-speed bicycles $10 per day (includes shuttle, if needed). AMEX, MC, VISA.
♥ ♨ ❊ ♦

After Dave Maynard, Boston's popular WBZ radio personality, conducted an on-air singing contest about why you want to go hot-air ballooning, the winner and her sister and the Maynards stayed at Silver Maple, took a balloon ride, and explored the area. Some other guests appreciate the Wrights' do-it-yourself tours (routes together with what to see and do) for cycling, for canoeing, and for walking—for 10 to 100 miles a day, from inn to inn, or from Silver Maple as a base.

The 1790s farmhouse had become an inn in the early 1900s. Pine-paneled cottages were added in the 1950s. When the Wrights decided to switch careers in the mid-1980s, they bought the inn and added baths, a common room fireplace, and crisp, simple country decor. Sharon is official baker. Scott, who grew up on a Vermont farm, wins prizes for his 150-pound pumpkins.

In residence: "Our cat, Albert Riley, has the life of Riley."
Bed and bath: Eight second-floor rooms (all with mountain views) in the inn; four rooms with sinks. Private baths (with tub or shower), except for two rooms that share a full bath. King, double, or twin beds. Cottages (nostalgic for some people) with private baths have three twins, a double bed and a twin, or two doubles and a twin. Two cottages have kitchenettes; one has working fireplace. Cot available.
Breakfast: 7–9. Juice, fruit, homemade breads and rolls, coffee or tea. Self-served in the dining room.
Plus: Ceiling fans in two guest rooms. Cottages air conditioned. Screened wraparound porch. Piano. Games. Horseshoes, croquet, badminton, shuffleboard, and volleyball. Picnic tables among the apple trees. Babysitting arranged.

Fair Meadows Farm B&B

802/285-2132

Box 430, Route 235, Franklin, VT 05457

Hosts: Terry and Phil Pierce
Location: In the land of "big sky," minutes to Canadian border. Three miles west of Franklin, 12 miles from I-89; 60 miles to Montreal.

Open: Year round.
Rates: $35 single, $45 double.
♥ ♨ ❊ ♦

Guests wrote: *"We even have a picture of the Pierces on our refrigerator. After 24 hours with them, we felt like family."*

Yes, indeed. That's just the way it is in the comfortable and immaculate farmhouse that has been in the family since 1853. Flowers and views are everywhere. But so are surrounding hills, as my cycling legs reminded me during a trip when the welcome B&B sign was in the right place at the right time. We noticed the window frame mounted in the hall with family pictures that tell of the widespread younger generation. The five Pierce children, educated at five different colleges, are now in five different states.

We enjoyed Phil's keen sense of humor and his perspective on the changes in dairying through the years. Although he is retired now, a nephew is continuing the family tradition. Terry continues her gardening and cooking and community involvement. Recipes are shared. And so are practical hints—everything from changing currency at a bank before entering Canada to alternative routes going south.

Foreign language spoken: French.
Bed and bath: Four rooms, each with a double bed except for one upstairs room with two twin beds. Rooms share two full baths, one upstairs and one downstairs. Room downstairs has a private half bath. Two cribs available.
Breakfast: At guests' convenience. A real farm breakfast including home-made muffins and butter. Served in the pine-paneled room off the kitchen and overlooking the meadow.
Plus: Large living room. TV. Bicycles can be kept in barn.

Cobble House Inn　　　　　802/234-5458

P.O. Box 49, Childrens Camp Ground Road, Gaysville, VT 05746

Hosts: Beau and Phil Benson
Location: Atop a mountain road, 20 miles from major ski areas. Near local golf on the river. Five miles from lake. Six miles west of Bethel. Nine miles from I-89.
Open: Year round. Two-day mini-

mum on most weekends and during foliage season.
Rates: Double occupancy. Per room, $80 or $100 including tax and service. Third person $40 in $80 room, $50 in $100 room.
♥ ♨ ❊ ✖ ✂

The trained chef must be a magician; when we spoke in June, Beau was looking for a pumpkin because a photographer was coming in a couple of hours to photograph a Thanksgiving magazine feature. My mailbag confirms that many guests believe that Beau does weave magic in the kitchen. And it all happens "off the beaten track, on a river and in the mountains." It was the very location the Bensons were searching for in 1985.

They bought this 1864 Federal-style house with cupola and huge barn, did the house (even the foundation) all over, and furnished with antique bed-steads and lots of country touches. Now they have an ardent following of diehard skiers, cyclists, and people who only want to relax. Now the "city boy" who was president of a small Washington-based research company is

(Please turn page.)

called "Farmer Phil." He raises livestock naturally and trains Morgan horses. He creates pastures and uses the felled trees for fencing. Next year's project: the barn. As guests can tell, you couldn't find a family that is happier doing what they do.

In residence: "Seven-year-old Sam is growing up with the inn and loves it." Barnyard with pigs, rabbits, horses, and cats.
Bed and bath: Six rooms on two floors, all with new private baths. Queen or double beds; rollaways available.
Breakfast: Usually 7–11. Belgian waffles, sourdough French toast, whole-grain pancakes. Bensons' own pork products. Outdoors in warm months. In bed, if you'd like.
Plus: Fireplaced guest parlors. Porch rockers. Perennial gardens. Wine or hot cider in winter. If requested, morning coffee outside your door. Flannel sheets. Option of dinner ($18–$25) Thursday–Saturday with advance arrangements. Sometimes, four-wheel-drive tours of the area. Three swimming holes (inner tube available) and miles of hiking and cross-country trails on the property. Two fishing rods. "We'll cook and store your catch for you." Use of refrigerator.

From Massachusetts: *"A treasure. . . . Perfect hosts."* From New York: *"One of our favorite places (we also liked Florence, Italy!) . . . words cannot describe the food . . . served with impeccable style and grace."*

The Hayes House   802/843-2461
Grafton, VT 05146-0092

Host: Margery Hayes Heindel
Location: Adjacent to an 1870 covered bridge. On a side street near the village center. Minutes' walk to cheese company (visitors welcome), historical society museum, Grafton Museum of Natural History, antiques shops, country store, printmaking workshop, blacksmith shop, ski shop, and trail system.
Open: Year round except April.
Rates: Single $30. Double $65 shared bath, $75 private bath. Child in sleeping bag in parents' room, $5 per bag per night.
♥ ♙ ♨ ✢

"I was a summer kid from Cambridge, Massachusetts, when this first became 'home.' I fell in love with my town then—and I'm still in love." Today Marge is clerk of the Board of Selectmen in this picturebook New England town. Twenty of the in-between years were filled with 28 moves while she was wife of a naval officer and mother of "two great children."

The house, built in 1803, "is furnished with many Oriental things that fit in well with old pieces—including me! I am gardener (flowers and vegetables), and good cook, enjoy arranging flowers, knit, sew, do stitchery, read far too many books—and I'm grateful to my cleaning lady because I hate to vacuum."

In residence: A Chesapeake Bay retriever, Velva. Three cats, Tyl, Grace, and Eric the Red.
Bed and bath: Four rooms. First-floor double-bedded room has four-poster bed high enough to require the stool provided to climb into it, working

fireplace, and private bath. On second floor, one single, one room with twin beds, and one with a double share one full guest bath (plus a half bath, spring through fall).

Breakfast: 8–10. Family style in the dining room. Continental with home-made breads, muffins, jellies and jams.

Plus: Fruit and cookies. Flowers in season. Babbling brook (toe-dabbling allowed) by the house. Porches. Kitchen privileges in winter or for bicyclists without a car. After 2 p.m. on winter afternoons, self-service for homemade soups. Babysitting arranged with advanced notice. Suggestions for back-road tours. Dogs are the only guests' pets allowed.

Carolyn's Bed & Breakfast
802/472-

15 Church Street, P.O. Box 1087, Hardwick, VT 05843-1087

Host: Carolyn Hunter Richter
Location: In the heart of a small Vermont town. Twenty miles north-east of Stowe. Five miles to mountain lake. Within five miles of three cross-country ski centers. Walk to tennis courts.

Open: Year round. Two-night mum in September and Octobe during holidays.
Rates: $45 single, $70 double each child six and older in par room, $10 under age six. MC,

♥ ⌂ ▄ ❅ ✗ ✄

From California: *"We feel we 'lucked out' when we found this charming . . . lively conversations on their front porch, afternoon tea, beautiful antiq ." From New York: "The fantastic piping hot breakfast was beautifully ser the lovely and homey dining room."*

Decorating is recent, but no one has disturbed the original cherry woodwork, built-in cupboards, or library in this Victorian house, where the Richters have lived for 17 years. Carolyn, an elementary school counselor and New Age therapist, enjoys "making something elegant with auction finds and a mini-mum of materials." Their B&B has been discovered and acclaimed by wedding guests, an Egyptian princess, and hundreds of tourists.

In residence: Anna is 15. Emily is home during college breaks.
Foreign languages spoken: A little French and Italian.
Bed and bath: Four second-floor rooms (accessible by two interior stair-ways) share one first- and one second-floor full bath. Two rooms have king beds, one with a crown canopy. One room with two twin beds. In the fourth room—a four-poster double bed, ceiling fan, sink. Rollaway, crib, and high chair available.
Breakfast: Usually 8–10. Maybe a souffle-like dish with baked French bread, cheese and sausage, or French toast, pancakes with blueberries or bananas, or Yorkshire pudding with raspberry syrup. Granola, fresh fruits, Vermont cider or orange juice. Homemade breads, coffee cake, or scones with butter and jam.
Plus: Tea and sweets upon arrival. Wine or sherry. Morning newspaper. Bedroom fans. Porch rockers. Children's wooden swing set. Dinner ($10)—homemade bread, soup, dessert, and beverage—with advance reservations. Victorian tea, by reservation, on porch or in dining room.

Kahagon at Nichols Pond   802/472-6446

Nichols Pond, Woodbury, VT
Mailing address: Box 272, Hardwick, VT 05843

Hosts: Lesley and Paul Smith
Location: Four miles along a dirt road east of Hardwick. Off Route 14 on a natural lake. Twenty miles to Stowe. "Just over the hill" to Cabot Creamery (free tours); 100 miles on scenic back roads to Montreal.

Open: Year round. By reservation only. Closed mud season.
Rates: $42 single, $65 double; 10 percent seniors' discount. MC, VISA.
♥ ♨ ⚶ ✈

> From Texas: *"Peace and tranquillity, wonderful food . . . tender loving care in what is surely one of the world's most beautiful spots."*

"We are out of the way but close to so much. There's beauty, loons on the lake, and just a few minutes up the trail is Nichols Ledge, 500 feet above the lake with vistas in all directions, even a glimpse of Mount Washington. You can hike on 400 acres and, in winter, ski on our 15 miles of cross-country trails. And lots of weddings take place here."

It's homey and peaceful at the 1870 farmhouse, the only sign of civilization on the road. Once a family farm and later an exclusive boys' camp, Kahagon became a retreat for families when Lesley's grandfather bought it in 1936. During the last nine years, it has been revived by two creative restauranteurs—Lesley, a former Colorado ski instructor, and Paul, a former university instructor. The redone self-contained cottages are still rented to families, but the main house, with its birch floors and handmade bird's-eye maple staircase, is now a B&B. The family tradition of hospitality lives on.

In residence: Two-year-old daughter, Morgan. Two horses, two cats, and two "well-behaved golden retrievers."
Bed and bath: Three second-floor cozy double-bedded rooms share a full bath. Cot and crib available.
Breakfast: (For B&B guests only.) 7:30–9:30. Juice, eggs, bacon or ham, homemade muffins or bread, pancakes or French toast, fresh fruit, hot beverages. In dining room overlooking fields that lead to lake.
Plus: Swimming, sailing, fishing, canoeing (no extra charge). Croquet. Babysitting. Option of dinner ($10–$15), gourmet picnics. Cocktails available. Fees for rides in a Meadowbrook cart from Amish country or antique fire engine; nearby horseback riding or scenic aerial tours in private plane.

The Andrie Rose Inn   802/228-4846

13 Pleasant Street, Ludlow, VT 05149

Hosts: Carolyn and Rick Bentzinger
Location: One-half block off Main Street, one-half mile to Okemo ski mountain. Ten minutes to Weston.
Open: Year round. Two-night minimum on fall and winter weekends.
Rates: Double occupancy. $90–

$110. Ten percent less for senior citizens and Sunday–Thursday stays of three nights. Single, $15 less. Cocktails extra (sold to guests only). AMEX, MC, VISA.
♥ ⚶ ♦ ✈ ✂

Welcome—via the guests' entrance—into the kitchen with hanging pots and pans and a granite counter shaped like the figure seven and lined with stools. Most of the time this is where guests "hang out" and watch Carolyn and Rick cooking and baking. (Much recipe swapping goes on.) Often, guests want to know why the young couple, both successful human resource directors with Fortune 500 companies, chose to leave Boston three years ago and completely redo this 1829 colonial-style house, which was a guest house in the 1950s and '60s. The answer: "For lifestyle and a chance to work together." Extended family members assisted with designing the pastel-colored wallpaper and refinishing floors. Others acquired oak auction pieces in Iowa.

Ceiling fans are everywhere. In summer, guests sip lemonade on the wraparound porch. They borrow a bicycle and take a picnic to a swimming area "with huge boulders and crystal-clear water." And almost year round, the living room fireplace beckons.

In residence: Aratusa, "Tusa," a Siberian husky.
Bed and bath: Ten rooms with antique double beds. Two rooms with skylights, sloping ceilings. All private full baths with pedestal sinks; five with whirlpool tubs, one with antique claw-footed tub.
Breakfast: 7:30–9:30 in winter, 8–10 rest of year. Perhaps buttermilk waffles or cinnamon walnut French toast. Oatmeal, cold cereals, fresh fruit platter, two kinds of sweet morning bread, yogurt, yeast slicing bread, juices. Buffet at tables for two by candlelight.
Plus: Jars filled with chocolate chip/raisin oatmeal cookies. Fresh fruit. Cocktail hour with Vermont cheese, fruits, breads, nuts. Individual thermostats. Down comforters. Mints on pillow. Hot chocolate, coffee, apple cider. Champagne for honeymooners. Option of dinner, $50 per couple, on Saturdays and holidays.

> A guest wrote: *"It's the first time I have been able to please my mother-in-law with accommodations. She raved about [this] place."*

Branch Brook Bed & Breakfast   802/626-8316

South Wheelock Road, P.O. Box 143, Lyndon, VT 05849-0143

Hosts: Ted and Ann Tolman
Location: In the village. Within walking distance of two covered bridges. Half a mile from I-91 exit 23. Two miles to Lyndon State College, 8 to Burke Mountain ski area, 35 to Canadian border. Near antiques shops and restaurants.

Open: Year round.
Rates: Double occupancy. $55 shared bath, $60–$70 private. $10 crib or rollaway. Singles $5 less. MC, VISA.
♥ ✖ ✂

"Our favorite place is our log cabin on 23 acres, located eight miles west. If guests want to cross-country ski, watch the maple sugaring operation, hike, or just relax there, we take them to it. To reach the cabin, we often passed by 'this old (1830s) house' which had been vacant for eight years. One day, in 1986, we saw a 'For Sale' sign in the tall grass. 'You don't want it,' said the realtor. We did. The renovations (rebuilding) took three years. The

(Please turn page.)

furnishings are primarily antiques, many of which we had in our restored 1760 Connecticut house. Guests are welcome to try using our AGA cooker, our only cooking source. Last May an AGA importer used our kitchen to film a video for an owner's manual."

In Connecticut Ted was assistant food service manager for an insurance company. Ann was director of the state's child nutrition programs.

Bed and bath: Five second-floor rooms. One room has queen canopied bed, private shower bath. Two rooms, each with two twin beds, share a shower bath (robes provided). Two queen-bedded rooms with beamed ceilings, private baths (one with tub and shower, one with claw-footed tub). Rollaway and crib available.

Breakfast: Served 8–9:30. Pancakes or French toast with "our own" maple syrup. Muffins or scones. Fresh fruit. Cereals. Yogurt. Eggs any style on toast. Bacon or sausage. Juices (five varieties). In fireplaced dining room with full-length windows.

Plus: Window fans. TV with cable, VCR. Puzzles. Games. Books. Late-afternoon coffee, tea, or hot cider. Cookies. Some rooms with phone jacks and individual thermostats. Babysitting upon request. Turndown service. Transportation to/from Vermont Transit bus stop or Lyndonville airport.

> From Florida: *"They love to cook and I love to eat . . . I think they introduced me to half the town of Lyndon, I'll have to go back to meet the other half."* From Canada: *"Spotless, charming decor . . . breakfast was a unique experience . . . but most important were the hosts, who made me feel special and right at home."* From Washington: *"The highlight of our trip."*

The American Country Collection Host #080
Manchester, VT

Location: Tranquil. On five acres with babbling brook at the foot of the Green Mountains. One mile from center of Manchester; 5 to Long Trail, 6 to Bromley, 10 to Dorset Play-house, 15 to Weston Playhouse or Stratton.

Reservations: Year round through The American Country Collection, page 335.
Rates: $55 single, $60 double.

> Guests wrote: *"Scones were superb. . . . The hospitality was beyond our expecta-tions. It was our first B&B and we loved it. . . . Talented people who added much to our stay."*

They were among many guests who are fascinated by the carvings done by the hosts, ex-advertising executives. He creates interesting pipes and does swordfish-bone scrimshaw. She carves birds. Their house, built for a tenant farmer in 1890 and added on to through the years, has wide board floors and beamed ceilings. It is furnished eclectically—with comfortable old pieces, antiques, sculpture, and art. The property includes a barn with many original features intact.

In residence: One dog.
Bed and bath: Two second-floor rooms. One with one double bed and attached private shower bath. One with king/twins option, private full bath on first floor at bottom of stairs.
Breakfast: Flexible hours. Juice, fresh fruit, homemade scones and muffins, coffee. Served in the dining room or on the deck.
Plus: Afternoon tea on the deck beside the brook, or by dining room wood stove or living room fireplace. Perhaps a tour of their workshop.

Brookside Meadows

802/388-6429
800/442-9887

RD 3, Box 2460, Painter Road,
Middlebury, VT 05753-8751

Hosts: Linda and Roger Cole
Location: On open meadow with view of pond, brook, and Green Mountains beyond. Within three miles of Middlebury College and center of town. Near Shelburne Museum, UVM Morgan Horse Farm, and many downhill and cross-country ski areas.

Open: Year round. Two-night reservations preferred. Two-night minimum on weekends.
Rates: $65–$85. $15 cot. $120–$150 suite (up to four people).
♥ ⚓ 🏠 ⁂ ◆ ✈ ⚡

> From Maine: *"Accommodations are excellent, modern, clean, efficient, comfortable. . . . Privacy is a priority. And price-wise, it can't be beat."* From Australia: *"Our family was made to feel so welcome . . . breakfasts were delicious . . . relaxed surroundings. . . . We spent three nights instead of the intended one . . . as we loved being with such beautiful people."*

Travelers from all over the world have declared the Coles gracious and helpful. Linda has been a teacher and Roger an administrator at Middlebury College. Their house is designed on the lines of a late-1800s colonial-style story-and-a-half farm home. Linda worked closely with the architect when it was built in 1979 and is responsible for the attractive decor and the beautiful gardens. The barn behind the house is an oldie built in 1876 and moved recently from 12 miles away. Whether you want to watch maple sugaring or find a local swimming hole (with view of covered bridge) or a lighted cross-country ski area, the hosts are prepared with more than directions.

In residence: Giant schnauzer Tux(edo). Two cats in the house. Outside, four white China geese.
Bed and bath: Two rooms plus a suite, all private baths. First-floor room with queen bed, old wide pine floors. Upstairs room has two twin beds, full bath, double sink. In suite, one room with queen bed, one with two twin beds, private entrance, bath, and living room with wood stove.
Breakfast: 7–9. Juice, coffee or tea, cereal and fresh eggs or French toast with local maple syrup.
Plus: Tea, wine or soft drinks. Wood stove in family room. Mints. Will meet guests at the local bus stop or provide transportation for bicyclists. Walking or cross-country skiing along brook with beaver dams.

October Pumpkin Inn

802/388-9525
P.O. Box 226, Route 125E   (US/Canada) 800/237-2007
East Middlebury, VT 05740

Hosts: Eileen and Charles Roeder
Location: "A quiet apple-pie-and-wooden-screen-door American village setting on an historic stagecoach road in Robert Frost country." Four miles south of Middlebury village; one mile east on Route 125.

Open: Year round.
Rates: Double occupancy. $50 shared bath. $75 private bath. $15 third person in room. Extended stay rates available.

They just love restoring and redoing, so six years ago they sold—as a private residence to previous guests—the farm where they had raised all their own produce and meats (and two teenagers) and redid this 1850 Greek Revival house into their second B&B. (They also have experience as inn managers and are immaculate housekeepers.) Restoration of "the charm of the old with amenities (including air conditioning) of the new" is complete with English and colonial antiques acquired during the hosts' days as dealers and auctioneers in New Jersey. Both Eileen and Charles did the stenciling seen throughout the inn.

In residence: "Three neurotic ducks and one chicken." Guests' polite pets accepted.
Bed and bath: Five rooms. Two first-floor rooms, each with queen bed, sitting area, private full bath. On second floor, canopied double bed, private full bath. Room with antique cannonball double bed and room with two single wicker beds share a bath with deep tub and hand-held shower. Cot available. Handmade quilts by Eileen.
Breakfast: At guests' convenience. Continental, featuring Charles's cast iron-baked corn sticks and homemade jellies and jams. Served by dining room wood stove.
Plus: Cozy parlor with piano and abundant reading material. Carriage house hosts guests' bicycles, skis, canoes, and vintage autos.

From Massachusetts: *"As inviting as the name and exterior color."*

Montpelier Bed & Breakfast

802/229-0878
22 North Street, Montpelier, VT 05602

Hosts: Karen and Warren Kitzmiller
Location: In a residential area, on a quiet side street. Ten-minute walk from downtown. Within walking distance of New England Culinary Institute and Vermont College.
Open: Year round.

Rates: $49 double, $38 single. $10 one-time charge for cot or crib. Child $0–$15 depending on age. Stays of two nights or more, 15 percent discount. Discount for cyclists who arrive on bikes.

When a cycling trip to Scotland showed them just how important local hospitality can be, the Kitzmillers realized that they had "the perfect house for B&B in the perfect location." Built in 1891 with massive one-piece granite steps, the B&B area has been completely done over for guests. Karen is a state legislator, nutritionist, and silk screen artist. Warren owns a sporting goods and bicycle store in town called Onion River Sports.

> From Philadelphia: *"An atmosphere that nourishes body and spirit . . . stimulating conversations . . . satisfying and nutritious breakfast . . . comfortable, clean, and graciously decorated room . . . close to nature walks and center of town."*

In residence: Amy, age 11, and Carrie, age 9. Tobler, "a lovable 116-pound Bernese mountain dog," not allowed in guests' quarters.
Bed and bath: Three second-floor rooms (with private exterior entrance) share one full bath. Two double-bedded rooms. One with two twin beds and an in-room sink. Cot and crib available.
Breakfast: 7:30–9. Homemade muffins or bread, homemade granola or cold cereal, fresh fruit and cheese or yogurt, juice, coffee or tea. Served in guests' second-floor sitting room.
Plus: Garden flowers. Window fans. Garage space for bicycles. Directions to four covered bridges within seven miles. Suggestions for restaurants, swimming holes, bike routes, cross-country ski trails, cultural events.

Rose Apple Acres Farm   802/988-4300

East Hill Road, RR 2, Box 300, North Troy, VT 05859-9719

Hosts: Jay and Camilla and (son) Courtney Mead
Location: Rural with spectacular views of Canadian Sutton Range. "To Canada, one mile as the crow flies." Near the end of the Long Trail. Ten miles from Jay Peak ski area. Less than a mile from Route 105. Near covered bridge and Big Falls on the Missisquoi River. "Within 10 miles, many restaurants with great chefs."
Open: Year round. Reservations recommended.
Rates: Per room. $42 shared bath. $52 private bath. $15 third person in room. AMEX.
♥ ⬛ ♦ ✈ ✄

> From Canada: *"Unspoiled charm, magnificent setting, reasonable rates, comfortable living arrangements, great food, myriad of activities—even sleigh rides right here, very relaxing, beyond our expectations . . . feel like you're staying with friends."*

"No, you don't have to dress for dinner," laughs Cam when she gets a call from someone who hasn't been to "a real B&B" before. "Here you can take a hayride, pick apples or berrries, swim in a farm pond, cross-country ski, or try spinning yarn. There are always changes. Courtney's Lincoln flock, a rare breed of sheep, has grown to 16. Clara and Gypsy just kidded, so hurray—goat milk again! Our horse population is up to eight. Haying is done with antique farm equipment. (Cort also has a sizable collection of antique sleighs.) And we continue to meet guests who fall in love with the area."

(Please turn page.)

On Cape Cod, where the Meads' four children grew up, Cam was a music and choir director. Jay, who is a toy train enthusiast, was a buyer for a building materials company.

In residence: Angel, a collie. Auger, a Himalayan cat. S.S., a barn cat. "Jimmy (should be called James) is an aristocratic Afghan."
Bed and bath: Three second-floor rooms. Two rooms, each with one double and two twin beds, share one full bath. Private full bath for one double-bedded room.
Breakfast: Flexible hours. "Bread pudding and fresh rhubarb sauce are favorites." Homemade granola, breads, jellies. Maybe mapled apples or blueberry buckle. Served in tin-ceilinged kitchen or candlelit dining room.
Plus: Living room with Franklin stove, TV, piano. Enormous barn for bicycle and ski storage.

Northfield Inn   802/485-8558
27 Highland Avenue, Northfield, VT 05663-1448

Hosts: Aglaia and Alan Stalb
Location: Overlooking the village and Norwich University, the country's oldest private military college. Five miles west of I-89. Nine miles south of Montpelier, 23 south of Stowe; 16 miles to Sugarbush.
Open: Year round. Minimum stays specified for special events such as quilt festival and art workshops.
Rates: Double occupancy $85 private bath, $75 shared, $115 suite. Single $75 private bath, $65 shared, $55 twin bed. Inquire about Sugarbush ski packages. MC, VISA.
♥ ❖ ◆ ✈ ⚲

From the porches there are panoramic views of mountains and sunsets. A welcoming fireplace blazes in the winter. The pride of the community, this restored 25-room Victorian (23 hours of videotape will tell all) has four gables with Palladian windows, lots of natural woodwork, and—now—baseboard heating. It is decorated with floral wallcoverings, Oriental rugs, antiques, and period lighting fixtures. Since the Stalbs opened in 1990, many international travelers have been among those who ask about the career change made by the innkeepers. Aglaia, former head of the computer resources department at Grumman Aerospace Corporation, has also worked as an interior designer, has owned and managed a construction company, and has worked in real estate sales and investments. Alan, the chef, was an engineer and aerospace product operations manager at Grumman. In the navy, he was a nuclear submarine specialist. "Our new lifestyle is more interesting, more intellectually stimulating and culturally fascinating than we thought possible."

Foreign language spoken: Greek.
Bed and bath: Eight large rooms (two are suites) on second and third floors. All private baths with glass-enclosed showers, one with claw-footed tub. Queen-sized beds include Victorian carved wood, four-posters, and brass—with feather beds.
Breakfast: 7–10. Crepes, stuffed French toast, German apple pancakes, eggs Benedict, souffle, or stuffed omelets. Special ethnic menus prepared. Served at table set with china and linen.

Plus: Afternoon tea. In winter, soup at noon. Butler's pantry with refrigerator, fresh fruit, home-baked goods, snacks. Ceiling fans. Down comforters and pillows. Two parlors. Game/exercise room. Library. Croquet. Horseshoes. Gardens. By reservation, dinners for groups and special events.

Sunning Hill   802/483-9402
Arch Street, P.O. Box 560, Pittsford, VT 05763-0560

Hosts: Betty and Lawson Stewart
Location: On a quiet side road, about seven miles north of Rutland. Pico is about 15 miles away; Killington, 20. Close to the Vermont Marble Museum, the New England Maple Museum, and golf, tennis, swimming.
Open: Usually year round.
Rates: $25 single, $40–$45 double. $5 crib. $10 cot.

♦ ♦ ❀ ✄

> From West Virginia: *"I liked entering right through the kitchen, just like real friends. My husband liked the furnishings. We both like the country silence. . . the neatest part was the place they told us to visit—all that marble!"*

And thanks to the Stewarts, we pedaled on a trafficless road during a spectacular foliage season. Since, they have discovered many hidden treasures while serving on the board of the Vermont Symphony. "What a way to learn Vermont!"

The warm ambiance of their 1806 farmhouse is comfortable and lovely, furnished with antiques, reproductions, and artwork. Lawson, a former engineer and editor in the corporate world, is a talented woodworker. Betty, a teacher and school administrator in Maryland, has a dream work space for sewing, needlework, and knitting projects. And because they have a sporting goods shop in nearby Mendon, "guests receive excellent service, particularly on ski work."

In residence: "Our son, his wife, and their children (ages 8 and 6) sometimes pop in from their home on the property." Niffer is a loving 10-year-old golden retriever.
Bed and bath: Two second-floor rooms, one double-bedded and one with two twins, share a full bath. Crib, cot available.
Breakfast: Time agreed upon the night before. 6:30–10. Waffles, pancakes, or omelets. Some home-baked breads, always fruits, juices, beverages. By kitchen fireplace or in gracious pine-paneled dining room.
Plus: Welcoming beverage. Babysitting can be arranged. Meadow and knoll for practice cross-country skiing. Five acres to explore. Good beginner alpine hill in yard for children; jungle gym. Brook has trout for anglers.

❀

Can't find a listing for the community you are going to? Check with a reservation service described at the beginning of this chapter. Through the service, you may be placed (matched) with a welcoming B&B that is near your destination.

Hickory Ridge House   802/387-5709
RD 3, Box 1410, Putney, VT 05346-9326

Hosts: Jacquie Walker and Steve Anderson
Location: Quiet. On 12 acres with woods for hiking, perennial gardens, views of rolling meadows and hills. Minutes' walk to swimming hole. Two miles to Putney village, I-91, and Connecticut River. Ten miles to Brattleboro.
Open: Year round. Two-night minimum on holiday weekends.

Rates: Double occupancy. Room with fireplace, $80 private bath, $68 shared. Without fireplace, $68 private bath, $45–$55 shared. $18 each additional person. $10 crib. Four or more days, 10 percent discount. MC, VISA.
♥ ❅ ✗ ⚊

Jacquie and Steve were chimney sweeps with previous careers in college teaching (political science), administration (Planned Parenthood), and parenting when they acquired this well-maintained and little-altered 1808 Federal brick country manor, which was once a college president's residence. This architectural gem features spacious rooms and halls, a grand stairway and Palladian window, country and Federal furnishings. The books, decor, cuisine, and music (recorder workshops and spontaneous performances) reflect the innkeepers' interests in other cultures and world affairs.

Often breakfast guests represent many parts of the United States and several countries. Since they became innkeepers six years ago, Jacquie and Steve's own extensive travels have taken them to China, France, the American Southwest, and Czechoslovakia. Nature lovers too, they, together with guests, sometimes ski on moonlit fields or swim at the nearby swimming hole. Eventually "everyone gravitates to the kitchen for tea and conversation."

In residence: "Trevor and Pupper are our aging but fun-loving golden retrievers."
Foreign languages spoken: "Steve can greet you in German, Russian, or French; now trying to learn some Czech."
Bed and bath: Seven rooms, three with private baths. Of the four with working fireplaces, the first-floor one is handicapped accessible and has a private shower bath. Rooms have queen, double, a double and a twin, or two twin beds. Rollaways, futons, and crib available. (Families with small children use rooms that can be a suite in wing.)
Breakfast: 8–9:30. Fruit compotes, hot applesauce, poached pears, or baked grapefruit. Homemade stollen, muffins, or coffee cakes. Eggs (gather your own here), pancakes, cheese souffle, or Belgian waffles. Served on large breakfast deck.
Plus: Wood stove. Fireplace. Hot cider or mulled cranberry-lemon drink. Tea and coffee always available. Guests' refrigerator. Piano. Croquet. Dogs' company on walks—maybe to wildflowers in hidden ravine. Dinners, receptions, and meetings arranged.

---

*T*hink of bed and breakfast as a people-to-people concept.

Quechee Bed & Breakfast

802/295-1776

753 Woodstock Road, Route 4, P.O. Box 0080, Quechee, VT 05059-0080

Hosts: Susan and Ken Kaduboski
Location: On 2½ acres with spectacular cliff-edge views of the Ottauquechee River. Half mile west of Quechee Gorge, within walking distance of village; 6.5 miles to Woodstock, 30–45 minutes to Killington, Pico, Okemo ski areas; 15 minutes to Dartmouth College.

Open: Year round. Two-night minimum during foliage and Christmas seasons, and weekends June through October.
Rates: Double occupancy. $85–$125 depending on view and room size. MC, VISA.
♥ ❄ ♦ ✈

As one Rhode Island innkeeper said, "There's only one word for it—'fabulous.'" And that was before the latest major changes were made by the Kaduboskis—"we think we got it right this time"—in the 1795 colonial that was once a coach stop. There's a combination of antiques and contemporary art, dried flowers and baskets, stenciled curtains and braided rugs. And there's Susan, who is overjoyed about learning to downhill ski—"at my age!"

Ken remembers, "Prior to this, we led a very corporate life. Our initial exposure to B&Bs was in England, where we lived for three years." Here they answer *Gourmet's* request for a recipe. They garden and feel lucky to live in this beautiful area. "And to meet such wonderful people."

In residence: "We named our cat Princess BB."
Foreign language spoken: "Slightly rusty fluent Spanish."
Bed and bath: Eight air-conditioned rooms on first and second floors. All private full baths. In main house, queen-sized four-poster or two twin beds. In renovated attached barn, king-sized bed, refrigerator, spectacular view; up steep stairway, queen-sized four-poster in cozy room. Sorry, no provisions for extra beds in a room.
Breakfast: Presented 8–9:30. Apple cinnamon pancakes, buttermilk waffles, or whole wheat French toast filled with cream cheese; Vermont cob-smoked bacon. Fresh fruit, homemade frozen yogurt or steel-cut oatmeal.
Plus: Living room with oversized brick-and-granite fireplace. Setups in each room. Refrigerator space. Lawn chairs.

Placidia Farm Bed and Breakfast

RFD l, Box 275, Randolph, VT 05060-9413   802/728-9883

Host: Viola Frost
Location: Six miles north of Randolph, 1½ miles up a dirt road. On 81 quiet acres with mountain views, trout pond, and brook. Near alpine and cross-country skiing areas.

Open: Year round. Two-night minimum on holiday weekends.
Rates: Double occupancy. $75–$85. $20 each additional guest in room. $8 per child ages 2–12.
♥ 🛥 ✈ ⚋

From Connecticut: *"A beautiful log home, surrounded by exquisite flower beds, a manicured lawn, and a breathtaking view of the hillside . . . a private apartment with a patio, welcoming goodies . . . hummingbirds sipping nectar just 10 feet away*

(Please turn page.)

. . . breakfast in a sun room with windows on three sides . . . gracious hostess who made us feel like family."

The hand-hewn log house was a weekend retreat for Vi and her husband when she was a tax adjuster for the federal government in Massachusetts. "Depending on the season, you might see a farmer harvesting hay. His cows graze in the meadow. And as of three years ago, we have a Christmas tree farm. Guests tell me they rest body and soul here."

In residence: Fawn, "a cat filled with personality."
Foreign language spoken: A little German.
Bed and bath: Private apartment: large room with double bed and rollaway, queen sofa bed in living room, fully equipped kitchen with microwave, full bath. Private entrance and deck.
Breakfast: Usually 8–9. Omelets, German apple pancakes, fresh eggs, or waffles. Popovers or homemade muffins. Fresh fruit and juices. Served on Vi's plant-filled sun porch, at table set with linen and fine china. Vi usually joins guests for coffee.
Plus: Living room with TV, radio, books, cards, and games. Forgotten items. Fans. Aquatic garden. Hiking. Make-your-own cross-country trails on property. "Recipes gladly shared."

The Richmond Victorian Inn   802/434-4440

Main Street, P.O. Box 652, Richmond, VT 05477   fax 802/434-4410

Hosts: Ron and Vicki Williamson
Location: Located in the village on Route 2, one mile east from I-89 exit 11. Fifteen miles to Shelburne Museum, 12 to Burlington, 30 to Stowe. Two miles from Long Trail at Jonesville.
Open: Year round. Two-night minimum last week in September through third week in October.
Rates: Double occupancy. $65 private bath, $50 shared. $95 large room with a double and a queen bed. $130 suite. MC, VISA.
♥ ❖ ◆ ⊁

"Well, we'll give it a try for one night," said the couple from Louisiana who came by in 1988, a month after the Williamsons had opened, when it was 90 degrees outside. "The professor and his wife stayed a week. We had a great time.

"We are old-car people, antiques and flea market nuts. We own and drive a 1931 Ford four-door sedan, and we are putting together a 1930 Model A pickup truck. We also restore old lighting fixtures. Five years ago, before moving in with our teenagers, we gave this 1880 Queen Victorian house a lot of TLC and decorated with comfort and warmth in mind."

Ron is an electrical contractor. Vicki, a property manager who does old-house restoration, owned and managed a natural food store.

In residence: Two cats. Callie "is an old hand at charming guests. Tigger is very curious and loves to play."

Bed and bath: Six second-floor rooms. Three rooms have private shower baths, three share a bath. A two-room suite has one queen bed and one room with two double beds. One room has a queen and a double bed. Others have a double or queen-sized antique Victorian or brass bed. Rollaway available.
Breakfast: Usually 8:30. Quiche, cheese souffle, sour cream coffee cake and cream cheese, walnut French toast, Harrington ham or Vermont smoked bacon, pancakes or waffles with pure Vermont maple syrup, and homemade muffins. Family style in dining room.
Plus: Welcoming beverage. Living room with TV, VCR. Champagne for newlyweds. Fresh flowers. Fans. Mints on pillows.

> From England: *"Nearly missed this charming house. Five rooms, each with own decor and character . . . immaculate . . . great breakfast. . . . Well recommended."*

Hillcrest Guest House   802/775-1670
RR 1, Box 4459, Rutland, VT 05701

Hosts: Bob and Peg Dombro
Location: Two miles from the junction of Routes 4 and 7, .3 mile from Route 7. About 20 minutes to Pico and a half hour to Killington ski areas.

Open: Year round. Advance reservations preferred. Two-night minimum during foliage season and ski weekends.
Rates: $40 single. $45 double.
🏃 ⊟ ✕ ⚡

> From New York: *"Never enjoyed a B&B more. Large, attractive, clean rooms; the atmosphere rejuvenating . . . restaurant suggestions and directions to points hitherto unknown. A sumptuous healthy breakfast. . . . A warm, homey place to stay."*

"We like to think of B&B as meeting new friends, exchanging ideas, learning about other hometowns, and sharing with guests our love of Vermont. Hosting here is in the style that we have experienced on travels through Great Britain, Portugal, and Ireland."

The Dombros' rambling mid-19th-century post-and-beam farmhouse has been their home for over 20 years. Their collection of country antiques enhances the New England flavor. Herb and vegetable gardens grow on the site of the old dairy barn. Plants thrive inside and out.

Bob has directed a school and rehabilitation agency for exceptional children. Now he is coordinator of an art gallery and a member of the district environmental commission. Peg is active in community theater, and then there's horticulture, her year-round love.

> From Massachusetts: *"Friends have never welcomed us with more warmth or more generous hospitality."*

Bed and bath: Three second-floor rooms share one full guest bath with tub and hand-held shower. Two double-bedded rooms. One room with one twin bed.
Breakfast: 7–9. Menu varies. Juice and fresh fruit, homemade muffins, Very Special French Toast served with maple syrup and Peg's original "little fruit things," fresh-brewed coffee. Served on screened porch or in country dining room.

(Please turn page.)

weather permits. Two porches. Wood stove and fireplace in living room. Fresh flowers. Down comforters. Packed lunches can be arranged for bikers, hikers, and skiers. Dinner by special request for guests only.

The Looking Glass Inn

802/748-3052

disconnected

RFD 3, Box 199, St. Johnsbury, VT 05819

Hosts: Barbara, Christopher, and Nancy Haas
Location: On 34 acres with views of mountains, pastures, and cows. Three miles from the center of town with its museum, library, art gallery, and Main Street old mansions. Near Maple Grove Farms (maple syrup products) tour. Just a few feet from I-93. Four miles from I-91. Within 20 minutes of Burke and Cannon mountains and two gourmet restaurants in restored old homes.
Open: Year round.
Rates: Double occupancy, $55–$60. Singles $35 (not available September, October, and December). MC, VISA.
♥ ☼ ✖ ✂

"People think we have been here forever because there are family collections and books everywhere. We had always wanted to live in the country and thought it would be ideal for an adult family to live together in a big old house that was a B&B. Our Second Empire brick Victorian with classic mansard roof was built in 1806 as a tavern with 15-foot-high first-floor ceilings."

The Haas family moved from Morristown, New Jersey, in 1986. Barbara, nursing supervisor at the community hospital, makes many of the dolls, quilts, and rabbits sold in the crafts shop, a converted garage on the property. Son Chris, a caseworker for New Hampshire, is studying to be an interpreter for the deaf. Daughter Nancy, a college tutor, is about to enter a PhD program in mathematics.

In residence: "Our five huskies and two cats are never ever allowed in the inn."
Bed and bath: Six rooms, each with an antique double bed. Two on first floor, rest on second. Three baths (one on first floor with original 1900 fixtures, including long tub and a shower). "If we are full, there are two rooms to a bath."
Breakfast: 7:30–9:30. "All you can eat." French toast, "Chris's secret recipe," with Vermont maple syrup. At least three kinds of fruit. Hot breads and muffins. Freshly brewed hazelnut coffee.
Plus: Wood-burning stove in guests' parlor. Coffee always available. Sherry in room. Mints on pillows. Down comforters. Volleyball. Badminton. Lawn chairs and swing. Dinner (at least three hours' notice required) $20 per person. Picnic baskets ($12.50).

Buckmaster Inn

802/492-3485

Box 118, Lincoln Hill Road, RD 1, Shrewsbury, VT 05738-9711

Hosts: Grace and Sam Husselman
Location: On a paved country road in the Green Mountains; 20 minutes to Killington and Okemo mountains. Two miles north of Cuttingsville.
Open: Year round. Reservations pre-ferred. Two-night minimum on holiday weekends.
Rates: Per room. $50 shared bath, $60–$65 private bath. $15 cot.
♥ ⚬ ⌂ ⁂ ⚞ ✁

Just as they dreamed, "It's country living at its best—with homemade breads and muffins and rural mountain scenery." In New Jersey Grace was a teacher and a director of a public library. Sam was an engineer. Their "gorgeous and functional" 10-room house, originally a coach stop and known as Buckmaster Tavern in the early 1800s, has a grand staircase and wide floorboards. Family heirlooms grace every room, yet Grace and Sam still "hunt for antiques."

Sam enjoys his horses, golf, chess, fishing, and "anything outdoors." In winter he (and guests) appreciate the extensive grounds for cross-country skiing. Grace enjoys knitting Icelandic sweaters as well as other handwork; many of her framed crewel pieces are throughout the house.

In residence: Patty Patience, an old English sheepdog. Two horses, Razalla and Marty.
Foreign language spoken: Dutch.
Bed and bath: Four rooms. On second floor, two rooms share a bath; one has a queen bed, the other has two twin beds. One room with four-poster double bed and private bath. On third floor, a huge beamed-ceiling hideaway with king bed, private bath with shower. Cot available.
Breakfast: 8–9. If later, self-service continental. Homemade Vermont jams and jellies, sweet breads and muffins and/or Vermont cheddar–and–egg casserole, hot beverages. Served in the country kitchen with wood-burning stove, in dining room, or on porch.
Plus: Tea and cookies upon arrival. "Special goodies and wedding bells, if we know honeymooners are arriving." Use of entire house, TV, library, and fireplace. Outdoor grills, picnic tables and umbrellas, and screened porches. Badminton. Croquet. In winter, use of toboggan on property.

> Guests wrote: *"Gracious hosts . . . immaculate home. . . . We wished our mini-vacation could have been longer!"*

Maple Crest Farm

802/492-3367

Shrewsbury, VT
Mailing address: Box 120, Cuttingsville, VT 05738

Hosts: Donna and William Smith
Location: Quiet. High in the Green Mountains, 10 miles south of downtown Rutland, 10 miles north of Ludlow. Near Killington and Okemo ski areas.
Open: Year round. Two-night minimum.
Rates: $25 single, $50 double. One night's deposit required.
♥ ⌂ ⁂ ✈

(Please turn page.)

This B&B has been discovered by *Country Living*. And by artists and photographers who comment about "true Vermont hospitality" where the major activities of farming and sugar making are carried on by a fifth generation. And now it's the home of quilting workshops—in a setting with antiques and personal treasures that reflect Smith activities through the years.

Except for the first 20 years, when it was run as a tavern, this 27-room landmark built in 1808 has been a private home, each generation welcoming guests on a small scale. Robert Frost and past governors slept here.

Donna met Bill when she was working at a nearby inn. In 1969 she started B&B at Maple Crest as a real home away from home. "This is the way B&B started. If I have to be commercial, I don't want to stay in B&B." She was town treasurer for many years and is a bank director.

In residence: K.C, a Labrador retriever. Tyler, an Airedale. About 80 cattle in the meadows.
Bed and bath: Six large rooms (two are suites with private half baths), each with a double and a single bed; some with wood stoves. One first-floor room with half bath shares full bath with second-floor rooms. Two apartments. Cot and crib available.
Breakfast: 8–9:30. Full country meal with bacon and eggs, pancakes with maple syrup made here on the farm, homemade muffins and jams.
Plus: Seasonal flowers. Beverage. Tour of farm and maple sugaring operation. Cross-country skiing and hiking on the property.

> From Washington, Rhode Island, and California: *"The most memorable part of the trip.... I had to arrive late at night and leave early in the morning, yet was met with great warmth. In that short time I knew it was a place that I wanted to return to with my family. . . . We were snowed in during an unusual October blizzard and loved it."*

Kelldarra, A Vermont Bed and Breakfast

P.O. Box 197, Jeffersonville, VT 05464-0197   802/644-6575

Host: Darra Kell
Location: Rural. On Route 109. On four hillside acres beside Lamoille River. Six miles to Smugglers Notch, 20 to Stowe, 1½ to village. Near many sugarhouses and a covered bridge.
Open: Year round. Two-night mini-mum; three nights for legal holidays and October weekends.
Rates: Per room. $50 double bed. $60 queen. $70 queen with Jacuzzi or room with two double beds. Single $10 less.
♥ ◂ ❋ ✘ ✂

> From New York: *"We felt so at home in this big, beautiful house sharing wonderful moments with Darra and her family."* From Arizona: *"Top quality of everything, from the freshly prepared gourmet food to the lovely furnishings, Waterford crystal. . . . "* From Canada: *"Told us about many interesting places to shop and visit . . . a wonderful place to call home."*

"A passion for cooking and people." Love of the outdoors. Joie de vivre. Darra brought all of that to her c. 1826 colonial brick post-and-beam farmhouse. There are wide floorboards, stenciled walls, and a welcoming kitchen with a wall of bricks from the original cooking hearth. Most of the antiques come from England. In the 1970s Darra lived in London and Paris, where she "entertained extensively." Here, since 1990, she has welcomed many guests who call this "the best B&B ever."

In residence: Daughters Shawn, 17; Hilary, 15; and Kendra, 9. "Our official greeter is Alex, a black cat, sometimes invited by guests to sleep in bed with them. He loves it!"
Bed and bath: Four large rooms. On first floor, one double-bedded room and one with two double (antique iron) beds share a full bath. On second floor, one with queen four-poster, private bath with Jacuzzi. One with queen bed, shared full bath.
Breakfast: Until 11. Perhaps pancakes with spiced apple-cinnamon sauce. Scones with jam and clotted cream. Fruited breads with savory butter. Vermont cheeses. Fresh fruit. Vermont smoked breakfast meats. Darra-blended and ground hazelnut coffee. Served by candlelight under early 18th-century English brass chandelier.
Plus: Fireplaced, brick-walled, and book-lined living room. Down comforters. Flannel sheets. Turndown service. Fresh fruit and flowers. Mints on pillows. Evening refreshments. Champagne for honeymooners. Sports equipment storage space.

Watercourse Way B&B
Route 132, P.O. Box 298, South Strafford, VT 05070

802/765-4314
800/562-5110

Hosts: Lincoln Alden and Anna Dewey Alden
Location: On a country road along the Ompompanoosuc River. Three miles south of the Strafford Meeting House and Old City Falls. Near "a mysterious copper field, and an amazing view on the hill behind us." Twelve miles north of Norwich, Vermont, and Hanover, New Hampshire.
Open: Year round. Reservations required.
Rates: $40 single, $60 double.

♥ ⚐ 🐾 ❄ ♦ ✈

> Guests commented: *"You feel very much at home. They live a casual lifestyle that makes you feel as if you are visiting with real Vermonters. . . . We were welcomed by a roaring fire, clean and comfortable surroundings. . . . Breakfast was superb."*

"Our guests come here to escape the city pace and to reacquaint themselves with nature and country life . . . in an undisturbed valley in the heart of Vermont."

Some from Texas came in wedding finery to be married in the calendar-picture-perfect town hall. Others remember falling asleep to the sound of the flowing river or walking through the cut-your-own Christmas tree farm to enjoy a view from the hammock.

The family lives in a restored 1850 Cape farmhouse. Anna teaches music in a public school. In the barn shop, Lincoln designs and builds custom

(Please turn page.)

contemporary furniture using select hardwoods with marble and granite insets.

In residence: Sons Orion, four, and Sterling, two. Three angora goats; Barney announces each arriving guest. Susie, a friendly dalmatian. Crystal, an outdoor cat.

Bed and bath: In guests' wing, three second-floor rooms share one full and one half bath. One room with a double bed, a twin bed, and a trundle; rocking chair and writing desk. One room with a double and a twin. And for those who like a hard bed, a futon set in a wood frame made by Lincoln. Original wide floorboards, country wallpaper, quilts, herbal wreaths.

Breakfast: Usually 8–9. Homemade applesauce (or lemon yogurt made almost famous in England by a guest), muffins, and eggs; thick French toast or puffed pancakes with Vermont maple syrup; egg souffle; waffles; or quiche. Freshly ground gourmet coffee, herbal teas from the garden, orange juice, fruit in season. Served by flagstone fireplace in common room.

Plus: Seven acres to roam. Swimming hole. Library. Piano. Fresh herbal teas from the garden. Sometimes, babysitting. Picnic table down by the river. Lounging chairs in perennial rock garden that overlooks the tree farm.

The 1860 House

School Street, P.O. Box 276
Stowe Village, Stowe, VT 05672

802/253-7351
800/248-1860
fax 802/253-9411

Hosts: Richard M. Hubbard and Rose Marie Matulionis
Location: In center of village, one block off the main street. A short walk to restaurants, shops, tennis courts, and award-winning Stowe Recreation Path.
Open: Year round. Two-day minimum on many weekends.

Rates: Per room, double occupancy. Summer $95–$105. Fall foliage and winter $105–$125. Postsnow–mid-June and postfoliage–ski season $85–$95. Five- and seven-day and ski packages (with lift tickets) available. MC, VISA.
♥ ✿ ◆

> From Massachusetts: *"We really think it's the most wonderful place in the world and would prefer not to tell anyone about it. Rick and Rose Marie are around when you need them. There's plenty of privacy and it's a good place to meet people. There's music, kitchen and laundry facilities. . . . The mattresses are so good that I peeked at the name. The rooms are beautiful and there's plenty of hot water."*

Other guests add praise for the voice-of-experience walking, cycling, and hiking information. Photographers, too, like the brown clapboard house with its gables, split rail fence, and extensive gardens. Since 1980 Rick, a lawyer, and his wife, Rose Marie, a Realtor, have hosted guests in their home, which is on the National Register of Historic Places. When they made extensive interior changes, they used the original wide pine board floors on the upper two floors and carpeting on the lower level. Throughout there are antiques, reproductions, Oriental and hooked rugs, and many plants.

Foreign language spoken: Some German.
Bed and bath: Five air-conditioned rooms on upper or lower levels with king, queen, or twin beds. All private baths; all but one have both tub and shower. Rollaways available.
Breakfast: From 7:30 on. Fresh fruit, orange juice, cereal, breads and pastry, coffee, tea, milk. A very social time. In dining room at expandable "Grandmother's dining room table."
Plus: Complimentary guest pass to health club located steps from the inn; facilities include outdoor pool in season, aerobic sessions, Nautilus, sauna, hot tub, steam room. Complimentary refreshments. Toiletries. Piano. Use of gas barbecue grill. Full kitchen privileges. Assistance with custom-designed day trips—walking, hiking, and cycling.

Guest House Christel Horman 802/253-4846

4583 Mountain Road, Stowe, VT 05672

Hosts: Christel and Jim Horman
Location: On Mountain Road (Route 108), 1½ miles from Mount Mansfield, 5¼ miles from Stowe village. Within Stowe's recreation path and near indoor and outdoor tennis.
Open: Thanksgiving to mid-April, mid-May through October. Two-night minimum preferred on weekends.
Rates: Per person, double occupancy. $34 summer, $40 winter. Holidays higher. $20 cot in same room. MC, VISA.
✣

Much of the old woodwork in this 1980 chalet-style house is from another lodge that was dismantled. Many of the decorative accessories, such as the kangaroo skin and the hand-painted ceramic plaques, are from "home"— Australia, where Jim was an auto mechanic and ski instructor. In the 1960s, after Christel, an accountant in her native Germany, had traveled and waitressed all over the United States, she met Jim in Stowe. (He still works for the Mount Mansfield Company.) In 1980, after they had the shell of their guest house built, the Hormans did the finishing work and decorating. They made corner benches, painted a mural of children sitting on a fence, and constructed all the headboards.

In residence: Neil, age 17.
Foreign language spoken: German.
Bed and bath: Eight carpeted rooms (on first and second floors), each with two double beds, private full bath, individual thermostat.
Breakfast: 8–10. Full breakfast, often with apple pancakes. Served outside in peaceful surroundings in summer.
Plus: Guest living room with hearthstone fireplace. Color TV and VCR. Cross-country skiing from the door. Small pool. Trout fishing in brook behind the house. Babysitting possibilities. Use of outdoor grill.

If you've been to one B&B, you haven't been to them all.

Inn at the Brass Lantern

717 Maple Street
Stowe, VT 05672-4250

802/253-2229
800/729-2980
fax: call to activate

Hosts: Mindy, Andy, and Dustin (age 12) Aldrich
Location: Half a mile from village center. Within 10 minutes of "everything," including restaurants, skiing, tennis, golf, hot-air ballooning, antique car show, dog show, theater, sleigh and surrey rides, antiquing, health spa.
Open: Year round. Two-night minimum during foliage peak and ski season weekends. Four- or five-day minimum Christmas–New Year's week.
Rates: Double occupancy. $65–$75 gable rooms, $75–$85 farmhouse rooms. $90–$120 fireplaced rooms. Off-season (April 1–June 15, October 20–December 10), $10 less. Third person in room $25. Singles, when available, $10 less. Packages include skiing, golf, honeymoon/anniversary, fly/drive. AMEX, MC, VISA.
♥ ⁂ ◆ ✄ ✂

It's home with a view of Mount Mansfield from the beamed living room. An active farm from 1800 until 1950, it was a lodge and then a restaurant before the Aldriches made it into an inn, an award-winning restoration, four years ago. Mindy, a nurse for 15 years, is living her father's fantasy. Andy continues his Burlington-based construction business. And Dustin pursues his interest in hockey.

There's stenciling, small-print wallpapers, wainscoting, and wide planked floors. The fresh country decor includes white ruffled curtains and locally made quilts. And there's spontaneity. Mindy's dad, the one who is responsible for all those fireplaces, is a mason (and antique car buff) who lives "on the other side of the mountain." He assists occasionally and has been known to bring his trumpet for a duet during an impromptu party when a piano player is a guest.

Bed and bath: Nine air-conditioned antiques-furnished rooms; some with canopied beds, most with view of Mount Mansfield. Cozy farmhouse double-bedded gable rooms have private shower baths. Larger rooms, some with fireplace, in farmhouse and attached renovated barn, have queen bed, private full bath.
Breakfast: 8–9:30. All homemade. Entree made with Vermont products might be French toast, apple crepes, blueberry pancakes, or omelets. Fruit, juice, hot beverages. Special diets accommodated.
Plus: Patio. Tea and dessert. Individual thermostats. Guest refrigerator. Down comforters. Maps for self-guided walking, hiking, and biking tours. Bath with shower for after checkout. Health club privileges (half mile away). Transportation to/from airport, train, or bus. Fresh fruit. Chocolates. Picnic baskets.

Innkeeping may be America's most envied profession. As one host mused, "Where else can you get a job where, every day, someone tells you how wonderful you are?"

Ski Inn   802/253-4050

Route 108, Stowe, VT 05672

Host: Harriet Heyer
Location: Set back from the highway on 27 wooded acres, 5.2 miles from Stowe village.
Open: Year round. May–November

as a B&B; dinners served in winter.
Rates: Double occupancy. Per person, $20–$25. In winter, $45–$60, including breakfast and dinner.
♦

A legend. An old-fashioned inn with a big fieldstone fireplace, knotty pine walls, and a Ping-Pong table. It was built by Larry Heyer in 1941 when Stowe was primarily a summer resort, when some folks weren't quite sure that skiing would be more than a fad. Fifty years later, Larry and Harriet, parents of Lyndall, a former U.S. ski team member, were still saying, "We started the trend of intimate country inns and have refused to expand."

In the 1940s Harriet had public relations experience in Manhattan. In the 1990s, between seasons, she bicycles in other parts of the country. In ski season she downhill skis every day.

> From New York: *"Into the driveway, over a wooden bridge, and you're into another world. . . . Roomy, charming, comfortable, spotless. . . . Harriet's unique ability to combine guests of varied and interesting backgrounds . . . excellent, plentiful food, not gourmet but touched up with homemade and homegrown goodies. . . . Location may be best in whole area."*

Bed and bath: Ten large rooms on two floors, each with a double and a single bed. Some rooms have private full baths.
Breakfast: In B&B season, continental with homemade jellies and preserves from homegrown elderberry, chokecherry, blueberry, or rhubarb/wild ginger. In winter, full meals with homemade everything.
Plus: Cotton sheets. Flat hiking on property. More than 15 miles of cross-country ski trails outside the back door. Outdoor fireplace and patio. Trout stream. Game room with piano.

Emersons' Guest House   802/877-3293

82 Main Street, Vergennes, VT 05491-1155

Hosts: John and Pat Emerson
Location: On the wide main street of this Champlain Valley city of 2,300. Skiing 45 minutes away at Sugarbush and Mad River Valley. Sixteen miles to Shelburne Museum,

eight miles on back roads to Morgan Horse Farm.
Open: Year round.
Rates: $35 single, $40–$50 double. $10 rollaway.
♥ 🖋 ⁂ ✈ ✄

Often heard upon guests' departure: "Your rates don't indicate just how nice this B&B is." And so it has been since 1980, since the day that Pat convinced John—a high school math teacher until 1988—that it would be a good idea to host B&B guests. It wasn't long before John, who wasn't too keen on "strangers" in the house, got used to being kicked under the table. As Pat says, "That would be my signal that it was time to stop the interesting conversation

(Please turn page.)

and get on with the day!" We have had one of those fascinating discussions. And so have hundreds of others—before and after a profile of the Emersons appeared in *Family Circle*.

The spacious 1850 home has refinished floors and fresh paper and paint— and is impeccably clean. The youngest of the Emersons' nine children is in college. And "Our lives continue to be enriched through guests from all over the world."

Bed and bath: Four second-floor rooms (three are very large) share two guest baths. One room has two single four-poster beds; each of the other rooms has a double. Rollaways available.
Breakfast: Usually 7:30–8:30. Eggs, pancakes, waffles, or French toast with Vermont maple syrup. Juice, homemade muffins and toast, jams and jellies from the hosts' berries. Bottomless cup of coffee or tea. Emersons usually join you in the country kitchen.
Plus: Bedroom window fans. Lawns. Porches. Babysitting can be arranged. Community pool, tennis courts, public playground nearby.

Strong House Inn   802/877-3337
RD 1, Box 1003, Vergennes, VT 05491-9531

Hosts: Michelle and Ron Bring
Location: Rural. On Route 22A with superb mountain views. One mile west of Vergennes center. Twenty-two miles south of Burlington. Access to nearby lake for windsurfing.
Open: Year round. Advance reservations recommended.

Rates: Double occupancy. $70–$90 private bath. $45–$55 shared bath. $15 third person in room. Singles $15 less. MC, VISA.
♥ ⅰ ∗⁎ ◆ ✗ ✂

> From Massachusetts: *"We were greeted with a complimentary bottle of wine and delicious homemade cookies. And oh, the breakfasts!"* From Canada: *"Michelle played with our five-year-old, who in turn became quite attached to her.... Warm and welcoming.... Perfect!"*

The 157-year-old Greek Revival house, on the National Register of Historic Places, is also a favorite with Vermont Bicycle Touring groups. When the Brings came here in 1987, they had experience as restorers of a Connecticut Victorian house and as a food service director and a retail buyer. Now they are caterers who try to keep up with the demand for their granola and blended coffee. Both ski and cycle. Ron is an avid windsurfer and snowboarder. Examples of Michelle's needlework, including cross-stitch and crewel, are displayed in the inn.

In residence: Two cats, Abbie and Arlo.
Bed and bath: Seven rooms with oak, maple, or mahogany furnishings. Private full bath for first-floor room with two double four-poster beds. On second floor, private full bath for two double-bedded rooms. Shared full bath for two double-bedded rooms (one has a twin bed also). Master bedroom has working fireplace, private half bath. Two-room suite with queen and double bed, working fireplace, private full bath, sun porch, outside entrance.

Breakfast: 8–9. Tea and coffee earlier. Local or homegrown produce. Fresh fruit. Juice. Homemade breads, muffins, granola. Buttermilk pancakes, frittata, souffles, quiches, French toast, or eggs Benedict. Breakfast meats. Served in dining room or outdoors.
Plus: Winter "baked delight" by fire. Summer lemonade and cookies. Bedroom window fans. Piano. Courtyard. Lawn games. Complimentary champagne for honeymooners.

Inn at Round Barn Farm   802/496-2276(B-A-R-N)
East Warren Road, RR 1, Box 247, Waitsfield, VT 05673-0247

Hosts: Jack and Doreen Simko and (daughter) AnneMarie deFreest; Alison Duckworth, assistant innkeeper
Location: Dramatic. Less than two miles from Route 100, through the covered bridge and over a hill to 85 acres of fields, ponds, meadows, and woods. Fifteen minutes from Sugarbush (North and South) and Mad River ski areas.

Open: Year round. Two-night minimum preferred on weekends.
Rates: Double occupancy. $90 double bed; $95 twin beds; $105 highback queen; $115 canopied queen, Jacuzzi; $130 canopied king, Jacuzzi. $145 with fireplace. Singles $10 less. MC, VISA.
♥ ✖ ✄

Colonial Homes is the latest magazine to feature the 19th-century farmhouse that the Simkos rebuilt to a style it had never known—with a blend of old and new, of fine and country antiques, of whimsy and contemporary crafts. Classical music plays in the fireplaced library, which has Oriental rugs and a grandfather clock. In some areas ceilings are insulated on the outside so that the original rustic beams show.

When the 12-sided barn had its grand (re)opening in 1989, the entire Vermont Symphony Orchestra played here. B&B guests have the opportunity to tour the trilevel barn, an award-winning restoration that is perfect for weddings, theater, and concerts. It is complete with spiral staircase to the top of the silo (what a view!) and a 60-foot-long lap pool kept at 78 degrees.

While a third generation of the Simkos runs the family's New Jersey–based floral business, Jack grows papyrus, water lilies, and organically grown edible pansies here in Vermont. Doreen and daughter AnneMarie are responsible for the decor and culinary delights of this acclaimed five-year-old B&B.

In residence: Patches, a calico cat. J.B., a black Lhasa terrier.
Bed and bath: Six rooms on first and second floors. All private baths—two with Jacuzzi—with brass fixtures and sinks in antique washstands. Canopied king or queen; four-poster twin beds; Victorian high-back queen; and an antique double spool bed (with shower bath).
Breakfast: 8:30–9. Specially brewed cinnamon coffee. Maybe cottage cheese pancakes with raspberry sauce, cinnamon raisin Belgian waffles, or French toast with Grand Marnier. Homemade muffins. Baked fruit in winter. Served with silver and antique dishes in sun porch or on terrace.
Plus: Hors d'oeuvres at tea/cider/cocktail time. Down pillows and comforters. Zoned heating. Wicker-filled solarium. Pool table. One mountain bike. Bedroom fans. Good-night chocolates.

Lareau Farm Country Inn   802/496-4949
Box 563, Route 100, Waitsfield, VT 05673-0563   800/833-0766

Hosts: Dan and Susan Easley
Location: In a large open meadow (with horses), one mile south of Waitsfield. Along "crystal clear Mad River" for swimming, canoeing, fishing. Near soaring, horseback riding, antiquing. Five miles to Mad River Glen and Sugarbush downhill skiing; 45 minutes to Shelburne Museum and Lake Champlain.
Open: Year round. Two-day minimum on weekends and holidays.

Rates: Per person, double occupancy. Spring and summer, $60–$70 shared bath, $70–$80 private bath. Fall and winter, $64–$80 shared bath, $72–$100 private bath. Discount on five-night (Sunday–Thursday) stays. Singles $10 less during nonholiday periods. ($1 of every reservation donated to Nature Conservancy.) MC, VISA.
♥ ♨ ❖ ♦ ✕

The Easleys are as much a draw as their inn, a farm that was in the same family for 40 years until Dan and Susan decided to leave their Pittsburgh jobs as bank training director and science teacher and move to their vacation town. Here these experienced house restorers created a comfortable country look with refinished floors and hand-tied quilts and have added a new large dining room and a columned wraparound porch.

Susan makes the quilts and designs the menus. Dan, an elementary school counselor, bales hay and cares for the horses and dogs. He drives an old-fashioned sleigh and carriages. The Easleys host memorable spontaneous happenings and lovely weddings. Guests hike and cross-country ski through the "enchanted forest." And many write to me about loving "the relaxed atmosphere" at their "home away from home."

In residence: "Our zoo": Dogs—Fannie, Fred, and Jasper. Cats—Fricky, Trixie, and Floozie. Horses—Holly and Dolly, "the driving duo."
Bed and bath: Fourteen rooms of various sizes. Ten with private baths (with tub or shower). Four rooms share two baths (one tub only, one shower only). Queen or double beds; one room has a twin bed also; another has two twin beds.
Breakfast: Generally 8–9. Fresh fruits, baked goods such as pumpkin muffins from Easleys' pumpkins, egg souffles, or "Dan's famous light-as-a-feather blueberry pancakes." Green Mountain coffee and farm-fresh eggs.
Plus: In winter, afternoon hors d'oeuvres. Cross-country skiing right here. Bocci. Horseshoes. Dinner usually available on Saturdays or for groups ($15–$18 per person); check when making reservations.

The tradition of paying to stay in a private home—with breakfast included in the overnight lodging rate—was revived in time to save wonderful old houses, schools, churches, and barns all over the country from the wrecking ball or commercial development.

The Mad River Inn Bed-n-Breakfast

Tremblay-Pine Road, P.O. Box 75　　　　　**802/496-7900**
Waitsfield, VT 05673-0075

Hosts: Luc and Rita Maranda
Location: Overlooking a dairy farm. Along the Mad River. On paved country road, one-fifth of a mile off Route 100. One mile north of village. Seven miles to Sugarbush, six to Mad River Glen ski area.
Open: Year round. Three-day minimum on holiday weekends. Four-night minimum during Christmas/New Year's week.
Rates: Per room, double occupancy. $95 private bath, $85 shared. $10 less weekdays. Singles $20 less. $20 more for triple or quad occupancy. Children under two free. AMEX, MC, VISA.
♥ ♨ ❀ ♦ ✈

Last year the O'Malleys came from all over the country to have their family reunion here. "We didn't know them, but we love having family around at holiday time," says Rita, who now refers to the first annual O'Malley/Skelly (Rita's maiden name) gathering. That was the year Annie Reed, Rita's sister, and Luc won the local Christmas decorating award.

In warm weather weddings are held in the gazebo. Year round there are fresh flowers as well as yards of floral print fabrics throughout the renovated 1860s farmhouse, which shows Rita's "love of the Victorian period." Each guest room reflects the interests of an ancestor—a railroad engineer, a colonel, the founder of baseball, and one grandmother. And to complete the picture, afternoon teas are a feature; all baked goods are prepared by sister Annie, the inn's chef. Before becoming innkeepers the Marandas lived in south Florida, where Luc was a nightclub manager and Rita marketed luxury real estate.

In residence: Son Jessee Roland, four.
Foreign languages spoken: French and some Spanish.
Bed and bath: Nine rooms, all with feather beds (unless you request otherwise). Two first-floor rooms with private baths; one has king bed, the other a queen. On second floor, four queen-bedded rooms with private baths. Two rooms share a hall bath; one has a king bed, the other a double bed. Another double-bedded room has private hall bath. Rollaway and crib available.
Breakfast: 8–9:30. Coffee at 7. Freshly squeezed orange juice, fresh-ground gourmet coffee, muffins made with homemade maple and berry butter. Fruit dish with colorful edible pansies. Main course may be oven-baked French toast, Mad River eggs with Vermont cheddar cheese sauce, blueberry and ginger pancakes, or fresh fruit crepes. In dining room or on back porch.
Plus: Big-screen TV in BYOB lounge. Ceiling or window fans. Knockabout rumpus room. Flower-bedecked back porch. Babysitting. Beach towels. Transportation to/from airport, train, or bus. Grill. Hammock. Organic gardens—herbs, vegetables, and edible flowers. Kitchen and laundry facilities. Heart-shaped almond cake for honeymooners. Dinner on Saturday evenings ($75/couple). Picnic baskets, $10 per person.

---

*T*o tip or not? (Please turn to page xii.)

Newtons' 1824 House Inn on the Mad River

Route 100, Box 159
Waitsfield, VT 05673-9802

802/496-7555
fax 802/496-5124

Hosts: Nick and Joyce Newton
Location: Along the Mad River on Route 100, one mile from town center. Surrounded by working farms. Minutes to Sugarbush and Mad River ski resorts.
Open: Year round. Two-night minimum during foliage, summer, and winter weekends. Two- or three-day minimum on holiday weekends.
Rates: $75 smaller double room. $85 standard double. $95 king, $105 queen suite. Singles $10 less. $20 additional person. AMEX, MC, VISA.
♥ ❖ ◆ ✈ ⚺

Incredible stuffed pears. Enormous muffins. Organic gardening (watermelons, berries, asparagus and more). Haying with a neighbor. A vintage tractor. A sledding hill. And sometimes, scheduled poetry readings. It's all a long way from the Manhattan lifestyle Nick knew as an investment banker and Joyce as a stockbroker. But not so far from the California farm life Nick knew as a boy, or from the horseback riding Joyce recalls from camp days.

The farmhouse has had many additions through the years and is filled with all kinds of collections—antiques, souvenirs, birds, and, in the living room, contemporary art.

In residence: Daughter Ashley, seven. Bonita, "a lovable golden retriever."
Foreign languages spoken: Spanish and limited French.
Bed and bath: Six carpeted rooms (various sizes), one on first floor, five on second. All private baths with tub and shower, except one that is shower only. King, queen, double, or twin-sized beds. Rollaway available.
Breakfast: Usually 8–9. Oatmeal souffle (a specialty), corn meal/buttermilk/blueberry pancakes, mango-filled crepes, bacon or sausage, homemade muffins, fresh fruits and freshly squeezed orange juice. In fireplaced dining room at table set with lace cloth.
Plus: Fireplaced living room with TV. Piano. At 5, hot spiced cider in winter, lemonade (served on terrace) in summer with homemade cookies. Evening sherry. Down comforters. Turndown service. Homemade truffles on pillow. Guest refrigerator. Babysitting. Outdoor hot tub. Swimming hole with rope swing. Dinners by advance arrangement.

Beaver Pond Farm Inn

802/583-2861

RD Box 306, Golf Course Road, Warren, VT 05674-9622

Hosts: Bob and Betty Hansen
Location: On a quiet dirt road, minutes from Sugarbush/Mad River Valley restaurants and shops. On 40 kilometers of groomed cross-country ski trails. One mile to Sugarbush downhill ski area; 200 yards from the first tee of Sugarbush Sports Center's golf course (open to the public), designed by Robert Trent Jones.
Open: Year round except May. Reservations required. Two-day minimum during fall and winter.
Rates: Per person, double occupancy. $32–$40 shared bath, $35–$45 private bath. Thanksgiving, ski (cross-country and downhill), golf, and summer concert packages available. MC, VISA.
♥ ❖ ◆ ✈

From New York: *"A real find . . . spent our honeymoon there . . . Betty and Bob have the gift of being able to offer warm hospitality as well as privacy. . . . Betty is an incredible cook—energetic and creative . . . not missed a trick in the decorating—down to hand-painted doorknobs . . . at the end of the day, the smell of home-baked chocolate chip cookies and hot mulled cider (in the winter) and shortbreads and ice tea (in the summer). It really feels better than home!"*

From all over—from England, Canada, and Arizona—come accolades about "the best of the best" that was in 1977 a vacant and boarded-up farmhouse. It became the Hansens' vacation home and eventually their B&B, "a backdrop for displaying the antiques that we have acquired over the years." I took a "narrated tour" and heard a fascinating account of all the changes and additions—from the front door found in the barn to the fireplaced living room that had been two smaller chimneyless rooms.

In New Jersey Betty was a caterer; Bob was a banker for 27 years. They ski, play golf (Betty wins championships), fish (Bob will guide you), travel, and enjoy classical music.

In residence: Jesse, a yellow Labrador retriever, and Jasper, a gray cat "who somehow found his way to our barn."
Foreign language spoken: French. (Betty attended the Sorbonne.)
Bed and bath: Six carpeted rooms, one on first floor with French doors, private deck. Queen or twin beds. Four private baths, one semiprivate; all with hair dryers. Cot available.
Breakfast: 8–9:30. Four choices offered each morning! Maybe smoked salmon "caught and smoked by Bob" and scrambled eggs. Or amaretto French toast. Or orange-yogurt pancakes. Or eggs Florentine. Homemade Danish pastries. Locally roasted coffee. Vermont sausage. Served on antique china with sterling silver in the dining room or on large deck.
Plus: Beverages. Setups and hors d'oeuvres. Bedroom ceiling fans. Down comforters. Suggested bicycle routes (15–70 miles) and trout-fishing streams. Will meet guests (fee charged) at Burlington airport. In winter, dinner served on Tuesday, Thursdays, and Saturdays and on Thanksgiving and Christmas.

The Sugartree Inn

802/583-3211
800/666-8907

RR Box 38, Sugarbush Access Road, Warren, VT 05674

Hosts: Howard and Janice Chapman
Location: Wooded. With panoramic mountain views. Three miles west of Waitsfield, one-quarter mile from Sugarbush resort area. Championship golf course sports center nearby.
Open: Year round. (Once they closed the inn to attend the wedding of guests.)

Rates: Per person, double occupancy. $40–$45 summer, $45 winter, $55–$60 during foliage season. $35 triple. Senior citizens 10 percent less. AMEX, Discover, MC, VISA.
♥ ♯ ❖ ♦ ✈

(Please turn page.)

Guests wrote: *"A super place. . . . Fun-loving hosts who make you feel welcome. . . . Lots of extra touches. . . . Eye-appealing and delicious breakfasts. . . . Antiques and crafts everywhere."*

A Montana worm and bait shop it is not. Second choice for a career change and escape from the city (Chicago) it is. So instead of flying around the world arbitrating construction disputes and claims, Howard is hosting in the inn Janice found in 1982 after she, who had never seen skiing, looked at 14 ski areas. An extensive conversion took place. Howard designed and built the landmark gazebo on the now-landscaped grounds "where chipmunks eat out of your hand in the summer." Janice made all the thick tied quilts and took courses at the New England Culinary Institute. Antiques are auction finds. On every door there's a grapevine wreath. Bows. Lots of ruffles. Oil lamps. New recipes. Handcrafted animals. Gardens. Window boxes. And plenty of guests who are happy that the Chapmans, native Virginians, love what they are doing.

Bed and bath: Ten carpeted and wallpapered rooms; one is wheelchair accessible. All private full or shower baths. Antique beds are canopied, four-poster, or brass. First-floor rooms have both a double and a single canopied bed. Second-floor rooms have a double and a single, a queen, or a double. Rollaway available.
Breakfast: 8:30–9:30 (8–9 in winter). Menu varies daily. Maybe French toast with raspberry sauce and whipped cream; buttermilk pancake creation with peaches and blueberries, Vermont maple syrup; scrambled eggs in pastry puff and cheese sauce. Fresh fruit. Local dairy and meat products. Homemade breads. Served at tables for four or more.
Plus: Late-afternoon soup for skiers. Tea, coffee always available. Bedroom fans. Ice machine. Forgotten toiletries. "Suggestions for romantic wooded swimming holes."

# *West Hill House B&B*		802/496-7162
West Hill Road, RR 1, Box 292, Warren, VT 05674-9620

Hosts: Bob and Nina Heyd
Location: Less than five-minute drive to Sugarbush ski area and golf course. On a country road with mountain views, meadows, pond, gardens. One and a half miles up from Route 100. Near gorgeous two-hour hiking trail, "unpublished in any book."

Open: Year round. Two-night minimum on weekends.
Rates: Double occupancy. $60 shared bath, $70 private. $5 more midweek in winter; $15 more during fall foliage, winter weekends, and holidays. Singles $10 less. Senior citizens 10 percent less. MC, VISA.
♥ ❖ ◆ ⋈ ✄

"A bigger place," thought the Heyds, until they realized that they wanted a B&B that was really home for the two of them—and a few guests. Four years ago, after Bob left his position as operations manager (of computers) at the *Boston Globe*, he became B&B cook and, at Sugarbush, a volunteer ski host. Groundskeeper Nina is the official "Ms. Fix-It."

Seemingly in the middle of nowhere, especially to those who arrive at night, this is a farmhouse that was turned ski lodge in the 1960s—and remodeled by the Heyds in 1988. As a casual B&B, it features a huge brick fireplace with beam mantel, refinished wide pine floors, and inviting guest rooms with handmade quilts. Cyclists are offered a ride up from town. For horses, there are apples from the small orchard. As one guest from New York wrote, "Their house is your house. The out-of-the-ordinary food, the music, and the company, together with Mitzi, are a winning combination."

In residence: Mitzi, an English springer spaniel "who smiles and talks to guests."

Bed and bath: Four second-floor rooms. Private full baths for room with double bed and one with queen bed. Two beamed and dormered rooms, each with a double bed, a twin bed, and a sink, share a full bath.

Breakfast: Usually 8 in winter, 8:30 in summer. Repertoire includes baked apples, spiced broiled grapefruit, bourbon or peach-and-strawberry-filled French toast, gingerbread pancakes, apple puffs, maple walnut or raspberry almond muffins. Served by candlelight with classical music.

Plus: Porch rockers. Summer flowers. Window fans. Late-afternoon cider, cold drinks, and goodies. Guest pantry with wet bar and telephone. Flannel sheets. Mints on pillows. Handmade sachets. Special occasions acknowledged. Dinners for groups, $15 per person.

From Massachusetts: *"Perfectly situated . . . inviting, welcoming . . . space for personal time and relaxation."*

Grünberg Haus Bed & Breakfast 802/244-7726
Route 100 South, RR 2, Box 1595   **800/800-7760**
Waterbury, VT 05676-9621

Hosts: Christopher Sellers and Mark Frohman

Location: In Ben & Jerry's hometown, on acres of meadows and woodlands with hiking trails. Within a five-minute drive of Green Mountain Chocolate Company. Twenty miles to Sugarbush, Stowe, Mad River Glen ski resorts, and over 900 kilometers of cross-country ski trails.

Open: Year round.

Rates: Per room, double occupancy. $55–$70 two double beds. $55–$65 one double bed or two twin beds. $35–$45 single. Extra person in room, $6 "permanent" bed, $15 rollaway. Private baths, $25–$35 more. Senior citizens, military personnel, and travel industry professionals 10 percent less. AMEX, MC, VISA.

♥ ♨ ❀ ◆ ✈ ✂

What a setting for a convention of harpists. Or for the annual Octoberfest. A long lane, a dramatic approach leads up to this Tyrolean-style chalet built by hand—surprise, just 20 years ago. In the living room, a massive fieldstone fireplace faces an eight-foot grand piano and a huge picture window with bird feeders beyond. Chris, a professional musician, plays and sings during breakfast and many evenings. As Mark says, "Full house turns into a party." And what about the chickens? Well, there's a story about the Vermont quarry worker, Fred Stone, who sells chickens. And the fact that both Mark and Chris

(Please turn page.)

had chickens when they lived in the Midwest. (They bought the inn three years ago.)

Chris substitute teaches in area schools, grades K–12. Sometimes, following checkout at the inn, Mark checks guests in at his Burlington airport job. In between times these two imaginative innkeeepers dream up events such as Christmas caroling to the animals at four different farms.

In residence: Two cats, Fritz and Mama. Chickens, doves, fancy pigeons, quail. Ike and Tina are turkeys who peek into the dining room (built on a hillside).

Bed and bath: Ten second-floor rooms, each with access to balcony. One shared bath between every two rooms. Double bed (one canopied), two twin beds (one pair in antique brass), or rooms with two double beds. Rollaways available.

Breakfast: 7:30–9:30. Fresh eggs, for sure. Entree might be ricotta-stuffed French toast or fresh spinach frittata. Fresh fruit creations. Carrot walnut muffins or peach yogurt bread. In dining room by a 21-foot-wide window.

Plus: Beams everywhere. Refreshments starting at 4 p.m. Hot tub, sauna, and tennis court. BYOB publike game room. Greenhouse and library. Guest refrigerator. Window fans. Transportation to/from airport, bus, or train. Babysitting. Monthly benefit concerts ($6). For groups, family-style dinners, $15 per person.

Inn at Blush Hill   802/244-7529
Blush Hill Road, RR 1, Box 1266, Waterbury, VT 05676   800/736-7522

Hosts: Gary and Pamela Gosselin
Location: At the top of a country road, overlooking golf course and mountains. One mile from I-89, off route 100. Within 20 minutes of Stowe, Sugarbush, and Bolton Valley ski areas. One mile to Ben & Jerry's ice cream plant; three to Cold Hollow Cider Mill.

Open: Year round.
Rates: Double occupancy. $85 or $95 private bath. $55 or $65 shared bath. $20 higher in foliage season (September 15–October 15) and Christmas week. $10 rollaway. AMEX, Enroute, MC, VISA.
♥ ❀ ♦ ✕

The grounds and gardens make this a perfect place for a wedding—according to Vermonters and people from many other states too. Honeymooners, skiers, and canoeists have also discovered the 1790s Cape with four fireplaces and wide board floors—all decorated with warm colors, country prints, and auction finds.

From New Hampshire and Washington, D.C., the Gosselins brought 25 years of experience in the hospitality field. Since arriving on a 20-below day in January 1988, they *almost* feel like natives. They have helped to develop a tourism association "to let people know how much is here." Gary is editor of the local newspaper, and Pam is a school volunteer. "And our whole family skis every chance we can!"

In residence: Christopher is eight. Tyler is three.
Bed and bath: Six rooms. The first-floor room has double bed, working fireplace, private shower bath. Upstairs, two rooms have double beds; one

has a queen; one has a double and a twin bed; one has queen four-poster bed, private bath, and view of the mountains and sunrise. Rollaway available.
Breakfast: 8–9. French toast or apple pancakes topped with Ben & Jerry's ice cream, Vermont maple syrup, and fresh fruit. Homemade breads and muffins. Juice and natural cereals. Served at 10-foot-long hired hands' table in country kitchen overlooking mountains.
Plus: Heated mattress pads. Porch rockers. Games. Piano. TV. Afternoon and evening refreshments.

> From Massachusetts: *"It's an incredible setting and a charming home, and the hosts are terrific."*

Weathervane Lodge   802/464-5426

Dorr Fitch Road, Box 57, West Dover, VT 05356

Hosts: Liz and Ernie Chabot
Location: One mile off Route 100, up a hill, in peaceful countryside with a panoramic view of mountains and valleys. Within minutes of Mount Snow, Haystack, and Maple Valley ski areas. Near Marlboro Festival, golf, tennis, lake swimming, horseback riding, hiking, museums.
Open: Year round.

Rates: Vary according to room and season. Double occupancy. Winter weekdays are lower than weekends and holiday weeks. Winter and foliage season rates with bunk facilities and shared bath $25–$32 per person. Suite with private bath $40–$44 per person. About 15 percent less in other seasons. Singles, add $10.
♥ ♨ ✿ ✕

"Returnees ask which room is available, and they know just where to settle in. That's the way my wife and I intended it to be. I built this Tyrolean-style place (with balconies) as my second home 30 years ago, and if you want, I can tell you how many nails there are, how I laughed, and how I cried. We have heating systems, but the four fireplaces—for atmosphere—burn 10 cords of wood a year. In summer there's a profusion of flower beds on the landscaped grounds. This place is loaded with antiques and charm. The homey, comfortable, tranquil feeling seems to work."

Ernie has just retired from his work in fine metals, work that took him all over the world.

In residence: Spooky, the cat, and Cooper, a golden retriever.
Bed and bath: Ten rooms and a suite. Most rooms have shared baths. Suite has a room with double bed, living room with double sofa bed, private bath. Another room has two doubles, a sleep sofa that makes up into a double, and a private bath. Others have two twins, double, set of twin bunks, double and a bunk, double and single, or four singles. Cot and crib available.
Breakfast: 7–9:30. Full. Could be pancakes, French toast, eggs any style—including poached in pure Vermont maple syrup. In beamed and fireplaced dining room with white cedar walls, plants, 30-gallon fish tank, antique clocks, lots of silver on the dry sink, atmosphere.
Plus: Beverages. Lounge with fieldstone fireplace and setup bar. Use of refrigerator. Trails, open field, and old town roads are on the property for walking and cross-country skiing.

Fox Hall Inn B&B   802/525-6930

Willoughby Lake, Westmore, VT
Mailing address: RR 1, Box 153E, Barton, VT 05822-9611

Hosts: Ken and Sherry Pyden
Location: Spectacular. On 76 rural acres bordering Lake Willoughby. Twenty miles to Burke Mountain, 40 to Jay Peak. Eight miles off I-91. Two hours from Montreal. "A naturalist's paradise. No shops. Only quaint country stores. (Gasoline available.) Great for water sports, hiking, walking, cycling, reading, cross-country skiing, ice fishing, snowmobiling, or just relaxing. Good restaurants within one mile."
Open: Year round.
Rates: Double occupancy. July–October 15 and December 24–January 2, $70 shared bath, $90 private. Other times, $60 shared bath, $74 private. Singles $10 less. Senior citizens' discount. Free use of boats. MC, VISA.

♥ ❖ ♦ ✈ ✀

This is the ultimate viewing spot, overlooking what is often called one of the world's most beautiful lakes. Guests sit for hours on the wide, partially covered wraparound veranda, which faces the fjordlike scene of Lake Willoughby flanked by Mounts Pisgah and Hor. A sweeping lawn leads to the private waterfront (swimming permitted) with boathouse, dock, canoes, paddleboat, and windsurfers.

The turn-of-the-century mansion with two domed towers (lots of bays inside) was part of a girls' camp that was unoccupied from 1975 until 1986, the year that Ken retired as a millwright with the Ford Motor Company. That's when the Pydens came "way out here to rehabilitate the property Sherry fell in love with." They opened in 1988 with ruffled tieback curtains on all the windows, plenty of comfortable chairs, and many moose items. "Sometimes guests feel so much at home, they want to help with dishes!"

In residence: Daughters Kristi and Carrie, in their twenties. Two dogs, Sugar Bayer and Aloysious. Four horses that complete the scene.
Bed and bath: Nine rooms. On first floor, room with a double bed and a three-quarter bed, private full bath. Second-floor rooms with private baths have a stall shower. Five rooms share a full bath plus a shower bath; marble sink in each of these rooms. Beds—queen and a twin; double; double and a twin; two twin beds.
Breakfast: 7–9. Juice, fresh-baked homemade muffins, fresh fruit salad, pancakes or French toast, hot beverages. Served in dining room or on the veranda.
Plus: Afternoon snack. Grand piano. Turndown service. Down comforters. Flannel sheets. Guest refrigerator. Mints on pillow. Gas grill, picnic table. Croquet. Volleyball.

***A**ccording to many hosts:*
"Guests come with plans and discover
the joys of porch sitting."

The Darling Family Inn   802/824-3223

Route 100, Weston, VT 05161-9801

Hosts: Chapin and Joan Darling
Location: Half mile north of village with panoramic view of mountains and farmland. Near Bromley, Stratton, Okemo, and Magic mountains, summer theater, antiques, crafts, art exhibits. Three miles from Weston Priory.

Open: Year round except Christmas eve and Christmas night. Two-night minimum on weekends.
Rates: $75–$95 per room, depending on size and location. Special rates for a stay of five or more nights.
♥ ❊

This style of country living was lauded by *Gourmet* magazine. American and English antiques are in a colonial setting created and recreated by Chapin, a skilled woodworker who was a Connecticut life insurance executive until 1980. To the 160-year-old farmhouse he has built an addition, "one that still allows us to stay small so that we can continue to provide surprises for our guests." The hardware is fashioned in the barn forge by son Jeff, a blacksmith. Another son, Eric, creates detailed handcrafted wooden items. Dried flower wreaths, hand-painted wood and tin items, even thimbles are examples of Joan's artistry. Also on the property—two housekeeping cottages where pets are welcome.

In residence: Son Eric. Mandy, the dog; Sasha, the cat. Any or all of the four grown Darling children might be visiting.
Bed and bath: Five second-floor rooms, all private full baths. Canopied queen and twin beds and double beds (one canopied) available.
Breakfast: 8–10. Juices (freshly squeezed orange juice); bacon, ham, and sausage; any style eggs, omelets, home fries, maybe French toast or berry pancakes and beverage. Cloth napkins. Chapin cooks. Joan serves by candlelight.
Plus: Beverages. Fireplaced living room. Library with wood stove. Chapin's guitar accompaniment for impromptu sing-alongs. Swimming pool. In season, hayrides and sleigh rides nearby (fee charged). Four-course candlelit dinners (extra charge) with advance notice.

The Wilder Homestead Inn   802/824-8172

Lawrence Hill Road, RR 1, Box 106D, Weston, VT 05161

Hosts: Roy and Peggy Varner
Location: Next to the historic Church-on-the-Hill. Just off Route 100; turn at post office, go over the bridge. Four miles south of Weston Priory.
Open: Year round. Two-night mini-

mum on July–October 21 and winter weekends.
Rates: Double occupancy. $75–$85 private bath. $55–$65 shared bath. $25 third person in room.
♥ ♯ ❊ ✗ ✂

(Please turn page.)

Roy helped to build the sets and Peggy's dream came true when she made her stage debut in *The Music Man*, produced around the corner at the Weston Playhouse.

The Varners chose innkeeping as a "real together" job following 33 years in their northeastern Pennsylvania construction business, where Peggy was secretary. In 1985 they bought this Federal brick house; since then it has been given *Gourmet* and *Country* magazine coverage. The dining room is beamed. There are colonial colors, quilts, tab curtains, and pierced lampshades. About the time the Varners' tenth grandchild arrived, Roy completed his two-year transformation of the old woodshed, using all original wood boards, into a crafts shop.

In residence: In hosts' quarters, two friendly cats love visitors who ask to meet them.
Bed and bath: Seven rooms on second and third floors. Five with private bath (all shower except for one full). Two rooms share hall full bath. Beds are twins/king, canopied queen, double, or twin-sized. One room has a queen and a twin bed, ceiling fan. Rollaway available.
Breakfast: 8–9. Fresh fruit, juices, homemade jams and biscuits, pancakes or French toast. Eggs ("try Roy's Vermont cheddar cheese omelet, yummy"), home fries. Brewed coffee. Teas. Served by dining room fireplace.
Plus: Tea or wine and cheese tray. Porch rockers.

> From Connecticut: *"Many antiques, books, huge fireplaces, a player piano . . . clean as a whistle . . . candoliers in every window . . . hale and hearty breakfasts . . . a change of pace."*

Golden Maple Inn   802/888-6614
Route 15, P.O. Box 35, Wolcott, VT 05680-0035

Hosts: Dick and Jo Wall
Location: On Route 15 in small village along the Lamoille River, "great for swimming, fishing, and canoeing. We are also near Fisher Covered Bridge, cross-country ski trails, and a classic 1930s single-screen movie theater that is complete with balcony and live piano music before the main feature." Eighteen minutes from Stowe and Craftsbury.
Open: Year round. Two-night minimum September and October weekends.
Rates: Private bath $45 single, $68 double. Shared bath $41 single, $58 double. $15 cot. AMEX, MC, VISA.
♥ ❖ ◆ ✈ ✂

> From Florida (and echoed by many): *"The personable and affable hosts restored this classic New England country house. An incredible ambiance! . . . comfortable antiques . . . fantastic breakfasts."*

Why Vermont? Dick is a retired competitive sailor and mountain climber who worked for many years in the ship- and yacht-building industry. He says, "I picked up an oar, put it on my shoulder, and walked inland until someone asked what it was. That's where I settled down in 1990."

In Yarmouth, Maine, Jo managed computer operations for a national footwear company. She and Dick are parents of three grown children and world travelers who, as guests can tell, love what they are doing.

In residence: In the carriage house—Missy, "our bashful calico."
Bed and bath: Three large rooms. One ground-floor double-bedded room, private full bath with Victorian tub and hand-held shower. On second floor, room with two twin four-posters and one with a double four-poster share a shower bath. Rollaway available.
Breakfast: 7–9. Oven-baked French toast, spicy baked eggs, or croissants filled with apples, eggs, and Vermont cheddar cheese. Fresh fruit. Juice. Cereals include hot oatmeal with apples, raisins, and cinnamon.
Plus: Flagstone terrace. Library. Tea and homemade sweets. Down comforters. Potpourri sachets. Ceiling fans. Turndown service. Flowers and vegetables from Jo's gardens. Picnic baskets ($8); option of Saturday and Sunday dinner ($19).

The Charleston House 802/457-3843

21 Pleasant Street, Woodstock, VT 05091

Hosts: The Houghs—Barbara and Bill, their son John, and his wife, Mary Ellen
Location: In historic district with shops, restaurants, and galleries within a four-block walk. Twenty minutes to Killington; 10 to Suicide Six. One mile to golf, tennis, and cross-country skiing at the Woodstock Country Club, a Robert Trent Jones golf facility open to the public.
Open: Year round.
Rates: Per room. $100–$135. AMEX, MC, VISA.
♥ ❖ ◆ ✖ ✁

"After living in Vail, Colorado; in Annapolis, Maryland; and on our sailboat, we became innkeepers in 1987. And all because a friend of a friend told us that the Charleston House might be for sale. With art and antiques befitting the 1835 frame and brick Greek Revival house, Barbara, a Virginian, embellished the southern charm for which the inn was known. Since we acquired the nearby 1880 Canterbury House, her recognized flair for elegance, using Laura Ashley fabrics and period furniture, has been extended to that acclaimed seven-room B&B."

Style, food, and hospitality have become Hough hallmarks. Bill, sometimes called the resident raconteur, is a former executive, stockbroker, salesman, and Realtor.

In residence: "Sander, our old resident golden retriever, works here when his presence is not required at Canterbury House."
Bed and bath: Seven air-conditioned rooms on first and second floors. All private full baths. Six queen-bedded rooms (one with private entrance, one with cable TV) plus one single room. Rollaway available.
Breakfast: 8:30 and 9:30. Varies. Entree repertoire includes baked strata and blueberry French toast. Served in dining room under crystal chandelier.
Plus: Patio. Champagne for anniversary and honeymoon couples. Profits from Barbara's cookbook, *Breakfast at the Charleston House*, are contributed to David's House, a charitable lodging facility for parents of hospitalized severely ill children.

Deer Brook Inn

802/672-3713

HCR 68, Box 443 (Route 4), Woodstock, VT 05091

Hosts: Brian and Rosemary McGinty
Location: Rural. On five acres by the Ottauquechee River. Four miles west of the village. Thirty minutes to Dartmouth College, 20 to I-89 and I-91; eight miles to Killington ski area.
Open: Year round.
Rates: Double occupancy. $65 Sun-day–Thursday, $75 Friday and Saturday, $85 foliage season and Christmas. Singles $15 less except foliage season and Christmas ($60). $10 extra person over five years old. MC, VISA.

♥ ♨ ⁂ ✈ ⅄

"The McGintys have restored the essence of New England and hospitality to their corner of Vermont," wrote some guests from Massachusetts. *Many* others concurred and added, "Brian and Rosemary put their hearts into redoing this [1820 colonial] farmhouse and keeping with the old style . . . exposed beams, beautiful stenciling, handmade (by Rosemary) quilts, wide pine floors . . . a creative home-style breakfast, a feast, in an atmosphere of charm . . . immaculate and decorated in simple country style . . . a roaring fireplace at the slightest chill. . . . You become part of the family. . . . The dogs, too, are great. . . . For dinner, a good family restaurant within walking distance . . . fall asleep to the sound of the brook across the road."

Restoration was a year-long task before the McGintys opened in 1988. In Breckenridge, Colorado, Rosemary, a nurse, and Brian were on the ski patrol.

In residence: James is four years old, Kelly, age one. Golden retrievers Sage and Nutmeg are mother and daughter.
Bed and bath: Four (two with skylights) second-floor river-view rooms, all private full baths. Two rooms with a queen bed, two each have a double and a twin bed. Rollaway and crib available.
Breakfast: 8–9. Hot entree may be baked egg strata or apple pancake (most-requested recipes). Fresh fruit. Juice. Homemade muffins, breads, or coffee cake.
Plus: Window fans. Individual thermostats. Complimentary champagne for honeymooners. Front porch.

Jackson House Inn at Woodstock

802/457-2065

Route 4 West, Woodstock, VT 05091-1243

Hosts: Bruce McIlveen and Jack Foster
Location: On three acres with gardens, a brook, a pond, mountain views to north and south. One and one-half miles west of Woodstock village.
Open: Year round. Two-day minimum on weekends and holidays.
Rates: Double occupancy. $120, $130, $160 (for suites).

♥ ♦ ✈ ⅄

"Outstanding. Really a marvelous place. And the innkeepers are wonderful too," said the world traveler, an antiques dealer we met in Canada. "Everything is done with such style," exclaimed the Bloomingdale's public relations director who is responsible for many *Bed & Breakfast in New England* programs.

Created by a banker from San Francisco and an airline director of marketing from New York, this elegant inn was built in 1890 as an exquisite example of colonial revival architecture. In 1984, following 14 months of renovation, Bruce and Jack furnished with museum-quality antiques—Oriental carved rugs; Baccarat and Lalique crystal; French Empire, Victorian, and New England country. Among accolades: *Glamour* magazine dubbed it one of the country's five most romantic inns.

In residence: A cat named Chester.
Bed and bath: Ten rooms, each in a different period or style, on three floors. All with ceiling fans. Double, queen, or twin beds. Two third-floor queen-bedded suites with French doors leading to decks that overlook landscaped grounds. All private baths, showers with glass doors.
Breakfast: 7:30–9:30. "Memorable." Varies. Santa Fe omelets, crab polenta, breast of chicken with poached egg on buttered fettucini with champagne sauce. Homemade scones, muffins, and banana bread. Fruit compote with peach schnapps. Freshly squeezed juice. Served family style in Queen Anne dining room.
Plus: A brochure that will make you want to book immediately. Wine and champagne with hors d'oeuvres at 6, with harpist on Saturdays. "Narrated" house tour. Godiva chocolates. Video library. Parlor and library. Pond for swimming. Walking trails. Free loan of French touring bikes and bike trail maps. Extra charge for gourmet lunch provided for Appalachian hikes; picnic baskets.

The Woodstocker Bed and Breakfast

61 River Street, Woodstock, VT 05091   802/457-3896

Hosts: Liza Deignan and Romano Formichella
Location: On the edge of the village, a five-minute walk away from restaurants and shops. Hiking trail up Mount Tom is just around the corner.
Open: Year round. Two-night minimum during foliage and holiday weekends.
Rates: Double occupancy. Spring, November, early December $65–$75 rooms, $75–$100 suites, $10 less midweek. Summer and winter $75–$80 rooms, $85–$100 suites, $5 less midweek. September, October, holiday weeks, $90 rooms, $100–$115 suites. $10–$20 additional person. MC, VISA.
♥ ✤ ◆ ✈ ⌖

What to do? Consult the innkeepers, who after just three years of residency now head the Woodstock Chamber's hospitality committee (in charge of the information booth on the green) and who are on several boards, including the Council on the Arts and Chamber of Commerce.

Liza and Romano came to this "wonderful community in which to live" after years of working together in the computer software field. They bought this B&B, a 150-year-old Cape with renovated attached barn, previously owned by someone in the plumbing business. (The cedar room with whirlpool is a big hit.) And they have surprised themselves (and Liza's mother) with their gardening and culinary skills. Enthusiasm is contagious here.

(Please turn page.)

In residence: Zucchina, "our black Lab, who doesn't go into the guest quarters but waits patiently for visitors outside."

Foreign languages spoken: Italian. Some French, German, Spanish.

Bed and bath: Nine rooms, all private full baths. On first floor, twins and doubles; suite with kitchen and two double beds. On second floor, doubles or queens. Two suites (one with TV, other with deck), each with a double-bedded bedroom, kitchen, living room, and dining area. Rollaway and crib available.

Breakfast: Usually 8–9:30. Homemade granola, cereal, muffins, breads, and coffee cakes. Quiche. Fresh fruit, juice, bagels, English muffins, Vermont-made jams and jellies, gourmet coffee. Buffet style with dining tables set in living room. For special occasions, breakfast in bed.

Plus: Teatime with homemade goodies. Some bedrooms air conditioned or equipped with window/ceiling fans. Books. Games. TV with VCR. Pickup at transportation points. Laundry facilities.

The Peeping Cow Bed & Breakfast

Route 106, P.O. Box 47, Reading, VT 05062-0047   802/484-5036
fax 800/484-9558

Hosts: Nancy and Frank Lynch

Location: Peaceful dairy country, 11 miles south of Woodstock. Surrounded by meadows, stone walls, brook, and forest. Five minutes to Mount Ascutney, 30 to Dartmouth College. Horseback riding and skiing down the road.

Open: Year round. Two-night minimum during fall foliage, Christmas week, and holiday weekends.

Rates: Per room. $60–$80 double occupancy. $5 one-night surcharge.
♥ ❀ ✖ ⅏

Along with some of the country's finest lodging places, this B&B participated in a Manhattan fund-raiser conducted by Christie's (fine art auctioneers). The c. 1830 farmhouse has been renovated over a 16-year period by Frank, a consulting engineer, who has been an old-car buff since his youth in Scotland. "Bovines peek through our Palladian living room window. Handmade nails are in the old pine random-width floors. Only wood heat is used. Fireside chats are the major indoor activity. Some guests browse in the nearby old cemeteries. Ogden's Grist Mill is a favorite of ours. So is '20 Foot,' our village swimming hole."

Nancy, a writer, occasionally attends European trade shows for her children, who export American patchwork. She was a film extra in a Fred Astaire film shot in Woodstock in 1982 and in *Funny Farm*, which was shot three miles south of here at the most photographed farm in the country.

From Ireland: *"A top-class B&B. No wonder the cows keep peeping!"*

Foreign languages spoken: Fluent French and Spanish, some German.

Bed and bath: Three rooms on first and second floors. One double-bedded room and one queen-bedded room, each with a private bath. Another queen-bedded room has a private bath, except in summer and foliage season, when it shares a bath with a room that has two twin beds.

Breakfast: Usually 8:15; earlier by request. Fresh fruits. House granola. Homemade rolls, muffins, jams, honey, fruit juice. Yogurt and cheeses. "We think our pure (well and spring) water is what makes the fresh-brewed coffee and steeped tea extra great." Served in dining room furnished with English antiques and oil paintings.

Plus: Handmade quilts in summer, down comforters in winter. No TV but plenty of books. Piano, mandolin, ukulele yours to use. Chess. Picnic lunch (advance notice, small fee). Orders taken for handmade quilts at discounted prices.

KEY TO SYMBOLS
♥ Lots of honeymooners come here.
✙ Families with children are very welcome. (Please see page xiii.)
✎ "Please emphasize that we are a private home, not an inn."
♣ Groups or private parties sometimes book the entire B&B.
♦ Travel agents' commission paid. (Please see page xii.)
✗ Sorry, no guests' pets are allowed.
✗ No smoking inside *or* no smoking at all, even on porches.

INDEX

MASSACHUSETTS

NEW HAMPSHIRE

ABOUT THE AUTHOR

Bernice Chesler, "America's bed and breakfast ambassador," has appeared on dozens of television and radio programs including "CBS This Morning," "CNN Travel Guide," and NPR's "Morning Edition." She is known for her personalized approach and attention to detail. Guests from all over the world write to her about their B&B experiences. She shares their impressions—and her own, gathered through hundreds of stays and extensive interviews—in her books, in Meet-the-Hosts programs conducted at major retailers throughout the Northeast, in workshops, and in lectures at bed and breakfast conferences from Maine to California.

Recipient of the nation's first B&B Achievement Award and first B&B Reservation Service Award, the author is a member of the Professional Advisory Board of the Professional Association of Innkeepers International. She has written for 'GBH, Yankee, Country Almanac, Family Circle, and Innsider magazines and for the Boston Globe and the Washington Post.

BBB—Before Bed and Breakfast—Ms. Chesler conducted thousands of interviews throughout the country for documentary films seen on national public television. As publications coordinator for the Emmy Award–winning television program "ZOOM," produced at WGBH, Boston, she edited twelve books emanating from the series. She is also the author of the classic guide In and Out of Boston with (or without) Children.